THE ARDEN SHAKESPEARE

THIRD SERIES
General Editors: Richard Proudfoot, Ann Thompson,
David Scott Kastan and H.R. Woudhuysen

THE MERCHANT OF VENICE

D0048964

THE ARDEN SHAKESPEARE

* Second series

THE ARDEN SHAKESPEARE

THE MERCHANT OF VENICE

Edited by
JOHN DRAKAKIS

Arden Shakespeare

1 3 5 7 9 10 8 6 4 2

This edition of *The Merchant of Venice*, by John Drakakis, first
published 2010 by The Arden Shakespeare

Editorial matter copyright © 2010 John Drakakis

Arden Shakespeare is an imprint of Methuen Drama

Methuen Drama
A & C Black Publishers Ltd
36 Soho Square
London W1D 3QY
www.methuendrama.com
www.ardenshakespeare.com

A CIP catalogue record for this book is available from the British
Library
ISBN: 978 1 903 43681 3 (paperback)
ISBN: 978 1 903 43680 6 (hardback)

Available in the USA from Bloomsbury Academic & Professional,
175 Fifth Avenue/3rd Floor, New York, NY 10010.
www.BloomsburyAcademicUSA.com

The general editors of the Arden Shakespeare have been
W.J. Craig and R.H. Case (first series 1899–1944)
Una Ellis-Fermor, Harold F. Brooks, Harold Jenkins and
Brian Morris (second series 1946–82)

Present general editors (third series)
Richard Proudfoot, Ann Thompson, David Scott Kastan and
H.R. Woudhuysen

Printed by Zrinski in Croatia

The Editor

John Drakakis is Professor of English Studies at the University of Stirling. He has taught widely in the field of Shakespeare studies and is currently the Director of the Scottish Institute of Northern Renaissance Studies, and of the M.Res in Renaissance Studies at Stirling. He is the editor of *British Radio Drama* (1981); of *Alternative Shakespeares*, New Accents series (1985); *Gothic Shakespeares* (with Dale Townshend), Accents on Shakespeare series (2008); *Tragedy* (with Naomi C. Liebler), Longman Critical Reader series (1998); *Shakespeare: The Tragedy of Richard III Q1*, Shakespeare Originals series (1996); *Shakespeare: Antony and Cleopatra*, Macmillan New Casebooks series (1994); *Shakespearean Tragedy*, Longman Critical Reader series (1991). He was the general editor of the Routledge English Texts series, and is currently the general editor of the Routledge New Critical Idiom series. He has recently assumed the general editorship of the revision of Geoffrey Bullough's *Narrative and Dramatic Sources of Shakespeare*, and he is completing a monograph on *Shakespeare's Discourses*. He has contributed a number of articles and book chapters to learned journals and volumes within the field of Shakespeare studies and literary and critical theory.

IN MEMORY OF

Elvira Sara Drakakis
(née Gentile)

1913–2002

CONTENTS

LIST OF
ILLUSTRATIONS

GENERAL EDITORS' PREFACE

The earliest volume in the first Arden series, Edward Dowden's *Hamlet*, was published in 1899. Since then the Arden Shakespeare has been widely acknowledged as the pre-eminent Shakespeare edition, valued by scholars, students, actors and 'the great variety of readers' alike for its clearly presented and reliable texts, its full annotation and its richly informative introductions.

In the third Arden series we seek to maintain these well-established qualities and general characteristics, preserving our predecessors' commitment to presenting the play as it has been shaped in history. Each volume necessarily has its own particular emphasis which reflects the unique possibilities and problems posed by the work in question, and the series as a whole seeks to maintain the highest standards of scholarship, combined with attractive and accessible presentation.

Newly edited from the original Quarto and Folio editions, texts are presented in fully modernized form, with a textual apparatus that records all substantial divergences from those early printings. The notes and introductions focus on the conditions and possibilities of meaning that editors, critics and performers (on stage and screen) have discovered in the play. While building upon the rich history of scholarly activity that has long shaped our understanding of Shakespeare's works, this third series of the Arden Shakespeare is enlivened by a new generation's encounter with Shakespeare.

THE TEXT

On each page of the play itself, readers will find a passage of text supported by commentary and textual notes. Act and scene divisions (seldom present in the early editions and often the product of eighteenth-century or later scholarship) have been retained for ease of reference, but have been given less prominence than in previous series. Editorial indications of location of the action have been removed to the textual notes or commentary.

In the text itself, unfamiliar typographic conventions have been avoided in order to minimize obstacles to the reader. Elided forms in the early texts are spelt out in full in verse lines wherever they indicate a usual late twentieth-century pronunciation that requires no special indication and wherever they occur in prose (except where they indicate non-standard pronunciation). In verse speeches, marks of elision are retained where they are necessary guides to the scansion and pronunciation of the line. Final -ed in past tense and participial forms of verbs is always printed as -ed, without accent, never as -'d, but wherever the required pronunciation diverges from modern usage a note in the commentary draws attention to the fact. Where the final -ed should be given syllabic value contrary to modern usage, e.g.

> Doth Silvia know that I am banished?
>
> (*TGV* 3.1.214)

the note will take the form

214 banished banishèd

Conventional lineation of divided verse lines shared by two or more speakers has been reconsidered and sometimes rearranged. Except for the familiar *Exit* and *Exeunt*, Latin forms in stage directions and speech prefixes have been translated into English and the original Latin forms recorded in the textual notes.

COMMENTARY AND TEXTUAL NOTES

Notes in the commentary, for which a major source will be the *Oxford English Dictionary*, offer glossarial and other explication of verbal difficulties; they may also include discussion of points of interpretation and, in relevant cases, substantial extracts from Shakespeare's source material. Editors will not usually offer glossarial notes for words adequately defined in the latest edition of *The Concise Oxford Dictionary* or *Merriam-Webster's Collegiate Dictionary*, but in cases of doubt they will include notes. Attention, however, will be drawn to places where more than one likely interpretation can be proposed and to significant verbal and syntactic complexity. Notes preceded by * discuss editorial emendations or variant readings from the early edition(s) on which the text is based.

Headnotes to acts or scenes discuss, where appropriate, questions of scene location, Shakespeare's handling of his source materials, and major difficulties of staging. The list of roles (so headed to emphasize the play's status as a text for performance) is also considered in the commentary notes. These may include comment on plausible patterns of casting with the resources of an Elizabethan or Jacobean acting company and also on any variation in the description of roles in their speech prefixes in the early editions.

The textual notes are designed to let readers know when the edited text diverges from the early edition(s) or manuscript sources on which it is based. Wherever this happens the note will record the rejected reading of the early edition(s), in original spelling, and the source of the reading adopted in this edition. Other forms from the early edition(s) recorded in these notes will include some spellings of particular interest or significance and original forms of translated stage directions. Where two or more early editions are involved, for instance with *Othello*, the notes also record all important differences between them. The textual notes take a form that has been in use since the nineteenth century. This comprises, first: line reference, reading adopted in the text and closing square bracket; then: abbreviated reference, in italic, to the earliest edition to adopt the accepted reading, italic semicolon and noteworthy alternative reading(s), each with abbreviated italic reference to its source.

Conventions used in these textual notes include the following. The solidus / is used, in notes quoting verse or discussing verse lining, to indicate line endings. Distinctive spellings of the basic text (Q or F) follow the square bracket without indication of source and are enclosed in italic brackets. Names enclosed in italic brackets indicate originators of conjectural emendations when these did not originate in an edition of the text, or when the named edition records a conjecture not accepted into its text. Stage directions (SDs) are referred to by the number of the line within or immediately after which they are placed. Line numbers with a decimal point relate to centred entry SDs not falling within a verse line and to SDs more than one line long, with the number after the point indicating the line within the SD: e.g. 78.4 refers to the fourth line of the SD following line 78. Lines of SDs at the start of a scene are numbered 0.1, 0.2, etc. Where only a line number precedes a square bracket, e.g. 128], the note relates to the whole line; where SD is added to the number, it relates to the whole of a SD within or immediately following the line. Speech prefixes (SPs) follow similar conventions, 203 SP] referring to the speaker's name for line 203. Where a SP reference takes the form e.g. 38+ SP, it relates to all subsequent speeches assigned to that speaker in the scene in question.

Where, as with *King Henry V*, one of the early editions is a so-called 'bad quarto' (that is, a text either heavily adapted, or reconstructed from memory, or both), the divergences from the present edition are too great to be recorded in full in the notes. In these cases, with the exception of *Hamlet*, which prints an edited text of the quarto of 1603, the editions will include a reduced photographic facsimile of the 'bad quarto' in an appendix.

INTRODUCTION

Both the introduction and the commentary are designed to present the plays as texts for performance, and make appropriate reference to stage, film and television versions, as well as introducing the reader to the range of critical approaches to the plays. They discuss the history of the reception of the texts within the theatre and scholarship and beyond, investigating the interdependency of the literary text and the surrounding 'cultural text' both at the time of the original production of Shakespeare's works and during their long and rich afterlife.

PREFACE

The Merchant of Venice is, of all of Shakespeare's plays, with the possible exception of *Othello* (the only other play set partly in Venice), the one that has most succumbed to the pressures of time and of history, particularly recent history. Anglo-American fiscal culture and even the culture of globalization itself depend upon the extension of spheres of political influence, and particular forms of 'usury' that would have horrified Elizabethans. One can only imagine what form an Elizabethan official inquiry might have taken into the western banking crisis of the past two years and the fates of those who engineered the irresponsible expansion of the sub-prime mortgage market, in a culture where hanging, drawing and quartering, not to mention the extraction of 'truth' through torture, were customary forms of punishment. Nor has this edition been exempt from such contemporary commercial pressures. It was begun in the 1990s in the period of what for some of us was the welcome decline of Thatcherism, though not, regrettably, of its attendant prejudices, and at the invitation of Jane Armstrong and Richard Proudfoot under the auspices of Routledge. It has subsequently been transferred to at least two other publishing companies – such are the ways of capitalism – before coming to rest, appropriately, under the imprint of Methuen Drama, Methuen being the original publishers of the Arden Shakespeare. Wheels have a habit of coming full circle.

During that time I have incurred many debts, too many to mention here. It is, however, a pleasure to be able to record a long overdue debt to Terence Hawkes, who has for many years undertaken the thankless task of playing William Camden to my Ben Jonson, and without whose unwavering support, encouragement and friendship I might have spent my life laying bricks, or even been moved to kill an actor or two. When I began this project it was under the sole general editorship of Richard Proudfoot, whose stern generosity and traditional textual scholarship I learned to appreciate. Since then the cast of general editors has grown into a quartet, and I am grateful to David Kastan for his enthusiastic encouragement at every stage, along with his many helpful suggestions, and to Ann Thompson for reminding me that there is a male chauvinist method of setting out a List of Roles that, despite my desire to observe a modicum of political correctness, I had overlooked. It has also been a pleasure to work again with Margaret Bartley, the current publisher, and to be able to call on her professional editing skills as well as her infectious humour when I needed them.

The international academic communities in Britain, Europe and North America have also been exceptionally generous. I am grateful to the Trustees of Amherst College who granted me a short-term fellowship at the Folger Library in the summer of 2000. The holdings of the Folger are impressive, and it was a privilege to work in a library where the materials I needed, and the bibliographical expertise, were all at hand, and where the library staff made their own scholarly expertise so freely available. I have also been fortunate over the years to have been part of a lively and innovative group of scholars who collectively have worked to change the study of Shakespeare and the ways in which we talk about his texts. Terence Hawkes, Alan Sinfield, Jonathan Dollimore, Catherine Belsey, Christopher Norris, Peter Hulme, the late Francis Barker, Stephen Greenblatt, Leonard Goldstein and Robert Weimann have all contributed to my thinking about *The Merchant of Venice* and about Shakespeare and Renaissance drama in general. I am also grateful to Stephen Orgel for providing me with a typescript of his lecture on 'Imagining Shylock' well before its publication in book form in 2003, and to Steven Mullaney for a wonderful (and long) conversation about the Dr Richard Lopez case, and its relevance to the dating of the play, in the garden of the Shakespeare Institute at Stratford in summer 2004. Professor Robert Stradling, formerly of the University of Cardiff, steered me in the direction of a number of historical studies of Venice that I found illuminating, and it is a pleasure to be able to record my heartfelt thanks for his friendship, interest and support. I owe a very special debt of gratitude to Naomi Liebler of Montclair State University, who invited me to lecture at Montclair on two memorable occasions, and who has been kind enough to share her considerable knowledge of Shakespeare and of Jewish culture with me as the edition developed. The staff at the Shakespeare Centre at Stratford-upon-Avon, in particular Helen Hargest, have been indefatigable in providing me with a range of illustrations of performances, and Michael Bogdanov, the director of the Wales Theatre Company, was kind enough to invite me down to Cardiff to a brilliantly thoughtful performance of *The Merchant of Venice* and to allow me to meet and talk with the cast of the production. I am also grateful to the Compass Theatre Company of Sheffield for providing me with details of their 1997 touring performance of the play.

At Stirling I have been fortunate to benefit from the support and friendship of colleagues, and generations of lively postgraduate and undergraduate students in the Department of English Studies. I am grateful to the Arts and Humanities Research Council for extending one period of institutional research leave, and to the University of Stirling for granting me a second to bring the edition to fruition. Colleagues in the University of Stirling Library have always responded to my requests for material with wonderful efficiency, and have provided me with all that I asked for and more. Dr Adrian Streete, formerly one of my PhD students, was for a short period of time my research assistant, and he made available to me his extraordinarily detailed knowledge of sixteenth-century religion along with a very wide knowledge of Renaissance literature. Dr Vance Adair and Dr Annie Doyle, also former research students, have provided the opportunities for many animated conversations over the years in connection with Shakespeare and the questions of 'theory' and I have learned much from them. They were, all three, part of my undergraduate Honours classes in 'Shakespearean Comedy' at different times, and they were an important part of a lively, critically sophisticated, sometimes sceptical, community of students who have provided the laboratory conditions for testing out some of the ideas in the following pages. All of them will doubtless be pleased to know that at least part of an obsession will now be laid to rest.

The list of those to whom I owe more general thanks is an extremely long one, and I have no doubt that a variety of influences can be easily traced in the pages that follow. Needless to say, the errors that remain are my own, and as Shakespeare's Gloucester would say when his bastard offspring appeared: 'the whoreson(s) must be acknowledged'. But the one person who has done more than any other to reduce the volume of error, and whom I only encountered at the copy-editing stage, is Linden Stafford. Her detailed work on the manuscript that I submitted, transforming it in the process, has been a lesson that all who have been fortunate enough to work closely with her, as I have done, will wish that they had learned earlier. Anyone who can make the business of copy-editing entertaining and, at the same time, maintain an unwavering commitment to the strictest accuracy and to very high standards of clarity commands respect. And to have had Linden's wide and encyclopedic editorial experience, as well as a formidable critical faculty, at my disposal during the final months of this project has been both a pleasure I had not expected and a source of my continued admiration. Of course, I should have known better; I have encountered her work before in ghostly form behind Harold Jenkins's superb edition of the Arden series 2 *Hamlet*.

It is at this stage of the process that I am conscious of the assistance of those who otherwise remain anonymous. I owe thanks to Zoe Ross, who assembled the index for me with professional speed and efficiency, and particularly to Kate Reeves, whose precision and sharpness of vision in proofreading proved invaluable.

My daughters Alexia and Helena, and their mother Christine, all have put in some sterling work to wean me from the alpha male eccentricities of a combined Calabrian and Cretan patriarchal inheritance, a process that would certainly have had my father wince in pain, and made even that arch-strategist, Shakespeare's Ulysses, blush. Finally, I am only sorry that the person to whom this edition is dedicated did not live long enough to see it come to fruition. She was not a literary scholar, although she had a passion for a good story, as well as an extraordinary compassion for others. I have been the beneficiary of her indefatigable and unwavering belief in the virtues of education, of her care, consideration and enthusiasm, and of her unostentatious but stern resistance to any form of prejudice. If there is one Shakespeare play to which I would venture to attach her name, it is *The Merchant of Venice*, and as someone of Calabrian descent I am certain that she would have known how to respond to Shakespeare's Venetians. If this edition fulfils any wider political aim beyond the numerical requirements of an increasingly bean-counting academy, it will have been to follow her example: to contribute to an understanding of the internal workings of prejudice – all prejudice – and to its eventual eradication, a commitment that she practised through her unstinting generosity during a long, modest but fruitful life.

John Drakakis
Stirling

INTRODUCTION

The Merchant of Venice is arguably Shakespeare's most controversial comedy because, for modern audiences, it broaches a topic that has become a touchstone of the political difference between tolerance and prejudice. Harold Bloom's chapter in *Shakespeare: The Invention of the Human* (1998) begins with the embarrassing admission that anyone now encountering the play 'would have to be blind, deaf and dumb not to recognize that Shakespeare's grand, equivocal comedy . . . is nevertheless a profoundly anti-Semitic work' (Bloom, 171). But he then describes the focus of the play's anti-Semitism, Shylock, as a figure who is 'at once a fabulous monster, the Jew incarnate, and also a troubling human uneasily joined with the monster in an uncanny blend' (6), whose 'realistic mimesis', compared to Marlowe's cartoon Jew Barabas in *The Jew of Malta*, 'is so overwhelming that it cannot be accommodated as a stage Jew' (73). The general contours of Bloom's argument are yet another version of the perennial claim to a liberal humanist universality that has informed centuries of Shakespeare commentary. What troubles Bloom, however, is that the play contains sentiments that are recognizably anti-Semitic, but at the same time a context is provided that invites us to read those sentiments critically.

Modern editors and commentators have responded variously to such claims about *The Merchant of Venice*, although the sense that this is primarily Shylock's play – indeed, his tragedy – is given added emphasis from the beginning of the eighteenth century onwards in criticism and performance, from Charles Macklin's 1741 stage realization to the present time, and has remained remarkably resilient. In his biographical account of Shakespeare (1709) Nicholas Rowe recalled that 'the incomparable Character of *Shylock* the *Jew*' was performed 'by an excellent Comedian', although he confessed that 'I cannot but think it was design'd

1

Tragically by the Author.'[1] In the twentieth century C.L. Barber's influential account of the play begins with the observation that 'Shylock's part is so fascinating that already in 1598 the comedy was entered in the Stationers' Register as "a book of the Merchant of Venice, or otherwise called the Jew of Venice"' (Barber, 167). For Barber, Shylock's role in the play is that of 'an embodied irony', who is 'troublingly like' the Venetians whom he opposes, but this does not explain the ambivalent attitude that we are persuaded to adopt to his fate. The ostensibly comic plot subscribes to a powerful Christian fantasy, but Barber is forced to concede that 'If one adds humanitarian and democratic indignation at anti–Semitism, it is hard to see from a distance what there can be to say for the play: Shylock seems to be made a scapegoat in the crudest, most dishonest way' (168–9). Despite these reservations, critical, and particularly theatrical, attitudes to Shylock have vacillated between perceiving the dramatic character as a source of tragedy, regarding him as a comic villain, or offering a Christian apology for the harsh treatment he receives (cf. Wertheim, 75ff.).

Lawrence Danson begins his full-length study, *The Harmonies of the Merchant of Venice* (1978), by observing that interest in the figure of Shylock has taken precedence in any discussion of the play (Danson, *Harmonies*, 2), while more recently John Gross's wide-ranging study of the social and theatrical history of Shylock argues: 'Not only does he stand out from his surroundings in peculiarly stark isolation; his myth has often flourished with very little reference to *The Merchant of Venice* as a whole, quite often with none at all' (Gross, 1–2). In an attempt to differentiate between the myth and historical reality, and between theatrical representation and the existence of actual communities of Jews in Renaissance London, James Shapiro sketches out 'the extent to which *The Merchant of Venice* had come to embody English conceptions of Jewish racial and national difference' (Shapiro, *Jews*, 2). But, if the figure of Shylock is a limit case, then the

1 Nicholas Rowe, *Some Account of the Life . . . of Mr William Shakespear* (1709), xix.

play itself becomes a test of our conceptions of genre and comic structure. In the form in which we have it, the *Merchant of Venice* also raises questions concerning the processes of composition and dramatic characterization, at the same time as it forces a reconsideration of the political myths surrounding Venetian republicanism that circulated in England during the late sixteenth century.

VENICE: MYTH AND REALITY

The *Merchant of Venice* is one of only two plays in the Shakespeare canon located in Venice, and the setting is topical. From the fifteenth century onwards Venice established itself as a dominant maritime power whose access to Turkey and to the trade routes of the eastern Mediterranean contributed to its reputation as a multicultural republic. James VI of Scotland's long poem *Lepanto*, a narrative of the Christian victory over the Turks in 1571, described Venice as 'This artificial town', that stood 'within the Sea' (l. 97) upon an island that was 'all her market place' (l. 107), that 'A Duke with Senate joyned doth rule' (l. 109) and whose citizens each year 'wed the Sea with rings / To be their sure reliefe' (ll. 111–12; Craigie, 206–8).

It was Venice's democratic institutions in particular that attracted the critical attention of Elizabethan commentators. For example, Elizabeth I's anti-Presbyterian Bishop of London, Richard Bancroft, began the second chapter of his *A Survey of the Pretended Holy Discipline* (1593) with a brusque dismissal of the threat of democracy that Venice posed. He firmly resisted popular calls for 'liberty' and he opposed republican sentiments, rejecting out of hand 'The canotoninge of kingdomes' and social equality, political concepts that were being disseminated by 'trauailers' to Europe. The 'vsual discourse' of such people was: 'what a notable thing it is to liue in *Venice*. There (forsooth) euery gentleman liueth with as great libertie as the *Duke* himselfe. They haue noe Earles, no Barons, no Noblemen, of whom their Gentlemen stand in awe' (Bancroft, 7–8). Whether the attraction for Renaissance commentators derived from its apparent continuation of an otherwise defunct Roman republican tradition (Bloom & Jaffa, 13–15), or whether its fame rested upon a reputation as 'the pleasure capital of Europe' (Honigmann, in *Othello*, 38), the Venice of Elizabethan popular imagination was a combination of fact and fantasy available as a convenient geographical location onto which English anxieties could be projected. By the 1590s Venice had clearly become a byword for the exoticism of travel. For the pedant Holofernes in *Love's Labour's Lost* it is a place of wonder: 'I may speak of thee as the traveller doth of Venice: / *Venetia, Venetia, / Chi non te vede, non ti pretia* [Venice, Venice, he that does not see thee does not esteem thee]' (*LLL* 4.2.94–6), but within the context of *Richard II* it is 'that pleasant country' to which the banished Thomas Mowbray, disgraced Earl of Norfolk, returns to die after 'Streaming the ensign of the Christian cross / Against black pagans, Turks, and Saracens' (*R2* 4.1.94–5). The tourist's view is substantially maintained in Thomas Coryate's *Coryate's Crudities* (1611).[1] In addition to noting buildings, places and courtesans, Coryate paid particular attention to the community of Jews dwelling in the Ghetto: 'an Iland: for it is inclosed around with water' (Coryate, 160). The community numbered 'betwixt fiue and sixe thousand' and comprised both Italian and Levantine Jews, each group distinguished by different styles of dress. Moreover, he observed that some of the Levantine Jews contradicted the English proverb, so that 'To looke like a Iewe (whereby is meant sometimes a weather beaten warp-faced fellow, sometimes a phrenticke and lunaticke person, sometimes one discontented) is not true' (Coryate, 231–3).

These varying impressions are anticipated by an earlier, more politically complex image of Venice that emerges in William

---

1   See also Gillies, 124, for the suggestion that Coryate's admiration may have been 'uneasy' due to the conflicting impressions of wonder and menace attendant upon the presence of different ethnic groups in the republic.

Thomas's *The History of Italy* (1549, 1561). In Thomas's essentially pre-Elizabethan account, what was a dominant military power had already begun to develop commerce and trade as instruments of political subjugation. He begins with the observation that:

> For sins Constantinople was gotten by the Turkes, theyr dominion hath decreased, both by reason (as the same goeth) they rather practise with money, to bie and sel countreys, peace and warre: than to exercyse needs of armes: and for that most Venetians are at these daies become better merchauntes than men of warre.
>
> (W. Thomas, sig. U3ᵛ)

Venetian judicial institutions, originally described by Thomas, were later to receive detailed attention in Lewis Lewkenor's translation of Gasparo Contarini's *The Commonwealth and Government of Venice* (1599), which appeared in print a year before the First Quarto of Shakespeare's play. Contarini remarked upon 'the wonderful concourse of strange and forein people, yea of the farthest and remotest nations, as though the city of *Venice* only were a common and general market to the whole world' (Contarini, sig. B1ʳ; see also Gillies, 123–4).

The Jews, who were central to the economic life of Venice, came originally from Germany, Spain and Portugal, and the Levant, and were allowed to settle in the Ghetto, named after the site of a foundry that had been built nearby, at the beginning of the sixteenth century. Fredric C. Lane has argued that the term 'ghetto' was not at this time primarily a symbol of racial segregation, since there was much 'friendly contact' between Jews and Christians, although the republic was not immune from occasional 'religiously coloured anti-Semitism' (Lane, 301). But it is the exotic, and politically questionable, Venice of the Elizabethan imagination enmeshed within its existence historically as an imperial maritime power that is the complex driving force behind Shakespeare's Venetian plays. John Gillies puts the contradiction that generated Elizabethan interest in Venice succinctly in his suggestion that 'Self consciously imperial and a "market place of the world", Shakespeare's Venice invites barbarous intrusion through the sheer "exorbitance" of its maritime trading empire' (Gillies, 125)

Venice was clearly a place of 'wonder' whose political institiutions were a source of fascination and suspicion for an Elizabethan culture wedded to autocratic monarchy but curious about other, less hierarchical, forms of government. Just as the history of imperial Rome furnished a series of safely distanced laboratory experiments in practical politics, so the Republic of Venice exemplified a modern economy apparently liberated from many of those constraints on the flow of capital and their attendant anxieties, which hampered economic activity in England. Elizabethan writers, and Shakespeare in particular, *read* Venice, and the result was a representation produced in response to cultural forces whose comparative novelty stood as a challenge to accepted modes of thinking. The ethnic variety of Venice, its much vaunted economic freedoms and its alleged sexual permissiveness,[1] all of which were the subjects of travellers' testimonies, entered the Elizabethan popular imagination and were interpreted according to the demands of an ideology struggling to contain its own social, political and economic contradictions. Coryate perceived a connection between Venetian courtesans and the theatre (Coryate, 247–8), which Shakespeare and his contemporaries, Thomas Middleton especially, developed thematically through the dramatization of the institutions of marriage and commerce. The resulting social and psychological tensions proved to be a fruitful resource for Elizabethan and Jacobean comedy, and has been much commented upon by feminist critics of the genre (cf. Leventen, 59–79).

---

1 Coryate, 246–7 and 261–4, where he describes the sexual permissiveness evident in Venice, and explains the role of the courtesan: 'As for the number of these Venetian Cortezans it is very great' (Coryate, 264).

Leslie Fiedler, anticipating some of the arguments now familiar in post-colonial discourse, suggests that in plays such as the *Merchant of Venice* 'the woman and the Jew embody stereotypes and myths, impulses and attitudes, images and metaphors grown unfashionable in our world'. But, in a perplexing psychological turn away from historical reconstruction that inadvertently exposes the dark origins of anti-Semitism, he claims that the play invites us to 'descend to the level of what is most archaic in our living selves and there confront the living Shylock' (Fiedler, 99).[1]

Post-structuralist theory has sharpened our awareness of representations of gender and race. Moreover, that Venice could provide an imaginative insight into the Elizabethan cultural unconscious indicates that its *meaning* could not easily be reduced to an accurate imitation of a particular geographical location. It was primarily a geographical space, perceived in part as a community of 'strangers'; but it was also, according to Contarini, 'a straunge and unusuall forme of a most excellent Monarchie', a 'Democrasie or popular estate' (Contarini, sig. A2ᵛ) that was a model of the operation of advanced mercantile activity. It was also a precariously founded foreign location, built, according to Contarini, upon 'Quagmires, and planted upon such unfirme moorish and spungie foundations' (sig. A3ᵛ). Venice furnished for English audiences and readers alike both a complex mediated image of themselves *and* the measure of a critical distance from perceived Elizabethan cultural practice. There is a kind of orientalism at work here that remains implicit even in John Gillies's account where the Venice of Shakespeare's two plays is perceived as being 'somehow complicit with the "exotic"' (Gillies, 123). But it was also an 'exotic' geographical space whose very 'moorish' foundations made it precariously artificial in a pejorative sense. This combination of exoticism,

---

1 Cf. Kristeva, 183, who argues that 'the archaic, narcissistic self, not yet demarcated by the outside world, projects out of itself what it experiences as dangerous or unpleasant in itself, making it an alien *double*, uncanny and demoniacal.'

political novelty and potentially anarchic force harmonized with Elizabethan perceptions of the human psyche, and raised questions of constitutional balance and temperamental difference that recall one of Aristotle's influential texts, the *Nicomachean Ethics*,[1] some of whose themes echoed insistently throughout the drama of the period. It was also the most materialistic of locations dependent upon commerce and money.

THE MENACE OF MONEY

The title of Shakespeare's play, 'The most excellent Historie of the *Merchant of Venice*', pinpoints the connection between geographical location and commerce (see Fig. 1). At the root of this complex dramatization of the social life of the republic is money itself and its historical significance for a society caught between a conservative past and new forms of commercial activity that threatened the stability of the social order.[2] The debate about money goes back to the distinction in Aristotle's *Politics* between money intended as a means of exchange dependent for its generation upon agricultural production, and commercial activity undertaken solely for the purpose of profit. Only when profit is linked to agricultural surplus can it be legitimately used to generate 'interest' in contrast to the use of money to make money. Aristotle describes the distinction thus:

> Interest or Vsury consisting in multiplying and encreasing of money from moneth to moneth, or yeare to yeare, is likewise comprehended vnder the artificiall getting of goods, and reprooued amongst all other meanes of getting, as contrary to the right vse of money, which was onely inuented for the

---

1   Aristotle's *Nicomachean Ethics* was translated into English from the Italian for R. Grafton and appeared in an octavo in 1547; a Latin octavo was published by H. Bynneman in 1581. The *Ethics* was of secondary importance, however, compared to *The Politics* in the late 1590s in England.
2   See Tawney; and also Weber. For a wider European perspective, see Wallerstein; Braudel; and Brenner.

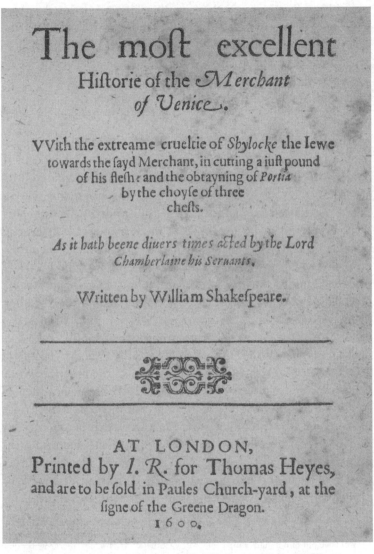

The most excellent

Historie of the *Merchant* *of Venice.*

VVith the extreame crueltie of *Shylocke* the Iewe
towards the sayd Merchant, in cutting a iust pound
of his flesh: and the obtayning of *Portia*
by the choyse of three
chests.

As it hath beene diuers times acted by the Lord
Chamberlaine his Seruants.

Written by William Shakespeare.

AT LONDON,
Printed by *I. R.* for Thomas Heyes,
and are to be sold in Paules Church-yard, at the
signe of the Greene Dragon.
1 6 0 0.

1   Title-page of the First Quarto of *The Merchant of Venice* (1600)

> furtherance of Trafficke, and according to the Nature thereof; and being a thing without life, neither ought nor lawfully may engender other mony, but should be employed to that purpose whereunto it was ordained: Though many men wholly imploy themselues to hoord vp mony without end, deeming that therein consisteth the principall and chiefe of richesse.
>
> (Aristotle, *Politics*, 38)

Martin Luther appreciated this distinction, and in the first part of his tract *Trade and Usury* (1524) described the idealistic concept of the 'just price': a merchant sells his commodities according to what is 'right' and 'fair' because selling 'ought not to be an act that is entirely within your own power and discretion, without law or limit, as though you were a god and beholden to no one'. Such activity, argued Luther, 'should be governed by law and conscience that you do it without harm and injury to him (the buyer, "your neighbour") your concern being directed more toward doing him no injury than toward gaining profit for yourself' (Luther, *Usury*, 248). Luther proposed a series of calculations designed to prevent the taking of excessive profit,[1] but he also identified a mercantile practice of direct relevance to *The Merchant of Venice*, that is, 'the practice of one person becoming surety for another' (252). Even though such an activity 'looks like a virtue stemming from love' it is the cause of 'ruin' because 'Standing surety is a work that is too lofty for a man; it is unseemly for it is a presumptuous encroachment upon the work of God' (252–3). Antonio's standing surety for Bassanio in the play is, within the Lutheran discourse of economic practice, a gesture whose effects are ambivalent,

---

1 'In determining how much profit you ought to take on your business and your labor, there is no better way to reckon it than by computing the amount of time and labor you have put into it, and comparing that with the effort of a day laborer who works at some other occupation and seeing how much he earns in a day. On that basis figure how many days you have spent in getting your wares and bringing them to your place of business, and how much labor and risk was involved; for a great amount of labor and time ought to have a correspondingly greater return' (Luther, *Usury*, 251).

just as his own involvement in trading practice generates both positive and negative interpretations. Antonio is engaged in an 'artificiall' activity, but he also uses his wealth to aid a friend in need with no thought of profit.

We need also to connect the ambivalence concerning the increasingly complicated operation of the flow of money with the practice of displacing certain necessary economic activities onto alien, that is non-Christian, groups or 'strangers'. Despite regional and national differences, the general structural patterns that were beginning to emerge throughout Christian Europe during the later sixteenth century were strikingly similar. It is precisely during this period that, as George Simmel argues, the figure of the 'stranger' comes into his own as a challenge to the social fabric of community (Simmel, 226). It is also the point at which a significant acceleration in the pace of economic practice takes place. Money ceases to have a purely instrumental value as a *means* to an end, and assumes an overriding power as a 'final purpose' that governs 'practical consciousness' (232), which now requires forms of legislation. Contarini's *Commonwealth and Government of Venice* (1599) outlines the Republic's political and judicial institutions that facilitated, underpinned and regulated mercantile activity, and it details the procedures for dealing with fiscal disputes between citizens and strangers, and also for the collection of taxes upon imports and exports (Contarini, sigs P2–3^v).

The Venetian economy was sufficiently developed to require a sophisticated range of monetary and credit facilities that were subject to the law, although by the end of the sixteenth century its supremacy was under threat from other European competitors, notably Holland, Portugal and England. Central to mercantilism in general were what Immanuel Wallerstein has called 'state policies of economic nationalism' that 'revolved around a concern with the circulation of commodities, whether in terms of the movement of bullion or in the creation of balances of trade (bilateral or multilateral)' (Wallerstein, 37).

In the *Merchant of Venice* both Antonio and the Jew are occupied in different but related branches of mercantilist practice, the one engaged in overseas trade and the other in facilitating the flow of capital through contractual means. Antonio is preoccupied with the process of exchange in which the relation between money and consumption and profit – what Marx would later call 'use-value' and 'exchange-value' (Marx, *Critique*, 27) – appears comparatively straightforward in the play, if a little mysterious in the details of its operation. The Jew, on the other hand, is concerned exclusively with the circulation of money in the form of loans and the interest to be derived from it. Indeed, his presence as a 'type' and his designation as a 'stranger' expose a politics of identity that extends beyond the sphere of the economic that Wallerstein describes. Antonio's role as the facilitator of Bassanio's project, in which wealth and life are combined, insists upon preserving the distinction between subject and object, between the human and the inanimate, that is undermined by the assignation of life and agency to money (cf. Hawkes, 121–5). The capacity of money to transform human society, both through the demand for forms of credit involving fiduciary guarantees and, in part, through its challenge to the limitations imposed upon exchange by the power of patriarchy, encouraged the perception of its danger. Nowhere was that danger more in evidence than in the practice of usury which, according to Thomas Wilson, involved men who 'rather seeke their owne gain, then any thing the benefit of theire Christian neyghbour' (T. Wilson, *Usury*, fols 4ᵛ–5).

USURY OR THE BUTLER'S BOX

Wilson's claim that usury challenged the ethos of Christian neighbourliness is typical of the Elizabethan propensity to situate economic practice firmly within the purview of religious discourse. In his tract on *Trade and Usury* (1524) Luther aligned the practice generally with the disposal of all temporal commodities, but especially in connection with the specifically Catholic activity of raising money to pay for church buildings. He equated profit with the term 'interest' which is translated as 'that which makes a difference' (*OED sb.*). But he used the Latin 'interesse' to identify the return on capital investment that tips the balance of 'interest' as a legitimate risk-determined form of compensation for a fiscal loan, into the comparatively risk-free practice of usury (Luther, *Usury*, 298). He advocated the feudal tithe as a differential form of loan repayment that involved both lender and borrower in the risks of productive activity (309), and he accused the usurer of absolving himself from any share in the risks of the borrower.

Shakespeare may not have been familiar with the details of Luther's text, but he was certainly familiar with the theologically saturated discourse of money, and its effects upon the behaviour and actions of those directly engaged, as he was to be himself, in fiscal practices. E.C. Pettet has argued that *The Merchant of Venice* 'contains one of Shakespeare's rare considerations of a major socio-economic problem of his time' (Pettet, 100). And he pinpointed the play's own investment in an economic practice that the sermon literature of the late sixteenth century had already vilified as a venal sin capable of undermining the very fabric of the social order.

Philip Caesar's *General Discourse Against the Damnable Sect of Usurers* (1578) was among the earliest of a number of tracts that regarded usury as 'the so beastlie and poysoned wickednesse' whose practitioners were 'worse then pagans, which are without Religion, wicked, not beleeuyng there is a God'. In his deployment of a series of images that were to become popular, he went on to conclude: 'thei are likened to poysoned serpentes, to mad Dogges, to greedie Wormes, to Wolues, Beares, and to such other rauening beastes' (Caesar, 4). In *The Death of Usury; or, The Disgrace of Usurers* (1594), published during the year of the revival of Marlowe's *Jew of Malta*, usury is defined as 'lending for *Gaine*', which was permitted in accordance with the Old Testament book of Deuteronomy. It was thought to have been forbidden by the New Testament Gospel according to St Luke, although it was later allowed by Calvin and Martin Bucer (*Death of Usury*, 5–6). The Puritan Henry Smith regarded the practice of usury as 'the vndoing of men' (7) and a manifestation of the biblical sin of covetousness.[1] Smith continued:

> Now, you long to heare what the Vsurer is like. To what shall I like[n] this generatio[n]? They are like the Butlers box: for as all the counters at last come to the Butler, so all the mony at last commeth to the Vsurer, ten after ten; and ten to ten, til at last he receiue not only ten for an hundreth, but an hundreth for ten. This is the onely difference, that the Butler can receiue no more than he deliuered: but the Vsurer receiueth more than he deliuereth. They are like a Moth; euen as a Moth eateth a hole in cloath, so Vsury eateth a hole in siluer.
>
> (H. Smith, 30–1)

Caesar had observed that usury was practised among Christians, and that 'amonge such as are called gentlemen' there was a tendency to sell their lands in order to take up the rootless, almost nomadic existence associated with usury (Caesar, sig. 4ᵛ). Indeed, Smith describes usurers as outsiders: 'Nonreside[n]ts, that is, such bad members, that no man speaketh for them but the[m]selues' (H. Smith, 31). In a series of sermons published in 1595 entitled *The Arraignment and Conviction of Usury* the churchman Miles Mosse advocates the 'fettering' of usurers 'with the vilest offenders, as those that deserued most shameful disgrace' (Mosse, 8). He advances a quasi-legal case against

---

1   See also Bell, who noted that 'usurie is prooued out of holy writ, to be one of the greatest sinnes', and asserts that usurers are 'unmercifull and very cruell men', that they are 'lyars and periured persons; as who by ioyning periurie to leasing, seeke to increase their sauage and brutish dealing' (Bell, sig. B4ᵛ).

usury and he cites both classical and biblical precedent in support of his argument:

> Tullie reckoneth Vsurers with Toll-takers and Customers, a kinde of men in those days of most base accompt and filthic conucrsation, as may be gatherd euen out of the holie scriptures. Aristotle sayth that Vsurers and Bawdes may well goe together: for they gaine by filthie meanes all they get. Saint Augustine coupleth them with Couetous men and Theeues. Musculus ioyneth Vsurie with Deceit, and Periurie. Lauater reciteth it with Drunkennes and Adulterie.
>
> (Mosse, 8)

Mosse hints at the latent sexual implications of usury as a profanation of all acts of exchange, and he goes on to outline a form of lending that is non-profit-making, that does not involve the process of objectifying value. This points us towards some of the possible motives for Antonio's willingness to loan Bassanio money: lending designed to 'gaine the fauor of God', to provide 'good example' or 'to purchase the loue or liking of another' (46). Mosse distinguishes between the activities of the usurer and 'the Merchant Adventurer', who, he argues, risks his wealth in the face of 'the ouerruling prouidence of God' that works 'when it pleaseth, sometimes beyond meanes, sometimes without meanes, sometimes contrarie to meanes: therefore is it that no man can say assuredly what the issue of any thing will proue' (56). This captures exactly the kind of uncertainty in which Shakespeare's Antonio finds himself, a potential Job at the mercy of divine providence, and a potential Christ-like scapegoat willing to risk all for someone other than himself for Christian love. In contrast, the usurer 'cloaks' his fraud and is both a many-headed monster and a serpent: 'Like are common vsurers unto the monster Hydra: for they haue many heades, that is, infinite deuises: and withall euery head is the head of a serpent: which serpent *was more subtile* (saith the scripture) *than*

15

any beaste of the fielde which the Lord God had made' (60). Deceit, monstrosity and animality provided the conceptual foundations for the specific figurations and representations of the usurer.

It is not until the fourth sermon that Mosse lumps together 'vsurers, Iewes, Disers, or gamesters, and blasphemers of God' (Mosse, 103). This distinction allows him to suggest at the end of his text that, despite the absence of Jews on English soil, usury continued to thrive. In the fifth sermon Mosse situates usury firmly in the realm of moral law and associates it with the prohibition of incest (Bell, 118–19).[1] For Mosse, of course, the animosity is fully justified, since what distinguishes the usurer from other men is his inhumanity, which he defines in terms which resonate in the text of the *Merchant of Venice*:

> It is no humanitie to drawe the dagger to stab a man, who is thine equall in yeeres and in valure of bodie. But for a man to drawe his weapon on a childe, who hath neither wisdome, nor strength to resist: is shamefull cowardnes, yea barbarous crueltie. So, it is inhumanitie for an vsurer to gripe a man that is rich and well able to pay: but with that sword of his, to runne quite thorough the heart of the needie (to whome it were more almes to giue the principall:) that, that is the horrible iniquitie which God specially, and by name hath as it were forbidden in those places of scripture, that make mention of the poore.
>
> (Mosse, 132–3)

The literal and metaphorical reference to the 'heart' and to the assault that usury mounts upon it, which is given a literal gloss in Shakespeare's play, affects both poor and rich alike. Moreover, the complex discourse that positions the usurer as the worldly

---

1   Both these claims are brought together in the allegation in the play that Salanio and Salarino level against the Jew's own response to the elopement of his daughter: 'My own flesh and blood to rebel' (3.1.31).

antithesis of all humane Christian values works to authenticate a network of social, political, economic and theological images that emerge as mythical formulations, and fuel what we now recognize as displaced forms of racism. It is these discourses that the *Merchant of Venice* dramatizes, emphasizing the stark contradiction inherent in the figure of the 'Jew' that Shakespeare identified as a 'type' but to whom he gave an English (Christian) name, 'Shylock' (Orgel, 'Shylock', 144–62).[1]

MARLOWE, SHAKESPEARE AND THE JEWS

The most popular dramatization of the figure of the Jew on the Elizabethan public stage was Marlowe's *The Jew of Malta* (*c*. 1592), a play that resurrected a number of anti-Semitic myths and situated them within an ethos of machiavellian intrigue. But Marlowe's play, like much of the contemporary writing of the period, makes only casual mention of the connection between Jews and usury. While communities of actual Jews in Elizabethan England have long been identified (see Wolf, 33–5, which contains a detailed list of names), there has always been controversy over whether they were engaged in espionage, or assimilated into the religious life of large cities such as London, or whether they continued to practise 'Jewish rites' privately (Wolf, 6–7). Above all, the figure of the Jew was associated throughout Europe during the Renaissance as someone whose religion allowed him to practise the lending of money at interest. Luther's poisonous diatribe *On the Jews and their Lies* (1543) posited a specific connection between Jews and usury, although it emerged as part of a more general expression of moral outrage and resentment at the Jewish claim to be God's chosen people:

> the Jews boast in their synagogues, praising and
> thanking God for sanctifying them through his law

---

1   I am grateful to Stephen Orgel for allowing me to see this chapter in advance of its publication.

and setting them apart as a peculiar people, although they know full well that they are not at all observing this law, that they are full of conceit, envy, usury, greed, and all sorts of malice. The worst offenders are those who pretend to be very devout and holy in their prayers. They are so blind that they not only practice usury – not to mention the other vices – but they teach that it is a right which God conferred on them through Moses. Thereby, as in all the other matters, they slander God most infamously.

(Luther, *Jews*, 168–9)

Luther goes on to identify the Jews as property-less exiles, who, through their usurious practices, 'skin and fleece' both Christian princes and their subjects (217–18). In this particularly offensive anti-Semitic invective Luther draws explicit attention to the Jews' preoccupation with usury that establishes this abiding stereotype[1] as the determining principle of religious, racial, moral and economic difference (see Fig. 2).

Luther's diatribe, which reaches its hideous apotheosis in Hitler's *Mein Kampf* (1933), locates the figure of the Jew within the discourses of economics and theology and it draws on a long-standing tradition of demonization that has been charted by a number of commentators (Trachtenberg; see also Sanders, 339–51). Jews had continued to be allowed to live and practise usury in Italian city-states such as Venice, but, even though they had been formally expelled from England in 1292, they continued to exert a powerful influence on the popular imagination. And it is within this tradition, where myth and fact jostled for supremacy, that the eponymous hero of Marlowe's *Jew of Malta* was firmly inscribed.

There is a general consensus amongst critics that Marlowe's play influenced Shakespeare, although M.M. Mahood represents

---

1 See Adolf Hitler, *Mein Kampf*, trans. Ralph Manheim (repr. 1996), which plumbs the depths of this Lutheran discourse.

2   Image of a Jew poisoning a well, from Pierre Boaistuau, *Certaine secrete wonders of nature* (1569)

a long line of critics who consider the *Merchant of Venice* to be 'a different kind of play and the product of a different kind of imagination' (Cam², 7–8). Some have argued that the later play stands in a critical, but unintentionally ironic, relation to the earlier one, and in particular that the figures of Barabas and

Ferneze in the *Jew of Malta* are transformed in the *Merchant of Venice* into Shylock and Antonio (Cartelli, 256–7). Others, such as James Shapiro, have taken a different tack altogether in claiming that Shakespeare simply failed either to successfully absorb or to contain Marlowe's powerful iconoclastic influence, with the result that a series of aesthetic and structural problems remain unresolved in the later play (Shapiro, '*Merchant*', 269ff.). Shapiro goes on to paint a picture of a nervous Shakespeare's psychological investment in 'the vicious circle of Girardian mimetic desire' as 'imitator and as shareholder in a rival company, implicated in a world of competitive appropriation' (270). Stephen Greenblatt identifies a 'disturbing perception of sameness' that is a characteristic feature of the Christian–Jew opposition in Marlowe's play, and that is converted 'into a re-assuring perception of difference' in the *Merchant of Venice*.[1] But in Shapiro's account this dialectical opposition ceases to be a feature of dramatic structure and becomes instead a question of authorial psychology resulting from a rationally disposed, possibly ironic, Shakespeare engaging with a subversive Marlovian quasi-carnivalesque energy that threatens to overwhelm the appropriator. These radically anarchic Marlovian energies are present in Shakespeare's play, but they are carefully, if not entirely successfully, embedded in a dramatic structure that owes less to the amoral impulses of machiavellian *realpolitik* than its predecessor.

The *Jew of Malta* was revived in the wake of the trial and execution in 1594 of Dr Roderigo Lopez, a Portugese Jewish physician and double agent who was accused of plotting to poison the queen. It is possible that a sense of theatricality infiltrated William Camden's account of the trial and execution of Lopez, and in particular the account of his final moments before execution in June 1594. Lopez was described by Camden as being 'of the *Jewish* sect', and having died 'affirming that

---

1 Stephen Greenblatt, *Learning to Curse: Essays in Early Modern Culture* (London and New York, 1990), 43.

he had loued the Queene as hee had loued *Iesus Christ*, which from a man of the *Iewish* profession was heard not without laughter' (Camden, 58–9).[1] Camden's straightforward linking of cause and effect makes more of Lopez's Jewishness than the actual accounts of his trial and especially his public execution, and does much to reaffirm the extent to which theatrical representation (possibly Marlowe's) influenced perception.[2] It is therefore unlikely that Shakespeare's imagination was stimulated primarily by the actual case of Dr Lopez, but rather by the complex theatrical and stereotypical representations of the figure of the Jew that could be deployed allegorically in order to focus upon a series of larger cultural questions.

Marlowe's play was again revived in 1596, and remained popular for some years after (*Jew of Malta*, 1). One of the evident objectives of the *Jew of Malta* was to submerge the difference between Christian, Jew and Turk in a machiavellian ethic that was universally applicable to them all. Marlowe also collapsed the difference between merchant adventurer and Jew that Shakespeare was concerned to emphasize. Barabas is wealthy but his usurious practice is only one of many commercial activities involving a long series of violations of morality: 'Then after that I was an usurer, / And with extorting, cozening, forfeiting, / And tricks belonging unto brokery, / I filled the jails with bankrupts in a year' (*Jew of Malta*, 2.3.192–5). Barabas's 'Of naught is nothing made' (1.2.105) gestures obliquely towards the sterile practice of generating money from money that Shylock will later seek to remystify, but he is shown to be initially sensitive to the ways in which his Christian persecutors justify their behaviour towards him. When the First Knight invokes the allegation of blood-guilt to justify Malta's attitude towards the Jew: ''Tis not our fault, but thy inherent sin' (1.2.110), Barabas

---

1   Stephen Greenblatt has suggested to me privately that the laughter of the crowd at Lopez's execution was provoked as much by their recollection of the theatrical figure of Marlowe's Barabas as it was by any ridicule of Lopez himself.
2   Cf. Stephen Greenblatt, *Will in The World: How Shakespeare Became Shakespeare* (2004), 277–8.

responds: 'What! Bring you scripture to confirm your wrongs?' (1.2.111). Shakespeare does not address this issue directly, but he does invert this sentiment in his ascription of the practice of quoting Scripture for devious purposes to the Jew. Here, as elsewhere, the *Merchant of Venice* enters into dialogue with the *Jew of Malta*, and the result is a critical discrimination of detail rather than an imitation.

The Barabas–Abigail relationship in Marlowe's play clearly provided a starting-point for Shakespeare's depiction of the Jew–Jessica relationship. Indeed, many critics have noted the verbal connection between Barabas's fulsome utterance at the moment when Abigail rescues his gold from a house that has been transformed into a nunnery: 'O my girl, / My gold, my fortune, my felicity' (*Jew of Malta*, 2.1.47–8). Salanio's reporting of Jessica's theft translates Barabas's sentiments into another key:

> I never heard a passion so confused,
> So strange, outrageous, and so variable
> As the dog Jew did utter in the streets:
> 'My daughter! O, my ducats! O, my daughter!
> Fled with a Christian! O, my Christian ducats!
> (2.8.12–16)

Further echoes, such as Ithamore's courting of the courtesan Bellamira with the line 'I'll be thy Jason, thou my golden fleece' (*Jew of Malta*, 4.2.96), may well have provided part of the inspiration for Bassanio's lines:

> her sunny locks
> Hang on her temples like a golden fleece,
> Which makes her seat of Belmont Colchis' strand,
> And many Jasons come in quest of her.
> (*MV* 1.1.169–72)[1]

---

1   The story of Jason's quest appears also in Ovid's *Metamorphoses*, book 7; see also Wheater, 16–36.

In each case Marlowe's savagely satiric tone, which serves to invoke a variety of stereotypes at the same time as he undermines their veracity, is transformed by Shakespeare into something more balanced, less exuberant and, at times, more conservative. Indeed, Irving Ribner noted that Shakespeare's play embodied 'an affirmation of ethical values basic to Christian belief', whereas Marlowe's play is anarchic in its refusal to offer any meaningful value at all (Ribner, 47; see also Greenblatt, *Renaissance*, 204–5).

Critics of the play have generally overlooked Barabas's identification of himself with the Old Testament figure of Job. In the opening scene Barabas is approached by three Jews, two of whom, Zaareth and Temainte, recall Job's comforters, Eliphaz the Temanite and Zophar the Naamathite. In the next scene the First Jew encourages Barabas to 'remember Job' (*Jew of Malta*, 1.2.181) as the model of patience when confronting adversity. But Barabas, unlike Job, curses his own birth and wishes 'for an eternal night, / That clouds of darkness may enclose my flesh, / And hide these extreme sorrows from mine eyes' (1.2.194–6). The biblical Job is also preoccupied with the organs of sight. For example, he laments that 'My face is withered with weping, & the shadow of death *is* vpon mine eies' (Job, 16.16); and when his tribulations end he acknowledges that he has hitherto been blind to God's providence: 'I haue heard of thee by the hearing of the eare, but now mine eye seeth thee' (Job, 42.5). This motif of suffering, announced with some seriousness in Marlowe's play, is adapted and dispersed in Shakespeare's narrative. The patriarchal Antonio becomes the temporary, Christian victim of misfortune, and is ultimately relieved by a mysterious providence, and Job's physical sufferings are relegated to the comic interlude of the Clown and Old Giobbe in the *Merchant of Venice* as an opportunistic variation on the theme of patriarchal adversity.[1]

1   See Levith, 95–106, where it is argued that the Clown–Iobbe episode, and other areas of the play, also owe much to Marlowe's *Dr Faustus*.

However, unlike Marlowe's play, which foregrounds the 'tragedy' of 'The Rich Jew of Malta', Shakespeare's play relegates the narrative of 'the extreame crueltie of *Shylocke* the Iewe' to a secondary role in the 'Historie of the *Merchant of Venice*'. Marlowe's Jew is destroyed by a machiavellian political practice of dissimulation and intrigue that infects Jew and Christian alike, whereas Shakespeare's Jew is ultimately incorporated (though unwillingly) into the Christian ethos of Venice. Marlowe's play conflates 'Jew' and 'merchant', whereas Shakespeare maintains a distinction between them, notwithstanding the apparent confusion that some critics have ascribed to Portia's question about identities at 4.1.170: 'Which is the merchant here, and which the Jew?'[1]

In representing two 'bogeymen' figures on the stage: the Jew and the Machiavel, Marlowe's dramatic technique is predominantly that of savage caricature. But the recent history of anti-Semitism has made modern audiences and readers more sensitive to the way in which both he and Shakespeare conceived the figure of the Jew. In the *Merchant of Venice* the Jew is a theatrical stereotype, a cultural fantasy, invoked as a manifestation of the principle of *otherness* against which Venice is made to define its own identity. He is also, as G.K. Hunter observed, part of 'a long patristic tradition' that regarded 'Jewishness as a moral condition', in a culture for which the epithet 'Jew', like that of 'Turk' or 'Moor', was 'a word of general abuse' 'dependent on a theological rather than an ethnographical framework' (Hunter, 65–6). This observation, however, masks the manner in which racial discourse such as anti-Semitism seeks to derive authority and legitimacy for its attitudes and actions. Moreover, Hunter implies that there is a historical break between the tradition that emanates from an essentially medieval conception of Judaism and modern anti-Semitism. Here the figure of the Renaissance stage Jew is characterized as a revenant from the past whose own

---

1   Cf. Moisan, 188–206. For an earlier contrast between Barabas and Shylock and between the Christians in Marlowe's and Shakespeare's play, see Poel, 1–12.

pedigree must be distinguished from the complex lives of 'real' Renaissance Jews, and whose identity is radically different from that of modern counterparts. This is a naïve historicization that Joshua Trachtenberg and others have sought to counter in his claim that the various allegations made against Jews, which are always the '*immediate* stimuli of active Jew hatred', have their ultimate source in a 'mass subconscious' that 'is still untouched' (Trachtenberg, 2–3). It is Shakespeare's innovation to present a composite being who is at one level true to 'type',[1] but who at another level is an individualized being who is able, for parts of the play, at least, to resist these cultural ascriptions.

Marlowe's *Jew of Malta* encapsulated a discourse that may have helped to shape the popular perception of actual events, but there is, however, a historical and critical tradition that has sought to establish the realistic origins of Shakespeare's depiction of the Jew.[2] David Lasocki's *The Bassanos: Venetian Musicians and Instrument Makers in England, 1531–1665* (1995) suggests a link between the family name 'Bassano' and Shakespeare's Bassanio. And he extends the connection to the historical figure of Emilia Lanyer, the younger daughter of Baptista Bassano, who is also a prime candidate for the identity of the Dark Lady of the Sonnets, and who was, in 1594, a mistress of Shakespeare's theatrical patron

1   See Harris, 80. Harris argues that Marlowe's Jew is 'a poisoning anal infiltrator as well as a dangerously effective mimic, against whom the Christian body politic must defend itself', but he also insists that the play 'utilises the disruptive potential of these stereotypes to perform a thorough critique of the Christian authorities who oppose themselves to him' (Harris, 80). Harris goes on to untangle the association of Jews with poison in his account of the Lopez affair and attempts to link Elizabeth's Portuguese Jewish physician with the figure of 'the dissembling Jew as theatrical, inconstant, slippery, impossible to pin down, but nonetheless luridly entertaining' (Harris, 106).

2   Shapiro, *Jews*, 46ff. Shapiro attempts to negotiate the historical distinction between the existence of ethnic Jews in Renaissance England, and the range of paranoid representations of the figure of the Jew as a focus of a series of social and psychological projections. He follows those commentators who seek to identify communities of Jews living in sixteenth-century England, and he draws attention to a number of circumstantial details that some have recently sought to align with elements of Shakespeare's play.

Lord Chamberlain Earl Hunsdon.[1] It is possible that Shakespeare had in mind the name 'Bassano' when he constructed the dramatic character 'Bassanio', and the associations that the play makes with the harmonizing power of music are suggestive.[2] But whether the name pointed to a covertly Jewish identity destined to disrupt the play's final image of circumscribed marital harmony, as Eric Mallin has suggested, is questionable on historical grounds, as are the connections that Lasocki and Prior make between the 'dark' Emilia Bassano, and the female Moor whom the allegedly sexually inadequate Lancelet is accused of impregnating (Lasocki & Prior, 134).

It is Shapiro's contention, and that of Joshua Trachtenberg before him, that in early modern England Jewishness was synonymous with criminality and 'invariably hidden and insidious, a secret waiting to be unearthed' (Shapiro, *Jews*, 9). Marlowe's Barabas exults in a catalogue of crimes that he shares with his slave Ithamore: they include killing 'sick people under walls', poisoning wells, murder generally, political duplicity, a host of deceptions and, of course, usury (*Jew of Malta*, 2.3.176–204).[3] However, Shakespeare's Jew initially rejects Bassanio's dinner invitation on the grounds that to eat pork would be 'to eat of the habitation which your prophet the Nazarite conjured the devil into' (1.3.30–1) In this he resembles the Jew Jonathas in the *Croxton Play of the Sacrament* (c. 1461) who rejects Christian social ritual, and who alleges the fraudulence of the Eucharist:

---

1 See Lasocki and Prior, 101ff. and 132. See also ch. 6, 'The Bassanos' Jewish identity', 92ff., although no clear evidence is adduced to confirm that the Bassanos were practising Jews: 'No single piece of surviving evidence proves conclusively that the Bassanos were Jews or of Jewish origin, yet a wealth of circumstantial evidence strongly suggests so' (Lasocki & Prior, 92).

2 See Eric S. Mallin, 'Jewish invader and the soul of state: *The Merchant of Venice* and science fiction movies', in Hugh Grady (ed.), *Shakespeare and Modernity* (London and New York, 2000), 163–4, for the suggestion that the name 'Bassano' suggests an alien presence whom Portia 'may have a harder time expelling . . . than she thought' (164).

3 For Ithamore's shorter but no less spectacular catalogue of crimes, see *Jew of Malta*, 2.3.205–14.

'And thus be a conceyte þe wolde make us blynd: / And how þat yt shuld be he that deyed upon þe Rode' (ll.123–4; Walker, 218).

In Shakespeare's play the process of demonization works both ways, since from the Jew's perspective the Christian Venetians are diabolical, whereas for the latter the Jew is the devil incarnate (1.3.94; 2.2.21–3). It was William Hazlitt who observed that, although Shylock was 'the depository of the vengeance of his race' whose bitterness has 'hardened him against the contempt of mankind', this contributed 'but little to the triumphant pretensions of his enemies' (Furness, 427). However, even though Shakespeare's play contains less of the inventive Marlovian detail that we find in the *Jew of Malta*, the invective directed against the Jew derives much of its malicious energy from a religious hostility that is the discursive register of an intolerant racism. For those who would rescue the play for a humanist perspective, it is possible to read the Jew's own reactions to his persecution as a principled critique of Christian Venice, although this position is not without its difficulties.

Stage representations that are not validated by actual social example, such as those of Barabas or Shylock, straddle an important conceptual divide. The stage-Jew looks backwards to a distant past and is the sum total of fantasies which emerge within what Benedict Anderson has called 'the religious community' (Anderson, 12ff.). These fantasies, these representations, are powerful and historically durable – child murder, well-poisoning, symbolic castration, apostasy, male menstruation, the commitment to money and to economic individualism – and they form part of that *otherness* against which communal identity asserts itself. Jean-François Lyotard insists that the figure of the 'jew' is an orientalist creation whose origins are rooted in a deeply Christian anxiety. He argues:

> 'The jews' are the irremissible in the West's movement of remission and pardon. They are what cannot be domesticated in the obsession to

dominate, in the compulsion to control domain, in the passion for empire, recurrent ever since Hellenistic Greece and Christian Rome. 'The jews' never at home where they are, cannot be integrated, converted, or expelled. They are also always away from home when they are at home, in their so-called own tradition, because it includes exodus as its beginning, excision, impropriety, and respect for the forgotten.

(Lyotard, 3)

Writing from the other side of the Holocaust, and with an acute awareness of the postmodern condition, Lyotard wrestles with the problem of how to represent that which, by definition, resists representation. For him, western anti-Semitism – what he calls 'the anti-Semitism of the Occident' – is not to be confused with xenophobia, but with the desire to incorporate a radical otherness into its structures. It is 'one of the means of the apparatus of its culture to bind and represent as much as possible – to protect against the originary terror, actively to forget it' (23). This challenge to an identity politics that perceives in the *Merchant of Venice* a mimetic representation of an actual Jew is an attempt to confront western Christian culture with its own discomforting limitations, in which the figure of 'the jew' functions as an excess that always escapes representation. Lyotard continues:

One converts the Jews in the Middle Ages, they resist by mental restriction. One expels them during the classical age, they return. One integrates them in the modern era, they persist in their difference. One exterminates them in the twentieth century.

(23)

The cultural mechanisms for which Lyotard seeks to offer an account emerge in late sixteenth-century England as a confrontation between a troubled Christianity and its own uncertain limitations, particularly those that impinge upon the proscription of certain kinds of economic activity. It also raises fundamental questions of what meanings the *Merchant of Venice* generates through the various conversions that take place in the play: from Jew to Christian, from bachelor to married man, from virgin to wife. Are these, as Leslie Fiedler once suggested, analogues of potentially disruptive energies that only the communal (and in this case theatrical) reaffirmation of social rituals can contain?

The shift of emphasis in much contemporary criticism of the *Merchant of Venice*, from an essentially mimetic commitment to social realism, to larger questions of representation, is a recent one. In a 1990 essay that attempts, sometimes uncomfortably, to straddle this divide, Stephen Greenblatt begins with the assertion that 'Marlowe and Marx seize upon the Jew as a kind of powerful rhetorical device, a way of marshalling deep popular hatred and clarifying its object' (Greenblatt, 'Marlowe', 41). But he also, and quite rightly, finds the diminution of 'a people' to the status of 'a rhetorical device' offensive, partly because he does not wish to forsake the important connection that we habitually sustain between language and the world:

> Our belief in language's capacity for reference is part of our contract with the world; the contract may be playfully suspended or broken altogether but no abrogation is without consequences, and there are circumstances where the abrogation is unacceptable. The existence or absence of a real world, real body, real pain, makes all the difference.
>
> (Greenblatt, 'Marlowe', 15)

This is an important caveat, but one that Greenblatt himself finds it difficult to maintain in the face of his tentative perception that Shylock is the embodiment of 'the abstract principle of *difference* itself' (15). Greenblatt is torn here between two contradictory experiences of Marlowe's play, in which the Jew's *otherness* is articulated as an unstable assembly of cultural meanings to which Marc Shell has drawn our attention (Shell, 48–9; see also Drakakis, '*Jew*', 114ff.) and a mimetic representation of an ethnic identity. James Shapiro formulates the historical ideational distortion that Greenblatt finds discomforting, and that Lyotard is at great pains to avoid, in his observation that in late sixteenth-century England 'theology is not juxtaposed with racial thinking; in fact it helps produce and define it' (Shapiro, *Jews*, 84).

What makes the *Merchant of Venice* a racist text is that the dramatic action turns upon an acknowledgement of *difference* that is, in Albert Memmi's pregnant phrase, used 'against someone to one's own advantage' (Memmi, 52), at the same time that it fuels a judgemental laughter. Not merely that, but Memmi goes on to describe it as '*a racism specific to its object*' (67) in which persecutor and victim exist in close proximity to each other as both 'familiar and alien'. It is, he says, 'an act of stigmatizing the other for one's own consolation, through the deployment of respective differences' (68).[1] Nowhere is that difference more obvious – in the play, but more often in critical practice – than in what Terry Eagleton has called 'a sophisticated piece of Christian anti-Semitism' whereby the Judaeo-Christian tradition makes a categorical distinction between a superseded 'Old' Testament legalism, replete with its emphasis on ritual observance, and a 'New' Testament commitment to 'love and interiority' (Eagleton, 165–6). Shakespeare's Jew, like his Christian Venetians, is heavily implicated in this racist economy, but in Shylock's case the stereotype is given a more perplexing gloss, indicating a greater range of meanings than the term 'Jew' as a signifier of racial difference alone would suggest.

1   But see also Greenblatt, 'Marlowe', 43, where he argues that Shakespeare 'compels the audience to transform its disturbing perception of sameness into a reassuring perception of difference'.

THE CON-TEXTS OF
THE MERCHANT OF VENICE

In addition to those narratives that centred on the Venetian republic, on the status of Jews and on usury, others circulated that are also directly linked to Shakespeare's play. In his eight-volume *Narrative and Dramatic Sources of Shakespeare* (1977) Geoffrey Bullough sought to produce 'a working collection of the sources and analogues' that the dramatist is thought to have used, although he subjugated them to the task of exploring 'the working of Shakespeare's mind' (Bullough, 1.x). Bullough's project is conservatively historical, but more recently scholars have forced a reconsideration of the figure of author 'within a heterogeneous dispersal' of discourses that Jonathan Goldberg designates as 'history' (Goldberg, 'Speculations', 242; repr. in Goldberg, *Hand*, 152–75). Such historicist and textualist manoeuvres invite reconsideration of the complex ways in which a variety of texts circulate and interact with each other. Francis Barker and Peter Hulme coined the term 'con-text' in order to capture this sense both of the text's inscription in history and of its dynamic interaction with other texts (Barker & Hulme, 191–4).

From the moment of its composition – some time after the midsummer of 1596 and the date of its appearance in the Stationers' Register in July 1598 – and its first performance, probably in the twenty months or so between autumn 1596 and July 1598, the *Merchant of Venice* can be shown to engage dynamically with a series of texts to which its relation is not strictly linear or hierarchical. Editorial speculation has extended from the positing of a lost play mentioned by Stephen Gosson in his *School of Abuse* (1578) as 'The *Iew*' played at the Red Bull theatre in Clerkenwell, to extant plays such as Robert Wilson's *The Three Ladies of London* (1584, repr. 1592), to prose texts such as Anthony Munday's *Zelauto* (1580) or Silvayn's *Declamation 95* from *The Orator* (1596), through to Giovanni

Fiorentino's *Il Pecorone*, published in Milan in 1558, and for which no contemporary English translation is known. Particular elements of the play, such as the 'casket' story, can be traced back to Boccaccio's *Decameron*, Richard Robinson's translation of the *Gesta Romanorum* (1575, repr. 1595) and to John Gower's *Confessio Amantis*, Book 5. Moreover, the introduction of a patriarchally controlled 'lottery' recalls the practice of election to political office in Venice that Contarini described in his *Commonwealth and Government of Venice* (1599). The lost play, *The Jew*, apparently represented 'the greedinesse of worldly chusers, and the bloody mindes of Usurers' (Bullough, 1.445–6; see also Burckhardt, 249–50), and along with the story of Ancelmus the Emperor from the *Gesta Romanorum* (Bullough, 1.511–14) may have helped to provide Shakespeare with the idea for the episodes involving the choice of caskets. What we do not know is precisely how allegorical the depictions of the individual characters in this lost play were, or indeed how, and in what form, they may have been accessible to Shakespeare.

In an influential account of the ways in which 'traditional forms of dramaturgy are turned into modern modes of characterization' on the Elizabethan stage, Robert Weimann develops the concept of *figurenposition*. This seeks to explain breaks in the dramatic illusion that inadvertently expose the traditional conventions of theatrical representation and characterization (Weimann, *Tradition*, 233). For example, Robert Wilson's late morality play *The Three Ladies of London* (1584, repr. 1592) anticipates in allegorical form some of the motifs of Shakespeare's play. Wilson's three ladies of the title are personified abstractions: Love, Lucre and Conscience, but it is Lucre and her 'secretarie' Usury who provide the stimulus for travel.[1] In a conversation with Usury, Lucre discloses her own pedigree, 'But Usurie didst thou never know my grandmother the old Ladie Lucar of Venice?' (sig. B1ᵛ), and then asks

---

1 'For Lucar men come from Italy, Barbarie, Turkie, / from Jurie: nay the Pagan him-selfe, / Indangers his bodie to gape for her pelfe' (*Three Ladies*, sig. A2ᵛ).

Usurie: 'But why camst thou into England seing Venice is a citie where Usurie by Lucar may live in great glorie?' (sig. B1ᵛ). Usury's response establishes a hereditary link between Italy and London,[1] although in a later play, *The Three Lords of London* (1590), Usury's parents are 'both Jewes, though thou wert borne in London' (STC 25783: sig. F4ʳ). Ultimately, one of the three lords, Policy, curbs the interest that Usury can charge, insisting that 'Londons Pomp is not sustained by Usury, / But by well-ventured marchandise and honest industrie' (sig. H3ʳ).

In *Three Ladies of London* Usury's role as Lucre's secretary is 'to deale amongst merchants, to bargen and exchange money' (sig. B1ᵛ). Wilson's play establishes a connection between the practice of usury and mercantilist practice, and it links these activities together, both genealogically and geographically, with the figure of the Jew Gerontius and the merchant Mercadorus. Indeed, in a legal judgement concerning Mercadorus's repayment of a debt to Gerontius, the latter's humanity prompts the judge to declare acerbically: 'One may iudge and speake truth as appears by this, / Jewes seeke to excell in Christianity, & Christians in Jewishnes' (sig. F1ʳ). Jews could imitate Christians in the same way that Christians could imitate Jews, a view that is echoed frequently in some of the usury tracts of the period. The *Merchant of Venice* recuperates these details, but also represents a decisive break with such traditional formal features of theatrical representation in its folding of the kind of dramaturgy that Wilson deployed into more sophisticated forms of characterization. But an Elizabethan audience watching Shakespeare's play would almost certainly have carried with it a knowledge of the moral abstractions situated just beneath the surface of characterizations that

---

1   'I have often heard your good grandmother tell / that she had in England a daughter which her farre did excell: / And that England was such a place for Lucar to hide, / as was not in Europe and the whole world beside: / then lusting greatly to see you and the countrey, she being dead, / I made haste to come over to serve you instead' (*Three Ladies*, sig. B1ᵛ).

we have become accustomed to reading primarily for their psychological verisimilitude.

Bullough identifies the *Three Ladies of London* as an 'analogue' (Bullough, 1.476), although the play disperses throughout its morality structure a number of elements that the *Merchant of Venice* draws together and individualizes. Shakespeare's text generates one kind of inflection of this material, while a nearly contemporaneous play, such as Marlowe's *Jew of Malta*, another analogue text, offers another. The *Three Ladies of London* was evidently popular and the text reveals evidence of having derived from the theatre. Moreover, the play's narrative involving an Italianate merchant, a Jew and a usurer, a marriage between Love and Money, along with sundry refinements developed in other texts, indicates how these interconnected details might have circulated in the Elizabethan popular consciousness.

Some of the narrative strands contained in the *Merchant of Venice* already had a long history by 1596–7. The so-called 'flesh-bond' may be traced back to the *Mahabarata* (Bullough, 1.446–7) but it was given a contemporary significance in Lazarus Piot's translation of Alexander Silvayn's *The Orator*, which appeared in print in 1596. Lazarus Piot was the pseudonym for Anthony Munday, whose own *Zelauto* (1580) also contained material relevant to Shakespeare's play (see Hamilton, 89–99). The circumstances in Munday's translation of Silvayn's *Declamation 95* of *The Orator* are, in part, similar to the episode in Wilson's play: a Turkish setting and a Christian merchant indebted to a Jew, who then defaults on the debt. But the Jew in Silvayn's narrative is not benign in his rejecting payment of a bond and demanding a pound of the merchant's flesh (Bullough, 1.484). It is tempting to conflate the Jew's allusion to castration with the act of circumcision: 'what a matter were it then, if I should cut of his privie members, supposing that the same would altogether weigh a just pound?' (Bullough, 1.484)[1]

In the *Merchant of Venice* it is Portia herself who reluctantly acknowledges the necessity of her father's 'law' as a means of curbing those libidinous impulses situated in her 'blood'. The play turns upon the semantic instability of 'flesh' and 'blood' and, despite the limited emphasis that James Shapiro places upon the word 'flesh' in the play (Shapiro, *Jews*, 121–2), it is 'blood' that is ultimately emphasized as the sign of patrilinear legitimacy. Blood is the bodily location of unrestrained carnal desire (the properties of youth but also the attributes of cultural otherness), and it also figures as the juridical absence that ultimately invalidates the Jew's bond. Portia emphasizes the generational instability of the meanings attached to 'blood' at 1.2 when she laments the cripplingly patriarchal restraint embodied in the brain's capacity to 'devise laws for the blood' that frustrates youth's venereal 'hot temper' to leap 'o'er a cold decree' (1.2.17–18). Salarino reiterates the point later in the play, and in a manner that suggests a perversion of youthful sexual energy, when he responds to the Jew's astonishment at his daughter's rebellion: 'My own flesh and blood to rebel!' (3.1.31).

> There is more difference between thy flesh and hers than between jet and ivory, more between your bloods than there is between red wine and Rhenish.
>
> (3.1.34–6)[2]

At issue here is the difference between the external marker of an identity that Jews shared with other infidels, and the internal sign of Christian salvation, which, thanks to a Pauline 'symbolic displacement', recuperated the ritual through the metaphor of

---

1 Shapiro, *Jews*, 119, comments on the emphasis placed upon the corruption of the 'flesh' in the Geneva Bible gloss on Genesis, 17.11, and the 1591 Bishops' Bible gloss on Deuteronomy, 30.3. For a fuller, psychoanalytical account of the meaning of circumcision, especially in Freud, see Sander Gilman, *Freud, Race, and Gender* (Princeton, NJ, 1993), 49–92.
2 See Appendix 1 for the suggestion that the parts of the Jew and Morocco might have been doubled.

the circumcised heart (Shapiro, *Jews*, 129).[1] Shylock's original bond specified 'an equal pound / Of your fair flesh, to be cut off and taken / In what part of your body pleaseth me' (1.3.145–7); and Antonio, deprived of his mercantile livelihood, later sees himself as 'a tainted wether [i.e. a castrated ram] of the flock' (4.1.113). By the time of the arraignment, however, the Jew's bond is made more specific: 'lawfully by this the Jew may claim / A pound of flesh, to be by him cut off / Nearest the merchant's heart' (4.1.227–9). We should be careful here not to read this narrative narrowly in terms of the Freudian account of castration anxiety. Silvayn's Jew gives his Christian debtor a choice that Shakespeare denies to Antonio and, in doing so, like Shylock, emphasizes the symbolic rather than the literal nature of the gesture. It is left to Silvayn's Christian, however, to expose the contradiction that lies at the root of the Jew's appeal to the law:

> But it is no marvaile if this race be so obstinate
> and cruell against us, for they doe it of set purpose
> to offend our God whom they have crucified: and
> wherefore? Because he was holie, as he is yet so
> reputed of this worthy Turkish nation: but what
> shall I say? Their own bible is full of their rebellion
> against God, against their Priests, Judges, & leaders.
>   (Bullough, 1.486)

The figure of the rebellious Jew who was responsible for the Crucifixion was re-enacted in myths of the mutilation of the Christian host as evidenced in the *Croxton Play of the Sacrament*, and provided a clear theological justification for racism. Remarkably, it also permitted a distinction to be made

---

1   Cf. Derrida, 'Translation', 431. Derrida views the Pauline 'circumcision of the heart' as part of a complex thematic network of 'translations' that the play negotiates involving 'the relation of the letter to the spirit, of the body of literalness to the ideal interiority of sense [that] is also the site of the passage of translation' ('Translation', 431).

between Jew and Turk that Shakespeare's later *Othello* (1604) all but conflates.

Silvayn's *Declamation 95* was one of a number of dialogues that were both exemplary and topical. We have no way of knowing if, or how, Shakespeare recalled or used it during the composition of the *Merchant of Venice*. But its interweaving of detail reveals a complex Renaissance psychopathology at some distance from Freud, and a discourse that implicates an 'officially discountenanced position'[1] such as that of the figure of the Jew, in the discourses of fiscal practice, religion, politics and the law. These elements receive different emphases in a series of fictional narratives within whose contours Shakespeare's text is embedded.

Almost all of the basic elements of the plot of the *Merchant of Venice* are contained in Ser Giovanni Fiorentino's *Il Pecorone* ('The Simpleton') (1558). They involve Giannetto (Bassanio), the third son of a rich Florentine merchant, Bindo, who is instructed by his dying father to go to Venice and to seek out his rich godfather, Ansaldo (Antonio), in the expectation of becoming his heir. While in Venice, Giannetto is persuaded to visit Damascus, but en route he encounters 'a sea-gulf with a fine port' which, he is told, belongs to the 'beautiful and capricious' lady of Belmonte (Portia),[2] a widow who has 'ruined many gentlemen' by persuading them to wager their wealth against their ability to afford her sexual satisfaction. Giannetto fails the test twice and in the process impoverishes his godfather, who is deceived into financing a third, successful, expedition with money borrowed from a Jewish usurer with whom he is forced to enter into a flesh-bond. Ansaldo is saved from the consequences of the bond by the interference of the lady, who, disguised as a lawyer, demands a ring as payment for her legal services. This provides both the means and the occasion for her

1   The phrase is Jonathan Goldberg's; see Goldberg, 'Speculations', 243.
2   Editors have consistently neglected to gloss 'Belmont' in Shakespeare's text, but the prefix 'Bel' may be taken to mean 'beautiful' and 'monte' is both a mountain or hill, and also signifies 'a banke of monie' (Florio, 321).

testing of the fidelity of her new husband. The quasi-parental relationship between Ansaldo and Giannetto eliminates from the narrative a sexual tension that many modern productions of Shakespeare's play, in particular Trevor Nunn's 1999 National Theatre production, and some commentators, have discerned in the Antonio–Bassanio–Portia triangle. Ser Giovanni's narrative embeds what is essentially a romantic plot in an ethos in which love is intimately connected with wealth, and where the ways of the world threaten to engulf the unwary. But the manner of securing an appropriate suitor for the Lady of Belmonte is very different from the casket test that the *Merchant of Venice* utilizes.

Another version, Munday's *Zelauto: The Fountain of Fame Erected in an Orchard of Amorous Adventures* (1580), concludes with the story of the amorous pursuit by the young scholar Strabino (Bassanio) of Cornelia (Portia), the sister of the 'martiall gentleman' Rodolpho (Lorenzo) and the daughter of a Veronese householder, Giorolamo Ruscelli. Giorolamo arranges for Cornelia to marry Truculento, a Christian usurer, described as a 'carpet knight' (Munday, 130), but, with the aid of Rodolpho and with money borrowed from Truculento to purchase a costly jewel as a present for Giorolamo, Strabino elopes with Cornelia, and Rodolpho with Truculento's daughter Brisana (Jessica). Here the usurer is implicated directly in the romantic plot, and this is the motivation for his insistence upon the precise terms of the loan, which, according to most modern theatre directors, motivates Shylock's insistence upon the literal terms of his bond. In Munday's version Rodolpho stipulates that the penalty for non-payment will be that Strabino will 'forfayte his patrimony, and besydes the best lym of his body' (139). But, because Rodolpho is willing to suffer the same penalty for his friend, Truculento stipulates that 'eache of your Lands shall stand to the endamagement, besides the loss of bothe your right eyes' (140). Giorolamo's opposition to Strabino carries with it an allegorical charge: 'You are a young Gentleman, youthfull and lyberall, and will spend more in a day: then he in a yeere, he is warie and wise, you youthfull and prodigal, therefore the match is otherwise determined' (144). It is this exercise of patriarchal power that provokes the elopements of Strabino and Cornelia, and Rodolfo and Brisana. Truculento proceeds to law, where he invokes 'firm affection and pure zeale of friendshippe, [that] mooued me to minde the destitute estate of these two Gentlemen, when as either they had not money to their contentment: or wanted such necessaries, as was to them needefull' (148). In court it is Strabino who vilifies Truculento, deploying a series of stock arguments against the usurer (150). The judge appeals to Christian love and compares Truculento's request with the cruelty of the Turk, 'whose tyranny is not to be talked of' (150). When the judge offers the defendants the chance of summoning 'Attourneyes', Truculento 'fared like a fiend, and curssed and banned like a Diuell of hell' (153), and it is Truculento's daughter Brisana, Shakespeare's Jessica, who pleads first, followed by Cornelia (Portia). At the end Truculento is defeated, but seeing no alternative he accepts Rodolpho 'for his lawfull sonne, and put[s] him in possession of all his lyvinges after his disease' (156). Munday's narrative partly resembles some elements of *The Taming of the Shrew* (Bullough, 1.453), but it anticipates particular details of the *Merchant of Venice*, in its account of the ambivalent identity of the usurer, in some of the language in which it describes usury and in certain elements of the plot that are similar to those of the later play.

In addition to these substantial narratives, there are others that share certain details with the text of the *Merchant of Venice*. Bullough cites the fourteenth story of Massucio's *Il Novellino*, one not translated into English, but which, along with Marlowe's *Jew of Malta*, contains the substance of the Lorenzo–Jessica plot. Also, some of the elements of the 'caskets' episode can be traced back to Boccaccio's *Decameron*, Richard Robinson's translation of the *Gesta Romanorum*, first translated into English in 1575 and reprinted in 1595, and John Gower's *Confessio Amantis*, Book 5. The introduction of a patriarchally

39

controlled 'lottery' echoes the procedures of election to political office that were followed in Venice, which Contarini outlines at considerable length in his *Commonwealth and Government of Venice* (1599).

Such is the dispersal of this narrative material that it is as likely that these stories were, in diverse forms, part of an Elizabethan folk consciousness, and hence accessible as part of a larger oral tradition to writers for the popular theatre who were eager to engage with their audiences. Indeed, they were part of a rich tapestry of collective fantasies, which could be moulded, embellished, inflected, adjusted and transformed, and which were capable of endlessly innovative repetition.

WHAT'S IN A NAME?

To the traces of other 'con-texts' that we may detect in the fictional narratives that comprise the *Merchant of Venice*, we must also add the narrative of the book's material production as the manuscript supplied to James Roberts passed through the hands of his compositors. Appendix 3 contains a brief history of the printing of Q1 (1600) and its relation to Q2 (1619) and F (1623), and the relevant bibliographical details that support the following argument. Each of the three texts of the *Merchant of Venice* diverges from one another in matters of minor detail, but common to all is a variation in a group of speech prefixes to whose significance literary commentators have hitherto given scant attention.[1] R.B. McKerrow noted the *Iew(e)/Shy(l)* variations (see Fig. 3) and the *Lancelet/Launcelet/Clowne* variations, and although he mentioned the Clown's surname Iobbe he did not discuss it further. Capell (1768) opted to normalize *Lancelet/Launcelot* as *Clowne*, and,

---

1   R.B. McKerrow, 'A suggestion regarding Shakespeare's manuscripts', *RES*, 11, 44 (1935), 45–65; repr. in George Williams. McKerrow was among the first to notice that there were both regularities and variations in the setting of early playtexts, and he posed the question of the meaning 'of this difference between regularity and irregularity in the way in which speakers' names were shown'.

178   *The Merchant of Venice.*

How dost thou like the Lord *Bassiano's* wife?
Iessi. Past all expressing, it is very meete
The Lord *Bassanio* liue an vpright life
For hauing such a blessing in his Lady,
He findes the ioyes of heauen heere on earth,
And if on earth he doe not meane it, it
Is reason he should neuer come to heauen?
Why, if two gods should play some heauenly match,
And on the wager lay two earthly women,
And *Portia* one: there must be something else
Paund with the other, for the poore rude world
Hath not her fellow.
  Loren. Euen such a husband
Hast thou of me, as she is for a wife.
  Ies. Nay, but aske my opinion to of that?
  Lor. I will anone, first let vs goe to dinner?
  Ies. Nay, let me praise you while I haue a stomacke?
  Lor. No pray thee, let it serue for table talke,
Then how som ere thou speakst 'mong other things,
I shall digest it?
  Iessi. Well, Ile set you forth.   *Exeunt.*

Actus Quartus.

Enter the Duke, the Magnificoes, Anthonio, Bassanio, and Gratiano.

  Duke. What, is *Anthonio* heere?
  Ant. Ready, so please your grace?
  Duke. I am sorry for thee, thou art come to answere
A stonie aduersary, an inhumane wretch,
Vncapable of pitty, voyd, and empty
From any dram of mercie.
  Ant. I haue heard
Your Grace hath tane great paines to qualifie
His rigorous course: but since he stands obdurate,
And that no lawful meanes can carrie me
Out of his enuies reach, I do oppose
My patience to his fury, and am arm'd
To suffer with a quietnesse of spirit,
The very tiranny and rage of his.
  Du. Go one and cal the Iew into the Court.
  Sal. He is ready at the doore, he comes my Lord.

Enter Shylocke.

  Du. Make roome, and let him stand before our face.
Shylocke the world thinkes, and I thinke so to
That thou but leadest this fashion of thy mallice
To the last houre of act, and then 'tis thought
Thou'lt shew thy mercy and remorse more strange,
Than is thy strange apparant cruelty;
And where thou now exact'st the penalty,
Which is a pound of this poore Merchants flesh,
Thou wilt not onely loose the forfeiture,
But touch'd with humane gentlenesse and loue:
Forgiue a moytie of the principall,
Glancing an eye of pitty on his losses
That haue of late so hudled on his backe,
Enow to presse a royall Merchant downe,
And plucke commiseration of his state
From brassie bosomes, and rough hearts of flints,
From stubborne Turkes and Tarters neuer traind

To offices of tender curtesie,
We all expect a gentle answer Iew?
  Iew. I haue possest your grace of what I purpose,
And by our holy Sabbath haue I sworne
To haue the due and forfeit of my bond.
If you denie it, let the danger light
Vpon your Charter, and your Cities freedome,
You'l aske me why I rather choose to haue
A weight of carrion flesh, then to receiue
Three thousand Ducats? Ile not answer that:
But say it is my humor; Is it answer'd?
What if my house be troubled with a Rat,
And I be pleas'd to giue ten thousand Ducates
To haue it bain'd? What, are you answer'd yet?
Some men there are loue not a gaping Pigge:
Some that are mad, if they behold a Cat:
And others, when the bag-pipe sings i'th nose,
Cannot containe their Vrine for affection.
Masters of passion swayes it to the moode
Of what it likes or loaths, now for your answer:
As there is no firme reason to be rendred
Why he cannot abide a gaping Pigge?
Why he a harmlesse necessarie Cat?
Why he a woollen bag-pipe: but of force
Must yeeld to such ineuitable shame,
As to offend himselfe being offended:
So can I giue no reason, nor I will not,
More then a lodg'd hate, and a certaine loathing
I beare *Anthonio*, that I follow thus
A loosing suite against him? Are you answered?
  Bass. This is no answer thou vnfeeling man,
To excuse the currant of thy cruelty.
  Iew. I am not bound to please thee with my answer.
  Bass. Do all men kil the things they do not loue?
  Iew. Hates any man the thing he would not kill?
  Bass. Euerie offence is not a hate at first.
  Iew. What wouldst thou haue a Serpent sting thee twice?
  Ant. I pray you thinke you question with the Iew:
You may as well go stand vpon the beach,
And bid the maine flood baite his vsuall height,
Or euen as well vse question with the Wolfe,
The Ewe bleate for the Lambe:
You may as well forbid the Mountaine Pines
To wagge their high tops, and to make no noise
When they are fretted with the gusts of heauen:
You may as well do any thing most hard,
As seeke to soften that, then which what harder?
His Iewish heart. Therefore I do beseech you
Make no more offers, vse no farther meanes,
But with all briefe and plaine conueniencie
Let me haue iudgement, and the Iew his will.
  Baf. For thy three thousand Ducates heere is six.
  Iew. If euerie Ducat in fixe thousand Ducates
Were in sixe parts, and euery part a Ducate,
I would not draw them, I would haue my bond?
  Du. How shalt thou hope for mercie, rendring none?
  Iew. What iudgement shall I dread doing no wrong?
You haue among you many a purchast slaue,
Which like your Asses, and your Dogs and Mules,
You vse in abiect and in slauish parts,
Because you bought them. Shall I say to you,
Let them be free, marrie them to your heires?
Why sweate they vnder burthens? Let their beds
Be made as soft as yours: and let their pallats
Be season'd with such Viands: you will answer
                                      The

3   The First Folio of 1623, sig. P5ᵛ, containing the speech prefix 'Iew': beginning of Act 4

more recently, Barbara Mowat and Paul Werstine (Folg) have opted for the Q1 spelling 'Lancelet'. However, the majority verdict has been that these variations have simply provided an indication of the provenance of Q1's manuscript source, Shakespeare's 'foul papers'.

This issue has been recently revisited in connection with a number of unstable speech prefixes in some of the other playtexts that Roberts printed: Q2 *Titus Andronicus* (1600), Q2 *Midsummer Night's Dream* (1619), Q1 *1 Henry IV* (1598) and Q2 *Hamlet* (1604–5) (R. Kennedy, 177–209). The conclusions that follow from Kennedy's detailed bibliographical account force a reconsideration of a group of speech prefixes that editorial tradition has hitherto sought to stabilize. Kennedy establishes a clear link between the variant speech prefixes *Shylocke/Iewe* and *Lancelet/Clowne*, although he does not extend this to *Iobbe/Gobbo*. Earlier editors of the play noticed these instabilities (Ard², xvii, 4n.; but see also Cam¹, 95), but only in one case, that of Capell, did it inform editorial choice. The present edition follows through the logic of Kennedy's argument and opts for the speech prefixes *Jew*, *Clown* and *Giobbe*, the last of which invites a radical reconsideration of one element of the play, and reinforces the wider significance of the Clown's name Lancelet. In the case of each of these names a theatrical or biblical 'type' coexists with an individual name, and it is important for modern readers and spectators to keep these two possibilities firmly in mind. One other case, the *Salarino/Salanio/Salerio* variation, rationalized by Dover Wilson but recently revisited,[1] does not involve type shortages, but does testify to Shakespeare's occasional casualness with the names of minor characters. Taken as a group, these cases traverse authorial and bibliographical narratives.

Even so, there are moments in Q1 when it is possible to detect the dramatist's own conception of the stage action as it might

---

1 Okamoto, 73. Okamoto offers an alternative argument for supporting Dover Wilson's conclusions in Cam¹. See also Mahood, 54, and Edelman, xiii.

percolate through stage directions. For example, descriptive stage directions such as 'Enter *Portia* with her wayting woman *Nerrissa*' (1.2) or 'Enter *Morochus* a tawnie Moore all in white, and three or foure followers accordingly, with *Portia, Nerrissa*, and their traine' (2.1), provide details about relative social status, and about a controversial racial stereotype, as well as rather vague instructions for a supporting cast ('three or foure followers'), most of which are characteristic of foul papers. Later entries such as '*Enter* Bassanio *with a follower or two*' (2.2.105.1), which omits 'Leonardo', or '*Enter Bassanio, Anthonio, Gratiano, and their followers*' (5.1.126.1), are also vague, while the double entry for Tubal at 3.1 (E2^v) is explained by Brown as an indication of a promptbook correction (Ard^2, xv).[1] However, Tubal's entry at this point is gradual in that it is the departing Salanio who first encounters him on one part of the stage, prompting his scurrilous characterization, and only then does he approach Shylock, who greets him. Could this be an early instance of a dramatist imagining a particular detail of stage blocking?

The evidence that the text furnishes is not consistent, and subsequent early printed editions do little to clarify the matter. Q2 (1619) attempts to correct errors and in the process generates others, and F (1623) adds its own theatrical accretions to the text in the form of musical stage directions. It is reasonable to suppose, the adjustments of bibliographical evidence notwithstanding, that the copy for Q1 (1600) was Shakespeare's own foul papers. Moreover, the manuscript may have been, in some respects, a little more consistent, especially in certain of its speech prefixes, than the pragmatic, but inadvertently obscuring, activities of Roberts's compositors might lead us to believe.

---

1 Mahood's explanation is more fanciful, involving a 'change of plan' that indicates 'joins in the text' (Mahood, 172), and she surmises that the repetition derives from Shakespeare's own failure to excise the first entry after having 'inserted a passage (57 SD to 62 SD)' designed to get Salarino and Salanio off the stage (Mahood, 110, n. 62, and 172).

FROM JEW TO SHYLOCK

We should resist the conflation of Shakespeare's dramatic rhetoric with an oversimplified social realism that is often assumed to be its objective, since the transition from social type to theatrical characterization is fraught with difficulty. Even so, one of Thomas Coryate's biblically glossed observations of Venetian Jews was that 'they obserue in their seruice which is vtterly conde[m]ned by our Sauiour Christ, Battalogia, that is a very tedious babling, and an often repetition of one thing, which cloied mine eares so much that I could not endure them any longer' (Coryate, 233).[1]

George T. Wright has argued that although we might question the claim that in a Shakespeare play 'different characters . . . have sharply distinctive metrical styles' we cannot overlook the fact that the dramatist 'devised unmistakably individual speaking voices' for particular characters, of whom, he insists, Shylock is one (Wright, 249). Wright's astute general observations about metre are underpinned by two related assumptions: that dramatic character is unitary and cohesive, and that the distinctiveness of Shylock's speech is indicative of an 'individuality' that distinguishes him from those around him. Even Greenblatt's observation that, although Shylock shares a language with his Christian adversaries, he inhabits it 'in a wholly different sense' (Greenblatt, 'Marlowe', 43) refuses either to explore the ramifications of this position or to relinquish it altogether. Of course, it would be counter-productive to dispense entirely with the concept of 'character', although it is important to register those textual effects that direct us towards the conditions under which some limited editorial cohesiveness and some degree of psychological verisimilitude are produced.[2]

---

1   See also Matthew, 6.7, for Christ's injunction: 'Also when ye pray, use no vaine repetitions as the heathen: for they thinke to be heard for their muche babling.'
2   See Sinfield, *Faultlines*, 63. Also, for a more extended commentary, see Marzola, 293–4.

At issue are both the Jew's meanings, and also the verbal repetitions in response to Bassanio's defence of what he takes to be Antonio's moral, as opposed to his financial, probity:

> JEW   Antonio is a good man.
> BASSANIO   Have you heard any imputation to the contrary?
> JEW   Ho, no, no, no, no. My meaning in saying he is a good man is to have you understand me that he is sufficient.
>
> (1.3.12–16)

The unfixing of meaning evident in this initial exchange is consistent with Antonio's own claim, later in the scene, that the Jew is a 'devil' who challenges the very probity and stability of language itself: 'An evil soul producing holy witness / Is like a villain with a smiling cheek, / A goodly apple, rotten at the heart' (1.3.95–7). The Jew's verbal repetitions, 'Ho, no, no, no, no', and his telling gloss on the adjective 'good', are neither evidence of idiosyncrasy nor 'reality effects' designed to imitate the speech patterns of 'real' Jews, however they may appear to modern sensibilities. Rather, they require to be read symptomatically as evidence of the propensity to a devilish duplicity that owes its scriptural origin to St Matthew's gospel, and its social ethic to Marlowe's Machevil in the *Jew of Malta*, who 'weigh[s] not men, and therefore not men's words' (Prologue, 8). Both legitimizing sources are symptomatic of a rich, varied and (to us) ethically dubious Elizabethan fantasy life in and through which cultural anxieties and scripturally authorized challenges to the political order manifest themselves.

The matter is complicated in the *Merchant of Venice* because the Jew's fiscal relationship to his Christian adversaries is sustained through a fiduciary process of negotiation. In the Venice of Shakespeare's play two opposed kinds of money-lending prevail: that which is 'natural' and is practised by Antonio, who, out of friendship, can say to Bassanio, 'My purse, my person, my extremest means / Lie all unlocked to your occasions' (1.1.138–9); and that which is 'artificial' and practised by Shylock, who lends 'not / As to thy friends, for when did friendship take / A breed for barren metal of his friend?' (1.3.127–9). The latter practice is, however, a necessary evil that the Christian Venetians need but can only represent in an estranged form. In almost every respect the figure of the Jew replicates in a distorted and alienated form the life of Venice, exposing the contradictions that lie beneath the surface of an allegedly multicultural society. This may be one of the reasons that Shylock is furnished with an unruly 'family', although not quite as unruly or perverted as that of the 'Jewish' eponymous hero of Jonson's *Volpone* (1605). The Shylock–Jessica relationship, along with the comic tribulations of the Clown journeyman Lancelet, discloses a 'hellish' version of the household that replicates in an ironic mode I.D.'s commentary at the end of the First Book of Aristotle's *Politics*, where this institution comprises 'Maister and servaunt . . . Husband and Wife . . . and . . . Father and the Children' and is described as 'like a kingdome, forasmuch as the father hath a care of his childre[n]' (Aristotle, *Politics*, 57). Children are expected to obey their fathers, who govern them 'regally, as well through friendship and prerogative of perfect age' (57), but also, 'The maisters gouernment ouer his slaues is tyrranicall, whereby all things are conueyed to the maisters profit: so that the one gouernement is lawfull, and the other which is after the Persian manner faultie' (58). This is very close to the distinction that Shakespeare's play maintains between the orderliness of Portia's 'family' where the law of a dead father continues to operate, *and* that of the Jew, where the bond between parent and child, and between master and servant, is strained to breaking point. In this context Shylock's is a recognizably 'Puritan' household that resists all forms of festive ritual. Initially, the Jew refuses Bassanio's invitation to dine, but his subsequent acceptance inverts a necessary social ritual and serves to emphasize the ways in which meanings themselves can be destabilized in the act of linguistic exchange: 'I am not bid for love; they flatter me, / But yet I'll go in hate, to feed upon / The prodigal Christian' (2.5.13–15). Christian and Jew invest the same linguistic sign, or social ritual, with different meanings. Shylock objects to 'masques' and he instructs Jessica not 'To gaze on Christian fools with varnished faces'; in a manifestly anti-festive vein he orders her to 'stop my house's ears – I mean my casements – / Let not the sound of shallow foppery enter / My sober house' (2.5.33–5). The Jew's apparent need to enunciate meaning – 'I mean', at the point where his own language risks straying into the realm of the metaphorical – indicates a linguistic parsimony that augments a questionable form of fiscal prudence. This is not so much the representation of an 'individual' as the *performance* of the values of an emergent 'class' whose hostility to theatrical practice is of a piece with representations of objectionable forms of financial exchange. Lancelet's departure from an exploitative household into a 'livery' is, in this context, both a criticism of the 'government' of Shylock's family and a conservative return to a domestic structure primarily dependent upon mutual obligation. Christian Venice is shown here to oppose its quasi-feudal generosity to a puritanical 'thrift' which is 'the maisters profit'.

This ambivalence is further underscored in the name 'Shylock', which Furness located in a document dated 4 July 1435, as the family name of one 'Richard Shylok of Hoo, co. Sussex' (Furness, ix–x). More recently, Stephen Orgel has confirmed that it was an English, not a Jewish, name whose etymology gives the meaning 'fair-haired' (Orgel, 'Shylock', 151–3). This gloss underscores Antonio's earlier description of the Jew as 'A goodly apple, rotten at the heart' (1.3.97) while the 'mixed' lineage that emerges is identical to the ambivalence that the writers of usury tracts discerned in the claim that it was Christians, not Jews, who practised usury in England. Christian Venice is society engaged in the early stages of self-alienation, but without a modern conceptual vocabulary to describe its trauma.[1] It is little wonder that Antonio should begin the play with a statement about a 'sadness' that cannot locate its own cause: 'In sooth I know not why I am so sad. / It wearies me; you say it wearies you' (1.1.1–2). And it is a debility that is contagious, since the play's fulfilment of a Christian fantasy – the conversion of the Jew – produces a split subject, Jew/ Shylock, who is clearly not at ease with himself: 'I pray you, give me leave to go from hence. / I am not well' (4.1.391–2). The multicultural Venetian republic, steeped in a venality that permeates all of its social institutions, produces subjects who are, in different ways, alienated from themselves, and, in the figure of Shylock especially, the medieval stereotype collides with an early form of modern subjectivity.

THE COMIC STRUCTURE OF THE PLAY

The title-page of the First Quarto of the *Merchant of Venice* announces three narratives: 'the Historie of the *Merchant of Venice*', 'the extreme crueltie of *Shylocke* the Iewe' and 'the obtayning of *Portia* by the choyse of three chests' (Fig. 1). In addition, two further thematically related narratives are included: the perfunctory meeting of the Clown Lancelet with his father, Old Giobbe, and his own change of allegiance from the house of the Jew to that of Bassanio; and the disobedience of Jessica and her elopement with the young Christian Lorenzo. The even more perfunctory courtship of Gratiano and Nerissa echoes that of Portia and Bassanio. The play also contains two scapegoats, one of whom, Antonio, is self-fashioned, while the other, Shylock, is the projection of Venice's deepest anxieties that are exposed before he is admitted to society. These narratives are connected to each other, and each offers a commentary on the others as they intersect in the wider structure of the play. But

---

1   Cf. Marx, 'Jewish question', 238–9, for the discussion of Jewish fiscal dealing as 'practical Christianity'.

in thinking of the structure of the *Merchant of Venice* we must take care that we do not invent the organic unity that we seek. And we need also to recall that, structurally speaking, the play is a comedy, even though we may be uncomfortable with some of the laughter that the comic action generates.

The content of the *Merchant of Venice* is deeply political and ideological, and it should not surprise us to find that its aesthetic structure is equally so. The genre of comedy might lead us to expect that the central characters succeed in surmounting the obstacles that beset them in order to reach a happy conclusion, but in this play that is not easily or satisfactorily achieved. Much of the action turns upon matters of a fiscal and a legal nature that have a particular relevance to the geographical setting of Venice, and it proves difficult to separate the laughter that they generate from the prejudices that these overlapping plots uncover.

Lawrence Danson seeks to account for the play's full, if not fulsome, expression of 'harmony' that emerges in the fifth act (Danson, *Harmonies*, 11). That this conclusion should require explanation is testimony to the difficulty that many critics have found in trying to align matters of structure with the play's generic identity. John Russell Brown argues that many of Shakespeare's texts talk about love as a commercial transaction: 'Shakespeare wrote of love as of a kind of wealth in which men and women traffic' (Brown, *Comedies*, 46), but he notes that, compared with the other comedies, '*The Merchant of Venice* is the most completely informed by Shakespeare's ideal of love's wealth' (61). Brown also contends that the play is structured around two radically divergent attitudes toward social relationship, the one built on love and friendship, and the other dependent upon financial gain; and that this duality is focused in the two mutually opposed meanings inherent in the term usury. Indeed, he sees the tension between these two meanings as 'part of a more general comparison of commerce and love which is likewise maintained throughout the play' (65; see also Leggatt, 122). Brown rightly identifies Venice in the play as the geographical location where this battle of opposed meanings is fought out, but he also notes the degree to which Belmont, superficially the alter ego of Venice, is infected with the same ambivalence. The play ends happily in Belmont with each of the three couples finding 'in their own way . . . love's wealth', although the action is shot through with a realism that qualifies that happiness.[1]

Brown's judicious commitment to the play's dominant ideology is further refined in Alexander Leggatt's *Shakespeare's Comedy of Love* (1974), which steers a careful path between the formal demands of comedy and what he takes to be an encouragement of 'a wider range of choices offered by the real world' (Leggatt, 118–19). For Leggatt, the play is 'more broken and disjointed' than the earlier comedies whose formal neatness is replaced by 'a more open and natural structure, with more loose ends' (121). Throughout his chapter on the play he emphasizes the realism and the naturalism of the representation of human relationships in the face of a temptation to read the dramatic action allegorically. Much of the subsequent criticism of the play has attempted to respond to this general discomfort, although the agenda set by some of the more recent, theoretically informed and more self-conscious modes of critical inquiry have found other ways of explaining the play's distinctive peculiarities.

For C.L. Barber the general comic movement 'through release to clarification' is complicated by the prominence given to the figure of Shylock and the difficulty we have in reading the tone of his presence in the play (Barber, 168). In contrast, Herbert Donow argues that the casket plot, along with the elopement of Jessica and Lorenzo, is the fulcrum of the play. He goes on to assert that, although the arraignment of Antonio

---

1   Brown, *Comedies*, 74: '*The Merchant of Venice* presents in human and dramatic terms Shakespeare's ideal of love's wealth, its abundant and sometimes embarrassing riches; it shows how this wealth is gained and possessed by giving freely and joyfully; it shows also how destructive the opposing possessiveness can become, and how it can cause those who traffic in love to fight blindly for their existence.'

is the most sensational element, 'the issues of usury and anti-Semitism are not, for all their interest to us, vital to the structure of the play' (Donow, 87). The quest for formal unity demands a harmonious interlocking of elements and a teleological thrust to the action that subsumes each strand into an aesthetically satisfying conclusion. But such are the complexities of the *Merchant of Venice* that we need to posit a model of structure, in which we can see the play in the process of constructing its own ideological solutions to the problems and contradictions that its multi-faceted narrative uncovers.

THE HISTORIE OF
THE MERCHANT OF VENICE

The central drama of the *Merchant of Venice* revolves around the relationship between the merchant Antonio and the Venetian Lord Bassanio. This is a genuine friendship that extends to an offer of financial assistance that will enable the Lord Bassanio to replenish his own coffers by a marriage to the wealthy heiress Portia. Antonio's 'historie' involves a particular narrative that combines both public and personal elements in a complex web of significations. The play begins in Venice with Antonio's expression of an unspecific world-weariness, paralleled by Portia's lament, a scene later, which serves to link Venice and Belmont: 'By my troth, Nerissa, my little body is aweary of this great world' (1.2.1–2). Portia's dissatisfaction derives from a specific cause, but Antonio's 'weariness' is more mysterious. He resists one explanation based on any financial anxieties he may have (1.1.40–4), and another alleging that he is 'in love' is met with a perfunctory rebuff, 'Fie, fie' (1.1.46) which in most modern productions of the play – and in Trevor Nunn's 1999 National Theatre production in particular – is enunciated with sufficient vigour to suggest that Antonio's 'love' for Bassanio is of a repressed homosexual, rather than homosocial, kind.

The poet W.H. Auden was one of the first to comment on the intimacy of the relationship between Antonio and his 'most noble kinsman' Bassanio (1.1.57),[1] although recent criticism has been more circumspect. For example, both Alan Sinfield and Bruce Smith have drawn attention to what the latter has described as 'The scenario of two male friends set at odds by a woman' (B. Smith, 66–7; see also Sinfield, 'How to read', 122–39), although both eschew as anachronistic any homosexual *identity* that might be ascribed to Antonio. Smith's reading of Antonio is intolerant of what he takes to be Bassanio's and Antonio's apparent failure to talk about love compared to the relatively uninhibited way in which Portia and Nerissa openly discuss the topic in the second scene of the play (B. Smith, 67–8). Sinfield puts the matter differently, suggesting that, while there may not have been a homosexual *subjectivity* during the early modern period, statements about its absence are misguided in that the modern reader or spectator may be confronted with 'ambivalent or partial signs of subjectivity' indicative of emergence rather than absence (Sinfield, *Queer Reading*, 13–14). Smith draws an important distinction between sexuality as a marker of identity and sexual activity within whose discursive purview homosexual acts came under the heading of 'the general depravity to which *all* mankind is subject' (B. Smith, 11). Moreover, by disentangling a Renaissance concept from a modern politics of oppression, Smith dispenses with a familiar model that 'overvalues the importance of sex' as part of the process of identity formation, while at the same time permitting him to view same-sex desire as a means of social empowerment (12) and as part of a more complex politics; the term 'desire' can thus be used – in the words of Eve Kosofsky Sedgwick – 'to name a structure'.

1 Auden, 231: 'It can, therefore, hardly be an accident that Shylock the usurer has as his antagonist a man whose emotional life, though his conduct may be chaste, is concentrated upon a member of his own sex.'

Sedgwick offers an important insight into the kind of relationship between males that confronts us at the opening of the *Merchant of Venice*. She argues that in certain Renaissance texts, such as Shakespeare's Sonnets, homosexuality is not an issue, but rather that 'we are in the presence of male heterosexual desire, in the form of a desire to consolidate partnership with authoritative males in and through the bodies of females' (Sedgwick, 38). This is made explicit in those of Shakespeare's Sonnets in which the narrator addresses the aristocratic young man. Here, as elsewhere in Shakespeare, the arrival of the woman threatens the severance of the homosocial bond between two men,[1] introducing division where there was once patriarchal harmony. Moreover, the interposing of the figure of the woman *between* two male friends of unequal social status is a threat to the desire of the socially inferior male, which in the case of Antonio has its own analogue in the jeopardizing of his mercantile enterprise. Antonio knows already that Bassanio is involved in the pursuit of a 'lady' (1.1.161) that will combine romance and profit. But Antonio's involvement in mercantile activity exposes him to a more general uncertainty that is inherent in the act of commodity exchange and that problematizes the concepts of 'use' and profit. The question in the play is not how these concepts operate historically so much as how they are internalized in the everyday behaviour of human subjects, and how that behaviour is theatrically represented.

Bearing this in mind, two kinds of desire are shown to come together in Antonio's project and both present different kinds of risk for Lord Bassanio's masculine merchant friend and his expressions of 'love'. It is in this tangled web of the play's discourses of desire, in which the economic, the social, the political and the personal overlap, that the figure of Antonio is

---

1 Cf. *WT* 1.2.67–86, where male friendship is described in pre-lapsarian terms by Polixenes: 'Had we pursu'd that life, / And our weak spirits ne'er been higher rear'd / With stronger blood, we should have answer'd heaven / Boldly "not guilty", the imposition clear'd / Hereditary ours' (*WT* 1.2.71–5). Both Polixenes and Leontes 'trip' and 'sin' when their respective spouses arrive on the scene.

inscribed. And it is the uncertainty that informs these activities that will be passed to the 'subjected' Shylock as part of his enforced conversion to Christianity later in the play. Antonio's 'historie' is germane both to the play's main narrative and to other histories that combine the spheres of the personal, the political and the economic.

The problem of what Smith takes to be a return to formal verse after Bassanio's temporary lapse into prose (1.1.114–18), which betrays a reluctance on Antonio's part to speak openly about his desire for Bassanio (B. Smith, 68), serves to introduce an important issue that emphasizes Antonio's power and Bassanio's indebtedness. The lady to whom Bassanio has already told Antonio that he has sworn 'a secret pilgrimage' (1.1.120) will also be the means whereby the prodigal aristocrat Bassanio will pay off his debts to Antonio, to whom he already owes 'the most in money and in love' (1.1.131). Bassanio has, by his own admission, been living beyond his means – 'By something showing a more swelling port / Than my faint means would grant continuance' (1.1.124–5) – and his capacity for conspicuous consumption provokes a desire that neither his nor Antonio's material means can satisfy. Both men are united in the patriarchal desire for the power that wealth brings. But it is only their mutual 'love' that protects the financial transaction from the possibility of censure, even though there may be a risk that the satisfaction of the desire for wealth will also introduce a tension into their male friendship.

In Bassanio's case the desire for money is expressed directly as the desire for Portia. One desire mirrors the other to the extent that the formalized discourse of wealth is infected with the erotic potential inherent in the discourse of sexual desire, and vice versa. Indeed, the consolidation of male homosocial desire through the body of the female is not an impersonal, objectively observable phenomenon so much as a subjectively *felt*, and hence emotionally charged, practice. In the case of Antonio, both these intertwined discourses jostle with a third, that of social status.

Antonio is a member of a subordinate class who by virtue of his access to money is able to hold a social superior in thrall.[1] What binds Venice together are love *and* money, friendship and erotic desire.[2] The love that Antonio and Bassanio share is mutual,[3] but the power of wealth to subjugate also accompanies, but cannot simply be reduced to, the libidinous drive for sexual satisfaction; nor can 'love' completely transmute these material concerns into exclusively spiritual equivalents. Money carries with it the taint of the mutable material world; it is a necessary and indispensable evil, a paradoxical substance that 'breeds' discontent in every area of social life that it touches. And it is these tensions that cause Antonio to feel ill at ease.

The metaphor of 'breeding' is crucial to our understanding of what is at issue in the 'historie' of the merchant of Venice, and it is Antonio himself who hints at the connection. It is *because* of his love for Antonio that Bassanio is able 'To unburden all my plots and purposes / How to get clear of all the debts I owe' (1.1.133–4); and it is this that prompts Antonio into making a remarkable offer: 'My purse, my person, my extremest means / Lie all unlocked to your occasions' (1.1.138–9). Antonio's 'purse' is, of course, the receptacle for his money, but it is also an Elizabethan term for the scrotum. He graduates from 'purse' to 'person' and moves from that punning association to 'extremest means'; all will be placed at Bassanio's disposal ('unlocked') in a gesture of complete love that is willing to relinquish the self and its material supports ('extremest means'). Antonio offers Bassanio his body as a kind of casket, although he is careful to preface this extravagant gesture with a reference to 'the eye of honour' within whose public gaze his generosity is both inscribed

---

1 See Marzola, 296–7, where Bassanio's status as an 'impoverished gentleman' and Antonio's as 'the emerging merchant' is shown to intersect with larger questions of gender identity, in which the penurious aristocrat is also in danger of losing his sexual potency (Marzola, 297).

2 Cf. Debora Kuller Shuger, *Habits of Thought in the English Renaissance: Religion, Politics, and the Dominant Culture* (repr. Toronto and London, 1997), 224–7.

3 See Aristotle, *Ethics*, 261–2, where the three types of 'friendship' are described: mutual affection, utility and pleasure.

and modulated. Later in the play Antonio will 'break a custom' by entering into an agreement with the Jew that involves the payment of interest ('excess') for the loan of a sum of money. The persistence of his outright rejection of the Jew's justification for his usurious practice through a punning invocation, 'I do never use it' (1.3.66), makes clear the distinction between the Jew's commitment to one meaning of the verb 'use' and the values that inform Antonio's generosity. And yet the inscription of the ambivalent 'purse' in the semantic field of 'person' indicates that he is willing to enter into an agreement that will assist, in part vicariously, in the generation of money *and* progeny. From the very outset two opposed types of generative patriarchal activity are brought into a differential relationship with each other that distinguishes the sterile 'breeding' of money (usury) as the demonized obverse of the act of biological generation.

The play's evident preoccupation with the material world has come to assume a central importance for a wide range of contemporary criticism. Indeed, Antonio's involvement with the question of breeding is so central to the action that Marc Shell can claim, with justification, that 'Generation, or production, is the principal topic of Shakespeare's *The Merchant of Venice*' (Shell, 48). The debate between Shylock and Antonio concerning the justification of usury permits us to distinguish between their respective theological commitments to Old Testament and Christian theology. It would, however, be a mistake to think of this struggle in Oedipal terms, although a number of psychoanalytical critics of the play have sought to identify its repressed material, whether at the level of dramatic character, authorial intention or Elizabethan culture itself (see, for example, Tennenhouse, 54–69; and Stephens, 91–129). For instance, Leonard Tennenhouse argues that the play's 'conversion of wealth into love is the fantasy that binds people together in forms of oral dependency', and he cites the crucial moment of Bassanio's response to his successful choice of the leaden casket as a signal 'that this submission of the woman to the man is the moment of oral fusion and bliss' (Tennenhouse, 63). However, the claim that Elizabethan social practice provides a set of cultural rules that 'offer possible coherence or relationship among symbols, institutions, social forms, professed values, and approved norms and thus enable us to identify a culture's paradigms' (55) is inadequately historicized. Tennenhouse consequently fudges the conflict between two divergent forms of patriarchy: the one dominant, and the other allowed to exist under the protection of the law, but marginalized as a destructive form of historically specific social energy.

Antonio is the link connecting two different kinds of social organization. The one is epitomized by the aristocratic Bassanio and implicates the merchant in the process of sustaining a particular social hierarchy, while the other, epitomized by the Jew, demonstrates the extent to which the power vested in circulating capital has shifted irrevocably from one social group to another. The play invites us to reflect upon the condoning of the one and the ridiculing of the other. Antonio's willingness to risk his total being as surety for his friend's debt is a demonstration both of love and of the proper 'use' of wealth, but it also positions him in the role of scapegoat in so far as he becomes the prey of the voracious usurer. Here his Christian 'flesh' and 'blood' take on a powerful symbolic significance as a type of Eucharist that neutralizes the negative aspects of trade, exchange and wealth accumulation. The price that Antonio is willing to pay positions him between the figure of a bankrupt and profligate aristocrat and a powerful usurer. This is, in effect, the position that the merchant has negotiated for himself between relying for his success upon the goodwill of a divine providence, on the one hand, and recognizing the need to ensure the circulation of capital, on the other. Antonio has neither the social status to disregard financial pressure by traditional means (such as an aristocratic marriage) nor the desire to engage in the practice of making money 'breed' by actively controlling the process of its circulation. His dependency upon the Jew, who in turn relies for his supply of money upon a fellow Jew, Tubal, disempowers him to the point where the only role open to him is that of Job-like sufferer at the hands of a providence that exacts exemplary punishment. What is also reinforced is the sense that money is a free-floating signifier that has the capacity to disengage itself from the material world of 'use' and 'need' in the business of exchange. It is no accident that, faced with the real prospect of losing the pound of flesh that he has risked to finance Bassanio's quest, Antonio can characterize himself as 'a tainted wether of the flock, / Meetest for death' (4.1.113–14). Here the suffering Job metamorphoses into the suffering Christ, and the 'historie' of the merchant is expanded exponentially.

It is, on the surface, providence that renders Antonio temporarily impotent, and not the allegedly castrating knife of the Jew. It is also deeply ironical that this same providence should engineer a reversal of roles, in that it is the patriarchal Shylock, forcibly 'converted' to Christianity, who ultimately comes to occupy the position from which Antonio has been providentially released. Indeed, in what might be regarded as a symbolic revision of the New Testament crucifixion narrative, the Christ-like Antonio is released and his role as sacrifice is transferred to the felon Shylock, who now comes to occupy the figure of the suffering Job. In the minor Lancelet–Giobbe plot the misfortunes of Old Giobbe can be rectified by the transference of Lancelet's allegiance from Jew to Christian. Shylock's 'conversion', on the other hand, entails a fantastical revision of the Christian narrative in which the Jew Barabas gets his just deserts, and Christ is released from his agony in the earthly world.

Initially deprived of his 'purse' and threatened in his 'person', Antonio is transformed from the role of financially fecund ewe into that of an impotent ram (a 'tainted wether') who is now confronted by the ravenous and wolfish usurer. His adversary is a figure whose allegorical significance received repeated emphasis in the numerous usury tracts as well as in texts such as Spenser's *Faerie Queene*, published a year before the appearance of the *Merchant of Venice* on the London stage.[1] The play shifts interestingly between two modes of representation, the one realistic and secular, the other deeply allegorical, and it is likely that an Elizabethan audience would have responded to both with equal fervour. It also shifts curiously between Antonio and Shylock, who are locked together in a network of mutually defining differences.

A number of commentators, taking their cue from Portia disguised as Balthazar, and seeking to account for the extent to which the play 'invokes the ideologically sanctioned mythologies of the time only to question and subvert them', have sought to determine who is the eponymous 'merchant' (see Moisan, 188–9). Clearly the differences are both religious and socio-economic, making these dramatic characters interdependent. Walter Cohen observes that in Shakespeare's sources there is no reference to 'any prior enmity between merchant and usurer, much less to a comparative motive for the antagonism' (Cohen, *Drama*, 201), and he argues that in Shakespeare's play 'English history evokes fears of capitalism, and Italian history allays those fears' (203). Cohen, like Thomas Moisan after him, is concerned to elucidate the ideological resolution of contradictions that the play uncovers, and in doing so to propose a political harmony that mirrors in certain respects the aesthetic harmony detected by commentators such as Lawrence Danson. But the play's production of ideology also involves the disclosure of those contradictions that it is the business of ideology to resolve. The Christianity that Venice asserts throughout the play seeks to incorporate the threat that the figure of the Jew poses to its moral and ethical foundations. Thus Venice becomes what

---

1   *FQ*, 69, where the Redcrosse Knight is enticed into the Babylonian kingdom of Queen Lucifera and her entourage of the Seven Deadly Sins including Avarice and Lechery: 'by him did ride, / Vpon a Camell loaden al with gold; / Two iron coffers hong on either side, / With precious metall full, as they might hold, / And in his lap an heape of coine he told; / For of his wicked pelfe his God he made, / And vnto hell him selfe for money sold; / Accursed Vsurie was all his trade, / And right and wrong ylike in equall ballaunce waide' (*FQ*, 1.6.27).

Marx would call 'a *hypocritical* state' in its refusal to engage with those imperfections that are exposed by the fiscal practices that constitute the lifeblood of its commercial activity (Marx, 'Jewish question', 223). To this extent, the anxieties that the play's characters register might be read as a critique of Venetian republicanism, whose more radical political effects Contarini (in Lewkenor's translation) had ameliorated by seeking to make it resemble a 'monarchy'.

As the 'merchant of Venice' Antonio registers all of the tensions that are generated as a result of the convergence of the obligations of friendship and economic activity. Venice is usually characterized, so Catherine Belsey has reminded us, as the place from which lovers flee to Belmont in what appears, at first sight, to be a straightforward opposition. She describes Belmont, ironically, as 'the location in the play of happy love' that attracts competing suitors. It is 'a refuge for eloping lovers, who flee the precarious world of capital interest and trade, to find a haven of hospitality, music, poetry . . . and the infinite wealth (without origins) which makes all this possible' (Belsey, 'Love', 41). But Belmont holds out the prospect of an imaginary fulfilment, the response to a demand that purports to be both aesthetic and, for Belsey, psychoanalytical. Indeed, she argues that Belmont domesticates desire, in that it attempts to minimize the negative effects of passion and suffering that were defining features of those 'classical and Italian narratives' whose hold on the popular imagination was fast receding at the end of the sixteenth century. It is Venice, she argues, that is the place of danger, anarchy and possible destruction, but the imperfect domestication that is finally effected in Belmont reflects 'the extent to which Venice is superimposed upon Belmont' (43).

This deep imbrication of two geographically distinct locations in each other's affairs is further emphasized in a detail from Robinson's translation from the *Gesta Romanorum* (1595). Here it is the King of Ampluy's daughter, sent to marry the only son of the Emperor of Rome, who is invited to choose from three caskets of gold, silver and lead: 'insculpt' upon the leaden casket is 'this posey. *Who so chooseth mee, shall finde that God hath disposed for him*' (Ard², 173).[1] Shakespeare's emendation of this source does, indeed, as Belsey argues, locate 'the meaning of the lead casket firmly in the realm of the secular and the sexual' (Belsey, 'Love', 45). But it also suggests an explicit and sustained link between Bassanio's romantic quest and Antonio's mercantilism. In placing his fortunes in the hands of providence, Bassanio, like Antonio, submits himself to a patriarchal power over which he has no control. This serves to distinguish all Venetian practice, commercial and sexual, from the activities of the usurer whose fortunes are determined by exclusively human calculation and for whom the realm of the sexual, and indeed of the patriarchal, is articulated as perversion.

Such contrasts – and the *Merchant of Venice* is full of them – are, of course, tendentious, but they reveal a series of very specific strategies of representation that disclose the operations of a dominant ideology in the play. The manifest opposition between Venice and Belmont figures forth an imaginary conflict between a political entity whose own self-knowledge, projected onto its legitimate subjects, is troubling, and a fantasy world that can never quite satisfy desire or shake itself free from quotidian concerns. Thus one of the major structural contrasts in the play turns out to be something other than it claims to be, rather like the leaden casket upon whose contents Bassanio risks his fortune.

Some of the ramifications of this complex structure emerge through the manner in which Bassanio is tested in Belmont. As in the case of Antonio, so with Bassanio faith is tested and the risks are as great in Belmont as they are in Venice. Like Antonio he is brought face to face with the prospect of death, and like Antonio he finds that his faith allows him to win through in the end. But the core of marriage, like the core of mercantilism, is dependent

---

1 Brown also notes the use of the word 'insculpt' that appears also in Morocco's description of the golden casket at 2.7.57, indicating that Shakespeare was familiar with Robinson's translation.

upon a faith that recognizes the inscrutable operations of nature only in their effects, while the vicissitudes and uncertainties of secular life present a constant challenge to those who are enmeshed in its unpredictable powers. In fact, immediately before making his choice of the caskets, Bassanio invokes a thesaurus of examples that assert the deceitful appearances of the world, of human behaviour and, crucially, of female beauty (3.2.88–101). The pathological fear of temptation – 'Thus, ornament is but the guiled shore / To a most dangerous sea; the beauteous scarf / Veiling an Indian beauty; in a word, / The seeming truth, which cunning times put on / To entrap the wisest' (3.2.97–101) – is linked here with death, at the same time that it echoes, in a different register, the suspicion attached to the Jew earlier. In the case of Job, the fear of misfortune or its actual occurrence is designed to test faith. For Antonio, the prospect of death is real, but, as in the case of Job, it is ultimately averted. In Bassanio's case, however, the confrontation is circumvented, only to be relocated in the institution of marriage itself where the dangers of infidelity are perennial, despite being circumscribed by a divinely sanctioned law. To complete the fantasy, the disruptive figure of the Jew is incorporated into a Christian ethos that will provide a justification for his suffering, offer him the prospect of release and convert his subversive fiscal practices into modes of exchange that are acceptable. The perfunctory appearance in the play of Old Giobbe offers a comic digest of these Job-like trials (see Fig. 4), although the prospect of his salvation lies, in part, in the hands of his son, just as Shylock's future well-being will be in the hands of his daughter. The trials of the suffering Job are recuperated in a light-hearted vein for a recognizably Christian narrative that emphasizes the conquest of death, not only through marriage and salvation, but through the overcoming of an impediment and on behalf of a figure who is integral to the pre-history of Christianity. The proximity of the woman and the Jew is nearer the surface of the Elizabethan masculine unconscious than appears at first sight.

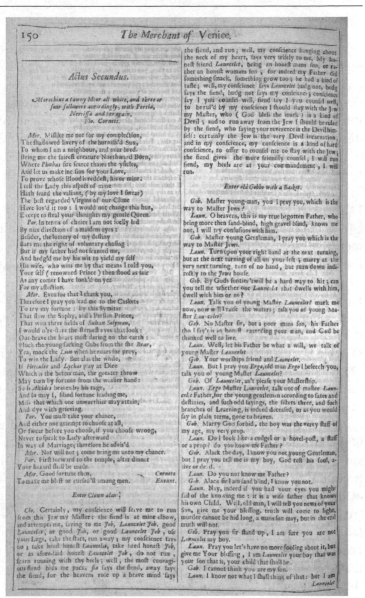

4   The Fourth Folio of 1685, which emends the name 'Iobbe' to 'Job' in Lancelet's prose soliloquy: beginning of Act 2

PARENTS AND CHILDREN

A major structural feature of the play, as indeed in a number of other Shakespearean comedies, is the relationship between parents and children. Lancelet's surname 'Giobbe' ('Iobbe') is a comic signifier of family allegiance, an amusing distortion. It is one of three family groupings in the play and it is an amalgamation of two distinct Old Testament narratives. Old Giobbe's 'sand' blindness (one of Job's afflictions) causes him to comment on what he takes to be Lancelet's beard: 'Lord worshipped might he be, what a beard hast thou got! Thou hast got more hair on thy chin than Dobbin, my thill-horse, has on his tail' (2.2.87–9). Lancelet is also momentarily reminiscent of the deceitful Jacob, who, at his mother Rebecca's instigation, is persuaded to place 'the skins of the kids upon his handes and the smooth of his neck' (Genesis, 27.11). Disguised to the touch as his brother Esau, he receives his father Isaac's blessing: 'And he knewe him not, because his handes were hairie, as his brother Esau's hands: and so he blessed him' (Genesis, 27.23). This narrative is linked to the Jew's invoking of biblical authority earlier at 1.3 to justify the practice of usury. Deceit and the capacity to interfere with the operations of nature require agency, although in the case of Old Giobbe the narrative of Jacob's deceit is not pursued.

Old Giobbe is a comic composite of two visually impaired Old Testament patriarchs, the one deceived (Isaac), the other suffering (Job), and offers a perfunctorily comic insight into the precariousness of what Aristotle identified as the 'three societies of persons, necessarie for the establishment of a perfect familie' (Aristotle, *Politics*, 57). In the larger structure of the play, familial relationships are represented in various forms, while deceit and suffering are located primarily, but not exclusively, in the figure of the Jew and Antonio respectively, as propensities of the infidel and the Christian Venetian.

The exercise of paternal and patriarchal power generates an anxiety that, in Shakespearean comedy generally, laughter attempts to dispel, and in the *Merchant of Venice* a network of analogous fathers and patriarchs is crucial to the play's dramatic structure. Modern productions sometimes assert the proximity in age of Antonio and Bassanio, although, before going to supper with Bassanio, Shylock distinguishes between himself and his host. He muses, 'Well, thou shalt see, thy eyes shall be thy judge, / The difference of old Shylock and Bassanio' (2.5.1–2), indicating the youth of Bassanio, but he also reveals to Jessica that he will 'go in hate, to feed upon / The prodigal Christian' (2.5.14–15). Prodigality is perceived by the Jew to be a contemptible Christian vice, but it also indicts Bassanio as a prodigal aristocratic son, for whom his provider, Antonio, stands in as a benevolent patriarch, as, indeed, is the case in Giovanni's version of the story. However, the disturbed relations between parent and child, patriarchal authority and subject, and the resultant challenge to the bonds of male society, indicate that there is something mobile and hence unstable in the foundational structures of Venetian society.

One modern editor of the play notes a 'certain radiance in the movement' from Venice to Belmont, but he also notes that at the heart of this 'fair upland retreat' there lies a similarity of mood to that which prevails in Antonio's Venice (Merchant, 38–9). Portia's melancholy (1.2.1–2) is the result both of an effort of personal suppression (1.2.17–20) and of external patriarchal prohibition (1.2.22–4). This traverses what one editor calls 'the business of Venice' (Merchant, 39) in that the law of the state embodied in the Duke, who later presides over the trial of Antonio, is, early on in the play, given a specific domestic analogue in 'the will of a dead father'. The 'dangerous rocks' and 'roaring waters' that beset Antonio's mercantile ventures are the properties of a patriarchal force that is at once hostile and seductive, paternal and maternal. In Belmont, the obstacles are analogous to the properties of 'youth' characterized as 'blood' and 'hot temper' and requiring a form of control that is literally an absent presence in the play, and they are figured forth in the imaginary danger that the female poses to the unsuspecting male. This is a multi-faceted providence, working both internally and externally, whose unpredictably protean operations permeate the entire ethos of the play.

The frailty of Antonio's aptly feminized vessel is recalled at the very moment when he ritualistically renews his faith. Moreover, the threat of violation by a wild masculinized nature, invoked as the constitutive 'other' of 'the holy edifice of stone', reduces to 'nothing' the worth of the merchandise, and so deprives the merchant of his financial probity. In what is effectively a domestic analogue, the youthful tempests in Portia's blood threaten to burst the straitjacket of parental 'will' that functions to protect 'worth' and guarantee another sort of probity, female chastity. These two forms of patriarchal control, which govern different kinds of material increase, generate anxieties that are common to both Venice and Belmont. Voracity of appetite, against which mercantilism tries to protect itself, poses a radical threat to Venetian stability embodied in the unrestrained fiscal greed of the usurer, who, despite his public parsimony, is allowed to generate wealth promiscuously.

The proximity of material 'worth' derived from financial generation and sexual value suggests that the discourses of sex and money are never very far apart in the *Merchant of Venice*, and the categorical imperative to restraint is common to both. It is Portia's waiting-woman Nerissa, conscious of the divinely inspired game of chance that lies at the root of Christian prosperity, who identifies the connection between a patriarchally driven hermeneutic practice and an ethically sanctioned success:

> Your father was ever virtuous, and holy men at their
> death have good inspirations. Therefore the lottery
> that he hath devised in these three chests of gold,
> silver and lead, whereof who chooses his meaning
> chooses you, will no doubt never be chosen by any
> rightly but one who you shall rightly love.

(1.2.26–31)

This still makes marriage *feel* like a 'lottery', even though Portia's affections are shown in the event to harmonize with the 'will of a dead father'. But, as feminist critic Lynda Boose has astutely observed, Portia has ultimately more control over the terms of the contract of marriage she formulates at 3.2 than might at first appear (Boose, 247–8). Nor, indeed, is patriarchy without its own uncertainties and anxieties, as the later trials of Bassanio, torn between an obligation to his friend and to his wife, make clear. It is an essentially patriarchal law that binds the elements of Christian society together in the play, and it is shown to function reciprocally. And yet those intricately anarchic forces it seeks to control by a process of subjugation and marginalization always threaten to return and undermine its efficacy. In one sense, this is the characteristic mechanism of comedy, involving a positioning, and a distancing of radical threat, through the mechanism of laughter. In this play it is the objects of laughter that are problematical.

The teleological thrust of the play is towards a resolution of the tensions between parent and child, and to this extent the *Merchant of Venice* traverses a familiar comic terrain. The relation between Lancelet and Old Giobbe lends a comic emphasis to the more serious theme of the care and provision that children are expected to make for parents, an issue that assumes a greater importance in the later tragedy *King Lear* (1606). Old Giobbe's unspecified misfortunes may well be ameliorated by the changing fortunes of his son, but, in the figure of the Clown, name and role complement each other, since he is both the source of a therapeutic laughter and, as 'Lancelet', the instrument capable of piercing affliction and relieving misery: 'Our house is hell and thou, a merry devil, / Didst rob it of some taste of tediousness' (2.3.2–3). This permits the distinction to be drawn between the play's licensed clowning and the usurer-Jew who is a more serious threat to Venice.

Notwithstanding this role, Lancelet appears to be capable, like Jessica herself, of violating the order of the family. The Clown's assertion, later in the play, that there will be no mercy in heaven for Jessica because of her Jewish birth is countered by Lorenzo's rejoinder that he can 'answer that better to the commonwealth' than the Clown, who is now charged with 'the getting up of the negro's belly: the Moor is with child by you, Lancelet' (3.5.34–6). Editors have speculated wildly about this detail (Cam^2, 32n.), assuming that this reference to the Moor represents either the remains of a lost source, or an excuse for the introduction of a pun (Ard^2, 99n.). In contradiction to providing for his parent, Lancelet is accused here of an extreme form of miscegenation analogous to that of the marriage between a Christian and a Jew. This allusion to unlawful increase might have provided a further strand to support the motif of fathers and children in the play that Shakespeare neglected to pursue.

The provocation for Lorenzo's remark is Lancelet's reduction of the sacrament of marriage to the status of a market transaction whereby an increase in the number of Christians in Venice will raise the price of pork. The playful accusation draws from the clearly nettled Lorenzo a counter-allegation that is both perfectly in keeping with the conservative, patriarchal and racist ethos that informs Venice, at the same time as it emphasizes the Clown's libidinal propensity to promiscuity. The freedom that Portia conditionally relinquishes on yielding to Bassanio as her 'lord, her governor, her king' (3.2.165) is realized negatively in the Jessica–Lorenzo subplot. Moreover, the Clown's alleged violation of the institution of marriage serves momentarily, as in the case of Touchstone in the later *As You Like It*, to draw the discourse of romantic courtship into the reductive purview of the material world of imperfectly regulated sexual activity and its possible consequences.

THE GENERATION GAME

The relations between parents and children intersect with the play's ideologically motivated concern to distinguish between different types of generation. Together they form a matrix in which authorized and demonized forms of biological generation and legitimate and demonized forms of generation of material wealth are brought into conflict with each other. Involved in the exchange and circulation of commodities, Antonio is caught between dizzying signs of competing values that his own activities depend upon for success, and their object is the accumulation of what Jean-Joseph Goux calls 'a primordial commodity', gold (Goux, 17), or more generally material wealth.

This figuration of an assembly of commodities engaged in a stately, erotic maritime dance that replicates the courtesies of the social order is a poetic attempt to negotiate the contradiction between the reductive 'petty traffic' of commodity exchange and the social hierarchy that restrains and institutionalizes its anarchic energies. Antonio's awareness that his control over his own fortunes is limited expresses a *desire* for that patriarchal authority to which his own social rank can give him only partial access. He can only realize that power and authority vicariously through furnishing his social superior, Lord Bassanio, with the material means to secure Portia. This vicarious 'fathering' – a form of generation at second hand that will later allow him to acknowledge his own sterility as a 'tainted wether of the flock', *pace* Aristotle's strictures on the sterility of fiscal 'breeding' – is displaced into friendship as a means of legitimizing the accumulation of material wealth. Antonio's wealth, which is all 'at sea' (1.1.177), is the precarious foundation of his 'credit' (1.1.180). It is the generative substance that reproduces itself and functions as a 'universal equivalent' (Goux, 16), since not only is it the currency of commercial exchange but it is internalized as an indicator of human worth. This wealth is characterized in the play as a transcendent metaphysical force, but it is also an earthly power subject to moral and ethical circumscription. And of course its latter identification drives the moral and ethical outrage that informs much of the writing about the most extreme and anarchic form of wealth accumulation, usury, in the late sixteenth century. Such is the complex nature of mercantile activity, its identity suspended between 'natural' and 'artificial' generation, and so volatile are its movements, that even Antonio himself at the outset of the play cannot 'know' himself. The 'gentle vessel' whose integrity is risked in the ritualized encounter with nature literally figures the larger fate of Antonio's argosies, but it is also a metaphor for Bassanio's project and the fate of Portia herself.

What remains unarticulated in the opening scene of the play is glossed in a more specific manner in 1.2, in which an absent primordial power is shown to be responsible for the generation of its earthly specular image. Portia's value as a potentially fecund commodity is expressed in terms of the multiple relationships that present themselves as possibilities figured in the international competition for her hand in marriage that we later see 'staged' in the casket game. But at the moment when it looks as though her value will be expressed in what Goux describes as 'one single commodity taken as a universal equivalent' (Goux, 16) the rules of the dead father's game demand the inversion of the traditional symbols of worth. In the casket scenes gold is not the 'universal equivalent' against which all commodities are valued but the key to a sterile existence, while it is the worthless lead that proves to be of greatest symbolic value. In Belmont, as indeed in the urbane and sophisticated Venice, nothing is quite what it seems. This inversion of the symbols of value drives a wedge between the material world and the sacrament of marriage, even as it incorporates both into its structures. The transcendent law of the dead father becomes the source of meaning itself, an alternative to that more volatile, earthly substance, material wealth, which makes of language a struggle for meaning, and threatens to subjugate the human world to its necessarily mutable and transitory practices. It is the patriarchal law of the father that contains the circulation of commodities, and that authorizes, guarantees and limits the generation of meaning.

However, the process of stabilizing meaning is shown to be a precarious one, always open to subversion from a libidinal energy that threatens order and hierarchy. Portia is one of the play's persistent indices of this tension, since having seen the contents of two of the three caskets (2.7 and 2.9) she must clearly be aware of the contents of the third (3.2) but is forbidden from disclosing them. This is certainly suggested in Michael Radford's film *The Merchant of Venice* (2004), and it has become a source of critical debate whether the end-rhymes 'bred', 'head' and 'nourished' actually direct Bassanio to choose the 'lead' casket (3.2.63–5). Of course, to rig the test would be to minimize the dramatic tension between the daughter's insistent desire and the dead father's injunction that is present from the very beginning, and Portia is forbidden from revealing the answer to any of her suitors. Indeed, it is important that ideologically and aesthetically the two contending forces are brought into alignment with each other, hence the model of harmony and reciprocity that the song performs with its binding rhymes and choral repetitions.

At the level of content, however, the song asks questions about the begetting, breeding and ultimate death of 'fancy' (3.2.63ff.). Bassanio's is the only suit to Portia that is interrupted in this way, and the dramatic postponement of his choice stages a public formal replaying of the earlier, more prosaic and domestic exchange between Portia and Nerissa (1.2.26ff.). Indeed, Portia recalls in an aside the very initial restraint that is required to curb her 'ecstasy': 'O, love, be moderate, allay thy ecstasy, / In measure rain thy joy, scant this excess. / I feel too much thy blessing; make it less / For fear I surfeit' (3.2.111–14). 'Excess' is a multiple signifier in the play that is applicable to the effects both of unrestrained sexual energy and of monetary 'interest'. Ironically in the play, the two activities are shown to be necessary in order for society to function, but they are also potentially dangerous unless they are properly regulated.

Marc Shell aligns the ethos of exchange with the trading of 'a human life for a human life', and argues that 'the essential dilemma of this play [is] about people and property' (Shell, 66). He goes on to suggest that the 'death' of Jessica – her conversion to Christianity – compels her father to seek revenge in accordance with an interpretation of the demands of Judaic law: '[for] the loss of his daughter – his own flesh and blood – he will take the flesh and blood of Antonio' (61). Jessica's elopement with the Jew's *raison d'être*, his money, contrasts with Portia's commitment to the injunction of her dead father, and signals the death of a future that it is the function of comedy to uphold. Indeed, at the end of the Sheffield-based Compass Theatre's 1997 production of the play, Carolyn Bazely, who doubled as Nerissa and Jessica, is deprived of her father's wealth, excluded from Belmont, and left weeping outside the gate. Brown has argued that Jessica's contribution is to the theme of 'love's wealth' in that her squandering of Shylock's wealth is an excusable fault and 'an understandable excess after the restriction of her father's precept of "*Fast bind, fast find; / A proverb never stale in thrifty mind*"' (2.5.52–3; Brown, *Comedies*, 70). However, this persuasive collapsing together of the material and spiritual worlds of the play is impossible to sustain, either critically or dramatically, because there remains a corrosive disjunction between biological generation and the generation of material wealth that cannot be expunged.

Antonio's initial telling conflation of 'purse' and 'person' initiates a linguistic promiscuity that infects the entire action of the play. It is intended to align a means with an end, to propose a *use* of money, in the Aristotelian sense, to express and facilitate friendship and to satisfy need. But, when Shylock collapses his own progeny into material wealth, the effects of the declension prove to be more sinister; Salanio registers 'a passion so confused', when he reports the 'dog Jew's' words: 'My daughter! O, my ducats! O, my daughter! / Fled with a Christian! O, my Christian ducats!' (2.8.12–16). Shell is correct to observe that ultimately 'the Venetian court cannot provide a satisfactory resolution to the ideological dilemma of property and person that gave rise to the action of *The Merchant of Venice* in the first place' (Shell, 74). But the problem arises from the ways in which the discourse of biological generation furnishes the metaphors for wealth creation. Nor is it simply a question of displacing the discourse of material wealth into the idealizing neo-Platonic discourse of romantic love in an attempt to remystify the act of generation. Jessica does what Portia refuses to do – she rebels, and it is her father who registers the enormity of her action: 'My own flesh and blood to rebel!' (3.1.31). Salanio utilizes this outburst to invoke the stereotypical allegation that Shylock is himself guilty of sexual promiscuity. And when the latter attempts to correct his interpretation, 'I say my daughter is my flesh and blood' (3.1.33), Salarino retorts with a shocking allegation of miscegenation that all but anticipates Lorenzo's accusation directed at the Clown later in the play at 3.5: 'There is more difference between thy flesh and hers than between jet and ivory, more between your bloods than there is between red wine and Rhenish' (3.1.34–6). The claim is not only that Jessica is 'legitimate' and that Shylock is the bastard, but that he is also, if not physically, then metaphorically 'black', and that, as the devil, his libidinal desires know no restraint.[1] This disturbing inversion proffers a fascinating insight into the economy of racial insult, but it also extends the comparison between the ways in which Shylock generates wealth, the way in which he is alleged to have begotten his own child and the way in which he now allegedly '(mis)uses' her. For Salarino 'usury' knows no decorum, and its libidinal energies carry generative excess to shockingly amoral extremes.

From the outset, lineage and the generation of money are closely interwoven in the narrative of the Jew's long history. In 1.3 the exchange between Antonio and Shylock, concerning the legitimacy and the details of the loan requested, turns

1 See Appendix 1 for the suggestion that Shylock and Morocco may have been 'doubled' in performance.

quickly to the authorization of usurious practice. The narrative involving Jacob's enterprising ruse to secure 'streaked and pied' lambs as payment for tending his uncle Laban's flock (1.3.67ff.) begins in deception. The Geneva Bible offers a marginal gloss that brands the young Jacob as a deceiver because he swindles his elder brother Esau out of his birthright: 'he was so called because he helde his brother by ye hele, as thogh he wolde ouerthrowe him & therefore, he is here called an ouerthrower, or deceyuer' (Genesis, 27.36). As in the story of Jacob's inheritance, so Shylock deceives nature in order to generate wealth (1.3.78–86). However, the Jew's citing of Scripture does the precise opposite of legitimizing his fiscal practices; in fact, it implicates him in a deceitful economy of generation in which increase of material wealth is literally animated. Gold and silver become 'ewes' and 'rams', while the pun on 'ewes/Iewes' (Shell, 48ff.) returns the material/animal to the racially divided human world of Venice. What is at stake here is not, as Brown argues, Antonio's 'impatience' (Ard², 25n.), but a dispute about the interpretation of lineage in which the 'stranger' inadvertently proffers a pastiche of Christian authorization.

Shylock will deploy a similar rhetorical strategy later in the play, when, stripped of all of the indicators of his identity, he seeks to align himself with his Christian tormentors. What begins as a plea for biological sameness – 'Hath not a Jew eyes? Hath not a Jew hands, organs, dimensions, senses, affections, passions?' – turns into a cultural critique that reverses the role of persecutor and victim:

> If you prick us do we not bleed? If you tickle us do
> we not laugh? If you poison us do we not die? And
> if you wrong us shall we not revenge? If we are
> like you in the rest, we will resemble you in that.
> If a Jew wrong a Christian, what is his humility?
> Revenge! If a Christian wrong a Jew, what should his

sufferance be by Christian example? Why, revenge!
The villainy you teach me I will execute, and it shall
go hard but I will better the instruction.

(3.1.53–66)[1]

It is important not to overlook the complexity of the Jew's
motivation here, since it crystallizes two events: the rebellion of
his 'flesh and blood' daughter and Antonio's failure to generate
the means to pay off his debt. This is not quite, as Stephen
Greenblatt claims, a case of the Jew appealing to a 'sameness'
that 'runs like a dark current through the play, intimating
secret bonds that no one, not even the audience, can fully
acknowledge' (Greenblatt, 'Marlowe', 43).[2] Rather, it seeks to
reverse the process of displacement by legal process, thereby
transferring the emotion generated by Jessica's filial rebellion
onto the business of Antonio's failure to fulfil the conditions of
the 'merry bond'. This turn from an earlier comic scenario to
what now threatens to become a deadly game further vindicates
the Christian claim that the Jew is a duplicitous 'devil' who cites
Scripture, and invokes his pedigree for sinister motives.

The problem, however, is that the Jew's defence exposes
an ethic of revenge that undermines the Christian claim to
tolerance. To a modern audience or reader this appears as a series
of rhetorical questions in an attempt to establish a common
humanity. Indeed, in Michael Bogdanov's 2004 production, this
is the moment when Shylock (Philip Madoc) begins visibly to
retreat into his own Jewish faith, a movement that is accelerated
by the engineering of a contrast with the casual, unconcerned
demeanour of Tubal (Bill Wallis). The speech, however, exposes
the very *structure* of racial prejudice, in that the disempowered,

1 Cf. Emilia's indictment of masculine authority and its allegations of female transgression in *Othello*: 'And have not we affections? / Desire for sport? And frailty, as
   men have? / Then let them use us well: else let them know, / The ills we do, their
   ills instruct us so' (*Oth* 4.3.99–102).
2 In a seductive rhetorical flourish, Greenblatt goes on to suggest: 'For if Shakespeare
   subtly suggests obscure links between Jew and Gentile, he compels the audience to
   transform its disturbing perception of sameness into a reassuring perception of difference. Indeed the Jew seems to embody the abstract principle of *difference* itself.'

emasculated 'stranger', who is deprived of his daughter and his money, responds by imitating what he perceives to be a Christian appropriation of Old Testament justice in which vengeance figures more prominently than forgiveness.

The Jew cannot be both the index of 'sameness' and an irreducible *difference* or 'the abstract principle of *difference*', since he too is constructed upon the axis of a series of differences, the most crucial of which revolves around the metaphor of generation. Salarino's 'There is more *difference* between thy flesh and hers [Jessica's]' (3.1.34–5) opens the word 'flesh' to a series of conflicting meanings that reveal a struggle between a socially approved method of generation and a hellish aberration that biologically and fiscally perverts an accepted natural order. And yet, paradoxically, in its biological manifestation the drive to generate threatens to expose fallen nature, while, in its fiscal manifestation, generation has become a recognized evil, necessary as the means to further legitimate economic activity. Far from being a transcendent principle of difference, the Jew is the very model of its differential economy, and the key to our understanding of a whole range of constitutive differences that the play uncovers in its path to resolution.

It is important for us to grasp how that system of differences is constructed, not in the abstract, but in its historically identifiable specificity. The Jew's appeal discloses what the post-colonial theorist Homi Bhabha would identify as an instance of 'mimicry' (Bhabha, 87–8), an imitation that exposes the nature of his irreducible *otherness* at the same time as it problematizes the system whose practices he now ventriloquizes. This conflict is embodied in Shylock's English name, and the implication that at the heart of English national identity is an otherness that is both racial and theological. This generative energy that is both libidinal and economic, which threatens all forms of stability, discloses in dramatic form that larger system of differences within whose aegis Elizabethan subjectivity was inscribed. It is no accident that in the trial scene Shylock should appeal to the feminized 'other' of reason: 'affection, / Maistrice of passion' that 'sways it to the mood / Of what it likes or loathes' (4.1.49–51).[1] Nowhere is this more evident than in the dysfunctional family over which Shylock presides, and which to some extent is a cruel parody of the family of which Portia is a part. The living Jew's patriarchal authority is questioned in his own house, whereas the wisdom of the dead Christian father's word (and his meaning) is adhered to in Belmont.

Curiously, it is the elopement episode in the *Merchant of Venice* along with its racial overtones that Shakespeare chose to return to in the later play, *Othello*. In Ser Giovanni's *Il Pecorone*, and *The Ballad of Gernutus*, no daughter appears. Jessica's role in the structure of the *Merchant of Venice*, however, is crucial in so far as it provides a mirror for the romantic plot involving Portia and Bassanio. Unlike Portia, who acknowledges her dead father's authority, Jessica asks 'what heinous sin is it in me / To be ashamed to be my father's child!' (2.3.16–17). Indeed, she draws an even finer distinction, admitting to a biological connection, but at the same time denying any cultural affiliation to her father: 'But, though I am a daughter to his blood, / I am not to his manners' (2.3.18–19). In short, this is a household in which the process of generation has gone awry, and where the customary frustrations of youth are supplanted by deeper, potentially more damaging forces, some of whose constraints generate more radical countervailing energies. Some productions have gone to some lengths to motivate Jessica's rebellion; for example, at the point when the Jew gives her the keys to his house and exhorts her to 'Do as I bid you' (2.5.51), in the 1978 RSC production Shylock (Patrick Stewart) strikes Jessica (Avril Carson) across the face. Moreover, at this point in the play, the Jew reveals a capacity for mimicry that we have already noted when he says that he is willing to yield only to the outward

---

1   Cf. *FQ*, book 2, 221, where the 'rational' Sir Guyon confronts the 'irrational' Pyrochles: 'Though somewhat moued in his mightie hart, / Yet with strong reason maistered passion raile, / And passed fairly forth', and also the figure of Mammon (*FQ*, 2.7.3).

form of Christian festivity, seeking secretly and usuriously 'to feed upon / The prodigal Christian' (2.5.14–15). Shylock's is a much more sinister manifestation of patriarchal 'will', since in its perverted form it cannot distinguish between devising 'laws for the blood' (1.2.17–18) and that more radical challenge to the very laws of Christian courtesy that enfolds the business of financial exchange in a series of social rituals. The exchange with Jessica allows us to see precisely what Shylock's 'manners' comprise, and, although few actors have gone as far as Patrick Stewart – and Stewart withdrew the gesture in later performances – the result is a lack of mutual trust between daughter and father to the point where she is prepared to negate the fact of her generation.

There is, however, a larger context in the play for this systematic inversion of the relation between generations evidenced in Shylock's household. Whereas in the later play *Othello* Desdemona's filial rebellion has deadly consequences in that it results in the death of her father, here Jessica's rebellion is given a positive motivation, in that her behaviour may be excused because she is the daughter of a Jew. At the end of 2.4 Lorenzo offers the following justification in his conversation with Gratiano:

> If e'er the Jew her father come to heaven,
> It will be for his gentle daughter's sake;
> And never dare misfortune cross her foot
> Unless she do it under the excuse:
> That she is issue to a faithless Jew.
>
> (2.4.34–8)

This is a rare moment in Shakespeare, where a daughter's rebellion is justified on religious grounds as a path to conversion, while the blame for any aberrant behaviour that she might display is displaced onto an alienated and alienating father. The linguistic opposition between 'Jew' and 'gentle' (gentile) here is part of a larger economy of *difference* whose function is designed, to use Albert Memmi's words, 'to denigrate the other, to the end of gaining privilege or benefit through the stigmatization' (Memmi, 37–8). The play's meticulous detailing of the elements of conflict allow us to read – though not, from a modern perspective, to endorse – these moments.

It is important to keep in mind, however, that Shylock is still a father, and, for late Elizabethan culture, the representation of a thwarted or deceived father requires careful negotiation. Sigurd Burckhardt's claim that 'Wherever we look, the Jessica–Lorenzo affair appears to be an inversion of true, bonded love' (Burckhardt, 253) exaggerates what in the play is much more ambivalent. Moreover, the name of the Jew's absent spouse, Leah, associates Shylock both with the Old Testament figure of Jacob's wife Leah, who is 'bleare eied' (Genesis, 29.17), and with Spenser's figure of Mammon, whose eyes are 'bleard' from watching over his money (*FQ*, 2.4). Jessica's exchanging of her father's ring for a monkey is even more tendentious in that it lays open to ridicule his courtship and subsequent marriage; it asserts an equivalence between 'ring' and 'monkey' that makes of Shylock's marriage an animalistic mimicry of a Venetian ritual.[1] And yet attached to this mimicry is a structure of feeling that qualifies the Jew's alienation in its privileging of the terms 'husband' and 'father'. The eloping Jessica, 'blinded' by love, had, herself, already expressed discomfort with her transformation into the figure of a boy:

> Here, catch this casket; it is worth the pains.
> I am glad 'tis night you do not look on me,
> For I am much ashamed of my exchange.
> But love is blind, and lovers cannot see
> The pretty follies that themselves commit,
> For, if they could, Cupid himself would blush
> To see me thus transformed to a boy.
>
> (2.6.34–40)

---

1 In the Michael Radford film (2004) the final shot is of Jessica looking out over the lake at Belmont fingering the ring that she is alleged to have exchanged for a monkey. This suggests that Tubal's earlier account has the status of gossip, and anti-Semitic gossip at that.

But this is but one of a number of exchanges in which she is involved, and each is aligned with one of the play's major motifs. Jessica's action is doubly significant because it exposes Shylock's imitative behaviour in such a way as to expand the lexicon of the play's dominant racist discourse, while at the same time allowing us to glimpse the material basis of the romantic discourse associated with Belmont.

Jessica is a Derridean *pharmakon*, in that she can poison her father's life through her wilfully reductive violation of those intimate rituals that authorize his patriarchal power, but by actually crossing over 'into the other' she becomes the vehicle through whom a Christian Venetian cure is administered.[1] Her actions, and her positioning in the play, replicate in a different register the position that the Jew himself occupies as *pharmakon*. The virulently anti-Semitic language of Venice is deployed as a means of focusing the threat that he poses, a personification of the disease that lies heavy on the heart of the state. The usurer holds in his power all those who come within his clutches, and he 'feeds' on his Christian victims while at the same time upholding the letter of the law. But he is also the cure for Venice's economic problems, since it is his control of the money supply – in particular his agency in the circulation of capital – that permits trade to flourish. The deep anxiety that this paradox generates begins in a playful vein when Gratiano offers to put a price on the act of generation itself: 'We'll play with them the first boy for a thousand ducats' (3.2.213–14). But it overflows the courtroom resolution of Act 4 and is finally brought to bear on the material foundation of the masculine fear of loss of possession: 'Well, while I live, I'll fear no other thing / So sore as keeping safe Nerissa's ring' (5.1.306–7). And at the root of the business of generation is the government of the household.

1   See Derrida, 'Pharmacy', 127, in which the '*pharmakon*' is described as 'the medium in which opposites are opposed, the movement and the play that links them among themselves, reverses them or makes one side cross over into the other, capable of effecting both a poison and a cure.'

CASKETS AND RINGS

Jessica is one of a number of characters whose function is to link two overlapping worlds of the play together. She elopes with a 'casket' (2.6.34) that, like one of the caskets in Belmont, contains her father's 'meaning', his wealth; she sells the ring he gave to Leah; and she is the agent of his metaphorical death, his enforced conversion to Christianity. The scene of Jessica's elopement is strategically positioned immediately before the entry of the first of Portia's two unsuccessful suitors, Morocco. But unlike Portia she gives way to the insistent demands of her 'blood' and, in a wilful rejection of her domestic role and the patriarchal authority of her father, chooses to be her own meaning.

Freud was well aware of the symbolism of caskets in the play, although he made no mention of Jessica. He noted that Portia becomes an object of choice whose qualities are displaced into the three caskets, and that, in a play where financial success is normally dependent upon forces outside human control, choice becomes a means of subverting destiny. He put the matter thus: 'Choice stands in the place of necessity, of destiny. In this way man overcomes death, which he has recognized intellectually. No greater triumph of wish fulfilment is conceivable' (Freud, 244–5). It is Freud's claim that the mythological goddess of death is transformed in the *Merchant of Venice* into 'the fairest and most desirable of women' but that she retains 'certain characteristics that border on the uncanny' (245). Freud's argument accounts in part for the odd combination of racist and nationalist sentiment that surrounds the episodes involving Morocco and Arragon, as well as for an even more perplexing combination of eagerness and diffidence that surrounds Bassanio's choosing.

Jessica drives through the fraught terrain of parental constraint, borrowing the appearance of an adolescent masculinity, and projects herself into a romantic entanglement that will ultimately limit her freedom. Indeed, Lancelet's joke at the beginning of the final scene of the play, 'Sola! Did you see Master Lorenzo and

Mistress Lorenza!' (5.1.41–2), goes some way to emphasizing this. Portia, by contrast, is compelled to act within a series of constraints that paradoxically restore agency to her. She is disempowered by patriarchy, but re-empowered as a consequence of acceding to its demands. Portia embodies what Freud describes as 'the three inevitable relations that a man has with a woman – the woman who bears him, the woman who is his mate and the woman who destroys him' (Freud, 247). Portia is described metonymically by Bassanio as a 'golden fleece' (1.1.170), but in a context in which all that glisters is not gold. Those who believe that the song and its allegedly tendentious rhymes are designed to steer Bassanio to the correct casket need only consider its effect upon him; it provokes a meditation upon the precarious nature of worldly surfaces. 'Outward shows' may be 'least themselves' (3.2.73), and this admission of the mutability that customarily infects choice is extended to cover all earthly practice:

> The world is still deceived with ornament.
> In law, what plea so tainted and corrupt,
> But, being seasoned with a gracious voice,
> Obscures the show of evil? In religion,
> What damned error but some sober brow
> Will bless it and approve it with a text,
> Hiding the grossness with fair ornament?
> There is no vice so simple but assumes
> Some mark of virtue on his outward parts.
> (3.2.74–82)

This long meditation is not usually an aside in performance; therefore what Portia hears should give her pause for thought – now, as Bassanio proceeds to muse on beauty and the hair that he had earlier reified, and later, when she deploys her 'gracious voice' in the service of the law:

> Look on beauty,
> And you shall see 'tis purchased by the weight,
> Which therein works a miracle in nature,

Making them lightest that wear most of it:
So are those crisped snaky golden locks,
Which maketh such wanton gambols with the wind
Upon supposed fairness, often known
To be the dowry of a second head,
The skull that bred them in the sepulchre.
Thus, ornament is but the guiled shore
To a most dangerous sea; the beauteous scarf
Veiling an Indian beauty; in a word,
The seeming truth, which cunning times put on
To entrap the wisest.

(3.2.88–101)

These axioms are directed initially to the golden casket, which is both 'guiled' and 'gilded', but they are applicable to the object of Bassanio's desire, since they recall linguistically, and in more detail, earlier evaluations of Portia's physical and material attributes. There is also the faint suggestion here that possession, and indeed marriage itself, is a risky proposition in that the suitor can never be sure of his prize. The complex metaphor of Portia's dowry functions as an index of death, 'a second head, / The skull that bred them in the sepulchre' (3.2.95–6), and of her beauty, as the deceitful object of the sailor's quest, and as a means of concentrating the play's main themes in the caskets. These caskets are symptoms of a self-deluded world that contains not only the duplicitous Jew but the potentially deceitful female, who is herself a kind of potentially duplicitous 'casket'. Venice and Belmont, for all the attempts of critics to separate them in the play's own imaginative ethos, are not what they seem, and are a little too close to each other for comfort.[1] Close, but not identical.

---

1 Cf. Belsey, 'Love', 45, where 'uncertainty' and 'enigma' are located in the riddle of the caskets as an enactment of 'desire'. Belsey regards the wooing of Portia as displaying 'a perfect appropriateness, a ceremonial decorum which endows it with all the traditional impersonality of the Anglican marriage service itself' (Belsey, 'Love', 46).

Bassanio's moral generalizations, however, are brought to bear literally on the caskets themselves, although his choice is circumscribed by an outright rejection of gold and silver, the two metals that, as symbols of monetary exchange, he sought from the outset. The dead father's legacy, as Freud astutely observed, encompasses the patriarchal fear of femininity, but it is also an acknowledgement of the desire for woman as the instrument through which male posterity may be secured. The play makes little of the discrepancy between the appearance of lead, 'thou meagre lead, / Which rather threaten'st than dost promise aught' (3.2.104–5), and the 'golden fleece' that adorns the beautiful Portia, except to hint at the danger that the latter poses. Portia is simultaneously the excess that threatens to escape patriarchal control and also its justification. Moreover, if lead is the receptacle of true beauty because it contains 'Fair Portia's counterfeit' (3.2.115), then it is important that the play should attempt to separate monetary from spiritual value in order to avoid the risk of the one contaminating the other. It is not just Bassanio who is shown to be in denial here but possibly an entire culture faced with a challenge to institutions whose capacity to mystify the relation between the sacred and the profane, the material and the spiritual, had hitherto managed to evade such radical questioning. It is as though the entire ideological fabric of Shakespearean comedy gapes momentarily to disclose a series of social contradictions that simply cannot contain the corrosive potential of the material wealth that it is so eager to accumulate.

It is also important for us to understand the larger context within which Bassanio is enjoined to play the game of choosing. The conditions are those of a wager – Portia calls it 'the lott'ry of my destiny' (2.1.15) – and the play views the prospect of marriage as just such a precarious enterprise that proscribes female choice. The first adventurer is Morocco, whose choice is postponed from the opening scene of Act 2 until scene 7. His Moorish pedigree would have struck a particularly Venetian chord with Elizabethan audiences, and it was to Morocco's slightly revised fortunes that Shakespeare returned in *Othello*. Morocco, like Othello, self-consciously dismisses his own 'complexion' (2.1.1) and asserts that his 'blood' is no different from that of 'the fairest creature northward born' (2.1.4). His appeal is not far removed from that of Shylock's to sameness at 3.1, and his utterance, like Shylock's, is distinct, betraying what Etienne Balibar calls a 'linguistic ethnicity' as opposed to a 'racial (or hereditary) ethnicity'. The openness of Morocco's linguistic ethnicity allows him to be identified with, though separated from, the characters around him in much the same way that Arragon will later be distinguished from the inhabitants of Belmont.

This cultural exclusiveness, to which Portia refers in her expression of relief at Morocco's failure of the casket test, is part of the mercantilist pressure that the play exerts upon the business of national identity. Outsiders traverse the gamut from the exotic to the ridiculous, as indeed stage portrayals of Morocco frequently demonstrate,[1] but they are deprived of those sophisticated skills required to interpret complex meaning, and as such can be dismissed summarily: 'A gentle riddance. Draw the curtains, go. / Let all of his complexion choose me so' (2.7.78–9). Destiny, it would appear, is on the side of a 'gentle'/'gentile' racial purity in the play. Portia will not be allowed to cohabit with a Moor whose name 'Morochus'/'Morrocho' in the quarto spelling would have recalled John Dando and Harry Hunt's popular tract *Maroccus Extaticus*, or *Bankes Bay Horse in a Trance* (1595), published by Cuthbert Burby. Maroccus was a talking 'Moorish' or Barbary horse that captured the imagination of Londoners in 1595, and was able to calculate monetary equivalences because he could 'tell just the number of pence in any piece of silver coin newly showed him by his master' (quoted in *Shakespeare's England*,

---

1 A number of modern productions depict Morocco as an extravagant, ornately dressed African, who flourishes his sword in a comically menacing manner especially at 2.1.24, where he swears 'By this scimitar'. Michael Radford's film (2004) recuperates these familiar gestures and augments them with an admiring and encouraging African retinue.

2.410). Even without the aid of extravagant theatrical flourishes, an Elizabethan audience would already have had a local as well as a stereotyped context in which to judge (and laugh at) Morocco.

This episode offers us an insight into how Belmont imagines itself, defined along the axes of differences between the exotic and the dangerous, the human and the animal, and the civilized and the barbaric.[1] The discourse that the theatrical figure of Morocco seeks to counter works against, but fails to overcome, the popular prejudices that interpret his 'otherness' in terms of blackness, promiscuity and animality, three attributions that are, at various points in the play, attached to the Jew. Arragon, another stereotyped 'foreign' suitor, is subjected to merciless ridicule, in which his Hispanic origin is brought into punning alignment with his demeanour: 'Arragon'/'arrogant'. Appropriately he seeks to distinguish himself from 'the barbarous multitudes', those 'common spirits' with whom he will not associate himself because he 'will not choose what many men desire' (2.9.30).

These two episodes draw on the verbal resources of a discourse of racial otherness that shapes the perceptions of its 'gentle' users, and within whose boundaries the Jew is vilified in Venice. In this, as in other respects, there is a reassuringly self-satisfied continuity between Venice's and Belmont's perceptions of the world in so far as both are capable of establishing their own racially inflected identities through a conservative laughter that banishes all that is 'foreign' to the margins. Up to a point this prejudiced reassurance invites acquiescence, but only up to a point, since it also exposes Venice and Belmont as internally divided states in which different nationalities do not, indeed cannot, coexist harmoniously. Not only that, but choice itself is shown to be over-determined by an active but absent metaphysical force committed to a combination of racial purity and social hierarchy. In the *Merchant of Venice* dead Christian

---

1   Cf. *Oth* 1.1.108–12: 'Because we come to do you service, you think we are ruffians, you'll have your daughter covered with a Barbary horse; you'll have your nephews neigh to you; you'll have coursers for cousins, and gennets for germans.'

fathers do not die; rather, they live on through their progeny and speak with authority from beyond the grave. Those who exist outside its boundaries must be either expelled or coerced. That an Elizabethan audience might have approved of this expulsion or coercion, whereas a modern audience would not, is an indication of a historical difference that the play itself repeatedly discloses.

IDENTITIES

The theatrical *frisson* that the casket game affords cannot be allowed to obscure a fundamental preoccupation with the identity conferred upon the individual by group membership in the play. Bassanio's success will guarantee his social status, since he will marry an heiress as well as replenish his impoverished purse. But in unlocking the leaden casket he also unlocks the 'meaning' of Portia that has been mediated through the continuing provision of her dead father, although, as Catherine Belsey observes, Portia is possessed of more than one identity in the play (Belsey, 'Love', 48). Bassanio does indeed 'come by note to give and to receive' (3.2.140), but in the light of his earlier strictures he remains uncertain of his prize:

> So, thrice-fair lady, stand I even so,
> As doubtful whether what I see be true,
> Until confirmed, signed, ratified by you.
>   (3.2.146–8)

This is the language of legal contract, of fiduciary exchange, that infects what is otherwise a successful romantic encounter, and its effect on Portia tellingly prompts a complex renegotiation of her identity. She responds to Bassanio by initially asserting her own split subjectivity, 'You see me, Lord Bassanio, where I stand, / Such as I am' (3.2.149–50), and wishes that she were better endowed to the point where she might 'Exceed account' (3.2.157). What was at the beginning of the play a potentially dangerous female excess

87

now becomes a desired 'interest' to be placed as profit at the feet of her successful suitor. It is difficult to know what to make, in this context, of the sudden regression that allows Portia to characterize herself as 'an unlessoned girl, unschooled, unpractised' (3.2.159). What is certain is that the transfer of chattels from one form of patriarchal control to another is undertaken in the full knowledge of the transformation that it will entail:

> Happiest of all, is that her gentle spirit
> Commits itself to yours to be directed,
> As from her lord, her governor, her king.
> Myself, and what is mine, to you and yours
> Is now converted. But now, I was the lord
> Of this fair mansion, master of my servants,
> Queen o'er myself; and even now, but now,
> This house, these servants and this same myself,
> Are yours, my lord's. I give them with this ring . . .
> Which, when you part from, lose or give away,
> Let it presage the ruin of your love,
> And be my vantage to exclaim on you.
>
> (3.2.163–74)

Portia sees this process as a 'conversion', although she seems to overstate the power that she now proposes to relinquish, since we know that her independence is carefully, if not entirely, circumscribed within the law of a dead father. From the outset she is aware of the dangers of sensuality, but here, confronted with a future husband, she adopts the posture of an ethically independent self, while at the same time acknowledging her subject position within a hierarchical order.

Portia's bestowal of the ring upon Bassanio, echoed in Nerissa's imitation of her mistress's actions, and in Jessica's reported perverse undermining of the ritual, asserts an ethical independence and possibly a power of sorts (Boose, 251–2),[1] and it also affirms the wisdom of her father. It is difficult to interpret Jessica's action as anything but transgressive, since it flies directly in the face of the very hierarchical order that the play strives to uphold, and plays fast and loose with the concept of fidelity. But it is, as we have seen, an exceptional case in that her transgression brings Shylock's dysfunctional family within the purview of a Christian order.

One of the analogues for Jessica that Shakespeare might well have had in mind was that of Marlowe's Abigail, whose securing of her father's wealth elicits ecstasy rather than apoplexy: 'O my girl, / My gold, my fortune, my felicity' (*Jew of Malta*, 2.1.47–8). Another may have been the figure of the Old Testament Rachel, sister of Leah, both wives of Jacob, who absconds from her father Laban's house: 'But Laban was gone to sheere his sheepe: and Rachel had stolen her fathers images' (Bishops' Bible; 'stale her fathers idoles' in the Geneva Bible) (Genesis, 31.19). John Coolidge argues that Jessica's elopement is a repetition of Jacob's absconding with Leah (Coolidge, 247), and if this is so then that knowledge would certainly modify any response to Shylock's subsequent anxiety. But Jessica's escapade is also a parody of the casket test (see Stephens, 120) in its literalizing of what in the test proper is a symbolic content. Moreover, it is her capacity for transgression that motivates her participation in the rehearsal of the catalogue of love's misfortunes at the beginning of the final act of the play, and allows her to make light of her actions.

Portia and Jessica treat the business with the caskets differently, in that Portia gives herself over to a game that takes the contradictions of the world fully into account and accepts that her future rests upon a gamble over which she has no control. Her domestic destiny is as precarious as Antonio's

---

1 See also Karen Newman for the claim that, when she gives herself to Bassanio, 'Portia objectifies herself and thereby suppresses her own agency in bestowing herself upon Bassanio' (Newman, 111).

commercial venturing, and she is, herself, caught up in it as the object of Bassanio's quest, which is itself dependent upon the sophisticated hermeneutic process of locating meaning. For Jessica, the contents of the casket she purloins are primarily a means to enter a market of material exchange that tendentiously ascribes equivalent value to rings and monkeys. For the one, identity is clearly circumscribed, and its instabilities are part of a process of transition from daughter to wife, but for the other identity is predicated upon an act of rebellion whose radical effects the play is quick to neutralize.

The stabilizing of Portia's identity at 3.2 follows hard upon the radical destabilizing of Jessica's identity that is underscored by her transformation (Derrida would say 'translation')[1] into the disguise of 'a boy' (2.6.40). Not merely that, but Jessica has already demonstrated her willingness to augment this disguise further, and in a manner that associates her with deceitful appearance: 'I will make fast the doors and gild myself / With some moe ducats' (2.6.50–1). Unlike Portia, Jessica does not bestow herself and her possessions through the ritual gift of a ring, and this is of a piece with her earlier self-division, when she wilfully refuses the curb of her father, to the point of rejecting her parentage at 2.3.17–19. After her elopement this becomes the subject of a light-hearted exchange with the Clown; Lancelet says that Jessica is now 'damned' (3.5.5), and that her only salvation lies in the hope that 'your father got you not, that you are not the Jew's daughter' (3.5.9–10). Jessica affects to be affronted at the Clown's implication of her bastardy, and this catches him between the forces of 'Scylla your father' and 'Charybdis your mother' (3.5.14–15). Her solution to this paradox is to airily invoke the power of Christian patriarchy – 'I shall be saved by my husband; he hath made me a Christian!' (3.5.17–18) – in a manner that is in direct contrast to the ritual

---

1 Derrida, 'Translation', 430–1, in which he notes the 'translation' of female identity into male identity, although at this point his concern is with Portia's disguise as a lawyer.

undergone by Portia and Bassanio and Nerissa and Gratiano. Jessica is here shown to inhabit a Christian identity differently from the inhabitants of Belmont and Venice. This is also, possibly, the source of animosity between Portia and Jessica displayed in the final act of the play in the Jonathan Miller production, where the actress Joan Plowright (Portia) disdains to acknowledge Jessica.

The racist animosity that is generated by the outsider's desire to be included achieves its crudest expression in the murderous hatred of Gratiano towards the Jew. Manipulative patriarchy elicits a degree of sympathy in so far as Portia's judiciously conditional will is made to conform to its demands, but in the case of Shylock's 'family', however, the discourse of gift-giving is transformed into a theologically sanctioned denigration. Jessica violates the symbolic significance of the exchange of love tokens, while the Jew himself declines into a Judas who is invited to re-enact part of the anti-Semitic narrative of Christian suffering: 'Beg that thou mayst have leave to hang thyself' (4.1.360). Either identity for Shylock would provoke the rigours of Venetian justice, since they would be directed against one accused of both betrayal and barbarism: 'In christening shalt thou have two godfathers. / Had I been judge, thou shouldst have had ten more, / To bring thee to the gallows, not to the font' (4.1.394–6). Gratiano's prejudice calls to mind a very different kind of 'ring' that would herald not birth but execution, and would condemn the Jew to the historic fate of those charged with the devaluation of the symbolic language of Christianity.

Jessica's exchange of her father's ring devalues it as a symbol of parental authority and conjugal unity. In contrast, Portia's bestowal of the ring upon Bassanio affirms the continuity of a choice initiated by her father, which she freely adopts as her own, and which allows a husband to occupy, in part, the role of father. But the gesture also serves to initiate a second test, of male fidelity, which gives back to the woman some of the power that she has ceded. Portia's giving of herself in accordance with the wishes of her dead father appears to be conditional, and prompts the question of precisely who is 'this same myself' that gives:

> This house, these servants and this same myself,
> Are yours, my lord's. I give them with this ring . . .
> Which, when you part from, lose or give away,
> Let it presage the ruin of your love,
> And be my vantage to exclaim on you.
>
> (3.2.170–4)

Portia not only cedes her inheritance here, but her behaviour is that of the female subject who internalizes – and challenges – the patriarchal values of her father, and who becomes, as a consequence, a split subject.

The metaphorical association between 'ring', 'honour', 'jewel' and 'vagina' was an Elizabethan commonplace,[1] but in the *Merchant of Venice* it becomes entangled in a further series of associations that indicate punning reference to 'Jew'/'jewel', and that permit a connection between material wealth, chastity and human sexuality. Even in the case of Jessica, who is most obviously associated with her father's 'jewels', the matter is handled gingerly, whereas in the case of Portia the decorum is absolute once she acknowledges the reality of carnal desire. Jessica's disguise accompanied with her father's purloined 'jewels' (including his ring) aligns her with a cupidity that Portia resists from the outset. Both disguises are temporary, and pragmatic, although that of Jessica initially poses a radical challenge to the play's complex construction of female subjectivity.

Portia's disguise as a lawyer, her 'translation', on the other hand, allows her entry into the social structures of the patriarchal world of Venice and provides the opportunity to test, albeit in

---

1 Cf. *AW* 4.2.40–51, a version of the incident in *Merchant of Venice* where Diana's request for Bertram's ring involves her making the association between 'ring', 'chastity' and 'jewel'.

a light-hearted vein, the substantial nature of those symbols of fidelity in which masculine Venice places such faith. In a world of mutability and change, 'jewels' are simultaneously capable of association with a fundamental human, and potentially anarchic, biological activity, and also with the most valued, spiritual forms of union that transcend the mutable world and transform identity. Portia's placing of the grateful Bassanio on the horns of a dilemma underlines the tension that lies at the heart of the competing obligations of homosocial and heterosexual love in the play. Indeed, the allegations of male infidelity that are turned back onto the women in the final scene occur *before* these two marriages have been consummated, and they are an attempt to forestall a masculine anxiety that derives from the desire to control female sexuality. Portia's and Nerissa's charge of male infidelity leads to an accusation of cuckoldry that allows Bassanio and Gratiano to display the very possessiveness that would make chattels of their wives. This momentary demystification of the Christian sacrament of matrimony effectively foregrounds the material supports of fidelity, although Bassanio and Gratiano display this anxiety in different registers. Indeed, at the end of the play it is not Portia or Bassanio who jokes about procreation but their social inferior, Gratiano, for whom Nerissa's 'ring' is both an index of possession and a titillating reminder of the sexual identity of the actor playing the female role.

The play does not eradicate the tension between heterosexual marriage and the bonds of male friendship that critics have occasionally detected in Portia's attitude towards Antonio in the latter stages of the play, although it does map this tension onto gendered subjectivities. However, we need to recall the clear distinction that Bruce Smith makes between 'homosexual *acts*' and the poetic discourse that concerns itself with 'homosexual *desire*' (B. Smith, 17). What the play does – and the 'ring' pun emphasizes the point light-heartedly – is to maintain a distinction between the sexual activity proper to heterosexual marriage while at the same time sustaining the homo-erotic desire that underpins the male bonding that is so evident throughout. The *Merchant of Venice* comically asserts limits to, and assiduously furnishes a context for, all those activities and subjectivities that support the economic and domestic life of Venice. In this large and complex interweaving of pressures and motifs, Portia is both the object of desire and the agency of its fulfilment. She is her father's 'meaning' but she is also the means whereby meanings (and commodities) circulate within the socio-political domain of the play. It is for this reason that hers and Nerissa's playful testing of their respective husbands' constancy has a serious side to it, analogous to the game with the caskets.

In the aftermath of the Jew's legal débâcle, the disguised Portia demands of Bassanio the ring that she had given him at the moment of their betrothal. Bassanio's resistance derives from an awareness of the added value that the object possesses: 'There's more depends on this than on the value' (4.1.430). That 'more' attracts a precise gloss two scenes later in the exchange between Nerissa and Gratiano where the latter asserts that their quarrel is

> About a hoop of gold, a paltry ring
> That she did give me, whose posy was
> For all the world like cutler's poetry
> Upon a knife: 'Love me and leave me not.'
>
> (5.1.147–50)

Nerissa rejects this reductive valuation for a much wider gloss that comes close to defining Bassanio's 'more'. The object in itself symbolizes an oath of fidelity, but what Bassanio and Gratiano have been persuaded to do is to use these symbols as payment for Portia's and Nerissa's legal services. In other words, the rings have been coerced from the domain of the symbolic into that of a promiscuous circulation that is both sexually suggestive and also the milieu of the money-breeding Jew as the play characterizes him. But, whereas an economy depends upon the free circulation of money, marriage depends upon the restriction of circulation, involving an irreducibly symbolic valuation that serves to control the plenitude of literal and figurative meanings.

After their earlier successes, Bassanio and Gratiano now find themselves at the mercy of their wives' deception, and are made to confront their worst patriarchal nightmare: female subjects who refuse subjection, and who circulate freely. Moreover, the 'boy' that Gratiano describes as the beneficiary of the ring brings to this final moment of the play the uncanny spectre of Jessica's earlier transgression at the same time as it offers a glimpse of the very homo-erotic desire that is the ideological fixitive of patriarchal power. But the audience shares the joke with Portia and Nerissa, so that the challenge to the institution of marriage that is momentarily proposed is carefully contained by the knowledge that the two ingenious perpetrators unite within themselves the identities of doctor, clerk and wife. The brief prospect of unlimited circulation (which in marriage signifies adultery, but in fiscal exchange is the necessary precondition of any transaction) that is raised here is neutralized by the distance that comedy maintains between the threat to harmony and satisfying resolution. In the play self-regulation, and the dilemmas that it frequently poses, are underwritten by the operations of the law. In the case of biological reproduction, a series of theologically grounded rituals, metaphors and symbols function to maintain the institution of marriage and hold human desire in check. In the case of fiscal 'breeding' that is capable of devouring the very foundations of power itself, the play argues that what is required is a stronger, more public, demonstration of control – colonization, even – that will involve both a punitive imposition and an internalizing of dominant values. By the end of Act 4 the 'outsider' Jew, whose hybridity has been in evidence throughout, is formally colonized by imperial Venice and transformed into a Christian subject. He is a divided subject, the seriousness of whose social position is rendered comic by the theatrically divided, and hence ontologically mobile, selves that the cross-dressed women – Portia in particular – display in their engagements with the patriarchal world of Venice.

BEFORE THE LAW

The *Merchant of Venice* initiates a sustained staging of the operations of law and represents dramatically and theatrically those values for which Venetian legal practice was admired, and whose detailed practices were described in Lewis Lewkenor's translation of Contarini's *Commonwealth and Government of Venice* (1599). The play does not follow faithfully the details that Contarini describes, but it does appear to affirm the view that the law itself is theatrical in essence.[1] Contarini distinguishes between those courts consisting of ten elected officials that dealt expressly with civil disputes between citizens of Venice (Contarini, 78), and the merchants' courts, consisting of forty elected magistrates, that dealt with legal disputes between merchants, and also between 'forayners and strangers':

> But if the question be betweene straungers, or if that
> any citizen will sue a stranger that cometh to lodge in
> *Venice* for some fewe dayes, those Iudges must then be
> repayred vnto that are appoynted to heare the cause
> of straungers, and haue thereof proper nomination
> and tytle.
>
> (Contarini, 107)

The *Merchant of Venice* conflates details of the Venetian judicial system that Contarini is at pains to keep separate, vesting authority, not in magistrates, but in the figure of the Duke, while emphasizing both the dialogic and adversarial nature of the proceedings. Also, what begins as the arraignment of a

---

1 Costas Douzinas, 'The literature of law', in Daniela Carpi (ed.), *Shakespeare and the Law*, Il Portico Biblioteca di Lettere e Arti 128 (Ravenna, 2003), 20.

Venetian citizen turns into a much more symbolically charged arraignment of a plaintiff, in the figure of the Jew.

It is this turn of events that, according to Sigurd Burckhardt, leaves audiences 'feeling distressed by Shylock's final treatment' (Burckhardt, 239–40), mainly because of what he calls Shakespeare's 'unequal dramatization' of Shylock and Antonio (241). He argues that in the scenes dealing with the choice of caskets it is 'the *styles* of metals conceived as modes of speech' (242) that are of crucial importance. But by the time we come to Antonio's trial it is the positivist precision of Shylock's speech (a 'plainness' that he associates with Bassanio's choice of the leaden casket at 3.2.104–7)[1] that sways our sympathies. It has become common practice in performance to emphasize that the transition from the initial light-hearted dismissal of the substance of the 'merry bond' to the serious and literal pursuit of its provision is motivated by the elopement of Jessica. Indeed, in Michael Bogdanov's innovative Wales Theatre production (2004), this is the moment when Shylock (Philip Madoc) retreats into his religious faith. In the exchange with Tubal at 3.1 the news of Jessica's profligacy is intercalated with that of Antonio's misfortune. But it is Burckhardt's contention that this would be to offer a psychological motive for an attitude that the play explains clearly as having its source in a longstanding enmity between Shylock and Antonio, which is reported by Jessica herself at 3.2.283–7 (252). The change that takes place involves a shift in the Jew's attitude towards the bond, a legally binding promissory note that he declares, contrary to the requirements of legal discourse, he will not perform. Indeed, Antonio's insistence on the performative implications of the bond is intercalated with his demonizing of Shylock, and with Bassanio's earlier identification of the gap between utterance and reference that threatens to undermine the performative capacity of law itself

---

1 Burckhardt, 1n. Burckhardt justifies the emendation of 'paleness' to 'plainness', proposed by editors since Warburton, on the grounds that it makes more interpretative sense than Q's 'paleness', and that it allows us to see more clearly the contrast between Antonio's 'eloquence' and Shylock's 'plain' speech.

(1.3.175). The 'merry bond' light-heartedly underplays the performative capacity of the law, but the later courtroom drama revolves around the conflict between its descriptive and its performative status. Whatever the disposition of our sympathies may be in this conflict, there lurks beneath the surface the distinct possibility that in Christian Venice equity before the law, especially in relation to 'strangers', may be an impossibility.

Clearly the theatrical display of legal process in the play fulfils a number of important dramatic and thematic requirements of the narrative that distinguishes it from many of its con-texts. In *Il Pecorone* the Jew is subjected to the entreaties of other merchants as part of an informal debate, arbitrated by 'the lady dressed as a lawyer'. In Munday's *Zelauto* the dispute between the usurer Truculento and Rodolfo is brought before a judge, while in Silvayn's *The Orator* claim and counter-claim are presented in the form of a quasi-legalistic dialogue in which the Jew's appeal is to an equity that he demands of others but is unwilling to practise himself. By comparison, the full theatrical display of legalistic process in the *Merchant of Venice* resonates within the wider linguistic and cultural context of Elizabethan public life and judicial practice.

Walter Cohen has observed that the ultimate legal authority in Venice 'rested not, as elsewhere in Italy, with a single ruler, but with a long established, highly legitimate, paternalistic oligarchy' (Cohen, *Drama*, 102–3),[1] but this is tangential to the play's apparent concerns. At a theological level, a number of commentators have sought to characterize the conflict between Shylock and Antonio as being between the letter of Old Testament law, and the Pauline spirit of the New Testament amelioration of Judaic practice. Lawrence Danson represents this as a matter of Shakespeare's

---

1 The precise details of the election of this oligarchy, and the various ways in which Venetian ducal authority was constrained, even though the office resembled in appearance that of a monarchy, are outlined in Contarini, sigs A2^r–2^v, and the election of legal officers is the subject of book 3 (Contarini, sigs K1^{r}ff.). See also Lane, 95–101. For an account of the legal restraints placed upon Jews in the 'ghetto' of Venice, see Sennett, 212–51.

own 'remarkable' decision 'to write about Christians and Jews' (Danson, *Harmonies*, 59), and in doing so he cedes to the solitary dramatist an independent, authorizing agency that minimizes the pressure of what must have been urgent non-theatrical social concerns. Not the least of these concerns is the general dilemma of a society steeped in theological precept, but forced to confront the potentially anarchic secular power of an increasingly complex economic practice, involving the circulation of money, in which the theatre itself was implicated.

Richard Halpern, in his reading of Marx's account of the pre-history of capital, puts the matter succinctly in his suggestion that 'primitive accumulation' is what lies *behind* the emergence of capitalism, forming part of its pre-history, rather than an instance of its being. Thus, he argues, 'Marx emphasizes that the dominance of merchants' capital, which prepares the way for capitalist production by encouraging the spread of markets and commodity production, is nevertheless structurally incompatible with the capitalist mode of production itself' (Halpern, 66). The focus upon the power of law as a means of resolving the conflict that the *Merchant of Venice* dramatizes (what Halpern calls, in a larger cultural context, 'politico-juridical force') represents the degree to which legal protection is afforded for those engaged in economic activity. But, as Halpern reminds us, we should be careful to observe that the social separation of classes that the play incorporates into its own structures are not, at this stage, as they would be in capitalism, reproduced 'primarily through economic means' (65). This provides us with a useful cultural context for the arraignment of Antonio in the play, and helps to distinguish the transitional nature of the relation between Jew and merchant that commentators have hitherto had difficulty in clarifying.[1]

---

1 Cf. Cohen, *Drama*, 203–4, where the distinction is made between 'usurer's capital' and capitalism itself that anticipates Halpern's critique, but does not quite explain the residually medieval discourse that the play deploys to articulate the threat that the Jew represents as other than elements of 'folklore': 'stipulation of a pound of flesh, after all, is hardly what one would expect from *homo economicus*' (Cohen, 199–200).

In the historical Venice the law mediated between the various interests of merchants, citizens and 'foreigners'. In the *Merchant of Venice* the law mediates between the economic interests of Antonio and Shylock; but patriarchal, oligarchic *will* articulates in the domestic sphere the economic and sexual interests of Portia and Jessica. It is also worth bearing in mind that in the case of Portia, and Jessica, Belmont and Shylock's household serve as what Richard Sennett (speaking of the significance of the 'ghetto' in Renaissance Venice) calls a 'geography of repression' (Sennett, 217). The arrest and subsequent arraignment of Antonio, therefore, becomes the focus of this overlapping series of proscriptions designed to place judicial and quasi-judicial curbs on all forms of 'excess' in Venice, and to test the efficacy of its laws.

Danson puzzles over Shakespeare's choice of material for the *Merchant of Venice* and argues that the evidence 'hardly points to any great Elizabethan hunger for Jewish plays, certainly not enough to make us attribute Shakespeare's choice to overwhelming popular demand'. He goes on to explain that Shakespeare knew 'his own culture's religious tradition', and that this would have led him to the fraught relationship between Old and New Testament law (Danson, *Harmonies*, 60). The play is, of course, shot through with Christian imagery; but the impetus for the drama emanated from the clash between religious precept and economic practice, for which there already existed a serviceable myth: the Jew, whose own performative language and economic practice were regarded as necessary evils. Perhaps it was this combination of fascination and scepticism about the freedom afforded to the citizens of a republic that was steeped in competitive overseas trade – the freedom to negotiate its own internal problems domestically and legally – that struck a chord with Shakespeare and his audiences.

The arraignment of Antonio is a trial with a difference, since it arises as a result of his initial agreement to participate in 'a merry sport' (1.3.141) whose tone changes. Curiously, Antonio himself does not perceive the bond as a form of trickery, notwithstanding his vitriolic critique, some forty lines earlier, of the Jew's capacity for perverse interpretation of Scripture (1.3.93–8). Indeed, when Bassanio urges Antonio to reconsider his decision it is the Jew who reminds his adversaries that their own capacity for suspecting others, like their propensity for 'hard dealings', derives from their own practice: 'what these Christians are, / Whose own hard dealings teaches them suspect / The thoughts of others' (1.3.156–8). This is the first of a number of occasions, as we have seen, when Venice's 'other' discloses that he merely imitates accepted Christian practice. Moreover, the circumstances in which the bond is formulated are also puzzling. In response to Shylock's complaint that he has been 'spurned' by Antonio, the latter insists upon entering into a usurious agreement to which he is ethically opposed:

> If thou wilt lend this money, lend it not
> As to thy friends, for when did friendship take
> A breed of barren metal of his friend?
> But lend it rather to thine enemy,
> Who, if he break, thou mayst with better face
> Exact the penalty.
>
> (1.3.127–32)

The Jew's response may be an attempt to accomplish what Charles Spinosa identifies as a more general strategy associated with the purpose of selling, whose function is 'to develop relationships and an identity within a local community'. Shylock's behaviour, consequently, is that of 'someone who conducts his business by instinct and gets results by developing relationships' (Spinosa, 378 and 393). This makes sense of lines such as 'I would be friends with you and have your love' (1.3.134), and it challenges the traditional reading of the legal conflict in the play,[1] although

---

1 See Tucker, 93ff., and Coolidge, 243–63. Mahood (Cam², 16–18) provides a brief résumé of the opposition between statutory law and equity in relation to the play, while Cohen, '*Merchant*', 49ff., touches on the folklore aspects of the conditions of the bond. Danson, *Harmonies*, 56–81, offers an account of the play's treatment of 'divine law'.

it does not fully address the context that the play provides for the Jew's remarks.

Spinosa's account provides a corrective to attempts to prove the veracity of 'the play's technical legal representations', and he locates the problem in Shakespeare's and the common lawyers' response 'to particular changes in social practices' (Spinosa, 372). These changes concerned the opposition between what legal institutions recognized as 'two forms of life – the customary and the contractual' as exemplified in Slade's Case (1597–1602), where the failure to make an agreed payment for a commodity at a date in the future was judged to be a breach of contract. By analogy, Shylock operates according to 'the customary forms of life' while the Venetians 'operate in the intentionalist, contractual manner implied in the understanding of the modern contract made determinative in *Slade's Case*' (Spinosa, 372). Consequently, the *behaviour* of the Venetians belongs to 'a newly contractual world that speaks in a chatty rhetoric where intentions are made explicit' – a world where the play's 'most paradigmatic figure' suffers from 'a sadness caused by his world's loss of simple trust and integrity', and which 'displays its greatest achievement in the calculative thinking of its second leading figure, Bassanio' (386). Spinosa notes the propensity for self-dramatization that permeates the fictional world of Venice (387)[1] and that begins with Antonio's 'I hold the world but as the world, Gratiano, / A stage, where every man must play a part, / And mine a sad one' (1.1.77–9).

However we attempt to trace the conflict enshrined in the debate between the allegedly literalist Shylock[2] and the legally

---

1 See also Lorna Hutson, *The Invention of Suspicion: Law and Mimesis in Shakespeare and Renaissance Drama* (Oxford, 2007), 5ff. Although Hutson does not mention *The Merchant of Venice*, her general argument that 'English participatory justice offers an epistemological model relevant to English Renaissance drama' is of direct relevance.

2 Cf. Danson, *Harmonies*, 89. This also informs a number of readings of the play: e.g. Burckhardt, 247; but note also the connection of Shylock with language and 'presence' or with writing and its metaphysical underpinnings that informs Marchitello, 241.

relativistic Portia,[1] we encounter contradictions that the play does not satisfactorily resolve. Howard Marchitello has noted that what he calls 'the same dream of presence-in-writing' informs the will of Portia's father, and the Jew's commitment to the letter of the law (Marchitello, 246). In fact, the play moves between referential, figurative and interpretative models of language, with the Jew, the alleged literalist, being accused of linguistic duplicity as a clear indicator of his demonic persona, and Bassanio eschewing appearances in his opting for the leaden casket. The emphasis placed upon the stability of the law as the foundation of Venetian social practice is invoked by Shylock:

> If you deny me, fie upon your law:
> There is no force in the decrees of Venice.
> I stand for judgement: answer, shall I have it?
> (4.1.100–2)

Ironically, this is the very law that binds 'stranger' and citizen in what would appear to be an equitable relationship. But it is clear from the outset of the trial that the law itself cannot be separated from the language in which it is enshrined or from the matter of interpretation. Moreover, the closer we observe the Venetian law in practice the less stable it becomes. For example, the disguised Portia admits that even though Shylock's suit is 'strange', it is 'in such rule that the Venetian law / Cannot impugn you as you do proceed' (4.1.174–5). In this context, if the Jew is a literalist, then his literalism is opportunistic rather than simply indicative of a commitment to Old Testament law, even though the conditions of the bond carry a heavy symbolic weight. Conversely, the bond is overturned by an equally opportunistic turning of literalism against itself: Shylock can have a just pound of Antonio's flesh, but the bond contains no mention of blood.

---

1 Marchitello, 248; a number of critics have associated the figure of Portia with the principle of 'equity', while at the same time noting how she exploits the literalism of the 'bond'.

At those points in the trial when Portia-as-Balthazar supports Shylock's case, he regards her as 'A Daniel come to judgement; yea, a Daniel!' (4.1.219), extolling what Thomas Luxon has described as her cleverness as a judge. But when she finally bests him it is Gratiano who appropriates the Jew's reference, thereby praising not her dexterity but her exemplification of God's providence (Luxon, 5). This reinforces the view that, as Daniela Carpi has argued, 'The struggle between Shylock and Portia is a struggle for the act of reading.'[1] But this is not simply a confrontation between the 'old' and the 'new', the medieval and the modern (Cohen, '*Merchant*', 51), but between the mercantilist state of Venice replete with its stabilizing laws, and a force that threatens that stability. The *discourse* rather than the figure of Shylock is what comes from the past, while the economic force he represents points towards a future that contemporary critics of usury were eager to sketch out in graphic detail. The play's own quasi-legal neutralizing of the force he represents looks backwards to an archetypal struggle, but also forward to the pressing need to subjugate a form of fiscal dealing endowed with the capacity to undermine the very fabric of society.

This is more than a trial scene, however, more than an exercise in the dangers associated with the separation of the operations of law from the exercise of mercy. Antonio's predicament arises from Bassanio's own involvement in merchant adventuring, and at the moment in the trial when it looks as though the Jew will get justice, and his victim will be a hostage to fortune, Antonio reminds his friend of the connection:

> Commend me to your honourable wife;
> Tell her the process of Antonio's end,

---

1 Daniela Carpi, 'The theme of interpretation in *The Merchant of Venice*', unpublished MS. I am grateful to Professor Carpi of the University of Verona for letting me see the typescript of this article. Danson, *Harmonies*, 122, emphasizes Balthazar's ability to 'intepret' the Law, but he also emphasizes the generic investment of the whole trial scene in the ethos of the 'fairy tale' where impossible demands are imposed on the participants. See also Freund, 48–75, for a full examination of the 'sequence of interpretive predicaments' that the play dramatizes, and their theoretical implications.

> Say how I loved you, speak me fair in death,
> And, when the tale is told, bid her be judge
> Whether Bassanio had not once a love.
> (4.1.269–73)

In addition to the self-dramatization ('when the tale is told') the speech is shot through with an unintended irony, since Portia will 'be judge'. But it also leads to Bassanio's extravagant gesture that would sacrifice his own life, his wife 'and all the world' (4.1.280) to 'this devil' (283) for deliverance. Gratiano joins in, and this elicits statements from the disguised Portia and Nerissa that the final act of the play will develop. But it is Shylock's aside that discloses a deeply embedded motive for his action that both affirms and challenges the Venetian impulse to demonize him:

> These be the Christian husbands! I have a daughter:
> Would any of the stock of Barabbas
> Had been her husband rather than a Christian.
> (4.1.291–3)

Of course, we might regard this punctuation of the legal proceedings as a dramatic signal that things are not quite so serious as they appear, but this light-hearted diversion betrays an anxiety that is of a piece with the entire play. The Jew's invocation of part of the crucifixion narrative, and of the machiavellian hero of Marlowe's play, serves to correct the impression that the trial has thus far conveyed, of the justice of Shylock's cause. But the Jew himself is not here the cause of the problem; rather he is the symptom of it, since it is Venice's own institutions that are shown to be built on insecure foundations. Antonio's plight becomes Bassanio's dilemma, and only the wealthy and ambidextrous Portia can rescue both. Moreover, in order to do so she has to adopt a role, a masculine persona, different from that which her father had decreed for her but which is, none the less, in keeping with the broad trajectory of his 'will'. In her disguise Portia wrests language from the body and in so doing saves Antonio, but she also initiates the project to convert Shylock. Justice in Venice, like the wind in whose powers the helpless mercantilist is forced to trust, turns about and in the process reaffirms the mystery of mercantile practice through a series of unauthored letters that legitimize Christian enterprise. The worlds of civil and theatrical law are here brought together as the homogenization of the juridical process of regulating social behaviour is shown to harmonize with the law of genre.

THE POLITICS OF HARMONY

In his essay 'The law of genre' Jacques Derrida observes: 'Every text *participates* in one or several genres, there is no genreless text, there is always genre and genres, yet such participation never amounts to belonging' (in Derrida, *Acts*, 230). What he takes to be an axiom of genre itself is particularly evident in the *Merchant of Venice*, in which, according to John Russell Brown, 'The comparison of the two usuries is part of a more general comparison of commerce and love which is likewise maintained throughout the play' (Brown, *Comedies*, 65). Brown's eloquent attempt to contrive a thematic coherence for the play is counterbalanced by Lawrence Danson's initial insistence that 'All Shakespeare's plays, then, are problem plays, but some problem plays are more insistently problematic than others', and that the *Merchant of Venice* is 'the most scandalously problematic of Shakespeare's plays' (Danson, *Harmonies*, 1–2). In a more recent study, which interpolates an important element of Derrida's more radical argument, Danson defines 'genre' as

> a system in which each new member changes the
> system: a form always in the process of reforming
> itself. The genre of a work is the idea we maintain
> in order to recognize the work's affinity with or,
> just as importantly, its distance from other works,
> while simultaneously we recognize that the idea – of

106

tragedy, of comedy, or any other genre – is never
equal to the shifting reality of actual theatrical or
literary practice.

(Danson, *Genres*, 5)

Viewed from one perspective, the *Merchant of Venice* is a comedy
that privileges domestic (and commercial) triumph over adversity,
in which a series of marriages are effected, at the same time
that a merchant, who is at the mercy of natural forces, is finally
favoured by a Christian providence. Within this general context,
it is possible to interpret the domestic triumphs as evidence of
the emerging power of women, through the figures of Portia,
Nerissa and, to a lesser extent, Jessica, as a number of feminist
critics have done. The relationship between Nerissa and Gratiano
echoes that of Portia and Bassanio, and both serve as examples of
the process of unification of a household within the rules that are
laid down by an absent patriarch. The lottery of the three caskets,
while directly affecting the relationship of Portia and Bassanio,
determines in part the fate of Bassanio's friend and benefactor
Antonio, while Bassanio's replenished household incorporates
into itself the figures of the Clown Lancelet, Nerissa and Gratiano
at the end, as well as Jessica and Lorenzo.

In this version of the play, Lorenzo's contrasting of the
'harmony' that is 'in immortal souls' with 'this muddy vesture
of decay' (5.1.63–4), and his appeals to the civilizing power
of music that can turn 'savage eyes' into 'a modest gaze'
(5.1.78), become central motifs, and appear to embody the play's
controlling aesthetic:

> The man that hath no music in himself,
> Nor is not moved with concord of sweet sounds,
> Is fit for treasons, stratagems and spoils;
> The motions of his spirit are dull as night,
> And his affections dark as Erebus.
> Let no such man be trusted. Mark the music.
>
> (5.1.83–8)

The association of the discordant man with 'affections dark as Erebus' may recall the household presided over by Shylock from which 'the vile squealing of the wry-necked fife' (2.5.29) is banished, just as the 'treasons, stratagems and spoils' serve to epitomize the Jew's behaviour (cf. Danson, *Harmonies*, 180–1). More importantly, the harmony that is in 'immortal souls', and that can only be *heard* by those who break through 'this muddy vesture of decay', is a consequence of the observer's capacity to *see* the constitution of the heavens:

> Sit, Jessica. Look how the floor of heaven
> Is thick inlaid with patens of bright gold.
> There's not the smallest orb which thou behold'st
> But in his motion like an angel sings,
> Still choiring to the young-eyed cherubins.
>
> (5.1.58–62)

Editors have variously commented on the similarity of these passages to sentiments expressed by Montaigne, and by the Old Testament book of Job (Ard[2], 128n.), but aside from glossing the meaning of 'patens' little effort has been made to explore the ramifications of the seductive image that Lorenzo deploys.[1] It is Jessica's marriage to Lorenzo that gives her access to the Christian salvation symbolized by the Eucharist, and it will allow her to throw off her Jewish past. It also, rhetorically and poetically, *performs* Jessica's transformation into a Christian wife after the earlier recitation of her dealings with her father. Danson is correct to make the connection between the music that precedes Bassanio's choice of the leaden casket earlier at 3.2 and music that accompanies Portia's homecoming (Danson, *Harmonies*, 184 and 188). But, in emphasizing its initial affective power, this argument overlooks the *ideological* investment in harmony that the play is desperate to assert in the face of an obstacle whose threat remains undiminished at the end. The

---

1 Danson, *Harmonies*, 186–8, begins with the correct gloss, but is diverted into thinking about the classical antecedents of the 'music' to which Lorenzo alludes.

affairs of the mutable world cannot be harmonized away, and so Shakespeare is not, in this case, simply repeating a series of classical maxims so much as commenting on the contradiction between their formal expression and the material reality that they attempt to transform. Although the Jew may have been coerced into conversion by the transgressive elopement of his daughter, there remains a residual threat that even Belmont's poetry cannot neutralize completely. As audience we may choose to laugh along with the victors, and to displace our anxieties onto the unstable terrain of male possession, and the accompanying threat of female sexual anarchy that marriage is designed to regulate. But that laughter is based upon a series of exclusions that are as political as they are formal.

The obstacles in this play are both patriarchal and, in a very special sense, racial. We may be invited to celebrate the marriage of Bassanio and Portia. We may even read Portia's cross-dressing as a theatrical expedient rather than a conceptually driven ruse, although, of course, it has been the object of much feminist critical attention, especially when considered alongside issues such as the symbolic exchange of rings and its consequence in the play. Karen Newman has noted that when Portia, as the disguised Balthazar, retrieves her ring from Bassanio she becomes her husband's equal rather than his possession.[1] The final ambivalence to which this leads cannot avoid the impression that among the Venetians, and even at Belmont (Venice's superficial other), there are too many stratagems in play to give us very much confidence in the power of music to curb the realities of social practice. It is as though we are offered a conventional comic ending, replete with a series of marriages, but also, at the same time, a critical commentary upon its now precarious efficacy. Form and content come together here in a combination that is unsettling, since the ending proposes, in Fredric Jameson's words, a history of the future that is a

---

1 Newman, 114: 'Bassanio gives away his ring in payment for services rendered and in so doing transgresses his pledge to Portia.'

fulfilment of desire but is also accompanied by an anxiety in the face of the unknown (cf. Jameson, 26).

What is often read as the aesthetic harmony of the *Merchant of Venice* is a dramatization of what Jameson has described, in another context, as a 'wider dialectic of continuity and rupture (or, in other words, of Identity and Difference)'. This enables us to rethink part of the play's original title, 'The most excellent Historie of the *Merchant of Venice*', as the repetition of the narrative of Christianity that both proposes itself as 'an absolute historiographic beginning' and discloses its own dramatic organization of the originary rupture that brings it into being (Jameson, 23). The presence of the Jew as a justification for Christianity itself is imbricated in another series of narratives that the play formulates which have to do with cultural anxiety about the status of Venice as a republic, and with the precarious ethics of economic exchange. According to this formulation, the aesthetic principle of harmony, combined with the pleasure of comedy, is irreducibly political.

So long as we keep the plight of Shylock at a distance, as Elizabethan audiences may have done, then the laughter that the play generates will be of a conservative kind. Such a position, however, is uncomfortable, especially for modern audiences and readers; critics since Rowe have laboured to humanize the figure of the Jew, and to think of the play as Shylock's tragedy. The 1985–6 East Berlin Deutschestheater production of *Der Kaufmann von Venedig* cast Holocaust survivor Fred Düren as Shylock, whose tragedy was played out against the carnivalesque decadence of a capitalist Venice. Indeed, although Shylock appears in only five scenes in the play (even though they are pivotal) and speaks a total of some 355 lines, the impact of his stage presence has been such that he fills the play. Perhaps the model for the Jew's tragic suffering, at least since the beginning of the twentieth century, is T.S. Eliot's poem 'The Journey of the Magi' in which the infidel's confrontation with the founding moment of Christianity is emphatically not a celebration but a metaphorical death. Elsewhere, Eliot's poetry betrays no sympathy for the figure of the Jew, but in the wake of post-colonial theory we are attuned to the process of domination that, in the play, an enforced conversion effects. The *Merchant of Venice* implicates the figure of the woman in the process of death, and it brings an exemplary Venetian, warts and all, to the brink of a re-enactment of Christian sacrifice. We should not underestimate the strain that the play's narrative is under to align Antonio's mercantilist practice with the theologically legitimized principles that govern commercial exchange. If we view the play from this perspective, then in purely ethical terms the Venetians secure a Pyrrhic victory, which only the most crude – and as it turns out ambivalent – appeal to biological increase might ameliorate. Questions of personal health admit of a nervous resolution, as Antonio's inexplicable 'illness' and Portia's 'world-weariness' are displaced onto the figure of the Jew, whose existence within the fabric of Venice is both tolerated and circumscribed. But that potentially disruptive otherness that helps to define the juridical and economic ethos of Venice, however, returns, via the romantic entanglements of Belmont, in the form of the ever-present prospect of marital infidelity as the ultimate threat to the model of production and increase. Love as desire fuelled by passionate intensity is shown in the catalogue of instances of infidelity, misfortune and uncontrolled emotion that Lorenzo and Jessica invoke at the beginning of the final act of the play as they compete to 'out-night' each other (5.1.23). The 'types' of lovers they invoke qualify all that follows, disclosing the potential for disruption that rests beneath the surface of the play's authorizing narrative that these two characters have, in their way, already subverted. They also lend an unexpected seriousness to the abiding fear that it is left to Gratiano to articulate as the play's closing sentiment. Whichever way we view the formal harmony of the ending of the play, its investments are social and political, domestic and public, and the discomfort that these tensions generate exceeds the capacity of the genre to contain them.

THE MERCHANT OF
VENICE IN THE THEATRE

The gulf between modern editorial practice and the performance of a theatrical text has become the focus of much recent debate, although the distinction was by no means as obvious during the early modern period. Stephen Orgel states the problem with characteristic clarity in his observation that 'The text in flux, the text as process, was precisely what Renaissance printing practice – whether for economic or philosophical reasons – preserved' (Orgel, 'Editor', 15). In his discussion of selected modern performances of the play, James Bulman concludes that the play has 'entered our historical consciousness as no other Shakespeare comedy has, converging with the pressures of history to yield meanings Shakespeare could never have imagined' (Bulman, 153).

We do not know how the parts for the original performances by the Lord Chamberlain's Men around 1596–7 were apportioned. Charles Edelman, in his otherwise comprehensive 'Shakespeare in Production' edition of the play, isolates the impact that the figure of the Jew would have had on its first audiences and quotes John Gross's speculative account of Shylock's 'fiery red wig', which would have identified him with Marlowe's Barabas and, before that, with 'both Judas and Satan in the old Mystery Plays' (Edelman, 3; see also Gross, 16–17, and Trachtenberg, 222, n. 26). H.H. Furness cited the posthumous elegy 'On the death of the famous actor Richard Burbage' as the source for the tradition that Burbage, the chief actor with the Chamberlain's Men, took the role of Shylock and wore a red wig (Furness, 370; see also Cam[1], 178). However, the appearance of Shylock in only five of the play's nineteen scenes, compared to Antonio's appearance in six, might indicate that Burbage may have taken the role of the dramatic character who lends his name to the play's title. The designation of 'Clown' for Lancelet indicates that this role was conceived for the company's resident clown, Will Kempe. If this is so, then the speculation that the role of the Jew was originally conceived as a comic one is placed in serious doubt (cf. Furness, 370).

In his edition of the play Jay Halio observes that it could have been performed by the doubling of parts using 'twelve men and four boys, or sixteen actors (including mutes)' and that this was not unusual for plays emanating from the Chamberlain's Men at this time (Oxf[1], 60). More recently, attention has turned to the mechanics of early rehearsal, and to the implications of providing the actors with only their parts and the appropriate cues. Tiffany Stern has ingeniously argued that in the exchange between Shylock, Antonio and Solanio at 3.3 Shylock's continual throwing out of Solanio's cue, 'I'll have my bond', has the effect of producing a constantly interrupted speech, and hence accounts for those repetitions that have usually been attributed to Shylock's 'character' (Stern, *Making Shakespeare*, 126–9). This may offer us a brief insight into the hypothetical dynamics of early performance, in that it draws our attention away from a quasi-Stanislavskian style of acting (see Brown, *Performance*, 71–90, esp. 88–9) towards the kind of ensemble playing that was the likely mode of Elizabethan theatrical performance. Initially the play was popular, and was revived in 1605 when Shakespeare's company, renamed the King's Men after 1603, acted it at Whitehall before James I on Sunday 10 February, and again at his request on the following Shrove Tuesday 12 February. After 1603, however, there is no evidence of performance of the *Merchant of Venice* until 1701 when George Granville, Lord Lansdowne revised and renamed the play.

Lansdowne's *The Jew of Venice: A Comedy* recast the play, emphasizing, according to the ghost of Shakespeare who acted as Prologue, the punishment of 'a stock-jobbing Jew' (Furness, 347). This affirmed the emphasis on the figure of Shylock that has become a consistent feature of the play ever since. Lansdowne's play was performed at Lincoln's Inn Fields by His Majesty's Servants, and the comic actor Charles Dogget was cast in the role of Shylock. It is likely that this was what Rowe reacted against when he suggested, some eight years later, that Shylock was more a tragic than a comic figure. Lansdowne's revision held the stage until 1741, when Charles Macklin resurrected Shakespeare's play, restored a number of minor roles that Lansdowne had excised, and reinterpreted the role of Shylock as a sinister, almost tragic, figure whose intensely ferocious malice evoked more fear than laughter.[1] Macklin's portrayal impressed an initially sceptical Alexander Pope and proved extremely popular for some fifty years, until finally, on 7 May 1789, at the age of about ninety-nine, he dried onstage, apologized to his audience, and was replaced by his understudy.[2]

Macklin's charismatic acting provided the yardstick until the advent of Edmund Kean in 1814. Richard Cumberland's *The Jew* (1794) – with its unmistakable echoes of Shakespeare's play – aimed, according to the Prologue, at 'but one species in the wide extent / Of prejudice, at which our shaft is sent',[3] and presented Drury Lane audiences with a surprisingly sympathetic portrait in the figure of Sheva. This noticeable shift in cultural perception helped to pave the way for Kean's performance. Kean forsook Macklin's red beard for a black wig that astonished his fellow actors (Furness, 378). According to the report of one of his biographers, F.W. Hawkins, Kean dispensed with 'the sullen gaol delivery common to the traditional Shylocks of the stage' to produce a more imaginatively flexible multi-faceted dramatic representation with 'the flexibility and indefiniteness of outline about it, like a figure with a landscape background' (Furness,

---

1   Cf. Gross, 94–101; see also Orgel, 'Shylock', 145–6, and Brown, *Performance*, 71–3. See also Edelman, 9–10, for a brief account of contemporary German performances of the play.
2   See Orgel, 'Shylock', 145–6 and 148–50, which traces Macklin's red skullcap to the distinction that Coryate made between Italian Jews, who wore red skullcaps during religious services, and Levantine Jews, who wore turbans (Orgel, 'Shylock', 148).
3   Richard Cumberland, *The Jew* (1794), sig. A1^r; see also Gross, 188–9.

379). William Hazlitt had expected to see a version of Shylock handed down by Macklin but he also noted that such was the vexatious obsession that Macklin's portrayal exerted over Kean that in performance he mixed up quotations from *Hamlet* and *Othello*, and mistook Bassanio for Antonio (Furness, 379–80).

Between the performances of Edmund Kean at the beginning of the nineteenth century and Henry Irving in 1879, the *Merchant of Venice* was frequently produced, in England, in New York and on the continent of Europe. Edelman lists a number of productions (Edelman, vxii–xviii), and John Gross puts the figure at 'over a hundred' for the century as a whole (Gross, 120–1). Those who were contemporary with or who followed Kean were William Macready (1823), whose dignified Shylock is thought by some to have anticipated that of Irving in a production that restored the part of Portia (Edelman, 16). Charles Kean's production of 1858 used Macready's promptbooks, but also restored for the first time, although in truncated form, the roles of Morocco and Arragon, and was noted not for its interpretation of the role of Shylock but for its spectacularly realistic scenery. But until Henry Irving, the interpretation of the role of Shylock, which had become the yardstick of the play's success on the stage, oscillated between those of Macklin and the elder Kean.

The *Merchant of Venice* was one of the plays that Irving put on in the second season after taking over the Lyceum Theatre, and its first performance was on 1 November 1879. Irving had previously acted the role of Bassanio to Edwin Booth's Shylock in Manchester in 1861 (Gross, 127), but his interest in the role of Shylock was rekindled in the summer of 1879 as a result of an encounter with a Levantine Jew (Bulman, 29). The figure of the Levantine Jew as exotic oriental was resurrected by Antony Sher in the 1987 Royal Shakespeare Company (RSC) production at Stratford, although by this time, and particularly in the 1980s, its political ramifications had changed considerably.

Irving's Lyceum production of 1879 was, as Bulman has argued, a model for Victorian imperial aspirations, while the assimilation of Jews into English public life underscored 'a Victorian interest in what we now call the Third World [and] those peoples whom the English had subjugated to their imperial will and whom they were now refashioning in their own image' (Bulman, 31). Irving's Shylock was provided with motives for his actions that pointed outwards beyond the performance to a larger social context in which the persecution of a race was foregrounded. And it was Irving who was responsible for the introduction of a non-Shakespearean scene, which had Shylock returning home across the stage bridge over which he had gone to dine with the Venetians, and, after the elopement of Jessica, knocking at the door of an empty house, a feature that Michael Radford's 2004 film of the play resurrects. In the interests of emphasizing the tragedy of Shylock, Irving curtailed the Belmont scenes and excised much of the play's anti-Semitic content in an attempt to 'preserve Shylock's decorum as a tragic figure by denying his affinity with earlier comic stage Jews' (Bulman, 40).

Before Irving's production the role of Portia was played by actresses who emphasized the frivolity of the Belmont scenes, but in Ellen Terry Irving discovered an actress capable of challenging his own stage presence. Terry had identified the potential of the role in 1875 when she played opposite Charles Coghlan's Shylock in the Bancrofts' production at the Prince of Wales Theatre. In her autobiography she recalls: 'never until I appeared as Portia at the Prince of Wales's had I experienced the awe-struck feeling which comes, I suppose, to no actress more than once in a lifetime – the feeling of the conqueror' (Terry, 115). She was helped on that occasion by Coghlan's weak and indecisive Shylock, but this was the first glimpse of a potential in the role that, almost a century later, feminist critics would explore further. But it was Irving's Shylock that held the stage, and he brought to the role a complexity that emphasized the tragedy of his plight at the hands of an insensitive Christian Venice.

The *Merchant of Venice* was the first new Shakespeare play that Irving staged at the Lyceum, was rehearsed in some three weeks and ran for 250 performances (Sprague, 107). Irving apparently played the role of Shylock over a thousand times, developing the portrait of a man whom, according to a review in the *Spectator* for 8 November 1879, 'none can despise, who can raise emotions both of pity and of fear, and make us Christians thrill with a retrospective sense of shame' (Edelman, 23–4). This was a view shared in large part by the novelist Henry James, who thought Irving's realization of the role 'a sentimental one, and he has endeavoured to give us a sympathetic and, above all, a pathetic Shylock' (quoted in Gross, 138). Irving's savage pruning of the text was accompanied by a comparative reduction in the amount of ancillary theatrical business, and a corresponding emphasis upon what others had found to be the actor's irritating mannerisms that were thought to be less conspicuous in his portrayal of Shylock (Sprague, 116–17). This readjustment of the balance of the play was to have a lasting effect in the modern theatre. It resulted in productions like that of Jonathan Miller in 1970, with its distinctly Victorian emphasis, and Peter Zadek's production of 1988–95 in which Shylock was portrayed as a Venetian businessman barely distinguishable (except, perhaps, in certain stereotypical speech mannerisms) from his Christian adversaries. This portrayal permeates the politically anodyne Tim Carroll RSC production of 2008.

Irving's *Merchant* reinforced the perception that the play's fifth act was indispensable, although a year later he cut it. Also, even though Portia's role continued to be heavily cut, it provided Terry with sufficient scope to explore some of its potential; indeed, her tactile portrayal caused considerable offence to refined Victorian sensibilities (James, 143). Moreover, critics found her performance to be self-conscious, especially in the trial scene, where even in disguise she made little attempt to hide her femininity. Irving's striving for a naturalistic effect was undermined by a combination of Terry's exposure of the play's own theatricality, alongside her own sense of a logic that foregrounded the spontaneity of feminine response underneath her male disguise.

Productions of the power of Irving's exerted a restraining influence upon those that followed, and the theatrical establishment is deeply conservative in the respect it accords to tradition. There were, as Charles Edelman notes, productions in the USA (in the wake of Irving's touring of his *Merchant*) that sought either to emulate his performance, or to return to earlier readings of the figure of the Jew. But the play was performed in Yiddish at the People's Theatre of New York in 1901 and 1903 (Edelman, 26–31). Jacob Adler's performance as Shylock contributed an ethnic verisimilitude to the role that must have produced a curious cultural effect in so far as it brought to the fore the historical plight of the figure of the Jew. As Avraham Oz has observed in his account of performances in Hebrew in Israel in the twentieth century, Shakespeare could not have anticipated productions of the *Merchant of Venice* in either Yiddish or Hebrew, or that Oz's own 1972 translation of the play would be used in courses on Jewish history (Oz, '*Merchant*', 57–60). Oz cites the more complex case of the 1987 RSC production in which Antony Sher, 'a South-African born Jew', played the role of Shylock, and which the actor perceived to be an attack on apartheid in which 'The former victims of racism (the Jews) turned racists themselves' (57).

Max Reinhardt's 1905 production of the play emphasized the festive atmosphere of Venice and Belmont (Edelman, 31–2), although in the Deutschestheater production of 1985 the carnivalesque elements were endowed with a contemporary political significance that extended well beyond the formal confines of the play itself. Generally, the beginning of the twentieth century saw little that was remarkable in productions of the *Merchant*. The division between Macklin's portrayal of Shylock as a comic villain (and the surgery carried out on the Belmont scenes) and Irving's tragic and intense revision effectively established the possibilities between which subsequent productions navigated. In an attempt to return to Elizabethan stage conditions William Poel dispensed with the lavish scenery that had characterized Victorian productions, but returned to the interpretation of Shylock as a comically grotesque villain, replete with red wig (Edelman, 36). The tradition of broad comedy and Elizabethan authenticity that had characterized Poel's production of the play was resurrected in Richard Olivier's 1998 production at the controversial New Globe theatre in London. Before the performance got under way, Marcello Magni's *commedia dell'arte* Harlequin was one of three figures who mingled with the audience before occupying particular roles on the stage, and the audience was encouraged to hiss Shylock when he appeared (in the interests of a spurious authenticity).

Poel's production represented an attempt to break from the tradition established by Irving, although Irving's performance continued to act as a yardstick by which others were measured. However, the cultural climate within which the figure of the Jew might be represented onstage had already begun to shift. James Shapiro has charted in some detail the political appropriation of Shylock, and of the play generally, by those opposing the Jewish Naturalization Act of 1753 (Shapiro, *Jews*, 195–224). By the end of the nineteenth century, Britain had been governed by a Jewish prime minister and novelist, the Tory Benjamin Disraeli (1874–80), and Dickens's demonic portrait of Fagin in *Oliver Twist* (1838), lasting though it proved to be, had been superseded by George Eliot's novel *Daniel Deronda* (1876). In Eliot's novel, in which the specific question of Jewish national identity was posed, issues of national origin were beginning to be associated with various offensively racial anthropological accounts of human evolution. As Daniel Pick has argued, 'Victorian depictions of the Jew shifted from an earlier more ramshackle racial rhetoric (evident in the mocking banter of the crowds to whom the young Disraeli spoke) to the harder-edged anthropological theories so evident by the 1870s', although an older demonic rhetoric survived with contemporary depictions of Disraeli as 'the devil himself in disguise' (Pick, 130),[1] and with the fictional character of Svengali in George du Maurier's novel *Trilby* (1894) represented in the magazine *Punch* as 'Shylock and Fagin, Mephistophesized' (Pick, 128). These changes and contradictions, along with their cultural deployment, provide an indispensable social context for theatrical performance, and particularly for the staging of the *Merchant of Venice*.

Herbert Beerbohm-Tree's 1908 production of the play emphasized spectacle, borrowed elements from Irving's production (most notably the invented scene of Shylock returning to his empty house) and augmented them with what John Gross has labelled 'Jewish, quasi-Jewish, or pseudo-Jewish effects' (Gross, 147). Tree had played the role of Svengali in the stage version of du Maurier's novel in 1895, and provoked the comment of one contemporary commentator on mesmerism that 'all London will be drawn to see a most remarkable presentment of the platform "mesmerist" outwardly at his best or at his worst' (Pick, 157–8). As representations of the figure of the Jew shifted in accordance with larger social shifts in political and cultural emphasis, so stagings of the *Merchant* exceeded those formal constraints that the limitations of an exclusively theatrical history might impose upon them. Max Beerbohm offers us some insight into his half-brother's interpretation of the role in his ambivalent suggestion that 'when we all have a very great admiration and sympathy for the Jews (the admiration which is always given to people who have us in their power), Shylock has become a romantically pathetic hero' (Gross, 148). It is precisely this mesmeric fascination with a dramatic character who could elicit contradictory responses from audiences that

1   I am indebted to Dr David Glover of the University of Southampton for drawing Daniel Pick's work to my attention.

allowed the play to hold the stage in a number of productions stretching from the end of the nineteenth century up to 1932 and the opening of the Royal Shakespeare Theatre.

During that period the tradition established by Irving was maintained in the productions of Frank Benson, who had followed closely upon the former's 1879 Lyceum production with performances at Stratford in 1887 and 1893–4, and in London in 1901 and 1905. The twin poles of definition consisted in either an emphasis upon serio-comic villainy designed to produce a hostile audience response, or alternatively one designed to elicit sympathy for the tragic victim of Christian prejudice. Edelman notes Oscar Asche's 1910 production that toured Australia, in which Asche played Shylock with 'a Whitechapel-Yiddish accent' indicating, possibly for the first time, an English perception of the Semitic identity of 'the East European Jews of London's East End' (Edelman, 38).

The variety of performances in the USA, on the continent of Europe and as far as Australia serves to illustrate the extent to which the *Merchant of Venice*, perhaps more than most Shakespearean texts, was submitted to the forms and pressures of the time. But, as John Gross observes, within the USA between the First and Second World Wars, it was the traditional portrayal of Shylock that distinguished performances (Gross, 168ff.). However, the 1925 Old Vic production drew attention once more to the figure of Portia, with Edith Evans in the role out-acting Baliol Holloway's Shylock. Also at the Lyric theatre, Hammersmith, in 1927, Lewis Casson played a heavily caricatured Shylock, whom he himself described as 'a mean little miser with some glimmerings of good in him' (Gross, 170), while Sybil Thorndike's Portia has subsequently been compared to that of Ellen Terry (Edelman, 40).

Anglo-American productions of the *Merchant* during the early part of the twentieth century need to be seen against a backdrop of Jewish diaspora and increasing economic crisis. The annual rate of Jewish emigration from eastern Europe declined considerably between 1901 and 1914, but there were large immigrant populations in the USA and, to a lesser extent, in Britain and in western Europe, and these attracted a virulent anti-Semitism fuelled in part by a petit-bourgeois hostility that increased in the wake of the financial crisis of 1929 (cf. Leon, 231–5; see also Edelman, 41ff.). The dilemma for theatre directors is best exemplified by Jürgen Fehling's production of the play at the Staatliche Schauspielhaus in Berlin in 1927. Fritz Kortner was torn between a humane conception of the role of Shylock advocated by Fehling and (at the risk of feeding an already widespread anti-Semitism) Kortner's own preference for a 'Shylock who had been treated inhumanly by Christianity, and so became inhuman himself' (Edelman, 46). This dilemma indicates the extent to which attitudes had hardened since Irving's time, and also it points to a new sophistication in the approach to the play within an rapidly deteriorating social milieu. Bearing this in mind, we can but wonder what Lewis Casson thought he was doing when in the same year he played a repulsively caricatured Shylock on the London stage.

Winthrop Ames's New York production of the play in 1928, with George Arliss in the role of Shylock, drew back from what Gross has labelled the depiction of 'traditional Shylocks' in favour of one who was 'steely, sardonic, well-spoken, well-mannered: a villain, but with an outward demeanour that might have been inspired by Irving's description of the character as "the only gentleman in the play"' (Gross, 168–9; Edelman, 47–8). Arliss had played the role of Disraeli in an earlier silent film and a year after his performance of Shylock he returned to make a sound version. It was the sound version of *Disraeli* (1929) that Laurence Olivier admitted had influenced his own 1971 portrayal of Shylock (Edelman, 47). The entanglement of the portrayal of Shylock with the historical figure of Disraeli, and with fictional characters such as du Maurier's Svengali, must also be set alongside some of the theoretical writings on racism and anti-Semitism that emerged during the nineteenth century. Combined with a growing awareness of the operations of capitalism, this emphasis was to be maintained throughout the twentieth century. Sher's Shylock, in the RSC production of 1987, did much to broaden the ethnographic implications of the role in order to address issues of 'racism' and 'orientalism' within a social context that had, by that time, become sensitive to questions of colonial domination.

Theodore Komisarjevsky's 1932 production of the *Merchant of Venice* initiated a radical break with those productions that had followed in the wake of Irving. Komisarjevsky was the first guest director at the newly built Shakespeare Memorial Theatre in Stratford-upon-Avon. He had been the assistant of Meyerhold in St Petersburg, and had directed Chekhov's plays to great acclaim at the Moscow Arts Theatre. The production opened in late 1932 with Randle Ayrton in the role of Shylock, Fabia Drake as Portia, John Wyse as Bassanio and Wilfrid Walter as Antonio, and included 'the three Sallies', Salerio, Salanio and Salarino. Lancelet appeared as a circus clown and the production purported to be a self-conscious critique of contemporary capitalism, with the Venetians distinguished by their capacity for racial prejudice and Shylock portrayed as a 'twisting comic devil' dressed brightly in the garb of 'a sinister pantaloon'.[1] The reviewer of the *Birmingham Gazette* for 21 April 1933 justified the transformation of the play 'into a fantastic pantomime' on the grounds that if it were played seriously it would amount to 'nothing more than a vulgar Jew-baiting by a number of Christians, most of whom are extremely ill-bred' (*Theatre Records*, 27.80).

The stage set was a caricature of the Venetian Rialto (see Fig. 5), while the transition from Venice to Belmont attracted the attention of one reviewer of the 1933 revival of the production who noted that 'The drunken bridges part and slide away into the wings; and up from the depths beneath the stage comes

---

1   *Theatre Records*, 27 (August 1932–June 1933), Shakespeare Centre, Stratford-upon-Avon, 18.

5 Ernest Daniels's set for Theodore Komisarjevsky's 1932 production of the play at the Shakespeare Memorial Theatre, Stratford-upon-Avon

a section of Portia's garden at Belmont, with the Prince of Morocco made up to look like a nigger minstrel with coal-black face and thick ripe red lips, sheltering from the sun beneath a red sunshade.' By this time George Hayes had replaced Randle Ayrton as Shylock, but the production remained 'light' and 'casual', intensifying the impression of his humanity in the face of the hatred it generated for 'the shallow Venetian youths who baited him' (*Theatre Records*, 27.80).[1] John Denis's Lancelet contributed to the depiction of a carnivalesque Venice whose reactionary excesses were to be viewed critically.[2] The neo-Brechtian style of performance did not please the anonymous reviewer of the *Stratford-upon-Avon Herald* for 16 September 1932, who thought that the production was likely to exert a pernicious influence on schoolchildren being introduced to Shakespeare for the first time (*Theatre Records*, 27.80).

The critical response to Komisarjevsky's production offers a convenient insight into the possible alternatives open to directors of the *Merchant of Venice* confronted simultaneously with a powerful indigenous theatrical tradition and an insistent contemporary politics whose course would ultimately transform the play's reception. In this history 1932–3 represents something of a watershed, since it was during this year that Hitler's *Mein Kampf* achieved a wide circulation in Europe, although its impact appears to have been confused upon a director of Komisarjevsky's political if not theatrical pedigree. When the play was revived in 1936 at Stratford by Ben Iden Payne, with Randle Ayrton once more in the role of Shylock and Valerie Tudor as Portia, there was a certain equivocation among reviewers combined with a peculiar political naïvety that was characteristic of the production itself. The reviewer in the *Times*

1 The baiting of Shylock, this time by a group of children, was introduced into the 1987 Bill Alexander RSC production at 3.1. See also D. Kennedy, 127ff., and also Edelman, 48–9.
2 Cf. the East German Deutschestheater production in which the Venetians were depicted as representatives of western capitalism, while Shylock became the tragic victim of capitalist (and implicitly fascist) insensitivity (see pp. 110, 135–6).

for 16 April 1936 tried to square the circle of the production's own studied ambivalence with the suggestion:

> Jew-baiters these Christians may be, but they have decency enough to bring out what is wolvish and distinctive in Shylock's hatred. Mr Randle Ayrton plays the Jew in such a way that we are neither in danger of giving him our sympathies nor of forgetting that he is a man. Shylock has good reason to hate Antonio, but Mr Ayrton makes it clear that before the end this hatred has been pushed to the verge of monomania.[1]

The *Birmingham Post* reviewer indicated that Shylock's behaviour after Act 3 may well have been motivated by the loss of his daughter (*Theatre Records*, 30.63), and future productions were to shed light on such moments – particularly the report of her having exchanged Shylock's ring for a monkey – as psychological motivation for his litigious intransigence.

The anonymous reviewer of the *Birmingham Gazette* for 16 April 1936 expressed surprise that the play was among the most popular in the Shakespeare canon, a 'fact', he noted, that is 'somewhat remarkable in these days, when Jew-baiting has ceased to be the sport of gentlemen'. However, he echoed William Hazlitt by observing that although Shakespeare *intended* Shylock to be repellent he 'put forward his view with such pointed argument, set in phrases so fine, that Shylock became one of the greatest of Shakespearean characters'. According to the myth of an even-handed Shakespeare, the dramatist began by being anti-Semitic, but 'before he had finished . . . found himself with his tongue in both cheeks' (*Theatre Records*, 30.63).

The provision of a subtextual motivation for Shylock's hostility to Antonio that is other than a response to the latter's manifest anti-Semitism brings to the fore a reactive prejudice that appears to threaten what many have identified as the comic equilibrium

1   *Theatre Records*, 30 (June 1935–July 1936), 63.

of the play. Indeed, in its eliciting of audience sympathy the play is balanced on a knife-edge: to side with the Venetians is to uphold anti-Semitic prejudice, while to sympathize with the plight of the Jew as victim is to threaten the play's formal comic ethos. The dramatist Arnold Wesker objected to the National Theatre production of the play in 1999. He had earlier rewritten the text as *The Merchant* in 1976 in response to what he regarded as the play's offensive 'humanizing' of Shylock that allowed its perpetrators to 'feel merciful and generous while enjoying their cherished image of the cruel Jew'.[1] The question is to what extent the play's discursive regimes – which depend in performance upon the larger social context – expose auditors to the *ideology* of racial prejudice in the very process of its own artistic production. At issue is the *structure* of prejudice and the theatrical display of its mechanisms of inclusion and exclusion, of legitimation and demonization, its rejections and its assimilations, and its irrational and inventive fantasies born of cultural anxiety that, as part of a strategy, reaffirm an anti-Semitic myth. In his *Anti-Semite and Jew: An Exploration of the Aetiology of Hate*, Jean-Paul Sartre exposes an irrationality that places 'the anti-Semite in the unhappy position of having a vital need for the very enemy he wishes to destroy' (Sartre, 40–1). The frequent theatrical representation of Shylock, particularly from 1970 onwards, as both an 'insider' and an 'outsider', goes some way, though in many cases unsatisfactorily, towards the theatrical exploration of this contradiction.

Recent theatrical criticism has finally scotched the myth that the *Merchant of Venice* was a favourite play of the Nazi regime in Germany in the years leading up to the Second World War.[2] Indeed, as Zoltan Markus has recently pointed out, the play was staged only once in Berlin during the Third Reich, and,

1 Arnold Wesker, 'Shame on you, Shakespeare', *Independent*, 21 July 1999.
2 See Edelman, 53ff. Also see Hortmann, 134ff. I am also indebted to Professor Zoltan Markus of Vassar College for a copy of his unpublished paper '*Der Merchant von Velence: The Merchant* in London, Berlin, and Budapest during World War II', delivered at the 'Shakespeare and European Politics' conference at the University of Utrecht, 7 December 2003.

following Wilhelm Hortmann, he cites its ambivalence as a reason, compared with the more rabidly propagandist potential of a play such as Marlowe's *Jew of Malta*. But Markus also cites a letter from *Reichsdramaturg* Rainer Schlösser to Goebbels written in July 1940, in which he recommends what is, in effect, a severely emended version of the play for performance:

> In this version Jessica is played as not the daughter but only as the foster-daughter of the Jew; race-political difficulties, therefore, are cleared out of the way. Since these modifications are not extensive, no philological offences occur at the delivery of the Shakespearean text, and Jessica performed by German actresses would never be played as a Jewess. I would see no reason why this classic work – which, moreover, in a talented performance, can offer support to our anti-Jewish fight – would not be allowed to return to Berlin.
>
> (in Markus, 9–10)

In some respects the *commedia dell'arte* style of the subsequent production recalls that of Komisarjevsky's 1932 Stratford production. Shylock was played by Georg August Koch with 'a yankable reddish beard, with sometimes greedy, sometimes timorous wandering eyes, with hands whose fingers open and close like claws'. One reviewer noted the actor's 'glued on hooked nose, and a red and woolly full beard' (Markus, 11), while another commentator quoted the evidence of eyewitnesses, that 'the director Paul Rose had placed a few extras in the auditorium who burst into loud abuse and cursing any time Shylock entered the stage' (10).[1] What made this production 'a harrowing kind of entertainment' was that it took place against a backdrop of the acceleration of the mass deportation of Jews from Berlin in July 1942 (12).

---

1   This appears also to have been the strategy adopted for the production of the play at the New Globe theatre in London in 1998 (see p. 119).

The events of the Second Word War have, as Dennis Kennedy rightly observes, 'completely transformed our ability' to read the play. Indeed, he argues that 'since 1945 we have been in possession of a new text of the play, one which bears relationships to the earlier text but is also significantly different from it' (D. Kennedy, 200). He describes Erwin Piscator's post-war production of the *Merchant of Venice* for the Freie Volksbühne theatre in West Berlin in 1962 in which Ernst Deutsche's Shylock broke with the German tradition of caricature to emphasize the character's 'humanity amid a corrupt and commercially antagonistic world' (200–1). Such discomfort was not exclusively German, as evidenced in Iden Payne's earlier revisitation in the 1940 production. Sidney Charteris, the *Birmingham Evening Despatch* reviewer, noted the embarrassment occasioned by the claimed convergence of the play's dominant ideological thrust, and wondered that the work of the national English poet might well be thought to be in collusion with the sentiments of a fascist enemy. Charteris observed:

> There was a too poignantly topical air about the production of 'The Merchant of Venice' at the Stratford Shakespeare Festival yesterday. Jew-baiting always found audiences a little shame-faced, and today it gives positive affront. B. Iden Payne's production, no less than Baliol Holloway's performance as Shylock, stresses the malignancy of the Jew to make his destruction just. It is not a pretty sight however cleverly the balance is weighted against him, and few could have avoided the thought that for Shakespeare's Venice might now be substituted Vienna, Prague or Warsaw. But however ill-advised we may consider the choice of 'The Merchant of Venice' at the moment, we cannot deny its host of opportunities for acting.[1]

1   *Theatre Records*, 34 (1939–41), 80.

The attempt here to separate politics from theatrical art is conspicuously uncomfortable. The play was performed on two further occasions at Stratford during the war, in 1942 and 1944, although reviewers made more of the difficulties encountered by audiences in getting to performances during the blackout than of any difficulty that the play itself might have posed. However, the 1944 production directed by Robert Atkins with George Hayes as Shylock and Helen Cherry as Portia provoked a more strategic response from reviewers. For example, the *Warwick Advertiser* reviewer sought refuge in universal categories with the observation: 'In this play we do not see Britons or Italians, Elizabethans or contemporaries, but humanity' (*Theatre Records*, 34.80). He went on to single out Anthony Eustral's Antonio as 'a gallant philosopher and free from self pity', while Hayes's Shylock was 'a Jew of fierce passions under powerful restraint' but possessed of 'unfaltering dignity', whose malice 'is never paltry' and who is 'magnificent in defeat'. The same reviewer thought Diana Wilson's Jessica 'an unfilial baggage with whom, one feels that, sooner or later, Lorenzo will have some trouble' (*Theatre Records*, 30.64). The *Birmingham Post* reviewer for 15 April 1944 thought the play 'good fun', and asserted disingenuously: 'After all, it is the Jew's nature, not his race, what [*sic*] we dislike.'[1] No mention was made by any of the reviewers of the savage cuts to Morocco's speeches at 2.7, or to the entire omission of Arragon and the decimation of the final scene with much of Gratiano's closing speech excised.

Charles Edelman has charted some eighteen separate productions of the *Merchant* between 1945 and 1970 in Britain, the USA and continental Europe, and he affirms the commonly held view that, after the revelations of the Holocaust, 'no production' could avoid 'some recognition . . . of its contemporary significance' (Edelman, xx–xxi and 55). Despite this sharpened historical emphasis, during this period there appears to have been little in the way of theatrical innovation. In

1   *Theatre Records*, 35 (August 1941–April 1947), 78.

Tyrone Guthrie's Shakespeare Festival production at Stratford, Ontario, in 1955, Frederick Valk's 'powerful' Shylock was counterbalanced by giving Antonio's affection for Bassanio 'a gratuitously homosexual motivation'. Robert Speaight records that 'Great tension was secured in the trial scene: Frances Hyland's fragile Portia moved in a Belmont of gauzy pink and white, and onlookers from the balconies watched Bassanio's choice of the right casket' (Speaight, 297; see also Edelman, 56–7). Speaight's puritanical dismissal overlooks a critical direction that W.H. Auden had inaugurated some years earlier in his essay 'Brothers and others' (Auden, 232ff.). Indeed, Auden's interpretation has consistently been espoused by directors, most recently that of Trevor Nunn's National Theatre production of 1999. Speaight was equally critical of the 1960 Michael Lanham Stratford production in which Dorothy Tutin played Portia and Peter O'Toole played Shylock. Influenced probably by the open stage at Stratford, Ontario, Lanham's production failed to accommodate itself to the physical constraints of the proscenium arch theatre at Stratford-upon-Avon. The result was an unusually mobile production in which, according to Speaight, 'instead of going straight up to his opposite number the actor stalks him like a deer', and in which 'the trial scene could not be saved by locomotion' (Speaight, 278).[1] Peter O'Toole's Shylock was without the malice that had characterized earlier Shylocks but for Speaight his 'flamboyant and arresting study [was] robbed of concentration by the St Vitus' dance through which he, too, had to waltz his way' (278). The actors were costumed in eighteenth-century dress.

Much has been written of the 1970 Jonathan Miller National Theatre production at the Old Vic in London with Laurence Olivier as Shylock and Joan Plowright as Portia. The production's Victorian setting, and the assimilation of Shylock into Victorian commercial society, a motif that later productions emulated and modified, allowed Olivier to introduce some

---

1 See Brown, 'Directors', 136, for further details of this production.

131

features that distinguished the figure of the Jew from his adversaries. Shylock's wearing of a yarmulke (again adopted by later productions as a distinguishing feature); Olivier's distinct appearance as a central European Jew, and his clipped accent that allowed him to introduce an obscene pun when he first drawls out 'Bass*ain*io's' name, left audiences in no doubt of the Jew's contempt for the Venetian society with which he was confronted. An unattractive and anti-Semitic Venice offset whatever maliciousness earlier productions had associated with Shylock. Quite striking, however, was the blocking in the final act of the play in which Portia refuses to acknowledge Jessica so that the latter's unwelcome assimilation into the comic world of Belmont is itself a kind of death that replicates the metaphorical death of her father. Indeed, the production ended with the intoning of the Jewish Kaddish, indicating, *pace* T.S. Eliot's Magi, that the acquisition of Christian faith involved painful death.

Miller's Old Vic production exposed the insidious roots of anti-Semitism in a Victorian setting, but John Barton's 1978 RSC production at The Other Place in Stratford-upon-Avon, though ostensibly in modern dress, sought to provide a justification for the Venetian hatred of Shylock. Patrick Stewart's Shylock was identifiably Semitic, with beard and yarmulke, though his frequent appearance in sleeveless waistcoat and occasional eyeshade established him as an accountant who guarded his money carefully. His small tobacco box and roll-up cigarettes, along with the paraphernalia of a parsimonious intelligence, reinforced a stereotyped miserliness. Stewart was openly contemptuous of the 'prodigal Christians' in 2.4, but his instruction to a dutiful Jessica, 'Do as I bid you' at 2.5.51, was accompanied in performance with a firm slap across Avril Carson's (Jessica's) face and by a movement across the stage to lock his money away in a desk. The shocking viciousness of this gesture (excised from later performances) was designed to generate sympathy for Jessica's elopement, while at the same time legitimizing the hatred of Shylock's Venetian adversaries. In the trial scene, Stewart pursued his goal relentlessly until finally bested, at which point he resorted to a Dickensian caricature of obsequiousness that fell short of suggesting a character whose stereotyped mannerisms were shaped by persecution and frustration (see Fig. 6).

The *Times* reviewer, Ned Chaillet, claimed that the play's more offensive elements were distanced in Barton's production,

6   John Barton's 1978 production at The Other Place, Stratford-upon-Avon, with Patrick Stewart as Shylock

and that the potentially sour racism was ameliorated by a tone that was 'lyrical and comic'. This observation, however, sits uneasily with the statement that 'Patrick Stewart's intelligent and occasionally explosive performance makes Shylock an opportunistic and avaricious maverick, content to give up his religion if it means saving his money and his life.'[1] The anonymous reviewer for the *Morning Star* (16 May 1978) saw Stewart's Shylock 'not [as] a detestable Jew, but a detestable human being', and went on to observe that in this production 'the often incompatible romantic interludes to the main action are here part of a cohesive development, the pivot of the play's movement from barren money-dominated relationships to those dependent on esteem, respect and love – from a winter darkness to a summer light' (*Theatre Records*, 100.91). The production was characterized by an understated Portia (Marjorie Bland), whose 'quality of mercy' speech (4.1) was 'not a beautiful Christian platitude but a profound statement of human needs' (100.91), and a Lancelet (Hilton McCrae) whose appearance resembled that of Harpo Marx. It is perhaps no accident that Arnold Wesker's radical revision of the play, which takes issue, among other things, with 'the play's contribution to the world's astigmatic view and murderous hatred of the Jew', should have received its English première at the Birmingham Repertory Theatre on 12 October 1978, a few months after Barton's production opened at the RSC.

In 1981 Jonathan Miller returned to the play as executive producer of a production directed by Jack Gold for the BBC Shakespeare series, and the upshot was a revision of his earlier version of 1970. Warren Mitchell's Shylock, replete with European accent, was an ethnic Jew, and the Victorian setting had been dispensed with in favour of one that was more authentically Elizabethan. Mitchell had established a TV reputation for himself as Alf Garnett, the excessively

---

1 Ned Chaillet, *Times*, 15 May 1978; in *Theatre Records*, Series A, 100 (April–June 1978), 88.

loquacious cockney bigot who was the centre of Johnny Speight's very successful sitcom *Till Death Us Do Part*, and his reputation as the outrageously comic spokesman of a working-class racism seeped into the portrayal of Shylock. James Bulman's account of this production is full and informative (Bulman, 101–16), but it fails to notice the intertextual significance of casting an actor whom British audiences had taken to its heart as the fictional Alf Garnett, while at the same time acknowledging the unpalatable nature of his views. To suggest, as Bulman does, that 'This squat, domestic, garrulous little man, this comic figure with a plaintive face, was the Shylock whom Gold and Miller called authentically Jewish' (103) is to miss the reason why Mitchell had been cast in the role in the first place, and was one of the main reasons why the production often teetered on the brink of caricature. Gold's sets were minimal and the actors occasionally addressed the camera, thus breaking through the naturalistic conventions of TV performance. Because Mitchell's presence took the edge off some of the play's more menacing concerns, the production risked falling into a sentimentality that obscured the problematic social and economic forces for which romance is an ideological disguise in the play. The result was a bland, inoffensive reading of the play that refused to dwell upon the contradictions present in Shakespeare's text. Moments of Chekhovian intimacy jostled in the trial scene with formal public perspectives, and, in an attempt to produce an unproblematically happy ending, characters such as Jessica (Leslee Udwin) were not allowed to dwell on the more serious implications of their actions.

The overall conservatism of the BBC Shakespeare series, punctuated only by some adventurous casting, contrasts with the fortunes of the *Merchant of Venice* in the theatre, where the traditions of performance had consistently been more controversial. For example, the former East Berlin Deutschestheater production of *Der Kaufmann von Venedig*

(1985–6) sought to explore the carnivalesque atmosphere of Venice, but in such a manner as to foreground its capitalist decadence. The role of Shylock was played with extraordinary sympathy by Fred Düren, himself a Jewish survivor of the Holocaust (see Fig. 7).[1] Indeed, in this production, which figured a wall that separated the carnivalesque Venetians from Shylock's house, it was Venice that represented capitalism in its most decadent form. Some of the Venetian carnival tableaux were reminiscent of the cartoons of George Grosz, while Düren's Jew was the focus of resistance to its technically fascist impulses. His potentially tragic post-Holocaust Shylock presented a dignified oppositional front to a Venice characterized by a decadent penchant for festivity. Shylock's house was separated by a wall from Venice, a barrier that emphasized the threat that its consumerism posed to the disciplined parsimony of a household in which everything was garnered and husbanded. When Ulrich Mühe's Lancelet decamped to Bassanio's employ, he went over the wall, and was next seen sporting a deckchair and a computer, and dressed in fashionable beachwear. Shylock generated money in order to survive, whereas Venice was obsessed with the trappings of consumer culture. Similarly, Jessica's elopement, again over a wall, emphasized the seductive but corrosive power of consumer capitalism, and her departure was accompanied by the flight of a bird on a wire diagonally across the stage. The topos of the wall figured to demarcate a community that prided itself upon an ordered existence, facing the threat of a crass materialism that had produced the very fascist mentality that could carry out the extermination of a race. The trial scene was designed to expose the vicious underbelly of Venetian decadence, and Düren's appearance in gaberdine and the dress of a concentration camp inmate, most powerfully in the trial scene, served to underline the inhuman logic that could displace

1   I am grateful to Professor Leonard Goldstein of the University of Potsdam for arranging for me to see this production in 1986, and also to the play's dramaturge Eva Walch for providing me with information on request.

the consequences of its own conspicuous consumption onto a social group that it could then proceed to persecute.

Bill Alexander's RSC production of 1987, coming as it did after the paperback republication of Edward Said's influential *Orientalism* (1985), appeared, in its actual visual portrayal of Shylock, to return to the costuming of Henry Irving (1879). But Antony Sher's Levantine Jewish Shylock communicated an alien otherness that appealed beyond the confines of anti-Semitism to a much broader, anxiously racist dynamic. In this production Shylock's habits and his costume were noticeably 'oriental' in Said's sense of the term (see Fig. 8). The hostility between Jew and Venetians was mutual, with the trial scene played out against the backdrop of competing religious and cultural icons inscribed on the brick wall at the rear of the stage: icons of the

7 The East German Deutschestheater production of *Der Kaufmann von Venedig* (1985), directed by Thomas Langhoff, 2.2, with Ulrich Mühe as Lancelet and Walter Lendrich as Giobbe

8   The Royal Shakespeare Company production of *The Merchant of Venice* in 1987, directed by Bill Alexander, with Antony Sher as an 'orientalist' Jew, and Deborah Goodman as Jessica

Madonna and the Star of David, which provided the ideological justification for virulent racial antagonism.

The reviewer of the *London Daily News* saw the production as 'a testament to Thatcher's England' in its exploration of the ethos of 'monetarism and imperialism'.[1] Much was made of the carnival atmosphere of Venice, to the point where children dressed in carnival costumes occasionally pursued Shylock, and this was augmented by the vicious jostling he got from Salanio and Salarino at 3.1. Similarly, Shylock's 'Hath not a

1   *Theatre Records*, 133 (March–May 1987), 80.

Jew eyes' speech later in the same scene was delivered in a tone that exactly captured the desperation of the underdog. At 2.7, Morocco's exaggerated mock-warlike gestures with his scimitar exposed him to comic ridicule, and asserted Portia's superiority; she returned the weapon to him only to have him fumble in the quasi-Freudian gesture of inserting the blade into its scabbard.

Throughout the production the virulence of the racial hatred between Jew and Christian was sustained. First Antonio, then Gratiano and then Bassanio all at various stages spat violently on Shylock, a feature that Michael Radford's film (2004) briefly resurrects in the un-Shakespearean opening shot of an encounter between Shylock (Al Pacino) and Antonio (Jeremy Irons). The acting space in both Venice and Belmont was that of a large oriental carpet, which also linked Jew and Christian in a series of economic activities that served to undermine some of the play's romantic motifs. The identity of Sher's Jew was shaped by a Christian hostility that was both religious and economic, involving a fear of the exotic other as well as an acknowledgement of its usefulness. The ritualistic nature of the conflict was demonstrated in the trial scene, whose deadly seriousness stood in contrast to the festive atmosphere in which the bond was initially agreed upon. In the later scene John Carlisle's Antonio was stripped to the waist and pinioned, as though about to be crucified, thus threatening a theatrical re-enactment of the biblical crime posited as the origin of anti-Semitism itself.

In Alexander's production the source of a mutual hatred was exposed, making it difficult to apportion sympathy to either side in the conflict. In the trial scene Shylock was encamped downstage – an alien nomadic presence – while his appeal to law ('I stand here for law') provoked Bassanio to spit at him. Moreover, Shylock's rejection of a financial settlement provoked a chanting in the court of 'Jew!' while the carnivalesque children who had earlier pursued him through the streets of Venice now sat at the upper level at the back of the stage. This was part of a series of much more heavily ritualized oppositions; for example, as he was about to exact punishment on Antonio, Shylock chanted a Seder night prayer in Hebrew at the same time as the Duke intoned the Catholic *Salve Regina* (Bulman, 117–18). At the crucial moment, however, the disguised Portia brought Shylock to his knees and pronounced that he must convert to Christianity while his adversaries augmented gestures of the sign of the cross with a cacophonous laughter. At the end of the scene the children descended and divided Shylock's belongings amongst themselves. This was, in effect, a Pyrrhic victory in which neither side fully evoked the sympathy of the audience.

Nor was Belmont any more tolerant. The production left no doubt about Portia's attitude to her suitors, and in the final scene of the play Gratiano's 'are we cuckolds' was met with a blow by Portia that floored him. Moreover, as if to emphasize the crass materialism that underpins the play's Christian ethos, as the characters depart at the end Jessica (played by Deborah Goodman as a recognizably ethnic Jew) returned to retrieve a crucifix necklace, and although she left with Antonio it was clear from his withholding of the necklace that she had yet to be fully assimilated into Venetian society. Antonio's petulance was but the stereotyped extension of a thwarted homosexual desire for Bassanio that was present from the beginning, and that surfaced particularly in the trial scene where the latter was reduced to tears at the possible fate of his friend.

Alexander's production did much to probe the dark forces that lie beneath the surface of what is formally a comedy, and it expanded the play's lexicon of prejudice well beyond the claim of anti-Semitism that it has usually attracted. Sher's persistent parodying of English jostled with the more familiar repertoire of the occasional punning that many productions have emulated ('pie-rats', for example, at 1.3.22), in an attempt to give Shylock a distinctive linguistic register. Many contemporary reviewers noted the absence of sentimentality in the production, and its reinforcement of the deep structural connection between the play's ostensible romance motif and the material contradictions of which it was nothing more than a mystification.

David Thacker's 1993 RSC production and Peter Zadek's 1995 Edinburgh Festival production (see Fig. 9) were in some ways similar. Both productions deployed modern hi-tech sets, and both resurrected the notion of a Shylock fully assimilated into the modern world of corporate business. Thacker's stage consisted of tubular steel platforms on three levels, stocked with office paraphernalia: desks, computers, fax machines. All that distinguished David Calder's attire from his Venetian business partners was his yarmulke. The *Times* reviewer, Heather Neill, regarded Shylock as 'the modern businessman, pillar of the community'[1] and Calder himself sought to diminish the distance between Shylock and the Venetians in the play. He observed, unironically, that 'The Christians in the play are not fascists, they are us', and went on to describe Shylock as 'a man deeply flawed, among flawed men, and ultimately he goes beyond the pale'. He continued: 'My aim is to show Shylock with dignity, not in an orange wig and funny accent' (*Theatre Records*, 167.4). Michael Arditti of the *Standard* was scathing in his dismissal of the production's ethos: 'This is soap-opera Shakespeare for devotees of Capital City; aimed at instant recognition and easy laughs' (167.7). Portia's (Penny Downie) racist sentiments were, as in earlier productions of the play, excised from the script, and the play's racial tensions were reduced to effects of character. Much emphasis in the production was placed upon the transformation in Shylock's behaviour that the elopement of Jessica effected, with the result that the complex tensions between Christian and Jew were oversimplified in the extreme. Thacker resorted to what has become a commonplace in locating the motivation for the shift of Shylock's behaviour in Jessica's elopement.

Charles Spencer of the *Daily Telegraph* observed a 'melancholy Antonio, settling the bill for a boozy business lunch with his

---

1   *Theatre Records*, 167 (May–September 1993), 4.

9 The set for the Berliner Ensemble production, directed by Peter Zadek, at the Edinburgh International Festival (1995), 4.1: Paulus Manker (Bassanio), Ignaz Kirchner (Antonio), Martin Selfert (Doge), Eva Mattes (Portia), Wiebke Frost (Nerissa), Gert Voss (Shylock)

gold credit card', looking like 'an elderly repressed homosexual, painfully in love with the handsome commodity broker Bassanio' (*Theatre Records*, 167.10), although there was little evidence in the performance to suggest such a reading. Thacker suppressed the play's anti-Semitic elements and trivialized its romantic elements, almost as though its racist contents were irrelevant to the commercial operations of the city. It was this production that elicited a strong response from the playwright Arnold Wesker, who refused to accept as anything other than patronizing the play's alleged attempt to enfold Shylock in the protective garment of a common humanity. Calder's Shylock permitted, so Wesker asserted, 'anti-Semites to feel comfortable with Shylock because he conforms to the myth they love, and to help assuage any guilt they might be experiencing while watching the play' (167.11). However, the discomfort, if not the anachronism, surfaced in the trial scene, when Shylock, now wearing gaberdine and yarmulke as though he had rediscovered his Jewish faith, pulled a knife from his executive briefcase (see Fig. 10); at his demise he was violently thrown to the floor, a feature of most modern productions. Left alone onstage as the court departed, Shylock then sat in the chair that Antonio had earlier occupied, a symbolic exchange of scapegoat roles, while Gratiano re-entered to vent insults upon him. Such moments jarred with the predominant values of the production and resulted in a degree of incoherence. Shylock availed himself of a Semitic identity only occasionally, when under pressure, and this did little to undermine the romance of Belmont.

Peter Zadek's Berliner Ensemble production of *Der Kaufmann von Venedig*, first performed at the Vienna Burgtheater in 1988 and in Berlin in 1993, was brought to the Edinburgh Festival in 1995. This was very different from his earlier 1972 Bochum Schauspielhaus production, which had offended the German Jewish community and had been, according to a number of commentators, 'in bad taste and politically grossly insensitive' (Edelman, 65–6). In the 1995 production Ignaz Kirchner

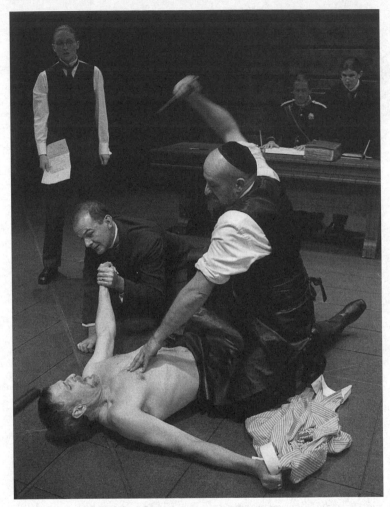

10   The Royal Shakespeare Company production at Stratford-upon-Avon,
     directed by David Thacker (2001), 4.1

doubled as Antonio and the Prince of Morocco, and Gert Voss
doubled as Shylock and the Prince of Arragon, a contrast that
underlined the extent to which both Jew and Venetian harboured
an interior 'foreign-ness'. More than in David Thacker's RSC

production of 1993, this Shylock was completely assimilated, as Zadek himself emphasized: 'My parents were completely assimilated, and thought of themselves as Jews in spite of having nothing to do with the Jewish religion; this was the picture I wanted to find in the play, a completely assimilated Jew who doesn't look like one, doesn't act like one, doesn't behave like one, but just happens to be a Jew.' The translator, Elisabeth Plessen, regarded the play as being about 'dealers in money and dealers in feelings',[1] underscored by the modern hi-tech set and Gert Voss's generally subdued demeanour that neither elicited the usual feelings of victimization nor provoked the impulse to demonize. Indeed, at the end of the trial scene, and after having scrutinized the small print of the bond, Shylock simply wrote his son-in-law and errant daughter a cheque and exited in dignified manner, 'in order', reviewer Michael Billington assumed, 'to phone his Swiss bank'. The director's refusal to come down on the side of either Antonio or Shylock represented an attempt to take cognizance of the historic shifts in world perception of the figure of the Jew. Billington lamented the absence of 'sexual pain' in the production: Jessica was welcomed in a Belmont characterized by 'rainbow-hued backdrops' (and contrasted with the hi-tech bank façade for Venice) simply because she brought money with her. Bassanio courted a mercenary Portia who was 'a spoilt daddy's darling' accompanied by his financial advisers, and there was no 'dawning realization on Portia's part that at the end she was married to a bisexual more passionately in love with Antonio than with her'. Billington observed the improvised clowning of Uwe Bohm's Lancelet, and the light-hearted portrayal of the casket scenes, but his judgement on Zadek's 'ironic' production was that its 'inventive irreverence' did not quite go far enough.[2]

---

1 Zadek and Plessen both quoted in James Woodall, 'The trick of the play: Peter Zadek on directing a German *Merchant*', *Edinburgh International Festival Programme*, Royal Lyceum Theatre, 29–30 August 1995.
2 Michael Billington, 'The romance of finance', *Guardian*, 31 August 1995.

The year 1997 saw two contrasting *Merchants*, one the Compass Theatre of Sheffield's touring version of the play, the other Greg Doran's RSC production. Neil Sissons's Compass Theatre production opened in February 1997 at the Gulbenkian Theatre in Canterbury and through an inventive sequence of doubling carried the play off with some six actors. David Westbrook's Antonio doubled as Lancelet and the Prince of Arragon, David Bowen doubled as Shylock and Lorenzo, Carolyn Bazely as Nerissa, Jessica and the Duke of Venice, Sarah Finch as Portia and 'Old Gobbo', and Richard Heap as Gratiano, the Prince of Morocco and Tubal. Set in the Depression years of the 1930s, and with a minimalist set, the production made no attempt to disguise the hostility of the Venetians towards a thoroughly demonized Shylock, envied for the wealth he possessed (see Figs 11 and 12). Sissons clearly borrowed the spitting motif from Bill Alexander's 1987 RSC

11   The Compass Theatre Company (Sheffield) touring production (1997), with Richard Heap (Gratiano), Carolyn Bazely (Jessica) and David Bowen (Lorenzo)

12   The Compass Theatre (Sheffield) touring production (1997), 4.1, with David Bowen (Shylock), David Westbrook (Antonio), Richard Heap (Gratiano), Carolyn Bazely (the Duke of Venice), Sarah Finch (Portia) and Simon Hunt (Bassanio)

production as part of what the *Yorkshire Post* reviewer Lynda Murdin described as 'an uncompromising and incisive picture of mutual hatred'.[1] The style of the production was mixed, moving from a harrowing seriousness to farce. The ruthlessness of David Bowen's gangster-like Shylock was counterbalanced by Simon Hunt's bisexual Bassanio in evening dress with his dim-witted aristocratic Venetian accomplices, and Sarah Finch's Portia who could not bring herself to utter the word 'Jew' without contempt. David Westbrook's Arragon cavorted around the stage to the incongruous strains of 'Viva Espana', and as Antonio and Lancelet prompted some questions about the nature of Antonio's initial disclosure of personal discomfort. But perhaps the most innovative element of the play occurred in Carolyn Bazely's interpretation of a Jessica who could be

1   Lynda Murdin, '*The Merchant of Venice*', *Yorkshire Post*, 14 February 1997.

affectionate to her father, deceitful and rebellious, but who, try as she might, was unable to break into the ranks of Christian Venetian society. In the final scene of the play, and as the victim of a racial contempt that went far beyond that of Jonathan Miller's 1970 production, she was spat upon by Antonio, and locked out from Belmont by a Lorenzo whose hostility towards her had been growing from the opening exchanges of the final act, to the point where, having secured her money, he left her sobbing at the bars of the gate into Belmont. This powerful moment did much to qualify any hostility that Shylock generated in performance, and reinforced Sissons's stated intention to explore the play's contradictions rather than smooth them over. Indeed, the complex figure of Jessica was shown to be as much a victim of Christian ruthlessness as her father, and her isolation at the end of the performance stood as a powerful testimony to the devastating effects of a prejudice capable of sustaining a thoroughly duplicitous bonhomie. The problem was chillingly amplified by David Bowen's doubling of Shylock and Lorenzo, leading to a conclusion that Jessica had become the victim of a double rejection far in excess of her original transgression.

Sissons's reading of the end of the play is one of the most adventurous of recent productions. Later in 1997 Greg Doran's RSC production sought to revitalize a number of familiar elements of performance, and Philip Voss's Shylock returned the figure of the Jew to a more recognizable ethnic type replete with gaberdine and yarmulke, although in a recognizably Renaissance setting. Doran himself had played the role of Solanio in Alexander's much more extreme 1987 version of the play, and in some ways his own production pulled back from the wider political perspective of its predecessor. All of the elements that we might expect from a modern production were present, but certain nuances were given an additional emphasis. The scenes between Shylock and Jessica (Emma Hardy), however, were too full of affection to suggest that the daughter could be utterly deceitful. For example, as Shylock entrusted the keys of his house to Jessica, both spoke in unison the line 'A proverb never stale in thrifty mind' (2.5.53), and, as he left, his daughter pulled him back and kissed him; the gesture indicated some affection between father and daughter, even though her final couplet re-emphasized her duplicity. The dark violence of Venice, encapsulated in Shylock's entry at 3.1, bloodied, Salarino's manhandling of him, and the spitting at Tubal that Shylock touchingly wiped away, reached its apotheosis in the trial scene where a significantly undernourished Antonio (Julian Curry) was brought to the brink of sacrifice. At the point when the tables were turned on Shylock, and after a bag containing 6,000 ducats has been emptied onto the floor of the court, Gratiano pushed him viciously to the ground. There he met the prostrate Antonio and when he tried to regain his feet he physically slid on the gold coins, and had to be assisted. Susan Fischer has noticed how 'the dreary metallic Venice of approaching carnival glistens and seethes with beclouded glory and squalor',[1] and it is this sense of a decaying Renaissance republic that did much to ameliorate our hostility to Voss's magisterial, but obsessive Shylock, who was finally rendered pathetic rather than tragic. (See Figs 13 and 14.)

Belmont presented something of a contrast, with its tower and an occasional cloud in an otherwise blue sky visible through a gauze screen at the back of the stage. Helen Schlesinger's Portia confronted her suitors in a light-hearted manner, and it was clear from her barely suppressed excitement that she knew already what was in the casket that Bassanio chose but was forbidden to disclose its secret. Yet even in Belmont money was central, as when in the final scene Jessica and Lorenzo sat amid the coins that had been left onstage at the end of the trial scene. Also, the final pairings were deftly managed at the end of the play, and in a manner that obscured the prospect of tension

1 Susan L. Fischer, '*The Merchant of Venice*', *Shakespeare Bulletin* (Winter 1999), 12. I am grateful to Susan Fischer for drawing my attention to her review, and for providing me with a typescript of her account of Hansgünther Heymes's 2001 co-production of the play presented in Madrid and Valencia.

13 The set of the Royal Shakespeare Company production at Stratford-upon-Avon (1997), directed by Greg Doran

14 The Royal Shakespeare Company's 1997 production by Greg Doran, 4.1, with Philip Voss as Shylock

between Antonio, Bassanio and Portia. After all, Antonio is reunited with his argosies and this did much to eliminate the contradiction between the relaxed homosocial love between the two Venetian men, and the heterosexual pairing of Portia and Bassanio.

Richard Olivier's 1998 New Globe production of the *Merchant of Venice* attempted to return the play to its 'original' conditions of performance. Much has been written on the questionable nature of this theatrical enterprise generally, but it appears to have been the policy of the theatre director Mark Rylance to encourage auditors to involve themselves in the performance. For example, in his programme note for this production he asserted, 'Shakespeare must have wanted you to look at each other sometimes while you listened . . . If you feel like playing as well, we would love to pass the ball to you, join in.' Most other productions of the play, from Komisarjevsky onwards, have been content to contain the carnivalesque atmosphere within the structure of the stage performance, but Rylance had a trio of *commedia dell'arte* figures roaming the audience prior to the opening of the play. Marcello Magni's Arlecchino, involved in whipping up the spectators into a suitable adversarial role before the beginning of the play, adlibbed his way around the auditorium, and the combination of mime, slapstick and verbal garrulousness extended to his performance of Lancelet, and to his periodic announcement of act intervals. Magni, along with fellow actor Lilo Baur who played Jessica, were members of Theatre de Complicite, a company specializing in slapstick comedy and mime, indicating the generally pantomimic atmosphere that the production sought to generate. The audience was encouraged to hiss Norbert Kentrup's Shylock whenever he appeared, and many of the subtleties that most productions have striven hard to preserve were sacrificed on the altar of a crude melodrama that rode roughshod over the play's performance history. One newspaper critic observed that the spectators were 'encouraged to behave as if Red Riding Hood and the Big Bad Wolf were on the stage',[1] an effect that does much to obscure what has become, for modern audiences, the play's difficult racist and religious content. The unpredictability of such a strategy might be gauged by the audience responses to Morocco and Arragon, the former receiving a more sympathetic reception than the latter. These episodes have often been handled lightly and with some exaggeration, but here, as elsewhere, the invocation of the ethos of pantomime did much to infantilize the audience and to deaden any awareness of the uncomfortable roots of the laughter. Such crass and mindless strategies reached their apotheosis in the elopement scene, where Lorenzo and his accomplices arrived and departed dressed in rabbit suits. In this production the novelty of the stage assumed a greater importance than the play itself, with actors circling pillars, leaning on them or hiding behind them, but, in the final analysis, appealing mainly to the same section of the audience within an arc at the front of the stage as they would have done in a traditional proscenium arch theatre.

Trevor Nunn's National Theatre production of 1999 remained, in part, within a mainstream theatrical tradition. The setting was the 1920s, and the ethos of Christian Venice was that of *Cabaret*; the play opened in an art deco café, with a middle-aged Antonio, evidently frustrated with the snippet of the Brahms sonata he was playing, and betraying a depression that hinted at an inner turmoil about his own sexuality. David Bamber's mannered northern English accent distinguished him from his companions, particularly Alexander Hanson's aristocratic Bassanio, with whom he was quite visibly infatuated. The frustration generated by this infatuation was later displaced onto the figure of Shylock, but it also provided the motivation for a masochistic desire in the trial scene to accept the role of scapegoat as proof of his love for the younger man. Bamber alternated the roles of suffering victim and eager sacrifice, and

---

1 Benedict Nightingale, *Times*, 3 August 1998, quoted in Edelman, 81.

in the final scene of the play brought the warring Portia and Bassanio together in a gesture that allowed him to retain some power in the matter of the disposing of the latter's affections to a suitable heterosexual partner.

Derbhle Crotty's Portia and Alex Kelly's Nerissa inhabited the fashionable world of 1920s café society, and Portia reviewed her suitors on silent black-and-white film as she sipped champagne. This is the world of F. Scott Fitzgerald's *The Great Gatsby*, whose inhabitants live opulent and aimless lives of conspicuous consumption, while beneath a glittering surface of fashion and glamour a more seedy world of commercial transaction continues. Richard Henders's boisterously youthful Gratiano was as adept at racial insult as he was at performing cabaret comedy, and Peter de Jersey and Mark Umbers as Salerio and Solanio (there were only 'two Sallies' in this production) fulfilled their roles as hangers-on. Derbhle Crotty was a clearly nervous Portia, and nowhere more so than when her own fate rested in the choices of Chu Omambala's Morocco, or Raymond Coulthard's outrageously Hispanic Arragon, who arrived accompanied by a flamenco guitarist and proceeded to dance his suit. Morocco managed a muted version of a *de rigueur* flourish with his scimitar, but, when rejected, Omambala's otherwise dignified figure resorted to a childish display of emotion. Venice and Belmont, from the outset, shared a dark melancholy that the play's romance was not entirely successful in relieving.

Into this fashionable world of whimsy and caprice Henry Goodman's Shylock brought a measure of dignity and, initially at any rate, benign tolerance. Goodman was identifiably Jewish, with his yarmulke, prayer shawl and middle-European accent (see Fig. 15), and his financial acumen showed up like good sense in the face of the wastefulness that he saw around him. The production placed some emphasis on the indignities that he had to withstand from his Venetian adversaries, with whom he sought to ingratiate himself merely as a way of surviving. Although Lancelet (Andrew French) complained of his master's treatment, and Gabrielle Jourdan's Jessica insisted that 'Our house is hell', there was very little evidence in this production to support the allegation. Indeed, at 2.5 the manifest affection that Shylock displayed to his daughter emerged in the prayer in honour of the woman of the house (*Eshes Chayic*), which they sang in duet. They also spoke Yiddish to each other, reinforcing their separateness from a Venice distinguished by a carnival profligacy. The only moment when Shylock became a stern and agitated parent was when he warned Jessica about protecting his house from carnival excess. At this moment he slapped her impetuously, in a manner that recalled Patrick Stewart's similar (though more extreme, and less evidently motivated) gesture in the 1978 RSC production. Gabrielle Jourdan's Jessica was insecure throughout the production, and her acceptance into the world of Belmont as Lorenzo's wife was not entirely

15   The 1999 National Theatre production in London, directed by Trevor Nunn, 1.3, with Henry Goodman as Shylock and David Bamber as Antonio

unproblematic. Though less hostile than Joan Plowright's Portia in Jonathan Miller's 1970 production, Derbhle Crotty's Portia displayed a certain coldness towards her that suggested there was as much prejudice in Belmont as in Venice. Moreover, as part of a revisionary ending of the play, Jessica herself performed the prayer that she had earlier sung with her father, but now her delivery was bitter and aggressive, full of regret and self-loathing, more reminiscent in mood of the Kaddish that accompanied the ending of Miller's production.

Henry Goodman's Shylock, as Michael Billington observed, is 'tortured by his own paradoxical impulses'.[1] This is nowhere more in evidence than in the trial scene, where in the face of a hostile Venetian court Shylock insists upon the conditions of his bond, but where sympathy oscillates from plaintiff to accused. Crotty's studious Balthazar displays her legal ingenuity but the stimulus is provided by Shylock's pang of conscience, since he cannot bring himself to exact the conditions of the bond at the first attempt. Even Tubal, present in this court scene, leaves in dignified disgust as his fellow Jew continues to insist upon the penalty. What motivates Shylock to pursue this extreme course is clearly not, in this production, the persecution he feels as a Jew, but the loss of his daughter. It is the destruction of his own closely guarded household that generates his murderous passion, but he is forced in the trial scene to steel himself against his own humanity in order to accomplish the conditions of the bond. The hesitation that accompanies Tubal's silent censure is crucial in that it permits Portia to turn the tables, although she only does so at the very last minute, even as the blade makes contact with Antonio's flesh. In the ensuing reversal Shylock then occupies the chair that had been Antonio's, and before he leaves he divests himself of his yarmulke and prayer shawl. We are left at the end of the scene feeling that this enforced renunciation of a faith that emphasizes prudence,

1   Michael Billington, 'The quality of melancholy', *Guardian*, 1 February 2000.

concern and respect for the orderliness of the household is a step down into a world of ephemerality and irresponsibility.

The mood at the end of the trial scene is too sombre to be alleviated by the problematic romance of the final act of the play. Portia and Nerissa's business with the rings seems frivolous by comparison, as indeed do the trials of constancy to which Bassanio and Gratiano are subjected. The dark courtship of Lorenzo and Jessica speaks more of the ambivalence of the examples of thwarted love that they cite than it does of the healing powers of moonlight and music. Gratiano's couplet that concludes the play is followed in this production by Portia's lines: 'This night, methinks, is but the daylight sick; / It looks a little paler. 'Tis a day / Such as the day is when the sun is hid.' There follows Jessica's moving and heavily ironic performance of the 'prayer for the lady of the household' that follows on from Nerissa's letter detailing her father's gift. Once the prayer is ended, Portia's concluding speech, 'It is almost morning', is followed by an ominous peal of distant thunder. It is this momentary shifting of emphasis that is characteristic of Nunn's conception of the play, a technique that led Billington to designate his style as 'deeply paradoxical', betraying an 'increasing tendency to invest Shakespeare with a mass of novelistic detail [that] clogs the narrative momentum'.[1] This version, which takes liberties with the text, is careful to avoid pandering to populist racism as it teases out the complex motivations of the figure of the outsider whose most horrific persecution is to be, given the setting, in the play's future. The storm clouds that gather at the end of the play and in Belmont, and the haunting aggressiveness of Gabrielle Jourdan's singing voice, point forward in an unmistakably Chekhovian manner to the Holocaust, and to an uncomfortable European complicity, in a way that few other productions have managed.

Michael Bogdanov's 2003 production of the play, first at Ludlow, and then in 2004 as part of the Wales Theatre

---

1 Billington, 'The quality of melancholy'.

Company's repertoire, which toured along with *Twelfth Night* and *Cymbeline*, mines the tension between what he has called romantic and cynical readings of the play (Bogdanov, 71). Set in the modern world of high finance, the Venetian Rialto is transformed into the Stock Exchange and the ethos is that of 'fast money, easy come easy go, desperate dealing, FTSE, NASDAQ, Dow Jones, names that jump straight out of a Potter spell'. Russell Gomer's flamboyantly prodigal Bassanio is 'a layabout lad-about-town' (72), while Paul Greenwood's mature, repressed, puritanical Antonio, whose displays of offensive anti-Semitism reach a climax when he is forced to strip to the waist in the trial scene, only allows his suppressed passion for the younger man to emerge in a lingering farewell kiss. The meticulous care with which Greenwood dresses himself after Balthazar's court victory augments and encourages the sentiments of the baying crowd in the gallery of the courtroom, who punctuate the proceedings with a barrage of offensive racist comments. Bassanio's entourage, Gratiano, Lorenzo, Solanio and Salerio (no Salarino in this production), display their promiscuity openly, and the production forces us to question both the ethos of Venice and the permanence of the romantic relationships that are established at the end of the play.

Into this hostile environment, Philip Madoc's benign and tolerant Shylock enters. His 'Jewishness' is downplayed, and what initial hostility there is between him and Antonio is dispersed in a gently sardonic humour that for the outsider indicates a way of life. It is only after the defection of Jessica that he takes refuge in a religious faith that exacerbates the gulf between Jew and Christian adversary. By contrast, Bill Wallis's Tubal, in an innovation on earlier productions, is content to live off his Christian clients, offering only the most perfunctory assistance to a calm, purposeful Shylock whose own self-discipline is contrasted with an undisciplined Venetian audience in the trial scene. Wallis's offhand account of Jessica's and Lorenzo's extravagance is a measure of the degree to which he has become assimilated into Venetian society. In Michael Radford's 2004 film, which aims at an historical verisimilitude, the final shot of Leah's ring on Jessica's finger suggests that Tubal, though here a more sympathetic figure, has himself been the victim of scurrilous gossip and that the motive for Shylock's intransigence resides in a pathological Venetian perfidy. Bogdanov's own comment on the episode is to enquire, 'What happened to the monkey?', at the end of the play (Bogdanov, 85).

In part Bogdanov's production recuperates certain of the features that have characterized a range of recent productions of the play. His Venetians are generally more aggressively acquisitive and far less stable in their affections than we have been accustomed to seeing, as evidenced in Heledd Baskerville's shocked response to the passionate kiss Bassanio shares with Antonio in the trial scene, and in Gratiano's (Richard Nicolls) and Lorenzo's (Morgan Rhys) incorrigible and frequently visible womanizing. There are some powerful innovations that include Portia's evident awareness of the contents of the caskets, resulting in an uncomfortable tension between comic playfulness, the fear of patriarchal error and racial prejudice. In a politically opportunistic gesture, the fool's head that Arragon removes from the casket is an image of George W. Bush. But, most poignantly, Shylock dons his prayer shawl and yarmulke only in the trial scene, and after the Duke's initial judgement he approaches Antonio, hesitates, gathers up his resolve to exact the penalty (see Fig. 16), only to be prevented and to have the signifiers of his faith unceremoniously removed. Unlike the Jonathan Miller (1970) and Trevor Nunn (1999) productions where the intoning of the Kaddish is left to augment Jessica's defection at the end of the play, here Madoc intones it at the moment when his fortunes are at the lowest ebb. His is a tolerant majesty, stripped of his Jewish accoutrements and forced brutally to the floor, which retreats for the last time into the consolation of his faith, but is brought low by the relentless persecution of a society that vilifies him even as it 'uses' him.

16   The 2003 Ludlow Festival production, directed by Michael Bogdanov, 4.1, with Philip Madoc as Shylock

A Shylock who is driven by the law that should protect him to insist upon justice is, in this challenging production, a tragic figure whose persecution is emphasized by the bitter tone of the disguised Portia's exchange with Bassanio at 4.2, and by the signal failure to engineer a genuinely comic closure. Indeed, the play ends with Jessica leaving the stage after Portia, followed by Bassanio and finally Antonio. Although the theatrical idiom and the social context are different, the mood of Bogdanov's trenchantly political reading of the play resembles that of the 1986 Deutschestheater production. It is a reading that challenges the enthusiastic claim to the global efficacy of a capitalist economy, and returns us to the historical moment of the genesis of civilization's discontents. In many ways Michael Radford's film reinforces this tendency, and, even though it is in some ways a costume drama, it addresses current economic, political and religious fundamentalisms in a way that forces the *Merchant of Venice* into the present.

THE MERCHANT
OF VENICE

LIST OF ROLES

ANTONIO	*a Christian merchant of Venice and friend of Bassanio*
BASSANIO	*a Venetian lord, friend of Antonio, and suitor to Portia*
LEONARDO	*servant to Bassanio*
GRATIANO	*a gentleman of Venice, friend of Antonio and Bassanio, and suitor to Nerissa*
LORENZO	*a gentleman friend of Bassanio and suitor to Jessica*
SALANIO SALARINO	*gentlemen of Venice and friends of Bassanio and Antonio*
DUKE of Venice	
SALERIO	*a Venetian emissary*
PORTIA	*a rich heiress of Belmont and beloved of Bassanio*
NERISSA	*Portia's waiting-woman*
Stephano, a MESSENGER	*a servant in Portia's household*
BALTHAZAR	*another of Portia's servants*
SERVINGMAN	*a menial in Portia's household*
Prince of MOROCCO	*a suitor to Portia*
Prince of ARRAGON	*a second suitor to Portia*
Shylock the JEW	*a Venetian usurer*
JESSICA	*daughter of the Jew and beloved of Lorenzo*
TUBAL	*a fellow Jew and his friend*
Lancelet Giobbe, a CLOWN	*a menial, first in the house of the Jew and later in the house of Antonio*
GIOBBE	*the father of the Clown*
MESSENGER	*a member of Portia's household*
MAN	*a menial in Antonio's household*

Jailer, Magnificoes, Attendants, Followers, Court Officials, Musicians, Servitor

LIST OF ROLES A list of 'The Actors Names' was first included in Q3 and arranged according to the social hierarchy of the characters, beginning with 'The Duke of Venice' and ending with 'Iaylor, and Attendants'. The list was emended by Rowe, who enumerated the male characters in order of status above female characters and menials. Departure from this editorial convention begins with Cam[1], which retains hierarchical order to some degree, and is followed in part in Oxf and Folg. In this edition the list is organized primarily in terms of affiliation and household and secondarily in order of appearance.

1 ANTONIO Q3 describes '*Anthonio*' as 'a Merchant'; in Rowe he is '*the Merchant*' and in Capell '*a noble Merchant*'. He is a 'burgher', who generates wealth by trade. Antonio is the Italianate form of 'Anthony', patron saint of swineherds, to whom one of each litter of pigs was usually promised. It was also popularly the name used for the smallest pig of the litter (*OED*) and later alluded to Antonio's claim that he is 'a tainted wether of the flock' (4.1.113). For the significance of Antonio's 'Christian' affiliation, see p. 341, 113n. The conflict between 'Christian' and 'Jew' harks back to Marlowe's *Jew of Malta*, which was performed some thirty-six times at the Rose theatre between February 1592 and June 1596. See *Jew of Malta*, 1, and also Henslowe, 16–47.

2 BASSANIO Q3 designates Bassanio 'a Venetian Lord'. Rowe transforms the relationship between Antonio and Bassanio by designating the latter 'his friend'. Dyce describes him as 'his kinsman and friend'. Bassanio is an aristocrat whose primary means of generating wealth is by borrowing and/or through marriage (Marzola, 295–6; Sinfield, 'How to read', 126–8).

4 GRATIANO the name given to the comic doctor in the Italian *commedia dell'arte*: 'a foole or self conceited fellow in a play or comedie' (Florio, 218). Gratiano refers explicitly to his own comic role at 1.1.79. He is a Christian foil to the

formal clown in the play, Lancelet, the Jew's man. See also Nickel, 325, who suggests that the Latin root of the name is *gratificari*, 'pleasing or gratifying'. Q3 designates Gratiano, Lorenzo, Salanio and Salarino as 'Gentlemen of *Venice*, and companions with *Bassanio*'. Rowe has 'Salanio', 'Solorino' and 'Gratiano' as '*Friends to Anthonio and Bassanio*'; Capell lists 'Gratiano', 'Lorenzo', 'Solanio' and 'Salerino' as '*noble Venetians; and Friends to the Merchant, and* Bassanio'.

6 SALANIO See 4n. Cam spells this as 'Solanio'.

7 SALARINO a messenger whose name, which was not in Q3 and first appeared in Cam[1], has confused editors (see p. 41). See 4n. Capell conflates Salerino and Salerio at 3.2.218ff., which is nonsensical, while Cam conflates the two roles throughout on the grounds that 'Salerio' is a corruption of 'Salerino' (Cam, 102–3). It is unlikely that the Salarino who appears in Venice with Salanio at 3.1.0.1 is the same character who appears in Belmont at 3.2.216.1. Q and F maintain an absolute distinction between Salerino and Salerio in these two scenes. Ard[1] surmises that at 3.2.218ff. Gratiano may be referring to one of three, rather than two, friends, and that 'A new actor would not be needed; two subordinate parts might be taken by the same man' (Ard[1], 4n.). See also 12n. below.

10 PORTIA a name that combines classical and biblical resonances. In Plutarch's *Lives*, Portia is Cato's daughter who committed suicide out of loyalty to her husband Marcus Brutus, referred to at *JC* 1.1.165–6 (Daniell, *JC*, 65–6). Plutarch referred to her as 'This young Ladie being excellentlie well seene in Philosophie, loving her husband well, and being of noble courage, as she was also wise' (Daniell, *JC*, 337). The name also has a biblical resonance: St Paul refers to a Porcius Festus who was a procurator of the Jews in Judea (Acts, 24.28). *OED* glosses 'procurator' as 'An advocate, defender, or supporter of the cause of any person, system, tenet,

163

proposal etc.' (*OED* 5) or 'a public administrator or magistrate' (*OED* 7); the term also contains a subsidiary meaning as 'procurer of a loan' (*OED* 6b). The semantic field of the name Portia expands through a number of biblical associations to incorporate the various roles that she adopts in the play. The Roman Portia (Porcia) was noted for her strength of mind and fortitude. In choosing the name Portia for his heroine Shakespeare takes selectively from Plutarch. See Daniell for the suggestion that in Plutarch's *Life of Cato the Younger* Portia's 'affectionate nature and fondness for her husband' contained a stronger sexual element than the modern 'affectionate' might suggest (Daniell, *JC*, 65–6). Portia's sexual desire (and the patriarchal requirement to control it) is evident at 1.2.12ff., and relevant to the comic action of the play in Acts 4 and 5. Shakespeare's Portia takes the name of Balthazar at 4.1, aligning her with one of the New Testament magi. The genealogies of the magi were thought by the Venerable Bede to extend back to the Old Testament, hence, in Portia's case, her being subject to the constraints of the past through the law of her dead father (1.2.23–4) by which she is bound, but also her looking towards the future which involves her voluntary submission to Bassanio as his wife (3.2.166–74). Portia, in her disguise as Balthazar, is a bringer of gifts to Antonio, and also to Lorenzo and Jessica, and she unites past, present and future. She is also herself the 'gift' for which Bassanio has competed.

11 NERISSA possibly derived from the Italian *nero* meaning 'black-haired'. Florio notes *Nericcio* or *Negriccio* as meaning 'blackish, suttie, dunne, swarte' (Florio, 330). A contrast may be intended here between the mistress, Portia, who is 'fair' (1.1.162), and Nerissa, who is 'dark'.

12 MESSENGER one of three 'messengers' in the play, two of whom are named, and one who is not. The first (unnamed) appears at 2.9.83.1. The second enters at 3.2.216.1, is named in the SD as 'Salerio' and is mentioned by name by Bassanio on entry; it is this Salerio who is confused with 'Solanio' in the SD at the opening of 3.3. The third messenger appears at 5.1.24.1 and identifies himself as 'Stephano' at 5.1.28. For the suggestion that these three parts were performed by the same actor, hence the need to identify the two characters who appear after the first unnamed 'messenger', see Hattaway, 71–2, and also Mahood, *Bit Parts*, 13–14.

13 BALTHAZAR here a messenger; but the name is given after the sixth century to one of the magi, and hence one of the bringers of gifts to the infant Christ. The Venerable Bede claimed that the three magi were descendants of the three sons of Noah, Shem, Ham and Japhet (*Oxford Companion to Bible*, 547).

15 Prince of MOROCCO In Q and F the designation is '*Morochus*' at 2.1.0.1. Morocco was part of Arabic north-west Africa, and the name derives from its chief city Marrakesh (*OED sb.*). But the term resonates with the Italian *Móro* meaning Moor, and possibly *Moróglie*, suggesting piles or haemorrhoids, and *Moróglo* meaning 'tipsie, wayward, full of wine and words' (Florio, 323). *Morochus* was also the name given to a horse popularly thought to be able to perform tricks, and whose exploits were recorded in a pamphlet of 1595 (see p. 85). Such secondary glosses are consistent with the practice in this play of having marginal characters condemn themselves either through their utterances or by virtue of their names. Another context is Elizabeth I's proclamation to the Lord Mayor of London in 1596 concerning the presence of 'Negars and Blackamoors' in London (Hall, 'Guess who', 94–5).

17 Shylock the JEW The emphasis on Shylock's name as opposed to his dramatic function begins with Q3, which describes him as '*Shylock*, the rich Jew, and Fàther of *Iessica*'. Marlowe combines social type and individualized

'character' in the *Jew of Malta*, where the name Barabas resonates with New Testament overtones. In *MV* Q1–4 and F1–4 the SPs remain unstable, but Rowe normalized the unstable SPs '*Iewe*'/'*Shy*[*l.*]' to '*Shylock*' (see p. 430). The Jew has an English name (see Furness, ix–x; Orgel, 'Shylock', 144ff.; and p. 47). For the significance of variant SPs, see p. 41; R. Kennedy; and Drakakis, '*Jew*', 105–21. For the alleged connection between Marlowe's play, the Dr Lopez affair and *MV*, see pp. 20–1.

There is some etymological uncertainty regarding the Jew's name, since the English surname 'Shylok' appears in a document of 1435 in the Battle Abbey deeds and refers to 'Richard Shylok of Hoo, co. Sussex' (quoted in Furness, ix; see also Orgel, 'Shylock', 144–62). Significantly, after Shakespeare's play, the name is associated with a Jew and appears in a ballad entitled *Caleb Shillocke, his Prophesie: or the Iewes Prediction*, thought to have appeared in 1607, though it may have been of much earlier provenance (quoted in Furness, x). The spelling 'Shilocke' appears in Q3 at sig. B2ʳ. The Old Testament book of Genesis, 10.24, mentions the name 'Selah': 'Arpharad begate Selah, and Selah begate Neber.' Cf. Oxf¹, 23, and also Cardozo, 219, and 223–4 for the suggestion that 'Shylock' may have been pronounced with a short *i* in order to facilitate a pun on the Clown's 'when I shun Scylla your father, I fall into Charybdis your mother' (3.5.14–15); cf. also Ard², 3. Bloom & Jaffa, 33, suggest that the form 'Shiloh' may well be the origin of Shylock's name. This appears as 'Silo' or 'Shiloh' in Genesis, 49.10: 'The scepter shall not depart from Juda, and the law giuer from betweene his feete, untill Silo come: and vnto him shall the gathering of the people be.' Some attempt may have been made to establish a connection between the figure of the Jew and a characteristically Old Testament name. Cam² cites Joseph Ben Gurion's *Compendious and most Marvellous History of the Latter Times of the Jews' Common Weal* (1593), in which a Roman defender of Askelon refers to one of the Jewish leaders as 'Shiloch' (Cam², 71). The name 'Shylock' or 'Shilocke' (or Q1's occasional variant 'Shyloch' at 1.3.48) is also close to 'shullock', an obscure dialect term meaning 'to idle about, to slouch. Used as a term of contempt' (*OED*). Cf. Thomas Cartwright, *A Confutation of the Rhemists Translation, Glosses and Annotations on the New Testament* (Leiden, 1618): 'M. Calvins great skill . . . could not without blushing be lacked of such schullockes and skipjackes as you be.' It seems likely that the two divergent etymologies are brought together in a name that carries with it both Old Testament connotations, along with the more colloquial suggestion of the usurer as one who gets rich but does no work. See also Gross, 51, for the suggestions that the name is close to 'shallach', 'the Hebrew word for cormorant', and 'shullock', 'a dialect word meaning "to idle about, to slouch"'. In modern English the colloquial term for a moneylender or usurer is a 'shylock' (*OED*). More recently, Laroque has suggested that in the figure of Shylock as 'a kind of amalgamation of the typical Jewish moneylender and the Puritan whose keen desire for profit had become proverbial in the Elizabethan period' the semantic components of the name 'Shy – *lock*' are combined to reinforce 'the theme of locking up and imprisonment in the play' (Laroque, 256–7).

18 JESSICA thought to be a version of the Old Testament Iscah or Jisca (see Furness, 15, and Ard², 3), who was the niece of Abraham. See also Genesis, 12.29 for confirmation of this genealogy: 'Abram and Nachor tooke them wiues: the name of Abrams wife was Sarai, and the name of Nachors wife was Milcha, the daughter of Haran, the father of Milcha, and the father of Jischah.'

19 TUBAL a name with wide biblical resonance, associated with unlawful religious activity and various forms of trade; the name of one of Noah's grandsons; see Genesis, 10.2. See also Genesis, 10.6, and 3.2.283–4: 'I have heard him swear / To Tubal and to Chus, his countrymen'. In 1 Chronicles, 1.5, Tubal is designated as a son of Japhet. In Ezekiel, 27.13, he is a merchant who traded in slaves and bondsmen, and who 'brought vessels of brasse for thy marchandize'. Tubal-Cain appears in Genesis, 4.22, as the son of Lamech and one of his two wives, Zillah, and Lamech is a descendant of the Cain who violated the law of monogamy. The association with 'Chus' aligns Tubal with the black son of Noah. See Hakluyt, 8.182, and Hall, 'Guess who', 105–6. In Bogdanov's 2004 production Tubal 'lives off' the culinary scraps of the Christian Venetians. A reference to '*Tuballs* musique' appears in the epistle 'To the reader' in Nashe's *Have with you to Saffron Walden* (1596), but may have been cited 'in part for its punning potential' (Tobin, 312–13).

20 CLOWN Since Rowe, with the exception of Capell, the figure of the Clown in the play has always been designated Launcelot/Lancelot Gobbo. Folg restores Q and F's 'Lancelet Gobbo', but in Q and F the speech prefix varies between 'Clown' and 'Launcelet'. *OED* defines 'lancelet' as a 'lancet', 'a small lance, a dart' (*OED* 1a (*obs.*)), and 'a surgical instrument of various forms usually with two edges and a point like a lance, used for bleeding, opening abscesses, etc.' (*OED* 2). For an exhaustive etymology of 'lancelet', see Parker. The 'lancelet' was a medical cutting instrument used in letting blood, and castration, and for other forms of medical incision (see William Clowes, *A Proved Practice for All Young Chirurgians* (1588), Nicholas Gyer, *The English Phlebotomy* (1592), and Peter Lowe, *The Whole Course of Chirurgerie* (1597), cited in Parker, 100). Parker cites Gyer's condemnation of 'mercenary bloodsuckers', 'Arabians,

barbarous physitions' and counterfeit 'Iews or Egiptians' who 'kill thousands' of 'faythful Christians' by bleeding (Parker, 100). Lancelet's role in the play is primarily that of the self-conscious 'clown' who 'pricks' his own and the pretences of others; his forename is descriptive of his role, and his surname is secondary, but it makes possible a comic reference to the unspecified tribulations of his father. The alternation of 'Launcelet' and 'Clown' as speech prefixes in Q and F is not unlike that of 'Shylock' and 'Jew', and the bibliographical reasons may also be similar. See pp. 40, 438.

21 GIOBBE pronounced Gi-ob-bè as trisyllabic. In SDs and full SPs the form that most frequently occurs is 'Gobbo', producing the disyllabic pronunciation, but the terminal *o* masks the biblical reference to the Italianate form of the name 'Job'. Lancelet's name at 2.2.3–5 in Q is '*Iobbe, Launcelet Jobbe*', good *Launcelet*', '*Iobbe*' and '*Launcelet Iobbe*'; F has '*Iobbe*' consistently here. F3 shortens '*Iobbe*'/'*Jobbe*' to '*Iob*'. Most editors have followed the practice of designating '*Iobbe*' as 'Gobbo'. Florio, 152, offers three meanings for 'Gobbo': (1) 'a kind of faulckon'; (2) 'a kind of shell fish'; and (3) 'a bunch, a knob or crooke backe, a croope'. There is no explicit reference to Old Giobbe's 'crook-back' in the play, although Parker argues that the Geneva Bible may contain a relevant gloss: 'Let their eyes be darkened that they see not, and bow downe their back alwayes' (Romans, 11.10, in Parker, 108 and 112). The title-page of Santi Marmochini's vernacular Italian translation of *La Bibbia* (Venice, 1545) refers to '*Et accio l'opera sia piu perfetta quanto alla dispta di Iobbe co suoi amici*', and as late as 1760 Italian versions of the Book of Job described their contents as *Ill libro di Giobbe*. Indeed, in the *Enclicope dia Italiana*, revised by Mario Cosati, Paulo Valentini and Pasquale Caropreso, vol. 17 (Rome, 1951), 150–2, 'Giobbe' is described as 'Vulgata *Job*', that is, '*Nomo del personaggio principali*

d'un libro della Bibbia e titolo del libro stresso' (150). Giobbe is 'sand-blind, high gravel-blind' (2.2.32–3), and the Old Testament Job reveals: 'Mine eye is dimme for very heauinesse, and all my strenth is like a shadow.' Satan afflicts Job with a plague of boils: 'So went Satan foorth from the presence of the Lorde, and smote Job with sore byles, from the sole of his foote, vnto his crowne' (Job, 2.7). Lancelet's name may refer obliquely to a cure for this affliction. See also p. 45.

That the original SP would normally have been *Iobbe* may be legitimately surmised because, like the SP *Iewe*, it would have made an additional demand on an already depleted supply of italic capital *I* types. The substitution of *G* for *I* and the misreading of terminal *e* for *o* produces *Gobbo*, and breaks the chain of Old Testament associations surrounding the names of Jobbe and Lancelet, associations that an Elizabethan audience would almost certainly have recognized. Dover Wilson noted the discrepancy between SPs and names in the dialogue (Cam[1], 99–100), surmising: 'The name should, we think, be "Giobbe", the Italian form of our English "Job" . . . but the point that we wish to make here is that, while the word in the dialogue represents the right sound, that of the SD seems to be a "correction" of the original by someone not unacquainted with Italian.' He observes the pointlessness of applying the epithet 'crook-back' to either Lancelet or his father, but cites Elze, who traces the reference 'Gobbo' to a statue in the Rialto in Venice, 'a stone figure which serves as a supporter to the granite pillar of about a man's height, from which the laws of the Republic were proclaimed' (cited in Cam[1], 100, n. 1).

24 **Followers** attendants who are members of the retinues of Bassanio and Morocco, and of the household of Portia

25 **Servitor** 'a (male) personal or domestic attendant (in early use chiefly, one who waits at table); a manservant' (*OED* 1)

THE COMICAL
HISTORY OF THE
MERCHANT
OF VENICE

[1.1]   *Enter* ANTONIO, SALARINO *and* SALANIO.

ANTONIO
In sooth I know not why I am so sad.
It wearies me; you say it wearies you;
But how I caught it, found it or came by it,
What stuff 'tis made of, whereof it is born,

TITLE See t.n. Rowe follows F's title *The Merchant of Venice*, adding the phrase '*a Comedy*'. In 1701 George Granville, Lord Lansdowne, published an adaptation of the play entitled *The Jew of Venice: A Comedy*. Oxf[1] conflates Q and Granville to produce the title *The Comical History of The Merchant of Venice, or Otherwise Called The Jew of Venice*. Mahood notes that only one play before 1600, Greene's *Alphonsus of Aragon* (1587), is designated a 'comical history' and suggests that the term 'history' may have been used to draw attention to the 'romance nature of the play' (Cam[2], 57). The combination of 'comedy' and 'history' in Q1 and Q2 emphasizes both the domestic and the narrative aspects of the action.

1.1 Theobald locates this scene in '*a Street in* Venice' and Cam[1] on '*A quay in Venice*'. Some modern productions (e.g. Nunn) prefer an indoor setting such as a café or a cabaret. Both in Venice and Belmont some scenes are 'outside' and others are 'inside'.

1   sooth truth
      sad an emotion for which the motivations are unclear. In *Pecorone* the merchant Ansaldo (Antonio) is 'grieved' when he hears of the death of Gianetto's (Bassanio) father, but that grief is mitigated by the joy he derives from Gianetto's presence. (See LN.)

4   stuff substance (*OED sb.*[1] II.3), but also with reference to 'inward character' (II.3b)

TITLE] *head title*: Q1, Q2 (The comicall History of the Mer- chant of Venice); The Merchant of Venice F; *title-page*: The most excellent Historie of the *Merchant of Venice* With the extreame crueltie of *Shylocke* the Iewe towards the sayd Merchant, in cutting a iust pound of his flesh: and the obtayning of *Portia* by the choyse of three chests *As it hath beene diuers times acted by the Lord Chamberlaine his Seruants.* Written by William Shakespeare Q1, Q2; *running title*: The comicall Historie of [*verso pages*] the Merchant of Venice [*recto pages*] Q1, Q2; The Merchant of Venice. F 1.1] *Rowe (ACT I. SCENE I.); Actus primus F* 0.1 SALARINO] F; Salaryno Q; Solarino F3; *SALERIO* Cam[1]

> I am to learn; and such a want-wit sadness makes of me,   5
> That I have much ado to know myself.
>
> SALARINO
>
> Your mind is tossing on the ocean,
> There where your argosies with portly sail
> Like signiors and rich burghers on the flood,
> Or, as it were, the pageants of the sea,   10

5 **I . . . learn** I do not know. This is set as a separate half-line in all editions after Pope, with the exception of Keightley, who attaches 'I am' to the previous line, and 'to learn' to the beginning of 5. In Q and F the whole of 5 is printed as a single line, with the phrase *makes of me* turned under in Q1.
   want-wit lacking in sense

6 **know myself** a proverb (Dent, K175) whose origin is classical but which appears frequently in 16th-century writings and throughout Shakespeare's work. Cf. Sir John Davies's poem *Nosce Teipsum* (1599): 'My selfe am *Center* of my circling thought, / Onely *my selfe* I studie, learne, and *knowe*' (Krueger, 11).

7 SALARINO the first encounter with one of three minor characters whose names appear inconsistently and who are collectively referred to as 'the three Sallies' (see pp. 426–7).

7–13 The convoluted syntax of these lines enacts the complex concerns that they articulate. As Antonio's 'mind is tossing on the ocean', so Salarino's description imitates his hypothesis in its movement between a series of metaphoric possibilities, each of which require some qualification and/or expansion.

8 **argosies** plural of argosy, a large merchant ship that takes its name from Ragusa, a city on the gulf of Venice. The earliest form was *ragusye* but it appears in English in the 16th century as *Aragouse, Arragouese* or *Arragosa* (*OED*). See *Jew of Malta*,

1.1.44: 'Mine argosy from Alexandria, / Loaden with spices, and silks, now under sail.' Malone (8) reverts to the original suggestion by Pope that the word derives its origin from the famous ship *Argo*, since there are two further references in the play to the story of Jason.
   portly majestic and dignified, but also corpulent (*OED adv.* b), indicating both status and an image of billowing sails (*OED sb.*[1] 2 sail; cf. *Tamburlaine 1*, 1.2.382: 'To be my Queen and portly Emperesse' (in Marlowe, 19).
   sail a collective noun that functions as a metonymy for the modern 'fleet' (cf. *Oth* 1.3.38: 'of thirty sail', and *Per* 1.4.61: 'A portly sail of ships make hitherward.' The image is one of a number indicating stately maritime progress, analogous to that of a civic pageant, hence the proliferation of similes in 9–13.

9 **signiors** members of the Signoria or governing body of Venice, but possibly (English) gentlemen
   burghers citizens (*OED* 1), though in this instance clearly dignataries
   flood literally, the flowing in of the tide (*OED* 1), hinting at Antonio's mental turmoil, but also a synecdoche for the sea

10 **as it were** a parenthetical phrase that reveals the self-consciousness of Salarino's description of Antonio's mind
   pageants theatrical shows; particularly floats drawn along in public processions dating back to the Middle Ages,

10 Or,] *Malone;* Or *Q*   were,] *Collier;* were *Q*

Do overpeer the petty traffickers
That curtsy to them, do them reverence
As they fly by them with their woven wings.

SALANIO

Believe me, sir, had I such venture forth,
The better part of my affections would   15
Be with my hopes abroad. I should be still
Plucking the grass to know where sits the wind,
Peering in maps for ports and piers and roads;

but also features of both Venetian festivals (Cam[2], 26) and pageants on the Thames (Chambers, *Elizabethan*, 1.138–9). Cf. also Stow, 713, for an account of the reception of the Earl of Leicester at Rotterdam on 23 December 1585.

11 **overpeer** look down on from above (*OED* 1), but also treat with contempt (*OED* 1b), rise above, excel or occupy a higher position (*OED* 2). All these meanings were current at the end of the 16th century. Ard[2] suggests a pun on 'peer of the realm' indicated by the reference to *signiors* and *burghers* (9). A sense of hierarchy is reinforced by the object of the sentence, *petty traffickers*. **petty traffickers** minor or insignificant tradesmen (*OED* 1: trafficker), possibly with the suggestion of intrigue or underhanded dealing (*OED* 2)

12 **curtsy** a stately bow effected by lowering the knees and bending the body (*OED* 3a), but also more generally an act of respect (*OED* 2), a courtesy; or the customary practice of smaller cargo ships lowering their topsails as a gesture of submission and mark of respect (Falconer, 22). The word perhaps suggests the rocking and dipping motion of the smaller ships in the wake of the argosies (Furness, 5)

13 **fly . . . wings** The argosies fly by like birds, but their wings, the sails, are artificial. (See L.N.)

14 **venture** an enterprise involving some degree of risk, anticipating the Jew's fuller description of the perils of trade later at 1.3.20–3.

15 **affections** emotions as opposed to reason, but in this instance more generally those external concerns that move or influence the mind (*OED* 2)

16 **still** continually and persistently, without change or interruption (*OED* 3)

17 **Plucking . . . wind** testing the direction of the wind by plucking grass and tossing it into the air, a means of emulating the operation of a weathervane: cf. *Jew of Malta*, 1.75 (*Works*, 243).

18 **Peering** F's 'Peering' combines the meanings of prying and peering into. Q's 'Piring' is an obsolete form of *peering* (*OED*), indicating careful scrutiny, with a view to calculating likely dangers. Furness notes, but is sceptical about, Halliwell's suggestion that Q3's 'Prying' was designed to avoid the possibility of phonetic repetition in relation to *piers* later in the same line (Furness, 5). Pooler thinks that Q3's 'Prying' (as opposed to Q2's 'Piering' and F's 'Peering') steers the meaning towards 'prying in', and he cites George Chapman, *Blind Beggar of Alexandria* (1598): 'And like an Eagle prying for her pray' (Ard[1], 7).
roads sheltered stretches of water or coves near the shore where ships might anchor safely (*OED* 3)

12 curtsy] *(cursie); curtsie F; curt'sy Ard[1]; cur'sy Ard[2]*   14 SP] *Salar. F; Sola F3*   venture] ventures *Hanmer*   18 Peering] *(Piring), F; Piering Q2; Prying Q3*

And every object that might make me fear
Misfortune to my ventures, out of doubt,   20
Would make me sad.
SALARINO   My wind, cooling my broth,
Would blow me to an ague when I thought
What harm a wind too great might do at sea.
I should not see the sandy hour-glass run
But I should think of shallows and of flats,   25
And see my wealthy *Andrew* docked in sand,
Vailing her high top lower than her ribs
To kiss her burial. Should I go to church

19 **object** obstacle or hindrance that impedes progress (*OED* 2)
20 **out of doubt** without question, certainly
21 **wind . . . broth** an adaptation of the proverbial 'Save your wind to cool your broth' (Tilley, W422).
22 **blow me** inflate me, but also allow to blossom (Onions), indicating that the breath Salarino would need to cool his broth would, if he had Antonio's responsibilities, remind him of what a gale at sea might do
ague a malarial fever, but associated figuratively with any disease that induced shivering
24 **sandy hour-glass** a sand-glass that ran for an hour and was used to estimate the passage of time
25 **flats** extended sandbanks or shallow areas. See Antony Ashley, *Mariner's Mirror* (1588), and also Falconer, 82–5; see also 3.1.3–5 for a later reference to a specific and notorious flat area, the Goodwins.
26 *Andrew* Johnson thought that this was the name of the ship to which Salarino is referring (Johnson, 386). Brown argues that this is a reference to one of two ships, the *San Andres*, captured in June 1596 by the Earl of Essex in his attack on Cadiz harbour

(Ard², xxvi–xxvii), important in the process of establishing the date of the play. Also, the name 'Andrew' is possibly synonymous with 'argosy' in denoting a type of ship rather than a particular vessel.
*docked stranded. The Q reading 'docks' makes little sense in this context; Furness suggests that the compositor may have misread the final letter 't' in his copy, because of 'the ease with which *s* in the old Court hand can be confounded with *d*' (Furness, 6).
27 **Vailing . . . top** stooping as in bowing as an act of submission. This continues the earlier series of metaphors that connect conduct at sea with social etiquette on land at 1.1.10, but now describes a ship so embedded in the sand that its topmast is lower than the level of its transverse timbers or ribs. Steevens cites Bullokar's *English Expositor* (1616), sig. O8ᵛ, where 'Vaile bonet' is defined both as a nautical term and as a social gesture: '*to putte off the hatt, to strike saile, to giue signe of submission*' (Steevens, 9).
28 **kiss her burial** Salarino personifies the shipwreck in an image of the vessel kissing in obeissance the sand that will be her grave.

21 SP] (*Salar.*); *Sal. F*   26 *Andrew*] *Andrew's / Collier*   docked] *Rowe;* docks *Q;* decks *Collier;* dock *Keightley*

And see the holy edifice of stone
And not bethink me straight of dangerous rocks,   30
Which, touching but my gentle vessel's side,
Would scatter all her spices on the stream,
Enrobe the roaring waters with my silks,
And in a word, but even now worth this,
And now worth nothing? Shall I have the thought   35
To think on this, and shall I lack the thought
That such a thing bechanced would make me sad?
But tell not me; I know Antonio
Is sad to think upon his merchandise.

ANTONIO

Believe me, no. I thank my fortune for it,   40
My ventures are not in one bottom trusted,

29 **holy . . . stone** the altar rather than the church itself; the 'eucharistic table' made of stone (*ODCC*, 40) that serves as a reminder both of life's perils (in this case the merchant's) and of the prospect of Christian salvation. This is more than just a synonym for *church* (28).

31 **but** merely
gentle delicate and therefore vulnerable, but also of superior social rank, belonging to the class of gentlemen (*OED* 2); a possible pun here on 'gentile', drawing an initial distinction between Christian merchants engaged in legitimate but vulnerable commercial activity and their Jewish counterparts who, in the play, are not; see also 2.6.52: 'Now, by my hood, a gentle, and no Jew.'

32–3 **spices . . . silks** Pooler cites *Jew of Malta*, 1.79–80, 'Mine argosy from Alexandria, / Loaden with spice and silks now under sail' (Ard[1], 8), and it seems likely that these lines are an expansion of Marlowe's.

34 **even . . . this** just now worth the full value of the cargo my argosy is carrying. Salarino emphasizes here the precariousness of Antonio's business venture, exposed as his ship is to the natural elements. Furness records Lettsom's view that there is something missing from the text between 34 and 35, but that the actor 'may be supposed to complete the sense by a gesture, extending his arms' (Furness, 7), presumably as he articulates the word *this*.

35 **thought** anxiety and care. Cf. *R3* 5.1.105, 'I'll strive with troubled thoughts to take a nap', and also, *Ham* 3.1.85, 'the pale cast of thought' (Furness, 7). The association of anxiety with melancholy recalls Antonio's initial inexplicable sadness, and seems to propose a connection between his frame of mind and the precariousness of his business venture.

37 **bechanced** happened by chance

41 I have not put all my eggs in one basket. Proverbial (Dent, A209); cf. More, *Richard III*, 41: 'For what wise merchant adventureth all his good in one ship?'
bottom keel, and hence ship. But note also the meaning of *bottom* as a 'ball of thread' (Onions); with the repetition of *fortune* at 40 and 43 this suggests a connection between the fate of Antonio's ship and the unravelling of his own fate or *fortune* for which he has made some provision.

32 her] the *Q2*   35 nothing?] *Q2;* nothing. *Q1,* F

Nor to one place; nor is my whole estate
Upon the fortune of this present year:
Therefore my merchandise makes me not sad.

SALANIO

Why then, you are in love.												45

ANTONIO

Fie, fie.

SALANIO

Not in love neither? Then let us say you are sad
Because you are not merry; and 'twere as easy
For you to laugh and leap and say you are merry
Because you are not sad. Now, by two-headed Janus,				50

45 SP See t.n. and p. 163. Q2 ascribes this speech, and Antonio's at 46, to Salarino; Furness misidentifies this edition as Q1 and supports the attribution of White (1854) to Salarino on the grounds that he is 'the more loquacious of Anthonio's two friends, and just after the entrance of Bassanio he declares that he had intended to banter Anthonio into good spirits' (Furness, 8).

46 Editors have occasionally commented on the irregular metre of this line. Hanmer conjectures: 'Fie, fie, away!' while Dyce (iii) believes that Shakespeare wrote: 'In love! fie, fie!' Cam[1] suggests that 'Anth. o no' may have been mistaken by the compositor for 'Anthonio', and that what Shakespeare 'intended Antonio to say was "O no! fie, fie!"' (Cam[1], 124). Ard[1] and Cam[1] speculate that the metrically imperfect line divided between the two speakers may suggest an embarrassed pause indicating Antonio's discomfort at Salanio's guess at the truth about his sadness. In Trevor Nunn's RNT production (1999), David Bamber's ostentatiously homosexual Antonio delivers these words in the form of a vehement denial.

47–8 sad . . . merry proverbial (Dent, S14). See also Nicholas Udall, *Ralph Roister Doister* (1566), 3.3.12–13: '*M. Mery:* . . . But why speake ye so faintly, or why are ye so sad? *R. Roister:* Thou knowest the proverb, because I cannot be had [glad].' See also *TGV* 4.2.28–9.

48 easy effortless, but in the light of 49 ironical

49 laugh and leap literally jump for joy, but Salanio's frustration with Antonio highlights a dialectic of happiness and sadness suggestive of a conflation of two proverbs: (1) to laugh and cry at once (Tilley, L92a) and (2) to laugh and lie down (Tilley, L92). See also *VA* 414: 'That laughs and weeps, and all but with a breath', and Florio, *Florio's Second Fruits* (1591): 'What game doo you plaie at cardes? At primero, at trump, at laugh and lie downe.' Oxf[1] cites Jonson, *Every Man Out*, 1.3.120–1, for the use of the phrase 'laugh and leap', although it is more likely that Shakespeare influenced Jonson in this usage.

50 two-headed Janus double-faced, as an attribute of the classical god Janus, who was the god of beginnings (*OCD*, 466), but here restricted to meaning both happy and sad. Pooler identifies

45 SP] (*Sala.*); *Sola. F; Salar. Q2* (also at 46)   45] Then y'are in love *Q2*   46 fie.] fie! *Theobald*
47 neither?   Then] *Q2;* neither: then *Q1, F*   50 Because you are] 'Cause you're *Hanmer*   two-headed]
my two-headed *F4*

Nature hath framed strange fellows in her time:
Some that will evermore peep through their eyes
And laugh like parrots at a bagpiper;
And other of such vinegar aspect
That they'll not show their teeth in way of smile   55
Though Nestor swear the jest be laughable.

Enter BASSANIO, LORENZO *and* GRATIANO.

Here comes Bassanio, your most noble kinsman,
Gratiano and Lorenzo. Fare ye well,
We leave you now with better company.

SALARINO

I would have stayed till I had made you merry,   60

Robert Greene's *Menaphon* (1589) as
the source of a connection between the
figure of Janus and 'chance': 'Chaunce
is like *Janus*, double-faced, as well full
of smiles to comfort, as of frownes to
dismay' (Ard[1], 9–10).

52 **evermore peep** always look, but with
partially closed eyes (*OED v.*[2] 1, peep)
because the face is contorted through
a disingenuous laughter. The following
adverbial phrase 'through their eyes'
releases the alternative meaning of
'peep' as 'to speak in a weak querulous
tone' (*OED v.*[1] 2, 3), where the 'eyes'
are also expressive of meaning.

53 **parrots . . . bagpiper** Pooler
establishes a connection between the
unintelligent imitative skill of the
parrot whose laughter is the sound of
screeching, and the melancholy sound
of the bagpipe (Ard[1], 10); see also the
Jew's later disparaging references at
4.1.48 and 55 to the nasal sound of the
bagpipe and to the *woollen* (possibly
'uillan') bagpipe. (See LN.)

54 **other** others
vinegar aspect sour appearance (*OED*
5B); *aspect* was usually accented on the
second syllable, as at 2.1.8 (Ard[1], 43).

56 **Nestor** King of Pylos noted for his
age and wisdom. The invocation of
Nestor by Salanio emphasizes the
extreme (and possibly unwise) persistence of Antonio's sadness no matter
how authoritative or how persuasive the
invocation to laughter might be.

57 **noble kinsman** In the main source for
the play, *Il Pecorone*, Antonio (Ansaldo)
is Bassanio's (Giannetto's) godfather
(*nonno*). The epithet *noble*, augmented
later by the title *lord*, indicates an
aristocratic lineage for Bassanio, reinforced by Q3's designation of Bassanio
as 'an Italian Lord' (sig. A1[r]), although
from Rowe onwards, and with the
exception of Dyce, who describes him
as 'His kinsman and friend', all editors simply designate him as Antonio's
'friend' (see Marzola, 296–7, for a
rethinking of the financial basis of this
'friendship').

60 **made you merry** made you happy.
Brown (Ard[2], 119ff.) notes that
Antonio's friends are persistent in
attempting to persuade Antonio out of
his sadness. He cites Burton, 2, mem. 6,
subs. 4, which incorporates a long history of mirth as a cure for melancholy.

53 parrots] *(Parrats)* bagpiper] *(bagpyper);* bag-piper *Q2, F;* Pagpiper *Q3*   54 other] others
Pope   58 Fare ye well] *Q3;* Faryewell *Q*   60, 65, 68 SP] *(Sala.);* Sola. *F3;* Salerio. *Cam[1]*

If worthier friends had not prevented me.

ANTONIO

Your worth is very dear in my regard.

I take it your own business calls on you,

And you embrace th'occasion to depart.

SALARINO   Good morrow, my good lords.   65

BASSANIO

Good signiors both, when shall we laugh? Say, when?

You grow exceeding strange: must it be so?

SALARINO

We'll make our leisures to attend on yours.

Exeunt Salarino and Salanio.

61 **worthier** a reinforcement of Salanio's comment at 57–8; meaning both distinguished by positive or good qualities (*OED* 2), but also of superior rank or standing in the community (*OED* 3). Significantly it is the first of these two meanings that Antonio will take up and develop in his reply at 62.
prevented forestalled or anticipated

62 **worth . . . dear** Although Antonio is clearly complimenting Salarino, the two different meanings of *dear* (*OED* †1) as noble, honourable and worthy (cf. *1H4* 4.4.31–2: 'And many mo corrivals and dear men / Of estimation and command in arms') and as expensive (*OED* 6c) (cf. *1H4* 3.3.45–6: 'as good cheap at the / dearest chandler's in Europe') may suggest an unintended irony here.
regard estimation

64 **occasion** opportunity, influenced by an external cause (*your own business*, 63)

66 **when . . . laugh** when shall we next be merry. Salarino has manifestly failed to relieve Antonio's sadness and now Bassanio, entering on a scene of some seriousness, takes up the challenge.

67 **exceeding   strange** very distant.

Furness notes only five usages in Shakespeare of the adverb 'exceeding(ly)' although he notes its frequency in Elizabethan writers (Furness, 9). Pooler glosses *strange* as unfriendly (Ard[1], 10), although a sense of controlling one's emotions is also implied, as in *RJ* 2.2.102–4: 'I should have been more strange, I must confess, / But that thou overheard'st e'er I was ware, / My true love passion.'
must . . . so? why must this be so? Mahood suggests either 'must you be so distant?' or, following Furness (9–10), 'must you go?' (Cam[2], 60), but Q's punctuation suggests that this clause relates directly to Salarino's 'strangeness'.

68 Mahood glosses this as indicating that 'Salarino and Solanio [*sic*] will make a point of being free at a time when Bassanio is at leisure too' (Cam[2], 60). Directed at Bassanio, Salarino's comment is not without irony, since it is the former who now takes on the task of alleviating the seriousness of the general mood. It is also, in part, aimed at Antonio, whose own sadness makes him unavailable for merriment.

68 SD *Salerino and Salanio*] *(Salerino and Solanio); Solar. and Sala. Rowe (at 71)*

LORENZO

My lord Bassanio, since you have found Antonio
We two will leave you, but at dinner-time   70
I pray you have in mind where we must meet.

BASSANIO   I will not fail you.

GRATIANO

You look not well, Signior Antonio;
You have too much respect upon the world:
They lose it that do buy it with much care.   75
Believe me, you are marvellously changed.

ANTONIO

I hold the world but as the world, Gratiano,

---

69 LORENZO Rowe wrongly ascribes this speech to Salanio (see t.n.), who has left the stage at 68. Furness notes Capell's restoration of this SP after the erroneous '*Lord.*' of *F2 1* (Furness, 10). Mahood takes the argument further by suggesting that 69–112 may be 'an inserted portion of Shakespeare's manuscript' (Cam², 60 and 171); her case rests (1) upon what are perceived as awkwardness produced by repetition, and (2) upon the alleged significance of a white space between Salarino and Salanio's exit and Lorenzo's address to Bassanio (Cam², 171).

70 **We two** Pooler suggests that this is a hint to an unwitting Gratiano (Ard¹, 11), and Brown amplifies this to indicate Gratiano's tactlessness in remaining unaware that Bassanio wishes to be left alone with Antonio (Ard², 8).

74 **respect upon** regard, or care for. The Latin origin of 'respect' is *respicere*, to look back at (*OED*). Furness notes that in the use of *upon* there is an allusion to this literal meaning of *respect* (Furness, 10), although Gratiano may also be alluding to Antonio's excessive preoccupation with temporal and hence transient matters, whereas he

should be giving more attention to his own spiritual well-being; cf. the proverbial *respice finem* (Tilley, E25), and also *CE* 4.4.43–4: 'Mistress, *respice finem*, respect your end, or rather to prophesy like the parrot, beware the rope's end.'

75 **lose . . . care** Q's 'loose' is a variant spelling of *lose* (Furness, 10). The general sense of this line is that he who observes the vicissitudes of the world too closely will expend too much anxiety to enjoy its (transitory) pleasures. Here the observation is cast in a form that is appropriate to Antonio's mercantile concerns. Brown notes the echo of Matthew, 16.25–6 (Ard², 8), and the suggestion in 74 that Antonio's gaze upon the world may be wrongly directed is reinforced by the biblical allusion.

76 **changed** The implication is that Antonio's moods change with his fiscal fortunes, so that his 'character' is constructed out of these commercial and religious tensions.

77–8 a 16th-century commonplace (Dent, W882). See John Withals, *A Short Dictionary for Young Beginners* (1584), sig. I5ʳ, for a connection between the metaphor of the stage and that of

---

69 SP] *(Lor.); Sola. Rowe*   73 Antonio;] *Rowe; Anthonio Q*   75 lose] *(loose)*

A stage, where every man must play a part,
And mine a sad one.
GRATIANO   Let me play the fool.
With mirth and laughter let old wrinkles come,   80
And let my liver rather heat with wine
Than my heart cool with mortifying groans.

dealing, with its implied reference to financial transactions (*OED* 3): 'vita haec est fabula quedam / Scena autem mundus versatilis, / histrio & actor Quilibet est hominum. This life is a certaine enterlude or play, the world is a stage ful of change euery way, Euerye man is a player, and therein a dealer.' The fullest statement of the commonplace connection between world and stage is in *AYL* 2.7.139–66, although Antonio seems to indicate (despite Gratiano's comment at 75) that his role is fixed. Possibly this is yet another example of the inadequacy of Antonio's own self-knowledge (see 5–6).

79 **sad** serious or sorrowful (*OED a.* 5, 5f)
    fool literally the role of the fool; in the Italian *commedia dell'arte* Gratiano was the name traditionally given to the comic doctor (see List of Roles, 4n.).

80 Let the wrinkles associated with old age come through mirth and laughter (rather than through care and anxiety). Cf. Tilley, O86: 'An ounce of mirth is worth a pound of sorrow'; see also *Locrine* (1594), 4.1.102: 'One dramme of ioy, must haue a pound of care.' Pooler offers two further glosses on the line: (1) May wrinkles of old age come as an accompaniment of mirth and laughter; (2) May an excessive number of wrinkles (*old* used as an intensifier) accompany mirth and laughter (Ard[1], 12).

81 **liver . . . wine** The liver was generally thought to be the organ of the human body where the blood was made and was hence the seat of the passions. In his *Prelections* (1616) William Harvey

noted that the liver was where heat was generated, and where the soul resided: 'The soul is in the blood. Innate heat is the author of life and where it most abounds there it exists principally and primarily' (quoted in Keynes, 109). Gratiano prefers to aid his liver in generating heat by drinking; cf. *AC* 1.2.25: 'I had rather heat my liver with drinking.'

82 **heart cool** In Aristotelian physiology the heart was the internal organ that generated heat, which then passed to the liver. Gratiano's contrast opposes the activities of liver and heart, and connects them with the production of mirth and laughter His method is one of 'analogical resemblance' (Sawday, 243) whereby the state of the physical organs is assumed to correspond to psychological and emotional states as well as to situations in the world at large (and, in this case, on the stage). See also *MND* 3.2.97: 'With sighs of love, that costs the fresh blood dear.'
    mortifying groans indicative of the mortification of desire. Cf. *H5* 1.1.25–7: 'The breath no sooner left his father's body / But that his wildness mortified in him, / Seemed to die too.' The semantic field of 'groan' extends from allusion to the pain of childbirth, through to the 'expression of sexual ecstasy' (Gordon Williams, 146–7). Gratiano prefers that *old wrinkles come* (80) through merriment, rather than pain, but the gesture towards the pain of childbirth *and* to the *petit mort* of orgasm, hints tactlessly, if vaguely, at other possible reasons for Antonio's sadness.

78 man] one *Q2*   79 mine] mine's *Hanmer*

Why should a man whose blood is warm within
Sit like his grandsire cut in alabaster?
Sleep when he wakes? And creep into the jaundice   85
By being peevish? I tell thee what, Antonio –
I love thee, and 'tis my love that speaks –
There are a sort of men whose visages
Do cream and mantle like a standing pond,
And do a wilful stillness entertain   90
With purpose to be dressed in an opinion
Of wisdom, gravity, profound conceit,

84 remain motionless like his grandfather's effigy carved in white stone. Q's spelling 'Alablaster' is a common form in the 16th century. Brown notes that the earliest sitting effigy in England is dated 1605, before which figures stood, lay or kneeled, and that *Sit* should therefore be glossed as 'continue or remain in a certain state' (*OED* 7) (Ard², 9).

85 **wakes** should be awake
jaundice a disease caused by an obstruction of bile, and characterized by a yellowing of the skin. Pooler compares *TC* 1.3.2: 'What grief hath set these jaundies in your cheeks?' (Ard¹, 13). Gratiano completes the connection in 85 in his warning that physical symptoms of disease are directly linked to particular forms of behaviour, one of which is *being peevish* (86), i.e. behaving in a perverse manner.

88 **sort** kind or type
visages faces

89 **cream and mantle** turn to the consistency and colour of cream, i.e. turn pale and yellow; one of a number of images here of unwholesomeness. *OED* 2c glosses 'mantle' as 'the part of a liquid which gathers on the top like the cream on milk; a "head" of scum, froth etc.', and this extends the reference in 85 to jaundice.

standing stagnant

90 **a . . . entertain** maintain a studied calm. Malone glosses this as to maintain an 'obstinate silence' (Malone, 12).

91–2 with the intention of conveying the impression that they are wise, grave and profound. The accumulated subordinate clauses qualify each other, so that *visages* (88, faces) resemble *a standing pond* (89) whose *wilful* (i.e. deliberate) *stillness* (90) is designed to communicate their *wisdom, gravity* and a depth to which their outward appearance points (*profound conceit*, 92). The use of *dressed* (91) implies the conscious assumption of a role and recalls Antonio's earlier reference (78) to his playing a part.

92 **profound conceit** deep thought but implying (mis)understanding of oneself; cf. Proverbs, 18.11, 'The rich mans goods are his strong citie, and as an high wall in his owne conceit', and Proverbs, 26.12: 'If thou seest a man that is wise in his owne conceite: there is more hope in a foole then in him' (Geneva Bible (1562), 252 and 255). The biblical allusions sustain the motif of studied deception that is, in fact, self-deception (cf. Furness, 12), which the glossing of *conceit* neutrally as 'understanding' or 'intelligence' (Ard², 9) only partially captures.

84 alabaster] *(Alablaster)*   87 'tis] *(tis); it is F*   89 cream] dream *Q2*

As who should say, 'I am Sir Oracle,
And when I ope my lips, let no dog bark.'
O, my Antonio, I do know of these   95
That therefore only are reputed wise
For saying nothing; when, I am very sure,
If they should speak, would almost damn those ears
Which, hearing them, would call their brothers fools.
I'll tell thee more of this another time.   100
But fish not with this melancholy bait
For this fool gudgeon, this opinion.

93 **As . . . say** as if one might say
Sir Oracle a source of divine utterance. See also *OED* 3a, where the
Oracle is 'That part of the Jewish
temple where the divine presence was
manifested; the holy of holies; also, the
mercy-seat within it'. F emends to 'sir
an Oracle' which is metrically unsound
and strips the epithet of its semantic
(and possibly anti-Semitic) resonance.
94 **when . . . bark** when I speak not
even a dog should bark; proverbial
(Dent, D526). See R.W., *Three Ladies
of London* (1584), 'All the dogs in the
town shall not bark at your doings
I trow' (Dodsley, 6.336); Pooler also
notes Exodus, 11.7: 'But amongst all
the children of Israel, shall not a dogge
mooue his tongue, from a man unto a
beast: that ye may knowe how that the
Lord putteth a difference betweene
the Egyptians and Israel' (Ard[1], 14).
Gratiano's allusion mischievously
hints that Antonio's behaviour is
'Jewish' in its studied combination of
anxiety and seriousness.
96–7 **reputed . . . nothing** thought
to possess wisdom because they say
nothing. Cf. Proverbs, 17.28: 'Yea a
very foole when he holdeth his tongue,
is counted wise: and he that stoppeth
his lips, is esteemed prudent', which
is clearly the source of the proverbial

'Fools are wise as long as silent' (Dent,
F531).
97 **when** Rowe (sig. E4[r]) emended this to
'who' in order to provide a subject for
the conditional verb 'would damn' at
98. Brown argues (Ard[2], 10) that the
loose syntax is indicative of Gratiano's
garrulity, and Mahood (Cam[2], 62)
suggests that the lack of a subject
indicates 'rapid, colloquial speech'.
98 **damn** Theobald (sig. B3[v]) cites
Matthew, 5.22: 'And whosoeuer shall
say unto his brother, *Racha*, shall be
in danger of a counsell: but whosoeuer
shall say, Thou foole, shall be in danger
of hell fire.' There may also be a pun
here on 'dam' as a form of obstruction,
indicating (1) that the words of a fool
would render the hearers damned and
(2) that a fool's speech is such as to
cause an obstruction in the ears of his
hearers.
101 **fish . . . bait** do not use your melancholy as a bait (to attract the claim
that your silence is a mark of wisdom).
Furness thinks that *melancholy bait* is
a genitive of apposition, and that it
should be printed 'melancholy-bait'
to indicate 'this bait of melancholy';
he glosses the line: 'fish not with this
melancholy as a bait' (Furness, 14).
102 **fool gudgeon** a small freshwater
fish normally used for bait. But *OED*

93 Sir Oracle] *(sir Oracle), Pope;* sir an Oracle *F*   95 Antonio,] *Rowe; Anthonio Q*   these] those
Q2   97 when,] *Dyce;* when *Q;* who *Rowe*   98 damn] *(dam);* dant *Q3*   102 fool gudgeon] *(foole
gudgin);* fool's gudgeon *Pope*

Come, good Lorenzo. – Fare ye well awhile,
I'll end my exhortation after dinner.

LORENZO

Well, we will leave you, then, till dinner-time.   105
I must be one of these same dumb wise men,
For Gratiano never lets me speak.

GRATIANO

Well, keep me company but two years more
Thou shalt not know the sound of thine own tongue.

ANTONIO

Fare you well, I'll grow a talker for this gear.   110

GRATIANO

Thanks, i'faith, for silence is only commendable
In a neat's tongue dried and a maid not vendible.

Exeunt [Gratiano and Lorenzo].

2 and 2b note a figurative usage: 'one that will bite at any bait or swallow anything: a credulous gullible person.'

104 **exhortation after dinner** Gratiano will leave the formal address (in this instance associated with religious observance (*OED* 2)) until after dinner. Warburton suggests that this is a reference to the practice of puritan preachers 'who being generally very long and tedious, were often forced to put off that part of their sermon called the *exhortation* until after dinner' (Warburton, 101)

108 *****more** Rowe's reading. Q has 'moe', meaning 'more in number', whereas *more* here indicates size or quality.

110 **for** 'for the purpose of' (*OED* 8)
gear discourse, or talk, used in a deprecatory sense as stuff and nonsense (*OED* 11a). But see also *OED* 9†b: 'possessions in general, wealth, money'. Antonio will become a talker in order to forestall any accusation associated with his erstwhile silence. However, the latent meaning of *gear* suggests that Antonio will deal with

Gratiano's *sententiae* as though he were conducting a business transaction, and it is this mercantile gloss that Gratiano picks up at 112.

112 **neat's tongue dried** a culinary delicacy. Gratiano makes an unusual association between *silence* and the combination of a dried ox-tongue and an unsaleable (because unattractive) virgin. Brown cites Nathan Field's *A Woman is a Weathercock* (1612), 1.2.146, 'But did that little old dried neat's tongue, that eel-skin, get him?', and *WT* 1.2.123–7 to indicate a bawdy reference, since the dried neat's tongue was a colloquial phrase for a withered penis, and hence for impotence (see Gordon Williams, 309–10).

maid not vendible a spinster who is no longer able to attract attention on the marriage market. Cf. *AYL* 3.5.60: 'Sell when you can, you are not for all markets.' Gratiano's primary concern here is with marriage as a sexual transaction, but it also has economic implications and keeps firmly in view Antonio's profession as a merchant.

103 Fare ye well] *Q3;* faryewell *Q*   108 more] *Rowe;* moe *Q*   112 tongue] *Q2, F;* togue *Q*   SD] *Exeunt* Gra. *and* Loren. *Theobald*

ANTONIO   Is that anything now?

BASSIANO   Gratiano speaks an infinite deal of nothing, more than any man in all Venice. His reasons are as two   115
grains of wheat hid in two bushels of chaff: you shall seek all day ere you find them, and, when you have them, they are not worth the search.

ANTONIO

Well, tell me now, what lady is the same
To whom you swore a secret pilgrimage,   120
That you today promised to tell me of?

BASSANIO

'Tis not unknown to you, Antonio,
How much I have disabled mine estate
By something showing a more swelling port
Than my faint means would grant continuance.   125

113 * In what is a compressed syntax, but one that does not require repunctuation, Antonio registers here the contradictory meanings released by Gratiano's departure from the stage. At the same time he evinces a certain weariness in the face of the complications that Gratiano's exit produces, which Bassanio takes up in 114. The phrase *that anything* may refer both to what Gratiano has been saying and also deictically to his leaving the stage. (See LN.)

114 **speaks . . . nothing** talks an incalculable amount of nonsense

115 **reasons** remarks or observations

116 **shall** must; stronger than the modern 'shall'. Cf. *R3* 4.4.292: 'Men shall deal unadvisedly sometimes.'

119 **same** one

120 **secret pilgrimage** Mahood suggests that this is a vestige of the play's source, *Il Pecorone*, where Gianetto keeps his quest for the Lady of Belmont secret (Cam², 63). The object of Bassanio's amorous attention is also elevated to a quasi-religious status; cf. *RJ* 1.5.97–100 and *PP* sonnet 3.5–8:

'A Woman I forswore; but I will prove, / Thou being a goddess, I forswore not thee: / My vow was earthly, thou a heavenly love; / Thy grace being gain'd cures all disgrace in me.'

122–5 These lines constitute a statement of Bassanio's aristocratic condition, which is, effectively, one of bankruptcy brought about by his living beyond his means.

123 **disabled mine estate** consumed my wealth (and hence rendered myself incapable of proceeding in any enterprise)

124 **something showing** displaying to some extent. *Something* is sometimes used adverbially to mean 'somewhat'; see 129.

swelling port inflated style of living; 'port' = bearing (Onions)

125 **faint means** slender resource

grant continuance permit (this inflated style of living) to continue. Mahood argues that the difficulty with the whole of this speech by Bassanio arises from his embarrassment (Cam², 63).

113 Is . . . now?] *Rowe;* It is that . . . now. *Q*   115 as] *om. F*   121 of?] *F; of. Q*

Nor do I now make moan to be abridged
From such a noble rate, but my chief care
Is to come fairly off from the great debts
Wherein my time, something too prodigal,
Hath left me gaged. To you, Antonio,　　　　　　　130
I owe the most in money and in love,
And from your love I have a warranty
To unburden all my plots and purposes
How to get clear of all the debts I owe.

ANTONIO

I pray you, good Bassanio, let me know it,　　　　135
And if it stand, as you yourself still do,
Within the eye of honour, be assured
My purse, my person, my extremest means

126 **make moan** complain
　　abridged curtailed or debarred Cf.
　　OED 5: 'to curtail, to lessen, to dimin-
　　ish (rights, privileges, advantages, or
　　authority)'.
127 **noble rate** aristocratic standard of
　　living
　　chief care main concern
128 **come fairly off** favourably acquit
　　myself
129 **my time** the time I have spent. Dover
　　Wilson takes this to mean more generally
　　'the time of, life, youth' (Cam¹, 126).
130 **gaged** pledged (*OED* †1b), but also
　　with the implication of being entan-
　　gled (Onions). Merchant emphasizes
　　the legal implications of 'gage' as 'an
　　anticipation of the Bond' (Merchant,
　　167).
131 **money . . . love** the first of a number
　　of connections between *money* and *love*
　　established in the play
132 **warranty** permission or authoriza-
　　tion (*OED sb*¹ 3c)
133 **unburden** disclose or reveal (as a
　　consequence of friendship)
　　plots and purposes schemes and
　　intentions

135 **it** may refer directly to Bassanio's
　　plots and purposes at 133, as in *TGV*
　　4.3.3–4. But also it may be an indefi-
　　nite object of the transitive verb 'to
　　know' (*OED* 9).
136 **it** refers generally to Bassanio's con-
　　dition (*OED* 3d)
　　still without change, interruption or
　　cessation, and hence constantly or con-
　　tinually (*OED adv.* 3). Cf. *TGV* 2.1.12:
　　'Well, you'll still be too forward.'
137 **eye of honour** visual field of
　　honour. Pooler cites Hooker's *Laws
　　of Ecclesiastical Polity* (1597), 5.9.2:
　　'General rules are no other in the eye
　　of understanding than cloudy mists
　　cast before the eye of common sense'
　　(Ard¹, 17).
138 **purse . . . person** The pun on *purse*
　　and *person* initiates a complex range
　　of fiscal and sexual associations con-
　　nected with the figure of Antonio;
　　purse means primarily a receptacle for
　　carrying money (*OED* 1), but there
　　is also a direct association between
　　purse and identity: one's *purse* and
　　oneself (*person*) (*OED* 2†b). However,
　　purse also means 'scrotum' (*OED* 8b);

133 unburden] *(unburthen)*

Lie all unlocked to your occasions.

BASSANIO

In my schooldays, when I had lost one shaft,   140
I shot his fellow of the selfsame flight
The selfsame way, with more advised watch
To find the other forth, and by adventuring both
I oft found both. I urge this childhood proof
Because what follows is pure innocence.   145

see Girolamo Ruscelli, *Alexis's Secrets*, trans. R. Ambrose (1569), 4.1.29: 'To remedie the itch of the purse of the testicles.' This implied reference to breeding is taken up later in the play (p. 56), but it also suggests a connection between fiscal and sexual commitment that is there from the outset but is never specified. On the more general issue of punning in the play, see Shell, 48.

139 **unlocked . . . occasions** available for all your needs. Pooler notes that *occasions* is a quadrisyllable (Ard[1], 18). The sexual ambiguity released by the pun on *purse* and *person* in 138 is extended in this line; Antonio will make *himself* available to Bassanio, although he defines himself metonymically in terms of his capacity to provide money. This also anticipates the ambiguity of the later 'casket scenes' (2.1, 2.7, 2.9 and 3.2) where the act of unlocking determines the future of the participants in a sexual *and* financial game. From the outset the critical connection between financial investment and 'breeding' (i.e. the increase of one's assets) is suggested.

140–4 **In . . . both** proverbial: 'Shoot one arrow after another' (Dent, A325)

140 **shaft** arrow

141 **selfsame flight** of equal trajectory and velocity

142 **advised** advisèd; well-considered, deliberate, judicious

143 **forth** out (*OED* †8). Cf. *3H6* 2.1.12: 'And watched him how he singled Clifford forth.'
adventuring risking. A number of editors follow Pope in emending this line by altering 'adventuring' to 'ventring' in an attempt to preserve the metre. Capell proposes 'advent'ring', which is clumsy. Brown suggests that the metrical irregularity indicates Bassanio's embarrassment at his request for money (Ard[2], 13), while Mahood suggests that the metrical irregularity may be a sign of foul papers (Cam[2], 64 and 171).

144 **urge . . . proof** put forward strongly an argument proved during childhood (*OED* 1: childhood); but also 'put forward a childish argument' (*OED* †3: childhood)

145 **pure innocence** Bassanio wishes here to emphasize the openness of his request to Antonio and he urges the innocence of childhood to support his case. But by regressing into childhood Bassanio implies another kind of relationship with Antonio: that of a prodigal (and possibly immature) son asking his father to supply his needs, a closer parallel to *Pecorone*. The connection with the biblical figure of the prodigal son (Luke, 15.11–13) is indicated at 129. Brown suggests two alternative glosses: (1) 'freedom from moral fault or cunning' and (2) 'childlike friendship and affection' (Ard[2], 13).

140 schooldays] *(schoole dayes)* 141, 142 selfsame] *(self same)*, *F* 143 forth, and by] foorth *Q2;* forth; and by *Rowe;* forth; by *Pope* adventuring] aduentring *Q2;* ventring *Pope;* advent'ring *Capell;* venturing *Dyce*

I owe you much, and like a wilful youth
That which I owe is lost; but if you please
To shoot another arrow that self way
Which you did shoot the first, I do not doubt,
As I will watch the aim, or to find both,   150
Or bring your latter hazard back again
And thankfully rest debtor for the first.

ANTONIO
You know me well, and herein spend but time
To wind about my love with circumstance,
And out of doubt you do me now more wrong   155
In making question of my uttermost
Than if you had made waste of all I have.
Then do but say to me what I should do
That in your knowledge may by me be done,

---

146 **wilful youth** obstinate or self-willed (*OED* 1) young man. In confessing to his own youthful prodigality Bassanio is attempting to excuse himself from a general claim that aristocrats are wasteful.

148 **self** same (*OED* B†1)

150 **watch the aim** Literally, Bassanio is proposing to observe Antonio aiming his metaphorical arrow (his investment); but see *OED* 6 for the sense of *watch* as something more than simple observance. Bassanio will not only observe the trajectory of Antonio's investment, but he will also do all he can to oversee the venture and hence help to secure its success.

150–1 **or . . . Or** either . . . or (Abbott, 136)

150 **find both** discover where both have gone

151 **latter hazard** second investment. Bassanio is already in debt to Antonio, having lost the first investment, as indicated at 147. A *hazard* is literally a stake in a game of chance (*OED* 1

and 1b), and emphasizes the precariousness of the business ventures in which a merchant such as Antonio is involved; *hazard* is 'a key word in the play, linking the choice of caskets with Antonio's risks' (Cam², 64).

152 **rest debtor** remain indebted (for the earlier investment)

153 **herein . . . time** in this matter spend only time, with the implication that Bassanio is expending time needlessly

154 **wind about** entwine (in the sense of 'twist about') (*OED* 7c)
   circumstance adjuncts of a fact (Onions) which limit action one way or another; also, more generally, prevarication or circumlocution (Bevington, 184). Antonio is accusing Bassanio of diffidence in making a request for further assistance, and risking insult by casting doubt upon the unconditional nature of Antonio's love for him.

156 **making . . . uttermost** casting doubt on the extent of my commitment to helping you

157 **made waste** squandered

And I am pressed unto it: therefore speak. 160

BASSANIO

In Belmont is a lady richly left,
And she is fair and, fairer than that word,
Of wondrous virtues. Sometimes from her eyes
I did receive fair speechless messages.
Her name is Portia, nothing undervalued 165
To Cato's daughter, Brutus' Portia.
Nor is the wide world ignorant of her worth,
For the four winds blow in from every coast
Renowned suitors, and her sunny locks
Hang on her temples like a golden fleece, 170

160 *pressed** The modernized spelling disguises the ambiguity. Pooler concludes that *pressed* is adverbial and has its root in the Old French *prest* (modern *prêt*) meaning 'ready', and for this reason retains the Q spelling 'prest' (Ard[1], 19). However, *OED v.*[1] *obs.* 2 glosses the verb *prest*: 'to advance (money) on account of work to be done or service to be rendered or not yet completed'. It may well be that Q's 'prest' combined with 'unto' indicates that this is a verb (Oxf[2], 111) that preserves the obsolete meanings, but also points forward to a more modern meaning, 'compelled' (*OED* †5). Antonio, therefore, says that he is compelled, and is prepared to lend his friend money once he knows what Bassanio expects of him. Furness cites *Per* 4 Prologue, 44–5: 'The pregnant instrument of wrath / Prest for this blow' (Furness, 19).

161 **richly left** who has inherited a fortune

162 **fairer . . . word** more than the word *fair* suggests. Bassanio is making a comparison based on the inadequacy of the adverb *fair* to describe Portia's *wondrous virtues* (163). Thus Portia's beauty is both outward *and* inward, and counters the proverbial 'Fair with-

out, false (foul) within' (Dent, F29).

163 **Sometimes** formerly (Onions). Bassanio may be referring here to a specific occasion in the past, or he may be suggesting that there was more than one, i.e. 'from time to time' (Onions). But see also *R2* 1.2.54–5: 'Farewell, old Gaunt; thy sometimes brother's wife.'

165 **nothing undervalued** of no less value than. See also 2.7.53.

166 **Cato's . . . Portia** the daughter of Marcus Porcius Cato, a noted opponent of the emperor Julius Caesar. See List of Roles, 10n. Merchant argues that there may be 'a light pun on "portion", with its implication of "inheritance" or "dowry"' (Merchant, 167–8).

169 **Renowned** renownèd

170 **golden fleece** the prize which Jason, the hero of Greek mythology and leader of the Argonauts, set out to obtain (*OCD*, 466–7). Portia's hair is likened to the *golden fleece* because she is the possessor of a rich inheritance, but the idea of the *golden fleece* has a wider commercial resonance. See also Marlowe, *Dr Faustus* (1604), 1.1.129–31: 'From Venice shall they drag huge argosies, / And from America the golden fleece / That early stuffs old

160 pressed] *Oxf*; prest *Q*   163 virtues.] *(vertues,)*   Sometimes] *(sometimes);* Sometime *Theobald*

Which makes her seat of Belmont Colchis' strand,
And many Jasons come in quest of her.
O my Antonio, had I but the means
To hold a rival place with one of them,
I have a mind presages me such thrift   175
That I should questionless be fortunate.

ANTONIO

Thou knowst that all my fortunes are at sea;
Neither have I money, nor commodity
To raise a present sum; therefore go forth:
Try what my credit can in Venice do,   180

Philip's treasury', where such fiscal enterprise is given a demonic gloss provided Faustus is prepared to be 'resolute' (1.1.132).

171 *Colchis' strand the shores of ancient Colchis on the eastern shores of the Black Sea, the home of Medea, and reputedly the location of the golden fleece, the object of Jason's quest. Q's 'Cholchos' may possibly be a Shakespearean spelling, but it distinguishes the name from its negative 'natural' associations as seen in Florio's gloss on 'Colchicòne: *a venemous hearbe*' (Florio, 108).

172 quest The image of 'the quest' serves to align Bassanio's project with an archetypal heroic action. Jason's original quest, however, was the result of a deception perpetrated upon him by Pelias, the ruler of Iolcus, who had usurped the throne of his father Aeson, and who wished to prevent Jason from claiming his inheritance by sending him in search of the golden fleece. There is a faint suggestion that Bassanio's heavily rhetorical account of Portia is the result of a self-deception of which he is unaware; his interest in Portia coincides with an aristocratic interest in acquiring her material wealth, and so she exists

as a financial 'interest': wealth gained through investment.

175 presages me [that] gives me an intuition of (*OED* 1 and 3)
thrift gain or advantage, in both a material and a non-material sense. Brown proposes two glosses, (1) material profit and (2) success or good fortune.

176 questionless without question. Bassanio knows that he is one of many suitors, and his intuition of good fortune may be a rhetorical ploy designed to persuade Antonio of the merit of his scheme.
fortunate literally, the recipient of future good (cf. *OED* 1), but also suggesting an improvement in material circumstances as a result of marriage (cf. *OED* 6); another example of the way in which material and non-material meanings jostle with each other throughout the play. Antonio picks up these meanings again in his use of the word *fortunes* at 177.

178 commodity wares or merchandise that might be exchanged for money. Cf. *TS* 2.1.322. Brown conjectures that 'opportunity' might also be meant here (Ard[2], 14).

179 present sum ready cash
180 Try prove (Onions)

171 Colchis'] *Riv; Cholchos Q; Colchos Theobald* strand] *Johnson;* strond *Q* 172 come] comes *Q2* 178 Neither] Nor *Pope* 179 forth:] *Folg;* forth *Q;* forth, *Q2;* forth; *Rowe*

That shall be racked even to the uttermost
To furnish thee to Belmont to fair Portia.
Go presently enquire, and so will I,
Where money is, and I no question make   184
To have it of my trust, or for my sake.   *Exeunt.*

[1.2]   *Enter* PORTIA *with her waiting-woman* NERISSA.

PORTIA   By my troth, Nerissa, my little body is aweary of
this great world.

181   **racked** stretched (as on the rack). Cf.
      LLL 5.2.811: 'You must be purged to
      your sins are rack'd.'
183   **presently** immediately
185   **of my trust** on the grounds of my
      being creditworthy (*OED* 4) and, con-
      sequently, to be entrusted as a guarantor
      with its use by someone whom I choose
      to nominate
      or ... sake or to secure it for my own
      use
1.2   Johnson is the first to locate the scene
      in '*A Room in Portia's House at Belmont*',
      specified further and embellished in
      Cam[1] as '*The hall of Portia's house*'.
      The action moves between Venice and
      Belmont throughout. In all but the
      final Belmont scene (5.1), which is set
      'outside', the action takes place 'inside'
      Portia's house.
0.1   Rowe here adds a description of the
      caskets (see t.n.) and he infers from
      Nerissa's 'these three chests of gold, sil-
      ver and lead' at 28–9 that they are visible
      onstage from the beginning, a conven-
      tion that prevailed up to Johnson. From
      Capell onwards, most editors and pro-
      ductions depart from Rowe. However,
      Dover Wilson stipulates their location:
      'at the back a gallery and beneath it the
      entrance to an alcove concealed by a
      curtain' (Cam[1], 9) and Miller's National
      Theatre production (1970) had the three
      caskets on a desk, referred to by Nerissa;
      in Nunn's production (1999) they were

absent until 2.7. Nerissa's 'these three
chests' may be deictic, although many
modern productions do not concur.
waiting-woman a female servant or
personal attendant (*OED*), possibly a
confidante. There is no textual evidence
to indicate kinship (as suggested in
Cam[2], 65–6), and Nerissa's social status
is closer to that of Emilia in *Oth* 4.3.7
who is described in F by Othello as an
'attendant', and who herself addresses
Desdemona on numerous occasions as
'madam'.
NERISSA See List of Roles, 11n.
Merchant emphasizes the contrast
between the swarthiness of complexion implied in Nerissa's name, and
the 'fairness' of Portia's complexion
(Merchant, 168).
1   **By my troth** literally, by my truth/
      faith/honesty; a mild oath or asservera-
      tion (*OED* 1b)
1–2   **little ... world** a familiar Elizabethan
      antithesis between the comparative
      insignificance of the human microcosm
      and the vastness of the physical uni-
      verse (Cam[2], 65). Furness conjectures
      that Portia's weariness may indicate
      'unconsciously, perhaps, the languor of
      hope deferred' in its anticipation of the
      'Venetian' to whom Nerissa refers later
      in the scene at 108 (Furness, 21). Portia's
      state of mind echoes that of Antonio,
      though her reasons are more in evidence.
1   **aweary** a verbal echo of Antonio's

1.2] *Rowe (*SCENE II.*)*   0.1] *Three caskets are set out, one of Gold, another of Silver and another of
Lead. Enter* Portia *and* Nerissa. *Rowe*

NERISSA   You would be, sweet madam, if your miseries
were in the same abundance as your good fortunes are;
and yet, for aught I see, they are as sick that surfeit   5
with too much as they that starve with nothing. It
is no mean happiness, therefore, to be seated in the
mean; superfluity comes sooner by white hairs, but
competency lives longer.

PORTIA   Good sentences, and well pronounced.   10

initial declaration of world-weariness at
1.1.2

3   **You** Throughout this scene Nerissa
addresses Portia as 'you', whereas Portia
addresses her as 'thou' ('thee'). The
differential use of 'the personal pronoun
maintain(s) difference of rank', despite
the use of prose indicating intimacy
(Kermode, 75); but see also Blake (55–7)
for information concerning the instability throughout Shakespeare's texts of
the marked and unmarked (formal and
intimate) uses of the second person
singular and plural pronoun.

5–6   **sick . . . nothing** possibly proverbial.
Cf. Tilley, S1011, 'Every SURFEIT
foreuns a fast', who cites *1H4* 3.2.71–2:
'They surfeited with honey, and began
/ To loathe the taste of sweetness.'
Nerissa insists that Portia's *good fortunes*
far outweigh her *miseries*, but that excess
of either produces sickness; cf. *TN*
1.1.2–3: 'Give me excess of it, that,
surfeiting, / The appetite may sicken,
and so die.' See also Dent, H560 ('Too
much HONEY cloys the stomach').

7–8   **mean . . . mean** small . . . middle
(Onions). F emends *mean* in 7 to
'smal', thereby losing the pun on
mean as 'undignified' (Clarendon, 85).
Cf. Proverbs, 30.8, 'giue me neither
pouertie nor riches, onely graunt me
a necessarie liuing' (Ard[1], 21), but see
also Dent, V80, 'VIRTUE is found
in the middle (mean)'; and Aristotle's
'Table of Virtues and Vices', where
liberality (*eleutheriotês*) is positioned

between prodigality (*asôtia*) at the level
of excess, and illiberality (*aneleutheria*)
at the level of deficiency (Aristotle,
Ethics, 104).
   seated situated. Cf. *Luc* 1144: 'Some
dark deep desert seated from the way'.

8   **superfluity** any action characterized
by excess or extravagance, 'immoderate
indulgence or expenditure' (*OED* †4
obs.)
   comes . . . hairs acquires the signs of
ageing sooner than it should; cf. Pooler,
who cites *The Cold Year* (1614), sig. A3ᵛ:
'Oh Sir! riots, riots, surfeits overnight
and early potting it next morning stick
white hairs upon young men's chins,
when sparing diet holds colour' (Ard[1],
21).

9   **competency** dexterity in managing to
maintain a balanced position between
two extremes; cf. *OED* 3 and †4: 'a
sufficiency, without superfluity, of the
means of life; a competent estate or
income'.

10   **sentences** from the Latin *sententia* (pl.
sententiae) meaning a maxim or an opinion (*OED* †1 and 2), but see also *OED*
3b, which explores the legal resonances
of the word. Nerissa counsels living
within the mean, but Portia understands
this as a punishment (*sentence*) imposed
upon her.
   pronounced articulated, but also in
the sense of declaring an opinion or
judgement. This is one of many occasions in Shakespearean texts when one
interlocutor's comments are, in part,

4 abundance] *(*aboundance*)*   7 mean] smal *F*   happiness, therefore,] *Dyce;* happines therefore *Q*
8 mean;] *F4;* meane, *Q*

NERISSA They would be better if well followed.

PORTIA If to do were as easy as to know what were good to
do, chapels had been churches, and poor men's cottages
princes' palaces. It is a good divine that follows his
own instructions: I can easier teach twenty what were   15
good to be done than to be one of the twenty to follow
mine own teaching. The brain may devise laws for the
blood, but a hot temper leaps o'er a cold decree; such
a hare is madness the youth, to skip o'er the meshes of

directed to the performance of another. Brown cites *LLL* 1.1.302, and notes that this is the beginning of a series of legal terms and phrases that Portia goes on to use in 17ff. (Ard[2], 15).

12–15 **If . . . instructions** Pooler suggests that this anticipates Ophelia's strictures against 'Some ungracious pastors' in *Ham* 1.3.47–51 (Ard[1], 22). Mahood argues that Portia here is trying out 'some "sentences" of her own' (Cam[2], 66), although the conditional *If* makes it very clear that Portia would have difficulty in living up to them herself.

13 **chapels** places of worship subordinate to and dependent upon the church of the parish (*OED* 3), sometimes located within larger ecclesiastical buildings (OED 2b)
had been conditional: 'would have been'; cf. *TGV* 4.1.34–5: 'My youthful travel therein made me happy, / Or else I often had been miserable.'

16 **than to be** F's omission of the conjunction 'to' was thought by Brown to correct a compositorial error in Q (Ard[2], 15). The repetition of the infinitive *to be* is clumsy, but not ungrammatical.

17–18 **brain . . . blood** The brain was thought to be the seat of reason. Cf. Burton, 1.153: 'the brain . . . is the most noble organ under heaven, the dwelling-house and seat of the soul,

the habitation of wisdom, memory, judgment, reason, and in which man is most like unto God.' (See LN.)

18 **hot blood** was thought to be a 'hot' humour, and overheating could lead to anger, and thence to madness, apparently a characteristic of women (Burton, 1.269).
temper 'the due or proportionate mixture or combination of qualities; the condition or state resulting from such combination' (*OED* I †1), but *temper* can also mean 'inclination' (*OED* 10).
cold decree Portia associates the absence of 'heat' with old age, and with prescriptive restraint. This train of thought is developed in 19–20, where *madness* is associated with youth, and the constraints of law ('meshes of good counsel') constitute a necessary net designed by those who are older and wiser, but less nimble ('good counsel the cripple'), to entrammel those who are youthful, inexperienced and, by implication, lacking the wisdom of age.

19–20 **hare . . . cripple** The allusion may be proverbial, deriving from the *madness* of the March hare (see Dent, H148). Portia's identification with the hare is appropriate, since it was popularly believed to be 'a melancholy meat' (Dent, H151), here emblematic of her 'weariness'.

16 than to] *(then to); than* F   18 decree;] *F4; decree,* Q

good counsel the cripple. But this reasoning is not in　20
the fashion to choose me a husband. O me, the word
'choose'! I may neither choose who I would, nor refuse
who I dislike, so is the will of a living daughter curbed
by the will of a dead father. Is it not hard, Nerissa, that
I cannot choose one, nor refuse none?　　　25
NERISSA Your father was ever virtuous, and holy men
at their death have good inspirations. Therefore the
lottery that he hath devised in these three chests of

20 **reasoning** discourse (as opposed to
the more modern 'ratiocination');
cf. *OED* †3: 'a statement, narrative,
or speech; a saying, observation, or
remark; an account or explanation *of*,
or answer *to* something'. F's emendation to 'reason' leads Furness to offer
the more modern gloss (Furness, 23).
Brown (Ard², 16) suggests that behind
Portia's 'sentences' lie a series of proverbial utterances concerned with the
opposition between youth and age (see
Dent, P537a and Y43).
20–1 **not . . . fashion** not of any use. See
OED 8, where 'fashion' is defined as
'a prevailing custom, a current usage',
and also *MA* 1.1.93–4: 'The fashion
of the world is to avoid cost, and you
encounter it.'
22–3 **who . . . who** whom . . . whom
(see also 25). In each case the relative
pronoun is the object of the verb; this
variation between 'who' and 'whom',
where both forms are acceptable
(Abbott, 274) continues to be used in
modern informal conversation.
23–4 **will . . . will** Portia quibbles on
the two meanings of *will* here: (1)
wilfulness (associated with her own
explicitly articulated desire for a lover
of her choosing), and (2) the 'will' or
last testament of her dead father which
restricts choice by imposing its own
authority upon desire.
26 **virtuous** good or efficacious, but also

with a suggestion of manly potency or
strength (*OED* 5). See also: 'Vertueso:
vertueus, honest, full of vertue'
(Florio, 596). In her attempt to justify
parental and, by implication, godlike
control, Nerissa inadvertently exposes
the mechanics of its operation.
27 **death . . . inspirations** proverbial
(Tilley, M514), but also cf. *R2* 2.1.5–6:
'they say the tongues of dying men /
Inforce attention like deep harmony.'
inspirations The *OED* 3a gloss on
'inspiration' makes clear that the
human mind has a capacity to receive
immediate divine influence. In the Old
Testament Book of Job, God furnishes
the human mind with understanding:
'Euery man no doubt hath a mind, but
it is the inspiration of the almightie
that giueth understanding' (Job, 33.8).
Nerissa hints that the law of Portia's
father has a divine origin, but she
also alludes to the Job-like suffering
imposed (by a harsh providence) upon
the fathers of female children.
28 **lottery** a game involving the distribution
of prizes by chance. Nerissa implies that
the game of chance involves the location
of a prize that is in one of *these three
chests* in the same way that 'meaning'
may be located in language. Merchant
perceives a pun on 'lottery'/'allottery',
where the latter term is glossed as 'portion' or 'share' (*OED obs.*) from the
French *allotier* (Merchant, 169).

20 reasoning] reason *F*　21 the fashion] fashion *F*　O me] *(ô mee)*　22–3 who . . . who] whom . . .
whom *F* 24 Is it] it is *F*　28 lottery] *(lotterie)* *F;* lottrie *Q*

gold, silver and lead, whereof who chooses his meaning
chooses you, will no doubt never be chosen by any   30
rightly but one who you shall rightly love. But what
warmth is there in your affection towards any of these
princely suitors that are already come?

PORTIA I pray thee over-name them and, as thou namest
them, I will describe them, and according to my   35
description level at my affection.

NERISSA First there is the Neapolitan prince.

PORTIA Ay, that's a colt indeed, for he doth nothing but
talk of his horse, and he makes it a great appropriation
to his own good parts that he can shoe him himself. I   40
am much afeard my lady his mother played false with
a smith.

NERISSA Then is there the County Palatine.

---

31 **rightly ... rightly** correctly ... properly (*OED* 1 and 2, but also cf. *R2*
2.2.18: 'Like perspectives, which, rightly
gaz'd upon'). Nerissa's elliptical statement attempts to align the correctness of
Portia's father's provision for his daughter's future with the injunction that she
will only love someone who chooses correctly. The meaning of *rightly* embraces
moral and emotional propriety (*OED* 1)
and emphasizes the limits placed upon
Portia's own freedom to choose.

32 **affection** feeling, fondness for, or
emotional attachment (to)

34 **over-name** to name over in succes-
sion (*OED*). Cf. *TGV* 1.2.7ff., which
provides a model in which the maid
(Lucetta) enumerates three of her mistress's (Julia's) suitors.

36 **level at** take aim at, or guess (*OED* †9a).
Mahood suggests that the phrase may
mean 'aim truly' (cf. *OED* †9b), indicat-
ing that Nerissa is being asked to infer
Portia's affections from her descriptions
(Cam², 67).

37 **Neapolitan prince** the prince from
Naples in Italy. Furness (25) notes
that during Shakespeare's time the
Neapolitans were noted for their horse-
manship.

38 **colt** a young horse (*OED sb.* 1), but also
someone who is young and inexperi-
enced (*OED fig.* 2). The pun reinforces
the prince's preoccupation with horses.

39 **great appropriation** special attribution or addition (*OED* †4)

40 **good parts** accomplishments

41–2 **afeard ... smith** Portia scandalously suggests here that the Neapolitan
prince's mother may have committed
adultery (*played false*) with a blacksmith
whose own preoccupation with horses
has been transmitted from father to
son. The motif of 'horses' extends to
Morocco (see pp. 85, 164), and later
to *Oth.*

43 **County Palatine** someone who has the
status of a count and who possesses regal
privileges that elsewhere belong only to
the sovereign (*OED* 2 and 2b). (See LN.)

---

30 will no doubt] no doubt you wil *Q2*   31 who] whom *Pope*   you] *om. Q2*   love. But] *Rowe;* loue:
But *Q;* loue: but *F*   34 pray thee] prethee *Q2*   41 afeard] afraid *F*   43 Then] *Q2;* Than *Q1, F*   is
there] there is *Q2;* is there *F*   Palatine] *Q2;* Palentine *Q1, F*

PORTIA He doth nothing but frown, as who should say,
'An you will not have me, choose.' He hears merry   45
tales and smiles not; I fear he will prove the weeping
philosopher when he grows old, being so full of
unmannerly sadness in his youth. I had rather be
married to a death's head with a bone in his mouth than
to either of these. God defend me from these two.   50
NERISSA How say you by the French lord, Monsieur Le
Bon?

44 **as . . . say** as if to say
45 **An . . . choose** an imaginary utterance
imputed mockingly to the frowning
count that makes him doubly unac-
ceptable: he stands accused of mis-
understanding both the test itself *and*
the consequences if he should fail. An
alternative, though not entirely satisfactory, gloss might simply be: 'If you
will not have me then you may choose
[someone else].' Ard² (17) glosses this
difficult conditional clause: 'have it
your own way, do as you please'.
*An the conditional 'if' in modern
English. Q prints an ampersand and F
emends to 'And', which some modern
editors have followed. In Q this is a
long line and the ampersand may have
been chosen by the compositor in
preference to 'An'.
46–7 **weeping philosopher** Heraclitus
of Ephesus, whose work flourished
around 500 BC. He was the first Greek
philosopher 'to explore the nature
of knowledge and the soul' (*OCD*,
415), but later acquired a reputation
in Rome based partly on a misinter-
pretation of his observation that the
flux of nature resembled the flow
of water, and was referred to as the
'weeping philosopher'. Brown cites
Batman upon Bartholome (1582), para.
3ᵛ: 'a Philosopher which alwayes wept
when he behelde the People, considering how busie they wer to gather

treasure, and how negligent in the
well bringing vppe of their children:
his workes, of purpose, were obscure'
(Ard², 17).
48 **unmannerly** impolite or rude
(*OED a.* 1), but also a possible pun
on 'unmanly' as 'dishonourable or
degrading to a man' (*OED a.* 1, 2:
'unmanly')
   sadness seriousness or gravity of
demeanour (*OED* †1, 2)
49 **death's head** the death's head or
memento mori, usually in the form
of a ring containing a depiction of
the human skull as a reminder of
death. Brown associates the image
of the skull with a bone in its mouth
with proverbial wisdom, and cites
Tilley, B517: 'he has a BONE in
his mouth', which would prevent the
act of speech (Ard², 17). Cf. *1H4*
3.3.29–30, 'I make as good use of it as
many a man doth of a death's-head, or
a *memento mori*', and in *Ham* 5.1.74ff.
51 **by** concerning; an obsolete use of the
preposition (*OED* 26 †c) as in *MA*
5.1.296–7: 'But always hath been just
and virtuous / In anything that I do
know by her.'
51–2 ***Monsieur Le Bon** a characteristic French name that has potentially sexual resonances elsewhere
in Shakespeare's plays. Q's spelling
'Boune' suggests a pun on 'bone',
explored in *LLL* 5.1.26–7, where the

44 frown, as] *Rowe;* frowne (as *Q*   45 An] *Capell;* & *Q;* If *Q2;* And *F*   choose.'] *Cam²;* choose, *Q;*
choose; *Q2;* choose: *F;* choose!' *Cam¹*   48 youth.] *Rowe;* youth.) *Q*   rather] rather to *F*   51–2 Le Bon]
Steevens; Le Boune *Q*

PORTIA God made him, and therefore let him pass for a
    man. In truth, I know it is a sin to be a mocker, but he!
    – why, he hath a horse better than the Neapolitan's, a   55
    better bad habit of frowning than the Count Palatine.
    He is every man in no man: if a throstle sing, he
    falls straight a-capering. He will fence with his own
    shadow. If I should marry him, I should marry twenty
    husbands. If he would despise me I would forgive him,   60
    for if he love me to madness I shall never requite him.

two words are clearly homophones;
see also *TC* 2.3.17–18 and Thersites'
reference to the 'Neapolitan bone-
ache', a euphemism for venereal disease. There is clearly a hint
of lewdness in the movement from
the Neapolitan prince, through the
County Palatine (both of whom
are associated in 49 with 'a death's
head with a bone in his mouth'),
to Monsieur Le Bon. France was
popularly associated with venereal
disease (see *H5* 5.1.82–3: 'Nell is dead
i'th' spittal / Of malady of France'),
and the association of *Bon* with *bone*
hints that, in addition to their other
deficiencies, each of these suitors is
both capable of sexual perversion
and a carrier of a disease that is the
consequence of sexual promiscuity.

57 **every . . . man** an imitator of other
men but has no qualities that are his
own
*throstle thrush. *OED* 1 identifies
'thrushel' as a south-western dialect
form; but the word 'thristill' appears
in 1375, and 'thrustylle', 'thrusshill'
or 'thrustyll' in 1440. Q's 'Trassell'
may be a variant of these Middle
English alternatives, but Brown
notes that 'Thrassel' is not recorded
in the *OED* before 1661; he suggests
that the Q spelling may be the result
of a compositorial misreading of 'o'
as 'a', which occurs elsewhere in the
text, at 1.3.18, 'Ryalta' for *Rialto*,

and 2.2.92, 'lost' for *last* (Ard², 18).
It is conceivable that Portia uses a
possible dialect form 'Trassell' as
a means of mocking Monsieur Le
Bon. That Shakespeare was familiar
with the word *throstle* is evident from
MND 3.1.122, 'The throstle with his
note so true', hence the likelihood
that the choice of an unfamiliar or
dialect word in this context would
have been deliberate.

58 ***a-capering** dancing in a frolicsome
way (*OED sb.²* b). But see also Florio
for the Italian derivation: 'capriolāre,
to caper', from 'capriōla, . . . a Sault
or Goates leape that cunning riders
teach their horses' (Florio, 83).

59 **should . . . should** By indicating the
multiple identity of Monsieur Le Bon,
Portia is expressing a hypothetical
condition that would normally be
represented in modern English by
the form 'should . . . would' (Quirk,
748). Brown thinks, in accordance
with Abbott, 322, that the second
should may be compulsive (Ard², 18)
in its denoting of contingent futurity.

61 **for if** for even if
shall F reads 'should', which Furness
(27) prefers to Q on the grounds
that Portia is humorously speculating
upon her inability to reciprocate the
love of twenty husbands.
requite repay, and hence reciprocate,
rather than Pooler's 'reward' (Ard¹,
26)

54–5 he! –] *Rowe;* he, *Q*   57 throstle] *Pope;* Trassell *Q*   58 a-capering] *Q3;* a capring *Q1, F*   61 shall]
should *F*

NERISSA What say you then to Falconbridge, the young
  baron of England?
PORTIA You know I say nothing to him, for he understands
  not me, nor I him. He hath neither Latin, French nor   65
  Italian, and you will come into the court and swear that
  I have a poor pennyworth in the English. He is a proper
  man's picture, but, alas, who can converse with a dumb-
  show? How oddly he is suited! I think he bought his
  doublet in Italy, his round hose in France, his bonnet in   70

62 **Falconbridge** Characters bearing this
name appear, or are referred to, in
five other plays of Shakespeare: *KJ*,
LLL, 1H6, 3H6 and *H5*. Honigmann
suggests that the later reference in *MV*
to 'Fauconbridge, the young Barron
of England' (Q), who is 'a "proper"
man but unlanguaged', is reminiscent
of the figure of the Bastard in the
earlier play (*King John*, xxiii–xxiv).
Also, the character 'Fauconbridge',
present in Q1 *2H4* but excised from F,
was a member of the Northumberland
circle; Honigmann suggests a connection in the early 1590s between
Shakespeare and the eminent Belasyse
family in Yorkshire who revived the
title of Earl Fauconberg in the early
17th century (*King John*, xxiv).
66 **come . . . swear** Brown cites Clarendon's gloss, 'bear me witness'
(Ard², 18), and, although this may be
a catchphrase (Cam², 68), the casual
reference to the judicial court points
forward to Portia's later appearance at
the court in Venice.
67 **poor pennyworth** small amount
(*OED* 1c). Pooler notes that the phrase
is often used 'of a bad bargain', and
cites Thomas Lodge's *Alarum against
Usurers* (1584): 'the youth hath a good
peniworth if in readie money he receive
twentie pound' (Ard¹, 26). Brown
detects a double meaning here that
incorporates the notions of 'a small
quantity' and 'a bargain' (Ard¹, 18).
67–8 **proper man's picture** the picture

or portrait of a fine-looking man. An
allusion to the provision of a portrait
as an aid both to courtship and to
remembrance; for example, Hamlet's
'pictures' of Old Hamlet and Claudius:
'Look here upon this picture, and on
this, / The counterfeit presentment
of two brothers' (*Ham* 3.4.53–4). See
also *Son* 16: 'With virtuous wish would
bear your living flowers, / Much like
than your painted counterfeit'. In the
1999 National Theatre production
(Nunn) Portia and Nerissa project the
film images of the former's suitors on
to a screen.
68–9 **dumb-show** usually a mime
involving actions but no words, frequently used as a dramatic device,
but here meaning simply an inert and
superficial picture
69 **suited** dressed. The specific detail of
this description suggests that Portia
may be describing an actual portrait
that she has in her hand. Brown perceives a pun here on 'dressed in a
suitable way', and compares it with
AW 1.1.152–3: 'richly suited but
unsuitable' (Ard², 18).
70–1 **doublet . . . everywhere** a
ridiculously eclectic amalgamation of
European dress characteristic of the
fashionable Englishman. Merchant
cites Robert Greene's *Farewell to
Folly* (1591) (Merchant, 170); but see
also Thomas Nashe, *The Unfortunate
Traveller* (1594): 'At my first coming to Rome, I, being a youth of

66 will] may *Pope* 69 suited!] *Rowe;* suted, *Q*

Germany and his behaviour everywhere.

NERISSA What think you of the Scottish lord, his neighbour?

PORTIA That he hath a neighbourly charity in him, for he borrowed a box of the ear of the Englishman and swore   75
he would pay him again when he was able. I think the Frenchman became his surety and sealed under for another.

NERISSA How like you the young German, the Duke of

the English cut, ware my hair long, went apparelled in light colours, and imitated foure or fiue sundry nations in my attire at once; which no sooner was noted, but I had all the boies of the citie in a swarme wondering about me' (Nashe, 2.281).

70 **doublet** a close-fitting body garment with or without sleeves, worn only by men (*OED* 1). See also *OED* 1b (with hose): 'the typical masculine attire; also, as a sort of undress, or dress for active pursuits, implying absence of the cloak worn for warmth and protection, or of the gown, coat or cassock befitting age or dignity'.
round hose padded breeches usually associated with French fashion. See Philip Stubbes, *Anatomy of Abuses* (1585): 'The Frenche hose are of two diuers makinges, for the common Frenche hose (as they list to call them) rounde. The other contayneth neyther length, breadth, nor side-nesse sufficient, and is made very rounde (being not past a quarter of a yarde side), whereof some be paned, cut, and drawen out with costly ornamentes, with Canions annexed, reaching down beneath their knees' (Sigs C2ᵛ–3).

72 **Scottish lord** a possible reference to contemporary events. Brown notes an outbreak of disorder on the borders with Scotland in 1596, around the time when *MV* was probably written;

a proclamation issued on 20 August 1596 commanded 'all persons vpon the Borders of England, to keepe peace towards Scotland', and another was issued on 13 August 1597 (Ard², 18).

75–6 **borrowed . . . able** an allusion to the antagonism between the English and Scots. Portia casts this as a comic, but not entirely analogous, version of the kind of relationship that will prevail between the participants in the later 'bond' between Shylock and Antonio, where Bassanio will be the borrower and Antonio the surety.

77 **Frenchman . . . surety** Portia compresses a series of references here. See LN.
surety guarantee or security; cf. *Son* 134: 'He learned but surety-like to write for me, / Under that bond that him as fast doth bind.'
sealed under entered into a separate signed agreement requiring both his signature and an official seal

79 **German** a native of Germany, but there is a barely disguised pun here on the meaning of 'german' as 'one sprung from the same stock; a brother, a near relative' (*OED* II.5†b *sb.*). Cf. *FQ*, 1.5.13: 'Thy selfe thy message doe to german deare', and also *Oth* 1.1.111–12: 'you'll have your nephews neigh to you, you'll have coursers for cousins and jennets for germans!'

72 Scottish] other *F*

Saxony's nephew?   80

PORTIA Very vilely in the morning, when he is sober, and
most vilely in the afternoon, when he is drunk. When
he is best, he is a little worse than a man, and when he
is worst he is little better than a beast. An the worst fall
that ever fell, I hope I shall make shift to go without   85
him.

NERISSA If he should offer to choose and choose the right
casket, you should refuse to perform your father's will
if you should refuse to accept him.

PORTIA Therefore, for fear of the worst, I pray thee set a   90
deep glass of Rhenish wine on the contrary casket, for

81 **vilely** Q prints 'vildlie' and F 'vildely', but *OED* records 'vildly' as a now
obsolete form of the adverb.
84 **little . . . beast** Portia's criticism
of the Duke of Saxony's nephew is
twofold: (1) that when he is sober
he has all the inadequacies associated with men and (2) that when he
is drunk he almost sinks to the level
of a beast. The latter is proverbial
(Tilley, M1219: 'Drunk as a mouse
(rat)', but see also Dent, M1237:
'To look like (As wet as) a drowned
MOUSE (rat)'. Cf. Thomas Wilson:
'As if one had . . . kept the Tauerne
till he had been as dronke as a Ratte'
(T. Wilson, *Rhetoric*, 128). See also
Thomas Nashe, *Pierce Penniless* (1592),
in which eight levels of drunkenness
are assocated with various beasts: 'Nor
haue we one or two kinde of drunkards
onely, but eight kindes. The first is
Ape drunke, and he leapes, and sings,
and hollowes, and daunceth for the
heauens: the second is Lion drunke,
and he flings the pots about the house,
calls his Hostesse whore, breakes the
glasse windowes with his dagger, and
is apt to quarrell with any man that
speaks to him: the third is Swine

drunke, heauy, lumpish, and sleepie,
and cries for a little more drinke, and a
fewe more cloathes' (Nashe, 1.207–8).
An if
84–5 **the worst . . . fell** the worst happens (befalls) that were ever to occur.
OED 1c notes a figurative usage of
'fall' involving a fall from a high estate
or a position of moral superiority.
85 **make shift** contrive or manage to
accomplish something (*OED* 6b)
91 **deep . . . wine** a large glass of wine,
similar to hock, from the Rhineland
area of Germany; *deep* refers to the
quantity rather than the colour; cf.
3.1.36, where the colour is contrasted
to 'red wine'.

contrary from the Latin *contrarius*,
meaning 'opposite' or 'hostile'. *OED*
2†b records a rare usage of the term
as meaning 'opposite to the proper
or right one: "the wrong"', and cites
KJ 4.2.198, 'Had falsely thrust upon
contrary feet'. Pooler thought there
might have been only two caskets in
the original form of the play (Ard[1],
28), while Brown, noting the reference
at 118 to 'four strangers', thought that
either this apparent confusion derived
from Shakespeare's foul papers or that

81 vilely] *(vildlie), Pope;* vildely *F*   82 vilely] *(vildly)*   90 pray thee] prethee *Q2*   91 Rhenish
wine] *(Reynishe wine)*

if the devil be within, and that temptation without, I
know he will choose it. I will do anything, Nerissa, ere
I will be married to a sponge.

NERISSA You need not fear, lady, the having any of   95
these lords. They have acquainted me with their
determinations, which is indeed to return to their home
and to trouble you with no more suit, unless you may be
won by some other sort than your father's imposition,
depending on the caskets.   100

PORTIA If I live to be as old as Sibylla, I will die as chaste

Portia, on this as opposed to the later
occasion, is not speaking precisely
(Ard², 19). This still leaves the question: does Portia *know* at this stage
which is the right casket? Certainly by
the time Bassanio comes to choose at
3.2.114, she *must* know, and this is the
reading offered in Michael Radford's
2004 film. Portia subtly manipulates
the very patriarchal law that holds in
check her freedom to act, a talent that
she will deploy later in the courtroom
in Venice.

92 **if . . . without** Even if the devil himself is inside the casket, the temptation
offered by the 'deep glass of Rhenish
wine' would not deter *the young
German*. The connection between
'German' and 'devil' appears in *MWW*
4.5.67: 'like three German devils, three
Doctor Faustusses', but see also Tilley,
D231, for the proverb 'The DEVIL
can transform himself into an angel
of light', and *LLL* 4.3.253: 'Devils
soonest tempt, resembling spirits of
light.'

94 **sponge** used figuratively here to
denote lack of moderation in drinking
(*OED* III. *fig.* 8). But see also *OED* 9b,
which extends the semantic field to
incorporate the sense of the appropriation or absorption of wealth; cf. *Ham*
4.2.13–15: '*Ros.* Take you me for a
sponge, my lord? / *Ham.* Ay, sir, that

soaks up the King's countenance, his
rewards, his authorities.'

95 **the having** a common grammatical
construction where the definite article
precedes the participial form of the
verb followed by an object (see Abbott,
93)

97 **determinations** fixed purposes or
intentions (*OED* 10)

98 **suit** pursuit of an object or quest
(*OED* †5 and †6), but also the act of
wooing (*OED* 12). Because the 'law'
of Portia's dead father carries juridical
weight, there is also a legal undertone
here in the sense that the suitor is
involved in the act of petitioning (see
OED 11†b).

99 **sort** manner or way. Clarendon suggests that it may also mean 'lot' from
the Latin *sors* and cites *TC* 1.3.375–7:
'No, make a lott'ry, / And by device let
blockish Ajax draw / The sort to fight
with Hector'. *OED* 2†b associates the
term with social rank and status; cf.
MM 4.4.15: 'Give notice to such men
of sort and suit.' In this compressed
comment Nerissa addresses Portia's
father's provision for his daughter,
which involves ensuring that she is
married to a suitor of appropriate
status.

101 **Sibylla** Deiphobe of Cumae, the
'longlyved Sybill' of Ovid, *Met.*, to
whom Apollo promised longevity, and

97 determinations] Determination *Rowe*   98 suit] *(sute)*; Suits *Rowe*   101 If] *(Yf)*

as Diana, unless I be obtained by the manner of my
father's will. I am glad this parcel of wooers are so
reasonable, for there is not one among them but I dote
on his very absence, and I pray God grant them a fair   105
departure.

NERISSA Do you not remember, lady, in your father's time,
a Venetian, a scholar and a soldier, that came hither in

whom Aeneas consults: 'At Cumye
landed, and / Went unto lonlyved
Sybills house, with whom he went
in hand / That he to see his fathers
ghoste mygt go by Averne deepe'
(Ovid, *Met.*, 13.122–4). But see also
Virgil's so-called 'messianic eclogue'
(Eclogue 4), where the Cumaean Sybil
prophesies the coming of a new age:
'*Ultima Cumaei venit iam carminis
aetas; / magnus ab integro saeclorum
nascitur ordo*' ('Now is come the last
age of Cumaean song; the great
line of the centuries begins anew')
(Fairclough, 48–9). Subsequent Jewish
and Christian readings accorded the
Sybil a position similar to the prophesies of the Old Testament (*OCD*, 835),
and this gives an added resonance to
what appears to be a casual remark
by Portia.

102 **Diana** goddess of chastity; cf. *MND*
1.1.89–90: 'Or on Diana's altar to
protest, / For aye, austerity and single
life.' But see also Virgil, Eclogue 4,
where the prophesy of the Cumaean
Sybil is connected with the return of
the 'Virgin' ('*iam redit et Virgo*' – 'Now
the Virgin returns'); the 'Virgin' in
this case was, significantly, Astraea or
Justice, the last of the deities to leave
the earth. Portia becomes the upholder
of 'justice', and these classical references both have a semantic density and
anticipate the later action.

103 **parcel** small party or group. Cf. *LLL*
5.2.160: '*A holy parcel of the fairest
dames*', although possibly used contemptuously here (*OED* 5†b *fig. obs.*).

103–4 **so reasonable** so amenable to the
restraints of reason, i.e. the conditions
imposed by Portia's dead father (cf.
OED 5), but ironic here, since none
of the suitors she has described is
endowed with 'reason'.

104 **for** because
but used in its preventative or adversa-
tive sense as a means of intensifying
Portia's disdain (see Abbott, 22)

105 **I pray God** F substitutes 'I wish' for
Q's 'I pray', in accordance with the
requirements of the 1606 Act against
the use of profanity in stage plays
and other entertainments. F's emendation effectively eliminates the irony of
Portia's utterance.
fair free from obstacles or unobstruct-
ed (*OED adj.* 15), but also, possibly, on
good terms; cf. *OED adv.* 2†b. Portia
is speaking ironically here in that she
herself is unwilling to extend this
courtesy to such unsuitable suitors.

108 **scholar . . . soldier** the ideal
Renaissance courtier. Cf. *Ham*
3.1.152–3, 'O, what a noble mind is
here o'erthrown! / The courtier's, soldier's, scholar's, eye, tongue, sword',
and also Castiglione: 'the more excellent our Courtier shall be in this arte
[of managing a weapon], the more
shall he be worthie of praise . . . But
because this is overlarge a scope of
matters, we wil holde our selves contented, as wee have said, with the
uprightnesse of a well-meaning mind,
and with an invincible courage, and
that he alwaies shew himself such a
one' (Castiglione, 36).

105 I pray] I wish *F*; wish *Rowe*

company of the Marquis of Montferrat?

PORTIA Yes, yes, it was Bassanio, as I think, so was he   110
called.

NERISSA True, madam. He, of all the men that ever my
foolish eyes looked upon, was the best deserving a fair
lady.

PORTIA I remember him well, and I remember him worthy   115
of thy praise.

Enter a Servingman.

How now, what news?

SERVINGMAN The four strangers seek for you, madam, to
take their leave; and there is a forerunner come from

109 **Marquis of Montferrat** The Marquis of Montferrato appears in Novel V of Boccacio's *Decameron* as 'a paladin of distinguished prowess' (Boccacio, 1.40). Montferrato was a detached possession of the Duke of Mantua, and Shakespeare would have encountered Mantua in Arthur Brooke's *The Tragical History of Romeus and Juliet* (1562), his major source for *Romeo and Juliet*. This geographical location also figures in *TGV* and *TS*. Mahood's suggestion that Shakespeare may have known of Gonzago the Duke of Mantua's campaign against the Turks in Hungary in 1595 (Cam[2], 69) establishes a connection between Mantua and the struggle against one of the number of enemies of Christianity ('the Turk') that becomes an issue in the later play, *Othello*. Both Montferrato and Mantua were also places in Italy where Jews settled (Edwards, 138).

110 **as . . . so** Q2's 'as *I* think he was so' may be more coolly deliberative than Q, which, as Pooler suggests, indicates a more impulsive Portia try-ing to check her eagerness (Ard[1], 30). Either way, Portia betrays a degree of disingenuousness here.

113 **the best deserving** Because he is the best, Bassanio deserves to have a *fair lady*. The grammatical awkwardness arises from the use of the participial *deserving* which in modern usage would normally be preceded by the definite article ('the') and then followed by the preposition 'of'. Abbott (93) suggests that 'of' 'seems to have been regarded as colloquial elsewhere in Shakespeare' (he cites Touchstone in *AYL* and the Gravedigger in *Ham*).

117 **How . . . news?** F and Rowe omit this, but Q emphasizes the comedy of Portia's dilemma: the appearance of a suitor who would be agreeable but about whose prospects of success she is constrained to say nothing.

118 **four strangers** Earlier in the scene there were *six* suitors, and this inconsistency is attributed by Brown to foul papers (Ard[2], xiv–xviii and 20–1).

119 **forerunner** literally, one who runs before (*OED* 1). The ambiguity is such

a fifth, the Prince of Morocco, who brings word the   120
prince his master will be here tonight.

PORTIA If I could bid the fifth welcome with so good
heart as I can bid the other four farewell, I should be
glad of his approach. If he have the condition of a saint
and the complexion of a devil, I had rather he should   125
shrive me than wive me. Come, Nerissa. – Sirrah,
go before.   [*Exit Servingman.*]
Whiles we shut the gate upon one wooer, another
knocks at the door.   *Exeunt.*

[1.3]   *Enter* BASSANIO *with* Shylock the JEW.

that it may mean simply a herald, but also a harbinger. The word appears in *KJ* at 2.1.2 in connection with ancestry: 'Arthur, that great forerunner of thy blood'. The pun on *fore/four* followed by *fifth* imitates numerical sequence, and sets up a comical context for the later entry of the Prince of Morocco.

122 **so as**, which is the modern form of the antecedent relative

124 **condition** disposition, qualities or character (*OED* 11)

124–5 **saint . . . devil** possibly proverbial; see Dent, D231: 'The DEVIL can transform himself into an angel of light.' This contrast appears earlier in *LLL* 4.3.250–2 in the form of a paradox, where good and evil oppose each other: 'Black is the badge of hell, / The hue of dungeons and the school of night; / And beauty's crest becomes the heavens well.'

126 **shrive** hear (Portia's) confession, that is, be the priest to whom she confesses rather than the one who officiates at the marriage ceremony **wive** marry. Portia emphatically will have him in neither role, hence rein-

forcing, for a modern audience, her racial prejudice.

126–9 **Come . . . door** not printed as verse in Q or F, although the rhyme on *before/door* suggests a clumsy couplet, conventionally observed until Keightley, and regarded as doggerel from Pooler onwards (Ard[1], 31). (See LN.)

1.3 Rowe was the first to set the scene outside in '*a publick Place in* VENICE', followed substantially by most editors, although Cam[1] adds '*before Shylock's house*'. Q is unspecific about whether this is an 'outside' or an 'inside' scene, and modern performances have set this and other similar scenes in both locations.

0.1 **Shylock the JEW** as in Q and F, but 'the Jew' was omitted in pre-20th-century editions and up to Pooler (Ard[1], 31). From 1870 onwards productions distinguish the Jew by means of costume, such as distinctive head-gear – Booth (1870), Irving (1879), Gielgud (1938), Olivier (1970) (Gross, 152–3), David Bowen (Compass Theatre, 1997), Phillip Voss (1998) and Henry Goodman (2000) – or a middle-

122 If] *(Yf)*   122–3 good heart] good a heart *Q2*   126–9 Come . . . door.] *Oxf* lines before. / wooer, / door. /   127 SD] *this edn*   128 gate] gates *Q2*   1.3] *Rowe (*SCENE III.*)*   0.1] *Enter* Bassanio *and* Shylock. *Rowe*

JEW   Three thousand ducats, well.

BASSANIO   Ay, sir, for three months.

JEW   For three months, well.

BASSANIO   For the which, as I told you, Antonio shall be
bound.   5

JEW   Antonio shall become bound, well.

BASSANIO   May you stead me? Will you pleasure me? Shall

European accent. Some modern productions have resisted this distinction,
e.g. Gert Voss (1995). Clearly from
the later reference to *Jewish gaberdine*
(108) the Jew was dressed distinctively,
although Bulman notes the 'doubtful tradition' according to which the
young Burbage played the part in a red
wig (Bulman, 8). See p. 112.

1–35 The scene begins with a prose
exchange between Bassanio and the
Jew. Vickers suggests that here prose
is reserved for 'the harsh world of
business' (Vickers, 968). The Jew's
prose is characterized by a 'brevity
of symmetry' in which the rhetorical
figures of *isocolon* [phrases or clauses
of equal length and structure], *parison*
[evenly balanced phrases, clauses and
sentences] and *epistrophe* [repetition
of words at the end of particular
phrases, clauses or sentences]' pre-
dominate (Vickers, 81–2). The Jew's
switch from prose to verse at 37ff.
signals an 'emotion' absent from the
prose (83).

1 SP For the reasons for adopting this SP
throughout, see p. 41 and the analysis
of Q's printing history (Appendix
2). Trachtenberg notes that the Jew
who appeared on the stage or in
other narratives from the medieval
period onwards 'was not an individual but a type . . . This Jew lacked
a name; rarely did he own personal
characteristics' (Trachtenberg, 13).
Shakespeare's Jew maintains a fine
balance, incorporating the stereotype,

but see Gross for an emphasis upon
his 'vivid individuality' (Gross, 51).

1 **ducats** coins of either gold or silver,
but also used to denote a sum of
money; cf. Coryate (228 and 253), who
notes that in Venice in 1608 the ducat
was worth 4*s.* 8*d*. Brown estimates
that Bassanio's request is for a sum of
around £700 (Ard², 22), the modern
equivalent of which would be very
large indeed.

3 **well** the repetition of this word in 6
is characteristic of the Jew's mode of
speech; *well* may simply be used as 'a
preliminary or resumptive word' (*OED*
VI.23 and 25) signalling both acceptance and qualification of a particular
situation. Pooler cites Dowden, who
suggests that *well* is an interrogative –
'well?' – and emends Q's punctuation
accordingly (Ard¹, 31); Vickers suggests that 'The presence of repetition
and parallelism is the dominant feature
of Shylock's prose' (Vickers, 82). See
also later at 2.8.15–22 in Salanio's
parody of the Jew's speech mannerisms.

5 **bound** contracted or placed under a
formal obligation (*OED* 7), with the
possibly subsidiary meaning 'captive',
which provides a sinister undertone
to the Jew's utterance (Cam², 71),
although the dominant meaning here
is a legal one.

7 **May you** are you able ('willing':
Furness, 53) to. See also Abbott, 307,
for the Anglo-Saxon derivation from
the verb *magan*, 'to be able'.

1+ SP] *this edn (throughout); Shy. Q*   1 ducats,] *(ducates)*   4–5] *Q3; Q lines* you, / bound. /
6 bound,] *Q, F;* bound. *Q2;* bound? *Pope*

I know your answer?

JEW   Three thousand ducats for three months, and Antonio
bound.   10

BASSANIO   Your answer to that.

JEW   Antonio is a good man.

BASSANIO   Have you heard any imputation to the contrary?

JEW   Ho, no, no, no, no. My meaning in saying he is a
good man is to have you understand me that he is   15
sufficient, yet his means are in supposition. He hath
an argosy bound to Tripoli, another to the Indies; I

---

stead help, be of use to, or render
service to (*OED v. trans.* 1a and 1c).
Cf. *TGV* 2.1.106: 'No, madam; so it
stead you, I will write', and also *Oth*
1.3.339–40.

12 **good** financially sound (*OED* 16a).
But see also *OED* II.5a and 7 for
suggestions of kindness and benevolence. The Jew may have in mind here
Antonio's financial circumstances but
there is also a submerged criticism of
the latter's financial dealings. Antonio
enlists the services of a usurer in
support of Bassanio but he is not a
usurer himself, and this is a bone of
contention from the outset.

13 **imputation** a charge of attributing
either a fault or a crime to a person
(*OED* 1). Mahood thinks that Bassanio
is responding to the Jew's imputation
that Antonio is 'dishonourable' (Cam²,
71), although this not clear.

14–15 **meaning . . . good** This repetition and explanation is another characteristic of the Jew's mode of speech
(Vickers, 82).

16 **sufficient** furnished with adequate
securities (against the loan Bassanio is
seeking). *OED* 2 emphasizes the legal
implications of the word (cf. Ard², 22),
but see also *OED* 1b (*b*): to provide for
the needs of, or to satisfy. Antonio's

earlier offer at 1.1.138–9 extends the
range of reference to more than simply
a legal sense of adequacy (*OED a.* 1).
supposition unrealized and, therefore, hypothetical (*OED* 2†b and 3).
See 1.1.177–9, where Antonio has
revealed that his business ventures are
at risk on the open seas because unlike
the Jew's they are exposed to the vicissitudes of nature.

17 **Tripoli . . . Indies** the port of Tripoli
in the Levant (eastern Mediterranean)
with which Venetian merchants traded
heavily. Mahood argues that this
multiplicity of trading ventures was
impossible for a Venetian merchant
of the time (Cam², 13 and 71). See
Wallerstein for the view that up to
the beginning of the 17th century
'the principal shipping lanes of the
Indian Ocean shifted from the northern half (the Red Sea and the Persian
Gulf) to the southern half (the Cape
route)' and that it was the Dutch
who were able to exploit the latter
because of superior maritime technol-
ogy (Wallerstein, 47). See also Braudel
(2.138–42) for a description of the
diversity of Venetian merchant trading
interests and the practical complications, as well as the uncertainties, to
which they gave rise.

---

8 answer?] *Rowe;* aunswere. *Q; answere.* *Q2, F*   9–10] *Pope; Q lines* months, / bound. /   10 bound.]
bound? *Pope*   13 contrary?] *Q2;* contrary. *Q*   14 SP] *this edn; Shylocke. Q*   Ho,] *(Ho); No, F2*
17 Tripoli] *(Tripolis)*

203

understand moreover upon the Rialto, he hath a third
at Mexico, a fourth for England, and other ventures
he hath squandered abroad. But ships are but boards,   20
sailors but men; there be land rats, and water rats, water
thieves, and land thieves – I mean pirates – and then
there is the peril of waters, winds and rocks. The man
is notwithstanding sufficient. Three thousand ducats: I
think I may take his bond.   25

BASSANIO   Be assured you may.

18 **Rialto** 'a high shore. Also a high place
for Princes seats. Also an eminent
place in Venice where Merchants
commonly meete, as on the Exchange
in London' (Florio, 432). See also
Coryate: 'The Rialto, which is at the
farthest side of the bridge as you come
from St. *Marks*, is a most stately building, being the Exchange of Venice,
where the Venetian Gentlemen and
the Merchants doe meete twice a
day, betwixt eleuen and twelue of the
clocke in the morning, and betwixte
fiue and sixe of the clocke in the
afternoone' (Coryate, 169; quoted in
Furness, 35).

19 **Mexico . . . England** an indication of
the diversity of Antonio's financial
interests, as well as the risks in which
he is currently involved, though possibly an exaggeration, designed to
produce a particular effect.

20 **squandered** scattered over a wide
area (*OED v.* 1a), although the Jew
may be alluding to more than this neu-
tral gloss permits. Cf. Thomas Nashe:
'Fooles shall squander in an houre all
the auarice of their ambitious wise
Auncesters' (Nashe, 1.91), where the
verb is used in a derogatory manner to
indicate waste and prodigality (*OED*
3). (See LN.)

    boards ships' sides (*OED* V.12), i.e.
made of timber planks

21–2 **land rats . . . pirates** bandits and

privateers, all of whom thrive by theft
on both land and sea. See Wallerstein,
48 and 158–61, for references to
piracy in the Mediterranean and in
the West Indies. Mahood notes that in
the Adriatic the pirates were Balkan
refugees from successive Turkish inva-
sions (Cam[2], 72). See 14–15n. on the
Jew's tendency to follow the use of
an image with an explanation. This
is also an example of the rhetorical
figure of chiasmus whereby the order
of words in one of two parallel clauses
is inverted in the other (*OED*). Brown
detects a bad pun, 'pir-*rats*' (Ard[2], 23),
and a number of modern productions
from Miller onwards emphasize this.

23 **peril . . . rocks** The Jew accentuates
the *natural* hazards that confront the
merchant; see 16n.

26–7 **assured . . . assured . . . assured**
The meanings here range from
Bassanio's 'certain' (*OED* A †1) and
'have confidence in' (assure: *OED v.*
8†c) to the Jew's requiring a formal
guarantee (assure: *OED v.* †7 and 7†c).
Cf. 1.1.137–8, Antonio's 'be assured /
My purse, my person, my extremest
means', which, in part, Bassanio now
echoes. Hence the different meanings
of 'assure' remain actively in play
throughout this exchange, obviating
the need to conclude that the Jew is
guilty here of 'twisting' Bassanio's
meaning (Cam[2], 72).

18 Rialto] *(Ryalto) F2;* Ryalta *Q*   21–2 water thieves . . . thieves] *Q;* land thieves . . . water thieves
Johnson

JEW   I will be assured I may; and, that I may be assured, I
will bethink me. May I speak with Antonio?

BASSANIO   If it please you to dine with us.

JEW   Yes, to smell pork, to eat of the habitation which your   30
prophet the Nazarite conjured the devil into. I will buy
with you, sell with you, talk with you, walk with you
and so following. But I will not eat with you, drink with
you nor pray with you. What news on the Rialto? Who
is he comes here?   35

28 **bethink me** devise or contrive (*OED*
†4 *obs.*). Cf. *3H6* 3.3.39: 'While we
bethink a means to break it off.'
Mahood punctuates 'me –' to suggest
that the actor has a choice whether to
articulate 'a half-formed thought of
some ingenious kind', or, following the
usage elsewhere, to deliver this as part
of a sentence which is 'complete' and
'decisive' (Cam², 72).

29 **dine** have dinner with. Furness
believes that this invitation to dinner was an unusual compliment
(Furness, 36), but it exposes a
distinction between the rituals of
courtesy characteristic of Venice
and those practised by the Jew. Yaffe
argues that refusal signifies Jewish
orthodoxy, but that later acceptance
of the invitation to dine signals that
the Jew has become a 'bad' Jew, and
that Shakespeare was aware of this
distinction (Yaffe, 6).

30–1 **habitation . . . into** a reference
to Matthew, 8.32–4, and to Christ's
expulsion of the devil from a dumb
man into a herd of swine (*habitation*).
The verb 'conjure' insinuates that this
was an act of supernatural trickery
(*OED v.* III.1 and 8) that incorporates
the very evil it would exorcise. But see
also *OED v.* II.†3 conjure: 'to charge
or call upon in the name of some
divine or sacred being'. The Jew turns
against the Christians the very rhetoric
of demonization directed against him,
and he mocks Bassanio and his friends

because they literally ingest *the devil*
each time they eat pork.

30 **habitation** dwelling place, used of
a human or an animal (*OED* 2); an
obsolete synonym for the Jewish
tabernacle (*OED* 2†b), which initiates a disdainfully ironic distinction
between the Old Testament faith and
Christianity and is distinctly 'biblical'
in its register

31 **Nazarite** literally, someone from
Nazareth. Before the Authorized
King James version of 1611, Bibles
used the term 'Nazarite' to describe
Christ. Furness cites Tyndale (1534),
Coverdale (1535) and the Bishops'
Bible (1595) among others that do
not make the distinction between
'Nazarite' and 'Nazarene' (Furness,
36–7).
conjured to summon by magical invocation (*OED* III.5). Cf. Marlowe, *Dr
Faustus* 1.1.149–50: 'Come, show me
some demonstrations magical, / That
I may conjure in some lusty grove.'
Furness cites Coryate, 215, to establish a distinction between the Jewish
respect for Christ as a 'great prophet'
and the rejection of the Christian
claim of his 'divinity'. The focus here
is upon the Jewish prohibition of the
eating of pork (30), but the two are
conflated in the Jew's counter-claim
that Christ is a demonic 'conjurer',
closer to Faustus than to the Christian
figure of the redeemer of mankind.

33 **so following** so forth

29+ If] (Yf)   30–4 Yes . . . with you.] *aside in Cam¹*   34 Rialto] (Ryalto)

205

Enter ANTONIO.

BASSANIO [*to the Jew*]   This is Signior Antonio.
JEW [*aside*]
  How like a fawning publican he looks.
  I hate him for he is a Christian;
  But more, for that in low simplicity
  He lends out money gratis, and brings down   40
  The rate of usance here with us in Venice.
  If I can catch him once upon the hip,
  I will feed fat the ancient grudge I bear him.

37–48 **How . . . him** See LN.
37 **fawning publican** a servile heathen.
Publicans were public officials, usually tax-gatherers (*OED* 1), but were
regarded with contempt because they
collected taxes on behalf of their
Roman rulers (*OED* 1*ß*) and were
oppressors of the Jews: 'If he will not
heare them, tel it unto the Church, if
he will not heare yᵉ Church, let him
be unto thee as an heathen manne
and a publicane' (Matthew, 18.17).
See also the association of the publican with profligacy: 'God, I thanke
thee that I am not as other men are,
extortioners, uniust, adulterers, or as
this Publicane' (Luke, 18.11). But note
a double irony in the Jew's aligning
himself with Pharisaical (or puritanical) restraint, since he inadvertently
invokes a Christian axiom: 'Verily I say
unto you, that the publicanes and the
harlots go into the kingdome of God
before you' (Matthew, 21.31).
39 **for that** because
  low literally, inferior of stature and
  hence a metaphorical description of
  his behaviour. But see Luke, 19.2–3,
  for the description of the tax-gatherer
  Zacchaeus who was 'the chiefe among
  the Publicanes, and was riche', but
  who was unable to see Jesus 'for the
  preasse, bycause he was little of stat-

ure' (Luke, 19.2–3). Mahood's gloss of
'humble foolishness' (Cam², 72) does
not quite encapsulate the persistent
and complex biblical resonances of
this insult. The Jew thinks Antonio's
behaviour is inferior, and by implication hints contemptuously that he is a
'little man' in every respect.
  simplicity free from artifice, deceit or
  duplicity (*OED* 3), but also ignorance
  or rusticity (*OED* 2). Brown (Ard²,
  24) cites Barabas's contemptuous dismissal of Christians in *Jew of Malta*,
  1.2.161–2: 'Ay, policy! that's their
  profession, / And not simplicity, as
  they suggest.'
40 **lends . . . gratis** literally, loans money
  freely. The implication is that Antonio
  does this out of friendship and for no
  reward. See pp. 45–6.
41 **rate of usance** rate of interest. The
  Jew deploys the more acceptable form
  usance rather than 'usury' as 'the more
  clenely name' for usury (see T. Wilson,
  Usury, 32; quoted in Ard¹, 34).
42 **upon the hip** at a disadvantage.
  Proverbial: 'To have one on the HIP'
  (Dent, H474). See *Oth* 2.1.303: 'I'll
  have our Michael Cassio on the hip.'
  The term is from wrestling; Brown
  suggests that there may be an allusion
  here to Jacob's nocturnal wrestling in
  Genesis, 32.24ff. (Ard², 24).

36 SD] *this edn*   37 SD] *Rowe*

He hates our sacred nation, and he rails,
Even there where merchants most do congregate,   45
On me, my bargains and my well-won thrift,
Which he calls 'interest'. Cursed be my tribe
If I forgive him.
BASSANIO   Shylock, do you hear?

44 **sacred nation** a reference to the Jew's own ancient lineage stretching back to Abraham; cf. Geneva Bible (1562): 'And I will make thee a great nacion, and will blesse thee and make thy name great, and thou shalt be a blessing. / I will also blesse them that blesse thee, & curse them that curse thee, & in thee shal all families of the earth be blessed' (Genesis, 12.2–3). The Bishops' Bible (1595) substitutes 'people' for 'nation'. But see Balibar: 'theological discourse has provided models for the idealization of the nation and the sacralization of the state, which make it possible for a bond of sacrifice to be created between individuals, and for the stamp of "truth" and "law" to be conferred upon the rules of the legal system' (Balibar, 95).
    rails utters abuse (*OED v.*[4] 1); ironic, since the Jew is himself involved in uttering abuse against Christians
45 **Even there** a deictic reference to the Rialto
46 **well-won thrift** earned reward (derived by conserving rather than consuming wealth). Mahood thinks that F's emendation 'well-worne' may be correct in that it denotes the Jew's usurious practice as time-honoured, and therefore validated by custom (Cam², 73). But Q1 and Q2's 'well-wone'/'well-won' makes perfect sense, suggesting 'hard-earned' success won directly through activity and in the face of Christian opposition.
47 **interest** The derogatory use of this term can be traced back to Luther,

where '*zinss kauf*' ('buying interest') is described as 'this slippery and newly-invented business [that] very frequently makes itself an upright and loyal protector of damnable greed and usury' (Luther, *Usury*, 2.295). Luther's emphasis upon the need for 'risk' in business allows for the intervention of God in human affairs, and he continues: 'money engaged in business and money put out at *zinss* are two different things, and the one cannot be compared with the other. The latter has a base which is constantly growing and producing profit out of the earth without any fear of capital losses; while there is nothing certain about the former, and the only interest it yields is accidental and cannot be counted on' (2.300). (See LN.)
'interest'. Cursed The spelling of 'interest' is not elided in Q, indicating that it is pronounced here as a trisyllable implying deliberate emphasis; the rhythm of the line demands that 'Cursed' be pronounced as a disyllable.
Cursed . . . tribe a reciprocation of the 'curse' traditionally placed upon all Jews. It is less likely that he means, as Mahood suggests (Cam², 73), one of the twelve tribes of Israel from which the Jews took their descent (Genesis, 49.1–28). Shakespeare may be recalling Ferneze's contemptuous reference in *Jew of Malta*, 1.2.62–4: 'No, Jew, like infidels. / For through our suffering of your hateful lives, / Who stand accursèd in the sight of heaven.'

46 well-won] well-worne *F*   48 Shylock] *Q2, F;* Shyloch *Q*

JEW [*to Bassanio*]
I am debating of my present store,
And, by the near guess of my memory,   50
I cannot instantly raise up the gross
Of full three thousand ducats. What of that?
Tubal, a wealthy Hebrew of my tribe,
Will furnish me. But soft, how many months
Do you desire? [*to Antonio*] Rest you fair, good signior,   55
Your worship was the last man in our mouths.

ANTONIO
Shylock, albeit I neither lend nor borrow
By taking nor by giving of excess,

49 **debating ... store** considering how much wealth I have accumulated (*OED sb.* 5). But see also *OED* 5† for the suggestion of the act of storing as 'hoarding'. In these exchanges the Jew's language is never free from the taint of implied accusation.

50 **near guess** rough estimate

51–2 **I ... ducats** Brown cites Bell, where the usurer protests his poverty and suggests another richer provider: '[he] sweareth and protesteth that hee hath no money at all, but that himselfe seeketh where to finde an vsurer' (Bell, B3ᵛ).

51 **gross** full amount; bulk (Onions)

54 **furnish me** supply me with what I need (Onions). See Deuteronomy, 23.19–20, where lending without interest among Jews is permitted, although this injunction facilitates a connection between the Jew and Tubal that is complex in the larger context of the play.

But soft But wait a moment

55 **Rest you fair** May you rest easy (*OED* 3†b). A greeting that is, in this context, ironic, particularly in view of the Jew's evaluation of Antonio earlier at 37ff. Here the Jew is depicted as 'two-faced', and this contributes to his overall portrayal as a machiavellian figure. Shakespeare may have had in mind the figure of Machevil, the Prologue in *Jew of Malta*: 'And let them know that I am Machevill, / And weigh not men, and therefore not men's words' (Prologue, 7–8), although the earlier portrait is much more consistently scurrilous, and in a context that is thoroughly ambivalent.

56 **the ... mouths** the most recent subject of our conversation; cf. *TS* 1.1.235: 'And not a jot of Tranio in your mouth.' There is, however, an irony in the Jew's greeting that may recall the sentiment expressed in the Geneva Bible (1562): 'Therefore the Lord said, Because this people come near unto me with their mouth, and honour me with their lippes but have remoued their heart far frô me, and their feare toward me was taught by the precept of men' (Isaiah, 29.13), a sentiment that appears in the Bishops' Bible at Job, 20.12–15.

58 **taking ... excess** taking or giving interest on capital borrowed or loaned. See Caesar, 'the gaine of fiue in the hundred, or of one pennie, yea of one Barley corne gotten by Vsurie, is vnlawfull' (Caesar, C2ᵛ) and 'Vsurie, or as the woorde of God doeth call it, excesse', and he concludes: 'if thou lookest to receiue more backe than thou deliueredst, thou art an Vsurer, and in this to bee blamed' (D1ᵛ).

50 guess] (gesse*)*   52 that?] *Q2, F;* that, *Q*   55 SD] *opp. 55 Rowe*   57 albeit] although *Q2*

Yet, to supply the ripe wants of my friend,
I'll break a custom. [*to Bassanio*] Is he yet possessed   60
How much ye would?

JEW   Ay, ay, three thousand ducats.

ANTONIO

And for three months.

JEW

I had forgot, three months, [*to Bassanio*] you told me so.
[*to Antonio*] Well then, your bond. And let me see – but
    hear you:
Methoughts you said you neither lend nor borrow   65

---

59 **ripe wants** pressing or urgent needs.
But Antonio also emphasizes the propriety as well as the urgency of Bassanio's quest (*OED sb.*³ 5, ripe: 'properly considered or deliberated').

60 **Is . . . possessed** does he know yet, i.e. is he in possession of. Q's spelling 'possest' confirms that this is pronounced as a disyllable. Q2 emends 60–1 to the unsatisfactory 'are you resolu'd, / How much he would haue?', where the substitution of 'resolu'd' for 'possest' reduces the threat posed by the Jew.

61 **ye would** you require. Q1's reading makes it clear that this question is directed to Bassanio but Q2's 'How much he would haue' and F's 'How much he would' confuse the issue. Bassanio has already made his requirements known to the Jew before Antonio's entry at 35, but up to this point Antonio is not sure if the Jew is in full possession of the details of the request; F's minimal emendation ('ye'/'he') and Q2's more substantive alteration both attempt, erroneously, to clear up, in an *ad hoc* manner, what they perceive to be an inconsistency.
three thousand ducats The Jew *may* be seeking to control the conversation

by answering for Bassanio, as Brown suggests (Ard², 25), but these deliberative repetitions and hesitations are part of a larger bargaining strategy that indicates duplicity. There is therefore no reason to posit, as Brown does, a missing half-line at 52 (Ard², 25). It is difficult for a modern audience or reader to appreciate the enormity of what is happening; the Jew is acting in direct conformity with Caesar's account, which describes the usurer as 'a deuill in the likenes of a man' (Caesar, *3ᵛ) who is 'a wonderfull framer of reprochfull speech, and can turne his tale at his pleasure' (Caesar, H1ᵛ). The nervously fragmented verse signifies the prospect of fragmentation of order, and hence wider disturbance.

64 **bond** the formal details of the agreement. The Jew's pause here is significant because it points up a contradiction in Antonio's customary practice and serves to emphasize the dangerous nature of this exchange.

65 **Methoughts** I thought (*OED v.* 2β). But note Onions, 'It seemed to me'; cf. *R3* 1.4.9: 'Methoughts that I had broken from the Tower'. Q2 and F emend to 'Methought'.

---

60 SD] *Cam*²   Is . . . possessed] are you resolu'd *Q2*   61 ye would?] he would haue? *Q2;* he would? *F;* you would? *Theobald*   63 SD] *Ard*²   you] he *Hanmer*   64 SD] *Riv*   65 Methoughts] *(*Me thoughts)*;* Me-thought *Q2*

Upon advantage.

ANTONIO   I do never use it.

JEW

When Jacob grazed his uncle Laban's sheep,
This Jacob from our holy Abram was,
As his wise mother wrought in his behalf,
The third possessor; ay, he was the third.   70

ANTONIO

And what of him, did he take interest?

JEW

No, not take 'interest', not as you would say
Directly 'interest'. Mark what Jacob did:

66 **Upon advantage** for profit, i.e. derived from the taking of interest, and thereby gaining an *advantage* over the borrower. Also, by borrowing at interest Antonio is placing himself at a *dis*advantage in relation to his creditor.

use Antonio says that he never 'uses' usury. This is part of a network of puns generated in the play around 'Iewes', 'ewes' and 'use' (see Shell, 48ff.), and they depend upon some homophonic resemblance between these terms. Antonio's comment leads in to the Jew's anecdotal justification for the practice of usury.

67 **Jacob . . . sheep** This story replicates the narrative in Genesis, 30.37–43, in which Jacob, the younger of Isaac's two sons, finds a way to increase his patrimony by interfering in the natural process of generation among his father's flock of sheep. (See LN.)

68 **holy Abram** the Abraham of Genesis, 17.1–22, with whom God made a covenant: 'Neither shall thy name any more be called Abram, but thy name shall be called Abraham for a father of many nations haue I made thee. / I will make thee exceeding fruitfull and will make nations of thee, yea & kings shall spring out of thee' (17.5–6). See also

Jew of Malta, 1.1.104–5, 'These are the blessings promised to the Jews, / And herein was old Abram's happiness', where clearly, as in Shakespeare's text, a metrically shortened version of the name is appropriate.

69 **wise mother** Jacob's mother Rebecca, working on his behalf, assisted her son in deceiving his father into giving the younger child his blessing; see Genesis, 27.13–23. Rebecca's 'wisdom' here is unintentionally ironic (from the Jew's point of view) but it establishes a connection between a stereotypical female duplicity and Jacob's 'subtiltie', and reinforces the Jew's capacity for devilish duplicity.

wrought fashioned or constructed artfully (*OED* †1b), with the suggestion of deceit

70 **third possessor** third generation from Abraham, through Isaac. Furness notes that this is a reinforcement of the Jew's pride in his own history (Furness, 42–3; cf. Ard², 25). It also indicates the desire for a mathematical and textual precision later underlined by his punctilious respect for the letter of the law.

73 **Directly** exactly or precisely; cf. *JC* 1.2.3–4: 'Stand you directly in Antonio's way / When he doth run

69 As . . . behalf,] *Rowe;* (As . . . behalf) *Q*   71 interest] *Q2;* interrest *Q1, F*   72 interest] int'rest *Pope*   73 interest] *Q2, F;* intrest *Q;* int'rest *Pope*

When Laban and himself were compromised
That all the eanlings which were streaked and pied   75
Should fall as Jacob's hire, the ewes, being rank,
In end of autumn turned to the rams;
And when the work of generation was
Between these woolly breeders in the act,
The skilful shepherd peeled me certain wands,   80
And, in the doing of the deed of kind,

his course.' However, the adverb has a wider resonance within the discourse of usury; for example, see the anonymous *Death of Usury* (1594), where the difference between 'direct' and 'indirect' interest is elaborated: '1. If a man takes aboue 10. pound in the 100. directly, he is coniucted by this branch [a clause governing the limiting of interest to 10%]. 2. If a man takes aboue 10. pound in the 100. indirectly [i.e. by accepting repayment before the due date], he is in great daunger' (*Death of Usury*, 23). The Jew goes on to describe the 'indirect' way in which Jacob obtains an increase on his investment.

74 **Laban** the brother of Jacob's mother and the father of two daughters, Leah and Rachel. Genesis tells the story of Laban's deception of Jacob. Jacob sought the hand of Rachel, the younger daughter, but Laban contrived to offer him Leah on the grounds that 'It is not the manner of this place to marrie the younger before the first borne' (Genesis, 29.26). This may be the source from which Shakespeare derived the Jew's wife's name Leah, and it associates him with a history of 'beguiling' (Genesis, 29.25: 'Wherefore has thou played thus with me? Did not I serue thee for Rachel? Wherefore then hast thou beguiled me?').
compromised come to terms (*OED v.* 2)

75 **eanlings** young lambs (*OED v. obs.*: 'of ewes: to bring forth lambs, to yean'). See

also *eaning time* (83): the time of birth.
streaked and pied faintly lined and blotched. 'Pied' originally meant dappled in black and white (*OED*), which may be read in this context as a visual metaphor of the Jew's allegedly dubious fiscal practice.

76 **hire** salary
rank lustful, licentious and in heat (*OED* †13)

77 **turned** turnèd

78 **work of generation** act of copulation

79 **in the act** in process

80 **peeled me** stripped off for me (*OED v.*[1] II.5). But see also the sense of pillage, rob and fleece; Q spells 'pyld' while F spells 'pil'd', presumably to emphasize that the word is pronounced as a monosyllable. Pope emended to 'peel'd', but a number of modern editors (e.g. Ard[2] and Cam[1]) have used the form 'pilled'. Modern usage has lost the pejorative sense reinforced here by the colour symbolism of black and white. The use of the ethical dative *me* (see Abbot, 147) calls attention to the Jew himself, who is the real focus of this narrative.
wands straight thin sticks (*OED sb.*)

81 **deed of kind** act of copulation. *Kind* here means 'nature' (*OED* †4); hence the modern idiom would be 'doing what comes naturally'. But, where usury is considered a human interference with the natural order of things, the reference to nature here reinforces, through irony, Jacob's and, by extension, the Jew's propensity to interfere with its operations.

74 compromised] *(compremyzd);* compremiz'd *F*   75 eanlings] *(eanelings);* euelings *F4;* Ewelings *Rowe*   77 In end] In th'end *Q2*   78 when] then *Hanmer*   80 peeled] *(pyld);* pil'd *F;* peel'd *Pope;* pilled *Cam*[1]

He stuck them up before the fulsome ewes,
Who, then conceiving, did in eaning time
Fall parti-coloured lambs, and those were Jacob's.
This was a way to thrive, and he was blest: 85
And thrift is blessing, if men steal it not.

ANTONIO

This was a venture, sir, that Jacob served for,
A thing not in his power to bring to pass,
But swayed and fashioned by the hand of heaven.
Was this inserted to make interest good?   90
Or is your gold and silver ewes and rams?

82 **fulsome** lustful or rank-smelling (*OED obs.* 2†c). The phrase *fulsome ewes* may also refer obliquely to the myth of the *foetor judaicus*, a bodily odour said to be produced by Jewish male menstruation (Sanders, 42), which Marlowe's Barabas is thought to have parodied in *Jew of Malta*, 2.3.45–8.

84 **Fall parti-coloured** drop (give birth to) mottled or dappled. See also Geneva Bible (1562) Genesis, 30.40: 'And Iaakob parted these lambes, and turned the faces of the flocke towards *these lambes* party coloured and all maner of blacke, among the shepe of Laban'; see also 31.8–12. Cf. Bishops' Bible Genesis, 31.10: 'But at ramming time I lifted vp mine eyes, and sawe in a dreame, & behold, the rammes leaped vpon the sheepe that were ring-straked, spotted, and partie.'

85 **blest** protected by supernatural influence (*OED* †3). See Genesis, 31.5, 'the God of my father hath bene with me', for an alternative way of describing the divine act of blessing.

86 **thrift** the act of thriving or prospering (*OED sb.*[1] †1), but in this context meaning profit or material gain; cf. 1.1.175.

87 **venture** undertaking of a hazardous or risky nature (*OED* 3)
served for rendered service for, or was obedient with the objective of achieving (*OED* †9). In the biblical narrative Jacob is in service to Laban, initially for

the hand of the latter's daughter Rachel (Genesis, 29–30). Antonio insists that Jacob's reward is the result of labour or toil that was generally thought to be inimical to the practice of taking of interest (cf. Cam[2], 75).

89 **swayed and fashioned** controlled and contrived. The emphasis upon the controlling power of God ('the hand of heaven'), is reinforced by the marginal gloss in the Geneva Bible (1562) to Genesis, 31.9: 'This declareth that the thing, which Jacob did before, was by Gods cōmandement & not through deceite.'

90 **inserted** introduced (into the narrative) (*OED* 1b). Antonio presses further the issue of the Jew's *reading* of Scripture, and hence questions the validity of the latter's interpretation of Jewish history.
make interest good justify the effectiveness of interest (cf. Onions, 95), but also *good* in a moral sense. The question insinuates contempt for an alleged 'gilding' of a narrative whose details Venice regards as disreputable, but there is an irony here because Antonio denies vehemently a practice to which he must now have recourse.

91 **gold . . . rams** Antonio is questioning the Jew's *allegorical* interpretation of Scripture by asking if *ewes and rams* are, metaphorically speaking, gold and silver, where 'ewes' might also echo the pronunciation 'Jews' ('Iewes').

JEW

I cannot tell, I make it breed as fast.

But note me, signior.

ANTONIO [*aside*]   Mark you this, Bassanio,

The devil can cite Scripture for his purpose.

An evil soul producing holy witness   95

Is like a villain with a smiling cheek,

A goodly apple, rotten at the heart.

O, what a goodly outside falsehood hath!

JEW

Three thousand ducats, 'tis a good round sum.

---

92 **I cannot tell** I don't know, or I have no opinion. Pooler glosses: 'a polite way of maintaining one's own view while seeming to refuse to dogmatize' (Ard¹, 37). The Jew's resistance takes the form of a pragmatic response to what is essentially a *theological* point proffered by Antonio.
breed The Jew establishes a circumstantial, if tentative, connection between the natural act of 'breeding' and the increase of his wealth. Comments on the unnaturalness of wealth accumulation stretch back as far as Aristotle. (See LN.)

93 **note me** observe me. But see *JC* 4.3.2–3, 'You have condemned and noted Lucius Pella / For taking bribes here of the Sardinians' (Daniell, *JC*, 350), where to 'note' is also to 'defame'. In what follows it is Antonio's contention that the Jew condemns himself out of his own mouth. Mahood suspects some stage business here, speculating that Antonio may have turned away from the Jew, who then needed to reclaim his attention (Cam², 75).

94 **devil . . . Scripture** In addition to being associated with beasts (*ewes*, 91), the Jew is also a *devil* who can manipulate meanings; cf. the proverbial 'The DEVIL can cite Scripture for his purpose' (Dent, D230). See

also *Jew of Malta*, 'And know that I am Machevil, / And weigh not men, and therefore not men's words' (Prologue, 7–8), and later, where the allegation of misuse of Scripture is turned against the Christians by Barabas: 'What! Bring you scripture to confirm your wrongs?' (*Jew of Malta*, 1.2.111). See also Strickland, 106–7.

95–7 The logic of Antonio's reasoning here begins from the assumption of the Jew's *evil soul* and then proceeds deductively to draw conclusions about his appearance.

95 **holy witness** sacred testimony, i.e. Holy Scripture. Ironically, in this response Antonio appeals to proverbial lore.

97 **goodly** having the appearance of beauty (*OED* 1 and †1 *obs.*). The image of fruit rotten from the inside out is present in *MA* 4.1.31–2: 'Give not this rotten orange to your friend; / She's but the sign and semblance of her honour.'

98 **goodly** as in Q, but Rowe emends to 'godly'. Brown prints 'goodly' but notes, following Dyce, that this may be a compositorial error emanating from the word having been caught from the line above (Ard², 27). See Genesis, 39.6, 'And Joseph was a goodly person and a well fauoured', glossed in the Geneva Bible (1562) as 'a faire personne'.

---

93 SD] *Keightley subst (after 98)*   98 goodly outside] *(goodly out-side), Q2, F;* godly outside *Rowe*   hath!] *Keightley;* hath. *Q*

Three months from twelve, then let me see the rate.   100

ANTONIO

Well, Shylock, shall we be beholding to you?

JEW

Signior Antonio, many a time and oft
In the Rialto you have rated me
About my moneys and my usances.
Still have I borne it with a patient shrug,   105
For sufferance is the badge of all our tribe.
You call me misbeliever, cut-throat dog,

---

101 **beholding** an obsolete form of 'beholden', meaning indebted or obligated (*OED* †1)

102 **many . . . oft** on a number of occasions. The Jew emphasizes that he has been very frequently harassed; cf. *1H4* 1.2.48–9: 'Well, thou hast called her to a reckoning many a time and oft.'

103 **rated** berated, reproved or scolded (*OED v.*² 1), but also with the pun on 'rate'. Cf. *rate of usance* (41) and the *OED v.*¹ 2 gloss: 'to reckon, calculate, estimate the amount or sum of'. The Jew implies that he has himself been *evaluated* because of his financial practices.

104 **moneys** sums of money, but also used as plural frequently in a legal sense (*OED* 4). See also *OED* 4¶ where it is suggested that this term was frequently attributed to Jews 'whose supposed pronunciation is sometimes ridiculed by the spelling "monish"'.

usances practices of lending or borrowing money at interest (*OED* †4). Cf. also *rate of usance* (41) and Lodge: 'I must haue ministers, wher by that which I look for may be brought to my hands: otherwise my stocke might lye without vsaunce to my vtter vndooing' (Lodge, 1.10).

105 **shrug** gesture of raising the shoulders, associated with forbearance. Malone cites *Jew of Malta*, 2.3.23–4:

'I learned in Florence how to kiss my hand, / Heave up my shoulders when they call me dog.'

106 **sufferance** patient endurance in order to withstand calumny (*OED* I.1–4). The sentiment is proverbial: Dent, S955, 'Of SUFFERANCE comes ease'. Cf. also *Jew of Malta*, 1.2.240: 'Be silent, daughter; sufferance breeds ease.' Q's spelling 'suffrance' requires it to be pronounced as a disyllable.

badge emblem or symbol but also an insignia of allegiance; cf. *Son* 44: 'But heavy tears, badges of either's woe'. The Jew identifies himself here as part of a group (*tribe*) whose insignia bear all the marks of persecution. See also Sanders, for the suggestion that since 1215 the formal badge of the Jew was 'a circle of yellow cloth on the arm' (Sanders, 351).

107 **cut-throat dog** inhuman murderer. The Jew is quoting the Christian myth of the thoroughly degenerate theological (as opposed to the actual) Jew, guilty of blood-lust and an agent of Satan in entrapping unwary Christians. See Trachtenberg, who also records the case of Münzmeister Lippold, the mint-master and financier of Elector Joachim II of Brandenberg. After the latter's death on 3 January 1571, Lippold was arrested, and confessed on 16 January 1573 to having conjured

---

101 beholding] beholden *Pope*   103 Rialto] *(Rialto)*   106 sufferance] *(suffrance), Q2*

And spit upon my Jewish gaberdine,
And all for use of that which is mine own.
Well, then, it now appears you need my help.   110
Go to, then, you come to me, and you say,
'Shylock, we would have moneys.' You say so.
You, that did void your rheum upon my beard
And foot me as you spurn a stranger cur
Over your threshold, moneys is your suit.   115

up the devil, who appeared 'once as a black dog, and again in human shape' (Trachtenberg, 84).

108 *spit Q's reading is 'spet', emended in F3 to 'spit' and subsequently modified by Rann to 'spat'. 'Spet' is a common form of the present or past tense of the verb, but *OED* notes that its modern usage is now only in dialect.
gaberdine a loose upper garment made of course material (*OED* 1); cf. *Tem* 2.2.36–7: 'My best way is to creep under his gaberdine.' Furness notes that this was not a specifically Jewish garment (Furness, 47–8). (See LN.)

109 use deployment or use in the modern sense, but also 'use' in the sense of advantage, or taking profit by way of interest (usury) (*OED* 5b). (See LN.)
that . . . own proverbial (Dent, 099), 'May we not do with our OWN what we list?', and also Matthew, 20.15: 'Is it not lawfull for me to doe that I wil with mine owne? Is thine eye euill, because I am good?' There is an irony in the Jew's quoting from the New Testament.

111 Go to normally an idiomatic gesture of protest (Onions) and perhaps also, as in this case, an expression of mild incredulity

112 Shylock the first time in the play that he articulates his own name. The Jew here parodies the speech of his Christian adversary, and this inaugurates a tension between 'Christian' name and stereotype that is sustained orthographically and ideologically throughout the play. See pp. 17 and 47.

You say so an apparently redundant sentence but both indicative of the Jew's distinctive repetitions and also possibly a gesture of mimicry

113 void your rheum evacuate or clear ('void': *OED v.* 2†b) bodily mucus ('rheum': *OED sb.*[1] 1–2); hence, spit phlegm
beard The Jew may be referring here to a part of his theatrical costume. See Trachtenberg, who suggests that the '*Zeigenbart*' (goat's beard, or goatee) 'is intended to identify the Jew as the human goat' (Trachtenberg, 46–7); and see also Strickland, 111.

114 foot kick or trample. This precise meaning is not recorded in *OED* but it combines the sense of trample underfoot (*OED sb.*[1] 33a) with the more general sense of subjection.
stranger cur alien dog (cf. 'cur': *OED* 1b). See Caesar for a series of related metaphors used to describe the usurer: 'a wolfe in Lambes skinne, a Mermaide with a man's voice, a Iudas among good men, and is seldome knowen till his bloodic purpose taketh place' (Caesar, 4ʳ).

115 your suit that for which you petition. This is more than a simple request (Cam², 76), since it implies a legal process (*OED* 11†b), but it also glances obliquely at the purpose for the loan, Bassanio's solicitation for the hand of Portia ('suit': *OED* 12). The tone of the following lines is one of contempt because the Jew has caught his Christian adversary in a contradiction.

108 spit] *F3;* spet *Q;* spat *Rann*   115 moneys] *(moneyes);* money *Q2*

What should I say to you? Should I not say,
'Hath a dog money? Is it possible
A cur can lend three thousand ducats?' Or
Shall I bend low and in a bondman's key,
With bated breath and whispering humbleness,   120
Say this: 'Fair sir, you spat on me on Wednesday last,
You spurned me such a day; another time,
You called me dog: and, for these courtesies,
I'll lend you thus much moneys.'

ANTONIO

I am as like to call thee so again,   125
To spit on thee again, to spurn thee too.
If thou wilt lend this money, lend it not
As to thy friends, for when did friendship take

119 **bend low** bow, but in the sense of abase or subject (myself) (*OED* 4†d)
bondman's key the tone of voice (*key*) of one who is legally bound in service to a superior, hence a slave ('bondman': *OED* 2)
120 **bated breath** restrained breathing (Onions)
121 **spat** See 108n. Q reads 'spet', but unlike the earlier example this spelling is sustained throughout F2–4; cf. also 126.
122 **spurned** treated with disdain by kicking (*OED v.*[1] †2)
such a day A modern gloss would be the relatively unspecific 'such and such a day' (contrasted with 121's *on Wednesday last*).
123 **courtesies** civilized behaviour, although the tone here is heavily ironic. The train of metaphors that the Jew pursues relies upon *inversions* of the social norm and emphasizes the Venetians' perception of him as an animal: *dog, spat, spurned*.
125 **as like** just as likely

127–8 **lend ... friends** a reference to the Old Testament injunction against loaning money at interest to kin; cf. Deuteronomy, 23.19–20: 'Thou shalt not hurt thy brother by usurie of money, nor by usurie of corne, nor by usurie of any thing that he may bee hurt withall. / Unto a stranger thou mayest lende upon usurie, but not unto thy brother: that the Lord thy God may blesse thee in all that thou settest thine hand to, in the land whither thou goest to possess it.' Brown (Ard[2], 29) quotes Wilson: 'God ordeyned lending for maintenaunce of amitye, and declaration of loue, betwixt man and man: wheras now lending is vsed for pryuate benefit and oppression, & so no charitie is vsed at all, as though there were no god to iudge, nor lyfe to come' (T. Wilson, *Usury*, N[7]).
128–9 **take ... friend** *take* = receive (Onions) or accept; deployed by Antonio as part of a commonplace distinction between lawful 'breeding' and the form of sterile breeding that was associated with usury. See LN.

117 money?] monies; *Keightley* 118 can] *Q*; should *F* 120 whispering] *(whispring)*, *Q3* 121] *Malone lines* Say this: / last / spat] *Oxf*; spet *Q*; spit *Pope* Wednesday last] wendsday last *Q2*; last *Wednesday* / *Pope* 122 day; ... time] *F*; day ... time, *Q1, Q2* 124 moneys.'] *(moneyes.)*; monies. *Q2*; monies? *Theobald* 126 spit] *F3*; spet *Q*; spat *Rann* 128 friends] friend *F2*

216

A breed for barren metal of his friend?
But lend it rather to thine enemy,   130
Who, if he break, thou mayst with better face
Exact the penalty.

JEW

Why, look you, how you storm.
I would be friends with you and have your love,
Forget the shames that you have stained me with,   135
Supply your present wants and take no doit
Of usance for my moneys, and you'll not hear me.
This is kind I offer.

129 **for** for the sake of gaining (cf. Abbott, 103). Although F emends to 'of', 'for' is used in Q as a preposition expressing a causal relation; see *R3*, 1.4.80–1: 'And for unfelt imaginations / They often feel a world of restless cares.'

131 **break** Onions glosses this as 'become bankrupt' (cf. *OED* 11), but see also *OED* 15b for the meaning of sever or default on a contract of any kind. Both meanings are active in a causal relationship in Antonio's utterance.
       better face with justification; a possible reference to the Jew's alleged capacity for deception as described by Bell: 'usurers be lyars and periured persons; as who by ioyning periurie to leasing, seeke to increase their sauage and brutish dealing' (Bell, B4).

133 **storm** make a fuss, or rage (*OED v.*3); possibly an implied stage direction indicating the manner of delivery of Antonio's speech from 125–32

134 This appeal for friendship may be pejorative. Brown (Ard², 29) quotes Bell's description of the usurer's change of manner once he has secured a deal with his victim: 'so soone as the silly poore man maketh mention of usurie, and willingly offereth the surplus aboue the principall, he abateth his sowre countenance, and he ginneth to smile; then at the length hee remembreth paternall [*illegible word*] and calleth him neighbour and friend' (Bell, B3ᵛ).

135 **stained** disfigured or disgraced, but also discoloured (*OED* 4 and 5c). Jews were sometimes associated with blackness; see Hall, who later neglects the figure of the Jew in the play and concentrates on Morocco (Hall, *Things*, 165–6). The Jew refers both to a moral *and possibly* a physical taint that the racial prejudices of the Venetians have constructed for him.

136 **doit** a former Dutch coin equivalent to half a farthing (Onions); in modern British money a quarter of an old pre-1971 penny, a derisory sum

137 **usance** See 104n.

138 **kind** generosity (kindness), but of somebody from the same family (*OED sb.* 11 and 12). This gesture of brotherly friendship to Antonio invokes a more sinister meaning in its inadvertent (and perhaps even perverse) allusion to the *deed of kind* (81n.). Any reading of this line must balance these competing meanings which are active in this context.

129 for barren metal] (for barraine mettaile*)*; of barraine metall *F*   132 penalty] penalties *F*   133 look you] *om. Pope*   storm.] (storme,*)*; storm? *Pope;* storm! *Malone*   136 doit] (doyte*)*; doite *F* 137–8] *Collier lines* monies, / offer. /   137 usance] (vsance*)*; Usage *Rowe*   138 is] sure is *Hanmer*   offer] offer you *Keightley*

BASSANIO

    This were kindness.

JEW   This kindness will I show.

    Go with me to a notary, seal me there   140

    Your single bond, and, in a merry sport,

    If you repay me not on such a day,

    In such a place, such sum, or sums, as are

    Expressed in the condition, let the forfeit

    Be nominated for an equal pound   145

    Of your fair flesh, to be cut off and taken

    In what part of your body pleaseth me.

139 **were kindness** would be kindness (in the sense of generosity).
Cf. *1H4* 5.2.1–2: 'O no, my nephew
must not know, Sir Richard, / The
liberal and kind offer of the King.'
The repetition of this word, in the
Jew's riposte in the second half of
the line, and Antonio's response later
at 149, ensures that the full range
of meanings, positive and negative,
of 'kind'/'kindness', remains in play
throughout this exchange.
140 **notary** clerk or secretary (*OED sb.*
†1), but also somebody in an official
capacity who has the authority to draw
up legal documents (*OED* 2), much in
the manner of a modern lawyer
141 **single bond** legally binding agreement given the name of *simplex obligatio* by Blackstone: 'whereby the obligor
obliges himself, his heirs, executors,
and administrators, to pay a certain
sum of money to another at a day
appointed. If this be all, the bond is
called a single one, *simplex obligatio*'
(Blackstone, 2.340).
    merry sport jocular game. The Jew
adds a condition to this bond (see
144–7) but follows closely the anonymous *Ballad of Gernutus* in which
'The Jew' proposes 'a merry ieast, /

for to be talked long'. This 'merry
sport' is endowed with symbolic overtones that are reminiscent of medieval
carnivalesque rituals (see Chambers,
Medieval, 1.157–9) and reach darkly
into the religious antagonism between
Jew and Christian in the play (see
Laroque, 274).
145 **nominated for** named as being
(Abbott, 148)
    equal exact or having identical value
(*OED a.*1), which is in itself an impossible concept, but also fair, just and
impartial from the Latin *aequus* (*OED*
†5). Cf. also *KJ* 2.1.483–5: 'If that
the Dolphin there, thy princely son,
/ Can in this book of beauty read "I
love", / Her dowry shall weigh equal
with a queen', where two incompatible
components are being forced into the
same standard of value.
146 **fair flesh** light-coloured flesh (*OED*
II.6). Furness suggests that this may
indicate that the Jew's physical appearance is of 'a darker, Oriental hue'
(Furness, 52). Cf. 3.1.34–6.
144–7 These are the terms the Jew
attaches to the bond, and their exag-
geratedly 'festive' nature makes the
bond preposterous from the outset.
(See LN, 'let . . . me'.)

139 SP BASSANIO] *(Bass.); Ant. Q3*   This . . . This] Ay, this *Capell*   142–6, 149, 153–5, 158–60,
162–3] *Verse lines begin with lower-case letter in Q*   147 body] bodie it *F*

ANTONIO

Content, in faith: I'll seal to such a bond
And say there is much kindness in the Jew.

BASSANIO

You shall not seal to such a bond for me;   150
I'll rather dwell in my necessity.

ANTONIO

Why, fear not, man, I will not forfeit it;
Within these two months, that's a month before
This bond expires, I do expect return
Of thrice three times the value of this bond.   155

JEW

O, father Abram, what these Christians are,
Whose own hard dealings teaches them suspect
The thoughts of others. [*to Bassanio*] Pray you tell
    me this:
If he should break his day, what should I gain

---

148 **seal to** authenticate or confirm (Onions). The process of sealing usually involved the act of appending a signature or affixing a wax seal (*OED* v.[1] 1b, 1c), but here it may simply mean 'come to a formal agreement'.

151 **dwell . . . necessity** continue or remain (Onions) within the constraining power of circumstance (*OED* 3) i.e. remain without the financial means to pursue my venture. Mahood notes that the end-rhymes *me*/*necessity* in 150–1 serve to add emphasis to Bassanio's words (Cam², 77).

154 **expect return** anticipate a profit (consequent upon the return of Antonio's argosies)

156 **father Abram** Abraham, the father of the Jews (see also 68n.). Cf. Genesis, 17.3–5: 'Abram fell on his face, and God talked with him saying, / It is I, beholde, my couenant is with thee, and thou shalt be a father of many nations.

/ Neither shall thy name any more be called Abram, but thy name shall be called Abraham: for a father of many nations haue I made thee.'

157 **teaches them suspect** teaches them to suspect; modern English would conjugate the verb in the singular case, but Abbott, 333, is of the view that this plural form, common in F, has its origin in the northern Early English dialect. The modern sense would be: 'teach them to be suspicious (of)'.

159 **break his day** fail to fulfil the conditions of the bond on the day specified. The double meaning of *break* allows the Jew to speculate rhetorically upon Antonio's failure to meet his obligation, and hence his inability to honour the conditions of the bond (*OED* III.15c), while also gesturing towards the possible consequences of that failure, i.e. his bankruptcy (*OED* 11b)

---

155 this] the *Capell*   156 Abram] *Abraham* / *Rowe*   157 dealings] dealing *F2*   suspect] to suspect *Pope*   158 others.] *(others:); others! Pope*   SD] *Oxf*

By the exaction of the forfeiture?   160
A pound of a man's flesh, taken from a man,
Is not so estimable, profitable neither,
As flesh of muttons, beeves or goats. I say
To buy his favour I extend this friendship;
If he will take it, so; if not, adieu,   165
And for my love, I pray you, wrong me not.

ANTONIO

Yes, Shylock, I will seal unto this bond.

JEW

Then meet me forthwith at the notary's;
Give him direction for this merry bond,

160 **exaction . . . forfeiture** demanding (*OED* 1) of the penalty for failing to honour the bond ('forfeiture': *OED* 2†b and 3)

162 **estimable** capable of being estimated or valued (*OED* †1), but also applied to persons in order to indicate worthiness of esteem or regard (*OED* 3). *Estimable* and *profitable* are not synonyms here, but distinctions that indicate the way in which the Jew is capable of returning with subtlety the insults of his adversary's low estimation of him.

163 **muttons . . . goats** at first sight, a series of common Elizabethan plurals (cf. Ard², 30). However, while 'beefs' and 'goats' are common forms, e.g. *2H4* 3.2.322, 'and now has he land and beefs' (derived from the French *boeuf*), 'muttons' is an unusual plural in Shakespeare. While the dominant sense here is 'sheep', the secondary meaning of 'prostitutes' reinforces the scandalous nature of the Jew's financial dealings as perceived by the Christians in the play; cf. *MM* 3.2.174–5: 'The Duke, I say to thee again, would eat mutton on Fridays.' Similarly, *goats* were associated both

with Jews (see 113n. on *beard*) and with lechery; cf. *Oth* 3.3.406: 'Were they as prime ['sexually charged', so *Othello*, ed. Honigmann, 235 and 338] as goats, as hot as monkeys'.

164 **buy his favour** purchase his good opinion (*OED sb*.1: 'favour'), but see also *OED sb*. 3†b for the gloss: 'lenity, mildness, mitigation of punishment'.

166 ***for . . . not** Q omits punctuation after 'love' (see t.n.), although modern editors follow Theobald and insert a comma. Mahood's gloss of the phrase *for my love*, 'for my sake' (Cam², 78), does not quite catch the full force of the line's symmetry, or of the apparent obsequiousness implied in the Jew's parenthetic clause *I pray you*, just as Clarendon rejects the gloss 'in return for my love'. It is clear that central to the line is a logic of exchange, but also there is an implication that the bargain agreed upon might not be kept, and that Christians are not to be trusted. The Q form submits to the following gloss: 'I beg you not to return a wrong to me for the love that I offer you [because this is not the bargain I intend].'

169 **merry bond** joke, parody of a customary financial agreement; see 141n.

162 profitable neither] or profitable *Pope*   163 beeves] *(beefs)*   goats.] *(Goates,)*; Goats, *Q2*   165 it, so;] *Rowe;* it so, *Q*   not,] *Q3;* not *Q*   166 love, I] *Theobald;* loue I *Q*   168 notary's;] *(Noteries,)*; Notaries, *F*

And I will go and purse the ducats straight,   170
See to my house, left in the fearful guard
Of an unthrifty knave, and presently
I'll be with you.   *Exit.*
ANTONIO   Hie thee, gentle Jew.
The Hebrew will turn Christian, he grows kind.
BASSANIO
I like not fair terms and a villain's mind.   175
ANTONIO
Come on, in this there can be no dismay,
My ships come home a month before the day.   *Exeunt.*

170 **purse . . . straight** straightaway place the ducats in a purse. The usual meaning of *purse* here would be to pocket, or confine (*OED v.* 1), but the Jew's use of a term earlier used by Antonio himself as a noun lends an additional resonance to *purse* (see 1.1.138); the Jew will now become Antonio's *purse*, suggesting a perverse (and sterile) repetition of the Antonio–Bassanio relationship.

171 **fearful** unreliable or timorous. See Abbott, 3, for examples of adjectives used in this way in both passive and active senses. Cf. *3H6* 2.2.30, 'Which sometime they have us'd with fearful flight', and *3H6* 5.6.86–7: 'For I will buzz abroad such prophecies / As Edward shall be fearful of his life.'

172 **unthrifty** good-for-nothing, but also with the subsidiary meaning of someone who is careless of the business of making profit and conserving his means, hence a prodigal (*OED* 2 and 3) **knave** male servant or menial (Onions)

173 **Hie thee** make haste (*OED* 2†b) **gentle** a possible pun on 'Gentile' (cf. Cam², 78), suggesting a contradiction in terms: a Jew who is a Gentile. But see Monsarrat for the suggestion

that 'gentle' and 'Gentile', though possibly homophonic, were clearly distinguished and that the meaning of the latter – 'of or pertaining to any or all of the nations other than the Jewish' (*OED* 1) – conflicts with the mood of this exchange, where the primary meaning of *gentle* seems to be 'kind' and 'generous' (Monsarrat, 4).

174 **he grows kind** *kind* in the sense of well disposed or benevolent (*OED* 3). But, bearing in mind the earlier play on *kind, kin* and *kindness* (138–9), the association of Christianity with generosity smacks of a certain self-congratulation.

175 **fair . . . mind** proverbial, as in Dent, F3, 'Fair FACE foul heart', and F29, 'FAIR without but foul within', for the contrast between outward attractiveness and inner corruption. Placed at the end of this exchange, Bassanio's reservation exposes to question the foregoing *bond*, but it also suggests that the Jew is associated with an inner 'blackness' that reinforces his position as an outsider.

176 **no dismay** no need to fear (*OED v.*[1] †3)

177 **month . . . day** month before their due date of arrival

173–4] *Q3; Q lines* turne / kinde. /   173 I'll] *Rowe*; Ile *Q; I will Warburton*   SD] *Exit* SHYLOCK. *(after* Jew.) *Capell*   174 The] This *F*   grows kind.] grows so kinde *Q2*   175 terms] teames *F*

[2.1]   *Enter [the* Prince of] MOROCCO, *a tawny Moor,*
         all in white, and three or four Followers accordingly,
             with PORTIA, NERISSA *and their train.*

MOROCCO
     Mislike me not for my complexion,
     The shadowed livery of the burnished sun,
     To whom I am a neighbour and near bred.
     Bring me the fairest creature northward born,

2.1 Rowe sets this scene in '*Belmont*' and Capell specifies '*A Room in* Portia's *House*'. Cam[1] adds '*The Hall of Portia's house*'.

0.1 *tawny Moor* a 'brown-skin native of foreign lands' (*OED obs.* but first usage dated 1603). See also the combination of 'tawny + moor' as 'blackamoor' (*OED sb.*[2]). Modern editors distinguish between 'blackamoor' or an Ethiopian African (*OED* 1), and *tawny* or brown-skinned Moor (Ard[2], 32).

0.2 *white* the visual contrast here is primarily moral and proverbial (Dent, B440: 'To make BLACK white'). See Hall for analysis of 'the various aesthetic possibilities of the juxtaposition of black and white' (Hall, *Things*, 247–8).

three . . . Followers imprecision suggesting Shakespeare's foul papers as manuscript copy

accordingly in accord or harmony with (Onions) Morocco's dress and complexion

0.3 *train* See t.n. Furness suggests that F's addition, '*Flourish cornets*', indicates a playhouse origin for F (Furness, 274–5).

1 **Mislike me not** do not disapprove of me ('mislike': *OED v.* 3). Mahood perceives a similarity between the opening three lines of Morocco's speech and

the biblical Song of Solomon, 1.5 (Cam[2], 79).

for because of

complexion pronounced com-plex-i-òn: the emphasis possibly indicating the 'foreign' nature of Morocco's diction (Cam[2], 79)

2 **shadowed livery** shaded uniform caused by the heat of the sun, here used metaphorically to refer to the colour of Morocco's skin; *shadowed* = 'obscured or darkened by shadow' (*OED a.* 3); *livery* = 'a suit of clothes . . . bestowed by a person upon his retainers or servants and serving as a token by which they may be recognized' (*OED sb.* 2). Cf. *LLL* 4.3.249–51 for the moral and religious symbolism attached to the 'black' face.

the burnished sun the sun made bright and glossy as if by being polished (*OED v.*[1] 2 and 4).

3 **near bred** literally, reared in close proximity to, since geographically Morocco situates himself near to the equator, and hence close to the sun. See Ovid, *Met.*, 2.39, for a mythological explanation of the cause of 'blackness' emanating from Phaeton's loss of control of Jove's chariot.

4 **fairest . . . born** the fairest-skinned creature whose complexion is the result of living further from the equator

---

2.1] *Actus Secundus.* F; ACT II. SCENE I. *Rowe*   0.1 *the* Prince of] *Capell subst.*   MOROCCO] *Capell;* Morochus *Q;* Morochius *F2*   0.3 *train.*] *train. Flourish cornets.* F   2 burnished] *(*burnisht*)*   4 Bring me] Bring *Q2*

Where Phoebus' fire scarce thaws the icicles,   5
And let us make incision for your love,
To prove whose blood is reddest, his or mine.
I tell thee, lady, this aspect of mine
Hath feared the valiant; by my love I swear,
The best-regarded virgins of our clime   10
Have loved it too. I would not change this hue
Except to steal your thoughts, my gentle queen.

PORTIA

In terms of choice I am not solely led
By nice direction of a maiden's eyes.

5   **Phoebus' fire** figuratively, the heat of
the sun, but reinforcing the implied
suggestion that Morocco is closely
aligned to a deity, since Phoebus is the
sun-god.
6   **make incision** make a surgical cut
(as part of the medical practice of
bloodletting)
7   **blood is reddest** i.e. more virile and
therefore more manly; Morocco's proximity to *the burnished sun* (2) marks
him as more lustful than his imaginary
Caucasian counterpart, hence the
emphasis on *blood* (sexual passion). Cf.
Burton, 1.147–8; cf. also Portia's reference to *blood* at 1.2.17–18 as passion
requiring to be controlled by law.
8   **aspect** aspèct; both appearance
(Onions) and gaze (*OED* †1) •
9   **feared** frightened or terrified;
an example of an intransitive verb
being converted into a transitive verb
(Abbott, 291)
10 **best-regarded** most highly thought of
clime country or region (*OED* 2 and
2b)
11 **hue** external appearance of the face
and skin (*OED sb.* 2); or colour (*OED
sb.* 3), claimed to be archaic by 1600,
and here reinforcing the notion of
Morocco as a 'stranger' preoccupied
with external evidence that will determine his choice of caskets

12 **steal** gain possession of (*OED* 4f)
queen a term of endearment suggesting perfection (*OED* 6), and associating Morocco with the conventions
of courtly love and regal pedigree;
but also 'quean' meaning harlot or
strumpet (*OED* 1), aligning Morocco
with the stereotypically licentious
figure of the Moor. Morocco *intends*
the first meaning, but the homo-
nym 'quean' releases an alternative
unintended meaning. See Wheatcroft
for reference to the alleged 'sexual
excess and perversity' of Moors and
Turks in contemporary Renaissance
representations (Wheatcroft, 260).
13 **In . . . choice** in so far as choice is
concerned; Portia tells Morocco that if
she were allowed to choose she would
not be fooled by appearances.
14 **nice direction** particular or precise direction (*OED* 7b and 7d), but
implying subtlety (*OED* 9b). There
is a subsidiary gloss here of wanton,
loose-mannered or lascivious (*OED*
†2 *Obs*). It is uncertain to what
extent Portia may here be referring obliquely to the alleged sexual
proclivities of the Moor, or indeed
to her own capacity for sexual desire
that has necessitated the implemen-
tation of her dead father's 'law' (see
1.2.17–18).

6 incision] *(incyzion) Q1, Q2;* ineision *F*

Besides, the lott'ry of my destiny   15
Bars me the right of voluntary choosing.
But, if my father had not scanted me
And hedged me, by his wit, to yield myself
His wife who wins me by that means I told you,
Yourself, renowned prince, then stood as fair   20
As any comer I have looked on yet
For my affection.

MOROCCO   Even for that I thank you.
Therefore, I pray you, lead me to the caskets
To try my fortune. By this scimitar,
That slew the Sophy and a Persian prince,   25

15 **lott'ry** a game in which prizes, usually of a monetary nature, are distributed by chance (*OED* 1). Because of her father's stipulation, Portia thinks of herself as a monetary prize, thus underlining the material foundation of marriage.

16 **Bars me** prevents me from. For the omission of the preposition in relation to verbs of ablation, see Abbott, 198. Portia expresses her frustration at the constraint imposed upon her freedom to choose for herself.
right Portia would normally have the *right* to choose for herself, but her *destiny* is controlled, unusually, by the 'will' of her dead father.

17 **scanted** restricted or confined (*OED v.* 6), but also in the sense of being deprived of adequate provision (*OED v.* II.3)

18 **hedged** hemmed in, and hence constrained (*OED v.* 5b)
wit wisdom, or prudence (*OED* II.6), but also ingenuity (*OED* II. 5†b). See Hulme for the suggestion that *wit* is an obsolete gloss on 'testament' (Hulme, 47–50).
yield myself surrender myself to be, implying a severely restricted choice. Mahood's gloss, 'bestow my hand upon the man who' (Cam[2], 80), credits Portia

with an agency in the process which she has been denied.

20 **renowned** renownèd
then . . . fair would then appear as fair (skinned). Morocco's success in the game will transform his appearance; cf. Desdemona's and the Duke's responses to Othello in *Oth* 1.3.252–4 and 1.3.291–2.

21 **comer** visitor (*OED* 1)
yet so far

22 **For my affection** for the purpose of securing my affection (Abbott, 149); see also Abbott, 150, for an example of the use of 'for' as an ellipse of the act of wagering.

22–38 **Even . . . grieving** The style of Morocco's speech recalls Marlowe's *Tamburlaine*; cf. *Tamburlaine 1*, 5.2.2227–45 (see also Shapiro, 'Merchant', 273).

24 **scimitar** a large curved sword used especially by oriental or Turkish soldiers (see Wheatcroft, 259–73). Morocco's oath is sometimes accompanied in performance by an extravagant gesture, although here it is also a synecdoche for his warlike character.

25 **Sophy** the king of Persia, derived from the name Ismael Safî, who founded the dynasty about 1500 (*OED*)
***prince,** See t.n. The absence of

15 lott'ry] *(lottrie)*; Lotterie *Q3*   destiny] *Q2*; destenie *Q*; Destinie *Q3*   18 wit] will *Hanmer*   20 renowned prince] *Rowe; in parentheses Q*   then] *F2*; than *Q*   24 scimitar] *(Symitare)*; Semitaur *Q2*   25 prince,] *Q2*; prince *Q*

That won three fields of Sultan Solyman,
I would o'erstare the sternest eyes that look,
Outbrave the heart most daring on the earth,
Pluck the young sucking cubs from the she-bear,
Yea, mock the lion when 'a roars for prey,   30
To win the lady. But, alas the while,
If Hercules and Lichas play at dice

punctuation in Q suggests that it was Morocco who killed the Persian prince who had won land from the Sultan, and who thus becomes the antecedent of the relative pronoun *That* in 25. Q2's punctuation makes clear what is ambiguous in Q, that Morocco is enumerating his own military exploits, rather than commenting parenthetically on those of his victims.

26 **fields** either specific pieces of land (*OED sb.* 4), or the grounds on which battles are fought (*OED sb.* 6). Morocco seems to be referring to 'battlefields' rather than to the *three fields* that might have been a feudal reward for killing the Sophy and his prince; both meanings are plausible, but Morocco's egocentricity suggests the first rather than the second.
   of While following Q's punctuation at 25, Mahood glosses 'for' rather than 'from' (*Cam²*, 80). This gloss seems accurate, since it indicates that the relative pronoun *That* refers back to *scimitar* in 24, emphasizing its instrumental value. But it also indicates that Q2's emendation of punctuation at 25 clarifies an ambiguity in Q. Morocco asserts that his military exploits have resulted in the acquisition of land in the service of Sultan Solyman, and that, having proved his masculinity in battle, he is now free to embark upon a romantic exploit where the quarry is *the lady* (31).
   Sultan Solyman an echo of Kyd's *Soliman and Perseda* (1592): 'Against the Sophy in three pitched fields, /

Under the conduct of great Soliman, / Have I been chief commander of an host, / And put the flint heart Persians to the sword.' Shakespeare's recollection of this detail confirms Morocco's expressions of bravery and loyalty, indicating that it was he and not the *Persian prince* who won *three fields* for Solyman.

27 **o'erstare** literally, stare over; see *OED prep.* 4, where spatial sense combines with that of purpose. Q2's 'out-stare' meaning 'to outdo in staring' (*OED v.*) restricts the resonance in Q.

28 **Outbrave** surpass in any act of bravery (*OED v.* 2)

30 **'a** he

31 **the lady** Some modern editors follow Rowe and emend to 'thee(,) lady' on the grounds that Portia is the addressee (Ard², 34). There seems to be no reason to depart from the Q reading, since Morocco is speaking in a generalized 'heroic' register (see Warren, 104–5).
   alas the while an exclamatory expression of unhappiness (*OED*), here for Morocco's present predicament

32 **Hercules** the ancient Greek hero Heracles or Alcides (cf. 35), one of the Nine Worthies, noted particularly for his Twelve Labours, which are referred to and parodied in *LLL* 5.2.583ff.; see Sidney's *An Apology for Poetry* for the image of Hercules in love as a source both of 'delight and laughter' (G. Smith, 1.200). He was also the focus of Seneca's *Hercules Furens* translated by Jasper Heywood

---

27 o'erstare] *(ore-stare);* out-stare *Q2*   30 'a] he *Q2, F*   31 the lady] thee lady *Rowe*   alas the while,] *(alas, the while);* alas the while! *Pope*

Which is the better man, the greater throw
May turn by fortune from the weaker hand.
So is Alcides beaten by his rage,   35
And so may I, blind Fortune leading me,
Miss that which one unworthier may attain,
And die with grieving.

PORTIA   You must take your chance,
And either not attempt to choose at all,
Or swear, before you choose, if you choose wrong   40
Never to speak to lady afterward
In way of marriage; therefore be advised.

MOROCCO
Nor will not. Come, bring me unto my chance.

and edited by Thomas Newton in *Seneca His Ten Tragedies* (1581).
Lichas the servant who was instructed by Hercules' jealous wife Deianira to give him a shirt that was stained with the blood of the centaur Nessus. Hercules had killed Nessus for attempting to rape Deianira after agreeing to carry her across a river; see Ovid, *Met.*, 9.129ff. The shirt was alleged to have magical properties as a love-charm but was actually poisoned. See also Seneca, *Hercules Furens*, where Lychas is a tyrant who usurps the throne of Thebes and who provokes Alcides' insane rage in retribution for his crimes. See LN, 'Lichas . . . dice'.

33 **Which** [as to] which, or to decide which; used here in a loosely adverbial manner; cf. Abbott, 272.
   throw cast of the dice; a quibble here on a wrestling term (Ard², 34), since Hercules literally 'threw' Lichas into the sea

34 **may**, by the intervention of fortune, transform the *weaker hand* into the stronger of the two participants in the game
   turn . . . from result fortuitously in a change of direction (*OED* IV.13)

35 **beaten . . . rage** overcome by his anger. Theobald emended 'rage' to 'page', on the basis of Lichas' alleged youthful servile status (Theobald, 19–20), but no corroborating textual evidence supports this emendation, since in Plutarch's narrative Lichas was a social inferior rather than a young attendant. In *Hercules Furens*, Lychas was a tyrant who, along with Hercules' own family, bore the brunt of his rage. Morocco appears to conflate the two narratives.

36 **blind Fortune** In Renaissance iconography the goddess Fortune appears blind in order to indicate the random nature of her actions.

41 typical of the conditions imposed upon intending lovers in Shakespearean comedy; cf. *MND* 1.1.65. But this anticipates the later, more serious, condition imposed upon the Jew at 4.1.343ff.

43 **Nor will not** Morocco agrees to the full consequences of choosing wrongly; the ambiguity here suggests both agreement *and* a recognition that (like the raging Hercules) there is a risk of loss involved in relinquishing control.

33 man,] man? *Rowe*   35 rage] Page *Rowe;* wag *Cam¹*   42 marriage;] *F4;* marriage, *Q*   43 Come . . . unto] Come . . . to *Q2;* therefore . . . to *Pope*

PORTIA

First, forward to the temple; after dinner
Your hazard shall be made.

MOROCCO   Good fortune, then,   45
To make me blest or cursed'st among men.   *Exeunt.*

[2.2]   *Enter the* CLOWN[, *Lancelet Giobbe,*] *alone.*

CLOWN   Certainly, my conscience will serve me to run from

chance 'opportunity' (Onions), but also including the sense of that opportunity being controlled by fortune or accident (*OED sb.* †3). Q2 changes the metre with its emendation of the phrase 'unto my chance' to 'to my chance'.

44 **temple** a synonym for 'church' and not 'Morocco's 'pagan' term for church' (Cam², 81); cf. *MA* 3.3.154–8: 'away went Claudio enraged; swore he would meet her as he was appointed next morning at the temple.' See LN.

45 **hazard** venture or risk (*OED sb.* 2 and †4); also a winning opening on a 'real' tennis court into which the ball is served (*OED sb.* 6), suggesting that this is part of a game. It is a question of how disingenuous Portia's deployment of this term might be in the circumstances.

46 **blest or cursed'st** most blessed or most cursed; see Abbott, 398, for other examples of ellipsis of superlative inflections.

2.2 Rowe sets this scene in '*Venice*' and Theobald specifies '*A Street in Venice*'. Cam¹ embellishes: '*The street before Shylock's house*'.

0.1 CLOWN The role was played by the resident 'clown', possibly the comic actor Will Kempe, who later played Dogberry in *MA* (see Humphreys, 22–3; and Armstrong, 194–5), and who was a member of Shakespeare's

company until 1599.

Lancelet the predominant spelling in Q2 and F, and the SP adopted throughout in Folg, but the obsolete form 'Launcelet' is used exclusively in Q. *OED* records an obsolete meaning for 'launce' as a balance or scale (*OED sb.*¹; *OED sb.*² glosses 'launce' as a sand-eel). See List of Roles, 20n.

*Giobbe the Italianate form of 'Job', whose misfortunes in the Old Testament Book of Job were proverbial. In the interaction between the Clown and his father some comic reference may be intended to the misfortunes of the biblical Job. The spelling 'Iobbe' occurs in Q at sig. C1ʳ and is taken over by F. See pp. 23, 41.

1 **conscience** the faculty of mind that distinguishes between right and wrong (*OED* II.4) rather than simply 'consciousness of' (*OED* I 1†c). Belsey cites William Perkins's *A Discourse of Conscience* (1596), which defines 'conscience' as 'a moral arbiter whose function is "to iudge of the goodnes or badnes of thinges or actions"' (Belsey, 'Conscience', 128). It serves as a counterbalance to passion, which 'may blind moral judgment' (142).

serve me furnish me with morally sanctioned evidence that will allow me (to transfer my service from the Jew's house elsewhere). The activation of the Clown's 'conscience' recalls the

this Jew, my master. The fiend is at mine elbow and
tempts me, saying to me, 'Giobbe, Lancelet Giobbe,
good Lancelet', or 'Good Giobbe', or 'Good Lancelet
Giobbe, use your legs, take the start, run away.' My   5
conscience says, 'No; take heed, honest Lancelet, take
heed, honest Giobbe', or, as aforesaid, 'Honest Lancelet
Giobbe, do not run, scorn running with thy heels.' Well,
the most courageous fiend bids me pack. '*Via*,' says the
fiend, 'away,' says the fiend, 'for the heavens, rouse   10
up a brave mind,' says the fiend, 'and run.' Well, my
conscience, hanging about the neck of my heart, says

morality psychomachia (Ard², 35) in
which good and evil confront each
other. Lancelet's parodic version
involves a choice between two evils:
remaining with the Jew, or running
away.

2 **fiend** devil; a gross parody of the
temptation of Christ (Luke, 4.3ff.)
  at mine elbow Satan is visualized as
standing alongside Lancelet tugging at
his elbow and prompting him to run
away.

5 **take the start** get going, as in making a sudden or decisive movement
(*OED sb.*² 2†c); also, more generally,
to begin a course of action (*OED sb.*²
5). Mahood cites the Bible, 1 Peter,
2.18–19, as a possible source for this
dilemma (Cam², 82).

6–7 **honest … Giobbe** a parody of
legalistic language, which emphasizes
the Clown's name and his lineage; see
LLL: '*For Jaquenetta, so is the weaker
vessel called which I apprehended with
the aforesaid swain*' (*LLL* 1.1.259–60).
The repetition of *honest* comically
reflects the biblical Job's 'honesty' in
the face of adversity: Job, 27.3–4.

8 **scorn … heels** treat the suggestion
of running away with contempt. The

opposite of the proverbial 'He shows a
fair (clean) PAIR of heels' (Dent, P31).
See also 28.

9 **pack** depart or be off
  ***Via** Used with a verb 'it signifieth
away' (Florio, 598); a modern translation of this Italian expression might
be 'Let's go' or 'Come on'. Q's 'Fia'
may be an English dialect form used to
exhort horses and oarsmen, or the spelling may be influenced by the possibility
of alliteration with *fiend* (Ard², 36).

10 **for the heavens** an exclamation or
petty oath (Ard¹, 47) for which a modern equivalent might be 'For heaven's
sake'. Comically inappropriate, but
not, as Malone claimed, a sign of
textual corruption (Malone, 38, n. 6).

10–11 **rouse up** arouse, as though from
sleep or inactivity; cf. *Luc* 540–1. With
the ensuing phrase, *a brave mind*, it
may simply be an exhortation to courage or it may suggest that Lancelet
should aspire to a higher action, since
rouse up is also a hunting term; cf. *1H4*
1.3.195–6.

12 **hanging … heart** The Clown imagines his *conscience* to be a restraint,
as a pendant hanging either around
his neck or around his heart itself, or

3 tempts] attempts *F3*   3, 4 Giobbe] *(Iobbe)*; *Gobbo Q2*; Job *F3*   Lancelet Giobbe] *(Launcelet
Jobbe)*; *Lancelet Gobbo Q2*; *Launcelet Iobbe F*; *Launcelet Job F3*   4 Lancelet] *Launcelot / Rowe*   4–5
Giobbe … Lancelet Giobbe] *(Iobbe … Launcelet Iobbe)*; *Gobbo …Lancelet Gobbo Q2*; *Iobbe …
Launcelet Iobbe F*   6, 13, 17 Lancelet] *Q2*; *Launcelot / Rowe*   7 Giobbe] *(Iobbe)*; *Gobbo Q2*   7–8
Lancelet Giobbe] *(Lancelet Iobbe)*; *Launcelet Gobbo Q2*; *Launcelet Job F3*   9 Via] *Rowe;* Fia *Q*

very wisely to me: 'My honest friend Lancelet', being
an honest man's son, or rather an honest woman's son,
for indeed my father did something smack, something   15
grow to – he had a kind of taste – well, my conscience
says, 'Lancelet, budge not.' 'Budge,' says the fiend.
'Budge not,' says my conscience. 'Conscience,' say I,
'you counsel well. Fiend,' say I, 'you counsel well.' To
be ruled by my conscience, I should stay with the Jew   20
my master, who, God bless the mark, is a kind of devil;
and, to run away from the Jew, I should be ruled by the
fiend, who, saving your reverence, is the devil himself.
Certainly the Jew is the very devil incarnation, and,

in close proximity to it. See also *MA*
2.1.176–7: 'What fashion will you wear
the garland of? About your neck like a
usurer's chain?'

15 **did something smack** tasted (*OED
vb.* 2) a little of (honesty); but see also
OED vb.[2] in which 'smack' is a sound
made by the lips 'in connection with
eating or drinking esp. as a sign of keen
relish or anticipation'. The Clown suggests that his father was not entirely
honest, though he aspired to honesty.

15–16 **something grow to** somewhat
(*OED adv.* 7b) increase in size (*OED v.*
6b); a bawdy reference to the Clown's
father's sexual appetite in a reference
to erection prior to intercourse, but
checked in the interest of propriety and
displaced into the association with food
rather than sex before he abandons this
digressive train of thought altogether.

17 **budge not** stand firmly (*OED v.* 1)

19 **well** Q2 needlessly emends the second
'well' to 'ill'; the Clown manipulates
the terms of the debate in such a way
as to receive good counsel from *both*
sides of the argument.

21 **God . . . mark** a formulaic utterance
and an exclamatory invocation ('bless':
OED IV.9) designed to avert the pos-

sible evil consequences of mentioning
anything improper or disagreeable; see
OED 18 for the suggestion that it
was used by midwives at the birth of
a child bearing a distinctive mark or
blemish.

kind of devil part of a larger
theological discourse of racism.
See Trachtenberg, 193–4, and also
Strickland, 95–155, for the medieval
background to this image.

23 **saving your reverence** another formula, usually an apology, preceding an
improper or indelicate remark (Ard[2],
37); a translation of the Latin *salva
reverentia tua* (Ard[1], 48).

24 **devil incarnation** devil incarnate (i.e.
embodied in the flesh); the Clown's
malapropism suggests, comically,
that the devil may be pink. Cf. *1H5*
2.3.30–1. Also a possible reference
to the Venetian red head-dress (see
Roth, 154–5), a feature of Radford's
2004 production. Q2's emendation
produces the suggestively nonsensical 'incarnall' (presumably gesturing
towards the 'carnality' associated with
the world of the flesh and the devil)
but misses the allusion that comprises
the point of the joke.

16 to] too *Q2, F*   17 Lancelet] *(Launcelet), Folg;* om. *Q2*   budge] *(bouge)*   19 well . . . well] well
. . . ill *Q2;* ill . . . ill *Theobald*   21 who, God   mark] *Rowe;* (who God   mark) *Q;* who (God . . .
mark) *Q2*   23 saving . . . reverence] *in parenthesis Q2*   24 incarnation] incarnall *Q2*

in my conscience, my conscience is but a kind of hard   25
conscience, to offer to counsel me to stay with the Jew.
The fiend gives the more friendly counsel: I will run,
fiend, my heels are at your commandment; I will run.

Enter Old GIOBBE *with a basket.*

GIOBBE   Master young man, you, I pray you, which is the
     way to Master Jew's?   30
CLOWN [*aside*]   O, heavens, this is my true-begotten
     father, who, being more than sand-blind, high gravel-
     blind, knows me not. I will try confusions with him.

25 **in my conscience** in fairness, or 'by all that is right or reasonable' (*OED* 10), where *conscience* is identified as the source of moral imperatives. The Clown plays upon the precise and colloquial meanings of *conscience* in this and the following line.

25–6 **but . . . hard conscience** a moral injunction that, in the circumstances, is difficult to obey. The adjective *hard* is normally used in 16th-century theological debates in connection with 'the heart', but here the *hard conscience* is morally sound. Calvin identifies 'hardness' with the consequence of God declaring the sinner a reprobate (Calvin, *Genesis*, 312), but the Clown inverts this association. See LN.

26 **offer** dare or presume; cf. *TS* 5.1.56.

28 **heels . . . commandment** proverbial (Dent, P31); see 8. Q's spelling, 'commaundement', emended in Q2 to 'command', suggests that the Clown may have been required by the playtext to pronounce the medial 'e' (see Abbott, 488), in accordance with his use elsewhere of an inflated formal language. This, aligned with Q's spelling 'Launcelot' (see 0.1) may also indicate the Clown's pronuncia-

tion of the vowel 'a' as a diphthong 'au'.

28.1 **Old** GIOBBE the Italianate form of 'Job' is preferred here. See p. 166, 21n.

30 **Master Jew's** Brown, following Roth, suggests that the question is 'ludicrous' in its imprecision, since the Jewish Ghetto in Venice housed such a large number of Jews (Ard², 37).

31 **O, heavens** a comically inappropriate oath in this context in the light of the Clown's decision to take *the fiend's* advice at 27–8

true-begotten legitimate; this is not as nonsensical as some modern editors have thought, although the Clown may simply be parodying formal discourse.

32 **sand-blind** half blind or dim-sighted (*OED*); cf. Job, 29.15 (Bible): 'I was an eye to the blinde, and a foote to the lame.'

32–3 **high gravel-blind** a jocular intensive synonym for sand-blind (*OED*) to be distinguished from 'stone-blind', which would mean completely blind; used possibly here as an invented intermediate term

33 **try confusions** attempt to clear the matter up, but also, paradoxically, try to confuse. Q2 emends to 'conclusions',

25 but] *om. Q2, F*   28 commandment;] *(commaundement,); commandment, F; command, Q2*   28.1 GIOBBE] *(Gobbo); Gobbo, his Father, / Capell*   29+ SP] *this edn; Gobbo. Q; Gob. F; Fat./ Capell throughout*   29 young man] *Q2; young-man Q*   31 SP] *Capell (Clo.); Launcelet. Q; Launce. Q2; Lan. F;* LANCELET *Folg*   31 SD] *Johnson*   33 confusions] conclusions *Q2*

GIOBBE   Master young gentleman, I pray you, which is the
way to Master Jew's?   35

CLOWN   Turn up on your right hand at the next turning,
but, at the next turning of all, on your left. Marry, at
the very next turning, turn of no hand, but turn down
indirectly to the Jew's house.

GIOBBE   By God's sonties, 'twill be a hard way to hit. Can   40
you tell me whether one Lancelet, that dwells with him,
dwell with him or no?

CLOWN   Talk you of young Master Lancelet? [*aside*] Mark
me now, now will I raise the waters. [*to Giobbe*] Talk
you of young Master Lancelet?   45

thus bringing the Clown's sentiments
more in line with *Ham* 3.4.196–7, 'and
like the famous ape, / To try conclusions, in the basket creep', where
'try conclusions' may be glossed as
'experiment'.

34 **Master young gentleman** ironic
in this context, since the Clown is
himself 'mastered' and is therefore
emphatically not a *gentleman*

36–9 Theobald notes that these directions, which are designed to confuse,
imitate Syrus's directions to Deinea
in Terence's *Adelphi*, 4.2.42, especially since the Clown is standing
outside the Jew's house.

37 **Marry** to be sure; originally the
name of the Virgin Mary, frequently
deployed as an oath, 'By Mary',
but used here as an interjection
(Onions)

38 **turn . . . hand** do not turn either to
your left or to your right

38–9 **down indirectly** not in a straight
line, circuitously (*OED* 1); nonsense,
since if Giobbe turns neither left nor
right then he must go in a straight
line.

40 ***By God's sonties** by God's saints;
by the sanctity of God: an oath of
obscure origin (*OED*: 'santy' meaning 'sanctity'). Furness suggests a
Scottish origin: 'sauntie' (Furness,
66). Q uses the dialect form 'Be', not
emended to 'By' until F4.

hit come upon, in the sense of
reach (*OED* II.11), but see also *OED*
IV.20c for the gloss 'to strike the
scent in hunting'; a possible covert
reference to the myth of the *foetor
judaicus* – alleged to be a distinctive
Jewish male body odour similar to
that of a 'he-goat' (Trachtenberg,
48–9), or produced allegedly by
menstrual fluid – which could only
be eliminated by Christian baptism
(cf. Sanders, 42).

41 **that . . . him** who is a member of his
household

43 **Master Lancelet** a title signifying responsibility, but the Clown is
preening himself on the status of
'master' now being attributed to him

44 **raise the waters** provoke him to
tears; also, more generally, cause confusion

35 Jew's?] *Q2, F;* Iewes *Q; Jew's / Rowe*   36 up on] vpon *F*   39 to] vnto *Q2*   40 By] *F4;* Be
Q   41 Lancelet] *(Launcelet), Q2; Launcelot / Rowe*   43 Lancelet?] *Q2; Launcelet, Q;* Launcelot?
Steevens SD] *Dyce, after now Johnson, after* waters *Keightley*   44 SD] *(To him.) Collier*
45 Master] *(maister);* M. *Q2*   Lancelet?] *Q2; Launcelot. Q; Launcelot? F*

GIOBBE   No master, sir, but a poor man's son. His father, though I say't, is an honest, exceeding poor man, and, God be thanked, well to live.

CLOWN   Well, let his father be what 'a will, we talk of young Master Lancelet.   50

GIOBBE   Your worship's friend and Lancelet, sir.

CLOWN   But, I pray you, ergo, old man, ergo, I beseech you, talk you of young Master Lancelet.

GIOBBE   Of Lancelet, an't please your mastership.

CLOWN   Ergo, Master Lancelet. Talk not of Master   55
Lancelet, father, for the young gentleman, according to Fates and Destinies and such odd sayings, the Sisters Three and such branches of learning, is indeed deceased, or, as you would say in plain terms, gone to heaven.   60

46 **No master** not a gentleman or an 'esquire' (Furness, 66). Old Giobbe inadvertently undermines his son's fantasy of social status.
48 **well to live** well off; cf. *WT* 3.3.119–20: 'if the sins of your youth are forgiven you, you're well to live. Gold! all gold!' Furness glosses the phrase as indicating general health, 'with every prospect of a long life' (Furness, 67), but most modern editors stress the comic paradox of Giobbe claiming to be both an *exceeding poor man* and, at the same time, materially comfortable.
49 **'a** he
51 **Your . . . Lancelet** Giobbe here corrects the appellation *Master Lancelet* by emphasizing the correct social status of his son, whom he assumes to be a friend of the *gentleman* he thinks he is talking to.
52 **ergo** therefore (Latin), marking the conclusion of a formal logical argument. The Clown reasons, parodically, that, *because* his sand-

blind father assumes a relationship between Lancelet and the *gentleman* he thinks he is talking to, *therefore* (*ergo*) his son must be a *gentleman* and hence entitled to be addressed as *Master*.
55 **Ergo, Master Lancelet** a further emphasis on the issue broached in 51; if Giobbe confers the title of *Master* upon the Clown, then his son must be *Master Lancelet*, who then proceeds to 'lance' the pretension of status (see Parker, 95ff.).
57 **Fates and Destinies** a parodic reference to the supernatural powers that govern human behaviour (*OCD*, 1–3). See LN.
59 **deceased** *Master Lancelet* has never existed and so the Clown suggests that he is dead; this leads to a further comic confusion.
59–60 **gone to heaven** The word *deceased* is plainer than the phrase *gone to heaven* but comical here, since the Clown has already thrown in his lot with *the fiend* (27–8).

46–8] *Q2 lines* sonne. / (though . . . it) / man, / liue. /   48 God be thanked] (God be thanked) *Ard²*   50 Master] *Q2;* Maister *Q*   45, 50, 51 Lancelet] *(Launcelet), Q2;* Launcelot. / *Rowe*   51 sir] *om. F*   53 Lancelet.] *Launcelet? Q3*   53–6 Lancelet] *Q2;* Launcelet *Q*   54 an't] *Q2;* ant *Q*

GIOBBE   Marry, God forbid, the boy was the very staff of
my age, my very prop.

CLOWN [*aside*] Do I look like a cudgel, or a hovel post, a
staff, or a prop? [*to Giobbe*] Do you know me, Father?

GIOBBE   Alack the day, I know you not, young gentleman!   65
But I pray you tell me, is my boy – God rest his soul –
alive, or dead?

CLOWN   Do you not know me, Father?

GIOBBE   Alack, sir, I am sand-blind, I know you not.

CLOWN   Nay, indeed, if you had your eyes you might fail   70
of the knowing me: it is a wise father that knows his
own child. Well, old man, I will tell you news of your
son. [*Kneels.*] Give me your blessing, truth will come to
light, murder cannot be hid long; a man's son may, but
in the end truth will out.   75

GIOBBE   Pray you, sir, stand up. I am sure you are not

61–2 **staff . . . age** an echo of Psalm 23.4; see also the Bible's apocryphal book of Tobit, 10.4, where it is Tobias's mother who bewails his death. There is also, however, a pun on the Clown's name with *staff* meaning 'lance' or spear: the Clown is lamented as both the 'lance' and support or *prop* (*OED sb.*[1] 1f) of Old Giobbe.

63 **cudgel** club or thick stick used as a weapon (*OED* 1)
hovel post door-post or door-jamb (Furness, 68)

65 **Alack the day** an exclamation of dissatisfaction which is articulated as a reproach to the day itself (*OED* b); cf. *RJ* 4.5.23: 'She's dead, deceas'd! She's dead! Alack the day!'

70–1 **if . . . me** even if you had the use of your eyes you might still fail to recognize me; elsewhere in Shakespeare's texts the preposition 'of' usually follows the participle (Abbott, 178).

71–2 **it . . . child** reverses the proverbial (Dent, C309): 'It is a wise CHILD (father) that knows his own father (CHILD)'

73 **Give . . . blessing** a familiar request from son to father, but sometimes the subject of parody; the Clown invokes a biblical frame of reference in an oblique allusion to the Jew's invocation at 1.3.67–84 of the story of Esau's deception of his blind father Jacob in Genesis, 27.35.

73–4 **truth . . . light, murder . . . hid** an amalgamation of two proverbs: Dent, M1315, 'Murder will out'; and Dent, T591, 'TRUTH will come to light (break out)', which Brown (Ard[2], 39) traces to Thomas Kyd's *The Spanish Tragedy* (1594).

76 **stand up** an embedded stage direction indicating that the Clown kneels at 73 before asking for Giobbe's blessing

76–7 **not . . . boy** Possibly some stage business, involving Giobbe's tracing the contours of the Clown's face, is implied here, leading to the father's expression of incredulity.

63 SD] *Collier*   64 SD] *Collier (to him.)*   66 – God . . . soul –] *Dyce;* (GOD . . . soule) *Q;* God . . . soule *F*   68 Father?] *Q2;* father. *Q*   73 SD] *Collier*   74 murder] *F;* muder *Q; Murther Q2*   75 in the end] at the length *Q2*

Lancelet my boy.

CLOWN Pray you, let's have no more fooling about it, but
     give me your blessing. I am Lancelet, your boy that was,
     your son that is, your child that shall be.   80

GIOBBE I cannot think you are my son.

CLOWN I know not what I shall think of that. But I am
     Lancelet, the Jew's man, and I am sure Margery your
     wife is my mother.

GIOBBE Her name is Margery indeed. I'll be sworn, if   85
     thou be Lancelet, thou art mine own flesh and blood.
     Lord worshipped might he be, what a beard hast thou
     got! Thou hast got more hair on thy chin than Dobbin,
     my thill-horse, has on his tail.

CLOWN It should seem, then, that Dobbin's tail grows   90

79–80 **your boy . . . be** a characteristically garbled reference to temporal
order (past, present and future) but also
an echo of the *Gloria* from the Book
of Common Prayer: 'As it was in the
beginning, is now, and ever shall be.'
In identifying himself as 'your child
that shall be', the Clown is expressing
the intention of behaving like a son in
the future (cf. *OED sb.* II.8).

81 **think** believe it possible or likely [that]
(*OED v.²* III.12)

82 **think** meditate upon or cogitate (*OED
v.²* B.3). The Clown appropriates his
father's word, but exploits an alternative meaning.

86 **thou** Up to this point in the dialogue
Giobbe has addressed the Clown as
you (69, 76, 81), but once he acknowledges him as his son he uses the more
familiar *thou* (see Hope, 73–8).

87 **Lord . . . be** May the Lord be worshipped; the verb *might* is used opta-
tively (see Abbott, 313, and also Hope,
143). However, Pooler suggests that

'Lord' is a blasphemous exclamation
and that the clause 'worshipped might
he be' is introduced to soften the
charge of irreverence (Ard¹, 53).

89 *****thill-horse** derived from the Old
English 'þylle' meaning a pole by
which a wagon or cart was attached
to a horse, hence a shaft (*OED*). But
see also *OED sb.²* 1 for the alternative
'fill-', which was also current in the
16th-century but is now obsolete. A
thill-horse is a horse placed between
the shafts or 'thills' of a cart; cf. the
modern 'cart-horse'. Q prints 'philhorse', and Q2 emends to 'pilhorse'.
With the exception of Theobald and
Malone ('phill-horse'), editors have
alternated between 'pill-horse' (Pope)
and 'fill-horse'(Ard¹, 53; Cam², 85).

90–1 **tail grows backward** evidently the
sand-blind Giobbe has mistaken the
hair on the back of his son's head for a
beard; see Mahood's glossing of *beard*
at 87 (Cam², 85). However, the Clown
pursues the logic of his father's error

78 fooling] *Q2, F*; fooling, *Q*   79 Lancelet] *(Launcelet); Lancelot Q2; Launcelot / Rowe (throughout)*   86 blood.] *Johnson*; blood: *Q*; blood [*Taking hold of Launcelot's back hair*] *Dyce*; blood . . .
[*he feels for Lancelot's face; Lancelot bows and presents the nape of his neck*] *Cam¹*; blood. / *He feels
Lancelot's head. Oxf*   89 thill-horse] *Theobald*; philhorse *Q*; pilhorse *Q2*; fil-horse *Capell*; phill-
horse *Malone*; fill-horse *Dyce*

backward. I am sure he had more hair of his tail than I
have of my face when I last saw him. [*Stands up.*]

GIOBBE Lord, how art thou changed! How dost thou and
thy master agree? I have brought him a present; how
'gree you now?   95

CLOWN Well, well: but, for mine own part, as I have set
up my rest to run away, so I will not rest till I have
run some ground. My master's a very Jew. Give him
a present? Give him a halter! I am famished in his
service. You may tell every finger I have with my ribs.   100
Father, I am glad you are come. Give me your present

and adds a further dimension to the
comparison, indicating that for it to
hold good then the horse's tail would
have to retract, since, as far as he can
recall, the Clown has less hair on his
face than Dobbin has on his tail.

91–2 **had . . . him** The mixture of tenses
of the verb *have* here is confusing,
but the line may be glossed thus:
'Dobbin *had* more hair on his tail
than the Clown now *has* on his face,
judging from the time when he last saw
him.' The difficulty is created by the
awkward positioning of the adverbial
clause 'when I last saw him'.
of . . . of on . . . on (Abbott, 175);
a possible indication of the father's
unfashionable rusticity compared with
his son's urban sophistication (Cam[2],
85)

94 **agree** get on with each other, in the
sense of living harmoniously together
(*OED* 11)

94–5 **how 'gree you** how do you like
that; but also, how will my giving your
master a present improve relations; a
contraction of 'agree' not restricted
to the discourse of any one social class
(Ard[1], 54)

96–7 **set . . . rest** made up my mind, or
resolved (*OED sb.[2]* 7c), but also a
gambling expression meaning to stake

or hazard, as in staking one's future
hopes upon (*OED sb.[2]* 7a). See LN.

98 **run some ground** put some distance
between (myself and my master's
house)
very an intensifier indicating 'utter' or
'real', in the sense of complete
Jew a person of the Hebrew race
(*OED sb.* 1), but also more generally a term of opprobrium applied to
one who is a usurer, who drives hard
bargains, and who is crafty (*OED sb.*
2). See also *MA* 2.3.253–5, 'if I do not
love her, I am a Jew', where the general
meaning of faithless rogue seems to be
intended.

99 **halter** hangman's noose (*OED sb.[1]*
2), but also a strap or cord by which a
horse was tethered or led (*OED sb.[1]* 1),
suggesting that another of the Clown's
grievances is the extent to which he is
constrained ('tethered') in the Jew's
house

100 **service** employment
tell count; cf. *KL* 3.2.89: 'When usurers tell their gold i'th' field'. While
the Clown counts his ribs as a consequence of his starvation, the Jew is
counting his wealth.

101 **me** ethical dative (Abbott, 220)
signifying 'on my behalf' (see also
Hope, 100)

91 of his] on his *F*   92 have of my] have on my *F*   last] *Q2;* lost *Q*   SD] *this edn*   93 changed!] *Q2*
(*chang'd.*)*; changd. Q*   94 agree?] *Q2;* agree, *Q*   95 'gree] (*gree*)*; agree Q2*

to one Master Bassanio, who indeed gives rare new
liveries: if I serve not him, I will run as far as God has
any ground. O, rare fortune, here comes the man. To
him, Father, for I am a Jew if I serve the Jew any longer.   105

Enter BASSANIO *with a Follower or two*[, LEONARDO *among them*].

BASSANIO [*to a Follower*] You may do so, but let it be so
    hasted that supper be ready at the farthest by five of the
    clock. [*Gives him letters.*] See these letters delivered, put
    the liveries to making and desire Gratiano to come anon   109
    to my lodging.   [*Exit Follower.*]
CLOWN   To him, Father.
GIOBBE [*to Bassanio*] God bless your worship.
BASSANIO   Gramercy. Wouldst thou aught with me?
GIOBBE   Here's my son, sir, a poor boy –

102–3 **rare new liveries** splendid new
    uniforms; part of the general opu-
    lence referred to in the description
    in *Pecorone* of Giannetto (Bassanio)
    (Bullough, 1.464).
103–4 **as far . . . ground** to the ends of
    the earth; possibly proverbial (Cam^2,
    86), but no source has been identified
104 **rare fortune** unusual (*OED a.*^{1} 5)
    good luck (*OED sb.* 1)
105.1 a general entry probably indicative
    of the authorial origin of the copy (see
    p. 43); from the dialogue at 164 later
    this is the only time when Leonardo
    can enter.
106 **You . . . do so** Bassanio is clearly in
    the middle of a conversation; this is
    thus a 'realism' effect.
106–7 **so hasted** accelerated in such a
    way
107 **farthest** latest
109 **liveries to making** servants to their
    work (i.e. the preparations for supper);
    liveries is a metonymy for servingmen.

109–10 **Gratiano . . . lodging** Dover
    Wilson (Cam^1, 135) suggests that, in
    view of Gratiano's appearance onstage
    later at 164, this instruction suggests
    a 'loose end', since the action of the
    scene takes place in the street. Mahood
    thinks that such compression is 'a not
    unusual feature of continuous dra-
    matic composition' (Cam^2, 86).
110 SD Q2 has '*Exit one of his men*', a
    feature that inclined Furness (71) to
    the erroneous view that Q2 was the
    superior, and hence the earlier text.
113 **Gramercy** a contraction of 'God
    grant you reward', from the Old
    French *grant merci*; but also simply
    meaning 'Thank you' (*OED* 1) and
    hence a polite response to Giobbe's
    invocation of God's blessing
114 **poor boy** possibly intended as a
    term of fatherly affection, with an
    emphasis on neediness, although the
    Clown responds to two other less com-
    plimentary meanings: (1) a servant or

103 not him] him not *Rowe*   105.1 LEONARDO . . . them] *Theobald subst.*   106 SD] *Oxf subst.*   108
SD] *this edn*   110 SD] *Exit one of his men. Q2; to a Follower, who bows, and goes out. / Capell; Exit
a Servant. / Malone; the servant goes Cam*^{1} 112 SD] *Oxf*   113 Wouldst] *(wouldst); would'st F;*
would'd F3; would F4   me?] *Q2; me. Q*   114 SP] *(Gobbe)*

CLOWN [*to Bassanio*] Not a poor boy, sir, but the rich Jew's   115
    man that would, sir, as my father shall specify –
GIOBBE He hath a great infection, sir, as one would say,
    to serve.
CLOWN Indeed the short and long is, I serve the Jew, and
    have a desire, as my father shall specify –   120
GIOBBE His master and he, saving your worship's
    reverence, are scarce cater-cousins.
CLOWN To be brief, the very truth is that the Jew, having
    done me wrong, doth cause me, as my father – being, I
    hope, an old man – shall frutify unto you –   125
GIOBBE I have here a dish of doves that I would bestow
    upon your worship, and my suit is –
CLOWN In very brief, the suit is impertinent to myself, as

a slave (*OED sb.*[1] †3); (2) a knave or a
rogue (*OED sb.*[1] †4)
116 **man** an assertion of maturity, as well
as status, and a correlative of 'master'
(*OED sb.*[1] II.4c and 10c); the Clown
emphasizes that he is employed by the
rich Jew but hints that his anticipated
reward for his service is not forthcoming.
117 **infection** affection; a malapropism
indicating Giobbe's lack of familiarity
with the formal language of such a
request. Ironically, Giobbe's conditional qualification 'as one would say'
exposes a latent meaning of 'affection'
in its verbal form as 'affectation, the
act of affecting or assuming artificial-
ity' (*OED v.*[1] V.†13).
119 **short and long** proverbial (Dent,
L419: 'The LONG (short) of it
and the short (long) of it'), again
in keeping with the Clown's style of
incorporating a variety of proverbial
utterances into his discourse, but see
also *MND* 4.2.36: 'for the short and
long is'.
120 **desire** wish, request or petition

(*OED sb.*[4]); physical or sensual appetite
(*OED sb.*[2])
122 **scarce** barely; Brown (Ard[2], 41) suggests that there may be a quibble on
the word indicating stingy or parsimonious (*OED* 2).
    cater-cousins cousins who are so
distantly related that they are not
considered to be family at all. *OED*
suggests a derivation from 'cater' *sb.*[1]
and *v.*[1], meaning 'being catered for or
boarded together'.
125 **frutify** The word intended is
'verify', although it is here confused
with 'fructify' meaning 'to bear fruit'
(*OED*).
126 **dish of doves** ostensibly a gift
of food, since doves were used as
food in the 16th century (Cam[2], 87);
doves were also associated with erotic
desire, and hence with Venus, goddess
of love, whose chariot doves were said
to draw.
128 **impertinent** The Clown means
'pertinent'; another malapropism that
is part of the comic deflation of the
aristocratic discourse of polite request.

115 SD] *Oxf*   116, 120 specify –] *(*specifie.*)*; specify, – *Johnson*   121–2 he, saving . . . reverence,]
Rowe; he (sauing . . . reuerence) *Q*; he (savin . . . reverence) *F3*   122 cater-cousins] *(*catercosins*)*
125 you –] *Oxf*; you. *Q*; you, – *Warburton*; you . . . *Keightley*   127 is –] *Q2*; is. *Q*

your worship shall know by this honest old man, and
– though I say it, though old man, yet poor man – my   130
father.

BASSANIO   One speak for both. What would you?

CLOWN   Serve you, sir.

GIOBBE   That is the very defect of the matter, sir.

BASSANIO

[*to Clown*] I know thee well. Thou hast obtained
     thy suit.   135
Shylock thy master spoke with me this day
And hath preferred thee, if it be preferment
To leave a rich Jew's service, to become
The follower of so poor a gentleman.

CLOWN   The old proverb is very well parted between my   140
master Shylock and you, sir: you have the grace of
God, sir, and he hath enough.

BASSANIO

Thou speak'st it well. Go, father, with thy son.
[*to Clown*] Take leave of thy old master and enquire

130 **though . . . it** The Clown's idiom
  parodies that of the aspiring gentleman in its attempt at logical precision.
132 **One . . . both** let one of you speak
  for both of you
134 **defect** intending 'effect' or 'purpose'; an unwitting quibble, since in
  order to serve Bassanio the Clown has
  to *defect* or revolt from his service to
  the Jew (*OED v.* †1 and 2)
135 **obtained thy suit** secured your
  request; *suit* here is something that
  is pursued or hunted after (*OED sb.*
  II.†5) but also a legal action of 'suing'
  or 'petitioning' (*OED* II.11). The
  terms of the Clown's request are frivolous, but their legality is serious, since
  the request involves formal obligation.
137 **preferred** recommended, but also

with the implication of being advanced
in status or rank, or being promoted
(*OED v.* I.1)
140 **parted** divided (*OED ppl.* I.1)
141–2 **you have . . . enough** proverbial:
  'The GRACE of God is (gear) enough'
  (Dent, G393), where 'gear' refers to
  wealth or possessions (*OED* III.9†b).
  The proverb has its origin in the Bible,
  2 Corinthians, 12.9 – an apposite choice
  that reinforces the distinction between
  Christian and Jew; cf. 2 Corinthians,
  23–4, where Paul speaks 'as a foole' who
  has been chastised by the Jews. This
  may also refer obliquely to the possibility that Bassanio has little material
  wealth compared to the Jew.
143 **well** properly (*OED a.* 8: 'well');
  heavily ironical in this context

129–30 man, and – though] *this edn;* man, and though *Q;* man and, though *Rowe;* man: and, though
Rann; man, and though *Ard²* poor man – my] *this edn;* poore man my *Q;* poor Man my *Rowe;* poor
man, my *Rann;* (poor man) my *Ard²* 135 SD] *Oxf* 136, 141 master] *Q2;* maister *Q* 141–2 the . . .
God] "the . . . God" *Cam¹* 142 enough.] "enough". *Cam¹* 143 speak'st] *F;* speakst *Q* 144 SD] *Oxf*

My lodging out. [*to a Follower*] Give him a livery   145
More guarded than his fellows': see it done.   [*Exit Follower.*]
CLOWN   Father, in. I cannot get a service, no! I have ne'er
a tongue in my head! [*Looks at the palm of his hand.*]
Well, if any man in Italy have a fairer table, which doth
offer to swear upon a book, I shall have good fortune.   150
Go to, here's a simple line of life; here's a small trifle of
wives. Alas, fifteen wives is nothing: eleven widows and

145 **livery** uniform; see 2.1.2n.
146 **guarded** decorated, embroidered or ornamented (*OED* 3). In John Day's *The Isle of Gulls* (1606) a distinction is made between 'a plaine foole' and 'the guarded foole' who is now 'out of request' (H3–3ᵛ). Brown suggests that Bassanio's plan may be to promote Lancelet from rustic servingman to professional Fool in his retinue (Ard², 42).
147 **I cannot . . . service** an ironic use of the negative that may be an appeal as much to an incredulous audience as to Giobbe, since the Clown *has* been successful in obtaining employment, despite his evident linguistic incompetence.
149 **table** a technical term in the art of palmistry to denote the quadrangular space between certain lines on the palm of the hand (*OED* II.14)
149–50 **which . . . book** This adverbial clause qualifies *man* in 149 from which it is detached, although Brown suggests that it can apply equally to the flat of the hand (*table*) itself (Ard², 43). It signifies the act of placing the hand upon the Bible as a means of verifying an oath.
150 **I . . . fortune** an exaggeration of the Clown's *good fortune* that seems to undermine his meaning; either he is saying that, if there are others whose palms are more auspicious than his, then *they* will have good fortune, or

that despite the attributes of others he will still himself be lucky. Theobald thought that the confusion here was due to the fact that a line had been lost (Theobald, 22). Mahood's repunctuation of the line: 'book! – I . . . fortune' (Cam², 88) unnecessarily tidies up the Clown's comically muddled syntax.
151 **Go to** an expression of disbelief (Onions: 'derisive incredulity'), which may express dissatisfaction, but which given the details that follow – 'a small trifle of wives' (151–2) – may also ironically understate the Clown's sense of his own virility. This is possibly a response to Giobbe's evident surprise that his son has succeeded in securing a part of that future, Bassanio's patronage.
simple ordinary (ironic)
small trifle insignificant number (*OED sb.* 2), ironic in the light of the catalogue that follows
152 **wives** In palmistry, long and deep lines that extend from the ball of the thumb towards the line of life in the palm indicate the number of wives (Furness, 76). Mahood perceives the Clown's alleged future marital exploits to represent a parody of 'his new employer's love quest' (Cam², 88).
*****eleven** Q2 emends Q's 'a leuen' to 'eleuen'; Q's spelling is common, though the 'a' is not to be regarded grammatically as an indefinite article.

145 SD] *Cam²; To his followers.* / *Johnson (after* livery*); To his followers.* / *Dyce (after* out,–) 146 SD] *Oxf subst.* 147 no!] *Cam¹; no, Q;* no; *Rowe;* no? *Pope;* no;– *Steevens;* – no; *Collier* 147–8 have . . . tongue] *(*haue nere a tong*);* ha . . . tongue *Q2;* haue . . . tongue *F* 148 SD] *Johnson (Looking on his palm.); looking on his hand.* / *Hanmer; Looks at palm of his hand. Cam²* 149 Well,] *Q2;* wel: *Q;* well, *F;* well; *Keightley* 152 eleuen] *Q2;* a leuen *Q*

nine maids is a simple coming-in for one man, and then
to scape drowning thrice, and to be in peril of my life
with the edge of a feather-bed. Here are simple scapes.   155
Well, if Fortune be a woman, she's a good wench for
this gear. Father, come; I'll take my leave of the Jew in
the twinkling.   *Exeunt Clown [and Giobbe].*

BASSANIO *[Gives Leonardo a shopping list.]*

I pray thee, good Leonardo, think on this:
These things being bought and orderly bestowed,   160
Return in haste, for I do feast tonight
My best esteemed acquaintance. Hie thee, go.

153 **coming-in** income or revenue; but
the Clown also inadvertently releases a
secondary meaning here (*OED sb.* 7),
implying a more literal form of *coming-in*
that contains a strong sexual innuendo
(Cam², 88; Gordon Williams, 76).

154 **drowning** meant literally but with
coming-in it may have 'a quibbling sense
of going bankrupt' (Ard², 43)

155 **edge . . . feather-bed** a euphemism
for the perils of or 'the troubles of the
marriage bed' (*CE* 2.1.27)
simple scapes straightforward trans-
gressions, especially with regard to violations of chastity (*OED sb.*¹ †2)

156 **Fortune . . . woman** proverbial:
'FORTUNE (Woman) is constant only
in inconstancy' (Dent, F605) and also
'FORTUNE is fickle' (Dent, F606).
Another proverbial strain involves
the association of Fortune and fools:
'FORTUNE favours fools' (Tilley,
F600; Dent, F617.1).

157 **gear** purpose or business (*OED* III.11
†c); but see also *OED* III.11a for a more
deprecatory gloss, 'nonsense'; the latter
is in keeping with the Clown's tone of
ironic dismissal.

157–8 **in the twinkling** Q2 emends Q's
reading to 'in the twinkling of an eye',
which Mahood regards as evidence of a
Q2 compositor trying 'to carry too many

words in his head' as he set the text
(Cam², 174). This is the idiomatic sense
of the phrase, although the Q form was
not uncommon (Ard², 43).

159 **this** a demonstrative pronoun that
seems to refer to the business Bassanio
was engaged in before encountering
the Clown and Giobbe. It could refer
specifically, as Mahood suggests (Cam²,
88), to the business being discussed
earlier at 106ff., or to the instruction
at 145–6, or even to additional business
to which the audience is not privy.

160 **orderly bestowed** properly accomplished or deposited (*OED v.* 1 and
2: 'bestow'). Furness thought that this
referred to Bassanio's stowing objects
on board ship (Furness, 77) and most
modern editors have glossed the phrase
'stowed on board ship'. This is plausible,
although there are a number of tasks
allocated at 106ff., and, since the initial
conversation between Bassanio and
Leonardo begins with a hypothetical
clause, 'You may do so', and is then
interrupted, the point of reference of the
demonstrative pronoun here is unclear.

162 **best esteemed** most valued. It is
not clear at this stage if this reference
includes the Jew but by 2.4.18–19 he is
included.
Hie thee hasten you

153 coming-in] *Warburton;* comming in *Q*   154 scape] escape *Q2*   158 twinkling] twinkling of
an eye *Q2*   SD] *Rowe subst.; Exit Clowne. Q; Lancelot and Old Gobbo enter Shylock's house Cam¹*
159 SD] *Bevington subst.*   162 best esteemed] *(best esteemd); best esteem'd Q2*

LEONARDO
My best endeavours shall be done herein.

Enter GRATIANO.

GRATIANO [*to Leonardo*] Where's your master?   164
LEONARDO Yonder, sir, he walks.   *Exit.*
GRATIANO Signior Bassanio!
BASSANIO Gratiano!
GRATIANO I have suit to you.
BASSANIO You have obtained it.
GRATIANO You must not deny me; I must go with you to   170
Belmont.
BASSIANO
Why then, you must. But hear thee, Gratiano,
Thou art too wild, too rude and bold of voice:

163 **herein** in this matter. In Q the SD
'*Exit Leonardo*' occurs as part of this
line, although this is the point at
which he begins to leave the stage;
he speaks another line at 165 after he
encounters Gratiano, who enters at
163.1. Furness (77) supposed, wrongly, that Q's positioning of Leonardo's
exit was evidence of the theatrical
origin of the printer's copy.
168 **suit to you** a request, or entreaty,
to make of you (*OED* II.11). Q
omits the indefinite article but
Q2 and F restore it. Elsewhere in
Shakespeare's texts 'suit' is usually
accompanied by an article or a possessive pronoun, although at 1.2.98
Nerissa uses the phrase 'trouble you
with no more suit'; Brown sets this as
a verse half-line (Ard[2], 44), but there
is no reason to set 167–8 as two verse
half-lines.
169 a courteous way of saying that

Gratiano's request is granted before
it is made. Furness (77), following
Abbott, 231, notes the initial use of
the formal address *You* here and in
170, before the change at 173 to the
more familiar *Thou* as he 'assumes
the part of a friendly lecturer'. But
see 69–81, and 86n., where the
forms *you* and *thou* denote different
relationships; Gratiano is both an
employee of Bassanio and a friend,
and this serves to reinforce a distinction between Christian and Jewish
'employment'.
170 **deny** refuse
172 **hear thee** listen
173 **rude** unrefined or unsophisticated
(*OED adv.* 3 and II.8)
bold of voice outspoken (*OED* 4);
Bassanio may be criticizing Gratiano
simply for his linguistic inadequacies
here, where *rude* and *bold* qualify the
noun *voice*.

163.1] SCENE III. *(after SD) Pope*   164 SD] *Oxf* Where's] Where is *Pope*   master] *Q2;* maister
Q   165 SD] *(Exit Leonardo opp. 163), Hanmer; Q2 (opp. 163); Exit. Le. F (opp. 163)*   168 suit]
(sute); a sute Q2, F   168–9] *Malone lines* you. / it.   170 You] Nay, you *Hanmer*   172 thee,] me
Q3   173 too . . . too] *Q2;* to . . . to *Q*

Parts that become thee happily enough
And in such eyes as ours appear not faults.   175
But where thou art not known, why, there they show
Something too liberal. Pray thee, take pain
To allay with some cold drops of modesty
Thy skipping spirit, lest through thy wild behaviour
I be misconstered in the place I go to   180
And lose my hopes.

GRATIANO   Signior Bassanio, hear me:
If I do not put on a sober habit,
Talk with respect, and swear but now and then,
Wear prayer-books in my pocket, look demurely,
Nay more, while grace is saying, hood mine eyes   185

174 **Parts** elements of bodily composition, used here metaphorically to indicate personal attributes, possibly punning, on the actor's 'part' or 'role' (Cam², 89)
become . . . enough are attractive enough in you
177 **Something too liberal** a little too unrestrained (Onions: 'liberal'). The epithet *liberal* also signifies 'indecent' or 'licentious', and while, as Furness (78) suggests, this does not seem to be the primary meaning here, it is hinted at (*OED adj.* †3).
178 **allay** temper or dilute in the sense of controlling the powerful effects of (*OED v.* II.7 and 8)
179 **skipping spirit** playful or wanton energy
180 **misconstered** misconstrued or misunderstood; pronounced as a trisyllable with the stress on the second syllable, as part of an imperfect pentameter line: 'miscònstered', confirmed in F's 'misconsterd'
182 **sober habit** modest demeanour rather than simply unostentatious

clothing, although this is a sumptuary metaphor: hence, the costume or outward show of modesty, which also follows on from the quibble on *Parts* at 174; cf. *RJ* 3.2.10–11.
183 **respect** due decorum
swear take a solemn declaration or an oath with an appeal to God or some such superhuman or sacred being (*OED v.* I.1 and †7) but also, more colloquially, to speak profanely
but . . . then only occasionally
184 **Wear prayer-books** carry holy books; a reference to the practice of carrying either the Bible or a prayer-book
demurely gravely but also with a modesty that is affected and unnatural (*OED adv.*)
185 **grace is saying** grace is being said; an apparent confusion between the active and passive participles; Furness (79) cites Abbott, 372, and suggests that the prefix 'a-' that would normally be attached to 'saying' may be missing.
hood mine eyes cover my eyes (with

176 thou art] they are *F*   177 liberal] *(liberall), F4;* lib'rall *Q2*   Pray thee] *(pray thee);* prethee *Q2*   178 To allay] T' allay *Pope*   179 lest] *Q2;* least *Q*   180 misconstered] *(misconstred), F (*misconsterd*);* misconster'd *F4;* misconstru'd *Rowe*   181 hopes] hope *Q3*   182 If I] *(Yf I), Q2;* If *F2*   183 then] *F2;* than *Q*   184 pocket] Pockets *Rowe*

Thus with my hat, and sigh and say 'amen',
Use all the observance of civility,
Like one well studied in a sad ostent
To please his grandam, never trust me more.

BASSANIO

Well, we shall see your bearing.   190

GRATIANO

Nay, but I bar tonight; you shall not gauge me
By what we do tonight.

BASSANIO   No, that were pity.

I would entreat you rather to put on
Your boldest suit of mirth, for we have friends
That purpose merriment. But fare you well;   195
I have some business.

GRATIANO

And I must to Lorenzo and the rest,
But we will visit you at supper-time.   *Exeunt.*

---

my hat); this would be an ambiguous
gesture, since it was also the distinguishing feature of the melancholy
lover.
187 **Use . . . civility** observe proper
decorum
188 **sad ostent** grave or serious (*OED
a.* I.†4: 'sad') appearance (*OED sb.*²
1: 'ostent')
189 **grandam** grandmother (*OED* 1),
but also an old woman generally
(*OED* 3). See also 'dam' (*OED sb.*²
3) for the contemptuous sense of
'mother' that Gratiano is deploying
in a speech whose tone is generally
parodic.
190 **bearing** carriage or deportment
(*OED sb.* 2), but also the action of
bringing forth (*OED* from 'bear' *v.*¹
IV: IV.18)
191 **bar** exclude from consideration
(*OED sb.*⁴ 8). Gratiano produces a

weak pun here on Bassanio's *bearing*.
gauge measure or evaluate (a person's worth) (*OED v.*¹ 4)
192 **were pity** would be a pity; a con-
densed conditional clause indicating
Bassanio's relief at not having to estimate Gratiano's worth on the basis
of festive behaviour that would be
inappropriate in Belmont
193 **entreat you** plead with you (*OED
v.* II.6)
194 **boldest** most audacious (as opposed
to a 'modest' or more sober alternative) costume of merriment (*OED
v.* 4)
suit of mirth festive costume; indicating a general demeanour, but also
sustaining the sequence of sumptuary
metaphors initiated by Gratiano at 182.
195 **purpose merriment** intend entertainment or amusement (Onions:
'merriment')

191 bar] *(barre) Q, F4*   195 fare you well] *F2;* far you well *Q;* faryewell *Q2*

[2.3]   *Enter* JESSICA *and* [Lancelet] *the* CLOWN.

JESSICA
I am sorry thou wilt leave my father so.
Our house is hell and thou, a merry devil,
Didst rob it of some taste of tediousness.
But fare thee well; there is a ducat for thee.
And, Lancelet, soon at supper shalt thou see   5
Lorenzo, who is thy new master's guest.
Give him this letter, do it secretly,
And so farewell. I would not have my father
See me in talk with thee.
CLOWN   Adieu. Tears exhibit my tongue. Most beautiful   10

2.3 Theobald introduced a scene division, but Mahood argues plausibly that 2.2–6 can be played continuously, with certain provisos (Cam², 90). Theobald locates the scene in '*Shylock's house*', and Capell specifies '*A room in* Shylock's *house*'. Cam¹ locates it outside the house: '*The door opens: Jessica and Lancelot come forth.*'

1 **so** in this way; an anaphoric intensifier (Abbott, 63), which alludes to a conversation that the audience does not hear but whose substance can be guessed from the Clown's account earlier at 2.2.1–28.

2 **hell** an association of the Jew's house with that of Satan (see 2.2), often used allegorically in connection with the Jewish synagogue (see Trachtenberg, 20–1). But see also Thomas Nashe, *Pierce Penniless* (1592), 1.161, for the connection between the devil and the usurer.
   merry devil playful demon. A major feature of hell was its population by anarchic demons; see Marlowe's *Dr Faustus*, scene 4ff., and also the Morality 'Vice' as 'the opponent of the Good, . . .

the corrupter of Man . . . [and] as the buffoon' (Cushman, 72).

3 **rob** proverbial; cf. Tilley, T108: 'One THIEF (merchant) robs (accuses) another'. Jessica justifies the Clown's 'robbery' as a consequence of the ethos of the Jew's house.
   taste of tediousness small quantity of (*OED sb.*¹ II.†3c) weariness (*OED* †2)

4 **there . . . ducat** monetary reward for the Clown's (professional) dexterity; cf. *TN* 2.4.667–70. Jessica's generosity here contrasts with the parsimony of the Jew.

10 **Adieu** a formal version of Jessica's *farewell* (8) but also a pun on 'A Jew' that is picked up in 11: *sweet Jew*.
   exhibit my tongue show what I would otherwise say. Editors have puzzled about this expression; Mahood, following Clarendon, thinks that the Clown means 'inhibit' (Cam², 90), in keeping with his earlier verbal imprecision, but Pooler (Ard¹, 61) quotes Thomas Kyd's *Soliman and Perseda*, 3.2.15: 'And here my swolne harts greef doth stay my tongue' (Kyd, 202). There is no reason to depart from the obvious gloss here,

2.3] *Capell subst.*; SCENE IV. *Pope*   0.1 Lancelet] *Rowe (*Launcelot*)*   1 I am] I'm *Pope*   2 merry] *om. F3*   4 fare] *Q2*; far *Q*   5 Lancelet] *(Launcelet), Q2; Launcelot / Rowe*   8 farewell] *F2*; farwell *Q*   9 in talk] talk *F*   10 SP] *Clo. F*; *Lance. Q2*   Adieu] *F4*; Adiew *Q*; Adue *F*   tongue.] *Cam²*; tongue, *Q*; tongue; *Theobald*; tongue. [*aside.*] *Johnson*

pagan, most sweet Jew! If a Christian do not play the
knave and get thee, I am much deceived. But adieu;
these foolish drops do something drown my manly
spirit. Adieu!   [*Exit.*]

JESSICA

Farewell, good Lancelet.   15

Alack, what heinous sin is it in me

To be ashamed to be my father's child!

But, though I am a daughter to his blood,

I am not to his manners. O, Lorenzo,

If thou keep promise I shall end this strife,   20

---

although the Clown is being melo-
dramatic in his display of grief.

11 **pagan** the primary sense of 'heathen'
(*OED* A *sb.* 1), which reinforces Jessica's
religious affiliation (and hence her
Semitism), but see also the secondary
meaning of prostitute (*OED* 2 †b). For
the ambiguity of the compliment that
reinforces a Christian prejudice, see
Trachtenberg, 76–7.

do F2's 'did', followed by most pre-
20th-century editors, suggests that
Jessica's father was not the Jew but
a Christian, and that therefore she is
illegitimate. Q's 'doe' anticipates the
forthcoming elopement of Jessica and
Lorenzo.

11–12 **play the knave** adopt the role of an
unprincipled or deceitful person (*OED*
sb. 3). There may, however, be a sexual
innuendo here, since *OED* †5 records a
rare and obsolete 1564 usage of 'knave'
as a 'reeling pin' around which a spool
revolves in spinning yarn, which in this
context would be unmistakably phallic.

12 **get** obtain or procure as in marriage
(*OED v. trans.* I.1 and I.17), but also
to obtain sexually and, by implication,
to impregnate and hence make plump.
This continues the train of barely submerged bawdy references.

13 **foolish drops** a euphemism for tears,
but also suggesting a display of feminine behaviour to be contrasted with
the Clown's *manly spirit* at 13–14

18 **daughter . . . blood** daughter issuing
from (in the sense of belonging to)
his blood, and therefore legitimate.
The usual construction would be to
use the preposition 'of' (cf. Abbott,
176). But contrast Portia's behaviour at
1.2.17–18, where patriarchal authority
is distinguished from youthful *blood*
(sexual ardour). In acknowledging her
lineage, Jessica casts a doubt on her
father's patriarchal 'virtue' and anticipates Salanio and Salarino's insults to
the Jew at 3.1.30ff.

19 **manners** customary behaviour (*OED*
sb.[1] 3). Brown suggests a probable
'word-play on "man"' (Ard[2], 46). This
reading sets up a plausible contrast with
daughter in the preceding line, contrasting Jessica's behaviour here with that of
Portia at 1.2.

20 **strife** antagonism or opposition (*OED*
1), but, in Jessica's case, divided loyalties;
she is the victim both of her father's
antagonism, which she assumes will
extend to Lorenzo but which she thinks
marriage will resolve, and also of the
opposition between Jew and Christian.

---

11 do] *(doe)*; did *F2*   12 adieu] *Rowe;* adiew *Q;* adew *Q2;* adue *F*   13 something] *(somthing), Q2,*
somewhat *F*   14 Adieu!] *(adiew.)*; adieu. *Q2;* adue. *F*   SD] *Q2; Exit Clown. Capell (opp. 15); Exit
Launcelot / Dyce; he goes Cam²*   15 Farewell] *F;* Farwell *Q;* Farewel *F4*   Lancelet] *(Launcelet), Q2;
Launcelot / Rowe*   20 If] *(Yf), Q2*

Become a Christian, and thy loving wife.					*Exit.*

[2.4]				*Enter* GRATIANO, LORENZO, SALARINO
					and SALANIO.

LORENZO

Nay, we will slink away in supper-time,
Disguise us at my lodging, and return,
All in an hour.

GRATIANO

We have not made good preparation.

SALARINO

We have not spoke us yet of torch-bearers.					5

SALANIO

'Tis vile unless it may be quaintly ordered,
And better in my mind not undertook.

2.4 Theobald locates the scene in *'the Street'*, and Cam[1] in *'Another street in Venice'*.

0.1 For the 'three Sallies' debate, see pp. 428–9; variations start to appear in F3–4, where 'Salarino' is accepted but 'Solania' is misspelt. Despite scene division variation throughout 18th-century editions, the Q SD remained until Dover Wilson (Cam[1]) elided 'Salarino' and 'Salerio' (27). Most recent editors have now returned to Q's reading.

1 **slink away in** steal away during

2 **Disguise us** put on our disguises

3 ***All . . . hour*** set as part of 2 in Q (see t.n.); thought by Dover Wilson to indicate 'that a passage about the masque has been "cut"', since 'we do not actually learn that a masque is afoot until l. 22 [23]' (Cam[1], 137). Brown thought it an imperfection that 'could equally well be a sign of foul-paper copy' (Ard[2], xvi and 47). The scene begins with two iambic lines, but the metre swiftly disintegrates.

5 **spoke us yet** have not yet engaged the services of; Rowe follows the F4 emendation 'as', and Dover Wilson suggests that the compositor misread the MS copy 'a' for 'u' (Cam[1], 137). Abbott, 220, confusingly cites this as an example of the old dative case, glossing as 'spoken for ourselves about'.

torch-bearers torch-bearers usually accompanied masquers; cf. *RJ* 1.4 SD: '*Enter* Romeo, Mercutio, Benuolio, *with fiue or sixe other Maskers, torch-bearers*' (Q1).

6 **vile** of poor or inferior quality (*OED adv.* 5 and 6), from the Latin *vilem* meaning common or base; Salanio is being critical of a vulgar or inferior performance, going further than simply saying it would be a bad idea if it were not *quaintly ordered*.

quaintly ordered skilfully or elegantly arranged (*OED adv.* †4: 'quaint')

7 **and better, in my view, not to be embarked upon;** *undertook* is an example of a curtailed form of the past

---

2.4] *Capell subst.;* SCENE V. *Pope*   **0.1** SALARINO] *(Salaryno); Slarino F; Solarino Rowe;* SOLANIO *and* SALARINO. *Capell;* salerio *Cam[1]*   **0.2** SALANIO] *Solania. F2*   **1–3]** *Capell;* time / houre. / *Q; prose Pope*   **5** us] *as F4*   **6+** SP] *Q2; Solanio Q*

LORENZO
    'Tis now but four of clock; we have two hours
    To furnish us.

        Enter Lancelet [*the* CLOWN, *with a letter*].

                Friend Lancelet,
    What's the news?   10
CLOWN   An it shall please you to break up this, [*handing
    letter to Lorenzo*] it shall seem to signify.
LORENZO
    I know the hand; in faith, 'tis a fair hand,
    And whiter than the paper it writ on
    Is the fair hand that writ.
GRATIANO   Love news, in faith!   15
CLOWN   By your leave, sir.
LORENZO   Whither goest thou?

participle ('undertaken') not uncommon in Shakespeare (Abbott, 343).
9   **furnish us** provide ourselves with the
things we need
11 **break up** open by breaking the seal;
breaking the 'seal' on the letter may
also allude to the immanent taking
of Jessica's virginity ('seal': Gordon
Williams, 270), and it is the first material exchange in what will become a
marriage contract.
12 **it . . . signify** literally, it will appear
to mean (something); a further parody
of the language of his social superiors,
but the question of signification is
apposite in the light of the metaphor
he deploys at 11, since the letter means
much more than it appears to signify.
13 **the hand** the handwriting
    fair clear, neat and legible (*OED a.*
    III.8c)

14 **writ on** has written upon (Abbott,
343); Hanmer emends: 'paper [that] it
writ on', which alters the emphasis in
the line (Ard[1], 63), and Furness (84)
suggests compositorial confusion over
the appearance of hypothetical MS
copy 'y^t' and 'yt' in the same line.
15 **fair** beautiful (*OED a.* 1 and 1a)
    Love . . . faith Gratiano's tone may
    be a sarcastic response to a 'faded
    conceit' (Cam[2], 91), but while it mocks
    Lorenzo it also betrays a sense of eager
    anticipation at the prospect of some
    private revelation.
16 **By your leave** a common phrase of
apology ('Will you permit me to?')
deployed usually by a servant to excuse
imminent departure; it cuts across
Gratiano's anticipation of *Love news*
and conveys a sense of mock embarrassment.

8 of clock] a clocke *Q2*; a-clock *Pope*; o'clock *Capell*   9 SD] *F; Enter Launcelet. after 10 Q; Enter
Lancelet. after 10 Q2; Enter Launcelot with a Letter. after 9 / Rowe*   10 news?] *Q2*; newes. *Q*   11 An
it shall] If it please *Q2*   11–12 SD] *Oxf subst.*   12 it shall seem] shall it seeme *Q2, F*   14 whiter]
whither *F2*   than] *F4*; then *Q*   it] that it *Hanmer*   15 Is] I *F*   Love news] *Q2*; Love, newes *Q*;
Love-newes *F2*   17 thou?] *Q2, F*, thou. *Q*

CLOWN   Marry, sir, to bid my old master, the Jew, to sup
tonight with my new master, the Christian.

LORENZO

Hold here; take this.   [*Gives money.*]

                    Tell gentle Jessica   20
I will not fail her; speak it privately.   *Exit Clown.*
Go, gentlemen,
Will you prepare you for this masque tonight?
I am provided of a torch-bearer.

SALARINO

Ay, marry, I'll be gone about it straight.   25

SALANIO

And so will I.

LORENZO   Meet me and Gratiano
At Gratiano's lodging some hour hence.

18–19 Dover Wilson cites this invitation to supper as part of the case for a 'lost' supper scene that was excised in revision (Cam[1], 110–11 and 138).

18 **Marry, sir** See 2.2.37n., but also suggesting its literal meaning, since the Clown will participate in the elopement plot.

   sup eat supper (*OED v.*[2] 1); contrast the Jew's earlier refusal of Bassanio's hospitality at 1.3.30–4; see Yaffe, 4–5 and 46, for the specific claim that the Jew's renouncing of customary dietary ritual bespeaks a 'willingness to transgress' Jewish law and a consequent sharing 'in the permissiveness that accompanies Venice's openness to commerce' (Yaffe, 46, 62).

21 **privately** confidentially (*OED* †8b)

22 ***Go, gentlemen** Q sets 22–3 as one

prose line; thought by Dover Wilson to be further evidence of cutting of a hypothetical masque scene (Cam[1], 138). Brown speculates, more plausibly, that this and other short lines indicate changes of tone in the dialogue as part of an overall impression 'of casual and fragmentary conversation, of many things about to happen' (Ard[2], 48).

23 **you prepare you** you prepare yourselves; the second *you* functions idiomatically as a reflexive pronoun.

24 **provided of** provided with; see Abbott, 171, for examples of the preposition 'of' used in connection with both the agent and the instrument. The *torch-bearer* will be the disguised Jessica.

25 **straight** immediately, straightaway

27 **some hour** about an hour

---

20 here; take this.] *this edn;* here, take this, *F;* heere take this *Q*   SD] *Dyce subst.*   21 SD] *Capell; opp.* 24 *Q   Exit Clown.*] *Exit Laun. / Rowe; Exit* LAUNCELOT. *Malone; Lancelot goes. Cam[1]; Exit Lancelot. Oxf; Exit* [LANCELOT *the*] *Clown. / Norton*   22–3] *Cam[1]; prose Q; Capell lines go.– / Gentlemen, / tonight? /; Collier lines* Gentlemen / tonight? /; *Oxf lines* Go. / Gentlemen, / tonight? /   23 prepare you] prepare *Q2*   this] th' *Hanmer*   25+ SP] *Q2 (Salar.); Sal. Q; Sol. / Rann; Salerio. Cam[1]*   26+ SP SALANIO] *Q2 (Salan.); Sol. Q; Sola. / Rowe; Sala. / Steevens; Solan. / Dyce*   26–7 Meet . . . hence.] *Pope; prose Q but capitalizes* Some

SALARINO
    'Tis good we do so.   *[Exeunt Salarino and Salanio.]*

GRATIANO
    Was not that letter from fair Jessica?

LORENZO
    I must needs tell thee all. She hath directed   30
    How I shall take her from her father's house,
    What gold and jewels she is furnished with,
    What page's suit she hath in readiness.
    If e'er the Jew her father come to heaven,
    It will be for his gentle daughter's sake;   35
    And never dare misfortune cross her foot
    Unless she do it under this excuse:
    That she is issue to a faithless Jew.
    Come, go with me, peruse this as thou goest.   39
    [Hands letter to Gratiano.]
    Fair Jessica shall be my torch-bearer.   *Exeunt.*

28 A modern equivalent would be: 'That's a good idea.'
30 **must needs** am compelled to
  directed communicated specifically (*OED v.* 1†b)
32 **furnished** supplied (*OED v.* 4), but additionally in the sense of being embellished with (*OED sb. c. colloq*)
35 **gentle** a pun on 'Gentile'; cf. 1.3.173.
36 **dare misfortune cross** an instance of the third person subjunctive used imperatively (Abbott, 364), but also alluding to the future (Furness, 85); grammatically the verb *dare* functions as a future subjunctive that mobilizes the subordinating conjunction *Unless* in 37 to emphasize that misfortune will never cross Jessica's path (*cross her foot* and hence trip her up) *unless* her Jewish parentage is invoked as an excuse.
37 **she** the female pronoun genders 'misfortune' at 36 by implication, since the goddess Fortune was regarded proverbially as a promiscuous female: 'FORTUNE is a strumpet (whore, huswife)' (Dent, F603.1).
38 **faithless** literally a non-believer, but also more generally 'untrustworthy'. The Jew is 'untrustworthy' because he does not share the beliefs of Christians; see also Matthew, 17.17–18.
40 **shall** is to be (Abbott, 315)

28 SD] *(Exit.); Exeunt SAL. and SOL. Capell; Exeunt Salar. and Salan. / Steevens; Exeunt Sala. and Solan. / Rann; Salerio and Solanio leave them Cam¹* 29 Jessica?] *Q2, F (Jessica?); Iessica. Q* 33 readiness] *(readines); readinesse Q2, F* 34 If] *(Yf), Q2, F* 35 It] *(Yt), Q2, F* 39 SD] *Oxf subst.* 40 Jessica] *(Jessica); Iessica Q2, F* SD] *(Exit.), Rowe, they walk on Cam¹*

[2.5]   *Enter* [Shylock the] JEW *and his man that*
                    was[, Lancelet] *the* CLOWN.

JEW

Well, thou shalt see, thy eyes shall be thy judge,
The difference of old Shylock and Bassanio.
[*Calls.*] What, Jessica! [*to Clown*] Thou shalt not gormandize
As thou hast done with me. – [*Calls.*]
                                   What, Jessica! –
[*to Clown*] And sleep, and snore, and rend apparel out.   5

2.5 Most editors follow Capell's embellishment of Theobald's 'Shylock's
house' to indicate an 'outside' scene:
'*The Same. Before* Shylock's *house*'.
This scene is often played *inside* the
house (e.g. Miller 1970; Barton).
However, Booth argues: 'an interior
is suggested, and Jessica is associated
with it, but no scene is evidently set
inside' (Booth, 23).

0.1–2 Almost all editors since Rowe have
emended the SD to '*Enter Shylock
and Launcelot.*' The absence of punctuation after '*was*' in Q (the phrase is
omitted completely in Q2) has indicated to some that this SD is ambiguous,
in that it means either 'Enter . . . and
the Clown who was formerly in his
employ' or 'Enter . . . and the man
who was formerly the Clown.' The
Clown may switch his allegiance but he
clearly does not switch his role. Brown
suggests that he is transformed from a
'rustic' clown to one who 'appears in
the long, motley "guarded" coat of a
fool of Bassanio's household' (Ard[2],
49). Ulrich Mühe's Lanzelot Gobbo
(Deutschestheater, 1985) entered
wearing beach-shorts, carrying a
deckchair and a portable computer,

signifying a new-found prosperity
after his escape (across the (Berlin)
wall represented on the stage) into
Bassanio's household.

1 thou . . . thy a form of address from
master to servant (Abbott, 232); the
first of two depletions of the Jew's
household and therefore dramatically
significant, as evidenced in the fragmentation of the Jew's language in
3–6.

2 of A modern idiom would gloss this
as 'between', but see *OED* 49 for the
possessive genitive 'of' indicating a
thing or quality belonging to a person.

3 What an exclamation that expresses
impatience (Onions)
gormandize feed to excess (*OED* 1
†3), a stark contrast with the Clown's
earlier version of his treatment by the
Jew at 2.2.98–100.

5 rend apparel out wear out your
clothes by tearing them (*OED v.*[1] 2c
cites this example of a rare usage);
usually a gesture accompanying
mourning, as in the Bible, Judges,
11.34–5, and also Job, 1.20–1, hence
deployed by the Jew, but perhaps
implying the Clown's profanation of
what was otherwise ritual behaviour

2.5] *Theobald subst.;* SCENE VI. *Pope;* SCENE V. *Capell subst.*   0.1] *Enter the Iew and Lancelet. Q2;
Enter Iew, and his man that was the Clowne. F2; Enter* Shylock *and* Launcelot. *Rowe; Enter* SHYLOCK, *and*
Clown. *Capell;* SHYLOCK *and* LANCELOT *come forth Cam[1]; Enter Shylock the Jew and his man that
was,* [LANCELOT] *the clown Oxf*   1 SP] *(Iewe); (Shy.) Q*   shalt] shall *F*   3 SD1] *Oxf subst.*   Jessica!]
Rowe; Iessica Q   SD2] *Oxf subst.*   4 SD] *Oxf subst.*   Jessica!] *Rowe;* Jessica, *Q;* Jessica? *Q2, F*
5 SD] *Oxf subst.*   apparel] *(apparaille); apparell Q2, F*

[*Calls again.*] Why, Jessica, I say!

CLOWN   Why, Jessica!

JEW

Who bids thee call? I do not bid thee call.

CLOWN Your worship was wont to tell me I could do
nothing without bidding.

Enter JESSICA.

JESSICA

Call you? What is your will?   10

JEW

I am bid forth to supper, Jessica.
There are my keys. But wherefore should I go?
I am not bid for love; they flatter me,
But yet I'll go in hate, to feed upon
The prodigal Christian. Jessica, my girl,   15
Look to my house. I am right loath to go;
There is some ill a-brewing towards my rest,
For I did dream of money-bags tonight.

8 **wont to** accustomed to
9 **bidding** being commanded (*OED*
   IV.10) or requested to. Cf. 7, where
   the semantic field of the verb *bid*
   ranges from 'ask' to 'command'; the
   Jew occupies the stronger form ('command'), whereas here the Clown may
   simply mean 'being asked to'.
11 **bid forth** invited out (*OED* III.8); as
   in 7–9, a further play upon the meaning of the verb *bid*, as evidenced at 13.
   Implicit in this invitation is a suggestion of compulsion that provokes the
   questioning of 12.
15 **prodigal Christian** an allusion to
   the biblical parable of the Prodigal
   Son (Luke, 15.11–32), but also to the

tendency to conspicuous consumption
of Christian Venice and in particular
the aristocratic ethos associated with
Bassanio (see Stone, 185–6)
16 **Look to** take care of
   right loath very reluctant
17 **ill a-brewing** misfortune fermenting
   (*OED v.* 4: 'brew')
   towards my rest threatening my
   repose, or peace of mind; *towards* is
   stronger than 'in the direction of',
   since the *ill a-brewing* indicates future
   danger.
18 **dream of money-bags** a reference to
   one of the play's source narratives, *The
   Ballad of Gernutus*. (See LN.)
   tonight last night (Abbott, 190)

6 SD] *Oxf subst.* Jessica . . . say!] *Capell; Iessica . . . say. Q; Jessica! . . . say. Theobald* Jessica!] *Rowe;
Iessica. Q* 7+ SP] *Shy. Q* do] did *Rowe* 8–9] *Q lines* me / bidding; *Q2 lines* no- / bidding / 15
girl] (*girle*); gyrle *Q2* 18 tonight] (*to night*); last night *Rowe*; to-night *Pope*

CLOWN   I beseech you, sir, go. My young master doth
expect your reproach.   20

JEW   So do I his.

CLOWN   And they have conspired together. I will not say
you shall see a masque, but, if you do, then it was not for
nothing that my nose fell a-bleeding on Black Monday
last, at six o'clock i'th' morning, falling out that year on   25
Ash Wednesday was four year in th'afternoon.

JEW

What, are there masques? Hear you me, Jessica,
Lock up my doors, and when you hear the drum
And the vile squealing of the wry-necked fife,

---

20 **reproach** In the manner of the mala-
propisms deployed at 2.2, the Clown
here intends 'approach', although the
meaning of 'reproach' as an act of
blaming, censuring or condemning
(*OED sb.* 3) inadvertently describes the
attitude of Christian Venice to the Jew,
and it is, in part, to this that the latter
responds at 21.

22 **conspired together** plotted together
(*OED v.* 1); again the Clown says more
than he means.

23 **masque** Masquerades took place
traditionally on Shrove Tuesday.
References to the general atmosphere
of misrule in the play have led some
commentators to conclude that the
predominant comic ethos is that of
a Shrovetide play (Laroque, 256–8;
Sohmer, 7).

24 **nose fell a-bleeding** an omen that
parodies the symbolic articulation of
the Jew's anxiety at 17–18; cf. Thomas
Nashe, *The Terrors of The Night* (1594):
'If he chance to kill a spider, he hath
suppressed an enemy; if a spinner [a
long-legged spider] creepe vppon him,
hee shall haue golde raine down from

heauen: if his nose bleede, some of his
kinsfolkes is dead' (Nashe, 1.358).
Black Monday Easter Monday; cf.
Stowe, 264, which refers to the occasion of 'the 14. day of Aprill, and
the morrow after Easter day, [when]
King Edward with his hoast lay before
the Citty of *Paris*; which day was full
darke of mist and haile, and so bitter
cold, that many men dyed on their
horsebacks with the cold, wherefore
unto this day it hath beene called the
Blacke Munday.'

25–6 **falling . . . afternoon** on Ash
Wednesday and at a time in the afternoon, during a leap year (every fourth
year) in which there was a conjunction
between Easter Monday and the first
day of Lent. (See LN.)

29 **vile** base or depraved (*OED adj.* A1),
suggesting a puritanical disposition in
keeping with the more general desire
to conserve rather than squander
wealth; see 2.4.6.
squealing Q2 emends the Q reading
to 'squeaking' and is followed by a
number of editors up to and including
Pooler (Ard¹).

19+ SP] *(Clo), Q2; Laun. / Rowe; Lancelot. Cam¹;* LANCELET *Folg* 19–20] *Pope; Q lines* Maister
/ reproch. /; *Q2 lines* go, / reproch. /   25 i'th'] *F4;* ith *Q;* in the *Q2*   26 Ash Wednesday] *F4;*
Ashwensday *Q;* Ashwednesday *F3*   in th'afternoon] *Q2, F;* in thafternoone *Q;* in the afternoon
F4   29 squealing] squeaking *Q2*   wry-necked fife] *(wry-neckt Fiffe), Q2 (wry-neckt Fife), F*

Clamber not you up to the casements then,   30
Nor thrust your head into the public street
To gaze on Christian fools with varnished faces;
But stop my house's ears – I mean my casements –
Let not the sound of shallow foppery enter
My sober house. By Jacob's staff, I swear,   35
I have no mind of feasting forth tonight.
But I will go. Go you before me, sirrah:
Say I will come.
CLOWN   I will go before, sir.

[*aside to Jessica*] Mistress, look out at window for all this;
There will come a Christian by   40

wry-necked fife a flute that required its player to bend his neck to the side and away from the instrument in order to play it, and hence the flute-player rather than the instrument. See also *OED*, which records a 1585 usage of the word 'wryneck' as a species of small bird 'distinguished by its habit of writhing the neck and head'. The word *fife* was also used to denote 'one who plays the fife' (*OED sb.* 3). Thus the depraved sound (*vile squealing*) is made by the musician craning his neck to the side (like the wryneck) in order to play his instrument.

30 **Clamber not you** don't you climb
casements literally, part of the window-frame (*OED* 2) but here used generally for windows

32 **varnished** painted (*OED* 1†), but also with the added implication of falsity suggesting simulation or pretence (*OED* 2b)

34 **foppery** folly, stupidity or licence; Q2 expands Q's 'fopprie' to 'foppery' while F prints 'fopperie'. The line is metrically imperfect even with the Q's elision, hinting perhaps at an unin-

tended irony in the Jew's appeal to musical harmony.

35 **Jacob's staff** an oath that is both relevant and appropriate in that it refers to the progress of Jacob in Genesis, 32.10, from lowly beginnings to prosperity. Calvin glosses this text: 'we must note the comparison betweene ye staffe, & the two droaues or bands, wherby he compareth ye former solitarinesse w^t the present abundance' (Calvin, *Genesis*, 669).

36 **no ... forth** no inclination or desire to go out to attend a feast; on the use of the preposition *of* to mean 'as regards', see Abbott, 174, and also Abbott, 41, for the use of *forth* in which motion is implied.

39 **for all this** in spite of all this, i.e. despite the warnings of your father (Abbott, 154). Pooler sets the Clown's speech at 38–9 as prose (Ard^1, 68), but Brown follows Malone in setting these lines as verse, although he thinks that the rhythm of 39 is nearer that of prose (Ard^2, 52); 38–9 are decasyllabic but they contrast with the iambic rhythm of the rhyming hexameters at 40–1.

34 foppery] *(fopprie), Q2;* fopperie *F*   37 sirrah:] *Rowe;* sirra, *Q*   38–9 I . . . this] *prose Collier*
39 at] at a *Q2*   this;] *F;* this, *Q*

JEW

Will be worth a Jewess' eye.   [*Exit.*]

JEW

What says that fool of Hagar's offspring, ha?

JESSICA

His words were 'Farewell, mistress', nothing else.

JEW

The patch is kind enough, but a huge feeder,
Snail-slow in profit, and he sleeps by day   45
More than the wildcat. Drones hive not with me,
Therefore I part with him, and part with him
To one that I would have him help to waste
His borrowed purse. Well, Jessica, go in;
Perhaps I will return immediately.   50

41 ***Jewess' eye** proverbial, signifying value; cf. Dent, J53: 'To be worth a JEW'S eye.' Throughout Q 'Iewes' is a disyllable, and is applicable to both male and female genders, and Pope was the first to emend to the female possessive. 'Iewes' as the modern 'Jewess' appears in Tyndale's Bible (1526), Acts, 24.24 (*OED*), although the Bishops' Bible utilizes the spelling 'Iewesse'.

42 **Hagar's offspring** the illegitimate son of the Egyptian bondswoman Hagar and Abraham, who is exiled for his 'mocking' the birth of Abraham's legitimate son Isaac in the Bible: Genesis, 21.9–10.

44 **patch** i.e. fool, possibly an allusion to the parti-coloured or 'patched' costume of the professional Clown (Ard[2], 52)

45 **Snail-slow in profit** as slow as a snail at learning (i.e. improving his behaviour), and, by implication, in doing anything useful. See *OED sb.* †3: 'profit'; but see Miles Mosse's *The Arraignment and Conviction of Usury* (1595), sigs C3–3[v]: 'This scripture therefore giueth

(as we see) direct occasion to intreate of vsurie: then which there are not many arguments more necessarie or profitable to be handled in these dayes.' The *OED* does not record a gloss on 'profit' as 'interest' until 1604 (*OED sb.* 5), and *Death of Usury*, 9, records a different sense of 'profit' – 'Yet we must take heed that we do not condemne all profitable and lawfull contracts' – indicating an instability in the meaning of the term.

46 **wildcat** a nocturnal cat that prowls at night (Clarendon, 97). The term is used figuratively to signify unruliness (cf. *OED fig.* 2).
Drones male honeybees who do no work but whose job is to impregnate the queen bee (*OED sb.*[1] 1)

49 **borrowed purse** literally, the sum of money that Bassanio has borrowed from Antonio; but cf. 1.1.138 for a series of subsidiary meanings that arise from the pun on the word *purse* in much the same way that they arise from the play on the word 'Iewes'.

50 **immediately** straightaway (*OED adv.* 3)

41 Jewess'] *Pope; Iewes Q;* Jewes *Keightley*   SD] *Dyce; Exit* Laun. *Rowe; Exit* Clown. *Capell; he goes Cam[1]; He exits. Folg*   42 ha?] *Hanmer;* ha. *Q*   45 Snail-slow] *Q2, F;* Snaile slow *Q*   and] but *F*

Do as I bid you; shut doors after you.
'Fast bind, fast find.'
A proverb never stale in thrifty mind.   *Exit.*

JESSICA

Farewell, and if my fortune be not crossed,   54
I have a father, you a daughter, lost.   *Exit.*

[2.6]   *Enter the masquers* GRATIANO *and* SALARINO.

GRATIANO   This is the penthouse under which Lorenzo
desired us to make stand.

SALARINO   His hour is almost past.

GRATIANO

And it is marvel he outdwells his hour,

51–2 *Q's lineation clumsily reduces two
lines to one (see t.n.), and may indicate
the state of MS copy. This a rare occasion when Q2's tidying up improves
the visual impression of the text by
isolating the proverbial utterance in
order to provide a couplet for the Jew's
exit, 52–3. Pope omits 'Do . . . you' (51)
as a way of trying to rectify the metre.

52 **Fast . . . find** proverbial: 'Fast (sure)
BIND fast (sure) find)' (Dent, B352).
This may be glossed as: that which is
safely (*fast*) secured will remain safe.

53 **stale** irrelevant, hackneyed or worn
out (*OED a.*[1] 2 and *fig.* 3)
thrifty intent on gain

54 **crossed** thwarted

2.6 Theobald locates the scene in '*The
Street*', but Cam[1] is unspecific as
to whether this is an 'inside' or an
'outside' scene: '*GRATIANO and
SALERIO come up, in masquing attire*'.

0.1 *masquers* This noun describes how
Gratiano and Salarino are dressed
(Ard[1], 53), and it does not imply that

other unnamed masquers are present
at the opening of this scene. Earlier, at
2.4.1–3, Lorenzo, Gratiano, Salarino
and Salanio plan to disguise themselves, and at the beginning of 2.6 two
of the four masquers now return to
assist in the elopement of Jessica and
Lorenzo.

SALARINO The 'three Sallies' problem
intensifies at this point. Rowe emended to 'Salanio', and Dover Wilson
emended to 'Salerio' (Cam[1], 139); one
of the few occasions when Q1 and Q2
are roughly in agreement with each
other (Salerino/Salarino) but not with
F (Salino). Pooler follows Q (Ard[1], 69),
but Brown follows Cam[1] (Ard[2], 53).
See 2.4.0.1n. and pp. 428–9.

1 **penthouse** the projecting eaves of the
upper storey of a house that were used
as shelter from sun or rain

2 **make stand** take up position in order
to wait

3 **hour** the arranged time of meeting

4 **outdwells** stays beyond (Onions)

51–2] *Q2; one line Q; Theobald lines* bid you.– / find. /   51 Do . . . bid you;] *om. Pope;* bid you.–
Theobald shut doors] Shut the doors *Pope, Theobald*   52 Fast . . . find.] *fast bind, fast find.* /
Theobald   2.6] *Capell subst.;* SCENE VII. *Pope*   0.1] *(subst.); Enter . . . Salino. F; Enter* Gratiano
and Salanio *in Masquerade. Rowe; Enter the masquers,* Graziano *and* Salerio, [*with torch-bearers*]
Oxf   1–2] *Rowe; Q2 lines* which / stand /   2 make] make a *F*

For lovers ever run before the clock.   5
SALARINO
O, ten times faster Venus' pigeons fly
To seal love's bonds new made than they are wont
To keep obliged faith unforfeited.
GRATIANO
That ever holds: who riseth from a feast
With that keen appetite that he sits down?   10
Where is the horse that doth untread again
His tedious measures with the unbated fire
That he did pace them first? All things that are,

5 **ever run before** always proceed in advance of, i.e. arrive early, a mark of the impetuosity of lovers

6 **Venus' pigeons** the doves that pull Venus' chariot, speeding her to the occasion of betrothal, emphasizing the urgency of newly declared promises of love; *pigeon* was sometimes used as a synonym for a young dove and lovers were referred to as 'turtles' or 'doves' (Ard², 53). There is a possible quibble here in that the urgency of youth is compared with the naïvety of lovers who become simpletons or gulls (*OED* 3b *slang*: 'pigeon': 'One who lets himself be swindled esp. in gaming; a simpleton, dupe, gull').

7 **seal love's bonds** consummate the relationship sexually
wont inclined to

8 **obliged faith** obligèd; formally agreed fidelity (as in marriage vows and the attendant sexual conduct, already undertaken)
unforfeited that is not lost through misconduct (*OED v.* 2b), but after the initial novelty and sense of anticipation have worn off

9 **ever holds** is always true; the cue for a series of truisms that Gratiano alludes to concerning the contrast between the novelty of infatuation and the consequences of satisfying desire, e.g.

9–10, which may be proverbial; there are possible allusions to two proverbial strands here: (1) Dent, M837, 'She is MEAT for your master', and (2) Dent, M850, 'All MEATS to be eaten, all maids to be wed.'

10 **sits down** the preposition 'to' is omitted at the end of the line, a common feature of relative sentences; see Abbott, 394.

11–13 **Where . . . first?** Gratiano alludes to a series of proverbs that point in different directions. The horse for whom the novelty of its actions is rendered tedious by repetition is like the satiated lover who loses his appetite for sex. See Dent, 657: 'He that has a white HORSE and a fair wife (woman) never wants trouble.'

11 **untread** retrace (*OED*)

12 **measures** steps, but see *OED sb.* III.20 for the gloss: 'a dance, esp. a grave or stately dance'
unbated fire ardour or enthusiasm that is undiminished. Cf. *OED v.²* 5: 'bate', 'to lessen in force or intensity; to mitigate, moderate, assuage, diminish'.

13–14 **All . . . enjoyed** possibly proverbial, although no source has been found; attached to the equestrian image at 11, this description recalls the heavily symbolic encounter between Venus and

6 pigeons] Widgeons *Warburton*   7 seal] steale *F*   than] *Rowe;* then *Q*

Are with more spirit chased than enjoyed.
How like a younger, or a prodigal,   15
The scarfed bark puts from her native bay,
Hugged and embraced by the strumpet wind!
How like the prodigal doth she return,
With overweathered ribs and ragged sails,
Lean, rent and beggared by the strumpet wind!   20

Adonis involving the tethering of her 'lusty courser' in *VA* 37–40: 'The studded bridle on a ragged bough / Nimbly she fastens – O how quick is love! – / The steed is stalled up, and even now / To tie the rider she begins to prove.'

14 **chased** chasèd; pursued
  enjoyed Q's 'enioyd' perfects the metre of the line.

15 **younger** youth, as in the Prodigal Son (Luke, 15.11–13); but also a submerged equestrian reference emanating from the interchangeability of the terms 'younger' and 'younker'. The 'younger'/'younker' alternative spellings prompted Rowe to emend Q's 'younger' to 'younker', and Brown does not exclude the confusion deriving from the Dutch/German word *younker* meaning young nobleman (Ard², 54).
  prodigal extending the motif of the return of the Prodigal Son in Luke, 15.20–1, an echo of the Jew's allegation against the Christian at 2.5.15 that Mahood reads as rousing 'a shiver of apprehension over Antonio's cargoes' as well as casting 'a doubt on the future happiness of the impetuous lovers' (Cam², 30–1)

16 **scarfed bark** scarfèd; a ship decorated with flags
  puts from sets out from
  native bay place of origin

17 **embraced** embracèd
  strumpet wind a wind (feminized) that is indiscriminate in the favours it bestows; this image of the strumpet

(prostitute) emphasizes both the erotic attraction of travel as well as the fickleness of a deceptive fortune, repeated at 20. The source of such sentiments is proverbial; cf. Dent, F606: 'FORTUNE is fickle.'

18 **prodigal doth she** a confusion of gender identity, since the Prodigal (the 'scarfèd bark'), now designated female, is figured as returning from a rough sexual encounter with a masculine 'strumpet wind': a mixture of metaphors and similes characteristic of the coarse indiscipline of Gratiano

19 **overweathered ribs** timbers worn or damaged by exposure to the weather (*OED*) or, more generally, weather-beaten but continuing the motif of the anthropomorphization of the figure of the ship, and the metaphor of travel as sexual encounter

20 **Lean** stripped, presumably of the scarves with which the ship began its voyage, but with the suggestion of 'ravaged' in keeping with the Prodigal Son motif
  rent torn apart (Onions)
  beggared made destitute (*OED v.* 1). *OED* gives the first instance of this usage as an adjective; the underlying theme of 15–20 is that of thwarted and deceived desire which informs both financial *and* romantic speculation, utilizing the rhetorical figure of epistrophe, a repetition designed to sharpen the contrast between departure and return (Cam¹, 96)

14 than] *Rowe;* then *Q* 15 younger] younker *Rowe* 17 Hugged] *Cam²;* hugd *Q;* Hugd *Q2;* Hudg'd *F* 18 the] a *F* doth she] she doth *F3* 19 overweathered] *(ouer-wetherd);* ouer-wetherd *Q2;* ouer-wither'd *F;* over-weather'd *Pope*

Enter LORENZO.

SALARINO

Here comes Lorenzo; more of this hereafter.

LORENZO

Sweet friends, your patience for my long abode.
Not I but my affairs have made you wait.
When you shall please to play the thieves for wives,
I'll watch as long for you then. Approach;   25
Here dwells my father Jew. Ho! who's within?

[*Enter*] JESSICA *above*[, *in boy's clothes*].

JESSICA

Who are you? Tell me for more certainty,
Albeit I'll swear that I do know your tongue.

LORENZO

Lorenzo, and thy love.

JESSICA

Lorenzo certain, and my love indeed,   30
For who love I so much? And now, who knows

---

22 **abode** delay (*OED sb.*[1] †1)

24 **play the thieves** take on the roles of thieves in order to obtain wives (just as Lorenzo is now doing)

25 The pause before the invocation to *Approach* led Dover Wilson to the conclusion that this short line, and another later at 47, disclosed evidence of cutting (Cam[1], 140). Pope attempted to regularize the line by inserting 'come' before 'approach'. See p. 255.

26 **father Jew** the juxtaposition of these two nouns suggests a tone of contempt for Lorenzo's future father-in-law. Mahood perceives an echo of *Jew of Malta*, 2.1, in this episode as a whole,

although she does not accept that the earlier play is a 'source' for the later one (Cam[2], 8).

*****Ho!** an exclamatory shout designed to attract attention (Ard[2], 55). *OED* records Q's 'Howe' as obsolete (*OED v.*[2] 1); Q2 prints the more modern 'Ho' and F prints 'Hoa'; all three forms were in use during this period.

27 **more certainty** so that I may be more certain; cf. Abbott, 11, for examples of the comparative degrees of adjectives.

28 **Albeit** even though
   know your tongue recognize your voice

31–2 These lines have an equal mixture of rhetorical question and exclamation.

20.1] *Enter* LORENZO, *masqu'd* / *Capell*; *after* 21 *Dyce*; LORENZO *approaches in haste Cam*[1]   21 SP] *Cam*[2]; *Sal. Q*; *Salino. F*; *Sol.* / *Rann*; *Salar.* / *Malone*; *Salerio Cam*[1]   23 I] I, *Q2, F*   25 then. Approach] *Keightley*; then: approch *Q*; then: approch, *Q2*; then: approach *F2*; then; come approach, *Pope*; then. Come, approach; *Capell*; therein. Approach. *Oxf*   26 Ho!] *Capell*; Howe *Q*; Ho, *Q2*; Hoa, *F*; How! *Ard*[2]   26.1 *Enter*] *Rowe subst.*   *Jessica*] Iessica *Q2, F*   *in boy's clothes*] *Rowe subst.*; *om. Q2, F*   31 For who] For whom *Johnson*

But you, Lorenzo, whether I am yours?

LORENZO

Heaven and thy thoughts are witness that thou art.

JESSICA

Here, catch this casket; it is worth the pains.

I am glad 'tis night you do not look on me,   35

For I am much ashamed of my exchange.

But love is blind, and lovers cannot see

The pretty follies that themselves commit,

For, if they could, Cupid himself would blush

To see me thus transformed to a boy.   40

LORENZO

Descend, for you must be my torch-bearer.

JESSICA

What, must I hold a candle to my shames?

And 'who' and 'whom' were often interchangeable as relative pronouns (see Abbott, 274; Blake, 62–3). An interrogative voice gives the following gloss: 'Who else is it that I love so much? And now who can know but you that I am yours?' An exclamatory voice produces this alternative reading: 'Lorenzo, with whom I am so much in love, and you are now the only one who knows that I am yours.' In performance the actor has a choice.

35 **glad . . . me** glad that because it is dark you are unable to see me. Omitted here is the relative 'that' meaning 'because' (Abbott, 284).

36 **much . . . exchange** feeling very guilty (*OED a.* 1: 'ashamed') because of my disguise. See p. 77.

37 **love is blind** proverbial (Dent, L506)

38 **pretty follies** contrived or artful foolishness (*OED sb.* II.2a: 'pretty'). However, the semantic field of *follies* extends from 'foolishness' (*OED sb.*[1] 1) to 'wickedness, evil or mischief' (*OED* †2), 'lewdness' or 'wantonness' (*OED*

†3), to 'madness' (*OED* †4).

commit do something reprehensible (*OED v.* III.6), but also to 'fornicate' (Gordon Williams, 76–7). Jessica's language combines both sexual and ethical taboos that reflect the seriousness of her action.

39 **Cupid** the son of Venus, goddess of love, who is characterized as a blind boy

40 **transformed** transformèd

41 **torch-bearer** light-bearer, but also the source of Lorenzo's sexual desire; cf. 2.4.24 and Lorenzo's earlier comment that he is already provided with a *torch-bearer*.

42 **hold . . . shames** illuminate my ignominy; referring both to the elopement itself, and to the future loss of Jessica's chastity under circumstances that are not entirely respectable. See Dent, C40, for the proverb: 'He that worst may must hold the CANDLE.' But see also Tilley, C51: 'A good candle-holder proves a good gamester', where the 'gamester' is promised participation in some lewd activity.

34 it is] tis *Q2*   36 I am] I'm *Pope*   ashamed] *(ashamde)*; asham'd *Q2, F*   40 transformed] *(trans-* *formed), Q2, F*   42 shames?] *F*; shames, *Q*; shame? *F2*

They, in themselves, good sooth, are too too light.
Why, 'tis an office of discovery, love,
And I should be obscured.
LORENZO   So are you, sweet,   45
Even in the lovely garnish of a boy.
But come at once,
For the close night doth play the runaway,
And we are stayed for at Bassanio's feast.
JESSICA
I will make fast the doors and gild myself   50
With some moe ducats, and be with you straight.
                                        [*Exit above.*]

43 **good sooth** truly ('sooth': *OED* 2)
   light illuminated in the literal sense of
   the term, and hence evident; but also
   light in weight and hence trivial (*OED
   a.*[1] I.1), or sexually immoral (Partridge,
   137)
44 **office of discovery** The function
   (*office*) of the 'light-bearer' is to discover with the aid of the candle's light.
45 **And ... obscured** And I [Jessica]
   ought to be hidden or darkened
   [whereas, as a torch-bearer, my shames,
   my disguise, and the impropriety of
   my actions, will be revealed]. This
   line condenses the tension between
   Jessica's identity [*I*] as the daughter of
   the Jew, her disguise in the identity of
   a 'boy', and the identity she is about
   to assume as a Christian wife who is
   defined by her *shames*, i.e. her elopement and imminent sexual 'fall'.
   So are you Indeed you are *obscured*
   (by your disguise). Lorenzo selects
   one of the competing meanings in
   order to allude primarily to Jessica's
   cross-dressing.
46 **lovely garnish** attractive outfit
   ('garnish': *OED sb.* †247)

47 This short line curtails further elabo-
   ration and effects an abrupt switch of
   focus.
48 **close** secret or hidden, and hence free
   from observation (Onions)
   runaway vagabond or rascal (Onions),
   but also one who runs away as in an
   elopement (*OED sb.* (*and a.*) I.2 and
   II.3b)
49 **stayed for** waited for or expected
   (Onions)
50 **make fast** secure or lock; Jessica has
   the keys to the house (see 2.5.12).
   gild cover with gold (*OED v.*[1] 1),
   but also supply or adorn with gold
   (*OED* 3 *fig.* and 5 *fig.*); *gild* is homonymically close to 'guilt', the feeling
   accompanying the act of committing
   an offence or a crime (*OED sb.* 4). In
   'gilding' herself with her father's gold,
   Jessica thus makes herself 'guilty'. Cf.
   Macbeth 2.2.55–6: 'I'll gild the faces of
   the grooms withal, / For it must seem
   their guilt.'
51 **moe** more in number; F's 'more' here
   would indicate size or quality. Cf.
   1.1.108n.
   straight immediately

45 are you] you are *F*   46–8] *Pope; Q lines* once, / runaway /; *Q2 lines* boy, / night / run-away
/   50 and] *Q2; & Q*   51 moe] *(mo); more F*   SD] *Dyce; Ex. from above / Theobald; She closes the
casement Cam*[1]

GRATIANO
    Now, by my hood, a gentle, and no Jew.
LORENZO
    Beshrew me but I love her heartily,
    For she is wise, if I can judge of her,
    And fair she is, if that mine eyes be true,   55
    And true she is, as she hath proved herself:
    And therefore like herself, wise, fair and true,
    Shall she be placed in my constant soul.

Enter JESSICA.

    What, art thou come? On, gentleman, away,
    Our masquing mates by this time for us stay.   60
                     [*Exeunt all but Gratiano.*]

Enter ANTONIO.

ANTONIO   Who's there?

52 **hood** the masquer's disguise that Gratiano is wearing
gentle both 'gentlewoman' (*OED sb.* 2) and 'Christian', since 'gentle'/'Gentile' were homophones Q2 emends to 'Gentile'.
53 **Beshrew me** may I be cursed, or may evil befall me (*OED v.* †3b)
54 **if . . . her** if I am able to judge her (Abbott, 307: 'can'); the use of the conditional *if* here reinforces a degree of uncertainty extended in 55.
55–7 **fair . . . true** typical of the conventional lover's praise of his mistress of the kind found in *Sonnets* (Cam², 97)
56 **true . . . proved** ironical, since, in order to be *true* to Lorenzo, Jessica has to be 'untrue' to her father
57 **like herself** heavily ironical, since

Jessica is still at this point in disguise, and therefore 'unlike' herself
58 **placed** placèd
constant steadfast (*OED a.* A1)
59 **gentleman** Q's singular 'gentleman' here, which Q2 and F emend to 'gentlemen', refers explicitly to the disguised Jessica, and extends light-heartedly Gratiano's earlier comment at 52.
60 **masquing mates** fellow masquers. There is a quibble on *mates*, sharpened by the fact that Jessica is disguised as a male who is also Lorenzo's intended marriage partner.
61–9 Mahood speculates that this passage was an authorial revision of a fuller 'masque scene' (Cam², 171–2). See 2.4.22n.

52 gentle] Gentile *Q2*   53 Beshrew] *Q2*; Beshrow *Q*   58.1] *Re-enter* Jessica. *Pope; Enter* Jessica, *to them.* / *Theobald; Enter* JESSICA, *below.* / *Capell*   59 come?] *Q2, F;* come, *Q*   gentleman] gentlemen *Q2, F*   away,] away; *Pope;* away! *Collier*   60 SD] *(Exit.); Exit, with Jessica.* / *Hanmer; Exit, with* JESSICA, *and* SALERINO. *Capell; Exit, with Jessica etc.* / *Johnson; He departs with Jessica and Salerio* Cam¹; *Exit with Jessica and Salerio Oxf; Exit with Jessica and Salerio; Gratiano is about to follow.* / *Bevington; All but Gratiano exit. Folg*   61 Who's] *Q2, F;* Whose *Q*

GRATIANO   Signior Antonio?

ANTONIO

Fie, fie, Gratiano. Where are all the rest?

'Tis nine o'clock; our friends all stay for you.

No masque tonight, the wind is come about.   65

Bassanio presently will go aboard;

I have sent twenty out to seek for you.

GRATIANO

I am glad on't. I desire no more delight

Than to be under sail and gone tonight.   *Exeunt.*

[**2.7**]   *Enter* PORTIA [*and* NERISSA] *with* [*the* Prince of]
                MOROCCO, *and both their trains.*

PORTIA [*to Attendant*]

Go, draw aside the curtains and discover

The several caskets to this noble prince.

[*to Morocco*] Now make your choice.

MOROCCO

This first of gold, who this inscription bears:

'Who chooseth me shall gain what many men desire.'   5

---

65 **come about** veered or turned around
(Onions) so that it is now in the right
direction for the ship to set sail on its
expedition

66 **presently** shortly

2.7.0.1 Capell added '*Flourish Cornets*';
Mahood explains the absence of a
musical direction in F at the opening
of 2.7 as unnecessary because Morocco
is already in residence (Cam², 98),

but argues that the 'flourish' when
Morocco leaves the stage at the end of
the scene in F may be an ironic comment on his hasty exit (Cam², 178).

1 **discover** reveal

2 **several** distinct or separate (*OED adj.*
A1. †1b)

4 **who** often used for the other relative forms, 'which' or 'that' (Abbott,
258)

---

62 Antonio?] *(Anthonio?); Anthonio. Q2;* Anthonio! *Hanmer*   63 Fie, fie,] Fie, *Pope*   64 o'clock;]
Capell; a clocke *Q*   65 tonight,] *(to night,); tonight; Theobald*   67] *om. Q2; after 64 Hanmer*
68 SP] *om. Q2*   I am] I'm *Pope*   69 under sail] *(undersaile);* vnder sayle *Q2;* vnder saile *F*
2.7] *Capell;* SCENE III. *Belmont. / Rowe subst.;* SCENE VIII *Pope*   0.1 *and* NERISSA] *this edn*
the Prince . . . MOROCCO] *Capell, Cam¹;* Morrocho *Q;* Morrochius *Rowe*   1 SD] *this edn*   curtains]
(curtaines); Curtain *F4*   2 prince.] *(Prince:);* prince . . . Servants draw back the curtains and reveal
a table and three caskets thereon Cam¹; The curtains are drawn aside, revealing three caskets Oxf*   3 SD]
Oxf   choice.] *(choyce.), Q2;* choice. *Three Caskets are discovered. / Rowe;* choice. *Morocco examines
the caskets Cam¹;* choice. *The curtains are drawn. / Bevington*   4 This] The *Q2, F*   who] which
Pope   5 many men] men *F*

The second, silver, which this promise carries:
'Who chooseth me shall get as much as he deserves.'
This third, dull lead, with warning all as blunt:
'Who chooseth me must give and hazard all he hath.'
How shall I know if I do choose the right?   10

PORTIA
The one of them contains my picture, prince.
If you choose that, then I am yours withal.

MOROCCO
Some god direct my judgement! Let me see,
I will survey th'inscriptions back again.
What says this leaden casket?   15
'Who chooseth me must give and hazard all he hath.'
'Must give', for what? For lead? Hazard for lead?
This casket threatens: men that hazard all
Do it in hope of fair advantages.
A golden mind stoops not to shows of dross;   20
I'll then nor give nor hazard aught for lead.
What says the silver with her virgin hue?

8 **dull** heavy and uninteresting (*OED a.* 3 and 5) but also blunt (*OED* 6) **all as** equally as
9 **hazard** risk or venture (*OED sb.* 2)
12 **withal** along with (Onions). Portia identifies herself with her *picture* in 11.
13 **Some god** Morocco's appeal to an unspecific *god* to direct his choice confirms his alien status.
14 **back again** in reverse order; a hint at a connection between Morocco and the practice of devil-worship
18–19 **men . . . advantages** men who venture everything do so in the hope of favourable benefits; but see 1.3.66, where the term *advantage* is a synonym for 'profit' or 'interest'.
20 **shows of dross** outward manifestation of worthless or impure matter; see

*OED sb.*1 for 'dross' as the extraneous impure matter thrown off from metal in the process of melting.
21 **nor give nor** neither give nor; the repetition of a conjunction that introduces both alternatives (*OED* 2b) **aught** anything
22 **virgin hue** pure and unsullied (*OED sb.* II.15b) colour, i.e. an exemplary paleness, possibly linked to the figure of the moon goddess, Diana, noted for her 'bright' appearance (*OCD*, 274). Morocco ascribes a female gender to silver (*her*) that he also associates with virginity, but he also reinforces his own sense of the hierarchical order of metals, and, by analogy, his sense of his own superior worth (gold) and status.

10] *printed twice* F   12 withal] *Rowe;* withall *Q;* with all *Capell*   13 judgement!] *Theobald;* iudgement, *Q;* judgment: *Pope*   14 th'inscriptions] *(*th'inscriptions,*);* the inscriptions, F   16] *italics Q3*   17 what? . . . lead?] *Q3;* what? . . . lead, *Q;* what? . . . lead! *Ard²* Hazard for lead?] *om.* F3   18 threatens: men] *Collier;* threatens men *Q;* threatens. Men *Rowe;* threatens. Men, *Theobald;* threatens: Men *Capell*

263

'Who chooseth me shall get as much as he deserves.'
'As much as he deserves.' Pause there, Morocco,
And weigh thy value with an even hand.   25
If thou be'st rated by thy estimation
Thou dost deserve enough; and yet, enough
May not extend so far as to the lady.
And yet, to be afeard of my deserving
Were but a weak disabling of myself.   30
As much as I deserve: why, that's the lady.
I do in birth deserve her, and in fortunes,
In graces and in qualities of breeding.
But more than these, in love I do deserve.
What if I strayed no farther, but chose here?   35
Let's see once more this saying graved in gold:

25 with . . . hand impartially
26 rated estimated
   thy estimation your own standard
   of value (*OED* †1 and 2†b); *estimation* sometimes means 'reputation', as
   in *CE* 3.1.102–3: 'Against your yet
   ungalled estimation, / That may with
   foul intrusion enter in'; here both
   meanings are active, since Morocco
   comes with a reputation which he
   immodestly announces.
27 enough sufficient, i.e. a quantity com-
   mensurate with worth; cf. *RJ* 3.1.97–8:
   'No, 'tis not so deep as a well, nor so
   wide as a church door, but 'tis enough,
   'twill serve.'
28 so as (Abbott, 281)
29 afeard . . . deserving doubt my own
   worth (Ard¹, 75); a doubt and a 'fear'
   that betrays an 'outsider's' lack of
   confidence in his capacity for success
30 disabling disparaging or belittling,
   but also to render incapable of action
   (*OED v.* 1b)
32–3 attributes of *birth*, wealth and
   courtly *breeding* that ironically echo
   the play's dominant discourse of racial
   purity

32 fortunes luck or chance (*OED sb.* 1),
   but also material wealth or substance
   (*OED* 6)
34 more . . . deserve I deserve because,
   more than the catalogue of deserts
   enumerated in 32–3, I can offer love;
   Morocco indicates that if he is successful then this will be more than
   a marriage of convenience. Furness
   (103–4) cites Capell as the source
   of the emendation whereby 'her' is
   implied here, on the grounds that it
   echoes the phrase *deserve her* at 32.
   Keightley, uniquely though unnecessarily, prints 'her' (Keightley, 129).
35 strayed wandered (*OED sb.* II.†4:
   'stray'); but see also *OED v.*² for the etymology of 'stray': '*extravagare*', meaning 'to wander outside'. Morocco's
   deployment of this idiom represents an
   unconscious indictment of a customary
   nomadic (and by implication subhuman
   and promiscuous) existence.
36 graved engraved, but also entombed.
   See *R2* 3.2.140, 'And lie full low,
   grav'd in the hollow ground', for the
   subsidiary meaning 'entombed', and
   also Freud, 235–47.

24 Morocco] *(Morocho)*; *Morrochius / Rowe*   29 afeard] afeared *Q2*; afraid *Q3*   34 deserve.] *Q2, F*;
deserue, *Q*; deserve her. *Keightley*

'Who chooseth me shall gain what many men desire.'
Why, that's the lady; all the world desires her.
From the four corners of the earth they come
To kiss this shrine, this mortal breathing saint.   40
The Hyrcanian deserts and the vasty wilds
Of wide Arabia are as throughfares now
For princes to come view fair Portia.
The watery kingdom, whose ambitious head
Spits in the face of heaven, is no bar   45
To stop the foreign spirits, but they come,
As o'er a brook, to see fair Portia.

39–43 Cf. *Tamburlaine 2*, 5.3.4617–20; see also Brooke, 42. Shapiro cites this and the earlier example at 2.1.24ff. as examples of Shakespeare's capacity for the burlesquing of 'Marlowe's aggressive over-reachers by relocating them within a comedy where their heroic visions are misplaced' (Shapiro, '*Merchant*', 273).

40 **shrine** a receptacle containing an object of religious veneration (*OED sb.* 2b), a reference both to the casket and to its hypothetical contents, although the usual association with the repository of human remains connects with the subsidiary meaning of *graved* at 36
mortal breathing saint a reference to the living Portia, but in its use of the idiom of idolatry it approaches blasphemy; cf. *Luc* 85: 'This earthly saint adored by this devil'.

41 **Hyrcanian deserts** a province of Persia situated to the south-east of the Caspian Sea, associated with the barrenness and the Caucasus but also notorious for its wild tigers. Cf. Virgil, 4.366ff., 'No, your parent was Mount Caucasus, rugged, rocky, and hard, and tigers of Hyrcania nursed you' (Knight, 108), but the place is also

used by Marlowe in *Dido Queen of Carthage* (1594), 5.1.158–9.
vasty vast or immense (*OED*), but in this instance emphasizing desolation (Furness, 104)

42 **throughfares** thoroughfares

43 **come view** come (to) view; on the absence of 'to' before the infinitive *view*, see Abbott, 349. Since this a decasyllabic line it is possible that Morocco might pronounce 'Portia' as a trisyllable both here and at 47 in performance; an example of epistrophe, used to emphasize the forced and extravagant nature of Morocco's speech.

44 **watery kingdom** the sea, ruled over by the classical deity Poseidon
ambitious head a ruler who has ambitions beyond his station, and who expresses them, in this case, through the turbulence of the sea. Poseidon was also thought to be responsible for causing earthquakes (*OCD*, 603), another facet of a general capacity for disturbance that augments an ambitious temperament.

45 **bar** impediment

46 **foreign spirits** adventurers of courage and determination who are also strangers (*OED sb.* III.13)

38 lady;] *Q3;* lady, *Q*   40 mortal breathing] *(*mortall breathing*);* mortal-breathing *Dyce*   41 vasty] *(*vastie*);* vaste *F;* vast *F3*   42 throughfares] through-fares *Q2;* through fares *F3;* through Fares *F4;* Thorough-fares *Rowe*   44 watery] *(*waterie*);* watry *Q2*   45 Spits] *Rowe;* Spets *Q*

One of these three contains her heavenly picture.
Is't like that lead contains her? 'Twere damnation
To think so base a thought; it were too gross   50
To rib her cerecloth in the obscure grave.
Or shall I think in silver she's immured,
Being ten times undervalued to tried gold?
O, sinful thought! Never so rich a gem
Was set in worse than gold. They have in England   55
A coin that bears the figure of an angel
Stamped in gold: but that's insculped upon.
But here, an angel in a golden bed
Lies all within. Deliver me the key.
Here do I choose, and thrive I as I may.   60

PORTIA

There, take it, prince, [*giving him the key*] and if my
     form lie there

---

49 **Is't like** is it likely
  damnation in Christian theology, the
  fact of being doomed to hell (*OED* 2),
  but here, for being guilty of heretical
  thought (Ard¹, 76)
50 **base** low, but also associated with the
  colour black; cf. *TA* 4.2.73: 'Zounds,
  ye whore, is black so base a hue?'
  gross coarse
51 **rib** wrap or enclose (*OED v.*¹ 1)
  cerecloth a shroud: a cloth impreg-
  nated with wax and used for enclosing
  a dead body, a winding-sheet (*OED
  sb.* 1)
  obscure dark or dismal (*OED a.* 1)
52 **immured** imprisoned or enclosed
  (literally, within walls (*OED v.* 2))
53 **ten times undervalued** the value
  of silver in relation to gold around
  the end of the 16th century (Furness,
  105); see also Braudel, 1.458–64.
  tried purified or refined (*OED* 1)

56 **angel** gold coin valued at ten shillings
  (*Shakespeare's England*, 1.341), and so
  called because it contained an image
  of the archangel Michael defeating a
  dragon
57 **insculped upon** engraved upon the
  surface (*OED v.* 1)
58 **angel ... bed** 'angel' as in celestial
  being; Morocco imagines Portia's picture lying inside the golden casket which
  is erotically figured as a 'golden bed'.
59 **Deliver me** give me, i.e. deliver (up)
  to me
59–60 **key ... may** possible rhymes
  (Kökeritz, 455) but Brown lists alternative pronunciations for *key* (Ard²,
  60). This may be yet another indication of the forced and formal idiom
  that characterizes Morocco's speech.
60 **thrive ... may** may I be as successful
  as I can
61 **form** portrait or likeness

49 her?] *F;* her, *Q*   51 rib] *Q2, F;* ribb *Q*   52 she's immured] *(*shees immurd*);* shee's immur'd *Q2;*
she's immur'd *F*   53 tried] *(*tride*)*   54 thought!] *Capell;* thought, *Q*   57 Stamped] *Pope;* stampt *Q;*
Stampt *Q2, F*   insculped] *(*insculpt*);* insculp'd *Johnson*   61 SD] *Oxf subst.*

Then I am yours!   [*Morocco unlocks the golden casket.*]
MOROCCO   O, hell! What have we here?
A carrion death, within whose empty eye
There is a written scroll. I'll read the writing.
   [*Reads.*]

> *All that glisters is not gold,*   65
> *Often have you heard that told.*
> *Many a man his life hath sold*
> *But my outside to behold.*
> *Gilded timber do worms infold.*
> *Had you been as wise as bold,*   70
> *Young in limbs, in judgement old,*

63 **carrion death** obviously a skull, but also an emblem for the mutable human body, and hence death (*OED sb.* 3) **empty eye** the eye-socket of the skull
64 **scroll** roll of paper or parchment (*OED sb.* 1)
65 proverbial, cf. Tilley, A146, and also Lodge, sig. B2ᵛ: 'The young Gentleman, vnacquainted with such like discourses, counting all gold that glysters, and him a faithfull friend that hath a flattering tongue, opens all his mind to this subtill vnderminer, who so wringeth him at last, that there is no secret corner in the poore Gentlemans heart, but he knoweth it.'
68 *But* only *my outside* a commonplace observation that refers to the exterior attraction of gold; cf. Lodge, sig. C2ʳ: 'Doe we buie ought for the fairenesse or goodnesse? Spangled Hobbie horses are for children, but men must respecte things which be of value indeede.'
69 *timber* as in Q, subsequently emended unnecessarily, on metrical grounds; Pope emended to 'wood', and Capell, following Johnson,

emended to 'tombs'. Q's 'timber' refers to the wooden painted coffin that contained the vermicular human body; *timber* was also regarded as a natural substance prone to distortion; cf. *AYL* 3.3.79–81: 'This fellow will but join you together as they join wainscot; the one of you will prove a shrunk panel and, like green timber, warp, warp.' The disruption of metrical embellishment here performs the sentiment of the line, indicating the deceptively cosmetic power of poetical language itself.
71 vigorous in body and mature in judgement. Possibly proverbial; see Tilley, O34: 'He that would be OLD long (well old) must be old betimes (Old young and old long).' For the larger, more severe context, see Lodge, sigs E2ᵛ–3: 'now if these men shuld in their enterprises be gazde into, I feare me yt as in the black Iet is seene no white: in the deadly poison is founde no preseruatiue: in the sprouting iuie no fruite: on the vnnecessarie thistle no grapes: so in these men the mischiefe woulde be so manifest, that the shew of vertue would be extinguished.'

62 yours!] *(yours?)*; yours. *Q2, F* SD] *Rowe subst.* 62–4 O . . . writing.] *Capell; Q lines* death, / scrowle, / writing. 62 here?] *Theobald;* heare, *Q;* here, *F* 63 death,] death? *Q2;* Death, *Rowe*
64 SD] *Riv* 69 timber] wood *Pope;* tombs *Capell;* woods *Keightley*

> Your answer had not been inscrolled,
> Fare you well, your suit is cold.

Cold indeed, and labour lost,
Then farewell, heat, and welcome frost.   75
Portia, adieu. I have too grieved a heart
To take a tedious leave: thus losers part.

Exit [with his train].

PORTIA
A gentle riddance. Draw the curtains, go.
Let all of his complexion choose me so.   *Exeunt.*

[**2.8**]   *Enter* SALARINO *and* SALANIO.

SALARINO
Why, man, I saw Bassanio under sail.

72 **Your answer** the response that you have received
73 **suit is cold** petition is devoid of passion; ironical, since earlier at 2.1.2 Morocco had proclaimed his close proximity to *the burnished sun*
75 **farewell . . . frost** a significant inversion, both of a proverbial saying (Dent, F769: 'Farewell frost'), and also of Thomas Nashe's farewell to Ireland in *The Terrors of the Night* (1594): 'Farewell frost: as much as to say farewell *Island*, for I haue no more to say to thee' (Nashe, 1.360).
76 **grieved** troubled or distressed (*OED* †1 and 4)
77 **tedious** long and tiresome (*OED* 1), a further reference to the dominant style of Morocco's language, and a final self-condemnation
part depart
78 **gentle riddance** polite deliverance (*OED* 4 and 5), but with a possible play on 'gentle'/'Gentile', to indicate that

the Christian Portia considers herself well rid of the infidel Morocco
79 **complexion** literally a reference to Morocco's blackness, but Brown links this with the larger context of 'temperament', i.e. 'the proportion in which the four humours (choler, blood, phlegm, and melancholy) were combined' in the human body to determine character type (Ard², 61).
2.8 Capell locates the scene in 'Venice. *A Street.*'
0.1 F adds '*Flo. Cornets*' in what may be an error (see 2.7.0.1n.). Brown follows Cam¹ in emending 'Salarino' to 'Salerio', but it is clear from the ensuing dialogue that a series of reported events at which Salarino was present have taken place offstage between his departure at 2.6.60 and his reappearance at this point. See p. 000.
1 **under sail** with sails set (*OED sb.*¹ 3d), ready to depart, or in the act of departing

72 *Your*] This *Rann (Johnson)*   73 *Fare you well,*] *(Fareyouwell)*   74 Cold] *Capell; Mor.* Cold *Q*   76 adieu.] *(adiew,); adieu, Rowe*   77 SD] *Dyce (Exit with his Train. Cornets.); he departs with his retinue Cam²*   **2.8**] *Steevens;* SCENE IV. *Rowe;* SCENE IX. *Pope;* SCENE VII. *Cam²*   0.1] *(Enter . . . Solanio.), Q2; Enter . . . Solanio / Flo. Cornets. F; Enter* Solarino *and* Solanio. *Rowe; Enter* Solarino *and* Salanio *Pope; Enter* SOLANIO, *and* SALERINO. *Capell;* SALERIO *and* SOLANIO *Cam¹*   1+ SP] *(Sal.), Cam²; Salar. Q2; Salerio Cam¹*

With him is Gratiano gone along,
And in their ship I am sure Lorenzo is not.

SALANIO

The villain Jew with outcries raised the Duke,
Who went with him to search Bassanio's ship.   5

SALARINO

He came too late, the ship was under sail.
But there the Duke was given to understand
That in a gondola were seen together
Lorenzo and his amorous Jessica.
Besides, Antonio certified the Duke   10
They were not with Bassanio in his ship.

SALANIO

I never heard a passion so confused,
So strange, outrageous, and so variable
As the dog Jew did utter in the streets:
'My daughter! O, my ducats! O, my daughter!   15

4 **raised** roused up. The Jew's dilemma is repeated and augmented in *Oth* 1.1 and 1.3, and in the conflict between Desdemona and her father Brabantio.
6 **under sail** See 1n., although the sense here is 'already departed'.
8 **gondola** a covered boat used for transporting passengers on the Venetian canals; cf. Coryate: 'none of them are open aboue, but fairely couered, first with some fifteene or sixteene little round pieces of timber that reach from one end to the other, and make a pretty kinds of Arche or vault in the Gondola; then with faire blacke cloth which is turned vp at both ends of the boate, to the end that if the passenger meaneth to be priuate, he may draw downe the same, and after row so secretly that no man can see him' (Coryate, 170–1).
9 **amorous** showing love or fondness

(*OED* 3), although suggesting an overtly sexual display of affection
10 **certified** attested in an authoritative manner (*OED* 1), a detail designed, possibly, to verify Antonio's non-involvement in the matter of Jessica's elopement
12 **passion** violent outburst of emotion (Ard[1], 80)
   confused made up of several ingredients mixed together (*OED* †4), here confusing 'family' and 'money'
13 **variable** liable to fluctuation (*OED adj*. A1 and A1b)
15 For the source of this line, see Masuccio's *Il Novellino* (Bullough, 1.504), and *Jew of Malta*, 2.1.47–8, 'O my girl, / My gold, my fortune, my felicity', and 254, 'O girl, O gold, O beauty, O my bliss!' What is a positive utterance in Marlowe is rendered negatively in *MV*. See p. 22.

3 I am] Ime *Q2;* I'm *Pope*   4 SP] *(Sola.),* *Q2 (Salan.); Sol. F; Solanio Cam[1]*   6 came] comes *F*   under sail] *(vndersaile), Q2 (*vnder saile*)*   8 gondola] *(Gondylo);* Gondilo *F;* Gondalo *Rowe*   9 amorous] armorous *Q2*   12 SP] *(Sal.); Salan. Q2; Sol. F; Sola. / Rowe; Solanio Cam[1]*   15 daughter! O . . . ducats! O . . . daughter!] *Theobald;* daughter, ô . . . ducats, ô . . . daughter, *Q;* daughter, O . . . ducats, O . . . daughter! *Pope;* daughter! O . . . ducats! O . . . daughter, *Warburton*

Fled with a Christian! O, my Christian ducats!
Justice, the law, my ducats and my daughter!
A sealed bag, two sealed bags of ducats,
Of double ducats, stol'n from me by my daughter!
And jewels, two stones, two rich and precious stones, 20
Stol'n by my daughter! Justice! Find the girl;
She hath the stones upon her, and the ducats.'

SALARINO
Why, all the boys in Venice follow him,
Crying 'His stones, his daughter and his ducats!'

SALANIO
Let good Antonio look he keep his day, 25
Or he shall pay for this.

SALARINO   Marry, well remembered.

16 **Christian ducats** *Christian* is used
as a transferred epithet because the
money has been transferred from the
Jew to the Christian Lorenzo, but
is also used as a straightforwardly
descriptive adjective that refers to
Christians both as the source of the
Jew's wealth and as practitioners of
usury. See p. 14.
18 **sealed . . . sealed** In order to make
this an orthodox iambic pentameter,
one of these must be pronounced as a
disyllable; Salanio is possibly parodying the Jew's loss of control, perfectly
expressed by variation in pronunciation. Puttenham labelled this device
'*Epizeuxis*' (Puttenham, 167) or the
'*cuckowspell*' (168) that foregrounds
(foolish) repetition and invokes the
practice associated with the cuckoo of
benefiting from the labour of others
(*OED* 3). See 1.3.1ff.
19 **double ducats** a coin of Spanish

origin worth ⅔ of an old English
£1 (i.e. 13s. 4d); see *Shakespeare's
England*, 1.342, and also Coryate, 285.
20 **jewels . . . stones** literally, references
to the stolen wealth, but also implicitly
bawdy, since *jewel* referred metaphorically to female chastity and *stones* to
testicles (Partridge, 128 and 192)
22 **stones upon her** literally, jewels in her
possession, but also bawdily suggestive
in the sense that Salanio puts into the
Jew's mouth words that suggest he is
unmanned by the loss of his jewels
(*stones*) and that imply that Jessica has
already had sexual intercourse with
Lorenzo
25 **look . . . day** make sure that he
repays his loan by the agreed time.
See Abbott, 368, for the omission of
the relative pronoun 'that' in connection with the appearance of the
subjunctive in a subordinate clause or
sentence.

16 Fled] Fed *F3* Christian!] *Dyce;* Christian, *Q;* Christian? *Pope* O] *(ô), Q2, F* ducats!] *F;* ducats. *Q* 17 Justice, . . . daughter!] *Pope;* Iustice, . . . daughter, *Q;* Iustice . . . daughter. *Q2;* Iustice . . .
daughter; *F; Justice! . . .* law! . . . ducats, . . . daughter! – *Capell;* Justice, . . . law – My ducats, . . .
daughter! *Johnson* ducats] ducats, *Q2, F* 20 two stones, two rich] two rich *Rowe;* two stones, rich
Pope; too, stones, rich *Warburton* 21 Stol'n] *Hanmer;* Stolne *Q;* stoln *F3;* Stoll'n *Warburton;* Stolen
Cam¹ 23+ SP] *(Sal.), Cam²;* Salar. *Q2;* Salerio *Cam¹* 24 ducats!] *(ducats.)* 25+ SP] *(Sola.), Q2
(Salan.);* Sal. *F;* Sol. / *Capell;* Sala. / *Steevens;* Solan. / *Dyce;* Solanio *Cam¹*

I reasoned with a Frenchman yesterday
Who told me, in the narrow seas that part
The French and English, there miscarried
A vessel of our country richly fraught.   30
I thought upon Antonio when he told me,
And wished in silence that it were not his.

SALANIO
You were best to tell Antonio what you hear.
Yet do not suddenly, for it may grieve him.

SALARINO
A kinder gentleman treads not the earth.   35
I saw Bassanio and Antonio part;
Bassanio told him he would make some speed
Of his return. He answered, 'Do not so,
Slubber not business for my sake, Bassanio,
But stay the very riping of the time;   40
And for the Jew's bond, which he hath of me,
Let it not enter in your mind of love.
Be merry, and employ your chiefest thoughts
To courtship, and such fair ostents of love

27 **reasoned** had a conversation (*OED v.* †2)
28–9 **narrow . . . English** English Channel between Dover and Calais
29 **miscarried** miscarrièd; perished (*OED v.* †1), but also in the sense of being unproductive (*OED* 4 and 4†b), while the subsidiary meaning of the premature delivery of its cargo (to the sea) may also be implied (*OED* 5)
30 **richly fraught** laden with valuable cargo (*OED* 1: 'fraught'). Pooler notes the echo of *Jew of Malta*, 1.1.54: 'The ships are safe, thou say'st, and richly fraught' (Ard¹, 81).
37–8 **make . . . return** aim to return quickly
39 ****Slubber not** do not perform in a hurried or careless manner; Q's 'Slumber', which Q2 and F correct to 'Slubber' (*OED v.* 3), is clearly an error.
40 **very . . . time** The primary meaning of this phrase is 'until Bassanio's project has fully matured', but it is connected to the subsidiary meaning: 'until the time has come for Antonio to fulfil the terms of his bond'.
41 **for** as for (Abbott, 149)
   of from (Abbott, 170)
42 **mind of love** preoccupation with romantic matters, but also a mind devoted to affection for Antonio (cf. 1.1.130–1) and therefore aware of his obligation
44 **ostents** displays (*OED sb.²* 1); cf. also 2.2.188.

33 SP] *(Sol.)*, *Q2 (Salan.)*; *Sola. / Rowe*; *Sala. / Steevens*; *Solan. / Dyce*; *Solanio Cam¹* 34 **for**] lest *Capell* 39 Slubber] *Q2, F*; Slumber *Q*

271

As shall conveniently become you there.'   45
And even there, his eye being big with tears,
Turning his face, he put his hand behind him,
And, with affection wondrous sensible,
He wrung Bassanio's hand, and so they parted.

SALANIO

I think he only loves the world for him.   50
I pray thee, let us go and find him out,
And quicken his embraced heaviness
With some delight or other.

SALARINO   Do we so.   *Exeunt.*

[2.9]   *Enter* NERISSA *and a Servitor.*

NERISSA

Quick, quick, I pray thee, draw the curtain straight;
The Prince of Arragon hath ta'en his oath,
And comes to his election presently.

45 **conveniently become you** be appropriate or fitting for you (*OED sb.* †4 and †b)
46 **even there** at that very moment; clearly not, as Dyce conjectured, an error of repetition from the previous line
48 **affection wondrous sensible** a remarkably intense display of emotion, but also capable of being perceived by those looking on (*OED adj.* I.3 and 4: 'sensible')
49 **wrung** pressed or squeezed (*OED v.* 1)
50 **he ... him** his (Antonio's) affection for the world derives exclusively from his affection for him (Bassanio)
52 **quicken** stimulate, or restore to life (*OED v.* 2a)
embraced heaviness embracèd; the sadness that has resulted from his

accepting responsibility for Bassanio's enterprise. Furness (112) draws attention to Portia's 'doubtful thoughts, and rash-embraced despair' at 3.2.109.
53 **Do we so** Let us go and do it, i.e. try to alleviate Antonio's sadness
2.9 Rowe locates the scene in 'BELMONT', but Ard[1] specifies '*A Room in Portia's House*'.
0.1 *Servitor* 'a (male) personal or domestic attendant (in early use chiefly, one who waits at table); a manservant' (*OED* 1)
1 **straight** straightaway or immediately
2 **ta'en his oath** has sworn (at the temple) to abide by the conditions governing his choice of casket, as stipulated at 2.1.40–2
3 **comes ... election** makes his choice (*OED* 2 and 2†b)

46 there] then *Dyce* 48 wondrous] wond'rous *Pope* 50 SP] *(Sol.), Q2 (Salan.); Sola. / Rowe; Sala. / Steevens; Solan. / Dyce; Solanio Cam¹* 2.9] *Capell subst.*; SCENE V. *Belmont. / Rowe;* SCENE X *Pope* 0.1 *Servitor*] *(Seruitor); Seruiture F; Servant / Rowe* 1 straight;] *(strait,)*

Enter [the Prince of] ARRAGON, *his train and* PORTIA.

PORTIA

    Behold, there stand the caskets, noble prince.

    If you choose that wherein I am contained,   5

    Straight shall our nuptial rites be solemnized.

    But if you fail, without more speech, my lord,

    You must be gone from hence immediately.

ARRAGON

    I am enjoined by oath to observe three things:

    First, never to unfold to anyone   10

    Which casket 'twas I chose; next, if I fail

    Of the right casket, never in my life

    To woo a maid in way of marriage;

    Lastly, if I do fail in fortune of my choice,

    Immediately to leave you and be gone.   15

PORTIA

    To these injunctions everyone doth swear

    That comes to hazard for my worthless self.

ARRAGON

    And so I have addressed me. Fortune now

---

5 **that** the one; the relative pronoun functions deictically to indicate any of the three caskets (see Blake, 3.3.2.6, 61ff.).

9 **enjoined** bound

10 **unfold** reveal

12 **Of** as regards, or what comes from (choosing) (Abbott, 173)

13 **in way of** in the direction of; cf. 1.1.55, where the phrase may be glossed 'with a view to'.
    marriage marriàge; cf. *TS* 3.1.138: ''Twere good methinks to steal our marriage'.

14 **Lastly** an addition to what is otherwise a decasyllabic line. Abbott, 511, suggests that these short lines either introduce or conclude a speech and

that their function is to heighten dramatic effect.

16 **injunctions** both directives (*OED* 1) and judicial constraints (*OED* 2)

17 **hazard** venture and put oneself at risk (*OED v.* 1 and 1b)
    worthless unworthy or without deserving (*OED a.* 2), in which case, an expression of feminine modesty; but also falsely modest in so far as Portia is not destitute in the material sense (*OED a.* 1)

18 **addressed me** prepared myself, or addressed myself to the task of

18–19 **Fortune ... hope** an invocation to Fortune to fulfil Arragon's hopes, stronger than the more modern 'Good luck' (Ard[2], 65)

3.1 *the* Prince of] *Capell* ARRAGON . . . PORTIA.] *(Arrogon . . . Portia.); Arragon . . . Portia / Flor. Cornets. F; Arragon . . . Portia, Flor. Cornets. The Caskets are discover'd. / Rowe* 5 If] (yf), *Q2* 6 rites] *Pope;* rights *Q* 7 you] thou *F* 9 enjoined] (enioynd); enioyn'd *Q2* to] t' *Pope* 13–14] *Capell lines* lastly / choice /; *Cam lines* marriage; / Lastly / choice / 13 woo] (wooe); woe *Q2* 14 Lastly,] (lastly,); Last, *Pope* do fail] fail *Pope*

To my heart's hope! Gold, silver and base lead.
'Who chooseth me must give and hazard all he hath.' 20
You shall look fairer e'er I give or hazard.
What says the golden chest? Ha, let me see:
'Who chooseth me shall gain what many men desire.'
'What many men desire': that 'many' may be meant
By the fool multitude that choose by show, 25
Not learning more than the fond eye doth teach,
Which pries not to th'interior, but like the martlet
Builds in the weather on the outward wall,
Even in the force and road of casualty.
I will not choose what many men desire, 30
Because I will not jump with common spirits
And rank me with the barbarous multitudes.
Why then, to thee, thou silver treasure house:
Tell me once more what title thou dost bear:
'Who chooseth me shall get as much as he deserves.' 35
And well said too; for who shall go about

24–5 **be meant / By** stand for; Rowe
emended to 'be meant of' but this does
not clarify the phrase; Furness (115)
cites Puttenham, 157: 'The good old
Gentlewoman would tell vs that were
children how it [a riddle] was meant
by a furd gloue.'
25 **fool** foolish or inferior (*OED sb.*[1])
26 **fond** infatuated or silly
27 **pries not** does not search inquisitively
into (*OED v.*[1] 1 and 2)
martlet swift, often confused with the
swallow and the housemartin (*OED*),
which builds its nest in the face of unan-
ticipated danger. See also Spurgeon,
187–90, who suggests that the quibble is
on 'martin' as a fool or a dupe (*OED* †2).
28 **in the weather** exposed to the vagar-
ies of the climate

outward wall exposed outer wall
29 **force . . . casualty** violence (of the
weather) and the path of mischance
or disaster. See *OED sb.*[1] 2 †d: 'force';
OED 1 and 2: 'casualty'.
31 **jump** agree; cf. *TS* 1.1.190: 'Both our
inventions meet and jump in one.'
common spirits energies associated
with the common people, and hence
undiscriminating
32 **rank me** class myself (*OED v.*[1] 2†b);
see also *OED adj.* III.12 for a subsidiary meaning of 'having an offensively
strong smell'.
barbarous uncultured or uncivilized
(*OED* 3) but with the subsidiary
meaning of 'not speaking the same
language' (*OED* 2)
36 **go about** attempt

---

19 hope!] *Theobald*; hope: *Q* 22 chest?] *Q2*; chest, *Q* 24 'many' may] *Cam*[1]; many may *Q*;
Many, may *Rowe*; may *Pope* 25 fool multitude] foole-multitude *Q2* 27 pries] payes *F3*; pry
Theobald th'interior] *Q2, F*; thinteriour *Q*; th'interiour *Q3* but like] like *Hanmer* 29 road] *Rowe*;
rode *Q* 32 barbarous] barbarious *F4* multitudes] multitude *Dyce* 36 too;] *F*; to; *Q*; too, *Q2*

To cozen Fortune and be honourable
Without the stamp of merit? Let none presume
To wear an undeserved dignity.
O, that estates, degrees and offices   40
Were not derived corruptly, and that clear honour
Were purchased by the merit of the wearer!
How many then should cover that stand bare?
How many be commanded that command?
How much low peasantry would then be gleaned   45
From the true seed of honour? And how much honour
Picked from the chaff and ruin of the times

---

37 **cozen** cheat
38 **stamp of merit** formal acknowledgement of worth
39 **wear . . . dignity** wear clothes that
  indicate an undeserved social status;
  a possible reference to the Sumptuary
  Laws that were revised in 1597, which
  contained details of appropriate attire
  (see Jardine, 142–4)
  undeserved undeservèd
40 **estates . . . offices** social classes,
  positions within the general system of
  social classification, and the holding of
  official positions within government
41 **derived** both gained and inherited
  clear honour evident worth, i.e. the
  outward manifestation of the integrity
  of the possessor
42 **purchased** acquired or obtained
  rather than simply bought; cf. *LLL*
  1.1.72–3: 'Why, all delights are vain,
  but that most vain / Which, with pain
  purchased, doth inherit pain.'
43 **cover . . . bare** cover their heads with
  their hats, and now doff them as a
  mark of respect for their (undeserving)
  social superiors
44 **be . . . command** would be subser-

vient when they are themselves at
present in positions of authority.
Arragon laments the disintegration
of the social order, though he is also
ironically building a case against his
own 'worth'.
45 **gleaned** gathered together (*OED v.*
  3), but also specifically to gather up
  ears of corn that have been separated
  from the chaff after reaping (*OED v.*
  1); see 47.
46 **true seed of** true beginning of the
  growth of (*OED sb. fig.* 2), but also
  a possible allusion to the biblical
  Parable of the Sower in Matthew,
  13.24–30
47 **chaff** technically the husks of corn
  separated as a result of threshing and
  winnowing (*OED sb.*[1] 1), but also figuratively, refuse or rubbish (*OED sb.*[1] 6)
  ruin what remains after decay (*OED
  sb.* 2b); an example of the rhetorical
  figure of hendiadys, i.e. the use of
  two terms to mean the same thing
  (Furness, 117)
  times a possible quibble on 'temse',
  which is a sieve used in winnowing
  (Ard[1], 86)

---

38 merit?] *Rowe;* merrit, *Q;* merit, *Q2*   41 and that] *Q;* that *Pope*   42 purchased] *Keightley;*
purchast *Q,* purchac'd *Q2*   wearer!] *Rowe;* wearer, *Q;* wearer; *F*   44 commanded . . . command?]
Q2, F; commaunded . . . commaund? *Q;* commanded . . . command . . . command! *Dyce*   45 peasantry] pezantry *Q2;* pleasantry *F*   46 honour?] honor? *Q2, F;* honour; *Collier;*
honour! *Dyce*   And how] *Q2, F;* and how *Q;* how *Pope*   47 Picked] (Pickt); Pick'd *Capell*   chaff]
Q2, F; chaft *Q*

To be new varnished? Well, but to my choice.
'Who chooseth me shall get as much as he deserves.'
I will assume desert; give me a key for this,   50
And instantly unlock my fortunes here.
    [*Unlocks the silver casket.*]

PORTIA
    Too long a pause for that which you find there.

ARRAGON
    What's here? The portrait of a blinking idiot
    Presenting me a schedule! I will read it.
    How much unlike art thou to Portia!   55
    How much unlike my hopes and my deservings.
    'Who chooseth me shall have as much as he deserves!'
    Did I deserve no more than a fool's head?
    Is that my prize? Are my deserts no better?

PORTIA
    To offend and judge are distinct offices,   60
    And of opposed natures.

ARRAGON   What is here?

---

48 **new varnished** newly refurbished (*OED* 1), or restored to former eminence; but not entirely distinguished, in this context, from the subsidiary meaning of simulated or pretended (*OED* 2b)

50 **assume desert** lay claim to merit, but in the formal sense of investing himself with (i.e. putting on) the insignia of his status (Cam[1], 144)

51 **And instantly unlock** Arragon asks for the key to unlock the casket for himself, so that he may learn his fate.

53 **blinking idiot** weak-eyed (*OED a.* 1: 'blinking') fool

54 **schedule** scroll of paper containing writing, often of a legal sort (*OED sb.* †1)

56 **deservings** deserts or due rewards

58 **fool's head** the prosthetic head of a fool, although gesturing also to the adornment of a professional jester that was, in the theatre, part of his distinctive appearance; see Henslowe, 5: 'ffor tremynge of the ffolles head as foloweth'.

60 In part, this is a version of the proverbial 'No man ought to be judge in his own cause' (Dent, M341). Portia ironically evades Arragon's question.

---

48 varnished?] *Johnson;* varnist; *Q;* vernish'd? *Q2;* varnisht: *F;* varnisht? *F4;* vanned? *Warburton;* varnish'd! *Dyce*   Well,] *F;* well *Q;* well, *Q2*   50] A key for this; I will assume desert, *Hanmer*   51 SD] *Dyce subst.; Unlocking the silver Casket. after 52 / Rowe*   52 Too . . . there.] "Too . . . there" *Capell*   53 here?] *Capell;* heere, *Q;* here, *F;* here! *Q3*   54 schedule!] *F4;* shedule, *Q;* sedule? *Q2;* schedule, *F*   55 Portia!] *Rann; Portia? Q*   57] *italics Q2*   have] get *Collier*   deserues!] *Ard²;* deserues? *Q;* deserues. *Q2, F*   58 head?] *Q2;* head, *Q*   59 prize?] *Q2;* prize, *Q*   61 SD] *(Hee reads) at end of line Q2*

[*Reads.*]

The fire seven times tried this;
Seven times tried that judgement is,
That did never choose amiss.
Some there be that shadows kiss;   65
Such have but a shadow's bliss.
There be fools alive iwis
Silvered o'er, and so was this.
Take what wife you will to bed,
I will ever be your head.   70
So be gone: you are sped.

Still more fool I shall appear
By the time I linger here.
With one fool's head I came to woo,
But I go away with two.   75
Sweet, adieu. I'll keep my oath,
Patiently to bear my wroth.   [*Exit with his train.*]

---

62 *tried* tested, but also in the sense of refined by fire (*OED v.* †3) and also proved (*OED v.* 7), as at 63

64 *did . . . amiss* has never chosen wrongly

66 *shadow's bliss* insubstantial pleasure such as that afforded by self-deception

67 *iwis* to be sure; certainly. Cf. *TS* 1.1.62: 'Iwis it is not half way to her heart.'

68 *Silvered o'er* coated in silver, with the implication that they lack substance. Aragon's pecuniary interest in Portia is affirmed by the contents of the silver casket.

69 *will* desire

70 *ever* always
head the fool's prosthetic head that Aragon now holds in his hand; but also, through the antecedent reference in 69 to consummating marriage, a bawdy gloss on the Geneva Bible (1562) Ephesians, 5.23: 'For the hus-

band is the wiues head, euen as Christ is the head of the Church, & the same is the sauior of *his* bodie.' The wordplay is upon *head*, meaning both prepuce and maidenhead (Partridge, 119).

71 *sped* dispatched, but used ironically here to indicate Aragon' s sterile quest (*OED v.* I.1: 'speed'). Also implied is the homophonic connection between 'sped' and 'spent', meaning to reach orgasm (Gordon Williams, 284), in this case prematurely and without issue.

73 **By the time** in proportion to the time; *by* is used here as a preposition (Abbott, 146).

77 ***wroth** possibly a combination of indignation (*OED a.* 1) and sorrow (*OED adv. obs.* 1: 'wrothe'). Q's spelling 'wroath' may have been employed to provide an eye-rhyme with *oath* at the end of 76 (Ard², 68n.).

---

66 *shadow's*] (shadowes); Shadow'd *Rowe*   71 *be gone:*] (be gone,); be gone, Sir, *Rowe;* farewel, Sir *Capell*   72 Still] *Q2; Arrag.* Still *Q*   77 wroth] *Rowe;* wroath *Q;* wrath *Warburton*

PORTIA
  Thus hath the candle singed the moth.
  O, these deliberate fools! When they do choose,
  They have the wisdom by their wit to lose.   80
NERISSA
  The ancient saying is no heresy:
  'Hanging and wiving goes by destiny.'
PORTIA
  Come, draw the curtain, Nerissa.

                    Enter Messenger.

MESSENGER
  Where is my lady?
PORTIA   Here. What would my lord?
MESSENGER
  Madam, there is alighted at your gate   85
  A young Venetian, one that comes before
  To signify th'approaching of his lord,
  From whom he bringeth sensible regreets:

---

78 *moth Q's spelling 'moath' may have
been intended as an eye-rhyme with
oath (76) and 'wroath' (77), where the
latter two rhymes indicate Arragon's
distortions of language. Q2 emends to
'Moth', and the sentiment expressed in
78 is proverbial: Dent, F394: 'The FLY
(moth) that plays too long in the candle
singes its wings at last.'

79 **deliberate** studied (*OED a.* 1), but
also a dismissive reference to the deliberative doggerel verse through which
Arragon announces his departure in
72–7

80 **by their wit** that is the consequence
of their wholly inadequate attempts at
reasoning; a possible inversion of the
proverbial 'Wit and wisdom is good

warison [provision]' (F. Wilson, 903).
Portia does not appear to be critical of
'reason' as such, but rather she objects
here to the combination of inadequate
reasoning and defective wisdom.

82 proverbial, as in Dent, W232:
'WEDDING and hanging go by destiny.'

85 **alighted** dismounted; more generally,
arrived (*OED † a. obs.*)

87 **signify** announce (*OED v.* 3)

88 **sensible** tangible, referring to the
'Gifts of rich value' at 90, and for
which, presumably, Bassanio required
Antonio's investment
  regreets greetings that are both felt
(*OED a.* I.1: 'sensible') and reasonable
(*OED* IV.14). *Regreets* may also mean

SD] *Exit.* / *Rowe; Exeunt* Arragon, *and Train.* / *Capell; Exit with his Train.* / *Dyce; he departs with
his train Cam¹* 78 moth.] *Q2;* moath: *Q* 79 fools!] *Rowe;* fooles *Q* 80 the] their *Q2* 81 ancient]
(auncient) 82 goes] go *Hanmer* 83.1] *Enter a Messenger. Q2; Enter a Servant.* / *Rowe* 84 lady?]
Q2, F; Lady. *Q* 85 alighted] *F4;* a-lighted *Q*

To wit, besides commends and courteous breath,
Gifts of rich value. Yet I have not seen   90
So likely an ambassador of love.
A day in April never came so sweet
To show how costly summer was at hand,
As this forespurrer comes before his lord.

PORTIA

No more, I pray thee; I am half afeard   95
Thou wilt say anon he is some kin to thee,
Thou spend'st such high-day wit in praising him.
Come, come, Nerissa, for I long to see
Quick Cupid's post that comes so mannerly.   99

NERISSA

Bassanio, lord, love, if thy will it be.   *Exeunt.*

'to greet again' (*OED* 1), indicating that Bassanio and Portia have met before. See *Pecorone*, where three visits to 'The port of the lady of Belmonte' are made (Bullough, 1.467ff.).

89 **To wit** namely
commends commendations (*OED sb.* 2)
courteous breath civil discourse

91 **likely** handsome (*OED* 5) and promising (*OED* 4a)

93 **costly** of great value (*OED a.* 1). *Summer* is of great value because it fulfils the promise of harvest heralded by April and springtime; a transferred epithet referring to Bassanio's being lavishly provided with 'Gifts of rich value' (90), which have been, and will become, *costly* in other, potentially more sinister ways

94 **forespurrer** forerunner (*OED* 2); someone who spurs their horse in order to arrive before anybody else. See 1.2.119n.

97 **high-day wit** extravagant inflated language of the sort associated with holiday excess (*OED sb.*[1] I.1: 'high-day')

99 **Quick** lively (*OED sb.*[1] A.I.1), but also hasty or impatient, and hence impetuous (*OED* A. 22a)
post messenger
mannerly decently or courteously (*OED adv.* †1)

100 Q punctuates: '*Bassanio* Lord, loue if thy will it be.' Rowe emended this to 'Bassanio, Lord Love, . . .', suggesting a connection with Cupid in the previous line. But 'Lord' may refer, ambiguously, both to Bassanio's social status and to an unspecified paternalist deity charged with determining the outcome, and of whose power Cupid would be the agent. The problem arises because of the uncertainty of the identity of the possessive *thy*, although the ambiguity that arises emphasizes both Bassanio's own agency and the limitations imposed upon it by forces beyond his control. This is reinforced by the echo here of Matthew, 6.10. Nerissa's severely compressed line can be glossed: '[Lord] Bassanio, [good] lord, may he love if he has a mind to, and if[, Father,] it is your will that

89 courteous] *Q2;* curtious *Q;* curteous *F;* curious *Q3*   95 afeard] *(a-feard), F4;* a-fear'd *Q2;* afraid *Pope*   96 Thou wilt] Thoul't *Pope*   97 spend'st] *(spendst)*   high-day] *F;* high day *Q*   98 Come,] *Q2, F;* Come *Q*   100 Bassanio, lord, love,] *(Bassanio* Lord, loue*)*   SD] *Exit. Q2*

[3.1]   [*Enter*] SALANIO *and* SALARINO.

SALANIO   Now, what news on the Rialto?

SALARINO   Why, yet it lives there unchecked that Antonio
hath a ship of rich lading wracked on the narrow seas.
The Goodwins, I think, they call the place: a very
dangerous flat, and fatal, where the carcasses of many a   5
tall ship lie buried, as they say, if my gossip Report be
an honest woman of her word.

SALANIO   I would she were as lying a gossip in that as ever
knapped ginger, or made her neighbours believe she
wept for the death of a third husband. But it is true,   10

he do so.' This seems a more likely
gloss than an alternative that would
make either Bassanio himself, or some
supernatural force, the primary agent
of his fortune.
3.1 Theobald locates the scene in '*A
Street in* VENICE', and Cam¹ specifies
'*The street before Shylock's house*'.
0.1 SALARINO one of the pair who discuss
events in Venice at 2.8. For the roles of
the 'three Sallies', see pp. 428–9.
1   Rialto See 1.3.18n.
2   yet it lives it is still current (*OED v.*¹
1b); the use of the adverb *yet* indicates
that Salarino's information is more
than a repetition of that provided at
2.8.28–30.
    unchecked not contradicted (Onions)
3   rich lading loaded with a rich cargo
(*OED v.* 1: 'lade'); cf. *richly fraught* at
2.8.30.
    wracked shipwrecked (*OED v.*² 2),
but also implying the downfall of
Antonio (*OED v.*² 3)
    narrow seas See 2.8.28n.
4   Goodwins dangerous sandbanks
situated off the Kent coast opposite
Sandwich and exposed at low water;

also proverbial: 'Let him set up SHOP
on Goodwin Sands' (Tilley, S393)
5   flat low-lying stretch of land, often a
marsh or swamp, but in this case an
area of quicksand (*OED sb.*³ 5b)
    fatal ominous or fraught with destiny
(Onions)
6   tall fine or gallant (Onions)
    gossip Report a gossip was a godpar-
ent (*OED sb.* 1a), and also someone
(usually female) who engaged in idle
chatter (*OED* 3). *Report* personifies
'common talk', but see also: 'FAME
(report) is a liar' (Tilley, F44). The use
of the conditional *if* in 6 underscores
the uncertainty, since *gossip Report* is
rarely thought to be 'an honest woman
of her word'.
9   knapped broke or snapped (*OED v.*¹
3: 'knap'), but also with the subsidiary
meaning 'to utter smartly or to chatter'
(*OED v.*¹ 4)
    ginger the root of a hot spicy tropical
plant used as a flavouring agent (*OED
sb.* A.1); *knapped ginger* can be glossed
as 'fabricated spicy stories'.
10 wept . . . husband mourned three
successive husbands, and had become

3.1] *F (Actus Tertius.)*; ACT III. SCENE *Rowe*   0.1] *Q2*; Solanio and Salarino. *Q*; Solanio and
Solerino. *F4*; Enter Salanio and Solerino. *Rowe*; SOLANIO *and* SALERIO *meeting Cam¹* 1+ SP]
Keightley; Solanio. *Q*; Salan. *Q2*; Sol. *F*; Sola. / *Rowe*; solarino *Pope*; Sala. / *Steevens*; Solan. /
Dyce   Now,] *Q2, F*; Now *Q*   2+ SP] *Cam²*; Salari. *Q*; Salar. *Q2*; Sal. *F*; Sol. / *Rann*; Salerio.
Cam¹   4 Goodwins, I think,] *F4*; Goodwins I thinke *Q*   5 carcasses] carkasses *Q2*   6 gossip] gossips
Q2, F   Report] *Q3*; report *Q*   7 honest] honst *F2*   8 lying a gossip] a lying gossippe *Q2*

without any slips of prolixity, or crossing the plain
highway of talk, that the good Antonio, the honest
Antonio – O, that I had a title good enough to keep his
name company! –

SALARINO Come, the full stop.   15

SALANIO Ha, what sayest thou? Why, the end is, he hath
lost a ship.

SALARINO I would it might prove the end of his losses.

SALANIO Let me say 'amen' betimes, lest the devil cross
my prayer, for here he comes in the likeness of a Jew.   20

Enter Shylock [the JEW].

How now, Shylock, what news among the merchants?

JEW You knew, none so well, none so well as you, of my

adept at feigning grief; possibly
proverbial, although no source
found

11 **slips of prolixity** lapses into ver-
bosity, or exaggerations that might
indicate insincerity. See *VA* 515–16,
'Which purchase if thou make, for fear
of slips, / Set thy seal manual on my
wax-red lips', where 'slips' is glossed
as counterfeit coins (Onions).

11–12 **crossing . . . talk** diverting from
the plain path of truth

13 **title** epithet and formal acknowledgement of status. Salanio laments both
his inability to find the appropriate
words to describe Antonio's qualities,
and his own inferior status.

15 **full stop** conclusion, as marked by
punctuation, but also an equestrian
metaphor indicating the checking of
the movement of a horse as part of
its training or manage (*Shakespeare's
England*, 2.414)

16 **end** conclusion (*OED sb.* II.7b)

18 **end** most extreme part (*OED sb.* II.7);
a quibble on *stop* and *end*, culminating
in *amen* at 19, the concluding formula
of a prayer and the sealing of a wish
(*OED sb.* A1 and A2)

19 **betimes** before it is too late (*OED adv.*
3)

19–20 **cross my prayer** intercept
the passage of my prayer (for the
safety of Antonio); see Lodge, sig.
D2ʳ: 'Beware therefore of this diuell-
ish SCANDALE, Rebellion, and
Detraction, and crosse you from this
Deuill, least he crosse you in your
walkes' (IV.25).

20.1 **Shylock** The Jew is named throughout this scene. See p. 422.

22 **none so well** no one as well as. See
Abbott, 275, for the interchange of 'so'
and 'as' in relative constructions. This
phrasal repetition is characteristic of
the way in which the Jew uses language
in the play (see Greenblatt, 'Marlowe',
43; see p. 44).

14 company! –] *F;* company. *Q*   16 Ha,] Ha! *Collier*   thou?] *Q2;* thou, *Q*   19 lest] *F4;* least
Q   cross] *(crosse);* erosse *F3*   20 my] thy *Theobald*   20.1] *Q2; at 21 Q; after 21 F*   the JEW]
this edn   21 Shylock,] Shylock? *Capell;* Shylock! *Dyce*   22+ SP] *this edn; Shy. Q*   22–5] *Q2 lines*
you, / flight. / Taylor / withall.   22 knew] know *Q2*

281

daughter's flight.

SALARINO   That's certain; I, for my part, knew the tailor
that made the wings she flew withal.   25

SALANIO   And Shylock, for his own part, knew the bird
was fledge, and then it is the complexion of them all to
leave the dam.

JEW   She is damned for it.

SALARINO   That's certain, if the devil may be her judge.   30

JEW   My own flesh and blood to rebel!

SALANIO   Out upon it, old carrion, rebels it at these years?

23 **flight** retreating or absconding (*OED sb.*² 1), and different from the technical usage at 1.1.141, where *flight* is associated with arrows of the same weight (*OED sb.*¹ 2†b)

24 **tailor** literally, a maker of clothes (*OED sb.* 1), but also an allusion to the proverbial 'The TAILOR makes the man' (Dent, T17), since Jessica is disguised as a male, and is therefore *made* or fabricated

25 **wings ... withal** a refinement of the image of flight, and also proverbial: 'The BIRD is flown' (Tilley, B364). In the Langhoff production, Jessica's *flight* was accompanied by a 'bird' traversing the stage diagonally from right to left and crossing the 'wall'.

27 *****fledge** fit to fly (*OED* 1), but also possibly high-spirited (*OED* 3). Q2 and F emend Q's obsolete spelling 'flidge' to 'fledg'd'. See t.n.

complexion temperament or disposition; cf. 2.7.79, where temperament and physical appearance coincide in the figure of the 'black' Morocco.

28 **dam** mother, although Salanio's comment echoes the proverbial 'The DEVIL and his dam' (Dent, D225), associating the Jew and his absent wife with Satan (Strickland, 122–30, esp. fig. 52 on 125); cf. Jessica's comment at 2.3.2: 'Our house is hell and thou, a merry devil.'

29 **damned** a Christian sentiment, since salvation and damnation are New Testament concepts; cf. John, 5.28–9. See also Calvin, *Institutes*, 1.1311, on the distinction between the corruption of earthly human nature and the promise of divine mercy.

30 **if ... judge** if the devil were to be her judge (as opposed to the Christian God). Salarino implies that God would not damn Jessica for her elopement.

31 **flesh and blood** progeny, as in the proverbial 'To be FLESH and blood as others are' (Dent, F367); the Jew's implicit claim, made more explicit in *Oth*, is that through her elopement Jessica has committed an act of treason.

32 **Out upon it** a phrase used to register indignation or impatience, although here it is an exclamation of disbelief; a modern equivalent might be 'Get away!'

carrion rotting flesh, applied contemptuously to a living person (*OED sb.* †4), but also indicating concupiscence (*OED sb.* 3b); Salanio links *flesh and blood* at 31 to *carrion* to imply morbid sexual desire.

rebels ... years? does it (your own flesh and blood) rebel at your age? Salanio is insinuating that the Jew may be scandalously promiscuous.

27 fledge] *Capell;* flidge *Q;* fledg'd *Q2, F;* fledged *Dyce*   29 damned] *(*damnd*);* damn'd *Q2, F*   30 judge.] *Q2;* Iudge *Q;* Judg. *F4*   31 rebel!] *Pope;* rebell. *Q;* rebel. *F4*   32 carrion,] carrion! *Capell*   years?] *Rowe;* yeeres. *Q;* yeares. *Q2*

JEW   I say my daughter is my flesh and my blood.

SALARINO   There is more difference between thy flesh and
hers than between jet and ivory, more between your   35
bloods than there is between red wine and Rhenish.
But tell us, do you hear whether Antonio have had any
loss at sea or no?

JEW   There I have another bad match: a bankrupt, a
prodigal, who dare scarce show his head on the Rialto,   40
a beggar that was used to come so smug upon the
mart. Let him look to his bond. He was wont to call
me usurer; let him look to his bond. He was wont to
lend money for a Christian courtesy; let him look to
his bond.   45

SALARINO   Why, I am sure if he forfeit, thou wilt not take

---

35 **jet and ivory** black and white; possibly both a literal and a metaphorical
ascription of 'blackness' to the Jew.
See Hall, *Things*, 39, for an account
of the 'rhetorical position' ascribed
to the alien.

36 **red . . . Rhenish** red wine and
white wine; *Rhenish* was a white
wine produced in the Rhine region.
Salarino extends the rhetorical claim
for Jessica's blood as 'white', at the
same time as he accuses the Jew's
of being the colour of red wine, and
hence darker.

37 **have had** has sustained; a curious
combination of past and present
tenses that combines a completed
action in the past (the shipwreck)
with the possibility of financial loss
in the continuous present as a consequence

38 **no** not

39 **match** bargain (*OED sb.*[1] †11), but

also 'match' as marital alliance

40 **prodigal** a characteristic allegation levelled by the Jew against the
comparatively profligate (or, more
exactly, unregulated) financial dealings of the Christian Antonio

41 **smug** neat and trim, or unruffled
(*OED a.* 3), but also, in this context,
self-satisfied or conceited (*OED
a.*1)

42 **mart** marketplace (Onions), but also
the Exchange. Coryate described the
Rialto as 'the Exchange of Venice,
where the Venetian Gentlemen and
the Merchants doe meete twice a
day, betwixt eleuen and twelue of the
clocke in the morning, and betwixt
fiue and sixe of the clocke in the
afternoone' (Coryate, 169).
look to pay attention to
wont inclined or accustomed

44 **courtesy** benevolence, generosity
and goodness (*OED sb.* 2)

---

33 my blood] blood *Q2;* bloud. *F*   35 hers] *(*hers,*);* hirs, *Q2*   37 hear] heare, *Q2*   37–8 any loss
at] at losse a *Q2*   39 bankrupt] *Rowe;* bankrout *Q*   39–40 a prodigal] for a prodigal *Warburton*   40
dare] dares *Pope*   41 beggar] beggar! *Rowe*   was] *om. Pope*   42 mart.] *(*Mart.*);* mart; *Rowe;* mart!
Pope   44 courtesy] *Capell;* cursie *Q;* curtsie *Q2, F;* courtesie *Rowe*   46+ SP] *Cam²; Salari. Q; Salar.
Q2; Sal. F; Sol. / Rann; Salerio. Cam¹*   46 forfeit] *Q3;* forfaite *Q;* forfet *Q2*

his flesh. What's that good for?

JEW To bait fish withal; if it will feed nothing else, it will
feed my revenge. He hath disgraced me and hindered
me half a million, laughed at my losses, mocked at   50
my gains, scorned my nation, thwarted my bargains,
cooled my friends, heated mine enemies, and what's his
reason? I am a Jew. Hath not a Jew eyes? Hath not a Jew
hands, organs, dimensions, senses, affections, passions?
Fed with the same food, hurt with the same weapons,   55
subject to the same diseases, healed by the same means,
warmed and cooled by the same winter and summer as
a Christian is? If you prick us do we not bleed? If you

---

47 **flesh** a reference to the condition of
the bond at 1.3.145–6, but also an
allusion to the legend that Jews fed on
the flesh and blood of Christians (see
Trachtenberg, 133–9; also Strickland,
96)
48 **bait** lure or entice (*OED sb.*[1] I.1)
48–9 **feed . . . revenge** a partial rejection
of the implicit claim that Jews ate
Christian flesh; cf. John Day, William
Rowley and George Wilkins, *Travels of
Three English Brothers* (1607): 'Sweet
gold, sweete Iewell! but the sweetest
part / Of a Iewes feast is a Christian's
heart' (Ard[2], 72). The 'revenge' motif
initiated here, but alluded to vaguely
at 1.3.42–3, is motivated by the news
of the elopement of Jessica and the
loss of a portion of the Jew's wealth;
made explicit in Bogdanov's 2004
production.
49–50 **hindered . . . million** prevented
(*OED v.* 2: 'hinder') me from making
half a million [ducats]. See Abbott,
198, for examples of the omission after
adjectives of prepositions that imply
value or worth. See also *OED v. trans.*

†1, where 'hinder' is glossed as 'to do
harm to, injure, or impair'; the list of
insults that follows at 50–2 catalogues
the indignities endured by the Jew.
51 **nation** See 1.3.44n.
54 **dimensions** bodily or material parts
that may be measured (*OED sb.* †4)
affections the origin of sensual
stimulation producing either pleasure
or pain, and involving the processes of
attraction and repulsion (see Burton,
1.161). The seat of all affections was
thought to be the heart (Burton,
1.251).
passions potentially rebellious feelings that originate in the body and
challenge the control of *reason*. The
Jew's invocation of *reason*, *affections*
and *passions* traverses the gamut of
Renaissance psychology in an attempt
to establish a similitude that at 49 he
appears to have rejected. See Plato,
4.134–5, for the source of this tripar-
tite division.
57 **warmed . . . summer** Cf. 1.3.21–2n.
note; another example of the rhetorical
figure chiasmus (Cam[2], 110)

---

50 half a] of a half a *Warburton*   52 his] the *F*   53 reason?] *F;* reason, *Q*   Jew. Hath] *Q2;* Iewe:
Hath *Q*   eyes?] *Q2, F;* eyes, *Q*   54 dimensions] *Q2;* dementions *Q*   passions?] *Q2;* passions,
Q   57 winter and summer] *Q2;* Winter and Sommer *Q;* summer and winter *Hanmer*   58 is?] *Q2;*
is: *Q*   bleed?] *Q2, F;* bleede, *Q*

tickle us do we not laugh? If you poison us do we not
die? And if you wrong us shall we not revenge? If we   60
are like you in the rest, we will resemble you in that. If
a Jew wrong a Christian, what is his humility? Revenge!
If a Christian wrong a Jew, what should his sufferance
be by Christian example? Why, revenge! The villainy
you teach me I will execute, and it shall go hard but I   65
will better the instruction.

Enter a Man *from Antonio.*

MAN   Gentlemen, my master Antonio is at his house and
   desires to speak with you both.

SALARINO   We have been up and down to seek him.

Enter TUBAL.

SALANIO   Here comes another of the tribe; a third cannot   70

---

62 **humility** the state of being meek or
   lowly (*OED* 1), and hence the condition in which he is expected both
   to receive and to respond to a *wrong*
   committed by a Jew
63 **sufferance** capacity for endurance
   or forbearance. See 1.3.106n. On the
   claim that the source of the Jew's self-
   justification may be Barabas's comment, see *Jew of Malta*, 5.2.115–16:
   'This is the life we Jews are used to
   lead, / And reason too, for Christians
   do the like' (see Ard², 73).
65 **execute** put into practice, carry out
   (Onions)
   go hard go forward with difficulty
66 **better** improve upon

   instruction knowledge learned (*OED*
   2) by Christian example
69.1 The direction '*Enter* TUBAL' is
   repeated after 71 in Q but corrected
   in Q2 and F; a possible clue to the
   copy supplied to the printer James
   Roberts, indicating promptbook correction (Cam¹, 147), or incomplete
   authorial emendation (Cam², 110).
   Possibly compositorial, involving a
   mistaken repetition, or arising from
   'a change of intention in writing the
   scene' (Ard², xv), but more likely an
   indication of the gradual entry of
   Tubal. See p. 309.
70–1 **cannot be matched** cannot be
   found to equal these two

---

59 laugh?] *Q2, F;* laugh, *Q*   60 die?] *Q2, F;* die, *Q*   62 humility?] *Rowe;* humillity, *Q;* humility, *Q2,
F*   Revenge!] *(Revenge?) Q;* Revenge, *Rowe*   64 by] by a *F3*   example?] *F3;* example, *Q*   Why,
revenge!] *(why revenge?);* why revenge. *F2;* Why Revenge. *Rowe;* why, Revenge. *Theobald;* why,
revenge. *Capell;* – why revenge! *Ard²*   66.1] *Enter a Servant from* Anthonio. *Rowe; Enter a Servant.
/ Capell; A servant accosts Solanio and Salerio Cam¹*   67 SP] *this edn; not in Q; Ser. / Rowe; Serv. /
Warburton; Servant. Cam¹;* SERVINGMAN *Cam²*   69.1] *repeated after 71 Q; after 71 Collier; Tuball
appears making for Shylock's house Cam¹*   70+ SP] *(Solanio.); Salan. Q2; Sol. F; Sola. Rowe; Sala.
/ Steevens; Solan. / Dyce*

be matched, unless the devil himself turn Jew.

Exeunt Gentlemen[, Salanio and Salarino, with Antonio's Man].

JEW   How now, Tubal, what news from Genoa? Hast thou
found my daughter?

TUBAL   I often came where I did hear of her, but cannot
find her.   75

JEW   Why, there, there, there, there! A diamond gone cost
me two thousand ducats in Frankfurt. The curse never
fell upon our nation till now; I never felt it till now. Two
thousand ducats in that, and other precious, precious
jewels. I would my daughter were dead at my foot, and   80
the jewels in her ear; would she were hearsed at my
foot, and the ducats in her coffin. No news of them?

---

71 **devil . . . Jew** an expansion of
connection between the devil and
the Jews (Trachtenberg, 42–3;
Strickland,, 95ff.) to include reference to usury. There may be more
than one proverbial saying behind
Salanio's suggestion: (1) Tilley, D314:
'The DEVIL'S mouth is the miser's
purse'; (2) Tilley, J51: 'To look like a
JEW', invoked negatively in Coryate,
232.

71 SD *See t.n. Greg regards Q's
'*Exeunt Gentlemen*' as 'rather scanty'
(Greg, *Editorial*, 123) and 'typical
of the author' (Greg, *First Folio*,
256–9). Brown concurs, suggesting
that there are similarities between
Q1 and *Hamlet* Q2 (1605) indicative
of the author's foul papers (Ard²,
xiv–xv, 74).

74 **I often came** on many occasions I
arrived at places (*OED adv.* 2: 'often')
cannot The shift from past (*came*) to
present (*cannot*) indicates that Tubal

continues to seek Jessica; see Abbott,
370.

77 **Frankfurt** situated on the river
Main in Germany and famous since
medieval times as a centre for commercial and monetary transactions; see
Coryate, 564.
curse the general curse placed upon
the Jews for having crucified Christ (see
Matthew, 27.24–5). See also Geneva
Bible (1562), Matthew, 27.25, marginal
gloss: 'If his death be not lawful let the
punishment fall on our heades & our
childrens, and as they wished, so this
cursse taketh place to this day'; alluded
to in *Jew of Malta*, 1.2.108–10: 'If your
first curse fall heavy on thy head, /
And make thee poor and scorned of all
the world, / 'Tis not our fault, but thy
inherent sin.'

81 **hearsed** entombed in a coffin (*OED
v.* 1c), used metaphorically in *Ham*
1.4.47: 'Why thy canoniz'd bones,
hearsed in death'

---

71 SD] *(Exeunt Gentlemen.); Exeunt Sala. and Solar. / Rowe; Exeunt* SOL. SAL. *and serv. Capell;
Exeunt Sal. and Salan. / Steevens; Exeunt SALAN. SALAR. and Servant. / Malone; Exeunt Solan.,
Solar., and Servant. / Dyce; Solanio and Salerio depart, followed by the servant / Cam²* 72 Genoa?]
Steevens; Genowa, *Q;* Genowa? *Q2;* Genowa? *F;* Geneva? *F4;* Genova? / *Rowe;* Genoa? / *Capell*
74 her] ster *F* 77 Frankfurt] *Oxf;* Franckford *Q;* Frankford *Q2* 79 precious,] *F;* precious *Q*
80 jewels.] *Q2;* jewels; *Q;* jewels: *F;* jewels! *Pope* 82 them?] *Capell;* them, *Q;* them; *Rowe*

Why so? And I know not what's spent in the search.
Why, thou loss upon loss! The thief gone with so much,
and so much to find the thief, and no satisfaction, no   85
revenge, nor no ill luck stirring but what lights o'my
shoulders, no sighs but o'my breathing, no tears but
o'my shedding.

TUBAL Yes, other men have ill luck too. Antonio, as I heard
in Genoa –   90

JEW What, what, what? Ill luck, ill luck?

TUBAL Hath an argosy cast away coming from Tripoli.

JEW I thank God, I thank God! Is it true, is it true?

TUBAL I spoke with some of the sailors that escaped the
wreck.   95

JEW I thank thee, good Tubal: good news, good news! Ha,

83 **Why so?** Q's punctuation, altered to
a colon in Q2, may be read as either
a question mark or an exclamation.
Pooler compares what he takes to be a
deliberative use of 'so' with an earlier
example at 1.3.165 (Ard[1], 96). But here
the Jew might, equally, be enquir-
ing why there is no news of Jessica,
considering the money he has spent
searching for her, or he may simply be
exclaiming on the thought that despite
the investment nothing has come of it.

84 ***loss upon loss!** Q's light punctuation after 'loss' (see t.n.), and F2's
emendation of 'thou' to 'then', makes
it difficult to gloss the context of
the Jew's remark. It seems unlikely
that the preceding *thou* refers to the
unnecessary expense incurred by
Tubal in the search (a possibility
suggested in Cam[2], 111); rather, it
indicates the exasperation both at the
loss of Jessica and at the subsequent
loss of the money invested in her
recovery. The ensuing sentence, 'The

thief gone with so much, and so
much to find the thief . . .' – a curious example of the rhetorical figure
epanalepsis involving the repetition
of the word *thief* – amplifies the Jew's
feeling of indignation.

86 **lights** falls or descends (*OED v.[1]*
II.6). See also *OED v.[1]* II.†7, where
it was sometimes used to denote a
descent into hell

87 **but o'my breathing** except those
that are the result of my breathing

92 **cast away** wrecked (Onions)
Tripoli Spelt 'Tripolis' in Q, this
is probably the thriving port on the
North African coast that was on one
of the trade routes between Venice
and the eastern Mediterranean (Lane,
341), now the capital of Libya; but
alternatively may refer to Tripoli on
the Mediterranean coast of modern
Lebanon, which, along with Antioch
and Beirut, functioned as an 'outlet
harbour' for Italian ships carrying
spices to Venice and Genoa (Parry, 43).

83 so?] so: *Q2;* so! *Pope*   what's] how much is *F*   84 thou loss] then loss *F2;* thou – loss *Ard[1]* loss!]
Theobald; losse, *Q*   86–8 o' . . . o' . . . o'] *Pope;* a . . . a . . . a *Q;* on . . . of . . . of *Q2*   90 Genoa –] *Rowe;*
Genowa? *Q;* Genoway *Q2*   91 luck?] *Q2;* lucke. *Q*   92 Tripoli] *(Tripolis)*   93 I thank God!] *Collier;* I
thank God, *Q;* thank God; *Pope*   Is it . . . is it] ist . . . ist *Q2*   true, . . . true?] *F;* true . . . true. *Q;* true? . . .
true? *Q2*   96 thee] the *Q2*   96–7 Ha, ha,] *Folg;* ha ha, *Q;* ha, ha! *Capell;* ha! ha! *Steevens;* Ha, ha! *Bevington*

ha, heard in Genoa!

TUBAL   Your daughter spent in Genoa, as I heard, one
night fourscore ducats.

JEW   Thou stick'st a dagger in me; I shall never see my gold   100
again. Fourscore ducats at a sitting? Fourscore ducats!

TUBAL   There came divers of Antonio's creditors in my
company to Venice, that swear he cannot choose but
break.

JEW   I am very glad of it. I'll plague him; I'll torture him.   105
I am glad of it.

TUBAL   One of them showed me a ring that he had of your
daughter for a monkey.

JEW   Out upon her! Thou torturest me, Tubal. It was my

---

97 *heard Brown believes that the confusion between 'e' and 'd' in Elizabethan
secretary handwriting was responsible
for the setting in Q of 'heere' rather
than 'heard', and emends accordingly;
the Jew is repeating Tubal's words *heard
in Genoa* in 89–90 (Ard², 75). Dover
Wilson, while retaining the F2 spelling
'here', suggested that a line of text
has been 'accidentally omitted, and that
'heere in Genoa' was the end of some
question like: 'What further tidings
didst thou *hear in Genoa*?' (Cam¹, 147).
98 heard Tubal's repetition of his earlier
usage at 89 draws together the two items
of news that converge in the geographical location of Genoa.
98–9 one night The preposition 'in' is
omitted (Abbott, 202).
99 fourscore eighty i.e. 4 x 20
101 sitting single meeting or occasion
(*OED sb.* 5a), in this case, of merrymak-
ing; cf. *WT* 4.4.562: 'The which shall
point you forth at every sitting'.
104 break fail or go bankrupt (Onions)
108 for a monkey This reference points
in two directions. (1) It may have had
a particular association for the Jew

beyond the usual frivolous associations
with 'aping'. Cf. Isaiah, 13.19–22, on
the fall of Babylon, esp. 13.20–1. (2)
The Geneva Bible (1562) Isaiah, 13.21,
uses the Hebrew '*Zim*' and '*Ohim*'
that Edward Topsell, *The History of
Four-Footed Beasts* (1607), 6–7, glosses
as 'monkeys': 'They haue a round
head, a face like a man, but blacke
and balde on the crowne, his nose in
a reasonable distance from his mouth
like a mans, and not continued like an
Apes, his stones greenish blew like a
Turkey stone.' Although the Jew is not
conscious of it, this echoes a Venetian
prejudice. The description of Shylock
as 'black' (3.1.35–6) confirms the dehu-
manizing Venetian image of him, and
Jessica's alleged bartering of Leah's ring
for a monkey reinforces the Venetian
prejudice that Jewish ritual imitates, and
thereby reduces to the level of animality,
a Christian sacrament. A 16th-century
English audience would have had no
difficulty in subscribing to these prejudices, but it might also have registered
that Jessica had eloped, thereby undermining patriarchal authority.

---

97 heard] *Neilson & Hill;* heere *Q;* here *F;* where? *Rowe*   Genoa!] *Cam²;* Genowa. *Q;* Genoway. *Q2;
Genova. F4; Genoua. / Rowe; Genoa? / Capell; Genoa? / Steevens*   98 one] in one *Q2*   99 night]
night, *Q2*   101 sitting?] *Oxf;* sitting, *Q, F;* sitting! *Q2*   ducats!] *Q2;* ducats. *Q*   102 creditors]
Creditours *Q2*   103 to] unto *Q2*   he] that he *Q2*   105 very] *om. Rowe*   him;] (him,)   106 of it.]
on't. *Q2;* of it, *F*   109 her!] *Theobald;* her, *Q;* her: *Q2*   torturest] tortur'st *Q2*

turquoise: I had it of Leah when I was a bachelor. I   110
would not have given it for a wilderness of monkeys.

TUBAL   But Antonio is certainly undone.

JEW   Nay, that's true; that's very true. Go, Tubal, fee me an
officer; bespeak him a fortnight before. I will have the
heart of him if he forfeit, for, were he out of Venice,   115
I can make what merchandise I will. Go, Tubal, and
meet me at our synagogue. Go, good Tubal, at our
synagogue, Tubal.   *Exeunt.*

[3.2]   *Enter* BASSANIO, PORTIA [*with* NERISSA],
            GRATIANO *and all their trains.*

110 *turquoise a ring containing a precious stone found in Persia and which
was either sky-blue or apple-green in
colour, known also as a 'Turkey stone', as
reflected in Q's 'Turkies', and with possible bawdy associations. Pliny (37.8.619)
valued the turquoise according to the
relative difficulty of obtaining it, the fact
that it was a mark of wealth, and that its
beauty derived from its frequently being
set in gold. But it was also the easiest
precious stone to counterfeit, cf. Ayres's
gloss of 'turquois' in *Sejanus*, 1.37, 'As
true as turquois in the dear lord's ring'
(*Sejanus*, 80), as a 'precious stone said
to change its colour in response to the
health of its wearer'. At the end of
Radford's 2004 film Jessica's evident
retention of the ring emphasizes that
this story is malicious gossip.
Leah the name of the elder daughter of
Laban, whose marriage to Jacob under
duplicitous circumstances is recounted
in Genesis, 29.20–8. Another part of
this biblical narrative is invoked earlier
at 1.3.73ff. to justify usury, but the invocation of the biblical Leah may have
ironic implications in that it associates
the Jew with the deceptions of Jacob.

R.F.H. [Herrey], *Two Right Profitable
and Fruitful Concordances* (1578), sig.
C7^v, indicates that the name meant
'painful or wearied' (Ard[2], 75–6).
111 **wilderness of monkeys** The association of 'monkeys', 'Turkies' and 'wilderness' extends the biblical echoes in the
Old Testament's Isaiah and reinforces
the Jew's perception that his daughter
has sunk to Babylonian depths.
113–14 **fee . . . officer** engage the services of a sheriff's officer for me (to
arrest Antonio)
114 **bespeak . . . before** request or
engage him a fortnight before the due
date of Antonio's repayment
115 **out of Venice** away from Venice,
though the Jew means that he wishes
Antonio dead
116 **make what merchandise** conduct
whatever business (*OED* 1c: merchandise)
3.2 Rowe specifies '*Belmont*', but Capell
locates the scene more precisely in '*A
Room in* Portia*'s house*'.
0.2 *trains* entourages; Mahood suggests
that Q's direction '*all their trains*' is
designed to make this scene 'outshine
2.7 and 2.9' (Cam[2], 112).

110 turquoise] *Rowe;* Turkies *Q*   113 Tubal,] *Q2, F;* Tuball *Q; om. Pope*   116 I will Go] *Collier;* I
will: goe *Q;* I will go: go *Q2;* I will: go: go *Pope;* I will: go, go, *Hanmer;* I will. Go, go *Johnson*   118
SD] *om. F4*   3.2] *Rowe* (SCENE II.)   0.1–2] *Cam²; Enter Bassanio, Portia, Gratiano and all their
trains. Q; Enter Bassanio, Portia, Gratiano and all Traines Q2; Enter Bassanio, Portia, Gratiano and all
their traine. F; Enter Bassanio, Portia, Gratiano, and Attendants. The Caskets are set out. / Rowe subst.*

PORTIA
   I pray you tarry. Pause a day or two
   Before you hazard, for in choosing wrong
   I lose your company; therefore, forbear awhile.
   There's something tells me – but it is not love –
   I would not lose you, and, you know yourself,   5
   Hate counsels not in such a quality.
   But, lest you should not understand me well –
   And yet, a maiden hath no tongue but thought –
   I would detain you here some month or two
   Before you venture for me. I could teach you   10

1 Portia's hesitation betrays anxiety, since by a simple process of deduction she must now know what the third casket contains, having seen the contents of the other two.
2 **in choosing wrong** if you choose wrongly. See Abbott, 372, on the general use of active participles.
3 **forbear awhile** postpone [your choice] for a while
4 **but . . . love** a public denial that some editors have compared with that of Beatrice in *MA* 4.1.268–72, although the two situations are not the same
5 **you know yourself** an appeal to Bassanio indicating that Portia is already favourably inclined towards him
6 Hatred does not inform this response (*OED v.* 1 and 2: 'counsel', 'to give advice to'; *OED sb.* II.7†b: 'quality', 'manner or style'). Portia's ambivalence derives from the fact that her dead father's decree overrides her own desires.
7 **lest . . . not** in the event of your not. This is not a double negative (see Blake, 6.2.9), since Portia knows the risk that Bassanio is about to take, and wants to keep him in Belmont for as long as possible.

understand me interpret who I am, i.e. comprehend the meaning of me (*OED* 1), as in Nerissa's comment at 1.2.29–30: 'who chooses his meaning chooses you.'
8 **maiden . . . thought** an impersonal expression of Portia's frustration, since, because she is inexperienced (*maiden*), the only proper weapon available to her is *thought*. This line brings together two mutually contradictory proverbs, both of which have a partial application to Portia's situation: (1) expressing the need for modest silence as in 'MAIDENS should be seen and not heard' (Dent, M45, quoted in Ard[1], 76); (2) expressing the duplicity of denial as in 'MAIDS say "nay" and take it' (Dent, M34).
9 **month or two** At 1 Portia asks Bassanio to remain 'a day or two'. Now she wishes to detain him for longer. This inconsistency is in keeping with Portia's agitated state of mind.
10 **venture for me** risk yourself (*OED v.* 1: 'venture') to obtain me. The repetition of *hazard* and *venture* sustains the connection with the financial risk that Bassanio is taking with Antonio's money and both their lives.

3, 5 lose] *F2;* loose *Q*   3 therefore] *om. Pope*   4 me – but . . . love –] *Keightley;* me (but . . . love) *Q;* me, but . . . love, *Rowe*   6 counsels . . . quality.] *Q2;* counsailes . . . quallity; *Q;* counsailes . . . quallitie; *F*   9 month] *F;* moneth *Q*

How to choose right, but then I am forsworn.
So will I never be, so may you miss me.
But if you do, you'll make me wish a sin,
That I had been forsworn. Beshrew your eyes,
They have o'erlooked me and divided me: 15
One half of me is yours, the other half yours.
Mine own, I would say: but, if mine, then yours,
And so, all yours. O, these naughty times
Puts bars between the owners and their rights:
And so, though yours, not yours. Prove it so,   20
Let Fortune go to hell for it, not I.

11 **I am forsworn** I will violate the oath that I have sworn
12 Therefore I will not violate my oath, and as a consequence you might not obtain me.
13 **But . . . do** But if you do fail (in your choice)
   a sin that which is a sin
14 **That . . . forsworn** that I had violated my oath
   Beshrew See 2.6.53n.
15 **o'erlooked** surveyed (*OED v.* 3) and bewitched (*OED v.* 7)
   divided me separated me into parts (*OED v.* I.3); but see also a suggestive gloss: 'to cleave or to penetrate by motion' (*OED v.* I.1c).
16 **half . . . half** a reference to Bassanio's analytical gaze; he has scrutinized Portia and she is already inclined to accept his mastery.
17 **Mine own** a reference to that half of Portia that she seeks to reserve for herself, but that after marriage she will relinquish to her husband
18 **naughty** bad or wicked (*OED a.* 3); not used frivolously in the 16th century
19 This refers to the active constraint placed upon Bassanio's choice. The subject of *Puts* is *these naughty times* (see Abbott, 333, on the use of the third person plural where the subject 'may be considered singular in *thought*').
   bars obstacles or barriers (*OED sb.*[1] II.12), but implicitly a legal obstacle (*OED sb.*[1] II.18). Portia resents her own powerlessness, as in 1.2.21–5, *and* the predicament of Bassanio, but she welcomes his ownership of her in advance of his choosing the correct casket.
20 **And . . . not yours** And, though it should be yours, it is not yours; Portia is anxiously aware that she will only be Bassanio's if he chooses the correct casket. Pooler mistakenly thinks that a distinction is being made here between *de jure* and *de facto* possession (Ard[1], 100).
   Prove it so if it transpires in that way; Portia puts the negative case if Bassanio should make the wrong choice.
21 Let the goddess Fortune be punished for it, not me.

11 then I am] I am then *Q2* 14 forsworn. Beshrew] *Q2*; forsworne: beshrow *Q* 16 the other] th'other *Johnson* half yours.] (halfe yours,)*;* halfe *F2*; yours, – *Capell*; half yours, *Johnson* 17 if mine] of mine *F*; first mine *F2* 18 yours.] *Q2*; yours; *Q* O,] *Capell*; ô *Q*; O *Q2*, *F*; Alas! *Pope* 19 Puts] (puts), *Q2*, *F*; Put *F2* 20 not yours.] *Keightley*; not yours, *Q*; not yours *Q2*, *F*; not yours; *Pope* Prove it so,] *Johnson*; proue it so *Q*; prove it so, *Rowe*; but prove it so *Hanmer*; Prove it not so! *Capell*

I speak too long, but 'tis to peise the time,
To eke it and to draw it out in length,
To stay you from election.

BASSANIO   Let me choose,
For, as I am, I live upon the rack.   25

PORTIA

Upon the rack, Bassanio? Then confess
What treason there is mingled with your love.

BASSANIO

None but that ugly treason of mistrust,
Which makes me fear th'enjoying of my love.
There may as well be amity and life   30
'Tween snow and fire, as treason and my love.

PORTIA

Ay, but I fear you speak upon the rack,

22 **peise** weigh down, and hence impede the flow of (*OED v.* †4)
23 **eke** prolong (*OED v.* 3b)
24 **stay** prevent (*OED v.*[1] 3)
   election choice (*OED* 2)
25 **live . . . rack** live in a state of acute anxiety or suspense (*OED sb.*[3] 1c), as though being tortured by having one's body stretched on a rack (*OED sb.*[3] 1)
27 **treason** crime against the state, in this case of love and marriage. Treason was regarded as the most serious of political crimes and confessions were extorted through torture (*Shakespeare's England*, 1.386 and 398–9); but Portia light-heartedly presumes that, if Bassanio *is* on the rack, then he has some treason to confess.
28 **ugly . . . mistrust** abhorrent betrayal associated with suspicion and sexual jealousy
29 **fear th'enjoying** be anxious or apprehensive about the possession (*OED v.*3: 'enjoy'), but also in a more carnal sense (*OED v.* 4†b). Bassanio's asser-

tion, that the *treason* of love is the fear of sexual betrayal and loss of possession, has a wider significance that will be taken up later in the play.
30 **amity** friendly relations (*OED*). Throughout this exchange the language of love deploys images from the world of politics (*treason* and *amity*), just as the ritual of the caskets is imbued with the language of mercantilist economics (*hazard* and *venture*).
   life organic, and therefore vital, connection (*OED sb.* I.1). 'Amity and life' is a phrase that occurs in *Tamburlaine 1*, 2.1.21–2, where it is opposed to 'death'. It is unnecessary to conjecture that this is a corruption of 'league' introduced by the compositor (Furness, 137–8).
32 **I . . . rack** a reference to the inaccuracy of information extracted through torture, but associated here with the habitual mendacity of the anxious lover. Cf. the trial of Roderigo Lopez, Elizabeth's Jewish doctor involved in

22 peise] *(peize); poize Rowe; peece Pope*   23 eke] *Johnson; ech Q; eck Q2; ich F; eech Q3; itch F4; eche Rowe*   draw it] draw out *Q2*   26 Bassanio?] *Pope; Bassanio, Q*   29 th'enjoying] *(th'inioying); the enioying F*   30 life] league *Dyce*   32 Ay,] *Rowe; I Q; I, F*

Where men enforcèd do speak anything.

BASSANIO

Promise me life and I'll confess the truth.

PORTIA

Well then, confess and live.

BASSANIO   Confess and love   35

Had been the very sum of my confession.

O happy torment, when my torturer

Doth teach me answers for deliverance!

But let me to my fortune and the caskets.

PORTIA

Away, then! I am locked in one of them: 40

If you do love me, you will find me out.

Nerissa and the rest, stand all aloof.

Let music sound while he doth make his choice;

Then, if he lose, he makes a swan-like end,

---

espionage; Lee claimed Lopez had been forced to confess 'to save himself from racking' (Lee, quoted in Furness, 398). On the marginal relevance of the Lopez plot to the play, see pp. 20–1.

33 **enforced** enforcèd

35 **confess and live** a reversal of the proverbial 'CONFESS and be hanged' (Dent, C587); versions of this appear in *Jew of Malta*, 4.1.146, and *Oth* 4.1.38–9.

36 **Had been** would have been; Bassanio further adjusts Portia's revision of the proverbial commonplace as a means of expressing his love for her.

very sum full extent or sum total; the idiom here is that of computation.

37 **happy torment** a common oxymoron indicating the coexistence of pain and pleasure associated with love, as in Edmund Spenser, *Amoretti and Epithalamion* (1595), Sonnet 42 (Spenser, *Works*, 569).

38 **deliverance** (my) release (*OED* 1) but also the act of giving up or surrendering (*OED* †3)

39 **let me** allow me to go; this is the sense of 'let' in Onions, and it is the dominant sense here. But see also *OED* *n*[2] 1 for the sense of 'let' as hinder or prevent. Bassanio wants to get on with the game, but at the same time he wishes to prolong his dialogue with Portia.

40 **Away, then!** Off you go! – although the tone here is one of mock disdain

41 **find me out** literally, discover the representation that is secreted in the correct casket, but also discover me and what I really think

42 **aloof** apart, at a distance (*OED* A3)

44 **makes . . . end** proverbial: 'Like a SWAN he sings before death' (Dent, S1028), and alludes to the legend of Cycnus, son of Poseidon, whom Achilles killed (*OCD*, 247). In Ovid, *Met.*, 12.79–165, 'Cygnet' is strangled

---

33 do] doth *F*   35 Confess and love] 'Confess' and 'love' *Cam¹*; 'Confess and love' *Oxf*   38 deliverance!] *Pope;* deliuerance: *Q*   39 caskets.] caskets. *Curtain drawn from before the caskets.* / *Dyce*   40 then!] *Theobald;* then, *Q;* then. *Pope*

Fading in music. That the comparison   45
May stand more proper, my eye shall be the stream
And wat'ry death-bed for him. He may win,
And what is music then? Then music is
Even as the flourish, when true subjects bow
To a new-crowned monarch. Such it is,   50
As are those dulcet sounds in break of day,
That creep into the dreaming bridegroom's ear

by Achilles, who is thwarted in his attempt to pierce his victim's armour because 'Neptune had as tho / Transformd him to the fowle whose name he bare but late ago' (Ovid, *Met.*, 303); this motif recurs in *Luc* 1611–12, *KJ* 5.7.21–2 and *Oth* 5.2.245–6: 'I will play the swan / And die in music.'

45 **Fading** losing its vigour and hence drooping (*OED v.*[1] 1), and also growing small or shrinking (*OED v.*[1] †2); a strong hint of the connection between failure and detumescence, although Portia refrains from using the participle 'dying', which would have made the image much more obvious
music This exchange initiates the role of music in the play that is later given such ideological force by Lorenzo at 5.1.53ff.
That so that

46 **stand more proper** be more appropriate; but Portia's playing on the verb *stand* (cf. 42, where its more literal meaning is employed) hints that her anxiety may have a sexual undercurrent. Bassanio's failure is imagined as a loss of erection.

46–7 **my . . . death-bed** Portia's tears will provide a *wat'ry death-bed* for her suitor should his quest fail (die), although she is also here imagining another kind of 'death' (a sexual 'death') for which her body will provide the necessary lubrication. Her *eye* may also be her vagina (Gordon Williams, 118), whose *wat'ry*

discharge quenches the lover's 'hot' penis; cf. Venus's invitation to Adonis: 'Graze on my lips, and if those hills be dry, / Stray lower where the pleasant fountains lie' (*VA* 233–4).

48 **what . . . then?** what will music signify then? Portia speculates here on the alternative meanings that music might have if Bassanio fails or succeeds in his choice.

49–50 **Even . . . monarch** thought by Malone to allude to the coronation of the French king Henry IV in the city of Chartres on 27 February 1594; but Brown confirms that this passage does not furnish sufficient evidence to support a date for the composition of the play (Ard[2], xxv).

49 **flourish** embellishment (*OED* †6B) or adornment that accompanies the act of bowing; Pooler thought this a reference to 'coronations on the stage, at which trumpets were blown' (Ard[1], 102).
true subjects Portia aligns herself with the figure of the *true subject* offering allegiance to a *new-crowned monarch*, and thus paves the way for her voluntary acceptance of a husband's sovereign power in marriage.

50 **crowned** crownèd
Such it is it is just like

51 **dulcet sounds** sweet sounds (*OED* 2) often associated with music or song
in at

52–3 **That . . . marriage** the music of the musicians that accompanies the bridegroom to the wedding ceremony (Halliwell, quoted in Furness, 139)

48 then?] *Q2;* than? *Q*   Then] *Q2;* Than *Q*   50 new-crowned] *Theobald;* new crowned *Q;* new crownd *Q2*

And summon him to marriage. Now he goes
With no less presence, but with much more love,
Than young Alcides, when he did redeem   55
The virgin tribute paid by howling Troy
To the sea monster. I stand for sacrifice.
The rest, aloof, are the Dardanian wives,
With bleared visages come forth to view
The issue of th'exploit. Go, Hercules!   60
Live thou, I live. With much, much more dismay
I view the fight, than thou that mak'st the fray.
    [*Musicians from Portia's train perform*] *a song the whilst*
    Bassanio comments on the caskets to himself.

54 **presence** handsome appearance, or
noble bearing (*OED* 5)
55–7 **Alcides . . . monster** a reference
to Hercules' (Alcides') rescue of
Hesione, the daughter of the Trojan
king Laomedon, from a punishment
decreed by Neptune, in return for the
king's horses (Ovid, *Met.*, 11.229ff.).
The Trojan king did not keep to the
bargain, and the result was the sacking
of Troy. Hercules undertook this task,
not for the love of Hesione, but for
her father's horses, and this reflects
ironically on Bassanio's motives, since
Portia is attractive in large part because
of her inherited wealth.
56 **virgin tribute** a reference to King
Laomedon's virgin daughter Hesione
howling lamenting
57 **I . . . sacrifice** Portia now places herself in the same situation as Hesione,
since she will be 'sacrificed' to her dead
father's wishes. In 'standing in for'
(*stand for*) Hesione, Portia proposes a
tableau in which the Trojan incident
will be re-enacted.
58 **Dardanian** Trojan

59 **bleared visages** blearèd; tear-stained
faces
60 **issue of th'exploit** outcome of the
adventure
61 **dismay** terror or anxiety (*OED sb.*
1: 'dismay'). The repetition of *much*
reinforces Portia's awareness of her
own lack of power in this situation.
62 **mak'st the fray** perform (*OED v.*[1]
V.57: 'make') the assault (*OED sb.*[1] †2:
'fray')
62 **SD** One of the musicians sings the
song and the whole troupe ('ALL')
repeat the refrains at 66 and 72,
while Bassanio considers the relative
merits of the caskets. It is not clear
whether Bassanio's deliberations
are silent, as Mahood thinks (Cam[2],
115), or whether they compete
with the song. Edelman notes the
theatrical tradition beginning with
Komisarjevsky of giving the song to
Nerissa, who intervenes as Bassanio
is about to choose the gold casket, and who emphasizes in 63–5
the words *bred*, *head* and *nourished*
(Edelman, 188n.).

56 virgin tribute] Virgin-tribute *F3*   60 Hercules!] *Theobald;* Hercules, *Q*   61 live. With] *Keightley;*
live with *Q;* live, with *F3;* live; with *Pope*   much, much] *(much much);* much *Q2, F*   62 I] To
Q2   than] *F2;* then *Q*   62 SD] *this edn; Here Musicke. A song the whilst . . . himselfe. F; Musick
within. A song whilst . . . himself. / Rowe; Musick; the whilst* Bassanio *comments on the Caskets to himself.
/ Capell*

Tell me where is fancy bred,
Or in the heart, or in the head,
How begot, how nourished? 65

ALL Reply, reply.

It is engendered in the eye,
With gazing fed, and fancy dies
In the cradle where it lies.
Let us all ring fancy's knell. 70
I'll begin it. Ding, dong, bell.

---

63 **fancy** a term often associated with the imagination and with fantasy (*OED sb.* 4), and, according to Burton, capable of producing material effects (Burton, 1.254; see also 3.100). The song poses the question whether fancy originates in the faculty of reason (*head*) or in the emotions (*heart*).

64 **Or** Either
head The rhyme with *bred* in 63 and *nourishèd* in 65 can be thought to offer Bassanio a clue to the choice of the correct casket (Weiss, 312). Pooler regards this as 'a charge against Portia's good faith' (Ard[1], 103), and Brown, emphasizing the impact of the scene on the theatre audience, notes that the song 'prevents a third recital of the mottoes on the caskets, dignifies and adds expectation to the dramatic context, and prepares the audience for Bassanio's following speech' (Ard[2], 80).

65 **nourished** nourishèd

66 ***Reply, reply** printed to the right of the page in Q as part of 65; omitted by Rowe, and accorded a separate line by Pope. Johnson thought this was a marginal direction, but Dover Wilson was the first modern editor to conclude that the song was sung as a solo and

that *Reply, reply* was the refrain to be sung by *all* (Cam[1], 150).

67 **engendered . . . eye** a neo-Platonic commonplace recounted in *Anatomy of Melancholy*, where the eye and the gaze are the stimuli to attraction (Burton, 3.85); however, the eye is also regarded as an enticement to lust (3.89–90) untrustworthy and capable of deception (3.91). The song induces the lover to think beyond the province of the *eye*, and hence to replace *fancy* with a more substantial commitment.
eye the Q reading, but F emends to 'eyes' in order to align the ending of 67 with 'dies' in 68. The imperfect rhyme in Q1, which Q2 does not improve, suggests foul papers, but F's reading may have been an attempt to tidy up the rhyme.

68 Through feeding (through *gazing*) to excess, the imagination dies. The imagery of food and satiety affirms the limitations of *fancy* as in *Luc* 803–4 and *TN* 1.1.1–3, where 'music' fulfils the same function.

69 **cradle . . . lies** Fancy, because it places its emphasis on the *eye*, is immature, hence its location in the *cradle*.

70 **fancy's knell** the sound of the bell that will announce the death of *fancy* (*OED sb.* 1b)

---

63 Tell] ONE FROM PORTIA'S TRAIN Tell *Oxf;* SONG / I.V Tell *Capell* is] his *Warburton* 64 Or in] In *Johnson* head,] head? *Q2;* head, head: *F* 65 nourished?] nourished. *F* 66, 72 SP] *Cam[1]; not in Q* Reply, reply.] *Pope; printed at 65 Q;* Reply. *Hammer* 67 It] 2.V. It *Capell* eye] eyes *F* 68 fed,] fed; *Capell* dies] *Rowe;* dies: *Q;* dies, *F* 69 lies.] *Collier;* lies *Q;* lyes, *Q2;* lies: *F* 71] *Johnson; Q lines* it. / bell. / I'll . . . it] *italics / Johnson*

ALL   Ding, dong, bell.

BASSANIO

So may the outward shows be least themselves,

The world is still deceived with ornament.

In law, what plea so tainted and corrupt,   75

But, being seasoned with a gracious voice,

Obscures the show of evil? In religion,

What damned error but some sober brow

Will bless it and approve it with a text,

Hiding the grossness with fair ornament?   80

There is no voice so simple but assumes

---

73 **outward shows** external appearances or displays that may lead to deception (*OED sb.* 2 and 3b)

74 **ornament** embellishment that reinforces the deception

75 **plea** petition or appeal presented in a court of law (*OED sb.* 1)
tainted blemished or stained (*OED a.* 1) but also infected with corruption (*OED v.* 10: 'attaint'); corruption is a consequence of the process of 'tainting' and not an example of hendiadys

76 **seasoned** flavoured; Spurgeon cites this as an example of the value Shakespeare attaches 'to seasoning and its effect on the attractiveness, and indeed on the essential goodness of food' (Spurgeon, 84). The context suggests otherwise, since seasoning is here being used to mask corruption, and alludes to the culinary practice of using spices to disguise the taste of stale or even rotting food (Cam², 116).
gracious pious (*OED a.* †6) but also endowed with charm or elegance (*OED v.* 2†b)

77 **show** appearance, but also in the sense of preventing disclosure of something less attractive (*OED sb.*¹ 2b); cf. *Luc* 506–7: 'In him the painter labour'd with his skill / To hide deceit and give the harmless show.'

78 **damned error** transgression or wandering (Latin *errare*: to wander from the path of good) that results in damnation, and, by implication, a wandering from religious orthodoxy (*OED* III.3); damnèd
sober grave and dignified (*OED* II.4); but see also *OED* I.1, 'not given to the indulgence of appetite', which extends the culinary imagery initiated in the song and sustained by Bassanio.

79 **approve . . . text** demonstrate or validate it (*OED v.*¹ †2) with reference to a biblical authority (*OED sb.*¹ †3: 'text')

80 **grossness** vulgarity but also lack of culinary refinement (*OED* 4)
fair beautiful or unspoilt

81–2 This refers to the discrepancy between the 'inner' person and *outward* appearance. The *voice* was usually assumed to be the means of uttering (or 'outering') inner being, but the connection was frequently regarded with caution. Bassanio exercises care because the *voice* of the singer that he has just heard may not reflect even outward *virtue*. The more familiar proverbial reference was limited to appearance; cf. 'VICE is often clothed in virtue's habit' (Tilley, V44), and also *R*7 2.3.17–18: 'Virtue itself turns vice being misapplied, /

---

73 So] (*aside*) So *Oxf*; (*addressing the golden casket*) So *Oxf*¹   75 tainted] tanted *F*   77 evil?] *F*, euill. *Q* religion,] *F*; religion *Q*   81 voice] (voyce); vice *F2*

Some mark of virtue on his outward parts.
How many cowards, whose hearts are all as false
As stairs of sand, wear yet upon their chins
The beards of Hercules and frowning Mars,   85
Who, inward searched, have livers white as milk;
And these assume but valour's excrement

And vice sometime's by action dignified.' Clearly 'voice' and 'vice' echo
each other phonetically and conceptually, but there is no need to emend Q's
'voyce' here.

81 **voice** Q's spelling 'voyce', emended
in Q2 and F to 'voice', was printed
as 'vice' in F2, maybe because the
two words were homophones. Brown,
following Kökeritz, notes that this
variant spelling of 'vice' occurs in *Cym*
2.3.33 (Folio text) and that 'smoyle' for
'smile' occurs in *KL* 2.2.80 (Ard², 81).
simple unmixed (*OED* III.11). Cf.
Son 125.7: 'For compound sweet for-
going simple savour'.

82 **his** The *voice* is gendered male here,
since Bassanio goes on to reprise
outward shows of masculinity ('The
beards of Hercules and frowning
Mars') that disguise cowardice.

84 *****stairs of sand** stairs that lack
solidity. Q's 'stayers' has been
thought by some editors to refer to
'stays' or supports (Ard¹, 105), and
this has led Mahood to restore Q's
spelling, and to posit an association
with George Herbert's phrase 'rope
of sands' in 'The Collar' (Cam²,
116). However, one of the themes
of Bassanio's speech is that of false
aspiration, and therefore *stairs* is an
appropriate modern emendation of
the now obsolete spelling 'stayers'
(*OED*). A more likely point of reference is in the Bible, Matthew, 7.24–8,
concerning 'a wise man, which built
his house upon a rocke' and 'a foolish
man, which built his house upon the
sand'.

85 **Hercules . . . Mars** For Hercules, see
55–7n.; Mars was the god of war
(see *Ham* 3.4.57). Both typify acts of
military heroism.

86 **inward searched** probed (*OED v.*
†8). The metaphor of surgical practice
is given currency within a wider ana-
tomical frame of reference that points
towards the difference between the
external appearance of the body and
the process of 'peering into a corrupt
world of mortality and decay', which
was to become 'a voyage into the very
heart of the principle of spiritual dis-
solution' (Sawday, 21).
livers . . . milk The liver was
thought to be the source of the blood
'whose office is to nourish the whole
body, to give it strength and colour,
being dispersed by the veins through
every part of it'. It also contains
the 'spirit' which is 'a most subtle
vapour, which is expressed from
the blood, and the instrument of
the soul, to perform all his actions'
(Burton, 1.148). Thus a *white* liver,
which produced blood that was the
colour of milk, signified a lack of
resolve or courage.

87 **valour's excrement** the outward
manifestation (*OED obs.* 1: excrement)
of bravery, but also waste matter (*OED*
†1) as exemplified by the prosthetic
beard of one who affects heroism.
See *LLL* 5.1.95–7, 'sometime to lean
upon my shoulder and with his royal
finger thus dally with my excrement,
with my mustachio', where both non-
scatological and scatological meanings
are present.

82 mark] *om. Q2*   his] its *Theobald*   84 stairs] *F4;* stayers *Q;* staiers *Q2*   86 milk;] *(*milke,*); milk?*
Capell

To render them redoubted. Look on beauty,
And you shall see 'tis purchased by the weight,
Which therein works a miracle in nature,   90
Making them lightest that wear most of it:
So are those crisped snaky golden locks,
Which maketh such wanton gambols with the wind
Upon supposed fairness, often known
To be the dowry of a second head,   95
The skull that bred them in the sepulchre.
Thus, ornament is but the guiled shore
To a most dangerous sea; the beauteous scarf

88 render them redoubted make them feared and respected (*OED*)
beauty the physical appearance of formal perfection (*OED* I.1) but also associated here with the kind of outward adornment (*OED v. obs.*: 'beauty') that masks a less attractive reality
89 purchased . . . weight bought according to weight just like cosmetics, which could be purchased by the ounce (Ard², 81)
91 lightest wanton or unchaste. See 2.6.43 for a similar quibble on 'light'.
92 crisped crispèd; curled
snaky serpentine, with a clear suggestion of seductive satanic deceit
93 maketh F emends to 'makes', preserving the singular verb even though the antecedent *locks* is plural (see Abbott, 247). Mahood notes F's improvement of the metre of the line (Cam², 117).
wanton gambols lascivious dancing (*OED sb.* 2: 'gambol'), here referring to the unruly hair at 92 that dances seductively as a consequence of being blown by the wind
94 supposed supposèd; imagined or presumed
95 dowry endowment (*OED fig.* 4), but more usually that portion of wealth acquired by the husband in marriage (*OED* 2). Here both meanings are

in play, since the seductive *supposed fairness* of the previous line is thought to bequeath to another woman the 'crisped snaky golden locks' (in the form of a wig), while the head from which they originally came is now in the grave (96). Pooler draws attention to *Son* 68 (Ard¹, 106), but other examples appear in *LLL* 4.3.255–6 and *TA* 4.3.146–7.
second head a reference to the emerging fashion of wigs, but also recalling Thomas Nashe, *Christ's Tears over Jerusalem* (1594): 'For thy flaring frounzed Periwigs lowe dangled downe with loue-locks, shalt thou haue thy head side dangled downe with more Snakes than euer it had hayres' (Nashe, 2.140).
97 guiled shore guilèd; dry land full of guile or treachery. Another version of the earlier *stairs of sand* (84) indicating lack of firm foundation, but here employing a metaphor that emphasizes the precariousness of maritime travel, which recalls Antonio's risks.
98 beauteous scarf a scarf, pleasing to the sight, and presumably covering the face; an extension of the imagery of ornamentation that permeates Bassanio's speech. For a general discussion of this topos, see Hall, 85–92.

92 crisped] crispy *Warburton*   93 maketh] makes *F;* make *Pope*   97 guiled] guilded *F2;* gilded *Rowe;* guilty *Warburton*

Veiling an Indian beauty; in a word,
The seeming truth, which cunning times put on   100
To entrap the wisest. Therefore, then, thou gaudy gold,
Hard food for Midas, I will none of thee;
Nor none of thee, thou pale and common drudge
'Tween man and man. But thou, thou meagre lead,
Which rather threaten'st than dost promise aught,   105
Thy paleness moves me more than eloquence,

99 **Indian beauty** an oxymoron that has exercised the ingenuity of a number of pre-20th-century editors (see Furness, 146). The Indian here is probably the West Indian whose colour is black (see Hall, 232), thus establishing a connection between a proverbial evil (Tilley, D 217: 'As black as the DEVIL') and voyages of exploration and colonization.

100 **cunning times** artfully contrived (*OED* 2b) but also deceitful (*OED* 5) contemporary practice. See also Nashe: 'Weomen, as the paines of the deuils shal be doubled, that goe about hourelie tempting, and seeking whom they may deuoure, so except you soone lay holde on grace, your paines in hell (aboue mens) shall be doubled, for millions haue you tempted, millions of men (both in soule & substaunce) haue you deuoured' (Nashe, 2.140).

put on dress themselves in

101 **Therefore, then, thou** Q's reading is marginally inferior to Q2's 'Therefore thou', but neither version is metrically sound. Dover Wilson suggests that 'then' was intended to replace 'Therefore' in Shakespeare's MS but was not erased (Cam[1], 151), although even in this conjecture the line would require the contraction 'T'entrap' and the replacement of the monosyllabic 'then' in order to restore the metre. Either the line is intended as an alexandrine, or it is, as Brown suggests, two short lines that

would accentuate a break in delivery (Ard[2], 82).

gaudy luxurious or ornate (*OED a.*[2] 1) but also possibly full of trickery (*OED a.*[2] †2)

102 **Hard . . . Midas** Midas was the King of Phyrgia who asked the god Bacchus, whom some of his subjects had captured, to transmute all that he touched to gold. The unforeseen effect of this was that Midas starved and came to hate wealth. The story is told in Ovid, *Met.*, 11.100–216, and is also the subject of John Lyly's play *Midas* (1592).

103 **pale** the subject of some editorial speculation, although Pooler quotes John Lyly's *Endymion*, 5.2.100: 'whose lippes might compare with silver for the palenesse' (Ard[1], 107). This might refer both to the paleness of the labourer or, metaphorically, to the concept of silver as a common form of monetary exchange.

common drudge one employed in menial or servile labour (*OED sb.*).

104 **meagre** poor or scanty (*OED* 1a), hence low in value

106 **paleness** Theobald emended Q's reading to 'plainness' in order to present a contrast with rhetorical ornament or *eloquence*, and/or to avoid the repetition of 103. The comparison between *lead* and *paleness* occurs in *RJ* 2.5.17, and the association between rhetoric and 'colour' is made in Puttenham, sig. C3[r].

99 beauty] dowdy *Hanmer;* feature *Keightley*   101 To entrap] T'entrap *Pope*   Therefore, then, thou] therefore thou *Q2;* Then thou *Pope*   102 food] foole *Q2*   103 pale] stale *Rann*   105 threaten'st] (threatenst); threatnest *Q2, F*   106 paleness] plainness *Theobald*

And here choose I; joy be the consequence.

PORTIA [*aside*]

How all the other passions fleet to air,
As doubtful thoughts, and rash-embraced despair,
And shuddering fear, and green-eyed jealousy.   110
O, love, be moderate, allay thy ecstasy,
In measure rain thy joy, scant this excess.
I feel too much thy blessing; make it less
For fear I surfeit.

BASSANIO [*Opens the leaden casket.*]
                              What find I here?
Fair Portia's counterfeit! What demigod   115
Hath come so near creation? Move these eyes?
Or whether riding on the balls of mine

108 **fleet to air** dissolve into the air
    (*OED v.*[1] 9b: 'fleet')
109 **As** such as
    rash-embraced impetuously accept-
    ed (*OED n.*[2] 2h: 'embrace')
    despair Despair was the cardinal sin
    of Marlowe's Faustus (Jump, 35), and
    Calvin explains it as a consequence of
    God's curse which 'seizes innocent
    creatures through our fault' (Calvin,
    Institutes, 1.341). Portia expresses
    her relief in the biblical terms of
    2 Corinthians, 4.8–9.
111 **allay** temper the force of (*OED* II.8)
112 **measure** moderation
    rain pour down. Q2 unnecessar-
    ily emends Q's 'raine' to 'range'; Q3's
    'rein' suggests 'rein in', i.e. control.
    Mahood cites a biblical allusion to
    Malachi, 3.10 (Cam[2], 118).
    scant diminish, limit or restrict (*OED
    v.*3c)
    excess extravagance of rapturous
    feeling (*OED* †1), but also usury or

interest; cf. 1.3.58n. Portia clearly
knows that Bassanio has made the
correct choice, but she cannot disclose
that knowledge.
114 **For . . . surfeit** I am afraid of
    becoming sick through excess (*OED*
    1: 'surfeit')
115 **counterfeit** picture or image rather
    than the modern gloss of false image
    demigod a being part human and part
    divine
116 **come . . . creation** come so close to
    its original
    Move these eyes? Do these eyes
    move?
117 **riding . . . mine** being reflected in
    my own eyes; literally, the act of rid-
    ing (as on a horse) with the possible
    bawdy subsidiary meaning of copulat-
    ing (*OED v.* B3: 'ride'); *balls* refers to
    eyeballs (*OED sb.*[1] 9) but also to horses
    with white streaks on their foreheads
    (*OED sb.*[3]) and hence, metaphorically,
    the whites of Bassanio's eyes.

108 SD] *Cam*[1]   109 rash-embraced] *Cam*[1]; rash imbrac'd *Q*; rash embrac'd *F3*   despair,] *Rowe;*
despaire; *Q;* despaire; *F4*   110 shuddering] *Capell;* shyddring *Q;* shuddring *F;* shudd'ring
Pope   112 rain] *(raine), F3;* range *Q2;* rein *Q3*   excess.] excess, *Q;* excess; *Capell;* excess!
Dyce   114 surfeit.] surfet *Q2;* surfeit! *Capell*   SD] *after* surfeit *Rowe; after* 115 *Malone*   What find
I] What do I find *Hanmer;* Ha! What find I *Capell*   115 counterfeit!] *Collier;* counterfeit. *Q;* coun-
terfeit? *Pope*   demigod] *Riv;* demy God *Q;* demie God *F;* demy-god *F4*   117 balls] ball's *Q2;* bals *F*

Seem they in motion? Here are severed lips
Parted with sugar breath; so sweet a bar
Should sunder such sweet friends. Here, in her hairs,   120
The painter plays the spider and hath woven
A golden mesh t'entrap the hearts of men
Faster than gnats in cobwebs. But her eyes!
How could he see to do them? Having made one,
Methinks it should have power to steal both his   125
And leave itself unfurnished. Yet look how far
The substance of my praise doth wrong this shadow
In underprizing it, so far this shadow
Doth limp behind the substance. Here's the scroll,
The continent and summary of my fortune.   130

118 **severed** parted (*OED v.* I.1b). The idea is repeated in the following line.
119 **bar** obstacle; the action of sweet breathing that separates the lips from each other
120 **sunder** separate
sweet friends Portia's two lips, here personified as two intimate friends. However, it is Portia who severs the intimate friendship between Bassanio and Antonio, so this image has a larger resonance in the play than either character may be aware of.
hairs plural used here; see Samuel Daniel, *Delia* (1592), 39.1: 'When winter snows upon thy sable haires'.
122 Underlying Bassanio's hyperbole is the recurrent idea of the spider's web as an instrument of deception; see Spenser's *Amoretti* (1595), Sonnet 27.1–2. Brown also notes Spenser, *Amoretti*, Sonnet 37.9–12 (Ard², 84); see also 92–3.
123 **Faster** more firmly
gnats in cobwebs a striking image that amplifies the power and fineness

of Portia's 'hairs' emphasizing their appearance as a mesh of such fine quality that they can entrap the most insignificant of flies. The gnat was sometimes associated with blindness; see Matthew, 23.24.
126 **unfurnished** unmatched with its fellow (Onions)
127 **substance** matter (*OED* 5); but also with a possible subsidiary reference to the notion of *substance* as the Real Presence within the Eucharist (*OED* 3c), as suggested by 115–16
shadow image, but in the Platonic sense of direct opposition to *substance*
128 **underprizing** underestimating or undervaluing (*OED v.*)
so far so to the same extent (Cam², 118)
129 **limp behind** walk with an impediment indicating an imperfect imitation of the original or real *substance*
130 **continent** container (*OED sb.* 1b); also a continuous tract of land associated with a voyage of exploration and for profit (*OED sb.* II.†3)

119 sugar breath;] *Rowe;* suger breath, *Q;* sugar'd breath; *Pope;* sugar breath: *Malone;* sugar-breath; *Keightley*   120 hairs] hair *Hanmer*   121 spider] *(Spyder,)*   122 t'entrap] *Collier;* tyntrap *Q;* t'intrap *Q2, F;* to entrap *Capell*   123 eyes!] *Collier;* eyes *Q;* eyes, *Q2;* eies, *F*   125 Methinks] *F4;* me thinkes *Q;* Me-thinks *Q2;* Me thinkes *F*   126 unfurnished] *(vnfurnisht);* unfinish'd *Rowe*   128 underprizing it] *(vnderprysing it);* underprising *F3*

302

[*Reads.*]

> You that choose not by the view
> Chance as fair and choose as true.
> Since this fortune falls to you,
> Be content and seek no new.
> If you be well pleased with this   135
> And hold your fortune for your bliss,
> Turn you where your lady is,
> And claim her with a loving kiss.

A gentle scroll. Fair lady, by your leave,
I come by note to give and to receive.   [*Kisses Portia.*]   140
Like one of two contending in a prize
That thinks he hath done well in people's eyes,
Hearing applause and universal shout,
Giddy in spirit, still gazing in a doubt
Whether those peals of praise be his or no,   145
So, thrice-fair lady, stand I even so,
As doubtful whether what I see be true,

---

132 **take** as favourable a risk and choose
as accurately. This statement enshrines
proverbial wisdom but also, as Mahood
notes, the sentiment has a particular
reference to Bassanio's manner of
choosing (Cam², 119).
133 *falls* descends (*OED sb.*¹ I.1b), with
the suggestion that it is bestowed upon
Bassanio by some higher power
136 *hold . . . bliss* consider your fortune
to be your joy (*OED sb.* 2: 'bliss');
also indicative of a state of beatitude
(*OED sb.* 2c)
140 **by note** according to the instruction
that he has just read; the *note* may
constitute 'a bill of dues' (Merchant,
193) but it authorizes (*OED sb.*² 7b)
Bassanio to kiss Portia, and to *receive*
all she has to offer.

141 **prize** contest (*OED sb.*² b)
144 **gazing . . . doubt** staring as though
in doubt
145 **peals** Q2 emended Q's 'peales' to
'pearles', although the reference to
applause at 143 makes clear that it
is the sound of the applause that is
referred to here.
146 **thrice-fair** a common hyperbole,
as in *1H4* 3.2.92–3. But here the
resonance is deeper, since Portia
is the object of Bassanio's quasi-
religious contemplation as *substance*.
The reference here is to Ovid's
'three-formed Goddesse' (*Met.*,
7.242), with the possible suggestion
that Portia wields divine influence
in heaven, the earth and the under-
world.

---

135 *pleased*] *F2;* pleasd *Q;* pleas'd *Q2*   139 A] *Bass.* A *F*   140 SD] *Collier subst.; at end of 139*
Rowe   142 eyes,] *Capell;* eyes: *Q;* eyes; *Q2;* eies: *F*   144 still . . . a] gazing still in *Pope*   145 peals]
(peales); pearles *Q2*

Until confirmed, signed, ratified by you.

[*Portia kisses him.*]

PORTIA

You see me, Lord Bassanio, where I stand,

Such as I am. Though for myself alone   150

I would not be ambitious in my wish

To wish myself much better, yet, for you,

I would be trebled twenty times myself,

A thousand times more fair, ten thousand times more
    rich,

That only to stand high in your account   155

I might in virtues, beauties, livings, friends

Exceed account. But the full sum of me

Is sum of something: which to term in gross,

Is an unlessoned girl, unschooled, unpractised.

---

148 **confirmed . . . ratified** extends the image of the *note* at 140 and underscores the formal contractual nature of their imminent union

153 **trebled twenty times** a quantitative gloss on Bassanio's *thrice-fair lady* at 146

155 **account** estimation (*OED sb.* IV.11), but also deploying the sense of financial statement (*OED sb.* II.2). What haunts Portia's discourse is also the figure of 'excess', i.e. what is acquired over and above the principal sum invested.

156 **livings** landed property (*OED sb.* †4) of the kind from which income might be derived

157 **Exceed account** Portia wishes herself to be 'in excess' of her intrinsic worth for Bassanio's sake, and that excess would be the 'interest' or 'increase' emanating from his investment.

full sum entire worth; Pooler notes the metaphor of computation, but also

notes the acquired meaning of *sum* as 'essence' (Ard¹, 110–11). Both meanings are operative here.

158 **sum of something** This Q reading is emended in F to 'sum of nothing', although the difficulty is compounded by the Q1 spelling 'sume', which Warburton emended to 'some'. Portia moves from an evaluation based upon a wish-fulfilment to a more modest *account* of her worth that she then proceeds to itemize, i.e. her worth amounts to *something*, where 'sum' is subsumed as a partial homophone.

term in gross express (*OED v.* 2: 'term') in general terms (*OED a.* 7: 'gross') or plainly (Onions); see 1.3.51, where *gross* is used by the Jew in relation to a large sum of money. Portia borrows the vocabulary of usurious practice in order to render ('sum up') in crude terms what she amounts to.

159 **unlessoned** uneducated

unschooled, unpractised untutored, undisciplined (*OED* 1 and 2); also

---

148 SD] *this edn*   149 me] my *F*   154–5] *Collier; Q lines* times / account /; *Malone lines* times / rich; / account /   154 A . . . more rich] a . . . more rich *Q;* A . . . More *Q2, F*   155 only] *om. F2*   158 sum of something:] *(*sume of something:*); summe of something; *Q2;* sum of nothing: *F*   159 unlessoned] *F;* vnlessond *Q;* vnlesson'd *Q2*   unpractised] *Q2;* vnpractized *Q;* vnpractiz'd *F*

Happy in this, she is not yet so old   160
But she may learn; happier than this,
She is not bred so dull but she can learn.
Happiest of all is that her gentle spirit
Commits itself to yours to be directed,
As from her lord, her governor, her king.   165
Myself, and what is mine, to you and yours
Is now converted. But now, I was the lord
Of this fair mansion, master of my servants,
Queen o'er myself; and even now, but now,

sexually inexperienced ('practice': Gordon Williams, 243). Although Portia may object to the constraints imposed upon her by her father, she is hardly undisciplined.

162 **bred so dull** brought up to be so unintelligent

164 **Commits** entrusts (*OED v.* 1), although the alternative meaning of *to* 'commit' adultery or to engage in an act of fornication (*OED* 6†c) is also present. Cf. *Oth* 4.1.72–3: 'What committed? / Committed? O thou public commoner!'

165 **As** such as that (see Abbott, 112)
lord . . . king an act of patriarchal fealty for which there is ample biblical support; see 1 Peter, 3.1, 'ye wiues bee in subiection to your husbands', and Ephesians, 5.22. Mahood compares Portia's submission to that of Kate in *TS* 5.2 (Cam², 120).

167 **converted** transformed (*OED* 11), but also with religious implications (*OED* 9)
But now just a moment ago (Abbott, 38)

168 **fair mansion** beautiful house, i.e. Belmont, from the Italian 'Bellamente', 'faire and softly, fairely. Also conueniently or with dexteritie' (Florio, 58); also her own body as that which

houses her soul (*OED sb.* 3c)
master an unstable gender category, since Portia (a male actor playing a female) is now relinquishing a limited control over her household; for a similar problematizing of gender categories, see *Son* 20.1–2, 'A woman's face with nature's own hand painted / Hast thou, the master mistress of my passion.'

169 **Queen** wife to a king (*OED* 1), but here an independent female authority who can exercise power
even now at this very moment; see Abbott, 38, for the Shakespearean emphasis on 'even' in this phrase to designate action of a very recent kind compared to the modern usage of 'even now' that 'is applied to an action that has been going on for some time and *still* continues, and where the emphasis is laid on "now"'.
but now clearly a different usage from 167, since the phrase emphasizes Bassanio's sovereignty over Portia from here onwards. Abbott, 38, uses this example to give an inadequate explanation of the distinction, since the gloss 'just at this moment' ignores the transformation in Bassanio's fortunes.

161 happier] more happy *Pope;* then happier *Dyce*   than this,] *(*then this,*);* then in this, *F2;* than this, *Johnson;* than this, in that *Capell;* in this, *Dyce*   162 bred] bread *F3*   163 is] in *Dyce*   167 But now, I] *Keightley;* But now I *Q;* I but now *Pope*   lord] Lady *Rowe*   168 master] *Q2;* maister *Q;* Mistress *Rowe*   169 o'er myself;] *Q2 (*ore my selfe;*);* ore my selfe: *Q;* o'er my self, *Rowe*   now, but now,] *Q2;* now, but now *Q;* now; but now *Rowe*

This house, these servants and this same myself,   170
Are yours, my lord's. I give them with this ring
    [*giving him a ring*]
Which, when you part from, lose or give away,
Let it presage the ruin of your love,
And be my vantage to exclaim on you.

BASSANIO

Madam, you have bereft me of all words.   175
Only my blood speaks to you in my veins,
And there is such confusion in my powers,
As, after some oration fairly spoke
By a beloved prince, there doth appear
Among the buzzing pleased multitude,   180
Where every something, being blent together,

171 *lord's The emendation of Q's 'Lords' to 'Lord' in Q2 and F is plausible but in this instance unnecessary; Dover Wilson argues that the Q1 reading 'underlines Portia's act of fealty' (Cam[1], 152) thus emphasizing her willing subjection. Despite his adoption of the Q1 variant, Brown suggests that it is not secure, and compares 1.3.157, arguing that 'Confusion of final 's' is a common [compositorial] error' (Ard[2], 30 and 86).
    ring an ornament symbolizing union, but having both conceptual and physical resonance. See Partridge, 175, for a gloss on 'ring' as female pudenda, and also *AW* 4.2.45–6 for the relationship between the object and its signification: 'Mine honour's such a ring; / My chastity's the jewel of our house.'
173 presage foreshadow or portend (*OED v.*)
174 vantage opportunity (*OED sb.* 4†b), but also in the sense of pecuniary profit or gain (*OED sb.* 1†b). Portia's

deployment of the discourse of love cannot separate itself from that of economics and the body.
    exclaim on protest against, denounce or decry; cf. *Jew of Malta*, 3.6.42: 'But I must to the Jew and exclaim on him.'
176 blood lineage (*OED sb.* 9), since Bassanio is an aristocrat, but also sexual passion (*OED sb.* 6)
177 powers faculties (*OED sb.*[1] 1b)
178 oration fairly spoke a speech beautifully crafted in the sense that it is both attractively balanced and rhetorically effective
179 beloved belovèd
180 pleased pleasèd
181 every something each element
    blent blended (*OED v.*[2] 4), but also dazzled (*OED v.*[1] 1b and 2). See also Edmund Spenser, *The Shepherd's Calendar* (1579), 'Aprill': 'Ah foolish boy, that is with loue yblent.' The line is awkward rhythmically and metrically imperfect, although it conveys the sense of Bassanio's searching for words to express his delight.

171 lord's] *Cam*[2]; Lords, *Q;* Lord, *Q2, F;* lord's! – *Cam*[1] SD] *Folg subst.; She puts a ring on his finger. after 174 Bevington* 172 lose] *Q2;* loose *Q* 176 veins] *Q2;* vaines *Q* 180 multitude,] *F;* multitude. *Q*

Turns to a wild of nothing, save of joy,
Expressed and not expressed. But when this ring
Parts from this finger, then parts life from hence;
O, then be bold to say, 'Bassanio's dead.'   185

NERISSA

My lord and lady, it is now our time,
That have stood by and seen our wishes prosper,
To cry, 'Good joy, good joy, my lord and lady!'

GRATIANO

My lord Bassanio, and my gentle lady,
I wish you all the joy that you can wish,   190
For I am sure you can wish none from me;
And when your honours mean to solemnize
The bargain of your faith, I do beseech you
Even at that time I may be married too.

BASSANIO

With all my heart, so thou canst get a wife.   195

GRATIANO

I thank your lordship; you have got me one.
My eyes, my lord, can look as swift as yours.

---

182 **wild** unruly or undifferentiated space denoting confusion (*OED sb.* II.6). Mahood's 'hubbub' (Cam², 120) seems more accurate in this context than Brown's suggestion of 'deserts and waste places' (Ard², 86).

183 **Expressed . . . expressed** articulated under pressure (*OED v.* 1b and 2), but also, paradoxically, not uttered.

186 **our time** an appropriate moment for us

191 **I . . . me** (1) I am sure that you do not need me to augment your wishes for your happiness by my adding to them; or (2) I am sure that your wishes will not stand in the way of my hitherto concealed wishes for my own

happiness. These two glosses combine 'conventional politeness' (Cam², 121) with a 'roguish' element characteristic of Gratiano (Cam², 153).

192–3 **solemnize . . . faith** marry. The idea of this union as a *bargain* returns the process of betrothal to the material world of mercantile dealing.

195 **so** provided that
get acquire in the sense of obtain possession of (*OED v.* I.1), but also with a possible quibble on 'beget' (*OED v.* III.26), meaning to father a child, which would underscore the element of surprise in what follows

196 **got** an extension of the play on *get* in 195

---

185 O] *Q2*; ô *Q*   Bassanio's] *F*; *Bassanios Q*; *Bassanio is Q2*   188 lady!] *Theobald*; Lady. *Q*   191 me;] *F2*; me: *Q*   193 faith,] *Pope*; fayth: *Q*   194 too.] *F*; to. *Q*   196 SP] *(Gra.)*, Cam²; *Cra. F4*   lordship;] *(Lordship,)*   have] gave *F*

You saw the mistress; I beheld the maid.
You loved, I loved, for intermission
No more pertains to me, my lord, than you.   200
Your fortune stood upon the caskets there,
And so did mine too as the matter falls.
For wooing here until I sweat again,
And swearing till my very roof was dry
With oaths of love, at last, if promise last,   205
I got a promise of this fair one here
To have her love, provided that your fortune
Achieved her mistress.

PORTIA   Is this true, Nerissa?

NERISSA

Madam, it is, so you stand pleased withal.

BASSANIO

And do you, Gratiano, mean good faith?   210

GRATIANO   Yes, faith, my lord.

198 **maid** Nerissa's status designated at 1.2.0.1 is 'waiting-woman', which, given Portia's social status, suggests 'lady-in-waiting' and not a menial. Gratiano deploys the title *maid* to designate that she is a young unmarried woman who is also a virgin (*OED sb.*[1] 1).

199 ***intermission** temporary cessation (*OED* 1b). Q's punctuation in this line appears nonsensical, since there is no recorded gloss of *intermission* as 'relief, pass-time' (Ard[2], 87). Gratiano is claiming for himself the same right to proceed as Bassanio.

200 **pertains** belongs or applies to (*OED* 1c)

201 **stood upon** depended upon

202 **as . . . falls** as it so happens

203 **until . . . again** without respite, i.e. repeatedly (see Abbott, 27: 'again')

204 ***my very roof** the actual roof of my

mouth. Q's spelling 'rough', emended to 'roofe' in Q2, was thought to have been a possible misreading of the MS copy 'tonge' (Ard[2], 87), but see *TS* 4.1.5–7: 'my very lips might freeze to my teeth, my tongue to the roof of my mouth'.

205 **at last . . . last** finally, if a promise will endure; a quibble on the two meanings of *last*.

207 **fortune** good luck (*OED sb.* 1), but also, possibly, a covert reference to the financial outlay that Bassanio has invested in this project (*OED sb.* 6)

208 **Achieved** succeeded in gaining (*OED v.* II.5)

209 **so . . . withal** provided that you are pleased with this state of affairs

210 **mean good faith** intend (*OED v.*[1] 1) to act in good faith

211 **faith** an abbreviation of the oath 'in faith', meaning 'on my honour'

199 I loved,] *this edn;* I lou'd *Q;* I lov'd: *Rowe;* I lov'd; *Warburton*   intermission] *(*intermission,*);*   intermission. *Q3*   201 caskets] Casket *Q2*   202 too] *(*to*);* too, *Q2*   203 here] *(*heere*),* Pope; heete *F2;* heat *F3;* Hard *Rowe*   204 roof] *Q2;* rough *Q*   207 love,] *Theobald;* loue: *Q;* loue *F4;* Love, *Rowe*   208 Is . . . Nerissa?] *Malone; prose Q*   209 is, so] so, *F*

BASSANIO

　Our feast shall be much honoured in your marriage.

GRATIANO　We'll play with them the first boy for a thousand

　ducats.

NERISSA　What, and stake down?　　　　　　　　　　215

GRATIANO

　No, we shall ne'er win at that sport and stake down.

Enter LORENZO, JESSICA *and* SALERIO, *a messenger from Venice.*

　But who comes here? Lorenzo and his infidel!

　What, and my old Venetian friend Salerio!

BASSANIO

　Lorenzo and Salerio, welcome hither,

　If that the youth of my new interest here　　　　220

　Have power to bid you welcome. By your leave,

　I bid my very friends and countrymen,

　Sweet Portia, welcome.

(Cam²), which plays on the literal meaning of the phrase in the previous line

213 **play** gamble. The stakes will be a wager of 1,000 ducats against which couple conceives the first male heir.

215 **stake down** put money down, as in making a bet. Commentators and editors have detected a bawdy double-entendre in this phrase, although Partridge, 189, is uncertain: 'The exact sense is somewhat doubtful.' Nerissa may be expressing surprise at the size of the bet (1,000 ducats), whereas Gratiano insists, bawdily, that, while his *stake* (penis) is *down* (flaccid), sexual intercourse cannot be performed.

216 **that sport** sexual intercourse

216.1 as in Cam¹; positioned after 217 in Q and F, and in most modern editions up to Dover Wilson; cf. the gradual entry at 3.1.69, where the SD 'Enter Tuball' is repeated in Q.

217 **infidel** one who does not hold to the Christian religion (*OED sb.* 2); a double-meaning, since Jessica has broken faith with Judaism and aligned herself with Christianity.

218 **Salerio** See p. 428 on the roles of the 'three Sallies'.

220 **If . . . interest** if the comparatively recent nature of my new status (as master of the house); also concern for property (*OED sb.* 1a: interest), and money received as a return on investment (*OED sb.* 10)

222 **very** true

215 What,] *Q2;* What *Q;* What! *Collier*　216.1] *after 217 Q; Enter . . . Salerio. after 217 F; Enter . . . Salanio. Rowe;* SCENE III. *Enter . . . Salanio. Pope; Enter . . .* SALERINO. *Capell; Enter . . .* SOLANIO. *Dyce;* LORENZO, JESSICA, *and* SALERIO *enter the chamber after 217 Cam¹*　217 infidel!] *(infidell?)*　218 Salerio!] *Cam²; Salerio? Q; Salanio? / Rowe;* Solanio? *Dyce*　219 Salerio,] *Salanio, / Rowe; Solanio, / Dyce*　hither,] *Q2;* hether *Q*　220 interest] *(intrest),* F　222 very] *om.* Q3

PORTIA   So do I, my lord.
They are entirely welcome.

LORENZO

I thank your honour. For my part, my lord,   225
My purpose was not to have seen you here,
But, meeting with Salerio by the way,
He did entreat me, past all saying nay,
To come with him along.

SALERIO   I did, my lord,
And I have reason for it. Signior Antonio   230
Commends him to you.   [*Gives Bassanio a letter.*]

BASSANIO   E'er I ope his letter,
I pray you tell me how my good friend doth.

SALERIO

Not sick, my lord, unless it be in mind,
Nor well, unless in mind. His letter there
Will show you his estate.   [*Bassanio*] *opens the letter.*   235

GRATIANO

Nerissa, cheer yond stranger; bid her welcome.
Your hand, Salerio; what's the news from Venice?
How doth that royal merchant, good Antonio?

224 **entirely** sincerely
228 **past . . . nay** beyond my attempts to decline (his entreaties)
231 **Commends him** wishes to be remembered to you, or sends his best regards to you
233 **unless . . . mind** unless he is mentally disturbed (because he is worried about his predicament), as opposed to being physically ill
234 **unless in mind** unless he has enough mental resilience (to withstand his present misfortune)
235 **estate** condition

236 **cheer** make happy (*OED v.* 4)
stranger Jessica is referred to as a *stranger* or a foreigner, i.e. one who is not a native of Venice
238 **royal merchant** Pooler suggests 'merchant prince' (Ard[1], 115), but see Braudel, 2.169, for the suggestion that 'royal merchandise' was a category of goods that was 'safe'. Gratiano is obviously referring to Antonio, but he may also be implying that his friend is a particular kind of trader whose ventures, normally secure, are, ironically, now at risk.

223–4 So . . . welcome.] *Capell; one line Q*   224 entirely] *Q2;* intirely *Q*   227 Salerio] *Salanio / Rowe; Solanio Dyce*   230 I have] haue *F2*   for it.] *(for it,); for it: Q2; for't; Pope*   231 SD] *Theobald; Gives him a letter. / Hanmer; delivering a letter / Capell*   his] this *F3*   235 SD] *Rowe; open the letter. Q; Bassanio opens a letter. / Johnson; Bass. reads the letter. / Dyce*   236 yond stranger;] *(yond stranger,); yon stranger, Q2*   237 Salerio;] *Capell; Salerio, Q; Salanio; / Rowe; Salerio: Collier; Solanio: Dyce*

I know he will be glad of our success:

We are the Jasons; we have won the fleece.   240

SALERIO

I would you had won the fleece that he hath lost.

PORTIA

There are some shrewd contents in yond same paper

That steals the colour from Bassanio's cheek:

Some dear friend dead, else nothing in the world

Could turn so much the constitution   245

Of any constant man. What, worse and worse?

With leave, Bassanio, I am half yourself,

And I must freely have the half of anything

That this same paper brings you.

BASSANIO   O, sweet Portia,

Here are a few of the unpleasant'st words   250

That ever blotted paper. Gentle lady,

When I did first impart my love to you,

I freely told you all the wealth I had

Ran in my veins – I was a gentleman –

And then I told you true. And yet, dear lady,   255

---

239 **glad** pleased to hear
240 **Jasons** See 1.1.170–2nn.
   fleece a possible pun on *fleece* and 'fleets' (Furness, 162), taken up at 241
242 **shrewd** harmful (*OED* †2), from Middle English 'schrewe': evil or malicious
   yond same that other (*OED a.*¹ †1). The letter from Antonio is one of two documents that Bassanio has, and Portia distinguishes between them. The other is the *scroll* at 139.
244 **else** otherwise
245 **turn . . . constitution** change the temperament in the sense of upsetting the equilibrium; a reinforcement of

the reference at 243 to the change in Bassanio's appearance; See 2.7.79n.
246 **constant** stable and steadfast (*OED* 1), hence one not prone to the vicissitudes of passion
247 **With leave** with your permission
251 **blotted** stained (*OED v.*¹ 1). The act of writing is deployed metaphorically to emphasize the serious nature of the contents.
253–4 **all . . . veins** my entire wealth lay in my lineage (i.e. noble blood); Bassanio identifies himself as an impoverished nobleman, and Mahood establishes a connection with *Son* 67. For a gloss on the syntactical complexity of this sonnet, see *Sonnets*, 251.

---

240 Jasons;] *(Iasons,)*   241 I would] Would *Pope*   242 yond] yon *Q2*   243 steals] *F3;* steales *Q;* steal *Pope*   Bassanio's] *F3; Bassanios Q*   247 Bassanio,] *Q2; Bassanio Q*   yourself,] *(your selfe,)*   248 I] *om. F2*   freely] *om. Q3*   254 veins – . . . gentleman –] *Ard²;* vaines, . . . gentleman *Q*

Rating myself at nothing, you shall see
How much I was a braggart. When I told you
My state was nothing, I should then have told you
That I was worse than nothing; for, indeed,
I have engaged myself to a dear friend,   260
Engaged my friend to his mere enemy,
To feed my means. Here is a letter, lady,
The paper as the body of my friend,
And every word in it a gaping wound
Issuing life-blood. But is it true, Salerio?   265
Hath all his ventures failed? What, not one hit,
From Tripoli, from Mexico and England,
From Lisbon, Barbary and India,
And not one vessel scape the dreadful touch
Of merchant-marring rocks?

SALERIO   Not one, my lord.   270
Besides, it should appear that if he had

---

256 **Rating** evaluating
257 **braggart** boaster or loud-mouth
258 **state was nothing** condition (but also 'estate') was worthless; a protracted statement of Bassanio's erstwhile financial probity
260 **engaged** bound myself by a pledge of the kind that one might make to a friend
261 **Engaged** exposed to risk (*OED* 2) and bound by contract (*OED* II.4), but also caused to be held fast, as in 'a snare, a net, or a bog' (*OED* III.a); more generally 'engage' means to involve, or get mixed up in (*OED* III.†13).
    mere sworn or deadly (*OED adj.* 4)
262 **feed my means** sustain my resources and my objectives (*OED sb.*[2] II.9†b)
263 **as the body** i.e. stained (blotted) and torn; refers literally to the letter, but

links its state with Antonio's mortal body. The imagery is quasi-religious, implying sacrifice, but the *life-blood* (265) is subliminally aligned with economic failure. These concerns are drawn together in the term *ventures* at 266.
265 **Issuing** pouring or gushing out (Onions)
266 **Hath** third person plural of the verb 'to have' (Abbott, 334)
    hit success (as in the modern colloquial sense of 'scored a hit')
267 **Tripoli . . . Mexico** See 1.3.17n. There appears to have been no recognized trade route between Venice and Mexico at this time (T. Elze, *Shakespeare Jahrbuch*, 14 (1879), cited in Furness, 164).
269 **scape** escape

---

257 braggart.] *(Braggart,)*; beggar, *F4* 258 have] bave *F3* 262 Here is] *(Heere is)*; Heer's *Q2* 263 as] is *Pope* 265 life-blood] *F4;* life blood *Q* Salerio?] *(Salerio); Salerio, F; Salanio? / Rowe; Solanio? / Dyce* 266 Hath] Have *Rowe* failed?] *(faild?) Q2;* faild, *Q;* faild! *F2;* fail'd! *F4* What,] *Q2;* What *Q* hit,] hit? *Q3;* hit! *F2* 267 Tripoli,] *(Tripolis,)* and] *om. Rowe* 269 scape] 'scape *Rowe;* 'scap'd *Pope* 270 SP] *(Sal.), Cam*[1]*; Solan. / Dyce*

The present money to discharge the Jew
He would not take it. Never did I know
A creature that did bear the shape of man
So keen and greedy to confound a man.   275
He plies the Duke at morning and at night,
And doth impeach the freedom of the state
If they deny him justice. Twenty merchants,
The Duke himself and the magnificoes
Of greatest port have all persuaded with him,   280
But none can drive him from the envious plea
Of forfeiture, of justice and his bond.

JESSICA

When I was with him, I have heard him swear
To Tubal and to Chus, his countrymen,

272 **present** immediately available
   discharge settle accounts with
   (Onions)
274 **bear** sustain, but also implied in the
   sense of carrying as a burden (*OED*
   *v.*¹ I.1)
275 **keen** fierce or savage (*OED a.* †2†c);
   a familiar allegation in a number of
   usury tracts of the period, e.g. Caesar,
   sigs. 3ᵛ–4
   confound destroy
276 **plies** exerts pressure on (*OED v.*¹ †2)
277 **doth impeach** calls in question
   (*OED* 3)
279 **magnificoes** Florio describes the
   dignitaries of Venice as 'nobly-minded
   magnificent; also a Magnifico of
   Venice' (Florio, 294). See also *Pierce
   Penniless* (1592): 'A stranger that
   should come to one of our *Magnificoes*
   houses' (Nashe, 1.200).
280 **port** high social status, dignity of
   bearing (*OED sb.*³ I.1)
   persuaded remonstrated, in the sense
   of attempted to convince (*OED* 2).
   Furness's 'argue', following Abbott,

194, does not quite encompass Salerio's
meaning here. Cf. *MM* 5.1.96: 'How I
persuaded, how I pray'd and kneel'd.'
281 **envious** malicious or spiteful
   (Onions)
282 **forfeiture** a loss that violates an
   obligation (*OED sb.* 2: 'forfeit')
284 **Tubal . . . Chus** the sons of Ham
   and Japhet respectively, who were
   themselves the two younger of Noah's
   three sons (Genesis, 10.2, 6). The
   Bishops' Bible has the form 'Chus',
   whereas the Geneva Bible (1562) has
   the form 'Cush' (Genesis, 10.6), indicating that for this name the former
   seems to have been the likely source.
   These names recall the larger narrative of the myth of Jewish origin (see
   Genesis, 9.25–7), but also 'Cush' was
   the Old Testament name for Ethiopia
   (Grant & Rowley, 194–5). Noble,
   161, notes that 'Chus also occurs in
   Hakluyt in the narrative of George
   Best, 'Cham and his blacke sonne
   Chus'. Cf. the connection between the
   Jew and 'blackness' at 3.1.35–6.

282 forfeiture] (forfaiture), *F;* forfeyture *Q2*   283 heard him] heard hiw *Q3*   284 countrymen,] *F4;*
country-men *Q;* Country-men *Q2;* Countri-men *F;* Countrimen *F3*

That he would rather have Antonio's flesh   285
Than twenty times the value of the sum
That he did owe him; and I know, my lord,
If law, authority and power deny not,
It will go hard with poor Antonio.

PORTIA
Is it your dear friend that is thus in trouble?   290

BASSANIO
The dearest friend to me, the kindest man,
The best-conditioned and unwearied spirit
In doing courtesies; and one in whom
The ancient Roman honour more appears
Than any that draws breath in Italy.   295

PORTIA
What sum owes he the Jew?

BASSANIO
For me three thousand ducats.

PORTIA   What, no more?
Pay him six thousand and deface the bond.
Double six thousand, and then treble that,

---

288 **deny not** do not prevent it, i.e. by withholding permission (*OED* 5)
289 **go hard with** be disadvantageous or hurtful to
292 **best-conditioned** most even-tempered (*OED sb.* I.1)
  unwearied indefatigable (*OED*)
293 **doing courtesies** performing good deeds. Cf. 3.1.44.
294 **ancient Roman honour** Roman honour was a yardstick of civilized behaviour; cf. Plutarch's 'Life of Marcus Brutus' (Plutarch, 102). Various elements of the Roman code of honour were frequently appealed to in Shakespeare; e.g. *2H4* 2.2.116: 'Peace! I will imitate the honourable Romans in brevity.'

296 Wright believed this short line to be part of a strategy 'to present credible and credibly various language on the stage' and was designed 'to make dialogue more convincing' (Wright, 137). This line returns Bassanio's hyperbolic language to the practical world of economics. The ensuing shared line, 297, has the effect of binding Bassanio and Portia together, and thus of 'realising more intently that condition of being bound together in a common action' (Wright, 139).
298 **deface** cancel or demolish (*OED* †2) rather than the more modern disfigure

292 best-conditioned and] *(*best conditiond and*) Q;* best condition'd and *Q2;* best condition'd, and *F;* best condition'd: An *Warburton;* best condition'd – *Johnson*   297–8 What . . . bond] *F; one line Q*   297 more?] *F;* more, *Q*

Before a friend of this description   300
Shall lose a hair through Bassanio's fault.
First go with me to church and call me wife,
And then away to Venice to your friend,
For never shall you lie by Portia's side
With an unquiet soul. You shall have gold   305
To pay the petty debt twenty times over.
When it is paid, bring your true friend along;
My maid Nerissa and myself meantime
Will live as maids and widows. Come away,
For you shall hence upon your wedding day.   310
Bid your friends welcome, show a merry cheer;
Since you are dear bought, I will love you dear.
But let me hear the letter of your friend.

BASSANIO [*Reads.*]   *Sweet Bassanio, my ships have all
miscarried, my creditors grow cruel, my estate is very low,*   315
*my bond to the Jew is forfeit, and, since, in paying it, it is
impossible I should live, all debts are cleared between you
and I if I might but see you at my death. Notwithstanding,*

301 **through** Q's reading renders this line metrically imperfect, though it is possibly pronounced as a disyllable; cf. Steevens's 'thorough'.

306 **petty** trivial (*OED* 2)

308 **maid** an affirmation of the social status of Nerissa that is persuasive, since it comes from Portia herself; cf. Gratiano's comment at 198.

311-13 Line 313 appears to be an afterthought, coming after the contents of the two preceding lines. Mahood suggests that 311-12 was a concluding couplet to the scene, and that 313 represents 'interpolated second thoughts' designed to strengthen Portia's motives for her intervention in the Trial scene' (Cam², 172). An equally plausible explanation emphasizes Portia's curiosity in relation to written

documents, although the reading of the letter itself augments Bassanio's description of the contents at 250-1

311 **cheer** countenance or disposition (Onions)

312 **dear bought** purchased at a high price, in terms of both Portia's relinquishing her wealth and the cost to Antonio; the phrase encapsulates the proverbial sentiment: 'Dear bought and far fetched are DAINTIES for ladies' (Tilley, D12).
love you dear love you with deep personal affection (*OED sb.* 2). The two competing meanings of *dear* signal an uneasy tension between the material and the emotional ethos of the play.

315 *miscarried* failed or perished (Onions)
estate state or condition (*OED sb.*1)

318 *if . . . but* if only I might

301 through] through my *F2;* thorough *Steevens*   309 away,] away; *F3;* away! *Theobald*   310 your] my *Rowe*   311–12] *om. Pope*   312 dear bought] *F3;* deere bought *Q;* dear-bought *Keightley*   314 SP] *Cam¹; not in Q*   314 SD] *Rowe subst.*   318 *and I*] and me, *Pope*   but] *om. F*

use your pleasure; if your love do not persuade you to come,
let not my letter.   320

PORTIA

O, love! Dispatch all business and be gone.

BASSANIO

Since I have your good leave to go away,
I will make haste. But, till I come again,
No bed shall e'er be guilty of my stay,   324
Nor rest be interposer 'twixt us twain.   *Exeunt.*

[3.3]   *Enter* [Shylock] the JEW, SALANIO, ANTONIO
and the Jailer.

JEW

Jailer, look to him. Tell not me of mercy.

319 *use your pleasure* do as you wish
321 **O, love!** a vocative addressed to
  Bassanio, imploring him to go to the
  aid of his friend
  Dispatch all business settle the
  present business with all possible
  speed (*OED v.* 5: 'dispatch')
322 **good leave** full permission
323 **come again** return again; although
  this is the literal meaning, the conjunction of *come*, *bed* and *guilty* suggests an
  alternative bawdy undercurrent, with
  'come' meaning 'to experience sexual
  emission' (Partridge, 81).
324 i.e. I will not rest; the projection of *guilt*
  onto *bed* links the postponement of the
  marriage consummation with the guilt
  that would result from failing to respond
  to Antonio's courteous summons.
325 **rest be interposer** rest (relaxation
  or sleep) intervene (*OED*). *Rest* is
  offered here as a potentially adulterous
  third member of a trio, ironical, since
  by extension, Antonio occupies this
  position in interrupting the betrothal
  ritual of Bassanio and Portia.

3.3 Theobald locates the scene in Venice,
  'SCENE *Changes to a street in* Venice';
  and Cam[1] specifies '*The street before*
  Shylock's house'.
0.1 *Q's error '*Salerio*' was emended in
  F to '*Solanio*' and in Q2 to '*Salarino*'.
  Salerio's presence in Belmont at
  3.2.218ff. confirms the impossibility
  of his presence in Venice, and thus distinguishes him from the two Venetian
  courtiers Salanio and Salarino (see p.
  429). This invites the conclusion that
  the confusion was compositorial, emanating from the abbreviation of speech
  prefixes. Q's emendation '*Sol.*' at 18 SP
  confirms the error in the SD (Ard[2], 92).
  JEW See pp. 420ff. Mahood suggests
  that the use of this as SP throughout
  the scene in Q is significant because
  'Shylock appears only as the moneylender not the father' (Cam[2], 126).
1 **Tell . . . mercy** The refusal to consider
  mercy is a violation of Ecclesiasticus,
  35.19: 'O howe fayre a thing is mercie
  in the time of anguish and trouble? It is
  like a cloude of rayne that commeth in

321 SP] *(Por.); om. Q2* gone.] gone! *Dyce* 325 Nor] No *Q2* twain] two *Rowe* 3.3] *Rowe (*SCENE
III.*); ACT III. SCENE IV. *Pope* 0.1 Shylock] *Rowe*; SHYLOCK *(at his door)* Cam[1] SALANIO] *F4*;
Salerio *Q*; Salarino *Q2*; Solanio *F*; Solarino *Rowe*; SOLANIO Cam[1] 1+ SP] *(Iew)*; Shy. / *Rowe* not
me] me not *Rowe*

This is the fool that lent out money gratis.
Jailer, look to him.

ANTONIO   Hear me yet, good Shylock.

JEW

I'll have my bond. Speak not against my bond;
I have sworn an oath that I will have my bond.   5
Thou call'dst me dog before thou hadst a cause,
But, since I am a dog, beware my fangs.
The Duke shall grant me justice. I do wonder,
Thou naughty jailer, that thou art so fond
To come abroad with him at his request.   10

ANTONIO

I pray thee, hear me speak.

JEW

I'll have my bond. I will not hear thee speak.
I'll have my bond, and therefore speak no more.
I'll not be made a soft and dull-eyed fool,
To shake the head, relent, and sigh and yield   15
To Christian intercessors. Follow not;
I'll have no speaking; I will have my bond.   *Exit.*

the time of drought.' The Jew departs from the positive emphasis on *mercy* in the Old Testament (see Monsarrat, 1–2).

2 **gratis** gratuitously, i.e. without charging interest (*OED* 1)

3 **yet** still, i.e. even though you refuse to listen to what I have to say

4–5 **bond . . . bond** a repetitive insistence upon the literal conditions of the agreement with Antonio that emphasizes the unchristian (and, by implication, inhumane) attitude of the Jew; also at 12–13.

6 This refers to the unjustified Christian habit of calling the Jew an animal (cf. 1.3.122–3); to which the Jew's appeal

in 3.1.53ff. is a response. For the connection between the usurer and a *dog*, see Caesar: 'On many places of the old Testament the word *Neschec* is read which signifieth Vsurie; it is deriued frô the verbe *Noschach*, which signifieth to bite, to gnawe, and deuoure as Serpentes, mad Dogges, and greedie Misers doe' (Caesar, 5).

9 **naughty** worthless or poor (*OED* 1) rather than wicked (*OED* 3)
    fond foolish, but implying that the Jailer favours Antonio

10 **come abroad with** accompany in public

14 **dull-eyed** easily deceived

2 lent] lends *F*   3 Shylock] Shylok *F*   5 I have] I've *Pope*   6 call'dst] cald'st *Q2;* call'st *F4*   7 But,] *(*but*)*   fangs.] *Q2;* phanges, *Q;* phangs, *F*   12 I'll] *Rowe;* Ile *Q;* I'le *F2*   12 bond.] bond: *Q2;* bond, *F*   14 dull-eyed] *(*dull eyde*) Q;* dull-ey'd *Q2;* dull ey'd *F*   16 not;] *Rowe;* not, *Q;* not: *F4*   17 SD] *(Exit Iew); Exit* Shylock *Pope*

SALANIO
  It is the most impenetrable cur
  That ever kept with men.
ANTONIO   Let him alone.
  I'll follow him no more with bootless prayers.   20
  He seeks my life. His reason well I know:
  I oft delivered from his forfeitures
  Many that have at times made moan to me;
  Therefore he hates me.
SALANIO   I am sure the Duke
  Will never grant this forfeiture to hold.   25
ANTONIO
  The Duke cannot deny the course of law;
  For the commodity that strangers have
  With us in Venice, if it be denied,
  Will much impeach the justice of the state,
  Since that the trade and profit of the city   30

18 **impenetrable cur** a dog impervious to (human) influence (*OED a.* 3). See 1.3.107, where the Jew alleges that Antonio has accused him of being a 'misbeliever, cut-throat dog'. The climate of anti-Semitic prejudice is sustained throughout the Radford film (2004).
19 **kept** lived
20 **bootless   prayers** unsuccessful prayers but also in the sense of unprofitable (*OED a.*[1] 3: 'bootless')
22 **forfeitures** penalties imposed for breach of contract
23 **made moan** complained
24 **Therefore . . . me** a justification for the Jew's hatred of Antonio that, Mahood argues, provides a more consistent motivation than the more recent elopement of Jessica (Cam[2], 127 and 185), emanating from the comparison with Proverbs, 26.18–19.

26 **deny . . . law** refuse to allow the law to take its course (Clarendon, 122). The Jew's emphasis is upon the *letter* of the law by which he claims protection. See Danson on 'the diabolic literalism of his flesh-bond' (Danson, *Harmonies*, 110), and Burckhardt for the suggestion that this opens a gap in the play between 'the private and utterly ineffectual speech of men as men and the deadening, unalterable letter of the law' (Burckhardt, 259).
27 **commodity . . . have** advantage granted to strangers. The connection between *commodity* and pecuniary self-interest is emphasized elsewhere in Shakespeare (*KJ* 3.1.581–2). See also Yaffe, 49.
29 **much impeach** call substantially into question

18+ SP] *Steevens (Sal.)*, *Malone (SALAN.)*; *Sol. Q*; *Sola. / Rowe*; *Salar. / Dyce*; *Solanio Cam*[1] 22 from] him *Q3*   24–5 I . . . hold.] *Pope*; *Q lines* grant / hold. /   29 Will] 'Twill *Capell*   the state] his state *Q2*

Consisteth of all nations. Therefore, go;
These griefs and losses have so bated me
That I shall hardly spare a pound of flesh
Tomorrow to my bloody creditor.   [*Exit Salanio.*]
Well, jailer, on. Pray God Bassanio come   35
To see me pay his debt, and then I care not.   *Exeunt.*

[**3.4**]   *Enter* PORTIA, NERISSA, LORENZO, JESSICA *and*
          [BALTHAZAR,] *a man of Portia's.*

LORENZO
Madam, although I speak it in your presence,
You have a noble and a true conceit
Of godlike amity, which appears most strongly
In bearing thus the absence of your lord.
But, if you knew to whom you show this honour,   5
How true a gentleman you send relief,
How dear a lover of my lord, your husband,
I know you would be prouder of the work

---

31 **Consisteth of** has its existence in (*OED v.* 6a, 6b, 6c), but also comprises. The operations of *trade and profit* (30), as well as justice, depend upon the equitable treatment of all those nationalities that comprise the state.
32 **bated** diminished (*OED sb.*[2] †1), but here also in the physical sense of loss of body weight.
3.4 Rowe locates the scene in '*Belmont*' and Ard[1] specifies '*A Room in Portia's House*'. Cam[1] sets it in '*The hall of Portia's house*'.
0.2 BALTHAZAR Editors since Theobald include the name of Portia's '*man*', but this is another duplicated name in the play, since it is also the name

that the disguised Portia adopts at 4.1.
2 **conceit** idea, conception or understanding (*OED sb.* 1), used here much more positively than in other examples where the verb form places emphasis upon imagination and fantasy
3 **godlike amity** divine friendship (*OED*: 'amity')
6 **gentleman . . . relief** *Gentleman* is the indirect object of the verb *send* and is thus an example of the dative case (Clarendon, 113); the relative 'to whom' is omitted (Abbott, 394).
7 **lover** friend; not to be confused with the modern sense of sexual partner

---

32 have] hath *Q3*   35 on.] *Keightley;* on, *Q;* on; *F4;* on. – *Johnson;* on: – *Capell*   3.4] *Rowe (*SCENE IV.*);* SCENE V. *Pope*   0.2 BALTHAZAR . . . *Portia's] Cam*[1] *(a man of Portia's, called balthazar); a man of Portiaes. F3; a Servant of Portia's / Rowe;* Balthazar. *Theobald; a* Servant. *Capell*   1 your] you *F2*   3 godlike] gold-like *Q3*   most] *om. Pope*   6 relief,] *F2;* releefe *Q;* Relief to *Rowe*

Than customary bounty can enforce you.

PORTIA

I never did repent for doing good,   10
Nor shall not now; for in companions
That do converse and waste the time together,
Whose souls do bear an equal yoke of love,
There must be needs a like proportion
Of lineaments, of manners and of spirit;   15
Which makes me think that this Antonio,
Being the bosom lover of my lord,
Must needs be like my lord. If it be so,
How little is the cost I have bestowed
In purchasing the semblance of my soul   20

9 than the formal obligation of kindness or benevolence demands of you. See *OED* †3, 4: *bounty* is associated with godlike benevolence or kindness. The emphasis is upon the capacity to surpass in generosity any formal obligation imposed upon her by a commitment sustained through her betrothal to Bassanio.

12 **waste** consume, spend or pass, but without any negative connotation (Furness, 173)

13 ***equal** Q's spelling 'egall' is an obsolete form of 'equal' (*OED*) that Q2 alters to 'equall'. Derived from Old French *egal*.
  yoke of love connection (*OED sb.* II.5b) through love; joined together in the way that two oxen might be harnessed. See Oz, *Yoke*, 181ff. for a fuller exploration of the significance of this phrase within the larger context of the play.

14 **needs** of necessity (Abbott, 25)
  proportion balance (*OED sb.* I.1)

15–18 **Of ... lord** This passage closely resembles John Lyly's *Euphues: The Anatomy of Wit* (1580): 'Doth not the sympathy of manners, make the coniunction of mindes? Is it not by a word, like will to like? Not so common as commendable it is, to see young gentlemen choose thê such friends with whom they may seeme beeing absent to be present, being a sunder to be conuersant, beeing dead to be aliue' (Lyly, 1.197). Editions of *Euphues* were printed by Roberts, *c.* 1595 and 1597 (1.102). See also Dent, L286, 'LIKE will to like', of which proverbial utterance these lines may be an extension.

15 **lineaments** physical attributes or features (*OED* †2).

17 **bosom lover** dear friend and confidant

19–20 **cost ... purchasing** money (and effort) I have expended in order to secure

19 **bestowed** laid out money for, or expended (*OED* 5†b)

20 **semblance ... soul** image (*OED* 2b) of my soul (i.e. Antonio). The logic of this comparison aligns Antonio, Bassanio and Portia as souls who 'bear an equal yoke of love' (13), and designates Antonio, curiously, as the image or likeness of Bassanio. See Sinfield, 'How to read', 138–9,

10 for] of *Pope*   11 Nor] And *Pope*   13 equal] *Q2* (equall)*;* egall *Q*   15 lineaments,] *Q2;* lyniaments, *Q;* lineaments *Warburton*   17 Being . . . lord,] (Being . . . lord) *Q2*   bosom lover] bosome-louer *Q2*   20 soul] *Rowe;* soule; *Q;* soul, *Q2*

From out the state of hellish cruelty.
This comes too near the praising of myself;
Therefore, no more of it. Hear other things:
Lorenzo, I commit into your hands
The husbandry and manage of my house   25
Until my lord's return. For mine own part,
I have toward heaven breathed a secret vow
To live in prayer and contemplation,
Only attended by Nerissa here,
Until her husband and my lord's return.   30
There is a monastery two miles off,
And there we will abide. I do desire you
Not to deny this imposition,
The which my love and some necessity
Now lays upon you.
LORENZO   Madam, with all my heart,   35
I shall obey you in all fair commands.

---

for the location of specifically 'early modern organisation of sex and gender boundaries'.

21 **out** out of
state . . . cruelty predicament or condition (Onions) of [the Jew's] devilish cruelty. Furness conjectured that Q2 emended 'cruelty' to 'misery' on the grounds that 'the phrase was too elliptical for Q2's editor' (quoted in Cam², 128).

23 ***Hear** F3 and F4 emend the Q spelling 'heere' to 'here', adopted by Rowe. Most modern editors follow Theobald in emending to 'hear'.

24 **commit . . . hands** metaphorical (1) to the extent of assigning general responsibility for and (2) carrying a sexual innuendo (see 3.2.164)

25 **husbandry and manage** the domestic management (*OED sb.*) and (metaphorically) the care of the horses (*OED sb.* 1, 2: 'manage'). The verbal associations of *commit* and *husbandry* communicate a bawdy undertone and point towards the sexual mastery of Jessica.

30 **husband . . . lord's** See Abbott, 397, where this example is offered of the application of the genitive case to both nouns.

33 **deny this imposition** refuse this command (*OED* 5b: 'imposition'); cf. 1.2.99.

34 **necessity** constraining power of circumstance (*OED sb.* 3)

36 **fair commands** courteously proffered (*OED sb.²* 1d), but also instructions emanating from a woman (*OED sb.²* 1a)

21 cruelty] misery *Q2*   22 myself;] *(my self,) F4;* my selfe, *Q*   23 Hear] *Theobald (hear);* heere *Q;* Here are *Rowe*   25 manage] *Q2;* mannage *Q*   house] *(house,)*   27 toward] tow'rd *Pope*   31 monastery] *(Monastry)*   two] too *F*   32 we will] will we *Q2*   35 lays] *F4;* layes *Q;* lay *Hanmer*   you] me *Q3*

PORTIA

My people do already know my mind
And will acknowledge you and Jessica
In place of Lord Bassanio and myself.
So fare you well till we shall meet again.   40

LORENZO

Fair thoughts and happy hours attend on you.

JESSICA

I wish your ladyship all heart's content.

PORTIA

I thank you for your wish, and am well pleased
To wish it back on you. Fare you well, Jessica.
                        Exeunt [Jessica and Lorenzo].

Now, Balthazar,   45
As I have ever found thee honest true,
So let me find thee still. Take this same letter,
And use thou all th'endeavour of a man,
In speed to Mantua. See thou render this
Into my cousin's hand, Doctor Bellario;   50
    [*Gives Balthazar a letter.*]

---

37 **people** household servants
39 This doubling of the Portia–Bassanio
   relationship represses the fact of
   Lorenzo and Jessica's elopement.
45 *Lines 45–6 are run together in Q;
   Dover Wilson thought that the short
   line 45 was an indication of 'adaptation' (Cam¹, 157), but Brown suggests,
   more plausibly, that it signals a pause
   'until the others are clear of the stage'
   before Portia addresses Balthazar
   (Ard², 96).
46 **honest true** See Abbott, 2, for examples of compound adjectives where the
   first functions as an adverb supporting
   or qualifying the second.

48 **th'endeavour . . . man** all the effort,
   i.e. strength (*OED sb.* 1), that a man
   may summon
49 **In speed** in order to travel quickly
   Mantua Editors since Theobald
   have emended 'Mantua' to 'Padua',
   since the text subsequently contains
   references to the latter location where
   there was known to be a famous law
   school. Shakespeare's own sense of
   Italian geography was imperfect and as
   a probable instance of Shakespearean
   confusion it should be allowed to stand.
   render give or deliver (*OED v.* II.7)
50 *cousin's hand** as in F (see t.n.); Q's
   'cosin hands' transposes the possessive

---

38 acknowledge] acknowledg *F4*   40 So . . . well] *F2;* So fare you well *Q;* And so farewell *Q2*   44
Fare you well] *F3;* far you well *Q;* farewell *Q2;* faryouwell *F*   SD *Jessica and Lorenzo*] *Rowe*   45–6]
Pope; one line Q   46 honest true] honest, true *Rowe;* honest-true *Keightley*   48   th'endeavour]
(*th'indeuour) Q;* the indeauour *F;* the endeavour *F3*   man,] man *Q2*   49 Mantua] *Padua Rowe*
50 cousin's hand] *(cosins hand) F;* cosin hands *Q;* Cosins hands *Q2*   SD] *Bevington subst. after 47*

And look what notes and garments he doth give thee,
Bring them, I pray thee, with imagined speed
Unto the traject, to the common ferry,
Which trades to Venice. Waste no time in words
But get thee gone; I shall be there before thee.   55

BALTHAZAR

Madam, I go, with all convenient speed.   [*Exit.*]

PORTIA

Come on, Nerissa; I have work in hand
That you yet know not of. We'll see our husbands
Before they think of us!

NERISSA   Shall they see us?

PORTIA

They shall, Nerissa, but in such a habit   60
That they shall think we are accomplished
With that we lack. I'll hold thee any wager,
When we are both accoutred like young men,
I'll prove the prettier fellow of the two,
And wear my dagger with the braver grace,   65

's', and Q2's 'Cosins hands' simply compounds the error in trying to offer a plausible solution.

52 **imagined speed** as quickly as possible, i.e. with all conceivable (*OED* 2: 'imagined') speed

53 ***traject** from the Italian *traghetto*, meaning 'any ferrie, a passage, a foard, or gozell ouer from shore to shore' (Florio, 572). To explain Q's 'tranect', Dover Wilson conjectures a compositorial misreading of 'ai' as 'an' (Cam[1], 157n.). It is conceivable that a compositor misread 'traiect', but it is also possible that 'tranect' is a Shakespearean neologism based on an imperfect English pronunciation of the Italian word for 'ferry' that was so unfamiliar as to require a gloss.

54 **trades to** goes to and from (*OED sb.* II.7)

56 **convenient** appropriate (*OED* †4)

60 **habit** dress or costume

61 **accomplished** accomplishèd; equipped

62 **that we lack** that which we do not possess, i.e. male genitalia
hold . . . wager take any bet

63 **accoutred** dressed, from the medieval French *accoustrer*, meaning to robe (*OED*); Q2 emends to 'apparreld'.

64 **prettier** more clever or skilful (*OED sb.* II.2a)

65 **braver grace** more refined ostentation. The sense of 'brave' is 'ostentatious' or 'showy' (Onions), but also indicates the kind of behaviour associated with masculinity; *grace* in this context is both 'ornament' and 'propriety' (Onions).

53 traject] *Rowe;* tranect *Q*   54 words] word *Q3*   55 thee gone] hee gone *F2*   56 SD] *Q2*   58 We'll] *Rowe;* weele *Q;* Wee'l *Q2;* wee'll *F*   59 us!] (vs?) *Q;* vs. *Q2*   62 that] what *Pope*   63 accoutred] *Q3;* accoutered *Q;* apparreld *Q2*

And speak between the change of man and boy
With a reed voice, and turn two mincing steps
Into a manly stride, and speak of frays
Like a fine bragging youth, and tell quaint lies
How honourable ladies sought my love,   70
Which I denying, they fell sick and died.
I could not do withal; then I'll repent,
And wish, for all that, that I had not killed them.
And twenty of these puny lies I'll tell,
That men shall swear I have discontinued school   75
Above a twelvemonth. I have within my mind
A thousand raw tricks of these bragging jacks
Which I will practise.

NERISSA   Why, shall we turn to men?

PORTIA

Fie, what a question's that,
If thou wert near a lewd interpreter.   80

66 **speak . . . boy** speak like an adolescent male whose voice is changing
67 **reed voice** squeaky voice (Onions); a reference to the reed used to make a musical pipe (*OED sb.*[1] II.7), hence the equivalent 'piping' to describe the pitch of the voice
mincing affectedly dainty or elegant (*OED* 2), here associated with a feminine gait
68 **frays** assaults (*OED sb.*[1] †2); a shortened form of 'affrays'
69 **bragging youth** literally a young male who boasts; Portia runs through the characteristics of the *youth* that 'she' proposes to imitate; see Orgel, *Impersonations*, 78–82, for a careful analysis of such moments in Shakespeare's plays.
quaint ingeniously elaborate (Onions)

72 **I . . . withal** which I could do nothing about (*OED v.* 54: 'do')
73 **for** in spite of (Onions)
74 **puny** weak or feeble (*OED* 4)
75 **discontinued** left
76 **Above a twelvemonth** more than a year ago, i.e. that I am not a schoolboy
77 **raw** immature or unsophisticated
bragging jacks boastful knaves
78 **turn to** become, in the sense of 'turn into', but also a play upon the alternative bawdy meaning of *turn*: to have sexual recourse to (Gordon Williams, 316)
79 Portia's dismissive response registers the bawdy gloss on Nerissa's question.
80 **near** approaching the position of
lewd base, vulgar or untutored (*OED a.* †2, †3 and †4), but also lascivious (*OED* 7)

67 mincing] *Q2;* minsing *Q*   68 stride,] *(*stride;*)*   69 youth,] *(*youth*)*   71 died.] *(*dyed.*)*; dyed: *Q2;* dy'd, *Pope;* dy'd; *Capell;* died; *Malone;* died, – *Dyce*   75 I have] I've *Pope*   76 twelvemonth] *F4;* twelue-moneth *Q;* twelue-month *Q2;* twelue moneth *F;* tweluemoneth *F3*   80 interpreter.] *(*interpreter:*) Q;* interpreter? *F2;* interpreter! *Theobald*

But come, I'll tell thee all my whole device
When I am in my coach, which stays for us
At the park gate; and therefore haste away,
For we must measure twenty miles today.   *Exeunt.*

[3.5]   *Enter* [Lancelet *the*] CLOWN *and* JESSICA.

CLOWN   Yes, truly, for, look you, the sins of the father are
to be laid upon the children; therefore, I promise you,
I fear you. I was always plain with you, and so now I
speak my agitation of the matter. Therefore be of good
cheer, for, truly, I think you are damned. There is but   5
one hope in it that can do you any good, and that is but
a kind of bastard hope neither.

JESSICA   And what hope is that, I pray thee?

CLOWN   Marry, you may partly hope that your father got
you not, that you are not the Jew's daughter.   10

interpreter one who explains, or puts a particular construction upon meaning (*OED* 1b)

81 all . . . device all the details of my plan

82 stays waits

84 measure travel (Onions)

3.5 Capell specifies '*A Garden*' in Belmont, but Cam¹ offers a much more lavish description of the location: '*An avenue of trees leading up to Portia's house; on either side, grassy banks and lawns set with cypresses*'.

0.1 Capell reverses the order: see t.n.

1–2 sins . . . children part of the Ten Commandments as set out in Exodus, 20.5. The invocation of Mosaic law underlines Jessica's transgression as a possible consequence of her father's 'misdeeds' (Jeremiah, 31.29–30.

3 fear you am fearful for you. For other examples of the omission of

the preposition before the verb, see Abbott, 200.

plain frank (*OED adv.* IV.11)

4 agitation . . . matter a possible malapropism, since the Clown appears to substitute *agitation* for 'cogitation' (Ecclesiastes, quoted in Furness, 182); but *agitation* neatly combines the sense of 'reflection' (*OED* 1: 'cogitation') and anxiety or perturbation (*OED* 4: 'agitation') both on Jessica's predicament and on her behalf.

4–5 be . . . damned a parody of John, 16.32–3; Jessica is *damned* because she has forsaken her father.

7 bastard unlikely, and therefore illegitimate; a pun on *bastard* that alludes to the carnal 'sin' of Jessica's mother

neither either (*OED* 3a, 3b), used to strengthen a preceding negative

9–10 got you not did not beget you

81 my] *Q2;* my my *Q*   3.5] *Capell subst.;* SCENE VI. *Pope*   0.1] *Enter* Launcelot *and* Jessica. *Rowe; Enter* JESSICA, *and the Clown.* / *Capell; LANCELOT and JESSICA approach in conversation* Cam¹   1+ SP] *Laun.* / *Rowe; Lancelot* Cam¹*; LANCELET Folg*   4 of good] *F;* a good *Q*   7, 11 bastard hope] bastard-hope *F4;* bastardhope *Theobald*

JESSICA   That were a kind of bastard hope indeed, so the sins of my mother should be visited upon me.

CLOWN   Truly, then, I fear you are damned both by father and mother: thus, when I shun Scylla your father, I fall into Charybdis your mother; well, you are gone both   15 ways.

JESSICA   I shall be saved by my husband; he hath made me a Christian!

CLOWN   Truly, the more to blame he; we were Christians enow before, e'en as many as could well live one by   20 another. This making of Christians will raise the price of hogs: if we grow all to be pork eaters, we shall not shortly have a rasher on the coals for money.

Enter LORENZO.

12 **sins . . . me** a gendered inversion of the injunction at 1–2, deploying biblical language and implying that in such a case Jessica's mother would have been guilty of a sexual infidelity that she would inherit

14–15 **Scylla . . . Charybdis** *Scylla* was a sea-monster that dwelt in a cave overlooking a whirlpool (*Charybdis*), two perils that Odysseus had to overcome in order to negotiate the narrow strait of water that separated Italy from Sicily (see Ovid, *Met.*, 13.865–74); proverbial (Dent, S169: 'Between SCYLLA and Charybdis').

fall into literally, and metaphorically in the sense of having sexual intercourse with

17–18 **saved . . . Christian** Jessica confirms her conversion by a reference to Corinthians, 7.13–14: 'And the woman which hath to her husband an infidel, and he consent to dwell with her,

let her not put him away. / For the unbelieving husband is sanctified by the wife, & the unbelieuing wife is sanctified by the husband: els were you children uncleane, but now are they holy.'

20 **enow** a form of 'enough' used to denote numbers rather than quantity (Clarendon, 114)

*****e'en as** Q2 corrects Q's 'in as' to 'e'ne as'; Brown notes a similar error in the Folio text of *TC* 1.3.355 (Ard², 99).

20–1 **one by another** together, but also upon (i.e. by exploiting) one another. Both meanings are implied here. Cf. John Marston, *The Malcontent* (1604), 4.4.4–5: 'do not turn player; there's more of them than can well live one by another already' (Hunter, 117).

23 **rasher** slice of bacon, often grilled over an open fire

for money at any price

14 I shun] you shun *Rowe*   I fall] you fall *Rowe*   17 husband;] *F4;* husband, *Q*   18 Christian!] *(Christian?) Q;* Christian. *F*   20 e'en as] *(e'ne as) Q2;* in as *Q*   23.1] *after 25 Dyce;* LORENZO is seen from the house *Cam¹*

326

JESSICA I'll tell my husband, Lancelet, what you say. Here
he comes.   25

LORENZO I shall grow jealous of you shortly, Lancelet, if
you thus get my wife into corners!

JESSICA Nay, you need not fear us, Lorenzo; Lancelet and
I are out. He tells me flatly there's no mercy for me
in heaven, because I am a Jew's daughter; and he says   30
you are no good member of the commonwealth, for,
in converting Jews to Christians, you raise the price of
pork.

LORENZO I shall answer that better to the commonwealth
than you can the getting up of the negro's belly: the   35
Moor is with child by you, Lancelet!

CLOWN It is much that the Moor should be more than

---

27 **into corners** into compromising
situations involving secretive meet-
ings (*OED sv sb.*[1] 6); cf. George
Whetstone, *A Mirror for Magistrates
of Cities* (1584), sig F4ᵛ: 'in euery corner, he had (secretly) such faythfull
Explorers, as mens proper Houses,
were no Couerts for naughtie practices, nor the Senat-house for partial
Judgementes.'

29 **are out** have quarrelled, i.e. have
fallen out with each other

29–30 **no mercy . . . heaven** Jews were
cut off from God's mercy, a divine
prerogative available to Christians
through the intercession of Christ.
For a general statement of the Jew's
position, see *Jew of Malta*, 1.2.114–16
(83) and also Romans, 11.30–2.

31 **the commonwealth** society in general (*OED* 2)

32–3 **raise . . . pork** a parodic and
materialist reduction of the Pauline
account of the Christian state of grace;
see Romans, 8.5–6, for the distinction
between the 'carnally minded' and the
'spiritually minded'.

35 **getting . . . belly** causing the negro
woman to become pregnant; an allegation that is never explained, since
there is no 'negro' woman in the Jew's
household. This further gloss on the
Clown's name, 'Lancelet', extends
the frame of reference to his capacity for sexual penetration. Lorenzo
uses the terms 'negro' and 'Moor'
interchangeably. At 2.1.0.1 Morocco
is described as a '*tawny Moor*', but
here the terms indicate an indiscriminate 'blackness'. It is puzzling that a
non-Christian should be present in
a Venetian (i.e. Christian) household,
albeit one that contains a converted
Jew, Jessica.

37 **much** a serious matter
Moor . . . more a quibble on a word
that in homonymic terms is both racial
and quantitative. Steevens (209) compares Thomas Heywood's *Fair Maid of
the West* (1615): 'And for your Moors
thus much I mean to say, / I'll see if
more I eat the more I may.'

37–8 **more than reason** quantitatively
bigger than she ought to be

24, 26, 28, 36 Lancelet] *Folg; Launcelet Q; Lancelet Q2, F; Launcelot / Rowe; Lancelot Cam*[1] 25
comes] *Q2;* come? *Q*   26 jealous] *(iealious) Q*   27 corners!] *(corners?);* corners. *Q2*   28 Lorenzo;]
F4; Lorenzo, *Q*   29 there's] there is *F*   36 Moor is] Moore's *Q2*

reason; but if she be less than an honest woman, she is
indeed more than I took her for.

LORENZO How every fool can play upon the word. I think   40
the best grace of wit will shortly turn into silence, and
discourse grow commendable in none only but parrots.
Go in, sirrah; bid them prepare for dinner!

CLOWN That is done, sir: they have all stomachs!

LORENZO Goodly lord, what a wit-snapper are you! Then   45
bid them prepare dinner.

CLOWN That is done too, sir; only 'cover' is the word.

LORENZO Will you cover then, sir?

CLOWN Not so, sir, neither; I know my duty.

LORENZO Yet more quarrelling with occasion. Wilt thou   50
show the whole wealth of thy wit in an instant? I pray
thee, understand a plain man in his plain meaning: go

38–9 **less . . . more** if she is less than honest, then that is more than I expected
her to be. The Clown asserts that the
woman (by her very nature) is disreputable to begin with, and that he was
under no illusion that she was otherwise.

40 **play . . . word** manipulate the meanings of words, but also suggesting that
this is symptomatic of a more general
promiscuity. Cf. *TN* 3.1.14–15: 'they
that dally nicely with words may
quickly make them wanton.'

41 **best . . . wit** the most attractive feature (*OED sb.* I.1: grace) of mental
agility

42 **discourse grow commendable**
conversation will be an acknowledged
feature
parrots noted for their repetitive and
meaningless babble; see Dent, P60,
'To prate like a parrot', and also *Oth.*
2.3.275–7.

44 **stomachs** appetites (*OED sb.* 5) i.e.
everybody is hungry; also a sexual
reference to the swollen belly of the
Moor at 35.

45 **Goodly lord** gracious lord; a modern
equivalent might be 'Good heavens'.
wit-snapper one who snaps up
every opportunity to indulge his wit
(Onions). Possibly a Shakespearean
neologism, but see *MA* 5.4.99–100 for
the variant 'wit-crackers'.

48 **cover** set the table, usually by covering
it with a cloth (Onions); there may
be a second possible allusion to the
legal issue of 'coverture' (Blackstone,
1.442).

49 **my duty** the obligation to remove his
hat in the presence of a social superior

50 **Yet . . . occasion** yet more quibbling,
i.e. by disputing and/or misunder-
standing what is being said (*OED sb.*[1]
III.†7: 'occasion')

---

40 the word.] *this edn;* the word, *Q , F;* the word! *F4;* a word! *Hanmer*   42 only] *om. Pope*   43 sirrah;]
(sirra,)   dinner!] *(dinner?);* dinner. *F4*   44 stomachs!] *Ard²;* stomacks? *Q;* stomackes. *Q2*
45 Goodly] Good *Pope*   lord,] *F (Lord,);* Lord *Q*   you!] *F4;* you, *Q;* you: *Q2*   Then] *Q2, F;* than
Q   46 dinner.] *Q2, F;* dinner? *Q;* dinner! *Ard²*   47 That is] That's *Q2*   too] *F2;* to *Q*   'cover']
Cam¹; cover *Q*   48 then] *F4;* than *Q*   50 occasion.] *this edn;* occasion, *Q;* occasion! *F4*   51 instant?]
Q2; instant; *Q*

to thy fellows, bid them cover the table, serve in the
meat, and we will come in to dinner.

CLOWN   For the table, sir, it shall be served in; for the meat,   55
sir, it shall be covered; for your coming in to dinner, sir,
why, let it be as humours and conceits shall govern.   *Exit.*

LORENZO
O, dear discretion, how his words are suited.
The fool hath planted in his memory
An army of good words, and I do know   60
A many fools that stand in better place,
Garnished like him, that for a tricksy word
Defy the matter. How cheer'st thou, Jessica?
And now, good sweet, say thy opinion:
How dost thou like the Lord Bassanio's wife?   65

---

55 **table** supply of food (*OED* 6c), and the equivalent of *meat* at 54, which is a further quibble on Lorenzo's more literal gloss on *table* at 53

56 **covered** brought in on covered dishes in order to preserve the heat

57 **humours** dispositions: the four constitutive elements that comprised the human body and were responsible for temperament and behaviour
conceits imaginative interpretations, poetic inventions, but also the capacity for understanding
govern control or determine

58 **dear discretion** precious discrimination (Onions). Furness quotes a reference to 'That faculty of the mind [discretion] most opposite to, and inconsistent with, this disposition to quibble, for which Launcelot was so remarkable' (Eccles, cited in Furness, 185).
suited adapted (*OED v.* 10), but also part of his outfit or dress (*OED v.* 9)

59 **hath planted** has placed, in the way artillery is placed on the battlefield ready to be discharged (*OED v.* 2b)

61 **A many** many (Abbott, 87)
stand . . . place have a better position or employment (Ard², 101)

62 **Garnished** furnished or dressed (Onions), but also alluding to tableware (*OED sb.* †1)
for . . . word by playing upon (the different meanings of) a word (Clarendon, 115); *tricksy* here is more than 'ambiguous' (Cam², 133), indicating 'artful, capricious' (Ard², 101) use of language.

63 **Defy the matter** confuse the issue, i.e. by resisting straightforward meaning (*OED sb.*¹ III.11b: 'matter': 'sense or substance')
How cheer'st thou How are you feeling. This resurrects some of the more unsavoury implications of Jessica's elopement.

64 **say thy opinion** say what you are thinking; an irony here, since the preceding dialogue has exposed the precariousness of firm 'discrimination', hence rendering a clear articulation of solid judgement difficult

---

56 covered] *(couerd)*   57 SD] *(Exit Clown.); Exit* Laun. *Rowe; Exit Launcelot. / Johnson*
58 suited] *(suted)*   62 Garnished] *(garnisht);* Garnish'd *Q2*   63 cheer'st] *F;* cherst *Q;* far'st *Q2*
Jessica?] *Q2; Iessica,* Q

JESSICA

    Past all expressing. It is very meet
    The Lord Bassanio live an upright life,
    For, having such a blessing in his lady,
    He finds the joys of heaven here on earth,
    And, if on earth he do not mean it, it   70
    Is reason he should never come to heaven.
    Why, if two gods should play some heavenly match
    And on the wager lay two earthly women,
    And Portia one, there must be something else
    Pawned with the other, for the poor rude world   75
    Hath not her fellow.

LORENZO   Even such a husband
    Hast thou of me, as she is for a wife.

JESSICA

    Nay, but ask my opinion too of that!

LORENZO

    I will anon; first let us go to dinner.

---

66 **Past all expressing** beyond the capacity of words to articulate
meet appropriate
67 **upright** honourable (*OED sb.* III.8)
70 **mean it, it** See t.n. Some 18th-century editors have followed Pope's 'merit it / In', a reading favoured by most modern editors. Q2's 'meane it, then' was adopted by some 19th-century editors. Clarendon (115) suggests that a gloss on *mean* approximating to 'appreciate' would make sense. But see *OED v.*[1] 1f: 'mean': 'to be well-intentioned or disposed'. Thus the sense would be that, if Bassanio is not well disposed towards the *blessing* conferred upon him (and embodied in the figure of Portia), then he should be deprived of the fruits of Christian salvation.
71 *Is Q's 'in' here is emended in F

to 'Is', which preserves the substantive reading in its emphasis on the Christian condition placed upon the attainment of eternal happiness. Q2 emends the terminal 'it' at 70 to 'then', and is followed erroneously by those editors who emend 'mean it, it' to 'merit it'.
73 **on the wager** for the bet
lay The context requires the meaning 'place', but, because of its association with *two earthly women*, the word *lay* also suggests coitus (Gordon Williams, 183).
75 **Pawned** staked (Eccles, cited in Furness)
rude ignorant or unrefined
76 **fellow** equal or match (Onions)
Even just
79 **anon** shortly

---

70 mean it, it] meane it, then *Q2;* meane it, *Q3;* merit it / In *Pope*   71 Is] *Q2, F;* in *Q*   heaven.] *Q4;* heauen? *Q;* heaven. heav'n. *Rowe;* heaven! *Cam*[1]   74 one,] *F4;* one: *Q*   75 Pawned] *(*paund*);* Pawn'd *Q2*   76–7 Even . . . wife] *Q2 lines* me, / wife. /   77 for a] *F;* for *Q*   78 too] *F2;* to *Q*   that!] *(*that?*);* that. *Q2*   79 anon] *Q2;* anone *Q*   dinner.] *Q2;* dinner? *Q*

JESSICA

    Nay, let me praise you while I have a stomach.   80

LORENZO

    No, pray thee, let it serve for table talk,

    Then howsome'er thou speak'st, 'mong other things

    I shall digest it.

JESSICA   Well, I'll set you forth.   *Exeunt.*

[4.1]   *Enter the* DUKE [of Venice], *the Magnificoes,*

        ANTONIO, BASSANIO, [SALERIO, *who remains*

        near the door,] *and* GRATIANO [*and three*

        or four Attendants].

DUKE

    What, is Antonio here?

ANTONIO   Ready, so please your grace.

80 **stomach** appetite and inclination

82 ***howsome'er** howsoever. Q's 'how so mere', emended to 'howsoere' in Q2, and 'howsom ere' in F2, is thought by Brown to indicate a pun on 'mere', meaning 'pure' or 'unmixed', usually associated with wine (Ard², 102), and to extend the culinary reference

83 **set you forth** publish your qualities (*OED* 144e, 144f), although playfully ironic in this context

4.1 Rowe specifies the geographical location in '*Venice*', but Theobald is more specific: '*the Senate-house in* VENICE'. Cam¹ indicates with characteristic detail: '*A Court of Justice; on a platform at the back a great chair of state with three lower chairs on either side; before these a table for clerks, lawyers' desks, etc.*'

0 1 *Magnificoes* members of the Venetian nobility, from the Italian *magnifico* meaning noble-minded (Florio, 295). The power vested in Shakespeare's Duke differs markedly from historical accounts of the operation of the Venetian judicial system (Furness, 189; Contarini, 107ff.).

1 An iambic hexameter that modern editors are inclined to set as two separate lines, in which there is a counterpoint between the conversational stress and the formal iambic organization of the line. **Ready** a customary formal reply to a call or a summons, suggesting 'Here' or 'Present' (Onions)

80 stomach.] Q2; stomach: *Q*; stomacke? *F*   82 howsome'er] *Rowe*; how so mere *Q*; howsoere Q2; how so ere Q3; howsom ere F2; howsome're F4   speak'st] *(speakst)* 'mong] *F*; mong *Q*; 'mongst F4   83 digest] *F*; disgest *Q*   it.] Q2; it? *Q*   SD] *F*; Exit. *Q*   4.1] *F (Actus Quartus.)*; ACT IV. SCENE I. *Rowe*   0.1–4] *Enter the Duke, the Senators,* Anthonio, Bassanio, *and* Gratiano. *Rowe; Enter, in State, the* Duke, *Magnificoes, Officers of the Court etc. and seat themselves; then enter* ANTONIO, *guarded,* BASSANIO, GRATIANO, SALERINO, Solanio, *and Others. / Capell;* ANTONIO *(guarded),* BASSANIO, GRATIANO, SOLANIO, *officers, clerks, attendants, and a concourse of people. The* DUKE *in white and six Magnificoes in red enter in state and take their seats* Cam¹; *Enter the* DUKE, *the Magnificoes,* ANTONIO, BASSANIO *and* GRATIANIO, SALERIO *and Others.* Ard¹   0.1 of Venice] *this edn*   0.2–4 who . . . Attendants] *this edn*   1–2] *Keightley; prose Q*   1 grace.] Q2; grace? *Q*

DUKE

   I am sorry for thee. Thou art come to answer
   A stony adversary, an inhumane wretch,
   Uncapable of pity, void and empty
   From any dram of mercy.

ANTONIO   I have heard   5

   Your grace hath ta'en great pains to qualify
   His rigorous course; but, since he stands obdurate,
   And that no lawful means can carry me
   Out of his envy's reach, I do oppose
   My patience to his fury, and am armed   10
   To suffer with a quietness of spirit,
   The very tyranny and rage of his.

DUKE

   Go one and call the Jew into the court.

SALERIO

   He is ready at the door; he comes, my lord.

3–5 A . . . mercy Cf. Thomas Lodge's account: 'your life be found sawced with crueltie, and no one action sauoring of mercie: the Lord shal place you among the goates' (Lodge, 1.20).

3 stony hard or obdurate (*OED a.* 5), as in the Bible, 2 Corinthians, 3.3: 'ye are the Epistle of Christ ministred by us, written not with inke, but with the spirit of the liuing God, not in stonie tablets but in fleshly tablets of the heart.'

4 Uncapable unable to hold or contain (*OED sb.* †1)

   void and empty another example of hendiadys, where both words share the same meaning

5 From This preposition is used in place of 'of' (Cam², 134); it denotes 'a condition which is changed or abandoned for another' (*OED* 7), i.e. one who possesses Christian mercy.

   dram the smallest quantity

6 qualify moderate, or ameliorate the effects of, through the exercise of judgement (*OED v. trans.* 1 and †2)

7 obdurate a polysyllable ending an imperfect iambic verse line; Abbott suggests that in this case sometimes the accent would fall on the middle syllable (Abbott, 491), but Mahood is the only modern editor to indicate 'obdúrate' (Cam², 135).

9 envy's malice's (*OED sb.* †1, 2)

10 armed provided with sufficient spiritual resolve (*OED v.*[1] 2); cf. St Paul's injunction, Ephesians, 6.11–12: 'Put on all the armour of God, that yee may stande against the assaults of the deuill. / For we wresstle not against blood and flesh; and [but] against powers, against worldly gouuerours of the darkness of this world, against spirituall wickednesse in heauenly places'.

12 tyranny violent and unmerciful action, associated with oppressive power (*OED sb.* 3a, 3b)

---

3 inhumane] *Q2;* inhumaine *Q;* inhuman *Rowe*   6–7] *Q2 lines* paines / course: / obdurate, /
6 ta'en] *F4* (ta'ne); tane *Q*   14+ SP] *Sal. Q2*

Enter Shylock [the JEW].

DUKE

Make room, and let him stand before our face.   15
Shylock, the world thinks, and I think so too,
That thou but leadest this fashion of thy malice
To the last hour of act, and then 'tis thought
Thou'lt show thy mercy and remorse more strange
Than is thy strange apparent cruelty;   20
And where thou now exacts the penalty,
Which is a pound of this poor merchant's flesh,
Thou wilt not only loose the forfeiture,
But, touched with humane gentleness and love,
Forgive a moiety of the principal,   25
Glancing an eye of pity on his losses
That have of late so huddled on his back,
Enough to press a royal merchant down,

17 **leadest this fashion** carries (*OED v.*[1] I.1b) this form or manifestation (*OED sb.* 2). It is not clear that the Jew's strategy or his behaviour is a pretence (Cam[2], 135), since there is no doubting the substantive nature of his *malice* towards Antonio, and its justification.
18 **last . . . act** last moment, brink
19 **remorse** pity or compassion
   strange remarkable, exceptional or wonderful (*OED* 10); cf. *Tem* 5.1.242–4: 'This is as strange a maze as e'er men trod, / And there is in this business more than nature / Was ever conduct of.'
20 **strange** alien (*OED sb.* †1)
   apparent manifest (*OED* 3). Johnson's gloss: 'seeming; not real' (452) is not appropriate here.
21 **where** whereas (Abbott, 134)
   exacts exact'st; a second person singular case of the verb (Abbott, 340)
23 **loose** relinquish or discharge (*OED v.*

1); similar to that of Matthew, 16.19, in its incorporation of the meaning 'lose' into that of 'release': 'and whatsoeuer thou shalt binde in earth, shall bee bounde in heauen, and whatsoeuer thou shalt loose in earth shalbe loosed in heauen.' Brown suggests that 'lose' may also be meant here because the spelling of the two verbs was not clearly distinguished (Ard[2], 104).
25 **Forgive** remit (*OED* 3)
   moiety portion or share of (*OED* 2†)
   principal the sum borrowed and the interest accrued (*OED sb.* II.6)
26 **Glancing** looking with
27 **of late** recently; cf. *H8* 2.1.146: 'Did you not of late days hear . . .'
   huddled crowded together unceremoniously (*OED* II.6)
28 **royal merchant** See 3.2.238n.; Antonio is not an aristocratic merchant, but one who deals in assured merchandise.

14.1] *(Enter Shylocke.)*   16 too,] *F3;* to *Q;* to, *Q2*   17 leadest] leadst *F2;* lead'st *F3*   19 Thou'lt] *Q2;* thowlt *Q*   21] *om. Rowe*   exacts] exact'st *F*   23 loose] lose *F4*   24 love,] *Q2;* loue: *Q*   25 moiety] *F3;* moytie *Q, F;* moity *Q2;* moyty *F2*   28 Enough] *(Enow)*

And pluck commiseration of his state
From brassy bosoms and rough hearts of flint,　　　　30
From stubborn Turks, and Tartars never trained
To offices of tender courtesy.
We all expect a gentle answer, Jew!

JEW

I have possessed your grace of what I purpose,
And by our holy Sabbath have I sworn　　　　35
To have the due and forfeit of my bond.
If you deny it, let the danger light
Upon your charter and your city's freedom!
You'll ask me why I rather choose to have

29 *commiseration . . . state sympathy for his predicament. Q's 'this
state', corrected in Q2 to 'his state',
is a manifest error emanating from a
compositorial misreading, as in *Ham*
Q2 (1605) at 4.4.89 and 5.2.148, a
text also printed in James Roberts's
printing shop (Ard², 104).
31 stubborn unyielding, inflexible,
obstinate (*OED* 1); refusing obedience, fierce, and applicable to animals as well as humans
Turks noted for the savagery of
their challenge to Christianity, and
thought during the period to be in
league with Jews; cf. *Jew of Malta*,
2.3.130–40, where Barabas takes as
his slaves both a Turk and a Moor,
and later seeks to give Malta into
the hands of the Turk Calymath
(5.2.85–95).
Tartars inhabitants of the region
of Central Asia (*OED* 1), but also
the inhabitants of hell (*OED sb.*⁴
obs.); 'tartar' was also a rich silk-like
cloth (*OED sb.*³ *obs.*) of the kind that
merchants traded in.
32 offices duties, from the Latin *officium*
meaning duty, obligation or service

33 gentle courteous, polite; with a quibble on 'gentile', as at 2.4.35; the Jew is
being asked to respond as a Christian.
34 possessed acquainted or informed
35 our holy Sabbath the Jewish Sabbath,
or seventh day (i.e. Saturday). See
Exodus, 31.16. Q's spelling 'Sabaoth',
reduced to the disyllabic 'Sabbath'
in Q2, is the Hebrew for 'armies',
implying the ferocity of response to
the Duke's expectation of a 'gentile'
answer from the Jew.
36 due and forfeit that to which
the Jew is entitled, and that which
Antonio must give up; Furness (192)
regarded this as an example of hendiadys, but there is also a quibble on
due/*Jew*.
37 danger light damage fall
38 charter . . . freedom Dover Wilson
regarded this anglicization of the
political order of Venice as being
inconsistent with earlier descriptions
at 3.2.276–9 and 3.3.26–31, and
hence evidence of partial revision
of a putative promptbook (Cam¹,
113–14): the phrase *your charter*
indicates the Jew's acceptance of his
position as a 'stranger' in Venice.

29 his state] *Q2;* this state *Q*　30 flint] *Q2;* flints *Q*　31 Tartars] *Q2;* Tarters *Q*　trained] *Cam¹;*
traind *Q;* train'd *Q2*　33 Jew!] *Ard²;* Iewe? *Q;* Iew. *Q2*　34+ SP] *Shy. / Rowe*　35 Sabbath] *Q2;*
Sabaoth *Q*　38 freedom!] *(freedome?);* freedome. *Q2, F*　39 You'll] *F3;* Youle *Q;* You'l *Q2, F*

A weight of carrion flesh than to receive   40
Three thousand ducats. I'll not answer that!
But say it is my humour. Is it answered?
What if my house be troubled with a rat,
And I be pleased to give ten thousand ducats
To have it baned? What, are you answered yet?   45
Some men there are love not a gaping pig!
Some that are mad if they behold a cat!
And others, when the bagpipe sings i'th' nose,
Cannot contain their urine: for affection,

40 **carrion** dead or putrifying (Onions)
42 **humour** inclination, derived from
    the temperament generated by the
    mixture of 'humours' or fluids in the
    body
45 **baned** poisoned (Onions)
46 **Some . . . are** there are some men
    [who]
    gaping pig roasted pig prepared for
    the table (Malone). See also Thomas
    Nashe, *Pierce Penniless* (1592): 'Some
    will take on like a mad man, if they
    see a pigge come to the table' (Nashe,
    1.188); a proverbial indication of an
    irrational dislike (Dent, P310: 'Some
    cannot abide to see a PIG'S head
    gaping'). Given the Jew's religious
    opposition to the eating of pork at
    1.3.30–4, the culinary image seems
    the more probable in this context
    (see Harrison, 312).
47 **Some . . . mad** there are some
    [men] who become mad [when].
    Here the use of the intransitive *mad*
    along with the conjugated verb 'to
    be' emphasizes the habitual nature
    of this particular action (see Blake,
    4.4.4(a), 145–6).

48 **bagpipe** Brown (Ard[2], 105) quotes
    Ben Jonson, *Every Man in His
    Humour* (1616), 4.2.19–22: 'E.KN.
    What ayles thy brother? can he not
    hold his water, at reading of a bal-
    lad? / WELL. Oh, no; a rhyme to
    him is worse than cheese or a bag-
    pipe' (Jonson, 3.364). This passage
    is not in Q (1598), indicating that
    Jonson took over the allusion from
    Shakespeare.
    sings i'th' nose a reference to the
    monotonous bass drone of the bag-
    pipe
49 **affection** often a synonym for
    passion, as in *FQ*, 2.4.34: 'Most
    wretched man, / That to affections
    must the bridle end; . . . Whiles they
    are weake betimes with them con-
    tend' (*FQ*, 204). But here *affection* is
    identified as the source of passion;
    cf. Burton: 'The good affections
    are caused by some object of the
    same nature; and if present they
    procure joy, which dilates the heart
    and preserves the body: if absent
    they cause hope, love, desire, and
    concupiscence' (Burton, 1.8.161).

40 than] then *F4*   41 not] now *Warburton*   that!] *(that?) Q;* that, *Q2;* that: *F*   42, 61 answered?]
Q2; aunswerd? *Q*   45 baned?] *(baind?);* bain'd? *F;* brain'd *Rowe*   answered] *Q2; aunswered Q*
46 pig!] *(pigge?) Q;* pig: *Q2;* Pigge: *F;* Pig, *Rowe*   47 cat!] *(Cat?) Q;* Cat: *Q2, F*   48 i'th'] *F3;* ith
Q; i'th *Q2, F*   49 urine: for affection,] *Dyce;* urine for affection. *Pope;* urine, for affection *Johnson;*
urine, for affection, *Capell;* urine for affection: *Malone*   affection] affections, *Steevens*

Maistrice of passion, sways it to the mood   50
Of what it likes or loathes. Now, for your answer:
As there is no firm reason to be rendered
Why he cannot abide a gaping pig,
Why he a harmless necessary cat,
Why he a woollen bagpipe, but of force   55
Must yield to such inevitable shame
As to offend himself being offended;

50 ***Maistrice of passion** the male/
female controller of passion. The
initial confusion is exacerbated by
Q2's emendation 'Masters of', which
attempts to clarify Q's 'Maisters of',
where 'maister' is a common spelling
for 'master' throughout. The sense
in Q is that *affection* determines and
controls (masters) *passion*, except
that *affection* is usually designated
as female. The spelling 'Maisters'
may owe something to the Middle
English spelling 'maistresse' found
in the Prologue to the F version
of Chaucer's *The Legend of Good
Women*, with which Shakespeare is
known to have been familiar. *OED*
glosses 'maistrice' as 'MASTERY in
various senses; superiority, superior
force or skill', and Shakespeare may
have been attracted to this spelling
because of its phonetic ambivalence
in combining 'master'/'mistress';
cf. *Son* 20.1–2: 'A woman's face
with nature's own hand painted /
Hast thou, the master mistress of
my passion.' There is no reason to
depart from the Q1 reading, and
the subsequent confusion that has
produced the phrase 'Masterless passion' (Rowe), 'Mistress of passion'
(Capell) or 'Masters oft passion'
(Cam²) may have been caused by the
choice of an obsolete word coupled

with the unusual designation of *affection* in the singular in 49.
  mood temper, disposition, inclination
(*OED sb.* 3)
52 **reason** explanation, which distinguishes between *affection* and *passion*
on the one hand, and rationality as the
seat of perception, understanding and
choice. See Burton, 1.9.164–5, for an
account of the distinction.
55 **woollen bagpipe** a reference that
baffled some 18th- and 19th-century
editors. Dover Wilson observed that
the bags of the pipes 'are quite commonly wrapped in baize or flannel'
(Cam¹, 161); Peter Holland has suggested privately that 'woollen' may
be an Elizabethan spelling of 'uillean' signifying 'uillean (elbow) pipes'
of Irish origin that were 'played by
wind supplied by bellows held under
player's arm' (*Oxford Dictionary of
Music*, 748).
  of force necessarily (because driven
by an irrational compulsion)
57 **offend himself** Q2 punctuates
'offend, himself'; the Q reading is
preferred because it preserves the
ambivalence of the line: the irrational
man (1) may offend himself by giving
way to his passionate inclinations, (2)
may *himself* be offended and hence
cause offence to others by his behaviour or (3) may do both.

50 Maistrice of passion] *(*Maisters of passion*)*; Masters of passion *Q2;* Masterless passion
Rowe; Mistress of passion *Capell;* Master of passion *Ard²;* Masters oft passion *Cam²* 51 it] she
Keightley 53 pig,] *Ard²;* pigge? *Q;* pig: *F4* 54 cat,] *Ard²;* Cat? *Q;* Cat: *F2* 55 woollen] swollen
Keightley; bollen *Dyce* 57 offend himself] offend, himself *Q2;* offend, himself, *F4*

So can I give no reason, nor I will not,
More than a lodged hate and a certain loathing
I bear Antonio, that I follow thus   60
A losing suit against him! Are you answered?

BASSANIO

This is no answer, thou unfeeling man,
To excuse the current of thy cruelty!

JEW

I am not bound to please thee with my answers!

BASSANIO

Do all men kill the things they do not love?   65

JEW

Hates any man the thing he would not kill?

BASSANIO

Every offence is not a hate at first!

JEW

What, wouldst thou have a serpent sting thee twice?

ANTONIO

I pray you, think you question with the Jew.

59 **lodged** deep-seated or implacable
certain steadfast
61 **losing suit** a case that will involve the
loss of money
63 **current** flow. The image alludes to
the Jew's evocation of the psychology
of the 'humours' in which irrational
hatred was thought to emanate from
an excess of black bile that flowed
into the blood; see Timothy Bright,
A Treatise on Melancholy (1586), sigs
A1ᵛ–2.
64 **bound** obliged; cf. 1.3.5 and 1.3.10,
for the reference to the conditions of
a formal contract (*OED v.* 6: 'bound'),
and also 2.5.52 for the proverbial: 'Fast
bind, fast find.'
65–7 examples of the rhetorical
device of stychomythia imitated

from Seneca's tragedies (Cam², 137),
made popular in English drama
through Kyd's *The Spanish Tragedy*
(1587), 2.2.25–31 and elsewhere.
67 **offence** feeling of being hurt (*OED sb.*
†4b), but also wrongdoing (*OED sb.* 7);
Bassanio argues that 'offences' in both
senses do not *begin* from hatred.
68 **serpent . . . twice** The Jew says that
he will not wait for a second offence
to be committed against him *and*
that he will not wait to be persecuted
again. Also the Christian Antonio is
demonized by being associated with
the figure of evil, the *serpent*, in a
contest of mutual recrimination.
69 **think you question** you are deluding
yourself into thinking that you can
debate

59 lodged] *Q2;* lodgd *Q;* lodg'd *F*   61 losing] *Q2;* loosing *Q*   him!] *(*him?*);* him; *Q2*   63 To excuse]
*(*to excuse*);* T'excuse *Pope*   cruelty!] *(*cruelty?*);* cruelty. *Q2*   64, 66, 68 SP] *Shy. Q2*   64 answers!]
*(*answers?*);* answere. *Q2*   65 things] thing *F2*   67 Every] Ev'ry *Pope*   first!] *(*first?*);* first. *Q2*   68
What,] *F3;* What *Q;* What! *Collier*   69 think you] stint your *Keightley*   the Jew] *(*the Iewe*);* a Jew *F3*

You may as well go stand upon the beach   70
And bid the main flood bate his usual height;
You may as well use question with the wolf
Why he hath made the ewe bleat for the lamb;
You may as well forbid the mountain pines
To wag their high tops, and to make no noise   75
When they are fretten with the gusts of heaven;
You may as well do anything most hard
As seek to soften that, than which what's harder –
His Jewish heart! Therefore, I do beseech you,

71 **main flood** Pooler glosses this as
'ocean' (Ard[1], 138), although Brown's
gloss 'high tide' (Ard[2], 106) seems the
more probable
     bate . . . height diminish its usual
height; the personification of *flood*
implies a connection with the superhuman power of the sea god Neptune.
72 **use question** enter into dispute; literally, engage in the act of questioning,
although, again, the 'use'/'Iewes' quibble remains firmly in the background
72–3 **wolf . . . lamb** proverbial; see
Dent, W602, 'Give not the WOLF
(fox) the wether (sheep) to keep', but
see also Terence, *Eunuchus*, 205: 'You
wretch, it was trusting the wolf with
the lamb [Ovem lupo commisisti].' See
also Sir Thomas Wilson's *Discourse on
Usury* (1572), fol. 142: 'so ye usurer
(like unto hel mowth) doth deuower &
gnaue, upon euery mans goods, as long
as there is a peny, or half peny worth in
the world to be had.'
73 *****bleat** Q's 'bleake' was emended in
F to 'bleate'. *OED* records 'bleak' as
a northern form of the verb 'to make
pale' (*OED v.* 1 and 2), and Pooler cites
the dialect form 'blake': to bleat (Ard[1],
138). Mahood thinks that the MS
may have contained the form 'blake'

(Cam[2], 138). However, this error seems
compositorial rather than authorial,
since Brown cites a case of *k/t* confusion in *Ham* Q2 (Ard[2], 107), and the
existence of variant states of these
lines in Q indicates some difficulty in
deciphering the MS at this point.
74–5 *****mountain . . . noise** Ovid, *Met.*,
15.677–9, was the probable source of
these images: 'Such noyse as Pynetrees
make what tyme the heady easterne
wynde / Dooth whiz among them, or
as from the sea dooth farre rebound:
/ Even such among the folk of Rome
that present was the sound.' F emends
Q's 'mountaine of Pines' to the more
metrically correct 'mountain pines'.
75 **wag** wave or move about
     and . . . noise and (bid them) to make
no noise; an example of an elliptical
expression (Abbott, 382) rather than
a double negative emanating from the
use in 74 of the verb *forbid*, in which
the verb 'bid' is implied
76 **fretten** annoyed or distressed. Abbott,
344, cites this as an example of an
irregular participial formation of the
verb 'fret', but *OED* records an obsolete form 'fretten' derived from the
Latin *fractus*, meaning to be broken in
pieces.

72 You may as] *Q(c)*, *Q2*; *om. Q(u)*; Or euen as *F*   wolf] *Q(c)*; Woolfe, *Q(u)*, *Q2*; Wolfe, *F*   73 Why
. . . made] *Q(c)*; *om. Q(u)*, *F*   bleat] *F*; bleake *Q*   74 mountain] *F*; mountaine of *Q*   76 fretten]
fretted *F*   78 that, . . . harder –] *this edn*; that then which what's harder: *Q*; that, then which what
harder? *F*; that, than which what harder? *F2*; that (than which what's harder!) *Theobald*; that – that
which what's harder? – *Cam*   79 heart!] *hart?*); heart. *F*

Make no moe offers, use no farther means,   80
But with all brief and plain conveniency
Let me have judgement, and the Jew his will!

BASSANIO

For thy three thousand ducats here is six!

JEW

If every ducat in six thousand ducats
Were in six parts, and every part a ducat,   85
I would not draw them; I would have my bond!

DUKE

How shalt thou hope for mercy, rendering none?

JEW

What judgement shall I dread, doing no wrong?
You have among you many a purchased slave,
Which, like your asses, and your dogs and mules,   90
You use in abject and in slavish parts,
Because you bought them. Shall I say to you,
'Let them be free, marry them to your heirs.
Why sweat they under burdens? Let their beds
Be made as soft as yours, and let their palates   95
Be seasoned with such viands?' You will answer:

---

80 **moe offers** i.e. more offers than those that have already been made; used here to intensify as a comparative rather than a superlative (Blake, 3.2.3.4, 46–7). F emends Q's 'moe' to 'more' here.

81 **brief . . . conveniency** speedy and simple propriety

86 **draw** take or receive (*OED* 45 cites this example)

87 **hope . . . none** an interrogative version of the New Testament Bible, James, 2.13: 'For hee shall haue iudgement without mercie, that hath shewed no mercie; and mercie reioyceth against iudgement.'

89 **many . . . slave** From the 15th century onwards, 'commercially adventurous' Italian cities such as Genoa, Venice and Florence had substantial slave populations (H. Thomas, 42–3).

91 **abject** base or degraded (*OED sb.* 3B)
   parts duties (*OED sb.* II.8)

93 **Let . . . free** Cf. Deuteronomy, 15.12: 'If thy brother an Hebrue sell himselfe to thee, or an Hebrue woman, and serue thee six yeeres, in the seuenth yeere thou shalt let him go free of thee.'

94 **burdens** heavy load

96 **such viands** food or victuals (*OED* 1) appropriate (to their new-found freedom)

---

80 moe] more *F*   82 will!] *(will?)*; will. *Q2*   83 six!] *(sixe?)*; sixe. *Q2*, *F*   84, 88 SP] *Shy.* / *Rowe*   86 bond!] *(bond?)*; bond. *Q2*   87 rendering] *(rendring)*   90 your asses] you Asses *F2*   91 parts] part *Rowe*   92 you bought] your bought *F2*   93–6 'Let . . . viands?'] *Oxf*; Let . . . viands, *Q*   94 burdens] *(burthens,)*

'The slaves are ours.' So do I answer you.
The pound of flesh which I demand of him
Is dearly bought; 'tis mine, and I will have it.
If you deny me, fie upon your law:　　　　　　　　　　　　100
There is no force in the decrees of Venice.
I stand for judgement: answer, shall I have it?

DUKE

Upon my power I may dismiss this court,
Unless Bellario, a learned doctor,
Whom I have sent for to determine this,　　　　　　　　105
Come here today!

SALERIO　　　　　　　　My lord, here stays without
A messenger with letters from the doctor,
New come from Padua!

DUKE

Bring us the letters! Call the messenger!　　　　*[Exit Salerio.]*

99 **dearly bought** bought at great cost; the meaning of the adverb *dearly* appears to be restricted in this context, but the Jew may also be invoking an obsolete meaning: 'from the heart' (*OED adv. obs.* †3); 'at great cost' (*OED adv.* 4) seems to be the manifest gloss, but the obsolete meaning has a particular application in this case.
100 **fie** an expression indicating indignation or disgust (*OED* 1); cf. 1.1.46.
101 **force** power to influence, effect or control, efficacy (*OED* 7, 7b)
102 **stand for judgement** Cf. 4.1.141, 'I stand here for law'; but contrast Portia's 'I stand for sacrifice' at 3.2.57. See Lewalski, 337–8, on the ambiguity of the verb *stand for*: (1) to occupy the position of and (2) to represent. In so far as the conflict is allegorical, this is an example of the opposition between

Old Testament law and Christian imperative.
103 **Upon my power** by the power vested in me; the Duke's assertion of his own power counters the challenge proffered by the Jew's allegation at 100–1.
105 **determine** resolve by legal dispute (*OED v.* 13)
106 **here stays without** there is waiting outside
107 **doctor** someone who is proficient in knowledge of the law (*OED sb.* 5b)
108 **Padua** at 3.4.49–50 Doctor Bellario's location is Mantua; here it is now Padua, indicating some inconsistency in the printer's copy. Padua was famous for its university, and was the centre of civil law in Italy (Cam[1], 157). See also *TS* 1.1.1–38.
109 This is clearly addressed to Salerio, who exits here and then re-enters with the disguised Portia at 117.

97 'The . . . ours'] *Cam[1]*; The . . . ours, *Q*　99 'tis] *F*; tis *Q2*; as *Q*; is *Capell*　106 today!] *(to day?)*; to day. *Q2*; to-day. *Pope*　SP] *Saler. Q2; Sal. F*　108 Padua!] *(Padua?)*; Padua. *Q2*　109 letters!] *(letters?)*; Letters, *Q2, F*; Letters. *Q3*　messenger!] *(messenger?)*; Messengers *F*　SD] *Oxf*

BASSANIO

Good cheer, Antonio! What, man, courage yet: 110
The Jew shall have my flesh, blood, bones and all,
Ere thou shalt lose for me one drop of blood!

ANTONIO

I am a tainted wether of the flock,
Meetest for death; the weakest kind of fruit
Drops earliest to the ground, and so let me.   115
You cannot better be employed, Bassanio,
Than to live still and write mine epitaph!

Enter [SALERIO *and*] NERISSA[*, disguised as a lawyer's clerk*].

DUKE

Came you from Padua from Bellario?

NERISSA [*Presents a letter to the Duke.*]

From both! My lord, Bellario greets your grace!

BASSANIO

Why dost thou whet thy knife so earnestly?   120

110 **Good cheer** an invocation to be optimistic; a modern equivalent might be 'Cheer up'.
courage yet have courage still
112 **for me** on my account
113 **tainted wether** literally, a diseased castrated ram; but see Bassanio's comment at 3.2.75–6, 'what plea so tainted and corrupt', where 'tainting' is the mark of a fallen nature ('evil') that *a gracious voice* may obscure. In substituting himself as a sacrifice for Bassanio, Antonio conflates both Old and New Testaments: (1) he replicates the action of Abraham, who sacrifices a ram in place of his son Isaac (Genesis, 22.13), and (2) he offers himself, Christ-like, as a sacrifice whose function is to take away 'the sin of the world'. Cf. John,

1.29: 'The next day, John seeth Jesus coming unto him, and sayeth, Beholde the Lambe of God, which taketh away the sinne of the world.' This conflation is in stark contrast to the Jew's earlier reference to the Old Testament narrative of Jacob and Esau, in which he justifies usury through an act of deception (1.3.67–84).
114 **Meetest** most suitable (*OED sb.* 3)
117 SD See 109n.
120 **whet . . . earnestly** a detail from one of the play's analogues, *The Ballad of Gernutus*: 'The bloudie Iew now readie is, / with whetted [i.e. sharpened] blade in hand, / To spoyle the bloud of Innocent, / By forfeit of his bond.' The uncertain date of the ballad clouds the issue of its provenance as a source for the play.

110 Antonio!] *Capell; Anthonio? Q; Anthonio, Q2;* Anthonio. *F; Anthonio; / Rowe*   112 blood!] *(blood?);* blood. *Q2*   113 wether] *Steevens;* vveather *Q*   115 earliest] soonest *Capell* and so] so *F2*   117 epitaph!] *(Epitaph?);* epitaph. *Q2*   117.1 *Enter*] SCENE II. *Enter / Pope* SALERIO *and*] *Oxf subst. disguised . . . clerk*] dress'd like a Lawyer's Clerk. */ Rowe*   119] *F* lines both. / grace. /   SD] *Capell subst.* both!] *(both?);* both, *Q2* lord,] *Rowe;* L. *Q;* Lord *F*   grace!] *(grace?);* grace. *F*

JEW

To cut the forfeiture from that bankrupt there.

GRATIANO

Not on thy sole, but on thy soul, harsh Jew,
Thou mak'st thy knife keen. But no metal can,
No, not the hangman's axe, bear half the keenness
Of thy sharp envy. Can no prayers pierce thee?   125

JEW

No, none that thou hast wit enough to make.

GRATIANO

O, be thou damned, inexecrable dog,
And for thy life let justice be accused!
Thou almost mak'st me waver in my faith,
To hold opinion with Pythagoras   130

121 ***bankrupt** (*OED v.*†1)

122 ***sole . . . soul** The Jew is whetting his knife on the sole of his shoe, and Gratiano's punning emphasizes the extent to which the Jew's intended action will be the source of his spiritual damnation. F distinguishes between 'soale' (*sole*) and 'soule' (*soul*), prompting Furness (205) to conjecture that the two words were pronounced differently.

123 **keen** sharp (*OED* 3); also, a transferred epithet applicable to the Jew's eagerness (*OED* 6), to which Gratiano refers at 125

124 **hangman's** executioner's; an allusion to the practice of execution by hanging as well as beheading, but also, possibly, to drawing and quartering, which was an added refinement used in the execution of those convicted of treason (see *Shakespeare's England*, 1.398)

125 **pierce** 'penetrate as a sharp instrument does' (*OED v.* 1), and 'touch or move deeply' (*OED v.* 5); the Jew's 'sharp envy' is given both a literal and a metaphorical realization.

126 **make** both 'compose' (*OED v.*[1] 5), and 'draw up' in the manner of a legal document (*OED v.*[1] 5d); the ambiguity reflects upon the Jew's commitment to legal process.

127 **inexecrable** deserving in the extreme to be cursed (*OED* 2), used as an intensifier of 'execrable'. F3 emends to 'inexorable', which alters the sense considerably to suggest one who is incapable of being persuaded (*OED sb.*: 'inexorable'). It is possible that both meanings are conflated in Q's spelling.

128 **for . . . accused** The meaning of this line is unclear; it can mean either (1) 'let justice stand accused for allowing you to continue to live', or (2) 'even though you are technically in the right, your inhumanity would provide the justification for taking your life at the risk of justice itself being arraigned for it.'

130 **hold . . . Pythagoras** Pythagoras, the son of Mnesarchus of Samos, flourished during the 6th century BC and was noted for his theory of the

121 SP] *Shy.* / *Rowe* forfeiture] *Q2;* forfaiture *Q;* forfeit *Pope* bankrupt] *Rowe;* Bankrout *Q* there.] *F;* there? *Q;* there *Q2* 122 sole, . . . soul,] *Hanmer;* soule: . . . soule *Q1, Q2;* soale: . . . soule *F;* soul! . . . soul, *Pope;* soale, . . . soul, *Theobald* 126 hast] hoast *F2* 127 inexecrable] inexorable *F3* 128 accused!] *Theobald;* accusd; *Q;* accus'd: *F;* accus'd. *Rowe*

That souls of animals infuse themselves
Into the trunks of men. Thy currish spirit
Governed a wolf, who, hanged for human slaughter,
Even from the gallows did his fell soul fleet,
And whilst thou layest in thy unhallowed dam,   135
Infused itself in thee; for thy desires
Are wolvish, bloody, starved and ravenous.

JEW

Till thou canst rail the seal from off my bond
Thou but offend'st thy lungs to speak so loud.

transmigration of human souls into animals. The doctrine is alluded to in Golding's Preface 'To the Reader', 95ff., in Ovid, *Met.*, 425, and also in Marlowe's *Doctor Faustus*, 19.174–6 (Jump). Gratiano reverses this doctrine in his suggestion that the Jew accommodates the soul of an animal.

131 **infuse** instil or insinuate from outside (*OED v.* 2) in what would be a parody of God's introduction of man's immortal soul into his body (*trunk*)

132 **trunks** bodies considered apart from souls (*OED sb.* †3)
currish dog-like, but here used as an expression of contempt (*OED* 1b: 'cur')

133 **wolf** a common allegation levelled against usurers; see 72–3n.; see also the fate of Lyceus, the King of Arcadia, who, for his sceptical irreverence, Jove transformed into a wolf (Ovid, *Met.*, 1.275–9: 'So is he made a ravening Wolfe: whose shape expressly drawes / To that the which he was before: his skin is horie graye, / His looke still grim with glaring eyes, and every kinde of waye / His cruel heart in outward shape doth well itselfe bewraye'). Some editors connect *wolf* with the Latin *lupus* and suggest an oblique topical reference to the execution of Elizabeth's Spanish physician, Roderigo Lopez; see the entry for

7 June 1594 in Stow, 768.
who ... slaughter regarded by Abbott, 376, as an example of a pronoun (*who*) used as a nominative absolute in conjunction with a participle (*Governed*)

134 **fell** savage or cruel (*OED adj.* 1: 'fell'); but 'fell' as a noun refers to the skin or wool of an animal (*OED sb.* 1), which recalls another element of the Jew's narrative justifying usury at 1.3.67–84, and the larger deception of Jacob at Genesis, 27.16: 'And she [Rebecca] put the skins of the kids upon his handes, and upon the smooth of his necke.'
fleet float or drift away (*OED v.* 9, 9b, and 10b)

135 **unhallowed dam** unholy mother. Gratiano implies that the Jew is the offspring of the devil, whose mother is the profane opposite of the Virgin Mary.

137 **starved** withered or famished (*OED*), but also spiritually dead (*OED v.* I.1)
ravenous voracious, like the raven (black) and hence devilish

138 **rail the seal** erase the official seal [from the bond] through heaping abuse or ridicule upon it (*OED v.* 3: 'rail')

139 **but offend'st** only causes an injury to

133 who,] *Theobald;* who Q   134 fleet,] fleet; *F*   135 layest] lay'st *Pope*   dam,] *Q2;* dam; *Q*   138 SP] *Shy. / Rowe*

Repair thy wit, good youth, or it will fall   140
To cureless ruin. I stand here for law.

DUKE

This letter from Bellario doth commend
A young and learned doctor to our court.
Where is he?

NERISSA   He attendeth here hard by
To know your answer whether you'll admit him.   145

DUKE

With all my heart. Some three or four of you
Go give him courteous conduct to this place.

                              [*Exeunt Attendants.*]
Meantime the court shall hear Bellario's letter.
[*Reads.*] *Your grace shall understand that at the receipt*
of your letter I am very sick, but, in the instant that your   150
messenger came, in loving visitation was with me a young
doctor of Rome: his name is Balthazar. I acquainted him

---

140 **fall** crumble as a decaying building might

142 **commend** present as being worthy of acceptance (*OED* 2); recommend (Onions)

143 **learned** learnèd

144 **attendeth . . . by** is waiting close at hand

147 **courteous conduct** gracious, or polite, escort (Onions)

149–62 The letter is delivered into the Duke's hands by the disguised Nerissa at 119, and he reads it silently during the exchange between Gratiano and the Jew at 121–41.

151 *in loving visitation* on a friendly visit (Mahood)

152 *Rome* This designation of geographical location compounds the earlier confusions about place at 108 and 3.4.48–9. Since Padua was the renowned centre of civil law (see 108n.), there seems

no reason why Balthazar should come from Rome that would suggest proficiency in the knowledge of theology (*OED sb.* 5). The ensuing judgement does, however, depend in part upon ecclesiastical knowledge, and it may be that Shakespeare simply wished to emphasize Balthazar/Portia's proficiency in both.

Balthazar Portia is not disguised as her servant Balthazar, who appears at 3.4 and whom she addresses at 3.4.45ff. The name she adopts here is a perfunctory disguise and is of a piece with the names of such supernumerary characters as Salerio and Salanio. Mahood (Cam², 141) rejects the suggestion that the name was meant to echo 'Beltashazzar', the Babylonian name for Daniel, but thinks that Kyd's *Spanish Tragedy* is a more likely source.

---

141 cureless] endlesse *F*   here] *om. Q3*   143 to] in *F*   147 SD] *Oxf; Exeunt officials Cam²; Exeunt some / Bevington*   149 SD] *Ard²; giving it to a Clerk. / Capell; He reads out the letter Cam¹*   149 *Your*] *Cle.* [Clerk reads.] Your *Malone*   150 *in*] at *Rowe*   152 *acquainted*] acquained *F*

*with the cause in controversy between the Jew and Antonio
the merchant. We turned o'er many books together; he is
furnished with my opinion, which, bettered with his own*   155
*learning, the greatness whereof I cannot enough commend,
comes with him at my importunity to fill up your grace's
request in my stead. I beseech you, let his lack of years be
no impediment to let him lack a reverend estimation, for I
never knew so young a body with so old a head. I leave him*   160
*to your gracious acceptance, whose trial shall better publish
his commendation.*

Enter PORTIA *[as] Balthazar[, with three or four Attendants].*

DUKE
You hear the learned Bellario what he writes,
And here, I take it, is the doctor come.
Give me your hand. Come you from old Bellario?   165

153 *cause in controversy* case in dispute
154 *turned o'er* have pored over, or consulted
155 *furnished* supplied
bettered with improved with the addition of
157 *importunity* urgent request
fill up satisfy or fulfil (Onions). Clarendon (118) suggests that the adverbial 'up' functions simply as an intensifier for the verb, but this locution implies the substantial performance of legal duty (*OED v.* 6) and is also a simple inversion of the part of the verb 'fulfil' (fill full).
158–9 *let . . . estimation* do not allow his comparative youth to prevent him from obtaining the respect that his reputation demands. The difficulty here arises from the exploitation of two meanings of *let*: (1) at 158 it means 'allow' or 'permit' but (2) at 159 it means 'prevent' or 'hinder'.

161–2 *whose . . . commendation* whose performance in the trial will provide a public display of the commendation that I have given him. In the light of what follows, Balthazar's skill is shown to exceed the description provided by Belario's 'letter'.
163 **what he writes** a modern gloss would be: 'You hear what the learned Bellario has written.' Abbott, 414, offers this as an example of a dependent clause that functions as an explanation of the object of the verb *hear*.
165 **Come** F emends to 'Came', presumably in order to distinguish Balthazar's present action at 164, 'is the doctor come', from an event in the past. The sense of 'Come . . .?' here is 'Have you come . . .?', where the auxiliary is omitted in the interests of the metre. Similarly Portia's response at 166 deploys the simple past *I did* to the same effect.

153 *cause*] Case *F3*   155 *bettered*] bettred *Q2, F*   158 *stead*] sted *F*   162.1 *as Balthazar*] *(for Balthazer); Dress'd like a Doctor of Laws. / Rowe; dressed as a doctor of civil law, with a book in her hand (after 163) Cam¹* with . . . *Attendants*] *Oxf subst.*   164 here, . . . it,] here (I take it) *F4*   165 hand. Come] *Cam¹*; hand, come *Q1, Q2*; hand: Came *F*; hand. Came *F4*

PORTIA

　I did, my lord.

DUKE　　　　　　　You are welcome: take your place.

　Are you acquainted with the difference

　That holds this present question in the court?

PORTIA

　I am informed throughly of the cause.

　Which is the merchant here, and which the Jew?　　　　170

DUKE

　Antonio and old Shylock, both stand forth.

PORTIA

　Is your name Shylock?

JEW　　　　　　　　Shylock is my name.

PORTIA

　Of a strange nature is the suit you follow,

　Yet in such rule that the Venetian law

　Cannot impugn you as you do proceed.　　　　　　　175

　[*to Antonio*] You stand within his danger, do you not?

---

167 **difference** essence of the conflict

168 **That . . . question** that is the subject of the present dispute

169 **informed throughly** informèd; *throughly* is a common Elizabethan contraction of modern 'thoroughly'; the line is an orthodox iambic pentameter. **cause** subject of litigation (Onions), but specifically, as in *Oth* 5.2.1, 'It is the cause, it is the cause, my soul', 'the case of one party in a law suit' (*Othello*, 305n.).

170 **merchant . . . Jew** In performance the question has been treated perfunctorily; for example, Joan Plowright (1970) and Derbhle Crotty (1999) both look away from Antonio and the Jew at this point. The question has proved more provocative for critics, cf. Moisan, who argues that the play 'blurs the distinctions on which the polarities' exemplified in the question

depend (Moisan, 188–9).

172 **Is . . . Shylock?** Joan Plowright (1970) addressed this question firstly to Antonio, as though Balthazar has mistaken the identities of the litigants. By contrast, Derbhle Crotty (2000) addressed the Jew directly as if simply to confirm his identity. **Shylock . . . name** For the curious conjunction of name and speech prefix 'Jew' in Q, see Drakakis, '*Jew*', 105–21.

173 **suit** lawsuit

174 **in such rule** because it is within the prescribed rules, i.e. because (the suit) is in such order (Onions)

175 **impugn you** find fault with you (*OED* 2b) **as you do** for the manner in which you

176 **stand . . . danger** stand within reach of his power to harm you; Furness (210) derives the phrase from the French '*être*

---

168 court?] *F4;* Court. *Q*　169 throughly] thoroughly *Steevens*　cause.] cause: *Q2; Case. F3*　172 SP2] *Shy. / Rowe*　175 impugn] impunge *Q2*　176 SD] *Rowe*　you not?] *F;* you not. *Q;* ye no? *Q2*

ANTONIO

    Ay, so he says.

PORTIA   Do you confess the bond?

ANTONIO

    I do.

PORTIA   Then must the Jew be merciful.

JEW

    On what compulsion must I? Tell me that.

PORTIA

    The quality of mercy is not strained: 180

    It droppeth as the gentle rain from heaven

    Upon the place beneath. It is twice blest:

    It blesseth him that gives and him that takes.

    'Tis mightiest in the mightiest; it becomes

    The thronèd monarch better than his crown.   185

    His sceptre shows the force of temporal power,

---

en son danger', where '*danger*' signifies both 'power' and 'debt'.

177 **confess the bond** acknowledge that (*OED v.* 2: 'confess') the agreement and the forfeit are legally valid

178 **must . . . merciful** Portia's *must* has the force of an appeal to the Jew's humanity rather than a statement demanding compulsion, so that a modern gloss might be: 'It is now up to the Jew to be merciful.'

179 **must** The Jew selects a more limited meaning of *must*, emphasizing compulsion.

180 **The . . . mercy** The competing claims of justice and mercy were a familiar topic of debate during the Renaissance, emanating from St Paul's distinction between Judaism and Christianity in Romans, 11.30–2. See also Declamation 95 of Alexander Silvayn's *The Orator* (1596), in which the Christian appeals against the legally just demand of his adversary: 'It may please you then most righteous Iudge to consider all these circumstances, hauing pittie of him who doth wholy submit himselfe vnto your

iust clemencie: hoping thereby to be deliuered from this monsters' crueltie' (Bullough, 1.486; see also p. 37).

not strained not produced under compulsion (*OED* 4), but also not passed through a strainer or colander (*OED* 7), and hence freely available to all

181 **droppeth . . . rain** Cf. Ecclesiasticus, 35.19 (Geneva Bible, 1560): 'Ó howe fayre a thing is mercie in the time of anguish and trouble? it is like a cloude of rayne that commeth in the time of a drought.'

182 **blest** consecrated or hallowed (*OED* 1) but also, possibly, endowed with healing virtues (*OED* 4b); Brown's gloss 'full of blessing' (Ard², 111) does not fully capture this dual function that incorporates both divine origin and effect.

184 **becomes** befits

185 **thronèd** thronèd

186 **sceptre** the ornamental rod that is the symbol of monarchical authority **temporal** secular as opposed to sacred (*OED* 3); cf. *H5* 1.1.9–10: 'For all the temporal lands which men devout / By testament have given to the Church.'

---

177 Ay,] *Rowe;* 1, *Q*   179 SP] *F; Shy. Q*   I?] *F;* 1, *Q*   180 strained] *(straind)*

The attribute to awe and majesty,
Wherein doth sit the dread and fear of kings.
But mercy is above this sceptred sway;
It is enthroned in the hearts of kings,   190
It is an attribute to God himself,
And earthly power doth then show likest God's
When mercy seasons justice. Therefore, Jew,
Though justice be thy plea, consider this:
That in the course of justice none of us   195
Should see salvation. We do pray for mercy,
And that same prayer doth teach us all to render
The deeds of mercy. I have spoke thus much
To mitigate the justice of thy plea,
Which, if thou follow, this strict court of Venice   200
Must needs give sentence 'gainst the merchant there.

JEW
    My deeds upon my head, I crave the law,

---

187 **attribute to** permanent distinction
of (*OED sb.* †2)
awe and majesty the feeling produced
in the subject by the *majesty* that is the
property of the monarch (Furness, 212)
189 **sceptred sway** rule or sovereignty,
symbolized by the magisterial wave of
the sceptre
190 **enthroned** enthronèd
192 proverbial: 'It is in their MERCY
that kings come closest to gods' (Dent,
M898)
193 **seasons** tempers (Onions), but a
culinary metaphor indicating that *justice* is made palatable by the addition
of *mercy*
195 **course** path; Portia gestures in the
direction of eternal death that would
be the lot of fallen humanity were it
not for God's mercy.
196 **salvation** the consequence of God's
mercy, and the guarantee of eternal
life offered to mankind through the
sacrifice of Christ, which emphasizes

the contrast between the Judaic commitment to the letter of 'the law' and
the Christian commitment to 'faith';
see Bible, Romans, 9.30–2.
197 **that same prayer** a reference to the
Lord's Prayer in the Bible at Matthew,
6.9–13, but also an echo of Matthew,
5.7, 'Blessed are the mercifull: for
they shall obteine mercie', and of the
Old Testament Ecclesiasticus, 28.2:
'forgiue thy neighbour the hurt he
hath done thee, & so shal thy sinnes
be forgiuen thee also when thou pray-
est.' See also accounts of the medieval
Processus Belial in which the Virgin
Mary's plea for mercy on behalf of
mankind defeats the devil (see Brown,
Ard[2], l–li; Danson, *Harmonies*, 95–6).
199 **mitigate . . . plea** moderate the
judicial strictness of your case
201 **Must . . . sentence** will be obliged
to pass sentence
202 **My . . . head** I will accept responsibility for my actions; Furness (213)

---

200 court] course *F*   202 SP] *this edn; Shy. Q*   head,] head. *Rowe;* head! *Hanmer;* head: *Capell*

The penalty and forfeit of my bond.

PORTIA

Is he not able to discharge the money?

BASSANIO

Yes, here I tender it for him in the court,   205

Yea, twice the sum. If that will not suffice,

I will be bound to pay it ten times o'er,

On forfeit of my hands, my head, my heart.

If this will not suffice, it must appear

That malice bears down truth. [*to the Duke*] And, I

    beseech you,   210

Wrest once the law to your authority;

To do a great right, do a little wrong

And curb this cruel devil of his will.

PORTIA

It must not be: there is no power in Venice

cites Henley's reference to Matthew, 27.25, but the Jew's utterance is closer to Old Testament Psalm 7.17, 'for his travaile shall come upon his owne head: and his wickednese shall fall on his owne pate', and Obadiah [Abdias] 15: 'for the day of the Lorde is neere upon all the heathen: as thou hast done, it shalbe done to thee, thy reward shall returne upon thine head.' **crave** demand (*OED v.* 1), earnestly request (*OED v.* 2); also, considering the allegation of the Jew's insatiable 'wolvish' appetite at 133, strongly desire (*OED v.* 5)

203 **penalty and forfeit** Cf. 36; a typically explicit formulation that covers both punishment and receipt; the penalty is what Antonio must pay, and the forfeit is what will come to the Jew as a consequence of the bond.

204 **discharge** deliver

205 **tender** offer (Onions)
    for him on his behalf, but also in order to have him released

207 **bound** under an obligation (Onions), but with the subsidiary meaning of constrained (*OED v.*[1] †1)

210 **malice . . . truth** malice overcomes (oppresses and defeats) truth. But see also *OED sb.* I.†2, where 'truth' is glossed as 'a solemn engagement or promise, a covenant', suggesting that if Bassanio's offer is rejected then it will be extreme animosity on the Jew's part that overrides the conditions of any formal agreement.

211 On this occasion (*once*) stretch (*Wrest*) the letter of the law so that it becomes subject to your own executive power.

212 Cf. *Luc* 528–9: 'A little harm done to a great good end / For lawful policy remains unacted.'

214–15 **no . . . established** establishèd; a reference to the rigour and consistency of the application of Venetian law; see *Pecorone*: 'Venice had a reputation as a place of strict justice, and the Jew's case was legal and formally made out, nobody dared to deny him, but only

206 twice] thrice *Dyce*   210 SD] *this edn*

Can alter a decree established.   215
'Twill be recorded for a precedent,
And many an error by the same example
Will rush into the state. It cannot be.

JEW

A Daniel come to judgement; yea, a Daniel!
O, wise young judge, how I do honour thee.   220

PORTIA

I pray you, let me look upon the bond.

JEW

Here 'tis, most reverend doctor; here it is.

PORTIA

Shylock, there's thrice thy money offered thee.

JEW

An oath, an oath, I have an oath in heaven!
Shall I lay perjury upon my soul?   225
No, not for Venice.

PORTIA   Why, this bond is forfeit,
And lawfully by this the Jew may claim
A pound of flesh, to be by him cut off
Nearest the merchant's heart. [*to the Jew*] Be merciful:

to plead with him' (Bullough, 1.472). Portia's language also echoes an Old Testament passage from Daniel, 6.8: 'Now, O king, confirme the decree, and seale the writing, that it be not changed, according to the law of the Medes & Persians, which altereth not.'

216 **precedent** case law in which one example might influence the outcome of future cases

217 **error** miscarriage of justice

219 **Daniel** the Old Testament prophet noted for his wisdom; see Ezekiel, 28.3: 'Beholde, thou thinkest thyselfe wiser then Daniel, that there is no secrets hid from thee.' (See LN.)

223 **thrice** This appears to conflict with the sum Bassanio has already offered at 206; it is an inconsistency that was not corrected, or a compositorial misreading, or, as Mahood suggests, a raising of the sum by Portia herself (Cam[2], 144).

229 **Nearest . . . heart** At 1.3.147 the Jew is unspecific about the location of the pound of flesh to be forfeited; Silvayn's *The Orator* (1596) speculates: 'what a matter were it then, if I should cut off his priuie members, supposing that the same would altogether weigh a iust pound?' A modern reader might perceive in this a displaced form of

215 alter] *F;* altar *Q*   216 precedent] President *F*   219 SP] *F; Shy. Q*   Daniell!] *Pope;* Daniell. *Q; Daniel. Q2, F*   220 I do] do I *F*   thee.] thee? *F4;* thee! *Rowe*   221 let me] *om. F3*   222 Here 'tis] *F4;* Heere tis *Q*   223 offered] *F;* offred *Q*   224 SP] *this edn; Shy. Q*   226 No,] *Q2;* Not *Q;* No *F*   229 SD] *Oxf*

350

Take thrice thy money; bid me tear the bond.   230

JEW

When it is paid according to the tenor.
It doth appear you are a worthy judge,
You know the law; your exposition
Hath been most sound. I charge you by the law,
Whereof you are a well-deserving pillar,   235
Proceed to judgement. By my soul I swear,
There is no power in the tongue of man
To alter me. I stay here on my bond.

ANTONIO

Most heartily I do beseech the court
To give the judgement.

PORTIA   Why then, thus it is: 240
You must prepare your bosom for his knife.

JEW

O noble judge! O excellent young man!

PORTIA

For the intent and purpose of the law
Hath full relation to the penalty
Which here appeareth due upon the bond.   245

JEW

'Tis very true. O wise and upright judge,
How much more elder art thou than thy looks!

castration; for the historical and biblical symbolism surrounding this, see
Shapiro, *Jews*, 113–30.
231 *tenor the substance of the bond
(*OED sb.*[1] I.1); Q2 emends Q's 'tenure'
to 'tenour'.
233 exposition explanation and interpretation (*OED* 5)
235 well-deserving pillar metaphorically, one who upholds
238 stay stand firm
on insistent upon, rather than depend-

ent upon (Abbott, 180)
243 intent and purpose design, or
purpose, and objective
244 Hath full relation is fully (and
hence appropriately) related to
245 here appeareth due is now clearly
due
upon as a consequence of (Onions)
247 more elder an addition to the comparative form of the adjective in order
to give it more emphasis (Abbott, 11,
cites this example)

231 tenor] *(tenour)* Q2; tenure Q   238 bond.] Q2; Bond, Q   240 then] Q2; than Q   242 SP] *F;
Shy.* Q   judge! O] *F4;* Iudge, ô Q; Iudge, O Q2   man!] *F4;* man. Q   246 SP] *Shy.* Q2   O] Q2; ô
Q   247 looks!] *Rowe;* lookes. Q; lookes? *F*

PORTIA [*to Antonio*]
   Therefore lay bare your bosom.

JEW   Ay, his breast.
   So says the bond, doth it not, noble judge?
   'Nearest his heart': those are the very words.   250

PORTIA
   It is so. Are there balance here to weigh
   The flesh?

JEW   I have them ready.

PORTIA
   Have by some surgeon, Shylock, on your charge,
   To stop his wounds, lest he do bleed to death.

JEW
   Is it so nominated in the bond?   255

PORTIA
   It is not so expressed, but what of that?
   'Twere good you do so much for charity.

JEW
   I cannot find it; 'tis not in the bond.

PORTIA [*to Antonio*]
   You, merchant, have you anything to say?

ANTONIO
   But little. I am armed and well prepared.   260

---

251 **balance** scales, used as a plural form (*OED* 2b); the scales have a symbolic function and are associated with the classical figure of Justice; cf. *MA* 5.1.202–3: 'Come you, sir, if justice cannot tame you she shall ne'er weigh more reasons in her balance.'
253 **by** in attendance, i.e. standing by
on your charge at your own expense (Onions), but also, possibly, with the subsidiary meaning of under your own instruction
255 **so nominated** designated explicitly

(*OED v.* 1)
256 **expressed** mentioned explicitly (*OED v.* 10)
257 **charity** one of the foremost Christian virtues; cf. 1 Corinthians, 13.1ff.: 'Though I speake wᵗ the tongues of men, and of angels, and haue not charitie, I am as sounding brasse, or as a tinckling cymbal.'
259 **You** F emends to 'Come', but the deictic *You* reinforces the distinction between *merchant* and 'Jew'
260 **armed** ready or fortified (*OED* 2)

248 SD] *Oxf* your] thy *F4*   250 'Nearest his heart':] *Cam¹*; Neerest his hart, *Q*; 'Nearest his heart,' *Ard²*   251–2 It . . . flesh?] *Capell; one line Q*   251 balance] Ballances *Rowe*; Scales *Theobald*   252, 255 SP] *Shy. Q2*   254 lest] *F4*; least *Q*   do] should *F*   255 Is it so] It is not *F*   259 SD] *Oxf*   You] Come *F*

Give me your hand, Bassanio. Fare you well,
Grieve not that I am fall'n to this for you:
For herein Fortune shows herself more kind
Than is her custom. It is still her use
To let the wretched man outlive his wealth,   265
To view with hollow eye and wrinkled brow
An age of poverty, from which lingering penance
Of such misery doth she cut me off.
Commend me to your honourable wife;
Tell her the process of Antonio's end,   270
Say how I loved you, speak me fair in death,
And, when the tale is told, bid her be judge
Whether Bassanio had not once a love.
Repent but you that you shall lose your friend
And he repents not that he pays your debt.   275
For if the Jew do cut but deep enough

262 **fall'n to this** brought low (as a
consequence of this misfortune)
264 **still her use** always the goddess
Fortune's way of dispensing her gifts.
Antonio is trying to console himself,
perhaps ironically, for his misfortune.
266 **hollow eye** eyes deeply sunk in their
orbits (*OED*)
wrinkled brow forehead wrinkled
because of anxiety; both are symptoms
of premature ageing brought on by
adverse fortune.
267 **age of poverty** *age* may be glossed
as 'old age' (Cam², 145), but Antonio
may be referring here to an epoch
comparable to the division that Ovid
outlines in *Met.*, 1.144ff: 'Of yron is
the last / . . . / For when that of this
wicked Age once opened was the veyne
/ Therein all mischief rushed forth:
then Fayth and Truth were faine /
And honest shame to hide their heades:
for whom crept stoutly in, / Craft,
Treason, Violence, Envie, Pride and

wicked Lust to win' (Ovid, *Met.*, 7).
lingering penance extended period
of atonement (for my sin of accumu-
lating wealth)
268 **cut me off** release me from
270 **process of** manner of, but also the
legal process that had led to
271 **speak . . . death** speak well of me
when I am dead; Abbott, 200, notes
the frequent omission of prepositions
in such constructions.
272 **bid . . . judge** ask her to judge.
There is a comic irony in this, since
the disguised Portia already occupies
this position in the courtroom.
273 **love** friend; this term of endearment does not necessarily carry the
modern connotation of sexual partner;
cf. *JC* 3.2.13: 'Romans, countrymen
and lovers'.
274 **Repent but** regret only; Bassanio's
acknowledgement of Antonio as a
friend makes his willingness to pay
this penalty worthwhile.

264 Than] *F4;* then *Q*   her custom] his custom *F2*   267 lingering] *(lingring)*   268 such] such a
F2   274 but] not *F*

353

I'll pay it instantly with all my heart.

BASSANIO

Antonio, I am married to a wife
Which is as dear to me as life itself;
But life itself, my wife and all the world   280
Are not with me esteemed above thy life.
I would lose all, ay, sacrifice them all
Here to this devil, to deliver you.

PORTIA

Your wife would give you little thanks for that
If she were by to hear you make the offer.   285

GRATIANO

I have a wife who I protest I love.
I would she were in heaven, so she could
Entreat some power to change this currish Jew.

NERISSA

'Tis well you offer it behind her back,
The wish would make else an unquiet house.   290

JEW

These be the Christian husbands! I have a daughter:
Would any of the stock of Barabbas

---

277 **instantly** shortly
   with . . . heart unreservedly; playing
   upon the word *pay*; Antonio's deployment of an aristocratic wit is regarded
   by Merchant (201) as an example of
   Renaissance *sprezzatura*.
279 **Which** who (Onions, 248); see also
   Blake, 44, who observes that '*Who,
   which* and *that* are used indiscrimi-
   nately as relative pronouns for animate
   and non-animate referents.'
285 **by** nearby
288 **power** deity
   currish dog-like (*OED* 1), hence
   bestial

290 **make else** make it otherwise
292 **stock of Barabbas** lineage (*OED
   sb.*[1] 3c) of Barabbas; Barabbas was the
   thief who was pardoned instead of
   Christ, but also the name of Marlowe's
   protagonist in *The Jew of Malta*
   (Barabas). 'Stock' also has a subsidiary
   meaning a sum of money or 'principal
   as distinguished from interest' (*OED
   sb.*[1] IV.†48). It is characteristic of the
   Jew that he should use a noun that has
   a financial resonance. As in Marlowe's
   play, the name is likely to have been
   pronounced with the accent on the
   first syllable: 'Bàrabbas'.

---

277 instantly] presently *Q2*   282 lose] *Q2;* loose *Q*   ay,] *Pope;* I *Q;* I, *Q3;* I'd *Rowe*   286 who]
whom *F*   291 SP] *Shy. / Rowe*   husbands!] *Collier;* husbands, *Q;* husbands; *F;* husbands: *F2;*
husbands. *F4*

Had been her husband rather than a Christian.
We trifle time; I pray thee, pursue sentence.

PORTIA

A pound of that same merchant's flesh is thine;   295
The court awards it, and the law doth give it.

JEW   Most rightful judge!

PORTIA

And you must cut this flesh from off his breast;
The law allows it, and the court awards it.

JEW

Most learned judge! A sentence! [*to Antonio*] Come,
prepare.   300

PORTIA

Tarry a little, there is something else.
This bond doth give thee here no jot of blood:
The words expressly are 'a pound of flesh'.
Take then thy bond: take thou thy pound of flesh.
But in the cutting it, if thou dost shed   305
One drop of Christian blood, thy lands and goods
Are by the laws of Venice confiscate
Unto the state of Venice.

---

294 **trifle** spend time to no purpose (Onions), i.e. waste
pursue proceed with (Onions)
300 **sentence** juridical pronouncement made as a result of deliberation (*OED sb.* 2)
302 **no jot** not the least amount (*OED sb.*[1]), from the Greek 'iota' meaning the letter 'i', the smallest letter in the alphabet
303 **expressly** clearly or explicitly (*OED adv.* 1†a), but also 'for the express purpose' (*OED adv.* 5)
305–7 Portia's 'reading' of the bond is

even more literally rigorous than the Jew's, but neither contradicts Venetian law as it is depicted in the play. For the origin of Venetian law in Roman law, see Shell, 66–8.
305 **the cutting it** A modern idiom would introduce the preposition 'of', 'the cutting of it', but the preposition was frequently omitted (see Abbott, 201).
307 **confiscate** confiscated (Onions); an example of the past participle from which the terminal -*d* is omitted because it ends in -*te* (Abbott, 342)

---

297 SP] *Shy. / Pope*   judge!] *Pope;* Iudge. *Q;* Judg. *F4*   300 SP] *Shy. / Rowe*   judge!] *Pope;* Iudge, *Q;* Judg, *F4;* judge – *Johnson*   sentence!] *Collier;* sentence, *Q;* sentence: *Pope*   SD] *Oxf*   303 'a . . . flesh'.] *Keightley;* a . . . flesh: *Q*   304 Take then] Then take *F*

GRATIANO   O upright judge!
    Mark, Jew – O learned judge!

JEW
    Is that the law?

PORTIA   Thyself shalt see the act,   310
    For, as thou urgest justice, be assured
    Thou shalt have justice more than thou desir'st.

GRATIANO
    O learned judge! Mark, Jew: a learned judge.

JEW
    I take this offer, then; pay the bond thrice
    And let the Christian go.

BASSANIO   Here is the money.   315

PORTIA   Soft!
    The Jew shall have all justice. Soft, no haste,
    He shall have nothing but the penalty.

GRATIANO
    O, Jew, an upright judge, a learned judge!

PORTIA
    Therefore, prepare thee to cut off the flesh.   320
    Shed thou no blood, nor cut thou less nor more

---

310 **act** operation (of the law) (Onions), but also decree (*OED* 5). The subsidiary meaning of 'performance' is also present, since it is the disguised Portia who will demonstrate the law's efficacy.

311 **justice** The emphasis here is on justice devoid of Christian mercy; cf. the Bible, Luke, 6.37–8, 'Judge not, and ye shall not be judged at all: condemne not and ye shall not be condemned at all: forgiue and ye shall be forgiuê. / . . . for the same measure that ye mete withall, it shall be giuen to you againe', and also James, 2.13: 'For hee shall haue iudgement without mercie, that hath shewed no mercie, and mercie reioyceth against iudgement.'

312 **desir'st** wish for; but also ask for (Onions)

316 **Soft!** an extrametrical expletive for which a modern gloss might be 'Hold on!' or 'Not so fast!' (Cam[2], 147)

317 **all justice** all the justice that the law permits, i.e. nothing but justice

319 **upright** morally just, honest, honourable (*OED* III. *fig.* 8)

308–9 O . . . learned judge!] *one line Pope*   308 O . . . judge!] *Rowe;* ô . . . Iudge, *Q;* O . . . Judg; *F4*   309 Jew – . . . judge!] *Johnson;* Iew, . . . Iudge. *Q;* Jew, . . . Judg. *F4*   310 SP] *this edn; Shy. Q*   312 desir'st] *(desirst);* desirest *Q2;* desirst *Q*   313 judge!] *F4;* iudge, *Q* judge.] *(iudge.);* judge! *Rowe*   314 SP] *Shy. / Rowe* this] his *Q3*   316–17] *Capell; one line Q1, Q2*   316 Soft!] *Capell, Collier;* Soft, *Q1, Q2;* Soft! *Cam[1] (as final syllable of verse line 315)*   317 haste,] haste *Q2;* haste:– *Collier;* haste! *Ard[2]*   319 Jew,] Jew! *F4*   judge!] *Pope;* Iudge. *Q;* Judg. *F4*

But just a pound of flesh. If thou tak'st more
Or less than a just pound, be it but so much
As makes it light or heavy in the substance
Or the division of the twentieth part   325
Of one poor scruple: nay, if the scale do turn
But in the estimation of a hair,
Thou diest, and all thy goods are confiscate.

GRATIANO

A second Daniel, a Daniel, Jew!
Now, infidel, I have you on the hip.   330

PORTIA

Why doth the Jew pause? Take thy forfeiture.

JEW

Give me my principal, and let me go.

BASSANIO

I have it ready for thee; here it is.

PORTIA

He hath refused it in the open court;
He shall have merely justice and his bond.   335

GRATIANO

A Daniel still, say I, a second Daniel!

---

322 **just** a an exact, but with the pun on
just that emphasizes here and in 323
the 'justice' of the action
323 **but so much** enough to
324 **in the substance** in its gross weight
326 **scruple** an apothecary's measure
equivalent to the weight of approxi-
mately one gram and consisting of 20
grains (*OED sb.*[1] 1), used here figuratively to denote the smallest amount
326–7 **if . . . hair** if the scale is tipped by
the weight of a hair, i.e. by the lightest
weight imaginable
329 **second Daniel** See 219n.; as a
result of his expertise as a judge in
the Apocryphal story of Susannah
and the Elders, Daniel was 'held in

great reputation in the sight of the
people' (Susannah, 64). Gratiano's
appropriation of the name from the
Jew draws together all the biblical
resonances that Daniel possessed for
a 16th-century audience. See also
Shaheen, 128–9.
330 **infidel** literally, a non-believer (*OED
sb.* 2), but especially apposite in this
context, since the representative of
judgement, Daniel, is claimed by
Gratiano for the Christian cause
on the hip See 1.3.42n.
331 **forfeiture** penalty (*OED* 3)
332 **principal** See 25n.
335 **merely** both entirely (Onions) and
only, i.e. without qualification

---

322 tak'st] *cutst Q2*   323 be it but] be it *F;* be't *Pope*   325 Or] On *Theobald*   326 do] *om. Pope*
330 you] thee *F*   331 pause?] *F4;* pause, *Q*   thy] the *Pope*   335 He] And *Q2*

I thank thee, Jew, for teaching me that word.

JEW

Shall I not have barely my principal?

PORTIA

Thou shalt have nothing but the forfeiture,

To be so taken at thy peril, Jew.   340

JEW

Why then, the devil give him good of it!

I'll stay no longer question.   [*Begins to leave.*]

PORTIA   Tarry, Jew,

The law hath yet another hold on you.

It is enacted in the laws of Venice,

If it be proved against an alien   345

That by direct, or indirect, attempts

He seek the life of any citizen,

The party 'gainst the which he doth contrive

Shall seize one-half his goods. The other half

Comes to the privy coffer of the state,   350

And the offender's life lies in the mercy

---

337 **that word** i.e. Daniel; heavily ironic, since Gratiano has appropriated it already for a Christian cause

341 **the devil . . . it** May the only good that comes from it be evil. This colloquial expression turns the accusation normally levelled against the Jew towards his adversary.

342 **stay . . . question** not remain to debate the issue any longer

344 **enacted** decreed; cf. *Luc* 528–9: 'A little harm done to a great good end / For lawful policy remains enacted'

345 **alien** stranger or foreigner (*OED sb.* B1)

348 **party** person, but used in the strictly legal sense of the term (*OED sb.* 5)
    contrive plot or scheme in the sense of planning evil as in treason (*OED*

$v.^1$ 1b); cf. *R2* 1.3.188–90: 'Nor never by advised purpose meet / To plot, contrive, or complot any ill / 'Gainst us, our state, our subjects, or our land.'

349 **seize** take legal possession of or confiscate; from the verb 'seisin' (*OED v.* 3)

350 **privy . . . state** the exchequer; see P. Williams, 39–43, for a brief description of this institution. The exchequer was presided over by the figure of the king, hence the phrase 'state treasury' (where 'state' was a synonym for the monarch), and is associated in this context with the authority and role of the Duke of Venice. See also Coryate, 169: 'In one of the higher roomes, which belongeth only to the State, there is kept wondrous abundance of treasure.'

338, 341 SP] *this edn; Shy.* Q   338 have barely] barely have *Pope*   340 so taken] taken so *F*
342 question] heere in question *Q2*   SD] *Bevington subst.*   345 an] any *Q2*   349 one-half] on half
Q2   350 coffer] coster *Q2*

Of the Duke only, 'gainst all other voice.
In which predicament I say thou stand'st,
For it appears by manifest proceeding
That indirectly, and directly too,   355
Thou hast contrived against the very life
Of the defendant, and thou hast incurred
The danger formerly by me rehearsed.
Down, therefore, and beg mercy of the Duke.

GRATIANO

Beg that thou mayst have leave to hang thyself,   360
And yet, thy wealth being forfeit to the state,
Thou hast not left the value of a cord;
Therefore thou must be hanged at the state's charge.

DUKE

That thou shalt see the difference of our spirit,
I pardon thee thy life before thou ask it.   365
For half thy wealth, it is Antonio's;
The other half comes to the general state,
Which humbleness may drive unto a fine.

---

352 **'gainst . . . voice** without the prospect of appeal. Such absolute power, associated more with the figure of the monarch, was not enjoyed by the historical Doge of Venice; see Contarini, sig. A2ᵛ.

353 **predicament** dangerous situation (*OED* 3), but also a term in logic for one of the ten categories of objects that are dependent upon a subject (*OED* 1). The term combines the Latin *praedicamentum* and *praedicatum* (*OED sb.* 1: 'predicate'). The Jew is now in the position of a 'predicate', dependent upon the mercy of the Duke.

358 **danger . . . rehearsed** the legal penalty, or threat, that I have just described

360 **leave** permission

362 **hast not left** do not have remaining

363 **charge** expense (Onions)

364 **our spirit** the corporate Christian essence of Venice; an implied contrast between the Jew's emphasis upon 'flesh' (and hence upon a literal judgement), and the court's emphasis upon the non-corporeal quality of 'mercy'. Brown notes here the use of the royal plural (Ard², 118).

365 **pardon** remit (Onions)

366 **For** as regards (Abbott, 149)

367 **general state** the exchequer, as in 350

368 **humbleness** modesty (*OED* 2), or even courtesy. The Duke's tactic here resembles the advice that Machiavelli offers in *The Prince* (1640): 'and whensoever hee should be forced to proceed against any of their lives, doe it when

---

355 too] *F2;* to *Q*   356 against] gainst *Q2*   358 formerly] *Q2;* formorly *Q;* formally *Hanmer*
364 difference] diffrence *Q2*   spirit] spirits *Q2*

PORTIA

Ay, for the state, not for Antonio.

JEW

Nay, take my life and all, pardon not that.   370
You take my house when you do take the prop
That doth sustain my house. You take my life
When you do take the means whereby I live.

PORTIA

What mercy can you render him, Antonio?

GRATIANO

A halter gratis, nothing else, for God's sake!   375

ANTONIO

So please my lord the Duke, and all the court,
To quit the fine for one-half of his goods,
I am content, so he will let me have
The other half in use, to render it

it is to be done upon a just cause, and apparent conviction; but above all things forbeare to lay his hands on other mens goods; for men forget the sooner the death of their father, than the loss of their patrimony' (17.131–2). **drive unto** bring to a settlement or conclusion in (*OED v.* IV.19); the Duke proposes, without wishing to be assertive (in *humbleness*), to levy half of the Jew's wealth as a fine, and not to exercise a full judicial entitlement to take his life, as a forfeit, in accordance with the Venetian law that Portia/Balthazar refers to at 351–2.

369 **for the state** Portia refers here to the half of the fine levied on the Jew that will come to the exchequer.

370–3 This speech echoes the Old Testament Ecclesiasticus, 34.23: 'Whoso robbeth his neighbour of his liuing, doth as great sinne as though he slue him to death: he that defraudeth the labourer of his hyre is a blood shedder'; see also *Jew of Malta*, 1.2.139–44.

375 **halter gratis** hangman's noose free of charge

377–9 **To . . . use** Antonio's proposal is not entirely clear. He is asking that the fine proposed earlier at 368 be remitted, and that he be allowed to administer the remainder of the Jew's wealth with the aim of handing it over to Lorenzo and Jessica on her father's death. The phrase *in use* means simply 'to hold in trust' (Ard[2], 119), with the possible subsidiary meaning of deploy in accordance with his own stated mercantilist principles. However, Mahood regards this part of the proposal as 'disturbing' (Cam[2], 149), since it resembles a kind of 'usury'. The first gloss effectively transforms the Jew into a beneficent patriarch through an act of Christian mercy, but the second leaves Antonio open to the charge that this demonstration of 'mercy' is less than generous.

377 **quit** remit (*OED v.* †4), but also absolve (*OED v.* †2†b)

376 and] *F;* & *Q*   court,] *Q2;* Court *Q*   377 quit] quite *F2*   for] from *Hanmer*

Upon his death unto the gentleman   380
That lately stole his daughter.
Two things provided more: that for this favour
He presently become a Christian;
The other, that he do record a gift
Here in the court of all he dies possessed   385
Unto his son Lorenzo and his daughter.

DUKE

He shall do this, or else I do recant
The pardon that I late pronounced here.

PORTIA

Art thou contented, Jew? What dost thou say?

JEW

I am content.

PORTIA   Clerk, draw a deed of gift.   390

JEW

I pray you, give me leave to go from hence.
I am not well. Send the deed after me
And I will sign it.

381 **stole his daughter** a surprisingly
frank statement that permits a brief
glimpse of the less 'romantic' aspect
of the Lorenzo–Jessica elopement in
that her father's permission has not
been sought
382 **favour** act of leniency; Antonio
clearly believes that his proposal is an
act of mercy.
383 **presently** immediately
Christian Coryate notes both the
reason why Italian Jews were reluctant
to convert to Christianity, and the consequences of their doing so: 'All their
goodes are confiscated as soone as they
embrace Christianity: and this I heard
is the reason, because whereas many of
them doe sometimes not only sheare,
but also flea many a poore Christians
estate by their griping extortion; it is

therefore decreed by the Pope, and
other free Princes in whose territories
they liue, that they shall make a restitu-
tion of all their ill gotten goods, and so
disclogge their soules and consciences,
when they are admitted by holy baptis-
me into the bosome of Christs Church'
(Coryate, 234).
384 **record a gift** legally bequeath (by
signing a deed of gift)
385 **all . . . possessed** all that he possesses when he dies
386 **son Lorenzo** son-in-law Lorenzo;
the Jew's *son* is named, but Jessica is
simply *his daughter*, and a portion of
the father's wealth now passes to the
son, reinforcing the patriarchal ethos
of Venice.
388 **late** recently
pronounced pronouncèd

380 Upon] Until *Hanmer*   385 possessed] *(possest)*; possess'd of *Keightley*

DUKE   Get thee gone, but do it.

GRATIANO

  In christening shalt thou have two godfathers.

  Had I been judge, thou shouldst have had ten more,   395

  To bring thee to the gallows, not to the font.   *Exit [Jew]*.

DUKE [*to Portia*]

  Sir, I entreat you home with me to dinner.

PORTIA

  I humbly do desire, your grace, of pardon;

  I must away this night toward Padua,

  And it is meet I presently set forth.   400

DUKE

  I am sorry that your leisure serves you not.

  Antonio, gratify this gentleman,

  For in my mind you are much bound to him.

                              Exeunt Duke and his train.

BASSANIO

  Most worthy gentleman, I and my friend

394 **two godfathers** i.e. the Duke and Antonio

395 **ten more** the number required to form a jury; a common quip, since the jury was often referred to as 'godfathers in law' because their decision dispatched the convicted criminal to God for final judgement; see Ben Jonson, *The Devil is an Ass* (1616), 5.5.10–11: 'If you be such a one Sir, I will leaue you / To your *God-fathers* in Law. Let twelue men worke' (Jonson, 4.258). In Venetian judicial practice an elected council of ten citizens were charged with judging cases of civil disagreement between citizens and foreigners (Contarini, 78).

397 **entreat you home** implore you to accompany me home

398 **your . . . pardon** The convoluted syntax expresses Portia's wish to decline the Duke's invitation; see Abbott, 166, and also 174, where this example is used to gloss the phrase *of pardon* as 'as regards' or 'concerning'. Q's capitalization of 'Grace' indicates that this is a parenthetical phrase that needs to be separated grammatically from the partitive construction 'of'. Portia desires a portion of the general power of pardon that the Duke had earlier demonstrated at 365.

400 **meet . . . forth** appropriate that I set out immediately

401 **that . . . not** that you do not have the time, i.e. that time is not your servant

402 **gratify** reward or requite (Onions)

403 **much bound** very much obliged, though with an obvious pun on *bound*

394 SP] *Q2; Shy. Q*   christening] *(christning)*   shalt thou] thou shalt *F*   396 not to] not *Q2*   SD *Jew] Rowe subst.*   397 SD] *Oxf*   home with me] with me home *F*   398 do] *om. Q2*   grace, of] Graces *Q3*   402 gratify] greatifie *F2*   403 SD] SCENE III. *Pope*

Have, by your wisdom, been this day acquitted   405
Of grievous penalties, in lieu whereof
Three thousand ducats due unto the Jew
We freely cope your courteous pains withal.

ANTONIO

And stand indebted, over and above,
In love and service to you evermore.   410

PORTIA

He is well paid that is well satisfied,
And I, delivering you, am satisfied,
And therein do account myself well paid;
My mind was never yet more mercenary.
I pray you, know me when we meet again.   415
I wish you well, and so I take my leave.

BASSANIO

Dear sir, of force I must attempt you further.
Take some remembrance of us as a tribute,
Not as fee. Grant me two things, I pray you:
Not to deny me, and to pardon me.   420

405–6 **acquitted / Of** absolved from, in the sense of freed from a criminal charge (*OED* 4)

406 **in lieu whereof** in return for which (Ard[1], 155)

408 **cope . . . withal** furnish you as compensation for the anguish that you have courteously withstood (*OED v.*[1] 'cope': furnish); the subsidiary meaning of 'cope': to give in exchange (*OED v.*[3]) may also be implied here, but the Duke's action is, in this context, primarily one of compensating Antonio for his suffering.

409 **over and above** i.e. beyond the sum of 3,000 ducats

412 **delivering you** releasing you from legal restraint (*OED v.*[1] 1b)

414 **was never yet** has never been. Portia alludes to the fact that she has never

desired more than she was entitled to, a reference to the contrary practice of 'usury' where the reward is always in excess of the loan.

415 **know** recognize (*OED v.* I.1b), but also possibly a play on 'know' in the carnal sense of the verb (*OED v.* 7), since the marriage has yet to be consummated

417 **of force** necessarily; also indicating a possibly submerged stage direction that requires Bassanio to physically prevent Portia from leaving
attempt try harder to persuade you (*OED* I.1), but possibly with the subsidiary meaning of to win over, seduce or entice (*OED* II.5)

418 **tribute** mark of esteem (*OED sb.* 2) as distinct from a mercenary payment (*fee*) for Portia/Balthazar's services

419 as fee] as a fee *Q2*

PORTIA

　You press me far, and therefore I will yield.

　Give me your gloves; I'll wear them for your sake,

　And, for your love, I'll take this ring from you.

　Do not draw back your hand; I'll take no more,

　And you, in love, shall not deny me this!　　　　　　425

BASSANIO

　This ring, good sir? Alas, it is a trifle;

　I will not shame myself to give you this!

PORTIA

　I will have nothing else but only this,

　And now, methinks, I have a mind to it!

BASSANIO

　There's more depends on this than on the value.　　　430

　The dearest ring in Venice will I give you,

　And find it out by proclamation;

　Only for this, I pray you, pardon me!

PORTIA

　I see, sir, you are liberal in offers.

　You taught me first to beg, and now, methinks,　　　435

421 press me far importune me in the extreme; because of Portia's disguise there may well be an element of innuendo in this exchange; there is a bawdy resonance in the use of the verb 'press' meaning 'to press down in the sexual act' (Partridge, 166), deriving possibly from the Latin *imprimendum* meaning to press or dig into (Gordon Williams, 244–5).

422 gloves Clarendon (123–4) suggests that Portia takes the gloves from Antonio and the ring from Bassanio, although there is no indication that she speaks to anyone but Bassanio. His *us* at 418 may be an aristocratic reference to himself (*OED* II.8) There is clearly

a pause while the gloves are removed from his hands, and it is only then that the ring is revealed. The emphasis on the pronoun *you* at the end of 423 is emphatic but not deictic.

425 love gratitude, but heavily ironical in the circumstances

429 have . . . it have a strong desire to secure it

430 more . . . value more depends on this than its monetary value. Bassanio alludes to the oath he swore to die before parting with Portia's gift to him (see 3.2.183–5).

432 by proclamation by general agreement (*OED* 1)

433 Only for this but (except) for this

425 this!] *(this?)*; this. *Q2*　426 sir?] *Collier;* Sir, *Q;* sir, – *Capell*　trifle;] *F4;* trifle, *Q;* trifle! *Keightley*　429 it!] *(it?)*; it. *Q2*, *F*　430 depends . . . than] *Warburton;* depends on this then *Q;* then this depends *Q2;* depends on this, than is *Theobald;* on this depends than is *Hanmer*　431 will I] I will *Q2*　433 me!] *(me?)*; me. *F*

You teach me how a beggar should be answered.

BASSANIO

Good sir, this ring was given me by my wife,
And when she put it on she made me vow
That I should neither sell, nor give, nor lose it.

PORTIA

That 'scuse serves many men to save their gifts!   440
An if your wife be not a mad woman,
And know how well I have deserved this ring,
She would not hold out enemy for ever
For giving it to me. Well, peace be with you.

Exeunt [Portia and Nerissa].

ANTONIO

My lord Bassanio, let him have the ring.   445
Let his deservings and my love withal
Be valued 'gainst your wife's commandement.

BASSANIO

Go, Gratiano, run and overtake him;
Give him the ring, and bring him, if thou canst,   449
Unto Antonio's house. Away, make haste.   *Exit Gratiano.*
Come, you and I will thither presently,
And in the morning early will we both
Fly toward Belmont. Come, Antonio.   *Exeunt.*

---

436 **how . . . answered** possibly proverbial; Halio cites Tilley, A345:
'A shameless beggar should have a
shameless denial' (Oxf¹, 209).
439 **neither . . . lose** Modern grammar
usually restricts the negative correlatives
neither/nor to single alternatives, but
occasionally in Shakespeare this may be
extended to three; on the general point,
see Blake, 207; cf. *Cor* 2.1.67: 'You know
neither me, yourselves, nor any thing.'
440 **'scuse serves** excuse (*OED*) permits

save hold on to
441 **An if** even if (Onions)
443 **hold out enemy** persist in her
enmity towards you
446 **withal** as well
447 **commandement** an archaic spelling ('commaundement' in Q) requiring pronunciation of the medial *e* in
order to preserve the iambic metre,
and hence its retention here: com-
mandèment.
453 **Fly** hasten (*OED v.*¹ 7)

441 An] *Capell;* And *Q*   442 this] the *Q2*   443 enemy] Enmity *Rowe*   444 SD] *Capell; Exeunt. Q;
Exit. / Rowe; Exit with* Nerissa *Theobald*   445 lord Bassanio] *Oxf;* L. *Bassanio Q;* Lord *Bassanio
Q2*   447 wife's] *Rowe;* wiues *Q*   commandement] *(commaundement)*   450 SD] *Exeunt Gratiano.
Q2; Exit Grati. F*

[4.2]   *Enter* [PORTIA *and*] NERISSA [*still disguised*].

PORTIA

Enquire the Jew's house out, give him this deed,
    [*giving paper to Nerissa*]
And let him sign it. We'll away tonight,
And be a day before our husbands home.
This deed will be well welcome to Lorenzo!

Enter GRATIANO.

GRATIANO

Fair sir, you are well o'erta'en.   5
My lord Bassanio, upon more advice,
Hath sent you here this ring and doth entreat
Your company at dinner.

PORTIA   That cannot be.
His ring I do accept most thankfully,
And so, I pray you, tell him. Furthermore,   10
I pray you, show my youth old Shylock's house.

GRATIANO

That will I do.

NERISSA   Sir, I would speak with you.
[*aside to Portia*] I'll see if I can get my husband's ring,
Which I did make him swear to keep for ever.

PORTIA

[*aside to Nerissa*] Thou mayst, I warrant. We shall have old
    swearing   15

4.2 Capell locates the scene in a '*Street before the Court*', and modern editors have substantially followed this. Pope begins 4.2 after 4.1.117, and 4.3 after 4.1.403.

1 **deed** deed of gift (Ard², 122); see 4.1.384.

5 This short verse line probably indi-

cates Gratiano's breathlessness.
you ... o'erta'en I am glad I have caught up with you

6 **upon more advice** on further consideration

12 **would** wish to (Onions)

15 **old** predictable; also abundant (Onions)

4.2] *Capell subst.*   0.1 PORTIA *and*] F   *still disguised*] *Oxf*   1 SD] *Bevington subst.*   9 His] This *Q2*   I do] do I *Rowe*   13 SD] *Ard¹; Aside to Portia at end of line Cam*   15 SD] *Oxf*

That they did give the rings away to men,
But we'll outface them and outswear them too.
Away, make haste, thou knowst where I will tarry.   [*Exit.*]

NERISSA

Come, good sir, will you show me to this house?   *Exeunt.*

[5.1]   *Enter* LORENZO *and* JESSICA.

LORENZO

The moon shines bright. In such a night as this,
When the sweet wind did gently kiss the trees,
And they did make no noise, in such a night
Troilus, methinks, mounted the Trojan walls
And sighed his soul toward the Grecian tents,   5
Where Cressid lay that night.

JESSICA   In such a night

17 **outface** defy, but also put on a brave face (Onions)
outswear them exceed them in their swearing of oaths
18 **tarry** be staying (*OED sb.* 2), but also with the subsidiary meaning of 'be waiting for you'
19 **this house** Shylock's house as stated at 11.
5.1 Rowe locates the scene in '*Belmont*' but it is Theobald who designates it as outside in '*A Grove or Green place before* Portia's *House*'.
1 **moon shines bright** an echo from Chaucer's *Troilus and Crisyede*: 'And every nyght, as was his owne to doone, / He stoode the brighte moone to byholde' (5.647–8, 569)
such a night The repetition of this phrase is the rhetorical figure epimone, which Puttenham nicknames 'the loueburden' and associates usually with the refrain in a lyric (Puttenham, 188). Wright argues that the half-lines

shared between the lovers signal 'the union of Lorenzo and Jessica, with the latter initiating the shared line-structure' (Wright, 140).
4–5 another Chaucerian echo: 'Upon the walles faste ek wolde he walke, / And on the Grekis oost he wolde se; / And to hymself right thus he wolde talke' (*Troilus and Crisyede*, 5.666–8). The relationship between Troilus and Cressida, to which Shakespeare returned in *TC* (*c.* 1602), was traditionally characterized by the infidelity of Cressida: 'And of Creseyde thou hast seyd at the liste, That maketh men to wommen lasse triste' (Chaucer, *The Legend of Good Women*, 332–3); an example full of irony in this context.
4 **Trojan** Q's spelling 'Troian' was emended in Q2 to 'Troyan', a spelling followed by some editors; but Brown notes that 'Trojan' is the most appropriate modernized form (Ard², 124).

18 Away,] Away! *Dyce;* [*Aloud*] Away! *Cam¹* SD] *Oxf subst.*   19 house?] *Q2;* house. *Q*   SD] *F; not in Q*   5.1] *F (Actus Quintus.);* ACT V. SCENE I. *Rowe*   0.1] *Lorenzo and Jessica pace softly beneath the trees Cam¹*   1] *Q2 lines* bright. / this, /   6 Cressid] (*Cressed.*); *Cressada Q2;* Cresseid *Pope*

Did Thisbe fearfully o'ertrip the dew,
And saw the lion's shadow ere himself,
And ran dismayed away.

LORENZO   In such a night
Stood Dido with a willow in her hand   10
Upon the wild sea banks and waft her love
To come again to Carthage.

JESSICA   In such a night
Medea gathered the enchanted herbs

7   **Thisbe ... dew** an episode comically
enacted by the 'rude mechanicals' in
MND 5.1.185ff. In Chaucer's *Legend
of Good Women*, the tales of Thisbe,
Dido and Medea follow each other in
the order replicated here. The story
of Pyramus and Thisbe is told in
Ovid, *Met.*, 4.68–210, and in both
this and Chaucer's version emphasis
is placed upon parental opposition to
the union of the lovers. Both versions
share a detail that may have provided
the inspiration for the reference to
dew: 'Next morning with hir cherefull
light had driven the starres aside /
And Phoebus with his burning beames
the dewie grasse had dride' (Ovid,
Met., 4.101–2).
     o'ertrip skip over (Onions)
8   **lion's ... himself** the shadow of the
lion before she saw the lion itself. In
Ovid, *Met.*, 4.120, and Chaucer, *The
Legend of Thisbe*, 805, it is 'lionesse', but
Chaucer's Pyramus refers to a 'lyon',
829, and does not see the lioness; in John
Gower's *Confessio Amantis*, 2.1392ff.,
'Leoun' is used throughout, as in *MND*
5.1.138ff. Jessica's invocation of this
story is appropriate in that, like Thisbe,
she has eloped, although the tale is also
concerned with mistaken action.
9   **dismayed** terrified (*OED sb.*)
10   **Dido** the widowed queen of Carthage
whom Aeneas rejected to fulfil his
destiny and conquer Italy: the subject
of Virgil's *Aeneid*, book 4, repeated in
Chaucer's *The Legend of Good Women*,

Gower's *Confessio Amantis*, 4.77–146,
and dramatized in Marlowe's *Dido
Queen of Carthage* (1594); a tale of
masculine infidelity, and ironical in
this context.
     willow ... hand absent in the source
narratives; however, the detail may
be symbolic, since the willow was
the symbol of unrequited love; cf.
Oth 4.3.39–58, Desdemona's 'willow'
song. The closest parallel appears in
Chaucer, 'The Legend of Ariadne',
from *The Legend of Good Women*,
2189–2203.
11   **wild** unconfined, but also desolate
(Ard[1], 125)
     waft beckoned (*OED v.*[2] 1, 1b); also in
the sense of guided or directed (*OED
v.*[1] †1)
13   **Medea** The story of Jason and Medea
appears in Ovid, *Met.*, book 7, and
is repeated in Chaucer's *Legend of
Good Women*, and Gower's *Confessio
Amantis*, 5.4070ff. Jessica does not
choose to emphasize the theme of
infidelity but focuses instead on the
rejuvenation of Jason's father Aeson.
This part of the tale, omitted in
Chaucer's version, is told at length
in *Met.*, 7.343ff., and in Gower; in
Ovid's version, it involves the cutting
of Aeson's throat, and the replacing
of his blood with the distilled juices
of the herbs she has gathered. This
emphasis upon death and rejuvenation
offers an analogue to Jessica's actions
in relation to her father.

11 wild sea banks] wide Sea-banks *Rowe*   waft] wav'd *Theobald*

That did renew old Aeson.

LORENZO   In such a night

Did Jessica steal from the wealthy Jew,   15

And with an unthrift love did run from Venice

As far as Belmont.

JESSICA   In such a night

Did young Lorenzo swear he loved her well,

Stealing her soul with many vows of faith,

And ne'er a true one.

LORENZO   In such a night   20

Did pretty Jessica, like a little shrew,

Slander her love, and he forgave it her.

JESSICA

I would out-night you did nobody come;

But hark, I hear the footing of a man.

Enter [Stephano,] *a* Messenger.

LORENZO

Who comes so fast in silence of the night?   25

MESSENGER   A friend.

---

15 **steal** run away, but also a reference to Jessica's theft of money and jewels from her father

16 **unthrift** prodigal, not eager for profit; a contrast with the Jew's emphasis upon *thrift* at 2.5.52–3

19 **Stealing** taking away dishonestly or secretly (*OED v.*¹) but also, homonymically, strengthening or fortifying (*OED v.* steel) by faith
   vows of faith promises of fidelity, but also an oblique reference to Jessica's conversion to Christianity as a religion dependent upon *faith* rather than upon law

21 **shrew** scold, or vexatious wife (*OED sb.*² 3)

22 **Slander** reproach or disgrace

23 **out-night** outdo in mentioning nights (Onions); the citing of these precedents develops into a competition between the lovers in a possible anticipation of future friction.
   did nobody come if nobody came; a conditional clause that heralds the imminent entry of Stephano at 24.1

24 **footing** tread or footsteps

25 **in silence** The definite article was often omitted in prepositional phrases; see Abbott, 89.

17 In] And in *Q2*   20 In] And in *F2*   21 Jessica, like . . . shrew,] *Johnson; Jessica* (like a little shrow) *Q*   shrew] *Q2*; shrow *Q*   23 nobody] *Q2*; no body *Q*   24.1] *Enter* Stephano *Theobald; Enter a Servant. / Capell*   26+ SP] *Ser. / Capell;* STEPH. *Malone*   26 friend.] *Q2, F;* friend? *Q*

LORENZO

    A friend? What friend? Your name, I pray you, friend?

MESSENGER

    Stephano is my name, and I bring word

    My mistress will, before the break of day,

    Be here at Belmont. She doth stray about   30

    By holy crosses, where she kneels and prays

    For happy wedlock hours.

LORENZO   Who comes with her?

MESSENGER

    None but a holy hermit and her maid.

    I pray you, is my master yet returned?

LORENZO

    He is not, nor we have not heard from him.   35

    But go we in, I pray thee, Jessica,

    And ceremoniously let us prepare

    Some welcome for the mistress of the house.

Enter [Lancelet *the*] CLOWN.

CLOWN   Sola, sola! Wo ha ho! sola, sola!

LORENZO   Who calls?   40

---

30 **stray about** roam around or wander (*OED v.*² 2)

31 **holy crosses** roadside crosses or shrines (Ard¹, 161)

33 **holy hermit** a religious recluse accompanying Portia in the activity described at 31. Johnson regarded this as evidence of an earlier draft (Johnson, 469); Dover Wilson thought this reference was a remnant from an older play (Cam¹, 167–8), but Brown is surely right in suggesting that this is a fabrication that 'fits well with Portia's feigned excuse for leav-

ing Belmont (cf. [3.4.26–32])' (Ard², 126).

37 **ceremoniously** 'in a ceremonious manner'(*OED*); Furness glosses the line: 'Let us prepare some ceremonious welcome' (Furness, 244).

39 **Sola . . . ha ho!** a combination of cries imitating the sound of the horn of a courier or post (*Sola*) and of a falconer (*Wo ha ho*: *OED* 1: 'Wo'). Brown notes that in *LLL* 4.1.148 Costard shouts, 'Sowla, sowla', 'on exit in a hunting scene' (Ard², 127); see also *LLL* Arden 3, 185.

---

27 A friend?] *Johnson;* A friend, *Q;* A friend! *Rowe; om. Pope* What friend?] *F;* what friend, *Q* 32 wedlock] wedlockes *Q2* 34 is] it *F* 37 us] vs vs *F* 38.1] *Folg; Enter* Launcelot. *Rowe; Enter Launcelot smacking a whip. / Rann;* LANCELOT'S *voice heard hollaing at a distance Cam*¹ 39+ SP] (*Clowne.*); Laun. / *Rowe;* Clo. / *Capell; Lancelot Cam*¹; LANCELET *Folg*

CLOWN Sola! Did you see Master Lorenzo and Mistress
Lorenza! Sola, sola!

LORENZO Leave holloaing, man! Here.

CLOWN Sola! Where, where?

LORENZO Here!   45

CLOWN Tell him there's a post come from my master, with
his horn full of good news. My master will be here ere
morning.   [*Exit.*]

LORENZO

Sweet soul, let's in, and there expect their coming.
And yet, no matter. Why should we go in?   50

41–2 *Mistress Lorenza Q has '& M.
Lorenzo', but F2 emends to 'and M.
Lorenza'. Lancelet clearly intends
his speech to *two* addressees and not
one, hence the ampersand as a familiar compositorial space-saving device
for 'and' in a long line. Q2's 'M.
Lorenzo, M. *Lorenzo*' accepts Q's
repetition of the name '*Lorenzo*' but
eliminates the ampersand meaning
'and', thereby missing the point of
Lancelet's joke at Jessica's expense,
since she is now no longer the Jew's
daughter but the wife of Lorenzo.
F2's 'and Mistress Lorenza' restores
Q's meaning and perceptively alters
the gender of the second addressee.
Furness (245) thought that the
ampersand was read in error for an
exclamation mark, while Clarendon
suggested, erroneously, that the
reference to 'him' later at 46 indicates that only Lorenzo is addressed
(Clarendon, 126).

46 **post** courier

47 **horn** literally, the postman's horn that
he blew to announce his arrival, but
also a reference to the horn of plenty
(cornucopia)

49 *Sweet soul part of the Clown's
speech in Q that Greg adduces as
evidence of an addition made in the
foul papers that served as printer's
copy (Greg, *Editorial*, 123). Mahood
conjectures that the Clown's speech
concluded with the phrase 'Sweet soul'
after some stage business (Cam[2], 156).
The attribution of the phrase 'Sweet
soul' to Lancelet as part of his address
to Lorenzo seems unlikely, unless,
implausibly in this context, it is considered as an expletive; nor is it a reference, almost in the form of an aside,
to Bassanio. There is clearly some
awkwardness here, but it is as unlikely
that the Clown would 'simply express
"kind" affection for Bassanio' (Cam[2],
156) as that he would address Lorenzo
with such intimacy. F2's emendation
'Sweet love', attributed to Lorenzo,
attempted to clear up the difficulty,
and Rann concurred in principle but
restored Q's wording, suggesting that
Lorenzo is more likely to have used
this mode of address to Jessica than to
any other character, especially to those
of superior social rank.
expect await

---

41 Master Lorenzo] *Cam;* M. *Lorenzo Q;* Mr. *Lorenzo / Rowe;* master *Lorenzo Q2, Pope* 41–2
Mistress Lorenza!] *F2* (M. *Lorenza);* & M. *Lorenzo Q;* M. *Lorenzo Q2;* Mrs. *Lorenza, F3;* mistress *Lorenza? Pope* 43 holloaing] *(hollowing);* halloing *Collier* 47–8 ere morning.] *Theobald;*
ere morning sweete soule. *Q;* ere morning sweet love. *F2* 48 SD] *Capell* 49 SP] *Rowe; not in Q*
Sweet soul, let's] *Rann;* Let's *Q;* Sweet Love, let's *Rowe* 50 in?] *Q2;* in. *Q*

My friend Stephano, signify, I pray you,
Within the house, your mistress is at hand,
And bring your music forth into the air.   [*Exit Messenger.*]
How sweet the moonlight sleeps upon this bank!
Here will we sit, and let the sounds of music   55
Creep in our ears. Soft stillness and the night
Become the touches of sweet harmony.
Sit, Jessica. Look how the floor of heaven
Is thick inlaid with patens of bright gold.
There's not the smallest orb which thou behold'st   60

51 **signify** indicate or announce (*OED v.* 3)
52 **mistress** The absence of a reference here to Bassanio is adduced by Mahood as evidence that 39–48 is an interpolation (Cam[2], 156). Earlier at 29–30 the Messenger refers to his 'mistress' and her imminent arrival, and Lorenzo's response is to that reference. It is important that Bassanio's and Portia's arrivals are treated separately, although this does not preclude the possibility that 39–48 are interpolated.
53 **music** musicians
   into the air outside
57 **Become** befit, are appropriate for
   touches . . . harmony the harmonious strains produced by the act of playing, or 'touching' a musical instrument. Pooler (Ard[1], 163) notes that 'touch' was the technical term for 'play'. See also Sir John Davies, 'A Hymne in Prayse of Musicke': 'Praise-worthy Musicke is, for God it prayseth, / And pleasant, for brute beasts therein delight: / Great profit from it flowes, and why it raiseth / The minde overwhelmed with rude passions might. / When against reason passions fond rebell, / Musicke doth that confirme, and these expell'

(Davies, 237).
58 **floor of heaven** the sky, but also the canopy over the stage popularly referred to as 'the heavens'. See Reynolds, 97–8.
59 **Is thick inlaid** has embedded thickly in its surface (*OED* 2: 'inlaid')
   patens small flat dishes on which is placed the Eucharist. Brown (Ard[2], 128) quotes Florio's *A World of Words* (1598), where 'Patena' is glossed as 'any kind of dish, platter or charger, a treene dish or wooden tray'. Q2's 'pattents' and F's 'pattens' move the gloss nearer to the homonymic 'patterns' preferred in F2 and followed by some editors. Lorenzo effects a further transformation symptomatic of the play's attempts to transmute the quotidian world of material wealth into the mystery of love. For a positive reading of this process, see Danson, *Harmonies*, 189ff.
60–1 This refers to the music emitted by the rotation of the eight concentric spheres that contained the planets and the stars; see Plato, 346. Furness (249) quotes Montaigne's essay 'On Custom' (Montaigne, 1.106); Clarendon (126) posits a connection with the Old Testament Job, 38.7, but he quotes from the King James

51 Stephano] *Q2; Stephen Q*   signify, . . . you] signify pray you *F;* I pray you signify *Keightley*   53 SD] *Hanmer; Exit* Stephano. *after* 52 / *Theobald*   54 bank!] *Theobald;* banke, *Q*   56 ears. Soft stillness] *Oxf[1];* eares soft stilnes *Q;* eares; soft stilnes *F2*   59 patens] *(*pattens*);* pattents *Q2;* pattens *F;* patterns *F2;* patines *Malone*

But in his motion like an angel sings,
Still choiring to the young-eyed cherubins.
Such harmony is in immortal souls,
But, whilst this muddy vesture of decay
Doth grossly close it in, we cannot hear it.   65

[*Enter Musicians.*]

Come, ho, and wake Diana with a hymn,
With sweetest touches pierce your mistress' ear,
And draw her home with music.   [*They*] *play music.*

JESSICA
I am never merry when I hear sweet music.

version; in the Bishops' Bible and
the Geneva Bible the wording is less
explicit: 'Where wast thou when the
morning stars praysed me together,
and all the children of God reioyced
triumphantly.'
62 **choiring** singing in a choir
 young-eyed cherubins an echo of
the *Te Deum*: 'To thee Cherubin
and Seraphin continually do cry.'
Cherubim were inferior to Seraphim
in the angelic hierarchy, and in
Shakespeare are sometimes associated with youthful femininity;
'young-eyed' may refer both to their
youthfulness and to the fact that
in the vision of the Old Testament
prophet Ezekiel their whole bodies were composed of eyes: 'And
their whole bodies, their backs, their
handes, and winges, yea, and the
wheeles also, were full of eyes rounde
about the foure wheeles' (Ezekiel,
10.12).
63 **harmony . . . souls** harmony is
the essence of the immortal soul;
cf. Timothy Bright, *Treatise of*

Melancholy (1586), where it is located
in the 'mindes of men' as 'a magicall
charme', indicating 'that the mind
was nothing else but a kind of harmo-
nie' (Ard[1], 129).
64 **muddy . . . decay** the human body,
made from the earth, and subject to
mutability
65 **grossly** materially (as opposed to
spiritually); see *OED adv.* †2).
[1]**it** i.e. the immortal soul
[2]**it** harmony
66 **wake Diana** awaken the goddess
of the moon and of chastity. Dover
Wilson glosses *wake* as 'keep vigil'
(Cam[1], 170). It is possible that two
frames of reference are operative here:
(1) the moon has become obscured
behind a cloud and requires to be
'wakened'; (2) the music requested to
produce this effect should also draw,
and welcome, Portia to Belmont. The
juxtaposition of these two frames of
reference aligns Portia with the goddess Diana.
69 **merry** given to mirth, or facetious
(*OED* 3, 3c)

62 young-eyed] *Q3;* young eyde *Q;* young eide *Q2;* young ey'd *F*   cherubins.] cherubims; *F3*   63
souls,] sounds! *Theobald*   65 it in] in it *Q2;* us in it *Rowe;* us in *Pope*   65.1] *Malone; Enter Musick,*
and Domesticks of Portia. Capell; Musicians steal from the house and bestow themselves among the trees;
they leave the door open behind them, and a light shines therefrom Cam[1]; Enter STEPHANO *with musicians*
Cam[2]   66 with a] with him a *Q2*   68 SD] *Musicke playes. Q2; Play musicke. after 69 F*

LORENZO

The reason is your spirits are attentive.   70
For do but note a wild and wanton herd,
Or race, of youthful and unhandled colts
Fetching mad bounds, bellowing and neighing loud,
Which is the hot condition of their blood;
If they but hear, perchance, a trumpet sound,   75
Or any air of music touch their ears,
You shall perceive them make a mutual stand,
Their savage eyes turned to a modest gaze
By the sweet power of music. Therefore the poet
Did feign that Orpheus drew trees, stones and floods,   80
Since naught so stockish, hard and full of rage
But music for the time doth change his nature.
The man that hath no music in himself,
Nor is not moved with concord of sweet sounds,

70 **spirits are attentive** faculties are preoccupied, and hence tranquil rather than unrestrained. 'Spirits' refers ostensibly to the soul (*OED sb.* I.1), the mind (*OED sb.* 17) and the intellect (*OED sb.* †18).

71 **wanton** unrestrained, but also sexually promiscuous

72 **race** herd or stud (Onions); also a rush or a charge (*OED sb.*[1] †2); and a group, used of animals as well as people (*OED sb.*[2] 1)
unhandled colts untamed stallions. 'Colt' was sometimes applied to someone lacking in experience, and also to one who is lasciviously inclined (*OED sb.* 2b).

73 **Fetching mad bounds** performing wild gambols or leaps

74 **hot . . . blood** heated, and hence unruly temperament; blood; an implicit reference to sexual ardour, since the blood is also the source of sexual passion

75 **perchance** perhaps, or by chance

77 **make . . . stand** all stop together; see *MND* 4.1.116, 'one mutual cry', for a gloss on *mutual* as 'common' (*OED* 4); but see also the sexual connotations of *stand* as applied to the male penile erection (Partridge, 190).

79 **the poet** usually identified as Ovid, who tells the story of Orpheus and Eurydice in *Met.*, 10

80 **feign** relate or represent in fiction (*OED v.* 3)
drew attracted. Ovid describes Orpheus' capacity to attract animate and inanimate nature through his music (*Met.*, 1.567)

81 **naught so stockish** nothing so insensitive or unfeeling (Onions: 'stockish')
hard obdurate (Onions)

82 **for the time** for the time during which it is playing

83–4 This refers to the commonplace analogy between the harmony of music and inner personal harmony that has its origins in the Pythagorean concept of the 'music' of the spheres;

75 but hear, perchance,] perchance but heare *Q2*   79 Therefore] Thus *Pope*   80 trees] teares *F2*   floods,] *F4;* floods. *Q*   81 stockish, hard] *F;* stockish hard *Q*   82 the] *om. F*

Is fit for treasons, stratagems and spoils;   85
The motions of his spirit are dull as night
And his affections dark as Erebus.
Let no such man be trusted. Mark the music.

Enter PORTIA *and* NERISSA.

PORTIA

That light we see is burning in my hall.
How far that little candle throws his beams!   90
So shines a good deed in a naughty world.

NERISSA

When the moon shone we did not see the candle!

PORTIA

So doth the greater glory dim the less.

cf. Sir John Davies, *Orchestra* (1596), stanza 46, where music is described as 'Loadstone of fellowship, charming rod of strife, / The soft minds Paradice, the sick minds Leach' (Davies, 102). Lorenzo's paean to music counters the Jew's rejection of music and dancing at 2.5.27ff.

85 **stratagems** tricks designed to gain advantage (*OED* 2), a term normally used in a military context (*OED* 1 and 1b)
    spoils goods or property confiscated from an enemy (*OED* 1)

86 **motions . . . spirit** impulses or desires of his vital energies. There is an implicit counter-reading of this phrase indicating sexual incapacity, i.e. 'the movements of his semen', and detumescence.

87 **affections** inclinations
    ***Erebus** the region of darkness situated between Earth and Hades. Q's error, 'Terebus', may have been due to the compositor's inability to distinguish between 'E' and 'T' in his copy (Ard[1], 130).

90 an echo of Matthew, 5.16 (Bible): 'Let your light shine before men, that they may see your good workes, and glorifie your father which is in Heauen.'

91 **naughty** morally bad or wicked (*OED* 3), but also worthless or nasty (Onions)

92 The effect of the candle-light is diminished by the superior light of the moon. Richard David (*LLL* Arden 2, 102) notes a passage from the *Gesta Grayorum* of 1594: 'At the Royal Presence of Her Majesty, it [attending star] appeared as an obscured Shadow: in this not unlike the Morning-star, which looketh very cheerfully on the World, so long as the Sun looketh not on it' (*Gesta*, 88). Nerissa qualifies Portia's comment in the previous line, and implies that good deeds are not always recognized; see also Dent, S826: 'STARS are not seen by sun shine (at midday)'.

93 proverbial (Dent, G437): 'The GREATER embraces (includes, hides) the less'. Horace's ode in praise of the Emperor Augustus Caesar may also be a source; Ode 12.18, '*nec viget quicquam simile aut secondum* [nor doth aught flourish like or even next to him]' (Horace, 34–5).

87 Erebus] *F2; Terebus: Q; Erobus, F*   88.1] *Enter* Portia *and* Nerissa *at a distance. / Johnson;* Portia *and* Nerissa *come slowly along the avenue Cam[1]*   92 candle!] *(candle?); candle. Q2*

A substitute shines brightly as a king
Until a king be by, and then his state   95
Empties itself, as doth an inland brook
Into the main of waters. Music, hark!

NERISSA

It is your music, madam, of the house!

PORTIA

Nothing is good, I see, without respect.
Methinks it sounds much sweeter than by day!   100

NERISSA

Silence bestows that virtue on it, madam.

PORTIA

The crow doth sing as sweetly as the lark
When neither is attended; and, I think,
The nightingale, if she should sing by day

95 **be by** is close by
 state both display of grandeur or majestical demeanour (*OED sb.* 19a); and the chair of state (Onions). The substitute's affected majesty is diminished and this effectively empties the chair of state of his presence.
96–7 **as . . . waters** proverbial (Dent, R140): 'All RIVERS (waters) run into the sea.' Portia uses this adaptable proverb in support of the concept of rank and hierarchy, though it is sometimes used to emphasize decline and mutability.
98 **music** musicians; see 53n.
 of coming from, but also belonging to
99 Nothing is considered good until it is compared with something else (*OED sb.* 7: 'respect'); hence, everything is relative. Portia's observation reprises a list of unstable comparisons that function to undermine the dominant discourse of 'harmony' prevalent in this scene.
101 **virtue** quality
102 This may be proverbial; see *TA*

3.1.159: 'Did ever raven sing so like a lark.' Portia is concerned to emphasize the consequences of inattentiveness (and hence lack of discrimination) to the relative merits of the singing of crow and lark. The lark was noted for its early-morning singing; cf. Tilley, L70: 'To sing like a LARK'.
103 **attended** the object of attention; but also expected or anticipated (*OED v.* III.13, 15); the *OED v.* 9 gloss 'accompanied', though questioned by Mahood (Cam², 159), cannot be ruled out, since Portia is concerned with relative values, so that difference is only discernible through comparison. There is also a suggestion that the lark occupies a superior hierarchical position on account of its capacity to achieve great height in flight, whereas the crow is distinguished for its black appearance.
104 **nightingale** The nightingale was thought to sing by night, compared to the lark, which was commonly thought to herald the dawn. The nightingale is

97] *Musicke. at end of line F* 98 your] the *Rowe* the] your *Rowe* house!] *(house?);* house. *Q2* 100 day!] *(day?);* day. *Q2* 101 that] the *Pope* madam.] *Q2;* Madam? *Q*

When every goose is cackling, would be thought   105
No better a musician than the wren.
How many things by season seasoned are
To their right praise and true perfection.
Peace! How the moon sleeps with Endymion
And would not be awaked.   [*Music ceases.*]
LORENZO   That is the voice,   110
Or I am much deceived, of Portia.

PORTIA

He knows me as the blind man knows the cuckoo:
By the bad voice!
LORENZO   Dear lady, welcome home.

PORTIA

We have been praying for our husbands' welfare,

also associated with the rape of Philomel by Tereus in the story told in Ovid, *Met.*, 6.527–854, and is alluded to in the prologue to Marlowe's *Jew of Malta*, 16–17: 'Birds of the air will tell of murders past? / I am ashamed to hear such fooleries!' Clearly Portia's emphasis is on the nightingale's musical accomplishments, but as with earlier analogies in this scene the allusion is ambivalent

106 **wren** the smallest of birds, whose song was thought to reverberate hollowly; cf. *2H6* 3.2.41–3: 'And thinks he that the chirping of a wren, / By crying comfort from a hollow breast, / Can chase away the first conceived sound?'

107 **by season seasoned** a play on two meanings: (1) at an appropriate or favourable time of the year (*season*); (2) garnished with spices or seasoning used in the preparation of food (*seasoned*)

108 **right** appropriate

109 **Peace!** an instruction to the musicians to cease playing

moon . . . Endymion the mythological figure of Endymion, beloved by the moon (Diana), and who sleeps eternally on Mount Latmos. Capell's SD at 110, '*observing Lor. and Jes. rising*' (Capell, 84), suggests that Portia is referring to the sleeping Jessica and Lorenzo, although this may be an elaborately witty way of saying that the moon has gone behind a cloud (Cam², 159). The emphasis already placed upon the philosophical importance of music makes it unlikely that the lovers would fall asleep during this time.

112 **as . . . cuckoo** a 16th-century proverbial commonplace (Dent, C894.1: 'You are like the CUCKOO, you have but one song'). Based upon this observation, Puttenham translates the Greek rhetorical trope Epizeuxis as the 'cuckowspell' (Puttenham, 167–8).

114 **welfare** well-being but also progress (*OED adv.* II.6b: 'well' associated with verb), since Bassanio and Gratiano have yet to arrive

106 wren] *Q2; Renne Q*   110 SD] *F; observing Lor. and Jes. rising. Musick ceases. / Capell*   112–13 He . . . voice!] *Q2 lines* knowes / voyce. /; *F lines* knows the / voice? /; *F2 lines* Cuc- / voyce? / 113 voice!] *(voyce?)*; voice. *Q2*   114 been] *F3;* bin *Q;* bene *F*   husbands' welfare] *(husbands welfare)*; husband health *Q2*

377

Which speed, we hope, the better for our words.   115
Are they returned?

LORENZO   Madam, they are not yet,
But there is come a messenger before
To signify their coming!

PORTIA   Go in, Nerissa.
Give order to my servants, that they take
No note at all of our being absent hence,   120
Nor you, Lorenzo; Jessica, nor you.   [*A tucket sounds.*]

LORENZO
Your husband is at hand, I hear his trumpet.
We are no tell-tales, madam, fear you not.

PORTIA
This night, methinks, is but the daylight sick;
It looks a little paler. 'Tis a day   125
Such as the day is when the sun is hid.

Enter BASSANIO, ANTONIO, GRATIANO *and their Followers.*

115 **Which speed** whose prosperity and
welfare; the relative pronoun attaches
the verb to the antecedent *welfare* and
to the plural noun; Portia's 'prayer'
has been for the two husbands'
expeditious and safe return, but, in
the light of our knowledge of where
she has been herself, this is heavily
ironical.
117 **before** in advance
119–20 **take / No note** make no mention
120 **hence** from here
121 SD ***tucket** from the Italian *toccato*,
meaning a trumpet flourish; it is exclu-
sive to F. Florio glosses 'toccata' as 'a
praeludium that cunning musitions
vse to play as it were voluntary before
any set lesson' (Florio, 566).
122 **his trumpet** the fanfare announcing
Bassanio's arrival, since he is already
a lord (see 1.1.69n.) and now, by mar-

riage, lord of Belmont. Mahood is
mistaken in the belief that Bassanio is
a 'private citizen' (Cam², 161) or that
his is possessive; a fanfare normally
announces a royal entry in F, but see F
AW 1.3.01, '*Flourish / Enter Countesse,
Steward, and Clowne*', and 3.5.01: '*A
Tucket afarre off. Enter old Widdow of
Florence, her daughter, Violenta, and
Mariana, with other citizens.*'
124 **but** only; Portia may be referring to
the dimming of her glory at 92–3 by
the imminent arrival of her husband.
The paleness at 125 may be a simple
observation that the moon (with whom
she has been associated) is now paler
than the sun (her husband) but it
may also be a reference to the complicated subterfuge in which she has been
involved, and which cannot as yet be
brought into the daylight.

118 coming!] *(coming?); coming.* Q2   in] *om. Pope*   121 SD] *F; A tucket sounded. / Collier;* '*A tucket
sounds'; voices are heard at a distance in the avenue* Cam¹   122 his] a *Rowe*

BASSANIO

We should hold day with the Antipodes,

If you would walk in absence of the sun.

PORTIA

Let me give light, but let me not be light;

For a light wife doth make a heavy husband,   130

And never be Bassanio so for me.

But God sort all. You are welcome home, my lord.

BASSANIO

I thank you, madam. Give welcome to my friend.

This is the man, this is Antonio,

To whom I am so infinitely bound.   135

PORTIA

You should in all sense be much bound to him,

For, as I hear, he was much bound for you.

ANTONIO

No more than I am well acquitted of.

PORTIA

Sir, you are very welcome to our house.

---

127 We would be like the Antipodes where their day is our night; Bassanio responds to Portia's superficial description of the poor quality of the light by suggesting that Portia's beauty could provide sufficient illumination.
hold maintain
128 if your presence were to replace that of the sun
129 ¹**light** radiance
²**light** wanton or promiscuous
130 **heavy husband** i.e. a husband weighed down with the fear that his wife might make him a cuckold; but also a possible allusion to a man's weight on a woman during sexual intercourse (Gordon Williams, 154 and 334)
131 **never . . . me** Bassanio will never be a *heavy husband* for me. Cf. *MA* 3.4.23–5: '*Hero.* God give me joy to

wear it, for my heart is exceeding heavy. *Marg.* 'Twill be the heavier soon by the weight of a man.'
132 **God sort all** May God take care of everything; a dismissive irony, since Portia has arranged what is to follow. In this speech, as elsewhere in the play, Portia alternates between masculine control and female submission.
135 **bound** obligated, though with echoes of its usage by the Jew beginning at 1.3.5ff. and resonating throughout 4.1.
136 **in all sense** in every sense of the word
137 **bound for you** obligated on your behalf; Portia emphasizes the relevance of the alternative meanings of *bound* in 136–7, distinguishing between its literal and legal applications.
138 **well acquitted of** exonerated from, both legally and personally

131 for] from *Rowe*   132 You are] y'are *Q2*

It must appear in other ways than words: 140
Therefore I scant this breathing courtesy.

GRATIANO [*to Nerissa*]

By yonder moon, I swear you do me wrong!
In faith, I gave it to the judge's clerk.
Would he were gelt that had it, for my part,
Since you do take it, love, so much at heart. 145

PORTIA

A quarrel ho! Already! What's the matter?

GRATIANO

About a hoop of gold, a paltry ring
That she did give me, whose posy was
For all the world like cutler's poetry

141 **scant . . . courtesy** cut short this formally courteous expression of welcome. Portia alludes to the difference between the mere courtesy of words of welcome and their being given substance through action, and she will shortly make good this promise by restoring Antonio to his merchandise.

142 **yonder moon** part of an oath, but significant in that up to this point the moon has been associated with Diana (66), with Portia (109), and hence with chastity

144 **gelt** castrated or emasculated (*OED v.*[1] 1)
  for my part as far as I am concerned

145 **at heart** to heart, i.e. so seriously

148 **posy** a short epigram used to adorn jewellery or dinnerware; Puttenham describes both the form and the custom: 'There be also other like Epigrammes that were sent vsually for new yeares giftes or to be Printed or put vpon their banketting dishes of suger plate, or of march paines, & such other dainty meates as by the curtesie & custome euery gest might carry from a common feast home with him to his owne house & were made for the nonce, they were called *Nenia* or *apophoreta*, and neuer contained aboue one verse, or two at the most, but the shorter the better, we call them Posies, and do paint them now a dayes vpon the backe sides of our fruite trenchers of wood, or vse them as deuises in rings and armes and about such courtly purposes' (Puttenham, 47).

149 **cutler's poetry** the kind of unsophisticated epigram that would be etched on the blade of a knife; a cutler is one who makes, deals in or repairs knives (*OED*). It is also a possible allusion to *cut*, the colloquial term for the female genitals (Gordon Williams, 90), and connects with 147. Williams notes that 'ring' is both a symbol of female chastity and a term for the vagina (Gordon Williams, 260), but it is also a familiar token of marital unity. All of these meanings are in play during these exchanges.

142 SD] *Capell; after 143 Rowe;* Gratiano *and* Nerissa *seem to talk apart. after 143 Johnson* 148 give] give to *Dyce* 148, 151 posy] Poesie *Q2, F*

Upon a knife: 'Love me and leave me not.'   150
NERISSA
What talk you of the posy or the value?
You swore to me when I did give it you
That you would wear it till your hour of death,
And that it should lie with you in your grave.
Though not for me, yet, for your vehement oaths,   155
You should have been respective and have kept it.
Gave it a judge's clerk! No, God's my judge,
The clerk will ne'er wear hair on's face that had it.
GRATIANO
He will, an if he live to be a man.
NERISSA
Ay, if a woman live to be a man.   160
GRATIANO
Now, by this hand, I gave it to a youth,
A kind of boy, a little scrubbed boy,
No higher than thyself, the judge's clerk,
A prating boy that begged it as a fee;
I could not, for my heart, deny it him.   165
PORTIA
You were to blame, I must be plain with you,

150 **leave** part with or from; Pooler's gloss, 'give away' (Ard¹, 169), suggests that the motto applies exclusively to the ring rather than to the giver, although it is likely that the pronoun *me* refers to both.
155 **Though . . . me** even if you would not on my account
156 **respective** considerate or respectful of [the gift]
157 **God's my judge** as God is my judge; a familiar oath, but emended in F to 'wel I know' as a consequence of the 1606 Act against the uttering of profanity onstage.

159 *****an if** if only. Q's 'and' is emended here because it is a conditional.
162 **scrubbed** scrubbèd; stunted or dwarfed (*OED* cites this example)
164 **prating** idle, chattering (*OED sb.*)
166 **to blame** at fault; Q2 and F's 'too' converts the infinitive construction to that of an intensifier indicating that *blame* is the adjectival equivalent of 'culpable' and suggesting the phrase 'too much to blame'. Both spellings were used interchangeably during the period, but Q's 'to' offers the more plausible reading.

150 'Love . . . not.'] *Collier; Loue . . . not. Q*   151 value?] *F4;* valew: *Q;* value; *Q2*   152 give it] *Q2;* giue *Q*   153 your] the *F*   157 clerk!] *F4;* Clarke: *Q;* Clarke; *Q2;* Clearke: *F*   No . . . judge] but wel I know *F*   158 on's] *Q2;* ons *Q;* on his *Capell*   159 an] *Pope;* and *Q*   160 Ay,] *Pope;* I, *Q;* If, *F2;* If! *Rowe*   166 to] too *Q2, F*

To part so slightly with your wife's first gift,
A thing stuck on with oaths upon your finger
And so riveted with faith unto your flesh.
I gave my love a ring and made him swear   170
Never to part with it, and here he stands.
I dare be sworn for him he would not leave it,
Nor pluck it from his finger, for the wealth
That the world masters. Now, in faith, Gratiano,
You give your wife too unkind a cause of grief.   175
An 'twere to me, I should be mad at it.

BASSANIO [*aside*]
Why, I were best to cut my left hand off
And swear I lost the ring defending it.

GRATIANO
My lord Bassanio gave his ring away

167 **slightly** carelessly (*OED adv.* 2), but also weakly (*OED* 3)
168–9 **oaths . . . faith** The emphasis on 'promises' and on 'faith' underscores the Christian context of marriage and refers to the linguistic and Scriptural foundations of its efficacy.
169 **so riveted** attached by rivets, and hence permanent; Dyce thought that the 'so' was repeated from 167 in error (see Furness, 261). However, Portia's repetition may simply be for rhetorical emphasis, even though the *so* before *riveted* may result in metrical clumsiness.
172 **I . . . him** I venture to swear on his behalf
    leave part with; cf. 150.
173–4 **wealth . . . masters** wealth that there is in the world; literally, wealth that the world is master of. As Nerissa suggests at 151, two different criteria of value are proposed here, (1) material value and (2) spiritual value, but they are not interchangeable.

175 **too unkind** clearly *too* is used here as an intensifier for effect and helps to produce a metrically imperfect line. Abbott, 462, notes this as an example where syllables ending in vowels are frequently elided before vowels in reading but not in writing. Brown suggests that the error may lie in the introduction of the indefinite article 'a' (Ard², 134). These suggestions may derive from the editorial desire for metrical perfection as against the text's rhetorical impact.
176 **An . . . me** if it were up to me
    mad angry, but also beside myself (Oxf², 222)
177 **I were best** it would be best for me
179 **ring** Throughout this exchange there is a tension between the *ring* as a symbol of marital unity and chastity and the sexual meaning of vagina (Gordon Williams, 260), but here there is a third layer of meaning to the word 'ring', since in Elizabethan performances female roles were played by young

169 so riveted] riveted *Pope;* riveted so *Capell*   175 a cause] cause *Dyce*   176 An] *Theobald;* And *Q*   177 SD] *Collier; at end of 178 Theobald*

Unto the judge that begged it, and, indeed,   180
Deserved it too, and then the boy, his clerk,
That took some pains in writing, he begged mine,
And neither man nor master would take aught
But the two rings.

PORTIA   What ring gave you, my lord?
Not that, I hope, which you received of me.   185

BASSANIO
If I could add a lie unto a fault,
I would deny it: but you see my finger
    [*holding up his hand*]
Hath not the ring upon it: it is gone.

PORTIA
Even so void is your false heart of truth.
By heaven, I will ne'er come in your bed   190
Until I see the ring.

NERISSA [*to Gratiano*] Nor I in yours
Till I again see mine!

BASSANIO   Sweet Portia,
If you did know to whom I gave the ring,
If you did know for whom I gave the ring,

males, suggesting what Orgel identifies here as the momentary emergence of a 'startling pederastic fantasy' (Orgel, *Impersonations*, 76). Sinfield notes Portia's 'purposefully heterosexist' strategy at work in this dialogue (Sinfield, 'How to read', 126); but Gratiano's volunteering of information in this way hints in comic fashion at the spectre of sodomy and also at its connection with various forms of reward, including, possibly, usury. Auden makes this connection and argues that 'Shylock the usurer has as his antagonist a man whose emotional life, though his conduct may be chaste, is concentrated upon a member of his own sex' (Auden, 231).

182 **took . . . writing** acted competently as a scribe in the court
186 **add . . . fault** supplement my original fault with a lie. Bassanio accepts responsibility for a deficiency (*fault*), but, as Orgel notes, he is bound to fail the test that Portia has set for him (Orgel, *Impersonations*, 76).
189 **void** empty
190 **come** both enter, and experience orgasm (Partridge, 81–2)
193–7 **ring** Bassanio's use of the rhetorical figures of anaphora (repetition of the same word at the beginning of a clause) and epistrophe (ending a clause with the same word) emphasizes the innuendo even more.

191 SD] *after 192* mine. *Capell*   191–2 Nor . . . mine.] *one line* F   192 mine!] *(*mine?*); mine. Q2; mine. *Capell*

And would conceive for what I gave the ring,   195
And how unwillingly I left the ring,
When naught would be accepted but the ring,
You would abate the strength of your displeasure!

PORTIA

If you had known the virtue of the ring,
Or half her worthiness that gave the ring,   200
Or your own honour to contain the ring,
You would not then have parted with the ring.
What man is there so much unreasonable,
If you had pleased to have defended it
With any terms of zeal, wanted the modesty   205
To urge the thing held as a ceremony?
Nerissa teaches me what to believe.
I'll die for't, but some woman had the ring!

BASSANIO

No, by my honour, madam, by my soul,
No woman had it, but a civil doctor,   210
Which did refuse three thousand ducats of me
And begged the ring, the which I did deny him
And suffered him to go displeased away:
Even he that had held up the very life

195 **conceive** understand or imagine (*OED v.* II. 8), but also to become pregnant (*OED v.* I.1)
198 **abate** stem or curtail
199–202 **virtue . . . ring** value of the ring. Portia's rhetorical parody of Bassanio's words at 193–7 indicate that she is morally superior to him.
199 **virtue** great worth or value (*OED sb.* II.9), but also chaste (*OED sb.* I.2c)
201 **contain** retain (*OED v.* II.†13c)
204 **had pleased** had been eager, i.e. had been pleased to have
205 **terms of zeal** enthusiastically articulated phrases
wanted the modesty lacked the decorum
206 **urge** persist in asking for
ceremony something sacred or symbolic
210 **civil doctor** doctor of civil law, but Brown (Ard[2], 135) suggests a possible pun on *civil* as polite (*OED* †9)
211 **Which** who; see Abbott, 265, for the interchangeability of 'which' and 'who'.
213 **suffered** allowed or permitted (*OED v.* II.13)
214 **held up** preserved

198 displeasure!] *(displeasure?)*; displeasure. *Q2*   200 Or] Of *Q2*   201 contain] retain *Pope*   206 ceremony?] *Q2;* ceremonie: *Q*   208 ring!] *(ring?)*, *Ard²;* Ring. *Q2*   209 my honour] mine honour *F*   211 Which] Who *Pope*   214 had held up] and vphold *Q2*

Of my dear friend. What should I say, sweet lady?   215
I was enforced to send it after him,
I was beset with shame and courtesy,
My honour would not let ingratitude
So much besmear it. Pardon me, good lady,
For, by these blessed candles of the night,   220
Had you been there, I think you would have begged
The ring of me to give the worthy doctor.

PORTIA

Let not that doctor e'er come near my house!
Since he hath got the jewel that I loved
And that which you did swear to keep for me,   225
I will become as liberal as you;
I'll not deny him anything I have,
No, not my body, nor my husband's bed.

217 **beset with** surrounded by [feelings of] (*OED v.* I.1†b)
220 **blessed** blessèd
   candles . . . night stars. Cf. *Son* 21.12: 'As those gold candles fixed in heaven's air'.
224 **jewel** literally, the ring as ornament, but also chastity or maidenhead (Gordon Williams, 173–4). Portia exploits here the suggestion of marital infidelity, by levelling an accusation at her husband.
226 **liberal** magnanimous, but also licentious; a quibble that extends the innuendo further and threatens Bassanio's own claim to authority over his wife
227–8 Portia parades in front of Bassanio the prospect of her own 'liberality' by laying claim to the freedom enjoyed by her husband to disregard her marriage oath. The audience is party to the joke she is playing on Bassanio, and they are invited to enjoy her exposure of a cherished tenet of masculine ideology

in which possession and control of the woman in marriage is paramount. In laying claim to equality with her husband – and this gesture, applied to Bassanio, is open to interpretation as a sign of human weakness (a foible) or as a mark of male promiscuity – Portia raises in a comic context an issue that, if applied literally to her, would be a very serious matter; indeed, in the later play *Othello* the mere unfounded allegation of female *liberal* behaviour leads to tragedy for Desdemona. Behind this exchange is, of course, the fact that Bassanio has given away a token of marital fidelity to a young man who has saved the life of his male friend, and Portia intends to remind him of what he has done. There remains some tension behind this whole comic exchange between the homo-social obligations of one male friend to another and the hetero normative obligations of a husband to his wife.

215 lady?] *Q2*; Lady, *Q*   220 For] And *F*   222 the] thee *F2*   doctor.] *Q2* (Doctor.); doctor? *Q*
223 house!] house *Q*; house, *Q2, F*

385

Know him I shall, I am well sure of it.
Lie not a night from home; watch me like Argus.   230
If you do not, if I be left alone,
Now, by mine honour, which is yet mine own,
I'll have that doctor for my bedfellow.

NERISSA
And I his clerk. Therefore be well advised
How you do leave me to mine own protection.   235

GRATIANO
Well, do you so; let not me take him then,
For if I do I'll mar the young clerk's pen.

ANTONIO
I am th'unhappy subject of these quarrels.

PORTIA
Sir, grieve not you. You are welcome notwithstanding.

BASSANIO
Portia, forgive me this enforced wrong,   240
And in the hearing of these many friends
I swear to thee, even by thine own fair eyes
Wherein I see myself –

229 **Know** recognize, but also have carnal knowledge of (Gordon Williams, 179–80)
230 **Lie not** do not sleep
from away from
Argus the legendary son of Aristor, who had 100 eyes 'of which by turne did sleepe / Alwayes a couple, and the rest did duely watch and warde' (Ovid, *Met.*, 1.776–7), and whom Juno engaged to watch over Io, the mistress of her husband Jove. Portia identifies herself with the concubine Io and in doing so exploits Bassanio's patriarchal fear of cuckoldry.
232 **honour . . . own** virginity that is still intact
233 *****my** Q's 'mine' was probably a printer's error caused by the compositor's eye catching the two instances of

'mine' in 232 (Ard², 136).
234 **be well advised** take great care, or take my advice
236 **take** catch
237 **mar** spoil
pen literally, his quill pen, but also his penis (Gordon Williams, 232)
239 **grieve not you** do not upset yourself
240 **enforced wrong** enforcèd; an error imposed upon me against my will
243 **Wherein . . . myself** in whose reflection I see myself; a Neoplatonic commonplace in which the virtue of the lover is reflected in the eyes of the woman. See *Son* 24.10–12: 'Mine eyes have drawn thy shape, and thine for me / Are windows to my breast, wherethrough the sun / Delights to peep, to gaze therein on thee.'

230 Argus.] *F2;* Argos, *Q*   233 that] the *F*   my] *Q2, F;* mine *Q*   239] *F lines* you, / notwithstanding. /
243 myself –] *F3;* my selfe. *Q;* my selfe. – *F2;* my self my selfe – *F4*

PORTIA   Mark you but that!
In both my eyes he doubly sees himself,
In each eye one. Swear by your double self,   245
And there's an oath of credit!
BASSANIO   Nay, but hear me.
Pardon this fault, and, by my soul, I swear
I never more will break an oath with thee.
ANTONIO
I once did lend my body for his wealth,
Which, but for him that had your husband's ring,   250
Had quite miscarried. I dare be bound again:
My soul upon the forfeit, that your lord
Will never more break faith advisedly.

244 He sees a reflection of himself in each of my eyes; but Portia may also be hinting at Bassanio's duplicity, since he is also open to the accusation of being 'two-faced'. Portia's argument depends upon her own duplicity in disguising herself as the lawyer Balthazar, and thus compounds the irony of this exchange.

246 **oath of credit** oath worthy to be believed; but also entrusting someone with goods or money on the faith of future payment (*OED v.* †3). The irony operates at two levels here: (1) Portia's mocking disbelief of Bassanio's narrative; (2) the fact that her suit was sought as part of a financial transaction for which Antonio has stood guarantor, so that she is the very source of Bassanio's financial and moral probity.

249 **wealth** There is something improperly suggestive lurking beneath Antonio's statement that he *did lend* his body for Bassanio's *wealth*, since the term has a double meaning: 'spiritual well-being' (*OED* †2) and 'worldly goods' (*OED* 3). In one sense Antonio has performed a sacrifice, but in another sense he has prosti-

tuted himself. With the emphasis upon 'duplicity' in the exchange between Portia and Bassanio, it is difficult to eradicate the secondary implications of Antonio's utterance.

250 **but for** except for
had . . . ring Here again the literal sense collides with the various meanings of the word *ring* that are active throughout this scene.

251 **Had quite miscarried** had come to destruction. 'Miscarry' was the term used by Salarino at 2.8.29 to describe the loss of a ship at sea, and by Antonio himself at 3.2.315. The frame of reference is complicated by the innuendo that surrounds *ring*. Its symbolic meaning encompasses Portia's chastity and, by implication, the fact that she is the source of both the acquittal of Antonio and the replenishing of Bassanio's material wealth, suggesting a 'rebirth' that would otherwise have been aborted (*OED* v. 5: 'miscarry').

251–3 **I . . . faith** in the circumstances, an ironic replication of the very dilemma from which the disguised Portia has already liberated Antonio

253 **advisedly** deliberately (*OED adv.* 4)

that!] *(that?);* that. *Q2*   244 my] mine *F2*   249 his] thy *F*   wealth,] wealth, *to* Bass. *Rowe;* weal; *Theobald*   250 husband's ring] *(husbands ring);* husband Ring *Q2;* husband's Ring *to* Por. *Rowe*

PORTIA

 Then you shall be his surety. Give him this,
  [*giving Bassanio the ring*]
 And bid him keep it better than the other.   255

ANTONIO

 Here, Lord Bassanio, swear to keep this ring.

BASSANIO

 By heaven, it is the same I gave the doctor!

PORTIA

 I had it of him. Pardon me, Bassanio,
 For by this ring the doctor lay with me.

NERISSA

 And pardon me, my gentle Gratiano,   260
 For that same scrubbed boy, the doctor's clerk,
 In lieu of this, [*showing Gratiano the ring*] last night
  did lie with me.

GRATIANO

 Why, this is like the mending of highways
 In summer where the ways are fair enough!
 What, are we cuckolds ere we have deserved it? 265

PORTIA

 Speak not so grossly. You are all amazed.

254 **surety** guarantor. Ironically, Portia invites Antonio to become involved in exactly the same kind of contractual relationship as that with the Jew and from which she had saved him.
259 **lay with** slept with; cf. *Oth* 4.1.35–7, where the alternative meanings of the verb 'lie' are explored. Portia places these doubts in Bassanio's mind as if to summon the spectre of male jealousy before dispelling it.
261 **scrubbed** scrubbèd; see 162n. Nerissa now returns Gratiano's words to him.
262 **In lieu of** in exchange for (*OED* 1), suggesting a pecuniary transaction;

the fiscal implications of the act of exchange are never absent from this dialogue.
263–4 **mending . . . enough** wholly gratuitous violations of marital fidelity. Roads required mending in the winter after bad weather, whereas in the summer this was usually unnecessary.
266 **grossly** stupidly and coarsely (*OED* 7a), but also possibly materially rather than spiritually (*OED* †5). Ironically, Gratiano's sexual coarseness (given graphic emphasis throughout Bogdanov's 2004 production), his emphasis upon what Portia and Nerissa have been doing with

254 SD] *Bevington subst. after 255* 255 than] *F4;* then *Q* 258 me] *om. F* 262 SD] *Bevington subst.* 264 enough!] *(*enough?*);* enough. *Q2;* enough: *F* 265 it?] *Q2;* it. *Q* 266 amazed] *(*amaz'd*)*

Here is a letter, read it at your leisure;
It comes from Padua, from Bellario.
There you shall find that Portia was the doctor,
Nerissa there, her clerk. Lorenzo here   270
Shall witness I set forth as soon as you
And even but now returned; I have not yet
Entered my house. Antonio, you are welcome,
And I have better news in store for you
Than you expect. Unseal this letter soon;   275
    [*giving Antonio a letter*]
There you shall find three of your argosies
Are richly come to harbour suddenly.
You shall not know by what strange accident
I chanced on this letter.

ANTONIO   I am dumb!

BASSANIO [*to Portia*]
Were you the doctor, and I knew you not?   280

GRATIANO [*to Nerissa*]
Were you the clerk that is to make me cuckold?

NERISSA
Ay, but the clerk that never means to do it,
Unless he live until he be a man.

their bodies, emanates directly from the linguistic ambiguity that both have exploited. They recall Lorenzo's description of the body earlier at 63–5 as 'this muddy vesture of decay' that *grossly* encloses the *immortal soul*.
  amazed bewildered, but also possibly terrified (*OED* †3), implying fear of some loss
277 **richly** in a splendid manner, sumptuously (*OED* 2)
  suddenly unexpectedly
279 **chanced** chancèd
281 **is to make** is going to make
282–3 **that . . . man** who does not intend to cuckold him (because he does not have the means, i.e. a 'will' or penis). The fictional Nerissa is, of course, female and could never expect to grow a penis, but the boy actor, if pre-pubescent, will eventually become a man, and the male actor will already be able to demonstrate his manhood sexually if given the opportunity. This deceptively complex joke permits a glimpse of the process of what acting the role of a female on the Elizabethan stage entails, and of the meanings that the female impersonator could generate.

272 even but] but ev'n *F*   275 SD] *Bevington*   279 dumb!] *(dumb?)*; dumbe. *Q2, F*   280 SD] *Bevington*   281 SD] *Bevington*   cuckold?] *Q2*; cuckold. *Q*   282 Ay,] *Rowe*; I *Q*; I, *Q2, F*

BASSANIO [*to Portia*]
  Sweet doctor, you shall be my bedfellow.
  When I am absent, then lie with my wife!   285

ANTONIO
  Sweet lady, you have given me life and living,
  For here I read for certain that my ships
  Are safely come to road.

PORTIA   How now, Lorenzo?
  My clerk hath some good comforts too for you.

NERISSA
  Ay, and I'll give them him without a fee.   290
  There do I give to you and Jessica
    [*giving the document to Lorenzo*]
  From the rich Jew, a special deed of gift,
  After his death, of all he dies possessed of.

LORENZO
  Fair ladies, you drop manna in the way
  Of starved people.

PORTIA   It is almost morning;   295
  And yet I am sure you are not satisfied
  Of these events at full. Let us go in,
  And charge us there upon inter'gatories,

---

286 **living** livelihood, i.e. the means to continue his commercial activities
288 **road** anchorage, or the stretch of sheltered water where ships wait before docking (*OED sb.* 3)
294 **manna** the bread dropped from heaven and gathered each morning to feed the Israelites during their journey through the desert after their escape from Egypt in the Bible's Exodus, 16.15ff.: 'And the house of Israel called the name thereof Manna and it was like Coriander seed and white: and the taste of it was like wafers made with hony' (16.31).

295 **starved** starvèd
296–7 **satisfied . . . full** fully satisfied with the account of these events, although the line-break that forces an emphasis on *satisfied* may gesture towards the postponement of sexual satisfaction (Gordon Williams, 267–8)
298 **charge . . . inter'gatories** question us under oath, as though we were offenders being formally examined in a court of law; a syncopated form of 'interrogatories' sometimes used in prose, as in *AW* 4.3.178; from the Latin *interrogo* (to examine

---

284 SD] *this edn*   284 Sweet doctor,] *Rowe;* (Sweet Doctor) *Q*   286 Sweet lady,] *Rowe;* (Sweet Lady) *Q*   288 road.] *Pope;* Rode. *Q;* Rodes. *F2;* Rhodes. *F3*   290 Ay,] *Rowe;* I, *Q*   291 SD] *Bevington after 290*   296 I am] Ime *Q2*   297 Let us] let's *Q2*   298 upon] on *Rowe*   inter'gatories] *Theobald;* intergotories *Q;* intergatories *F;* interrogatories *F3*

And we will answer all things faithfully.

GRATIANO

Let it be so. The first inter'gatory   300
That my Nerissa shall be sworn on is:
Whether till the next night she had rather stay,
Or go to bed now, being two hours to day.
But, were the day come, I should wish it dark
Till I were couching with the doctor's clerk!   305
Well, while I live, I'll fear no other thing
So sore as keeping safe Nerissa's ring.   *Exeunt.*

FINIS

judicially), from which the noun *interrogatum* is derived. See also *OED* B. *sb.* 1.

301 **sworn on** required to answer under oath. Gratiano takes up Portia's momentary return to the language of the court at 298, and offers a bathetic parody of it.

302 **next night** i.e. tomorrow night

303 **being ... day** since it is only two hours until dawn

304 Gratiano wishes for the night to come so that he can consummate his marriage; a 'gross' version of the Ovidian commonplace. Cf. *Amores*, 1.13, where Aurora, the goddess of the dawn, is upbraided for interrupting the lover's pleasure.

305 **couching** lying down to sleep (*OED v.*[1] I. †1), but also, in a quasi-military sense, lowering himself to the position of (sexual) attack

306 **fear ... thing** a play on 'no thing' as the vagina (Gordon Williams, 219), since this is the very *thing* whose possession Gratiano (and, by implication, Bassanio) has been afraid of losing in this final scene

307 **sore** grievously, but in the sense of 'as much as'
    ring The final word of the play underlines through innuendo Gratiano's sexual fears; the possession of his wife's sexual organ is both an onerous task, and is fraught with uncertainty and anxiety.

300 inter'gatory] *Theobald;* intergory *Q(u);* intergotory *Q(c),* Q2; intergatory *F;* interrogatory *F3*   303 being ... day.] *F4;* being   day: *Q;* being ... day, *F;* being ... to-day *Malone*   305 Till] that *Q2*   FINIS] *om. F4*

LONGER NOTES

1.1.1 sad Another reason for Antonio's sadness may be the knowledge of Bassanio's imminent departure for Belmont. Explanations have variously included suggestions that this detail is an unresolved remnant of an earlier version of the play (Schücking, 171; Stewart, 16); that Antonio is secretly in love with Bassanio (Auden, 233–4); that his feelings for Bassanio are 'intense', though difficult to describe in sexual terms (Sinfield, 'How to read', 124); or that Antonio's own alienation from himself is connected, as Salarino suggests (7–8), with the uncertainty of his financial transactions. A less convincing speculation identifies Antonio's sadness with dramatic foreboding (Ard², 4). Clearly in this context *sad* refers to a feeling of greater intensity than straightforward seriousness (*OED* 4a, 4d). Cf. *MA* 3.2.17–19 for the connection between sadness and lack of money, and also *Cym* 1.7.61–3 for the uncertain source of sadness. Burton, 3ff., contains an extensive account of 'Love melancholy', and Babb, 158, argues that there is a connection between 'amorous languor' and 'melancholy' – hence the tendency to diagnose Antonio's sadness as melancholy. There are only two clear examples of the association of melancholy with love in Shakespeare's plays: *LLL* 4.3.11–14 and *MA* 3.2.48–50.

1.1.13 fly . . . wings Cf. 3.2.120–2, where Portia's picture is described in the following way: 'Here, in her hairs, / The painter plays the spider and hath woven / A golden mesh t'entrap the hearts of men.' This is possibly a proleptic irony in that human imitations of nature are sometimes prone to its vicissitudes. The classic instance is Marlowe's Faustus, who, 'swollen with cunning of a self-conceit, / His waxen wings did mount above his reach, / And, melting, heavens conspir'd his overthrow' (*Dr Faustus*, Prologue, 20–2, in Marlowe, 146). See also Wallerstein, 37–40, for a concise description of the operation of mercantilism as 'only a short moment in time when a given core power can manifest *simultaneously* productive, commercial, and financial superiority *over all other core powers*' (Wallerstein, 39). Salarino suggests that Antonio may be worried about those vicissitudes that beset his trading ventures which are beyond human control, but the oblique reference to Icarus insinuates that the merchant may have over-extended his financial powers.

1.1.53 parrots . . . bagpiper Clearly the association here is with unrestrained festivity, although the appropriateness of the bagpipe as an instrument in this context may owe something to the melancholy drone against which the

392

chanter develops a varied pattern of sounds. The bagpipe was a wind instrument for all occasions, and was distinguished by a combination of chanter and drone(s), the latter providing a sustained single note (see Arnold, 1.140, and also Abraham,742–3. In *The Image of Ireland with a Discovery of Wood Karne* (1581), John Derricke notes the connection between the rebellious 'Wood Karne' and the sound of their bagpipes as they retreat:

> Now goes the foes to wracke,
> the karne apace do sweate:
> And bagge pipe then in stead of Trompe,
> doe lulle the backe retreate,
> Who eares the Bagpipe now,
> the pastyme is so hotte:
> Our valiant Captens will not cease
> till that the feeld be gotte.
>
> (STC 6734, sig. Gii^r)

This image of retreat to the sound of the bagpipe augments Salanio's perception of Antonio's withdrawal in the face of the investigation of the possible causes of his sadness.

1.1.113 *Mahood's suggestion that, if *that anything* is intended to refer to Gratiano's bawdy account of silence, then the sentence means 'Peace at last!' (Cam², 62) fails to account for the proliferation of meanings that are released at this precise moment in the action. Bevington, 184, glosses: 'Was all that talk about anything?' A number of editors follow Rowe's emendation, which makes this line a question: 'Is that anything now?' (sig. E4^v). Collier preserves the Q reading but repunctuates – 'It is that: – any thing now.' – signalling Antonio's weary agreement with the garrulous Gratiano, followed by a melancholy dismissal. It is conceivable that the compositor misread his copy, corrected his misreading but did not remove the initial 'It'. Stanley Wells concurs, but emends 'It' to 'Yet' on the grounds that 'the compositor may have misread a hastily written "yet" as "yt"' (see *TxC*, 324). On the other hand, the line may, in the final analysis, represent an idiom that a modern gloss cannot fully recover.

1.2.17–18 **brain . . . blood** Portia's identification of the brain in the process of constructing laws which regulate and control behaviour may be read in terms of the modern Freudian opposition between the 'superego' and the 'id' (Laplanche & Pontalis, 138). In its Elizabethan context *blood* refers, among other things, to the human body as such and its libidinal drives. Thus the opposition between the rational and the physiological, here reformulated as the opposition between the libidinal energy of youth and the prohibitions of old age, is common in Shakespearean texts; cf. *LLL* 5.2.72–3, 'The blood of youth burns not with such excess / As gravity's revolt to wantonness', and also *Ham* 1.3.116–17: 'When the blood burns, how prodigal the soul / Lends the tongue vows.' These axioms are underpinned by the theory of 'humours' which stated that the human body contained four 'humours', described by Burton as 'a liquid or fluent part of the body' – blood, phlegm, yellow bile (or choler) and black bile (or melancholy) – and these released 'spirits', 'a most subtle vapour, which is expressed from the blood, and the instrument of the soul, to perform all his actions' (Burton, 1.147–8).

1.2.43 **County Palatine** This office was also associated with the court of the German emperors (*OED* A). Mahood thinks that this dramatic character 'corresponds to the Elizabethan stereotype of the Spaniard' but that Shakespeare recalled that a Spanish suitor 'was to figure in the play' and consequently 'substituted this unspecific title which was held by various Hungarians, Poles, Germans and Burgundians' (Cam², 67). Pooler cites Johnson's suggestion that this was an allusion to Albertus a Lasco, a Polish Palatine who visited England in 1583 (Ard¹, 24), although Furness (26) is sceptical that an audience would have grasped the reference. The title could be used more generally, although in this instance it almost certainly depicts a figure of Teutonic origin. The title 'county' is generally thought to retain its final syllable from the Old French *counte* or Italian *conte*. The Q1 spelling is 'Palentine', and before 1611 there is no recorded instance of 'palatine' meaning 'of the palate', derived from the Latin *palatum* (*OED* A *adj.*), but Q2's 'Palatine' indicates that this was a variant spelling, suggesting that Portia may be hinting that as far as she is concerned the 'County Palatine' is unpalatable and hence not to her taste.

1.2.77 **Frenchman . . . surety** Clearly the Frenchman is a less attractive 'type' of Antonio, though Pooler cites Warburton, who claims that this alludes to the promises of assistance that the French customarily gave the Scots during this period (Ard¹, 27). The fact that the Frenchman also contracted separately for 'a box of the ear' that has gone unreciprocated extends the allusion to include reference to past famous English victories over the French; cf. Thomas Nashe: 'if you tell them what a glorious thing it is to haue *Henrie* the fifth represented on the Stage, leading the French King prisoner, and forcing both him and the Dolphin to sweare fealty' (Nashe, 1.213). But see Lodge's description of the relationship between 'merchant' and 'usurer', which suggests a form of collusion that may have been more common: 'In short space, our Marchant beginneth to looke after more assuraunce, and where to fore he was content with obligation, he now hunteth after statutes . . . The force whereof our youth considering not, so he haue foyson of money: the world to be short, at the last falleth out thus, both land, mony, & all possibiulities, either by father or friends, are incroched vpon, by this gentle master Scrape-peny, for that now our youth finding neither suretie nor similitude, by his flattering vsurer is laid vp close for escaping' (Lodge, 1.26).

1.2.126–9 **Come . . . door** Dover Wilson's suggestion that these lines date back to a 'pre-Shakespearean' version of the play (Cam¹, 128) is unconvincing. Brown cites *CE* 3.2.143–5 as an example of a rough couplet completing a prose speech, but this does not occur at the end of a scene;

his second example, at *1H4* 4.2.79–80, is a much better one (Ard², 21). The practice of reserving such devices for 'low-life' characters is not consistent in Shakespeare; see *R2* for examples of the formal closing of scenes generally with rhyming couplets irrespective of status (at *R2* 3.4.106–7 the final rhyming couplet is given to the Gardener). Similarly in *LLL* 4.1.146–7 a bathetic final couplet is given to Costard, but see also *LLL* 5.1.145 6, where a final couplet in a prose exchange is divided between Dull and Holofernes. Evidently couplets could be used for moments of formal closure in serious scenes, but in comic scenes they may be self-consciously undermined to achieve a humorous effect. 'Come, Nerissa. – Sirrah, go before' promises a formal rhyme, but, in the contrived awkwardness of what follows, Portia's utterance effectively *performs* the formal clumsiness of all of her suitors except one.

1.3.20 squandered Implied here may be an allusion to the New Testament parable of the Prodigal son (Luke, 15.13–32), which would cast the Jew in the role of patriarch now being asked to make provision for his successor, Antonio. This archetypal conflict between Judaism and Christianity, between the religion (and economic practices) of the Father (Old Testament) and of the Son (New Testament), provides a larger context for Antonio's later claim to the status of a Christ-like scapegoat (4.1.113–14). It also initiates a complex antagonism between the Jew who is the focus of racial hatred in Venice because he is alleged to be historically 'guilty', and the Christians who, in contemporary economic terms, regard themselves as being in danger of becoming his 'victims'. For a detailed account of the process of scapegoating see Girard, 1–12 and 112–24.

1.3.37–48 How . . . him The Jew's soliloquy is spoken in verse and as an 'aside' to the audience; Vickers, basing his observation upon a humanist conception of 'character', regards this as offering entry into an emotional inner life that elicits contradictory responses of sympathy and distrust (Vickers, 83). However, the duplicity that this soliloquy initiates has more in common with the practices of the Vice figure of earlier Tudor drama (see Weimann, *Tradition*, 153ff.). The Jew's comparatively unselfconscious temporary disruption of the illusion emphatically does not 'criticise from the audience's point of view', although he embodies the 'paradox of the vice', whose 'vicious' action retained its fascination, which was 'at once free of the fears and horrors of hell and also allied with them, a vitality that becomes both ugly and attractive because it has been branded as evil' (Weimann, *Tradition*, 153). Shakespeare's dramatic technique represents a complex innovation upon the figure of the stage Vice. See p. 48.

1.3.47 interest Lutheran economic thinking, and its theological implications, were available through texts such as Caesar's 1578 *General Discourse Against the Damnable Sect of Usurers*; see sig. B4ᵛ, and also sig. F3: 'if one is bounde to paie me twentie crownes at the Calendes of Maye, and doth not: if I through his disapointing mee runne into any daunger, as if I sould hauc paied the same to another at that very tyme, here is it meete that

equalitie be obserued, in that he gained by nine: but equalitie is not obserued, if he by my lending be made ritche, and I by his breaking daie bee
made poore: that is called Interest for the damage arising.' Brown cites
Death of Usury, sig. F3ᵛ: '*Vsurers* are ashamed at this day of their title . . .
they are ashamed of the name and word of *usurie*' (Ard², 24). In the tradition of Luther the term 'interest' was stigmatized, and as part of his own
justification for a financial practice detested by his adversaries the Jew
prefers *thrift* (46), since it suggests economical management of resources
and a careful expenditure of means (*OED* 3), but even this choice of alternatives may have laid him open to criticism, since the *OED* records an
obsolete meaning of 'thrift' to suggest euphemistically parsimony and
niggardliness. All of these terms deployed in the context of the play are
double-edged.

1.3.67 **Jacob . . . sheep** This is the second occasion on which Jacob has sought
to undermine a natural order, the first being when he, with the aid of his
mother Rebecca, usurps his elder brother Esau's position by persuading
his blind father Isaac that he is Esau. See Genesis, 27.13–23, where the
emphasis is upon Jacob's 'subtiltie' (27.35) and Esau's subservience.
Significantly Isaac predicts that Esau will be the beneficiary of the natural
properties of the earth: 'thy dwelling place shall be the fatnesse of the
earth, and of the dewe of heauen from above' (27.39). The Jew's deployment of this biblical anecdote designed to justify his practice of usury is
thus ironical in that it reinforces his 'unnatural' practice compared to
Antonio's Esau-like faith in the abundance of the natural world.

1.3.92 **breed** In *The Politics* Aristotle observes: 'Money-making then, as we
have said, is of two kinds; one which is necessary and acceptable, which
we may call administrative; the other, the commercial, which depends on
exchange, is justly regarded with disapproval, since it arises not from
nature but from men's dealings with each other. Very much disliked is the
practice of charging interest; and the dislike is fully justified, for interest
is a yield arising out of money itself, not a product of that for which
money was provided. Money was intended to be a means of exchange,
interest represents an increase in the money itself. We speak of it as a
yield, as of a crop or a little; for each animal produces its like and interest
is money produced out of money. Hence of all ways of getting wealth this
is the most contrary to nature' (Sinclair, 46). Aristotle's *Politics* appeared
in a translation by I.D. a year after Shakespeare's play was performed. See
also Francis Bacon, *Of Usury*, which recapitulates this position before
offering a more tolerant strategy (Bacon, 23–6). Bacon perceives the
practice of usury as a '*a concessum propter duritiem cordis* [a thing allowed
on account of the hardness of men's hearts]' (Bacon, 123), a sentiment
partially justified in Matthew, 19.8: 'He sayde vnto them, Moses, because
of the hardnesse of your hearts, suffered you to put away your wiues, but
from the beginning it was not so.' This concentration of biblical references
in these exchanges brings Old Testament Semitic lore and the New

Testament into conflict, with the Jew playing the role of the devilish 'tempter' and Antonio his Christ-like victim.

1.3.108 **gaberdine** See Nashe, *Pierce Penniless* (1592), for a description of a usurer's garments: 'At length (as Fortune served) I lighted vppon an old stradling Vsurer, clad in a damaske cassocke, edged with Fox fur, a paire of trunke slops, sagging down like a Shoomakers wallet, and a short thridbare gown on his backe, fac't with moatheaten budge; vpon his head he wore a filthy, course biggin [cap or hood (*OED* 2)], and next it a garnish of night-caps, which a sage butten-cap, of the forme of a cow-sheard, ouer spread very orderly: a fat chuffe it was, I remember, with a gray beard cut short to the stumpss, as though it were grimde, and a huge, woorme-eaten nose, like a cluster of grapes hanging downwardes' (Nashe, 1.162–3). In Leviticus, 16.4, Aaron prepares to offer a sacrifice by dressing in a 'holy linen coat', 'linen breeches', 'a linen girdle' and a 'linen mitre'. It is possible that there was a stage costume for the figure of the usurer/Jew; cf. Brown, who follows Reynolds, 175, in suggesting that the Jew's stage costume, like that of 'Turks, Italians, and other nationalities', was probably standard (Ard², 28).

1.3.109 **use** See *Death of Usury*, 8: 'when one comes to borrowe money, the *usurer* asketh him if he will giue vse for it, the borrower saith he will, this is so called, because the *usurer* depends vpon the borrower what he will giue'. Cf. also *MA* 2.1.261–2, 'he lent it me awhile, and I gave him use for it', and also *Son* 6.6: 'That use is not forbidden usury.' Sonnet 6.6 distinguishes between, on the one hand, the exchange that takes place as part of the mutual pleasure of sexual love – in that both lovers receive an 'excess' of what they give – and, on the other, 'usury' as an unequal, and potentially sterile, exchange that always favours the usurer. The Jew's *use* is scandalous partly because the exchange is in principle unequal, but also because, unlike Antonio at 1.1.135–9, the Jew will, on principle, separate himself from his money, thus condemning himself out of his own mouth as a false friend. See *OED* 10b, where 'use' carries a strong sexual connotation as in *Son* 4.13–14, 'Thy unused beauty must be tombed with thee, / Which us'd lives th'executor to be', and also *Oth* 5.2.69: 'That he hath – ud's death! – used thee.'

1.3.128–9 **take . . . friend** The concept begins with Aristotle's *Politics* in which he observes: 'Money was intended to be a means of exchange, interest represents an increase in the money itself. We speak of it as a yield, as of a crop or a litter; for each animal produces its like and interest is money produced out of money. Hence of all ways of getting wealth this is the most contrary to nature' (Sinclair, 46). Cf. 1.3.92 LN. See also Caesar, who notes the 'madnesse' of 'men in these doting daies of this worlde, that to a thyng frutlesse, barren, without seede, without life, will ascribe generation: and contrary to nature and common sense, will make that to engender, whiche beeyng without life by no waie can encrease' (Caesar, B1ᵛ).

1.3.144–7 **let . . . me** Blackstone's account of such a legal condition is illuminating. He observes that to the *simplex obigatio* 'there is generally a condition added, that if the obligor [i.e. Antonio] does some particular act, the
obligation shall be void, or else shall remain in full force: as payment of
rent; performance of covenants in a deed; or repayment of a principal sum
of money borrowed of the obligee [the Jew], with interest.' If this condition remains unperformed, 'the bond becomes forfeited, or absolute in
law, and charges the obligor while living' (Blackstone, 2.340). However,
Blackstone details an important corollary that is germane to the later
action of the play: 'If the condition of a bond be impossible at the time of
making it, or be to do a thing contrary to some rule of law that is merely
positive, or be uncertain, or insensible, the condition alone is void, and the
bond shall stand single and unconditional: for it is the folly of the obligor
to enter into such an obligation, from which he can never be released. If
it be to do a thing that is *malum in se*, the obligation itself is void: for the
whole is an unlawful contract, and the obligee shall take no advantage from
such a transaction. And if the condition be possible at the time of making
it, and afterwards becomes impossible by the act of God, the act of law, or
the act of the obligee himself, there the penalty of the obligation is saved:
for no prudence of or foresight of the obligor could guard against such a
contingency' (Blackstone, 2.340–1) If, as Blackstone's legal conditions
imply, the bond is legally impossible from the outset, then the issue
becomes one of the *ritualistic* value of the sacrifice of flesh, and the resultant tension is one between a *literal* reading of the obligation [the Jew] and
a *symbolic* one [Antonio].

2.1.32 **Lichas . . . dice** The episode in which Hercules and Lichas 'play at
dice' is the result of a complex narrative conflation. In *The Life of Romulus*
which appears in North's translation of *Plutarch's Lives*, Hercules is
invited to play at dice with 'The clerk or sexten of Hercules' temple'
(North, 1.92). The purpose of the game was, initially, to pass the time, but
the emboldened sexton 'did desire the god Hercules to play at dice with
him, with the condition that if he did win, Hercules should be bound to
send him good fortune: and if it were his luck to lose, then he promised
Hercules he would provide him a very good supper, and would besides
bring him a fair gentlewoman to lie withal' (North, 1.92–3). See also
Honigmann, 32, who first drew attention to this passage. In Morocco's
narration of this episode, the roles of Lichas and the sexton are conflated,
to suggest that Hercules' rage is provoked as a consequence of his being
thwarted in his amorous intentions by someone of lesser worth who, in the
original narrative, Hercules had vanquished by throwing into the sea.
Morocco's invocation of this narrative is directed towards an emphasis
upon Hercules' (Alcides') *rage* (35), and directs attention to another version of the Hercules/Lichas narrative that appears in Jasper Heywood's
translation of Seneca's *Hercules Furens* (1581). The goddess Juno enumerates Hercules' labours, and asks: 'Seekes thou a match t'Alcides yet? /

Thers none, except hymselfe: let him agaynst himselfe rebell' (Seneca, 1.11). In Seneca's version Lychus is a tyrant who attempts to destroy Hercules's family, and who 'of Alcides enmies all let Lycus be the last' (1.29). At the end of the fourth act Amphytrion offers himself as a sacrifice, and Hercules collapses, provoking the following question: 'Liv'ste thou? or els to death doth thee betake / The selfe same rage, that hath sent all thy famyly to death? / It is but sleepe, for to and fro doth goe and come his breath. / Let tyme bee had of quietnesse, that thus by sleepe and rest / Great force of his disease subdew'de, may ease his greeved brest' (1.42–3). The emphasis here is on the debilitating effects of Alcides' *rage*, suggesting that Shakespeare conflates two versions of the narrative in Morocco's speech.

2.1.44 **temple** In *MND* 4.1.179–80 the 'temple' is the place where marriage is solemnized: 'For in the temple, by and by, with us, / These couples shall eternally be knit' – although the Athenian setting of the play may suggest a pagan rather than a Christian ritual. Q1 prints 'temple', whereas Q2 prints 'Temple'; it is conceivable that since Morocco is about to enter into a legally binding agreement (see 40) the 'Temple' in Q2 may be thought of as a place similar to one of the Inns of Court (*OED sb.*[1] II.5). On the other hand, see *OED sb.*[1] I.1c for a more specific gloss, where the 'temple' is 'the seat of the Jewish worship of Jehovah' cleansed from the activities of merchants in the New Testament's Matthew, 21.12: 'And Jesus went into the Temple of God, and cast out them that sold & bought in the Temple, and ouerthrew the tables of the money changers, and the seates of them that sold Doues.'

2.2.25–6 **but . . . hard conscience** The joke is that the Clown confuses *conscience* with the desire for venal comfort and, consequently, conflates the worldly desires of the flesh with the demand of the 'spirit'. This distinction is clearly maintained in Nathaniel Woodes's *Conflict of Conscience* (1581), in the dialogue at 4.3 between the allegorical Philologus, Conscience and Sensuous Suggestion (Schell & Schuchter, 526–31). Moreover, afflictions of 'conscience' were also associated with the figure of Job; cf. William Perkins, *The Whole Treatise of The Cases of Conscience* (1606), 57: 'it must be considered, that the best seruants of God, haue beene in their times molested by the Deuill. Christ in his second temptation, was carried by the Deuill, from the wildernesse, to a wing of the Temple of Ierusalem. The children of Iob, were destroied by the Deuill, & he himselfe was filled with botches, and sores.'

2.2.57 **Fates and Destinies** The Clown's mock-heroic tone allows him to invoke and ridicule some of the classical and scholastic explanations of death, hence his reference at 57 to 'such odd sayings' and at 58 to 'such branches of learning'. His reduction of this complicated explanation to *plain terms* at 59 invokes a Christian explanation: *gone to heaven*. There are two levels of irony here. First, the explanation of a human existence replete with offspring is echoed in the Book of Job, 13.5ff.: 'The dayes of man surely are determined, the number of his moneths are knowen onely unto thee, thou hast appoynted him his boundes which hee cannot goe beyond . . . For if a tree be cut downe, there is some hope yet that it will sprowt, and shoote forth the branches againe.' This reinforces the comic play on Giobbe's name. Secondly, the joke lies in the fact that none of these explanations is true, since his son is alive.

2.2.96–7 **set . . . rest** Two further possible meanings may be hinted at in the Clown's utterance. In one sense, 'rest' may refer to taking up residence (*OED sb.*[1] 5); cf. *RJ* 5.3.109–10, 'O here / Will I set up my everlasting rest', and also Thomas Lodge's *Rosalynde or Euphues Golden Legacie* (1590): 'The next morne they lay long in bed, as wearied with the toyle of vnaccustomed trauaile: but assoone as they got vp, ALIENA resolued there to set vp her rest, and by the helpe of CORIDON swept a barga[]ne with his Landlord, and so became Mistres of the farme & the flocke' (Lodge, 1.50). Another meaning of 'rest' is a support used in the firing of an old heavy musket (*OED* II.11a). Partridge compares 'set up one's rest' to the practice of setting 'one's lance against the check that holds the butt of a tilter's lance when it is couched for the charge against the tilter's opponent' (Partridge, 181); this provides a further gloss on the Clown's name 'Lancelet' to indicate an action that will demonstrate his manly fortitude, hence the paradox involving 'resting' and 'not resting'.

2.5.18 **dream of money-bags** See also Thomas Nashe, *Terrors of the Night* (1594), for the more general connection between the activities of the day and dreaming: 'A Dreame is nothing els but the Eccho of our conceipts in the day' (Nashe, 1.356); and, further, 'Dreames to none are so fearfull, as to those who accusing priuate guilt expects mischiefe euerie hower for their merit. Wonderfull superstitious are such persons in obseruing euerie accident that befalls them; and that their superstition is as good as an hundred furies to torment them' (Nashe, 1.358). The Jew's fear anticipates the future in precisely the same way that in the later play, *Othello* (1604), Brabantio dreams the elopement of Desdemona with Othello at 1.1.140–1: 'This accident is not unlike my dream, / Belief of it oppresses me already.' Both the Jew and, later, Brabantio dream different versions of the radical challenge to patriarchal authority, where the emphasis of the former is upon the challenge to his monetary power. The ethos here is also reminiscent of Marlowe's *Jew of Malta*, where Barabas has 'one sole daughter whom I hold as dear / As Agamemnon did his Iphigen: / And all I have is hers' (*Jew of Malta*, 1.1.136–8), and where Abigail wishes 'gentle sleep' for her tormented father dispossessed of his wealth: 'Give charge to Morpheus that he may dream / A golden dream, and of the sudden walk, / Come and receive the treasure I have found' (2.1.36–8).

2.5.25–6 **falling . . . afternoon** Steve Sohmer has suggested privately that, in accordance with Venice's own calendar, the *More Veneto*, the year 1595 ended on 29 February 1596, and that Shrove Tuesday fell on Tuesday 27 February 1595/6. See also Sohmer, 17ff., and 105ff. for the confusion

of feast-days produced by the conflict between the Gregorian and Julian
calendars. However, see also Cheney, 142, where it is suggested that
Shrove Tuesday fell on 4 March and Easter Day on 20 April; see also
Cheney, 124, for the suggestion that in the leap year 1596 Shrove Tuesday
was on 23 February and Easter Day on 11 April. The Clown's reference
may, in its parodying of this debate, provide what Sohmer (26) calls a
'temporal marker' in that it may allude to an historical date, which, taken
in conjunction with other evidence, may point to 1596 as the possible date
of the play's composition, although this is not a temporal marker that we
can take literally (see pp. 20–1).

4.1.219 **Daniel** Daniel is also the name given to the figure of the judge in the
Tudor interlude *Nice Wanton* (1560) who resists the invitation to bribery
offered by the figure of Iniquity with the words: 'Should I be a briber?
Nay! He shall have the law, / As I owe to God, and the king obedience and
awe' (Wickham, 156). This is clearly what the Jew means by the epithet,
but also current was the narrative of Susannah and the Elders, from the
Apocrypha, referred to in Thomas Nashe's *The Return of the Renowned
Cavaliero Pasquill* (1589): 'Heerin I see the Churches case, is *Susannaes*
case: this accusation of incontinencie is framed against her by such as
haue sought to be incontinent with her themelues. Had *Susanna* prosti-
tuted her body to the Elders, her credit had neuer beene called into
Question by her accusers . . . but as the storie saith, that *Daniell* was raysed
by GOD to acquite her, and conuince euery scatterer of false reports, I
thinke before I end, Signor *Pasquill* of Englande wyll prooue the man that
must sette a gagge in the mouth of *Martin* the great, and cut vp an
Anatomie of all his knauerie' (Nashe, 1.91–2). The Old Testament
prophet Daniel was a renowned interpreter of two of King
Nebuchadnezzar's dreams; see Daniel, 2.26, 'Then answered the king and
sayde to Daniel, whose name was Baltassar, Art thou able to shew me the
dreame which I haue seene, and the interpretation thereof?', and also
Daniel, 4.18: 'This is the dreame that I king Nabuchodnosor haue seene:
therefore thou, O Baltassar, declare the interpretation thereof for so much
as all the wise men of my kingdome are not able to shewe what it meaneth:
but thou canst do it, for the spirit of the holy god is in thee.' Ironically,
however, it was to the prophet Daniel that the coming of Christ, and
hence the beginnings of Christianity, were revealed (see Daniel, 12.1–13,
and also Calvin's commentary on the book of Daniel (Calvin, *Commentaries*,
5.678–9).

APPENDIX 1

CAST LIST

The narrowing down of the date of *The Merchant of Venice* to the period 1596–7 suggests that it was one of the last plays to be performed at Burbage's established playhouse, The Theatre, or that it was one of the first at the newly leased Curtain. There is no way of knowing what connection there might have been between the 'urban' concerns of Shakespeare's play, the Chamberlain's Men's financial difficulties, and James Burbage's intention to secure a playing space at Blackfriars, within the city, in the months leading up to his death in February 1597 (Gurr, 283, 285). Evidently the play appeared during a period of intense business activity for the Chamberlain's Men, a company whose 'principall Comoedians' were, according to the list supplied by Ben Jonson in 1616, describing the actors who participated in the 1598 production of *Every Man in His Humour*: Shakespeare, Augustine Philips, Henry Condell, William Slye, Will Kempe, Richard Burbage, John Heminges, Thomas Pope, Christopher Beeston and John Duke (Jonson, 3.403). Richard Cowley was also a member of the company, 'because he is named as playing Verges against Kemp's Dogberry in the text of *Much Ado About Nothing*', as was John Sincler, who was 'evidently a distinctly skinny player'. According to Andrew Gurr, Sincler's roles range from Nym and Slender in *2 Henry IV*, *Henry V* and *The Merry Wives of Windsor*, to Shift in Jonson's *Every Man Out of His Humour* and Nano the dwarf in *Volpone* (Gurr, 280).

Will Kempe almost certainly played the role of the Clown in the *Merchant of Venice*, and it is possible that, given the characteristics of the Dogberry–Verges coupling in the later *Much Ado*, Richard Cowley took the role of Old Giobbe. The difficult decision might well have been who to cast as Antonio, and who as the Jew. James Burbage might reasonably have been expected to take the role of Antonio, but, if the role of the Jew was intended to be comic, would it be possible that an actor such as John Sincler took the role of Shylock? If he did, then it would have been a more substantial role than any of those that Sincler had played up to this point (cf. Ringler, 112). Ringler argues that 'We should start with the major speaking parts, and seldom or never assign more than one role to an actor with a large number of lines to memorise' (120), although he goes on to suggest that the actor who played Theseus in *Midsummer Night's Dream* in 1.1 could have doubled as the Faerie in 2.1 (132). On matters of change of costume, Ringler cites Jessica's transformation at the end of 2.5; the change from 2.5 to 2.6.26 takes 'about a minute of acting time, for her costume change' (120–1). Ringler continues: 'Changes involving a complete change of identity probably took somewhat longer, but not much longer. Elizabethan actors apparently prided themselves on being quick-change artists, and like some actors today – such as Alec Guinness – delighted in playing multiple roles' (121).

T.J. King notes that the *Merchant of Venice* requires some ten actors to play twelve 'principal male roles' (King, 84–5), and 'three boys to play three principal female roles'. He notes that thirteen actors speak 98 per cent of the lines, and he goes on to observe that 'Six men can play seven small speaking parts and thirteen mutes' and that 'three boys play three mute attendants on Portia' (84–5). King proceeds to arrange these results in two tables – 49 (184–5) and 80 (254). Of the major speaking parts in the *Merchant of Venice* 'Shylock–Jew' has a total of 335 lines and he appears in five scenes; Bassanio, who appears in six scenes, speaks 329 lines, and Antonio, who also appears in six scenes, has 188 lines, some 14 lines more than Lorenzo (who appears in seven scenes) and some 19 lines less than Gratiano, who appears in eight scenes (184–5). Aside from the obvious suggestion that in this play the character who lends his name to the title speaks a little less than half the lines of his adversary, we may note that the largest number of lines is divided between six actors, and each of the totals is modest compared with roles in other plays. The boy actor who played Portia has the largest number of lines (557) and appears in some nine scenes. If we accept Ringler's claim that Elizabethan actors prided themselves on taking on multiple roles, then each of the six principal roles in this play might, when available, take on other minor roles. The two that are of particular interest are those of the Jew and Morocco (who speaks a total of 103 lines and who appears in only two scenes). The nature of the connection arises as a consequence of a chance remark from Salarino at 3.1.34–5: 'There is more difference between thy flesh and hers than between jet and ivory.' This may, of course, be a metaphorical utterance, but the various associations of the Jew with 'the devil' indicate that Shylock may indeed have been 'black'. This leads to the speculation that Shylock and Morocco may have been doubled, a practice that would require only one quick change, near the end of 1.3, where Shylock, dressed in a 'gaberdine' or loose garment, leaves the stage some five lines before Antonio and Bassanio, and Morocco appears '*all in white*' at the beginning of the next scene (2.1). What is common to both is the possibility of a 'black face' that brings together on the stage the 'Moor' and the Jew as types of outsider, a practice worthy of Salarino's punning reference.

The following cast list, with suggestions for doubling, and based on the availability of actors to fulfil more than one role during actual performance, is necessarily speculative. But, in addition to Shakespeare having in mind particular actors for particular roles, the problem of 'the three Sallies' may well have arisen as a suggestion for doubling. The 'three Sallies' confusion arises between 3.1 and 3.2. Clearly from a speech prefix at sigs E2–2ᵛ '*Solanio*' and '*Salari.*' indicate the presence of the two familiar 'Sallies' in 3.1. The '*man from* Anthonio' who enters at sig. E2ᵛ could well have been the actor who played Lorenzo (who may also have doubled as 'Leonardo' in 2.2). Either of the two 'Sallies' could have doubled as Salerio in 3.2, but the problem arises in 3.3 where the 'Salerio' who came from Venice in 3.2 is back in Venice in 3.3. The speech prefix '*Sol.*' on sig. F4^r prompts the plausible speculation that the doubling of this role was anticipated, and that the name 'Salerio' in the speech heading at 3.3 may well have referred to the actor who played the roles of both Salerio and Salanio. It is conceivable that, as with the anticipation of which actors might take certain roles, the manuscript that lies behind the *Merchant of Venice* might also have contained information concerning doubling of some of the parts.

CASTING CHART

Adult actor	1.1	1.2	1.3	2.1	2.2	2.3	2.4	2.5	2.6	2.7	2.8
1	Antonio		Antonio						Antonio		Salarino
2	Salarino	X (Serv)		X			Salarino		Salarino		Salanio
3	Salanio			X			Salanio		X	X (?)	
4	Bassanio		Bassanio		Bassanio						
5	Lorenzo			X	X (Leonardo)		Lorenzo		Lorenzo		
6	Gratiano			X	Gratiano		Gratiano		Gratiano		
7			Jew					Jew			
8				Morocco						Morocco	
9					Clown	Clown	Clown	Clown			
10					Old Giobbe				X	X	
Boy actor											
1		Portia		Portia						Portia	
2		Nerissa		Nerissa						X	
3	X (?)			X (?)		Jessica					

Adult actor	2.9	3.1	3.2	3.3	3.4	3.5	4.1	4.2	5.1
1	X			Antonio			Antonio		Antonio
2		Salarino			X Balthazar (?)		X		X (Messenger)
3		Salanio	X Salerio	Salanio			X		X
4	X		Bassanio				Bassanio		Bassanio
5	X Messenger	X Servingman (?)	X		Lorenzo	Lorenzo			Lorenzo
6	X						Gratiano		Gratiano
7		Jew	Jew	Jew			Jew		X
8	Arragon		X				X		X
9			X (?)			Clown	X		Clown
10	X	Tubal (?)		X Jailer (?)			X Duke (?)		
Boy actor									
1	Portia				Portia		Portia	Portia	Portia
2	Nerissa				Nerissa		Nerissa	Nerissa	Nerissa
3					Jessica	Jessica	X		Jessica

APPENDIX 2

TYPE SHORTAGES

There were type shortages throughout the setting of Q1 involving, in particular, roman capital 'W' sorts and roman capital 'I' sorts, and occasionally lower-case 'w' sorts. In those parts of the text where the figure of Shylock appears, the variation of speech prefix forms was determined by the availability of italic capital 'I' sorts; where there was a clear demand, or where they were in short supply, then the speech prefix '*Shy(l).*' was set. In the case of the '*Launcelet*'/'*Clown(e)*' variation, both prefixes may well have been in the manuscript from which Q1 was set, but it is clear that the role was intended for the resident 'clown' of the company, Will Kempe. For a fuller account of the bibliographical peculiarities of the *Merchant of Venice* Q1, see Brown, 'Compositors' (27–32), and R. Kennedy (191–202).

Type shortages	A1	A2ᵛ	A3	A4ᵛ		A1ᵛ	A2	A3ᵛ	A4
Comp.	X	Y	Y	Y		Y	Y	Y	Y
Roman cap W	X	X		X			X	X (1 VVsubstit.)	X
U. case W substit. vv	X	X		X			X	X	X
L. case w sub vv									
Roman cap I									
Italic cap I substit. Y/y									
Iew(e)									
Shy(l)									
Launcelet									
Clown(e)									

Type shortages	B1	B2ᵛ	B3	B4ᵛ		B1ᵛ	B2	B3ᵛ	B4		C1	C2ᵛ
Comp.	Y	Y	Y	Y		Y	Y	Y	Y		X	X
									*			
Roman cap W			X						X			
U. case W substit. vv			X (VV sub)						X			
L. case W substit. vv							X					
Roman cap I	X	X	X	X (top)		X	X	X	X			
Italic cap I or substit. Y/y/i	X	X	X	X (top)		X	X	X	X			X (ile)
Iew(e)												
Shy(l)		X	X	X				X	X			
Launcelet												
Clown(e)											X	

Type shortages	D4v	D3	D2v	D1		C4	C3v	C2	C1v		C4v	C3
Comp.	Y	Y	Y	Y		X	X	X	X		X	X
	*	*	*	*								
Roman cap W	X	X	X									
U. case W substit. vv	X	X	X (VV substit.)									
L. case W substit. vv				X								X
Roman cap I	X	X	X	X		X	X				X	X
Italic cap I or substit. Y/y/i	X (substit. yf (1))	X	X	X		X	X				X (substit. Y (2))	X
Iew(e)				X							X	
Shy(l)								X				
Launcelet									X			
Clown(e)				X		X					X	X

Type shortages	D1^v	D2	D3^v	D4		E1	E2^v	E3	E4^v		E1^v	E2
Comp.	Y	Y	Y	Y		X	X	X	X		X	X
	*		*	*								
Roman cap W	X	X	X	X		X			X			
U. case W substit. vv		X (top)	X	X		X			X			
L. case W substit. vv	X		X									
Roman cap I				X		X		X	X		X	X
Italic cap I or substit. Y/y/i				X		X		X	X		X	X
Iew(e)												
Shy(l)							X					X
Launcelet								X				
Clown(e)												

Type shortages	E3ᵛ	E4	F1	F2ᵛ	F3	F4ᵛ		F1ᵛ	F2	F3ᵛ	F4
Comp.	X	X	Y	Y	Y	Y		Y	Y	Y	Y
	*	*	*	*	*	*		*	*	*	*
Roman cap W	X	X	X	X		X		X		X	
U. case W substit. vv	X	X	X	X		X		X		X	
L. case W substit. vv											
Roman cap I	X		X	X	X	X			X	X	X
Italic cap I or substit. Y/y/i	X		X		X	X			X	X	X
Iew(e)											X
Shy(l)											
Launcelet											
Clown(e)											

413

Type shortages	G1	G2^{v}	G3	G4^{v}		G1^{v}	G2	G3^{v}	G4		H1	H2^{v}
Comp.	X	X	X	X		X	X	X	X		Y	Y
	*	*	*	*		*		*	*		*	*
Roman cap W	X		X			X			X			X
U. case W substit. vv	X		X			X		X	X			X
L. case W substit. vv	X			X			X		X		X	
Roman cap I	X		X	X				X	X		X	X
Italic cap I or substit. Y/y/i	X		X (ile)	X				X	X		X	X
Iew(e)				X				X	X		X	X
Shy(l)												
Launcelet												
Clown(e)		X				X	X					

Type shortages	H3	H4ᵛ	H1ᵛ	H2	H3ᵛ	H4		I1	I2ᵛ	I3	I4ᵛ
Comp.	Y	Y	Y	Y	Y	Y		X	X	X	X
	*	*	*	*	*	*		*	*	*	*
Roman cap W	X		X			X			X	X	X
U. case W substit. vv	X		X						X	X	X
L. case W substit. vv			X					X			
Roman cap I	X	X		X	X	X		X	X	X	X
Italic cap I or substit. Y/y/i	X	X		X	X	X		X	X	X	X
Iew(e)	X										
Shy(l)		X	X	X	X	X					
Launcelet											
Clown(e)											

Type shortages	I1ᵛ	I2	I3ᵛ	I4		K1	K1ᵛ	K2
Comp.	X	X	X	X		X	X	X
	*	*	*	*		*	*	*
Roman cap W	X		X			X	X	X
U. case W substit. vv	X		X			X	X	X
L. case W substit. vv								
Roman cap I	X		X	X		X	X	X
Italic cap I or substit. Y/y/i	X		X	X		X (ile (2))	X	X
Iew(e)								
Shy(l)								
Launcelet								
Clown(e)		X						

APPENDIX 3

THE QUARTO OF 1600, ITS INSTABILITIES, AND EDITORIAL PRACTICE

Printed playtexts are unstable documents bearing the marks of every agency involved in their production, from the author and the playhouse, through to the printer and publisher. Editors search out and distinguish between the different kinds of evidence available from these sources, and they base their decisions to emend texts upon the conclusions they draw from this evidence. *The Merchant of Venice* is a comparatively clean text, first printed in quarto form in 1600 (Q1), then again in 1619 (Q2) as one of the notorious Pavier quartos, the title-page of which is erroneously dated 1600 (see Fig. 17), and again in the 1623 Folio. Q1 is thought to derive from Shakespeare's foul papers (Ard², xx; Cam², 169–72; Oxf¹), and Q2 and F are now generally agreed to have been set from variously annotated copies of Q1.[1] Roberts entered the play in the Stationers' Register on 22 July 1598 as 'a booke of *the Marchaunt of Venyce or otherwise called the Iewe of Venyce*' but on 28 October 1600 'A booke called *the booke of the merchant of Venyce*' was entered by Thomas Hayes with the 'Consent of master Robertes'. Whether the delay in printing was due to the absence of permission from the Chamberlain's Men is not certain, although editors have

---

1 Greg, 'False dates', 115–18; see also Ard², xviii. Until the twentieth century the order of Q1 and Q2 was reversed, with Furness's New Variorum edition of the play (1888) and Charles Pooler's original Arden edition opting for the primacy of the Pavier quarto. However, editors are now agreed that Q1 is authoritative and that Q2 is one of a group of ten quartos printed for Thomas Pavier in 1619 by William Jaggard, to whom Roberts had sold his business in 1608.

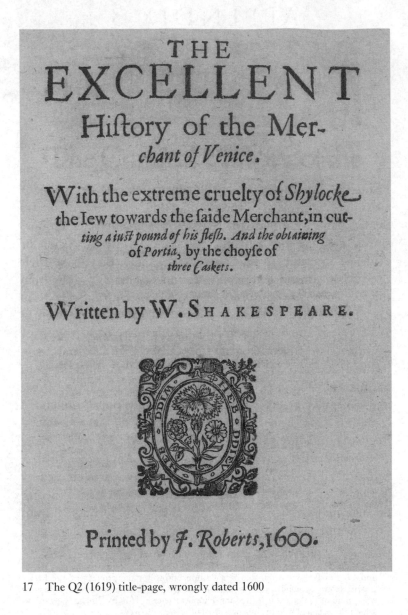

THE
EXCELLENT
History of the Mer-
chant of *Venice*.

With the extreme cruelty of *Shylocke*
the Iew towards the saide Merchant, in cutting a iust pound of his flesh. And the obtaining
of *Portia*, by the choyse of
three *Caskets*.

Written by W. SHAKESPEARE.

Printed by *J. Roberts*, 1600.

17   The Q2 (1619) title-page, wrongly dated 1600

speculated upon Roberts's motives (see Ard[1], viii–ix). Brown conjectures that Roberts had temporarily secured a manuscript from the playhouse in 1598 and entered it on the understanding that he would not print the play until further permission was granted. The apparent repetition, 'A booke called the booke of . . .' in Hayes's entry, he takes to indicate that the publisher had secured a copy of the promptbook which he then presented, with Roberts's permission, to the Stationers' Company' (xvii–xviii). W.W. Greg was certain that 'the copy submitted was the actual promptbook from the theatre' (Greg, *Editorial*, 106), but although some of the stage directions contained in Q1 suggest a theatrical source there are others that were thought to have derived from Shakespeare himself (Greg, *Editorial*, 123; see also Ard[2], xiv–xvii). The wording of Roberts's initial entry yields two conflicting motives: either that he had secured a manuscript, possibly foul papers, that antedated the promptbook, with the intention of securing the right to print the play at a later date; or that this was an attempt to safeguard the actors' interests against the possibility of unauthorized publication while the play was in performance (Mahood, 168). A third possibility is that Hayes's 'copie' was the actual 'booke' that Roberts had already printed, and that was subsequently marked up for the compositor, probably Jaggard's Compositor B, who set Q2 and who made some 3,200 minor changes to his copy.[1] Whatever the reasons for these two entries in the Stationers' Register, and for both the misdating of Q2 and the interval before its appearance, Q2 (1619) was evidently set from an annotated copy of Q1 (1600) in which sig. G4[r] was in the corrected state, and F (1623) from a copy in which this page was in an uncorrected state (see Figs 18 and 19).[2]

---

1 See D.F. McKenzie, 'Compositor B's role in *The Merchant of Venice* Q2 (1619)', *Studies in Bibliography*, 12, ed. Fredson Bowers (Charlottesville, 1959), 75–90, esp. 75, where McKenzie refers to B's 'handling of printed copy in 1619'.
2 *TxC*, 323ff. Wells misidentifies the page as sig. G4[v].

18 Q1 (1600) with uncorrected sigs G3ᵛ–G4ʳ

Of particular relevance to editorial practice is the perceived instability of a number of speech prefixes in Q1. After comparing Q1 with other texts that James Roberts printed, Richard Kennedy concludes that the two compositors who set Q1, known as X and Y, variously exhausted their supplies of type, in particular, italic capital '*I*' and roman capital 'I' types, and were forced, in Y's case, to depart from the copy spelling '*Iew(e)*'. Compositor Y was responsible for setting sheets A

19 Q1 (1600) with corrected sigs G3ᵛ–G4ʳ

(minus the title-page), B, D, F and H, and he began setting the outer forme of sheet B[1] with an exhausted supply of roman capital 'I' types, forcing him to substitute italic '*I*' types. He began by setting the speech prefix '*Iew(e)*' but the depletion

1 In quarto printing compositors setting was by formes: the inner forme comprising pages 2 (sig. 1ᵛ), 3 (sig. 2), 6 (sig. 3ᵛ) and 7 (sig. 4), and the outer forme comprising pages 1 (sig. 1), 4 (sig. 2ᵛ), 5 (sig. 3) and 8 (sig. 4ᵛ). For a full description of the process, see Gaskell, 78–117, 89 and 106.

of roman capital 'I' sorts, along with that of roman capital 'W' sorts, forced him to substitute a capital 'Y', a lower-case 'vv' and a lower-case 'i' at the beginning of lines B2ᵛ21, B2ᵛ27 and B2ᵛ28. At B2ᵛ30 he substituted the speech prefix '*Shyl.*' but continued to substitute italic capital '*I*' for roman capitals for the remainder of the forme until he obtained a supply of Roman sorts at around B4ᵛ2 (Gaskell, 191–4).[1] Kennedy pursues the general pattern of shortages throughout the quarto and in the work of both compositors, explaining the variations in speech prefixes to which this led, and the occasional substitutions of 'Y' for 'I' and of lower-case sorts at the beginning of verse lines, as a practical compositorial solution to the problem of depleted type-cases and the attendant possibility of concurrent printing (Gaskell, 194) that has little bearing on the manuscript source itself. The implications of this for an editor of the play is clear: that Compositor Y began by following his copy and setting the speech prefix '*Iew(e)*' and did so throughout where his supply of italic capital '*I*' types permitted him to do so. He departed from that practice whenever his supply became depleted. In so far as we can speculate upon Shakespeare's intention from these details, they point inescapably towards the conclusion that the dramatic character that we have come to know as Shylock was designated throughout the manuscript by the speech prefix 'Jew'. As a further disincentive to dismissing this textual instability as evidence of an unsystematic compositorial pragmatism, the following line at sig. H1ʳ34, on a page set by Compositor Y in which there are numerous substitutions of italic capital '*I*' sorts from H1ʳ10 onwards, should act as a caution (see Drakakis, '*Jew*', 105–21):

> *Iew. Shylocke* is my name.

1   A cursory glance at sig. B2ʳ of Q2 (1619) indicates a severe shortage of roman capital 'I' types before the entry of the Jew, necessitating an earlier response than in Q1 (see Appendix 2). The issue does not arise in F (1623), where one of the three compositors responsible began by setting '*Shy.*' (Gaskell, 163) but designated '*Iew.*' in the catchword and resorted to the latter on three occasions immediately following (166). See Hinman, 2.423–6, for a summary of the setting of Quire O.

This line escapes even Q2's practice of normalizing speech prefixes, and it also remains in F. This is anything but the case of either dramatist or compositor failing to make up his mind.[1] Rather, it points to something much more complex and it challenges what we may call, following Jonathan Goldberg, the traditional scene of Shakespearean writing where ideas are thought to precede representation (Goldberg, *Writing*, 287). It prompts the question of what might have driven Shakespeare to write '*Iewe*' at the same time as he named the stereotype '*Shylocke*'. For the moment, it is sufficient to say that the present edition reinstates a tension that these variant speech prefixes disclose and that editors and commentators have long overlooked.

A second consequence of type shortages during the setting of Q1, this time involving Compositor X, but, as in the case of the '*Iew(e)*'/'*Shy(l)*.' substitution, also involving Compositor Y, emerges in relation to the variant speech prefix '*Clo(wne)*'/'*Laun(celet)*'.[2] The shortages of italic capital '*C*' necessitated the alteration of the manuscript '*Clo(wne)*' to '*Laun(celet)*', and here again the editorial consequences are significant. It is likely that Shakespeare thought primarily of the role rather than the character, and, since Lancelet would probably have been played by Will Kempe, the resident clown in the Chamberlain's Men, it was clearly the actor's capabilities that motivated the dramatist's imagination. Kempe's name and also his role, Andrew ('merry andrew'), both appear in another Shakespeare quarto of 1600 set from authorial manuscript, *Much Ado About Nothing*,[3] and this offers us a unique insight into the fundamentally collaborative nature of Shakespeare's own writing

---

1   Cf. Barton, 88, where she notes that in the case of 'Iobbe'/'Gobbo' 'it seems to have taken [Shakespeare] some time to make up his mind.'
2   R. Kennedy, 199ff. Brown (Ard[7], xvii, n. 4) doubted the claim originally made by Dover Wilson (Cam[1], 95) that the prefix '*Clowne*' arose from a shortage of italic capital *L* sorts, but he took the matter no further.
3   Humphreys, 75, and 187–8, where at 4.2.4 the speech prefix is '*Andrew*' rather than '*Dogberry*', and at 4.2.9 and 12, 24, 29, 33, 38, 41 and 47, where the speech prefix is '*Ke(mp)*'.

practice. The choice of 'Clown' for this edition restores to view a dynamic ambivalence inherent in the opposition between what Robert Weimann has identified as theatrical presentation and a 'new self-contained mode of impersonation' (Weimann, *Author's Pen*, 169–70), from which all but one of the previous editions of the *Merchant of Venice* have sought to cleanse the text.

A third consequence of type shortage in Q1 affects the treatment of the character of the Clown's father, 'Old Gobbo', which takes us further than Kennedy's conclusions (see Figs 20 and 21). Dover Wilson (Cam[1]) thought that the name should have been 'Giobbe', the Italian form of our English 'Job', but that the '*old Gobbo*' of the stage direction at sig. C1[v] in Q1–2 'seems to be a "correction" of the original by someone not unacquainted with Italian' (Cam[1], 99–100).[1] Brown (Ard[2]) conjectured further that the initial repetition of the Clown's patronymic '*Iobbe*' at sigs C1–1[v] in Q1 (normalized to '*Gobbo*' in Q2) indicated that 'Shakespeare intended to use the Italianized form of Job' (Ard[2], xxii),[2] and he dismisses E.K. Chambers's suggestion that the dramatic character of Old Gobbo may have been inspired by a malicious allusion to St Gobbo in letters of 1596 'to an unnamed enemy of the Earl of Essex, who can only be the hunch-backed Robert Cecil' (quoted in Ard[2], xxii). Again, Brown pursued the matter no further, but Mahood, following Dover Wilson in assuming 'Gobbo' to be accurate, ascribes the inconsistency to Shakespeare's failure to tidy up his text (Cam[2], 171). We cannot rule out the possibility of either a covert reference to Cecil or

1 Dover Wilson also draws attention to an observation by the nineteenth-century commentator, Karl Elze, that the 'Gobbo' reference might be traced to the Gobbo di Rilato in Venice, 'a stone figure which serves as a supporter to the granite pillar of about a man's height, from which the laws of the Republic were proclaimed' (Cam[1], 100, n. 1).

2 The title-page of Santi Marmochini's vernacular Italian translation of *La Bibbia* (Venice, 1545) refers to '*Et accio l'opera sia piu perfetta quanto alla dispta di Iobbe co suoi amici*' and as late as 1760 Italian versions of the Book of Job described their contents as '*Ill libro di Giobbe*'. Indeed, in the *Encliclope dia Italiana*, revised by Mario Cosati, Paulo Valentini and Pasquale Caropreso, vol. 17 (Rome, 1951), 150–2, 'Giobbe' is described as '*Vulgata Job*' – that is, '*Nomo del personaggio principali d'un libro della Bibbia e titolo del libro stresso*' (150).

a mischievous pun, but it is clear from the initial spelling that the Italianate *Iobbe/Giobbe* was uppermost in Shakespeare's mind from the outset. Old *Iobbe* began as a vernacular, low-life parody of the biblical Job, whose Italian spelling was unfamiliar to Roberts's compositor, who himself was beset with problems of type shortage that he solved in a manner that has since

The comicall Historie of

...or good *Launcelet Iobbe*, vse your legges, take the start, runne away, my conscience sayes no; take heede honest *Launcelet*, take heede honest *Iobbe*, or as afore-saide honest *Launcelet Iobbe*, doe not runne, scorne running with thy heeles; well, the most corragious fiend bids me packe, *fia* sayes the fiend, away sayes the fiend, for the heauens rouse vp a braue minde sayes the fiend, and runne; well, my conscience hanging about the necke of my heart, sayes very wisely to mee: my honest friend *Launcelet* beeing an honest mans sonne, or rather an honest womans sonne, for indeede my Father did something smacke, something grow to; he had a kinde of taste; well, my conscience sayes *Launcelet* bouge not, bouge sayes the fiend, bouge not sayes my conscience, conscience say I you counsaile well, fiend say I you counsaile well, to be rulde by my conscience, I should stay with the Iewe my Maister, (who God blesse the marke) is a kinde of deuill; and to runne away from the Iewe I should be ruled by the fiend, who sauing your reuerence is the deuill himselfe: certainely the Iewe is the very deuill incarnation, and in my conscience, my conscience is but a kinde of hard conscience, to offer to counsaile mee to stay with the Iewe; the fiend giues the more friendly counsaile: I will runne fiend, my heeles are at your commaundement, I will runne.

Enter old Gobbo with a basket.

Gobbo. Maister yong-man, you I pray you, which is the way to Maister Iewes?
Launcelet. O heauens, this is my true begotten Father, who being more then sand blinde, high grauell blinde, knowes me not, I will try confusions with him.
Gobbo. Maister yong Gentleman, I pray you which is the way to Maister Iewes.
Launcelet. Turne vp on your right hand at the next turning, but at the next turning of all on your left; marry at the very next turning turne of no hand, but turne downe indirectly to the Iewes house.
Gobbo. Be Gods sonties twill be a hard way to hit, can you tell me

the Merchant of Venice.

mee whether one *Launcelet* that dwels with him, dwell with him or no.
Launcelet. Talke you of yong Maister *Launcelet*, marke mee nowe, nowe will I raise the waters; talke you of yong Maister *Launcelet*.
Gobbo. No Maister fir, but a poore mans Sonne, his Father though I say't is an honest exceeding poore man, and God bee thanked well to liue.
Launce. Well, let his Father be what a will, wee talke of yong Maister *Launcelet*.
Gob. Your worships friend and *Launcelet* fir.
Launce. But I pray you *ergo* olde man, *ergo* I beseech you, talke you of yong Maister *Launcelet*.
Gob. Of *Launcelet* an pleafe your maistership.
Launce. Ergo Maister *Launcelet*, talke not of maister *Launcelet* Father, for the young Gentleman according to fates and destenies, and such odd sayings, the fifters three, and such branches of learning, is indeede deceased, or as you would say in plaine termes, gone to heauen.
Gobbo. Marry God forbid, the boy was the very staffe of my age, my very prop.
Launcelet. Doe I looke like a cudgell or a houell post, a staffe, or a prop? doe you know me Father,
Gobbo. Alacke the day, I knowe you not yong Gentleman, but I pray you tell mee, is my boy G O D rest his soule aliue or dead.
Launcelet. Doe you not know me Father.
Gobbo. Alacke sir I am sand blind, I know you not.
Launcelet. Nay, in deede if you had your eyes you might fayle of the knowing mee: it is a wise Father that knowes his owne childe. Well, olde man, I will tell you newes of your sonne, giue mee your blessing, trueth will come to light, murder cannot bee hidde long, a mannes Sonne may, but in the ende trueth vvill out.
Gobbo. Pray you sir stand vp, I am sure you are not *Launcelet* my boy.

C 2   *Launce.*

20 Q1 (1600) with the speech prefix *Gobbo/Gob* at sigs C1ᵛ–C2ʳ

425

The comicall Historie of

Launce. Pray you let's haue no more fooling, about it, but giue mee your blessing: I am *Launcelet* your boy that was, your sonne that is, your child that shall be.

Gob. I cannot thinke you are my sonne.

Launce. I know not what I shall thinke of thar: but I am *Launce-let* the Iewes man, and I am sure *Margerie* your wife is my mo-ther.

Gob. Her name is *Margerie* in deede, ile be sworne if thou bee *Launcelet*, thou art mine owne flesh and blood: Lord worshipt might he be, what a beard hast thou got; thou hast got more haire on thy chinne, then Dobbin my phill horse hate on his taile.

Launce. It should seeme then thar Dobbins taile growes back-ward. I am sure hee had more haire of his taile then I haue of my face when I loft faw him.

Gob. Lord how art thou chang'd: how doost thou and thy Ma-fter agree, I haue brought him a present; how gree you now?

Launce. Well, well, but for mine owne part as I haue fet vp my reft to runne away, fo I will not reft till I haue runne some ground: my Maifter's a very Iewe, giue him a prefent, giue him a halter, I am famifht in his feruice. You may tell euery finger I haue with my ribs: Father I am glad you are come, giue me your prefent to one Maifter *Baffanio*, who in deede giues rare newe Lyueries, if I ferue not him, I will runne as farre as God has any ground. O rare fortune, heere comes the man, to him Father, for I am a Iewe if I ferue the Iewe any longer.

Enter Baffanio with a follower or two.

Baff. You may doe fo, but let it be fo hafted that fupper be rea-dy at the fartheft by fiue of the clocke : fee thefe Letters deliuered, put the Lyueries to making, and defire *Gratiano* to come anone to my lodging.

Launce. To him Father.

Gob. God bleffe your worfhip.

Baff. Gramercie, wouldft thou ought with me.

Gobbo. Heere's my fonne fir, a poore boy.

Launce. Not a poore boy fir, but the rich Iewes man that would fir as my Father fhall fpecifie.

Gob.

the Merchant of Venice.

Gob. He hath a great infection fir, as one would fay to ferue.

Lan. Indeede the fhort and the long is, I ferue the Iewe, & haue a defire as my Father fhall fpecifie.

Gob. His Maifter and he (fauing your worfhips reuerence) are fcarce catercofins.

Lau. To be briefe, the very truth is, that the Iewe hauing done me wrong, dooth caufe me as my Father being I hope an old man fhall frunfie vnto you.

Gob. I haue heere a difh of Doues that I would beftow vpon your worfhip, and my fute is,

Lau. In very briefe, the fute is imperinent to my felfe, as your worfhip fhall know by this honeft old man, and though I fay it, though old man, yet poore man my Father.

Baff. One fpeake for both, what would you?

Lau. Serue you fir.

Gob. That is the very defect of the matter fir.

Baff. I know thee well, thou haft obraind thy fute,
Shylocke thy Maifter fpoke with me this day,
And hath preferd thee, if it be preferment
To leaue a rich Iewes feruice, to become
The follower of fo poore a Gentleman.

Clowne. The old prouerb is very well parted betweene my Mai-fter *Shylocke* and you fir, you haue the grace of Godfir, and hee hath enough.

Baff. Thou fpeak'ft it well, goe Father with thy Sonne
Take leaue of thy old Maifter, and enquire
My lodging out, giue him a Lyuerie
More garded then his fellowes: fee it done.

Clowne. Father in, I cannot get a feruice, no, I haue nere a tong in my head, wel: if any man in Italy haue a fayrer table which dooth offer to fweare vpon a booke, I fhall haue good fortunes goe too, heere's a fimple lyne of life, heere's a fmall trifle of wiues, alas, fifteene wiues is nothing, a leuen widdowes and nine maydes is a fimple comming in for one man, and then to fcape drowning thrice, and to be in perrill of my life with the edge of a featherbed, heere are fimple fcapes: well, if Fortune be a woman fhe's a good wench for this gere: Father come, ile take my leaue of the Iewe in the

C 3

21   Q1 (1600) with the speech prefix *Gobbe/Gob.* at sigs C2ᵛ–C3ʳ

sent editors on a wild-goose chase. There are a number of inconsistencies in the text of the play that we may fairly attribute to Shakespeare, but the bibliographical evidence for this one directs our attention, in part at least, elsewhere.

'*Clowne*' and '*Gobbo*' appear together only in the inner and outer formes of sheet C of Q1, both of which were set by Roberts's Compositor X. Compositor X began by setting the inner forme of sheet C with a limited supply of italic and roman capital '*I*' sorts along with a small number of capital *C* sorts. He had already anticipated the consequences of running out of roman capital 'I' sorts, and so even from the start of setting C2^v he substituted a lower-case 'i' ('ile') at C2^{v}8, and an italic capital '*G*' for '*I*' in what was in the manuscript either '*Iobbe*' or '*Gobbe*'. He knew he would be in trouble by the time he came to set C4^v because with an exhausted supply of roman capital 'I' sorts he would be forced to substitute italic capital '*I*', even though he would go on to set '*Iewe*' at C4^{v}33 and 34 and '*Iessica*' at C4^{v}36. Despite the fact that '*Shylocke*' was referred to by name at C4^{v}35, this did not prompt him to adjust his speech prefix '*Iewe*'. He replenished his stock after setting sig. C3^r but by this time he had exhausted his supply of roman capital 'I' sorts. The repetition of '*Iobbe*' in the last line of sig. C1^r and in the first half of C1^v indicates that this was clearly the spelling that he encountered in his copy, although in the second of the three repetitions in the last line of C1^r he set '*Jobbe*' using a swash '*J*'. From the entry of '*old Gobbo*' at C1^{v}22 onwards, and with one exception at C2^{v}34, where the speech prefix is '*Gobbe*', he set either '*Gobbo*' or '*Gob*'. He required no other italic capital '*I*' sorts and in any event none was available until after he had set sig. C3^r. The substitution of italic capital '*G*' for '*I*' seems fairly straightforward, but the issue is clouded by his setting a terminal *o* rather than *e* in the name '*Gobbo*' once the Clown's father appears. It is not inconceivable that Shakespeare may have changed his mind, but the more likely bibliographical explanation for this inconsistency lies in the manuscript itself and in the secretary-hand formation of lower-case 'e'. In Hand D of the addition to *Sir Thomas More*, thought generally to be Shakespeare's, 'e' sometimes consists of two oblique semicircles, one beneath the other, which is similar to lower-case 'o', where the circle sometimes remains uncompleted (Thompson, 95–6). Having already resolved to substitute italic capital '*I*' for '*G*', Compositor X read '*Iobbe*' or '*Gobbe*', which, taking into account his nervousness about the possibility of type shortages, he abbreviated as '*Gob*' throughout the remainder of the forme in the speech prefixes with the single exception of '*Gobbe*' at C2ᵛ34. When he came to set the inner forme of sheet C he was confronted with '*Iobbe*' in the Clown's prose soliloquy, which he retained, but the periodic occurrence of an indistinct terminal '*e*' in *Gobbe*, especially in the stage direction at C1ᵛ22, led him to set '*Gobbo*' in the extended form of the speech prefix, and to continue doing so for the remainder of sigs C1ᵛ–2. What is clear from this is that the character that we have come to know as Gobbo, and whose name means hunchback, is, in fact, Iobbe or Giobbe, the Italianate version of the Old Testament figure of Job, whose disyllabic name the Clown probably pronounced in an anglicized form as 'Jóby'.

A third category of names involves the notorious case of what Dover Wilson, taking his cue from Capell, thought was 'the muddle of the three Sallies' (Cam¹, 100). Q1 opens with three characters onstage, '*Anthonio, Salaryno*, and *Salanio*', and the latter two are initially designated either in full on sig. A2ʳ as '*Salanio*' and '*Salarino*', or in abbreviated form as '*Salar.*' in speech prefixes. However, on A2ᵛ the abbreviations become '*Sala.*' and '*Sola.*', evidently a solution that Compositor Y, who set A2–4ᵛ, deployed as a means of distinguishing between them. But this uncertainty remains on C4–4ᵛ, in a sheet set by Compositor X, where on C4ʳ the stage direction reads '*Enter Gratiano, Lorenso, Salaryno, and Salanio*', but where the speech prefixes are '*Salari*' and '*Solanio*', suitably abbreviated to '*Sol.*' and '*Sal.*' on C4ᵛ. By sig. E2ʳ, in another sheet set by Compositor X, '*Salanio*' has become '*Solanio*', and '*Salarino*' remains the same, though with a variant spelling both in the stage direction and in the abbreviated speech prefixes. After sig. E2ᵛ we hear nothing more of these two characters and we may conclude that either there was an instability in the spelling of '*Salanio*'/'*Solanio*' in the copy that both compositors were working from, or that this alteration was made by the compositors themselves in order to make clear the distinction in print. That the variant '*Salanio*' should be common to both compositors suggests that this was

the spelling they encountered initially and that this is the form
nearest to Shakespeare's own spelling.

The problem is compounded by the appearance in Belmont
of a character named '*Salerio*' at sig. F2ᵛ, who is designated 'a
messenger' in the stage direction (3.2), and who is abbreviated
to '*Sal.*' consistently at F2ᵛ–3, but who has the same name as
the character who appears in the scene immediately following
at sig. F4ʳ: 'Enter the *Iew*, and *Salerio*, and *Anthonio*, / and the
Iaylor.' The confusion is exacerbated by the appearance in 3.3
of two variant speech prefix abbreviations: at sig. F4ʳ the speech
prefix abbreviation is '*Sol.*', while at F4ᵛ it is '*Sal.*'. At sig. F2ᵛ
(3.2) 'Salerio' is addressed by name both by Gratiano – 'vvhat,
my old Venetian friend *Salerio*?' – and by Bassanio: '*Lorenzo*
and *Salerio*. welcome hether.' We can be fairly sure that the
character's name here is Salerio, but it is very doubtful whether
the familiarity of Gratiano's address, 'my old Venetian friend',
indicates that the character being referred to is either Salanio
or Salarino. Compositor Y, who set sheet F, seems to be quite
clear, however, that the character who is in Venice is Salanio but,
since he recalled the possibility of confusion that he resolved
earlier in sheet A, he resorted to setting the speech prefix '*Sol.*'
at F4ʳ30. It seems clear that '*Salerio*' in the stage direction is
either an authorial or a compositorial error and that the character
intended here is, in fact, Salanio. Since only *one* of the Salanio/
Salarino pair appears in 3.3, the speech prefix '*Sal.*' at F4ᵛ5 may
simply be a variant of '*Sol.*' that escaped Y's attention.

Q2 (1619) compounds the difficulty by emending the F4ʳ
entry SD to '*Salarino*' in an attempt to resolve the inconsistency
of having one character appear in two divergent geographical
locations on successive occasions, while F opts for '*Solanio*'. In
his review of the evidence, Dover Wilson thought it inappropriate
that Gratiano's familiar address should be to a character who
has, so far, not appeared before, and so he concluded that this
was 'far more likely to have been "Solanio" or "Salarino" than
a new character of whom we have previously heard nothing'.

Once having embarked on this path, Wilson could not avoid the conclusion that '"Salerio" must be the true form and "Salarino" merely a corruption of it' (Cam[1], 102–3), a solution that Capell had first proposed. F appears to be correct in this instance, while Q2 offers a more or less educated guess at what was, in the manuscript from which the Q1 Compositor Y set the text, a piece of authorial carelessness; this may, as Yasumasa Okamoto has suggested, be evidence of 'Shakespeare's quite interesting writing process'.[1] Mahood was among the first to restore the three characters of Salanio, Salarino and Salerio to the text, although she acknowledges that her evidence is not strong (Cam[2], 179). Notwithstanding what we may deduce from the evidence available about Shakespeare's occasional casualness with the names of minor characters, the bibliographical traces that the text of the play has left direct our attention to another kind of narrative within which compositorial practice is embedded. It is the pressure from this alternative narrative, deriving from a non-authorial source, that suggests that the reasons for conflating Salarino and Salerio are not convincing. Salarino must not, therefore, be the victim of editorial surgery.

In his review of the evidence for the printer's copy that lay behind Q1, John Russell Brown concluded that the variations of '*Shylock*'/'*Jew*' and '*Iobbe*'/'*Gobbo*' are 'more readily explained as the inaccuracies and inconsistencies of an author's manuscript (Ard[2], xvii). He rejected Dover Wilson's suggestion that the variations in the forms of certain speech prefixes were caused solely by type shortages (Ard[2], xvii, 4n.; see also Cam[1], 95) on the grounds that in the case of *Clown/Lancelet* the evidence for shortages of italic capital '*L*' is weak. The instability of this and other speech prefix forms in the play was taken to indicate foul papers as against scribal copy, although Brown correctly concludes that in the case of *Jew/Clown* 'the variations between character name and character *genre*' would not have presented

---

1   Okamoto, 73. Okamoto offers an alternative argument for supporting Dover Wilson's conclusions.

a theatrical prompter with any difficulty (Ard², xvii). Mahood has also suggested that the inconsistent decrease in the use of capital letters to set the beginnings of verse lines may indicate that the text was set from Shakespeare's foul papers, since this was a feature of Hand D in the manuscript of *Sir Thomas More*. But she regards the frequent substitutions of italic for roman type, and occasionally the substitution of roman capital 'Y' for 'I', as indications of type shortage (Cam², 172). Mahood reviews the evidence from punctuation and spelling, and compares it with Roberts's setting of *Titus Andronicus* Q2 (1600) and *Hamlet* Q2 (1605), and she concludes that, 'a few venial printing errors apart', what we have in *The Merchant of Venice* Q1 is a text 'almost certainly . . . as it came from Shakespeare's hand' (Cam², 173).

Neither Brown nor Mahood extends the argument to speculate upon the process of dramatic composition. For example, we know that in *Much Ado About Nothing* Q1 (1600) at 4.2.4 and 9, and the lines following, the variant speech prefixes '*Andrew*' and '*Kemp*' are used instead of the character's name Dogberry, in a text that, according to A.R. Humphreys, 'shows every sign of having been set up from Shakespeare's manuscript' (Humphreys, 75). Evidently, even when composing, Shakespeare had in mind both particular actors (in the case of Dogberry, the resident clown Will Kempe), and also the character type, which suggests that in certain instances the individuality of the character was secondary to both the stereotype and the manner of representation. The *Merchant of Venice* introduces a further complexity into this process in that *Jew*, *Clown* and *Giobbe* each represent different stereotypes – cultural, religious, theatrical and biblical – and that Shakespeare, like his audiences, could move between them with an imaginative flexibility that causes problems only to the normalizing editor.

ABBREVIATIONS AND REFERENCES

Place of publication in references is London unless otherwise stated. Quotations and references to Shakespeare plays other than *The Merchant of Venice* are from *The Arden Shakespeare Complete Works*, ed. Richard Proudfoot, Ann Thompson and David Scott Kastan (Walton-on-Thames, England, 1998), unless otherwise stated. Biblical quotations are from the Bishops' Bible (1595) unless otherwise indicated.

ABBREVIATIONS

ABBREVIATIONS USED IN NOTES

c	corrected state
dir.	directed by
LN	longer note
n.	(in cross-references) note
sig., sigs	signature, signatures
SD	stage direction
SP	speech prefix
subst.	substantially
this edn	a reading adopted for the first time in this edition
t.n.	textual note
u	uncorrected state
*	precedes commentary notes involving readings altered from the text on which this edition is based
( )	enclosing a reading in the textual notes, indicates original spelling; enclosing an editor's or scholar's name, indicates a conjectural reading

WORKS BY AND PARTLY BY SHAKESPEARE

AC	*Antony and Cleopatra*
AW	*All's Well That Ends Well*
AYL	*As You Like It*
CE	*The Comedy of Errors*
Cor	*Coriolanus*
Cym	*Cymbeline*
E3	*King Edward III*
Ham	*Hamlet*

1H4	*King Henry IV, Part 1*
2H4	*King Henry IV, Part 2*
H5	*King Henry V*
1H6	*King Henry VI, Part 1*
2H6	*King Henry VI, Part 2*
3H6	*King Henry VI, Part 3*
H8	*King Henry VIII*
JC	*Julius Caesar*
KJ	*King John*
KL	*King Lear*
LC	*A Lover's Complaint*
LLL	*Love's Labour's Lost*
Luc	*The Rape of Lucrece*
MA	*Much Ado about Nothing*
Mac	*Macbeth*
MM	*Measure for Measure*
MND	*A Midsummer Night's Dream*
MV	*The Merchant of Venice*
MW	*The Merry Wives of Windsor*
Oth	*Othello*
Per	*Pericles*
PP	*The Passionate Pilgrim*
PT	*The Phoenix and Turtle*
R2	*King Richard II*
R3	*King Richard III*
RJ	*Romeo and Juliet*
Son	*Sonnets*
STM	*Sir Thomas More*
TC	*Troilus and Cressida*
Tem	*The Tempest*
TGV	*The Two Gentlemen of Verona*
Tim	*Timon of Athens*
Tit	*Titus Andronicus*
TN	*Twelfth Night*
TNK	*The Two Noble Kinsmen*
TS	*The Taming of the Shrew*
VA	*Venus and Adonis*
WT	*The Winter's Tale*

REFERENCES

EDITIONS OF SHAKESPEARE COLLATED

Ard[1]	*The Merchant of Venice*, ed. Charles T. Pooler, 3rd edn, Arden Shakespeare (1916)
Ard[2]	*The Merchant of Venice*, ed. John Russell Brown, Arden Shakespeare (1964; repr. 1972)
Bevington	*Works*, ed. David Bevington, 4th edn (updated) (1997)
Brown	*See* Ard[2]
Cam	*Works*, ed. William George Clark and William Aldis Wright, 9 vols (Cambridge and London, 1863)
Cam[1]	*The Merchant of Venice*, ed. John Dover Wilson (Cambridge, 1926)
Cam[2]	*The Merchant of Venice*, ed. M.M. Mahood (Cambridge, 1987; repr. 1992)
Capell	*Comedies, Histories, and Tragedies*, ed. Edward Capell, 10 vols (1767–8), vol. 3 (1768)
Clarendon	*Shakespeare Select Plays*, ed. W.G. Clark and W.A. Wright, vol. 2 (Oxford, 1888)
Collier	*Works*, ed. John Payne Collier, 8 vols (1842–4), vol. 2 (1842)
Dyce	*Works*, ed. Alexander Dyce, 9 vols (1864–7)
Edelman	*The Merchant of Venice*, ed. Charles Edelman, Shakespeare in Production series (Cambridge, 2002)
F, F1	*Comedies, Histories and Tragedies*, the First Folio (1623)
F2	*Comedies, Histories and Tragedies*, the Second Folio (1632)
F3	*Comedies, Histories and Tragedies*, the Third Folio (1663)
F4	*Comedies, Histories and Tragedies*, the Fourth Folio (1685)
Folg	*The Merchant of Venice*, ed. Barbara Mowat and Paul Werstine, New Folger Library Shakespeare (New York and London, 1992)
Furness	*The Merchant of Venice*, ed. Horace Howard Furness, New Variorum Shakespeare (Philadelphia, 1888)
Halio	*See* Oxf[1]
Hanmer	*Works*, ed. Thomas Hanmer, 6 vols (Oxford, 1743–4)
Johnson	*Plays*, ed. Samuel Johnson, 8 vols, vol. 1 (1765)
Keightley	*Plays*, ed. Thomas Keightley, 6 vols (1864)
Mahood	*See* Cam[2]
Malone	*Plays and Poems*, ed. Edmond Malone, 10 vols, vol. 5 (1821)
Merchant	*The Merchant of Venice*, ed. W. Moelwyn Merchant, New Penguin Shakespeare (Harmondsworth, England, 1967)
Mowat & Werstine	*See* Folg
Neilson & Hill	*The Complete Plays of William Shakespeare*, ed. William Allan Neilson and Charles Jarvis Hill (1942)

Norton	*The Norton Shakespeare*, ed. Stephen Greenblatt, Walter Cohen, Jean E. Howard and Katherine Eisaman Maus (New York and London, 1997)
Oxf	*Works*, ed. Stanley Wells, Gary Taylor, John Jowett and William Montgomery (Oxford, 1986)
Oxf¹	*The Merchant of Venice*, ed. Jay Halio (Oxford, 1993)
Pooler	*See* Ard¹
Pope	*Works*, ed. Alexander Pope, 6 vols (1723–5)
Q, Q1	*The Merchant of Venice*, the First Quarto (1600)
Q2	*The Merchant of Venice*, the Second Quarto (1619)
Q3	*The Merchant of Venice*, the Third Quarto (1637)
Qq	Q1 and Q2
Rann	*Works*, ed. Joseph Rann, 6 vols (1786–94)
Riv	*The Riverside Shakespeare*, ed. G. Blakemore Evans and J.M. Tobin, 2nd edn (Boston and New York, 1997)
Rowe	*Works*, ed. Nicholas Rowe, 6 vols (1709)
Signet	*The Merchant of Venice*, ed. Kenneth Myrick (1965)
Steevens	*Plays*, ed. Samuel Johnson and George Steevens, 10 vols, vol. 3 (1778)
Theobald	*Works*, ed. Lewis Theobald, 7 vols (1733)
Warburton	*Works*, ed. William Warburton, 8 vols (1747)
Wells	*See* Oxf
Wilson	*See* Cam¹

OTHER WORKS CITED

Abbott	E.A. Abbott, *A Shakespearian Grammar*, 3rd edn (1870)
Abraham	*The New Oxford History of Music*, vol. 4: *The Age of Humanism 1540–1630*, ed. Gerald Abraham (Oxford, 1954)
Anderson	Benedict Anderson, *Imagined Communities* (1991)
Aristotle, *Ethics*	Aristotle, *The Nichomachean Ethics*, trans. J.A.K Thompson (Harmondsworth, England, 1976)
Aristotle, *Politics*	Aristotle, *The Politics*, trans. I.D. from the French of Loys Le Roi (1598)
Armstrong	W.A. Armstrong, 'Actors and theatres', *SS 17* (1964), 191–205
Arnold	Dennis Arnold (ed.), *Oxford Companion to Music*, vol. 1 (Oxford, 1983)
Auden	W.H. Auden, 'Brothers and others', *The Dyer's Hand and Other Essays* (1975)
Babb	Lawrence Babb, *The Elizabethan Malady: A Study of Melancholia in English Literature from 1580 to 1642* (East Lansing, Mich., 1951)
Babbington, *Brief*	Gervaise Babbington, *Certain Plain Brief, and Comfortable Notes upon every Chapter of Genesis* (1592)
Babbington, *Commandments*	Gervaise Babbington, *Exposition of the Commandments* (1583)

References

Bacon	Francis Bacon, *Essays* (1962)
Balibar	Etienne Balibar, 'The nation form: history and ideology', in Etienne Balibar and Immanuel Wallerstein (eds), *Race, Nation, Class: Ambiguous Identities* (1991)
Bancroft	Richard Bancroft, *A Survey of the Pretended Holy Discipline* (1593)
Barber	C.L. Barber, *Shakespeare's Festive Comedy* (Cleveland, Ohio, and New York, 1963)
Barker & Hulme	Francis Barker and Peter Hulme, 'Nymphs and reapers heavily vanish: the discursive con-texts of *The Tempest*', in John Drakakis (ed.), *Alternative Shakespeares* (London and New York, 1985), 191–4
Barton	Anne Barton, *The Names of Comedy* (Toronto, 1990)
Bell	Thomas Bell, *The Speculation of Usury* (1596)
Belsey, 'Conscience'	Catherine Belsey, 'The case of Hamlet's conscience', *SP*, 76 (Spring 1979), 127–48
Belsey, 'Love'	Catherine Belsey, 'Love in Venice', *SS 44*, ed. Stanley Wells (Cambridge, 1992), 41–55
Bhabha	Homi K. Bhabha, *The Location of Culture* (1994)
Blackstone	William Blackstone, *Commentaries on The Laws of England*, 4 vols (1769)
Blake	Norman F. Blake, *A Grammar of Shakespeare's Language* (Basingstoke, 2002)
Bloom	Harold Bloom, *Shakespeare: The Invention of the Human* (New York, 1998)
Bloom & Jaffa	Allan Bloom with Harry Jaffa, *Shakespeare's Politics* (Chicago and London, 1964)
Boccacio	Boccacio, *The Decameron*, trans. J.M. Rigg (1930)
Bogdanov	Michael Bogdanov, *The Director's Cut* (Edinburgh, 2003)
Boose	Lynda Boose, 'The comic contract and Portia's golden ring', *SSt*, 20, ed. J. Leeds Barroll (1988), 241–54
Booth	Roy Booth, 'Shylock's sober house', *RES*, 50 (1999), 22–31
Braudel	Fernand Braudel, *Civilization and Capitalism 15th–18th Centuries*, 3 vols, trans. Siân Reynolds (1985), vol. 1: *The Structures of Everyday Life*; vol. 2: *The Wheels of Commerce*
Brenner	Robert Brenner, *Merchants and Revolution: Commercial Change, Political Conflict, and London's Overseas Traders 1550–1653*, 2nd edn (London and New York, 2003)
Brockbank	Philip Brockbank, 'Shakespeare and the fashion of these times', *SS 16*, ed. Allardyce Nicoll (1963), 30–42
Brooke	Nicholas Brooke, 'Marlowe as provocative agent in Shakespeare's early plays', *SS 14* (1961), 34–45
Broughner	D.C. Broughner, 'Red wine and rhenish', *Shakespeare Association Bulletin*, 14 (1939)
Brown, *Comedies*	John Russell Brown, *Shakespeare and his Comedies*, (1957)

Brown, 'Compositors'	John Russell Brown, 'The compositors of *Hamlet Q2* and *The Merchant of Venice*', *Studies in Bibliography*, 7, ed. Fredson Bowers, 17–40 (1955)
Brown, 'Directors'	John Russell Brown, 'Three directors: a review of recent productions', *SS 13*, ed. Allardyce Nicoll (1961), 137–46
Brown, *Performance*	John Russell Brown, *Shakespeare's Plays in Performance* (1966)
Bullough	G. Bullough, *Narrative and Dramatic Sources of Shakespeare*, vol. 1 (1977)
Bulman	James Bulman, *Shakespeare in Performance: The Merchant of Venice* (Manchester, 1991)
Burckhardt	Sigurd Burckhardt, '*The Merchant of Venice*: the gentle bond', *ELH*, 29 (1962), 239–62
Burton	Robert Burton, *The Anatomy of Melancholy* (1621), ed. Holbrook Jackson (1932)
Caesar	M. Philippus Caesar (Philip Caesar), *A General Discourse Against the Damnable Sect of Usurers* (1578)
Calvin, *Commentaries*	John Calvin, *Calvin's Commentaries*, 22 vols (Grand Rapids, Mich., n.d.)
Calvin, *Genesis*	John Calvin, *A Commentary of John Calvin upon the First Book of Moses called Genesis* (1598)
Calvin, *Institutes*	John Calvin, *Institutes of the Christian Religion*, ed. John T. McNeill, 2 vols (Philadelphia, 1970)
Camden	William Camden, *The History of the Most Renowned and Victorious Princess Elizabeth, Late Queen of England*, STC 4500 (1630)
Cardozo	J.L. Cardozo, *The Contemporary Jew in Elizabethan Drama* (Amsterdam, 1925)
Cartelli	Thomas Cartelli, 'Shakespeare's *Merchant*, Marlowe's *Jew*', *SSt*, 20, ed. J. Leeds Barroll (1988), 255–60
Castiglione	Baldassare Castiglione, *The Book of the Courtier*, trans. Sir Thomas Hoby (1561), Everyman's Library (1928)
Chambers, *Elizabethan*	E.K. Chambers, *The Elizabethan Stage*, 4 vols (Oxford, 1923)
Chambers, *Medieval*	E.K. Chambers, *The Medieval Stage*, 2 vols (Oxford, 1903)
Chapman	George Chapman, *The Comedies of George Chapman*, ed. T.M. Parrott (1914)
Chaucer	Geoffrey Chaucer, *The Riverside Chaucer*, ed. Larry Benson (Oxford, 1998)
Cheney	C.R. Cheney, *A Handbook of Dates for Students of English History* (1978)
Cheyette	Brian Cheyette, *Constructions of the Jew in English Literature and Society: Racial Representations 1875–1945* (Cambridge, 1993)

Cohen, *Drama*   Walter Cohen, *The Drama of a Nation: Public Theatre in Renaissance England and Spain* (Ithaca, NY, and London, 1985)

Cohen, '*Merchant*' Water Cohen, '*The Merchant of Venice* and the possibilities of historical criticism', *The Merchant of Venice: Contemporary Critical Essays*, ed. Martin Coyle, New Casebooks (1998)

Contarini   Gasparo Contarini, *The Commonwealth and Government of Venice*, trans. Lewis Lewkenor (1599)

Coolidge   John Coolidge, 'Law and love in *The Merchant of Venice*', *SQ*, 27, 3 (Summer 1976), 243–63

Coryate   Thomas Coryate, *Coryate's Crudities* (1611)

Craigie   *The Poems of James VI of Scotland*, ed. James Craigie (Edinburgh, 1955)

Cushman   L.W. Cushman, *The Devil and the Vice in English Dramatic Literature before Shakespeare* (1900)

Daniell, *JC*   William Shakespeare, *Julius Caesar*, ed. David Daniell, Arden Shakespeare, 3rd series (1998)

Daniell, *Tyndale* David Daniell, *William Tyndale's Translation of the New Testament* (1534; New Haven and London, 1989)

Danson, *Genres* Lawrence Danson, *Shakespeare's Dramatic Genres* (Oxford, 2000)

Danson, *Harmonies* Lawrence Danson, *The Harmonies of the Merchant of Venice* (New Haven, 1978)

Davies   Sir John Davies, *The Poems of Sir John Davies*, ed. Robert Krueger (Oxford, 1975)

Davis   Ralph Davis, 'England and the Mediterranean 1570–1670', in F.J. Fisher (ed.), *Essays in Economic and Social History of Tudor and Stuart England* (Cambridge, 1961)

Death of Usury *The Death of Usury; or, The Disgrace of Usurers* (1594)

Dennis   *The Oxford Companion to Music*, ed. Arnold Dennis (Oxford, 1983)

Dent   R.W. Dent, *Shakespeare's Proverbial Language: An Index* (Los Angeles and London, 1981)

Derrida, *Acts* Jacques Derrida, *Acts of Literature*, ed. Derek Attridge (New York and London, 1992)

Derrida, 'Pharmacy' Jacques Derrida, 'Plato's pharmacy', *Dissemination*, trans. Barbara Johnson (Chicago and London, 1981)

Derrida, 'Translation' Jacques Derrida, 'What is a "relevant" translation?', trans. Lawrence Venuti, in Lawrence Venuti (ed.), *The Translation Studies Reader* (New York and London, 2004)

Dodsley   Robert Dodsley, *A Select Collection of Old English Plays*, ed. W.C. Hazlitt, 15 vols (1875)

Dollimore   Jonathan Dollimore, *Radical Tragedy: Religion, Ideology and Power in the Drama of Shakespeare and his Contemporaries*, 2nd edn (New York and London, 1989)

Donow	Herbert S. Donow, 'Shakespeare's caskets: unity in *The Merchant of Venice*', *SSt*, 4, ed. J. Leeds Barroll (1968), 86–93
Dowden	Edward Dowden, *Shakespeare: A Critical Study of his Mind and his Art* (1875)
Drakakis, 'Afterword'	John Drakakis, 'Afterword', in Andrew Murphy (ed.), *A Concise Companion to Shakespeare and the Text* (Oxford, 2007)
Drakakis, 'Jessica'	John Drakakis, 'Jessica', in John W. Mahon and Ellen Macleod Mahon (eds), *The Merchant of Venice: New Critical Essays* (New York and London, 2002)
Drakakis, '*Jew*'	John Drakakis, '*Jew*. Shylock is my name: speech-prefixes as symptoms of the early modern', in Hugh Grady (ed.), *Shakespeare and Modernity: Early Modern to Millennium* (2000)
Drakakis, 'Patriarchy'	John Drakakis, 'Historical difference and Venetian patriarchy', in Nigel Wood (ed.), *The Merchant of Venice: Theory in Practice* (Buckingham and Philadelphia, 1996)
Drakakis, 'Venice'	John Drakakis, 'Shakespeare and Venice', in Michele Marrapodi (ed.), *Italian Culture in the Drama of Shakespeare and his Contemporaries: Rewriting, Remaking, Refashioning* (Aldershot, England, 2007)
Duffy	Eamon Duffy, *The Stripping of the Altars: Traditional Religion in England 1400–1580* (New Haven and London, 1992)
Eagleton	Terry Eagleton, *Sweet Violence: The Idea of the Tragic* (Oxford, 2003)
Edwards	John Edwards, *The Jews in Christian Europe 1400–1700* (1988)
ELH	*English Literary History*
ELR	*English Literary Renaissance*
Every Man Out	Ben Jonson, *Every Man Out of His Humour* (1600)
Fairclough	*Virgil: Eclogues, Georgics, Aeneid, Minor Poems*, trans. H.R. Fairclough, 2 vols (Cambridge, Mass., 1960)
Falconer	A.F. Falconer, *Shakespeare and the Sea* (1964)
Faversham	Anon., *Arden of Faversham*, ed. M.L. Wine (1973)
Ferber	Michael Ferber, 'The ideology of *The Merchant of Venice*', *ELH*, 20 (1990)
Fiedler	Leslie Fiedler, *The Stranger in Shakespeare* (1973)
Florio	John Florio, *Queen Anna's New World of Words* (1611)
FQ	Edmund Spenser, *The Faerie Queene*, ed. A.C. Hamilton (1977)
Freud	Sigmund Freud, *Art and Literature*, Pelican Freud, 14 (Harmondsworth, England, 1985)
Freund	Elizabeth Freund, 'Binding and unbinding: the summons to interpretation in *The Merchant of Venice*', *Hebrew University Studies in Literature and The Arts: Essays in Honour of Ruth Nevo*, 19 (1991), 187–210

Gaskell Philip Gaskell, *A New Introduction to Bibliography* (Oxford, 1972)

Gesta *Gesta Grayorum* (1594), ed. W.W. Greg (Oxford, 1914)

Gillies John Gillies, *Shakespeare and the Geography of Difference* (Cambridge, 1994)

Girard René Girard, *The Scapegoat*, trans. Yvonne Freccero (Baltimore, 1986)

Goldberg, *Hand* Jonathan Goldberg, *Shakespeare's Hand* (Minneapolis and London, 2003)

Goldberg, 'Speculations' Jonathan Goldberg, 'Speculations: *Macbeth* as source', in Jean E. Howard and Marion F. O'Connor (eds), *Shakespeare Reproduced: The Text in History and Ideology* (New York and London, 1987); repr. in Goldberg, *Hand*

Goldberg, *Writing* Jonathan Goldberg, *Writing Matter from the Hands of the English Renaissance* (Stanford, Calif., 1990)

Goux Jean-Joseph Goux, *Symbolic Economies after Marx and Freud*, trans. Jennifer Curtiss Gage (Ithaca, NY, 1990)

Gower John Gower, *The Complete Works of John Gower*, ed. G.C. Macaulay (Oxford, 1901)

Grant & Rowley F.C. Grant and H.H. Rowley, *Dictionary of the Bible*, 2nd edn (Edinburgh, 1963)

Greenblatt, 'Exorcists' Stephen Greenblatt, 'Shakespeare and the exorcists', in Patricia Parker and Geoffrey Hartman (eds), *Shakespeare and the Question of Theory* (New York and London, 1985)

Greenblatt, 'Marlowe' Stephen Greenblatt, 'Marlowe, Marx and anti-Semitism', *Learning to Curse: Essays in Early Modern Culture* (New York and London, 1990)

Greenblatt, *Renaissance* Stephen Greenblatt, *Renaissance Self-fashioning from More to Shakespeare* (Chicago, 1980)

Greene Thomas Greene, *Menaphon*, ed. G. Harrison (Oxford, 1927)

Greg, *Editorial* W.W. Greg, *The Editorial Problem in Shakespeare* (Oxford, 1942)

Greg, 'False dates' W.W. Greg, 'On certain false dates in Shakespearean quartos', *Library*, 2nd series, 9 (1908)

Greg, *First Folio* W.W. Greg, *The Shakespeare First Folio* (Oxford, 1955)

Gross John Gross, *Shylock: Four Hundred Years in the Life of a Legend* (1992)

Gurr A.J. Gurr, *Shakespearean Playing Companies* (Oxford, 1996)

Hakluyt Richard Hakluyt, *The Principal Navigations, Voyages, Traffics and Discoveries of the English Nation*, 8 vols (London and New York, 1927)

Hall, 'Guess who' Kim Hall, 'Guess who's coming to dinner? Colonisation and miscegenation in *The Merchant of Venice*', in *The Merchant of Venice*, ed. Martin Coyle, New Casebooks (Basingstoke, 1998), 92–116

Hall, *Things* Kim Hall, *Things of Darkness: Economies of Race and Gender in Early Modern England* (Ithaca, NY, and London, 1995)

Halpern Richard Halpern, *The Poetics of Primitive Accumulation: English Renaissance Culture and the Genealogy of Capital* (Ithaca, NY, and London, 1991)

Hamilton Donna B. Hamilton, 'Anthony Munday and *The Merchant of Venice*', *SS 54* (Cambridge, 2001), 89–99

Harris Jonathan Gil Harris, *Foreign Bodies and the Body Politic: Discourses of Social Pathology in Early Modern England* (Cambridge, 1998)

Harrison G.B. Harrison, *A Description of England*, ed. George Edelen (New York, 1968)

Harvey Gabriel Harvey, *Works*, ed. A.B. Grosart (1884–5)

Hattaway Michael Hattaway, *Elizabethan Popular Theatre: Plays in Performance* (1982)

Hawkes David Hawkes, *Idols of The Marketplace: Idolatry and Commodity Fetishism in English Literature 1580–1680* (New York and Basingstoke, 2001)

Henslowe *Henslowe's Diary*, ed. R.A. Foakes, 2nd edn (Cambridge, 2002)

Hinman, *Facsimile* *The Norton Facsimile: The First Folio of Shakespeare*, ed. Charlton Hinman, 2nd edn (New York and London, 1996)

Hinman, *Printing* Charlton Hinman, *The Printing and Proof-reading of the First Folio of Shakespeare*, 2 vols (Oxford, 1963)

Holaday Allan Holaday, 'Antonio and the allegory of salvation', *SSt*, 4 (1969)

Homer Homer, *The Iliad*, trans. A.T. Murray (Cambridge, Mass., 1925)

Honigmann E.A.J. Honigmann, 'Shakespeare's Plutarch', *SQ*, 10 (1959)

Hood John B. Hood, *Aquinas and the Jews* (Philadelphia, 1995)

Hooker Richard Hooker, *Of The Laws of Ecclesiastical Polity*, ed. Christopher Morris, 2 vols (1907)

Hope Jonathan Hope, *Shakespeare's Grammar* (2003)

Horace Quintus Horatius Flaccus, *Odes and Epodes*, trans. C.E. Bennett (1914)

Hortmann Wilhelm Hortmann, *Shakespeare on the German Stage: The Twentieth Century* (Cambridge, 1998)

Hulme Hilda Hulme, 'Wit, rage, mean: three notes on *The Merchant of Venice*', *Neophilologus*, 41 (1957)

Humphreys *Much Ado About Nothing*, ed. A.R. Humphreys, Arden Shakespeare, 2nd series (London and New York, 1981)

Hunter G.K. Hunter, 'The theology of Marlowe's *The Jew of Malta*', *Dramatic Identities and Cultural Tradition* (Liverpool, 1978)

Hutson Lorna Hutson, *The Usurer's Daughter: Male Friendship and Fictions of Women in Sixteenth-Century England* (1994)

James	Henry James, *The Scenic Art: Notes on Acting and the Drama* (1949)
Jameson	Fredric Jameson, *A Singular Modernity: Essays on the Ontology of The Present* (London and New York, 2002)
Jardine	Lisa Jardine, *Still Harping on Daughters: Women and Drama in the Age of Shakespeare* (Brighton, 1983)
Jew of Malta	Christopher Marlowe, *The Jew of Malta* (*c.* 1592), ed. N.W. Bawcutt (Manchester, 1978)
Jonson	Ben Jonson, *The Complete Works*, ed. C.H. Herford and P. Simpson, 11 vols (Oxford, 1952)
Jump	*Christopher Marlowe: Doctor Faustus*, ed. John Jump (1962)
Kennedy, D.	Dennis Kennedy, *Looking at Shakespeare* (Cambridge, 1993)
Kennedy, M.	Michael Kennedy, *Oxford Dictionary of Music* (Oxford, 1985)
Kennedy, R.	Richard F. Kennedy, 'Speech-prefixes in some Shakespearean quartos', *PBSA*, 92 (June 1998)
Kermode	Frank Kermode, *Shakespeare's Language* (Harmondsworth, England, 2000)
Keynes	J.M. Kenyes, *The Life of William Harvey* (Oxford, 1966)
King	T.J. King, *Casting Shakespeare's Plays: London Actors and their Roles 1590–1642* (Cambridge, 1992)
King John	William Shakespeare, *King John*, ed. E.A.J. Honigmann, Arden Shakespeare, 2nd series (1967)
Knight	G. Wilson Knight, *The Crown of Life* (1958)
Kökeritz	Helga Kökeritz, *Shakespeare's Pronunciation* (New Haven, 1953)
Kristeva	Julia Kristeva, *Strangers to Ourselves*, trans. Leon S. Roudiez (Hemel Hempstead, 1991)
Krueger	*The Poems of Sir John Davies*, ed. Robert Krueger (Oxford, 1975)
Kyd	Thomas Kyd, *Works*, ed. F.S. Boas (Oxford, 1941)
Lane	Fredric C. Lane, *Venice: A Maritime Republic* (Bal-timore and London, 1973)
Lanham	Richard Lanham, *A Handbook of Rhetorical Terms* (Berkeley, 1991)
Laplanche & Pontalis	J. Laplanche and J.B. Pontalis, *The Language of Psychoanalysis* (1985)
Laroque	François Laroque, *Shakespeare's Festive World* (Cambridge, 1991)
Lasocki & Prior	David Lasocki with Roger Prior, *The Bassanos: Venetian Musicians and Instrument Makers in England 1531–1665* (Aldershot, England, 1995)
Lee	S.L. Lee, 'The original of Shylock', *Gentleman's Magazine*, 246 (1880), 185–200
Leggatt	Alexander Leggatt, *Shakespeare's Comedy of Love* (1974)

Leon	Abram Leon, *The Jewish Question: A Marxist Interpretation* (New York, 1970)
Le Roy Ladurie	Emmanuel Le Roy Ladurie, *Carnival in Romans*, trans. Mary Feeney (Harmondsworth, England, 1981)
Leventen	Carol Leventen, 'Patrimony and patriarchy in *The Merchant of Venice*', in Valerie Wayne (ed.), *The Matter of Difference* (New York and London, 1991)
Levith	Murray J. Levith, 'Shakespeare's *Merchant* and Marlowe's other plays', in John W. Mahon and Ellen MacLeod Mahon (eds), *The Merchant of Venice: New Critical Essays* (New York and London, 2002)
Lewalski	Barbara K. Lewalski, 'Biblical allusion and allegory in *The Merchant of Venice*', *SQ*, 13 (1962), 327–43
Lodge	*The Complete Works of Thomas Lodge*, ed. Edmund Gosse, 4 vols (Glasgow, 1883)
LLL Arden 2	William Shakespeare, *Love's Labour's Lost*, ed. Richard David, Arden Shakespeare, 2nd series (1968)
LLL Arden 3	William Shakespeare, *Love's Labour's Lost*, ed. H.R Woudhuysen, Arden Shakespeare, 3rd series (1998)
Luther, *Jews*	Martin Luther, *On the Jews and their Lies* (1543), *Luther's Works*, vol. 47: *The Christian in Society*, ed. Franklin Sherman (Philadelphia, 1971)
Luther, *Usury*	Martin Luther, *Trade and Usury* (1524), trans. C.M. Jacobs, *Luther's Works*, vol. 45: *The Christian in Society*, ed. Walther I. Brandt and Helmut T. Lehmann (Philadelphia, 1962)
Luxon	Thomas Luxon, 'A second Daniel: the Jew and the "true Jew" in *The Merchant of Venice*', *Early Modern Literary Studies*, 4, 3 (January 1999), 1–15
Lyly	John Lyly, *The Complete Works*, ed. R.W. Bond, 3 vols (Oxford, 1902)
Lyotard	Jean-François Lyotard, *Heidegger and 'The Jews'*, trans. Andreas Michael and Mark Roberts (Minneapolis, 1990)
Mahood, *Bit Parts*	M.M. Mahood, *Playing Bit Parts in Shakespeare's Plays* (1998)
Malcontent	John Marston, *The Malcontent*, ed. G.K. Hunter (Manchester, 1975)
Marchitello	Howard Marchitello, '(Dis)embodied letters and *The Merchant of Venice*: writing, editing, history', *ELH*, 62, 2 (Summer 1995), 237–65
Markus	Zoltan Markus, '*Der Merchant von Velence*: The Merchant in London, Berlin and Budapest during World War II', unpublished paper delivered at the Shakespeare and European Politics conference at the University of Utrecht, 7 December 2003
Marlowe	Christopher Marlowe, *The Complete Works*, ed. C.F. Tucker-Brooke (Oxford, 1910)

Marston, *Poems*	John Marston, *The Poems*, ed. Arnold Davenport (Liverpool, 1961)
Marx, *Critique*	Karl Marx, *A Contribution to the Critique of Political Economy*, trans. S.W. Ryazanskaya (Moscow, 1977)
Marx, 'Jewish question'	Karl Marx, 'On the Jewish question', *Early Writings*, trans. Rodney Livingstone and Gregor Benton (Harmondsworth, England, 1975)
Marzola	Allessandra Marzola, 'Which is the woman here and which the man: economy and gender in *The Merchant of Venice*', *European Journal of English Studies: Current Shakespeare*, 1, 3, ed. John Drakakis (1997), 291–309
Masten	Jeffrey Masten, *Textual Intercourse: Collaboration, Authorship, and Sexualities in Renaissance Drama* (Cambridge, 1997)
Maus	Katherine Eisaman Maus, *Inwardness and Theater in the English Renaissance* (Chicago and London, 1995)
Melbancke	Brian Melbancke, *Philotimus: The War Betwixt Nature and Fortune* (1583)
Memmi	Albert Memmi, *Racism*, trans. Steve Martinot (Minneapolis and London, 2000)
Moisan	Thomas Moisan, '"Which is the merchant here? And which the Jew?" Subversion and recuperation in *The Merchant of Venice*', in J.E. Howard and M.F. O'Connor (eds), *Shakespeare Reproduced: The Text in History and Ideology* (1987), 188–206
Monsarrat	Gilles Monsarrat, 'Shylock and mercy', *Cahiers élisabéthains*, 67 (Spring 2005), 1–13
Montaigne	Michel de Montaigne, *Essays*, trans. John Florio, ed. L.C. Harmer, 3 vols (1965)
Mosse	Miles Mosse, *The Arraignment and Conviction of Usury* (1595)
Munday	Anthony Munday, *Zelauto: The Fountain of Fame Erected in an Orchard of Amorous Encounters* (1580)
Nashe	Thomas Nashe, *The Complete Works*, ed. R.B. McKerrow, 5 vols (Oxford, 1958)
Newman	Karen Newman, 'Reprise: gender, sexuality and theories of exchange in *The Merchant of Venice*', in Nigel Wood (ed.), *The Merchant of Venice: Theory in Practice* (Buckingham and Philadelphia, 1996)
Nickel	John Nickel, 'Shylock in Washington', *Textual Practice*, 15, 2 (2001)
Noble	Richmond Noble, *Shakespeare's Biblical Knowledge* (1935)
North	*Plutarch's Lives Englished by Sir Thomas North*, ed. W.H.D. Rouse, 10 vols (1898)
N&Q	*Notes and Queries*

OCD	*The Oxford Classical Dictionary*, ed. M. Cary, J.D. Denniston, J. Wight Duff, A.D. Nock, W.D. Ross and H.H. Scullard (Oxford, 1961)
ODCC	*The Oxford Dictionary of the Christian Church*, ed. F.L. Cross (1957)
OED	*Oxford English Dictionary*, 2nd edn
Okamoto	Yasumasa Okamoto, 'The three Sallies reconsidered: a case study in Shakespeare's use of proper names', *SSt*, 15, ed. Jiuro Ozu, Shakespeare Society of Japan, 1979 (1976–7)
Onions	C.T. Onions, *A Shakespeare Glossary*, 2nd rev. edn (Oxford, 1972)
Orgel, 'Editor'	Stephen Orgel, 'What is an editor?', *The Authentic Shakespeare and Other Problems of the Early Modern Stage* (New York and London, 2002)
Orgel, *Impersonations*	Stephen Orgel, *Impersonations: The Performance of Gender in Shakespeare's England* (Cambridge, 1996)
Orgel, 'Shylock'	Stephen Orgel, 'Imagining Shylock', *Imagining Shakespeare: A History of Texts and Visions* (Basingstoke, 2003)
Othello	William Shakespeare, *Othello*, ed. E.A.J. Honigmann, Arden Shakespeare, 3rd series (1997)
Ovid, *Heroides*	Ovid, *Heroides*, trans. Harold Isbell (Harmondsworth, England, 1990)
Ovid, *Met.*	Ovid, *Metamorphoses*, trans. Arthur Golding (1567), ed. John Frederick Nims (London and New York, 1965)
Oxford Companion to Bible	Bruce M. Metzger and Michael D. Coogan (eds), *The Oxford Companion to the Bible* (1994)
Oz, '*Merchant*'	Avram Oz, '*The Merchant of Venice* in Israel', in Dennis Kennedy (ed.), *Foreign Shakespeare* (Cambridge, 1993)
Oz, *Yoke*	Avram Oz, *The Yoke of Love: Prophetic Riddles in The Merchant of Venice* (Newark, NJ, 1995)
Parker	Patricia Parker, 'Cutting both ways: bloodletting, castration/circumcision, and the "Lancelet" of *The Merchant of Venice*', in Diana E. Henderson (ed.), *Alternative Shakespeares 3* (London and New York, 2008)
Parry	J.H. Parry, *The Age of Reconnaissance: Exploration and Settlement 1450–1650* (2000)
Partridge	Eric Partridge, *Shakespeare's Bawdy* (1968)
Patterson	*The Most Excellent History of The Merchant of Venice*, ed. Annabel Patterson, Shakespeare Originals (Hemel Hempstead, 1995)
PBSA	*Papers of the Bibliographical Society of America*
Pecorone	Giovanni Fiorentino, *Il Pecorone* (Milan, 1558)
Pettet	E.C. Pettet, '*The Merchant of Venice* and the problem of usury', *The Merchant of Venice*, Macmillan Casebooks, ed. John Wilders (Basingstoke, 1969)

Pick   Daniel Pick, *Svengali's Web: The Alien Enchanter in Modern Culture* (New Haven and London, 2000)

Plato   Plato, *The Republic*, ed. F.M. Cornford (Oxford, 1941)

Pliny   Pliny the Elder, *The History of the World*, trans. Philemon Holland (1601)

Plutarch   Plutarch, *Lives*, ed. T.J.B. Spencer (Harmondsworth, England, 1964)

Poel   William Poel, 'Shakespeare's Jews and Marlowe's Christians', *Westminster Review* (Bedford, n.d.)

Puttenham   George Puttenham, *The Art of English Poesie* (1589)

Quirk   Randolph Quirk, *A Grammar of Contemporary English* (1972)

RES   *Review of English Studies*

Reynolds   G.F. Reynolds, *The Staging of Elizabethan Plays at the Red Bull Theatre* (New York, 1940)

Ribner   Irving Ribner, 'Marlowe and Shakespeare', *SQ*, 15 (Spring 1964)

Richard III   Sir Thomas More, *The History of King Richard III* (1976)

Ringler   William A. Ringler, Jr, 'The number of actors in Shakespeare's early plays', in Gerald Eades Bentley (ed.), *The Seventeenth-Century Stage: A Collection of Critical Essays* (Chicago and London, 1968)

Roth   Cecil Roth, 'The background of Shylock', *RES*, 9 (1933)

Rougement   Denis de Rougement, *Love in the Western World*, trans. Montgomery Belgion (Princeton, NJ, 1983)

Rozmovits   Linda Rozmovits, *Shakespeare and the Politics of Culture in Late Victorian England* (Baltimore and London, 1998)

Sanders   Wilbur Sanders, *The Dramatist and the Received Idea* (Cambridge, 1968)

Sartre   Jean-Paul Sartre, *Anti-Semite and Jew: An Exploration of the Aetiology of Hate*, trans. George J. Becker (New York, 1976)

Sawday   Jonathan Sawday, *The Body Emblazoned: Dissection and the Human Body in Renaissance Culture* (1995)

Sedgwick   Eve Kosofsky Sedgwick, *Between Men: English Literature and Male Homosocial Desire* (New York, 1995)

Sejanus   Ben Jonson, *Sejanus*, ed. Philip Ayres (Manchester, 1990)

Seneca   *Seneca His Ten Tragedies Translated into English by Thomas Newton anno 1581*, ed. Thomas Newton, 2 vols (London and New York, 1927)

Sennett   Richard Sennett, *Flesh and Stone: The Body and the City in Western Civilization* (Boston and London, 1994)

Shaheen   Naseeb Shaheen, *Biblical References in Shakespeare's Comedies* (Newark, NJ, 1993)

Shakespeare's England   *Shakespeare's England: An Account of the Life and Manners of his Age*, 2 vols (1916)

Shapiro, *Jews*   James Shapiro, *Shakespeare and the Jews* (New York, 1996)

Shapiro, '*Merchant*'	James Shapiro, 'Which is the *Merchant* here, and which the *Jew*', *SSt*, 20, ed. J. Leeds Barroll (1988), 269–79
Schell & Schuchter	Edgar T. Schell and J.D. Schuchter (eds), *English Morality Plays and Moral Interludes* (New York, 1959)
Schücking	Levin Schücking, *Character Problems in Shakespeare's Plays* (1922)
Shell	Marc Shell, *Money, Language and Thought: Literary and Philosophical Economies from the Medieval to the Modern Era* (Baltimore and London, 1982)
Shuger	Debora Kuller Shuger, *Habits of Thought in the English Renaissance: Religion, Politics and the Dominant Culture* (Toronto and London, 1997)
Simmel	George Simmel, *The Philosophy of Money*, trans. Tom Bottomore and David Frisby, ed. David Frisby, 2nd edn (London and New York, 1990)
Sinclair	*Aristotle: The Politics*, trans. T.A. Sinclair (repr. Harmondsworth, England, 1979)
Sinfield, *Faultlines*	Alan Sinfield, *Faultlines: Cultural Materialism and the Politics of Dissident Reading* (Oxford, 1992)
Sinfield, 'How to read'	Alan Sinfield, 'How to read *The Merchant of Venice* without being heterosexist', *Alternative Shakespeares 2*, ed. Terence Hawkes (1996)
Sinfield, *Queer Reading*	Alan Sinfield, *Cultural Politics – Queer Reading* (1994)
Smith, B.	Bruce Smith, *Homosexual Desire in Shakespeare's England: A Cultural Poetics* (Chicago and London, 1994)
Smith, G.	Gregory Smith (ed.), *Elizabethan Critical Essays*, 3 vols (Oxford, 1904)
Smith, H.	Henry Smith, *The Examination of Usury in two Sermons* (1591)
Sohmer	Steve Sohmer, *Shakespeare's Mystery Play: The Opening of the Globe Theatre 1599* (Manchester, 1999)
Sonnets	*Shakespeare's Sonnets*, ed. Stephen Booth (New Haven and London, 1977)
SP	*Studies in Philology*
Speaight	Robert Speaight, *Shakespeare on the Stage: An Illustrated History of Shakespeare Performance* (1973)
Spenser, *Works*	Edmund Spenser, *Works*, ed. J.C. Smith and E. de Selincourt (1961)
Spinosa	Charles Spinosa, 'The transformation of intentionality: debt and contract in *The Merchant of Venice*', *ELR*, 24 (Spring 1994)
Sprague	A.C. Sprague, *Shakespearean Players and Performances* (Cambridge, Mass., 1953)

Spurgeon	Caroline Spurgeon, *Shakespeare's Imagery and What it Tells Us* (Cambridge, 1935)
SQ	*Shakespeare Quarterly*
SS	*Shakespeare Survey*
SSt	*Shakespeare Studies*
STC	Short Title Catalogue
Stephens	Lyn Stephens, 'A wilderness of monkeys: a psycho-dynamic study of *The Merchant of Venice*', in B.J. Sokol (ed.), *The Undiscover'd Country: New Essays on Psychoanalysis and Shakespeare* (1993)
Stern, 'Globe'	Tiffany Stern, 'Was *Totus mundus agit histrionem* ever the motto of the Globe theatre?', *Theatre Notebook*, 51 (1997)
Stern, *Making Shakespeare*	Tiffany Stern, *Making Shakespeare: From Stage to Page* (2004)
Stewart	J.I.M. Stewart, *Character and Motive in Shakespeare* (1949)
Stone	Lawrence Stone, *The Crisis of the Aristocracy* (Oxford, 1965)
Stow	John Stow, *The Annals or a General Chronicle of England from Brutus until the Present Year of Christ* (1615)
Strickland	Debra Higgs Strickland, *Saracens, Demons, and Jews: Making Monsters in Medieval Art* (Princeton, NJ, and Oxford, 2003)
Stritmatter	Roger Stritmatter, '*Old* and *new* law in *The Merchant of Venice*: a note on the source of Shylock's morality in Deuteronomy 15', *N&Q*, n.s., 47 (March 2000), 71–2
Strong	Roy Strong, *The English Icon: Elizabethan and Jacobean Portraiture* (1969)
Tamburlaine 1	Christopher Marlowe, *Tamburlaine the Great* (1590), Part 1, in Marlowe
Tamburlaine 2	Christopher Marlowe, *Tamburlaine the Great* (1590), Part 2, in Marlowe
Tawney	R.H. Tawney, *Religion and the Rise of Capitalism* (Harmondsworth, England, 1938)
Tennenhouse	Leonard Tennenhouse, 'The counterfeit order of *The Merchant of Venice*', in Murray M. Schwartz and Coppélia Kahn (eds), *Representing Shakespeare: New Psychoanalytical Essays* (Baltimore and London, 1982)
Terence	Terence, *The Comedies*, ed. Betty Radice (Harmondsworth, England, 1965)
Terry	Ellen Terry, *The Story of My Life: Recollections and Reflections* (New York, 1907)
Theatre Records	*Shakespeare Birthplace Trust Theatre Records*, Shakespeare Centre, Stratford-upon-Avon
Thomas, H.	Hugh Thomas, *The Slave Trade: The History of the Atlantic Slave Trade 1450–1870* (1997)

Thomas, W.	William Thomas, *The History of Italy* (1561)
Thompson	E. Maunde Thompson, 'The handwriting of the three pages attributed to Shakespeare compared with his signatures', in A.W. Pollard, W.W. Greg, E. Maunde Thompson, J. Dover Wilson and R.W. Chambers (eds), *Shakespeare's Hand in Sir Thomas More* (Cambridge, 1923)
Three Ladies	Robert Wilson, *The Three Ladies of London* (1592), STC 25785
Three Lords	Robert Wilson, *The Pleasure and Stately Moral of the Three Lords and Three Ladies of London*, STC 25783 (1590)
Tilley	Morris Palmer Tilley, *A Dictionary of Proverbs in England in the Sixteenth and Seventeenth Centuries* (Ann Arbor, Mich., 1950)
Trachtenberg	Joshua Trachtenberg, *The Devil and the Jews* (Philadelphia, 1983)
Tobin	J.J.M. Tobin, 'Nashe and Shakespeare: some further borrowings', *N&Q*, n.s., 39 (September 1992), 309–20
Tucker	E.J.F. Tucker, 'The letter of the law in *The Merchant of Venice*', *SS 29*, ed. Kenneth Muir (Cambridge, 1976), 93–101
Tucker-Brooke	*The Shakespeare Apocrypha*, ed. C.F. Tucker-Brooke (Oxford, 1908)
TxC	Stanley Wells and Gary Taylor, with John Jowett and William Montgomery, *William Shakespeare: A Textual Companion* (Oxford, 1987)
Vickers	Brian Vickers, *The Artistry of Shakespeare's Prose* (1968)
Virgil	Virgil, *The Aeneid*, trans. W. Jackson Knight (Harmondsworth, England, 1958)
Walker	Greg Walker (ed.), *Medieval Drama: An Anthology* (Oxford, 2000)
Wallerstein	Immanuel Wallerstein, *The Modern World System II: Mercantilism and the Consolidation of the European World Economy 1600–1750* (Boston and London, 1980)
Warren	Michael J. Warren, 'A note on *The Merchant of Venice* 2.1.37', *SQ*, 32 (1981)
Watt, 'Breed'	Gary Watt, 'Breed of metal and pound of flesh: faith and risk in metaphors of usury', *Polemos*, 2 (2007), 95–116
Watt, 'Law'	Gary Watt, 'The law of dramatic properties in *The Merchant of Venice*', in P. Raffield and G. Watt (eds), *Shakespeare and the Law* (Oxford, 2008), 237–52
Weber	Max Weber, *The Protestant Ethic and the Spirit of Capitalism*, 2nd edn (London and Boston, 1976)
Weimann, *Author's Pen*	Robert Weimann, *Author's Pen and Actor's Voice: Playing and Writing in Shakespeare's Theatre* (Cambridge, 2000)

Weimann, *Tradition*   Robert Weimann, *Shakespeare and the Popular Tradition in the Theater: Studies in the Social Dimension of Dramatic Form and Function*, trans. Robert Schwartz (Baltimore and London, 1978)

Weiss   John Weiss, *Wit and Humour in Shakespeare* (1876)

Wertheim   Albert Wertheim, 'The treatment of Shylock and thematic integrity in *The Merchant of Venice*', *SSt*, 6, ed. J. Leeds Barroll (1972)

Wesker   Arnold Wesker, *The Merchant* (1983)

Wheatcroft   Andrew Wheatcroft, *Infidels: A History of the Conflict between Christendom and Islam* (New York, 2004)

Wheater   Isabella Wheater, 'Aristotelian wealth and the sea of love: Shakespeare's synthesis of Greek philosophy and Roman poetry in *The Merchant of Venice*', *RES*, 173 (February 1993)

White   R.G. White, *Shakespeare Scholar* (1854)

Wickham   Glynne Wickham (ed.), *English Moral Interludes* (1976)

Williams, George   George Walton William (ed.), *Shakespeare's Speech-headings: Speaking the Speech in Shakespeare's Plays* (Newark, NJ, and London, 1997)

Williams, Gordon   Gordon Williams, *A Glossary of Shakespeare's Sexual Language* (1997)

Williams, P.   Penry Williams, *The Tudor Regime* (Oxford, 1979)

Wilson, F.   F.P. Wilson (ed.), *Oxford Dictionary of English Proverbs* (Oxford, 1970)

Wilson, T., *Rhetoric*   Thomas Wilson, *The Art of Rhetoric* (1585)

Wilson, T., *Usury*   Thomas Wilson, *A Discourse on Usury* (1572)

Wolf   Lucien Wolf, 'Jews in Elizabethan England', *Transactions of the Jewish Historical Society of England*, 11 (1928)

Worthen   W.B. Worthen, *Shakespeare and the Authority of Performance* (Cambridge, 1997)

Wright   George T. Wright, *Shakespeare's Metrical Art* (Berkeley, 1988)

Yaffe   Paul Yaffe, *Shylock and the Jewish Question* (Baltimore and London, 1997)

MODERN PRODUCTIONS CITED

Alexander   RSC, Stratford-upon-Avon, dir. Bill Alexander, 1987

Atkins   RSC, Stratford-upon-Avon, dir. Robert Atkins, 1944

Barton   RSC, Stratford-upon-Avon, dir. John Barton, 1978

Bogdanov   Wales Theatre Company, dir. Michael Bogdanov, 2004

Carey   RSC, Stratford-upon-Avon, dir. Dennis Carey, 1953

Carroll   RSC, Stratford-upon-Avon, dir. Tim Carroll, 2008

Doran	RSC, Stratford-upon-Avon, dir. Greg Doran, 1997
Gold	BBC TV, Shakespeare, dir. Jack Gold, 1980
Guthrie	Stratford, Ontario, dir. Tyrone Guthrie, 1955
Hands	RSC, Stratford-upon-Avon, dir. Terry Hands, 1971
Iden Payne 1936	Stratford-upon-Avon, dir. B. Iden Payne, 1936
Iden Payne 1940	Stratford-upon-Avon, dir. B. Iden Payne, 1940
Ingram	Swan theatre, Stratford, dir. Loveday Ingram, 2001
Komisarjevsky	Stratford-upon-Avon, dir. T. Komisarjevsky, 1932
Langhoff	Deutschestheater, East Berlin, dir. Thomas Langhoff, 1985
Luscombe	English Shakespeare Company, dir. Tim Luscombe, 1991
Miller 1970	National Theatre, London, dir. Jonathan Miller, 1970
Miller 1973	Film, dir. Jonathan Miller, 1973
Nunn	National Theatre, London, dir. Trevor Nunn, 1999
Olivier	New Globe theatre, London, dir. Richard Olivier, 1998
Poel	St George's Hall, London, dir. William Poel, 1898
Radford	Film, dir. Michael Radford, 2004
Sissons	Compass Theatre, dir. Neil Sissons, 1997
Thacker	RSC, Stratford-upon-Avon, dir. David Thacker, 1993
Zadek	Berliner Ensemble, dir. Peter Zadek, 1995

INDEX